To
A Marxi

Ian Birchall

To Chanie Rosenberg,
Cliff's "companion in struggle" for over half a century

Bookmarks Publications

Tony Cliff: A Marxist for His Time
Ian Birchall

Published by Bookmarks Publications in 2011
Copyright © Bookmarks Publications

ISBN 9781905192809 (pbk)
    9781905192793 (hbk)

Cover design by Ruth Pallesen-Mustikay
Typeset by rpmdesign
Printed by Halstan Printing Group

Acknowledgements

The following gave me interviews, in person or by telephone. Many of them also gave me additional information or made useful suggestions. People with names marked (†) have sadly died since I conducted the interviews.

Peter Alexander
Tariq Ali
Dave Ayre
Chris Bambery
Colin Barker
Ewa Barker
Hanna Ben Dov
Weyman Bennett
Willie Black
Helen Blair
Alan Borrell
Eileen Boyle
Geoff Brown
Sue Caldwell
Alex Callinicos
Ray Challinor (†)
John Charlton
Choi Il-Bung
Pete Clark
Bob Clay
Ken Coates (†)
Nigel Coward
Roger Cox
Sarah Cox
Edward Crawford
Jim Cronin
Ralph Darlington

Chris Davison
Shaun Doherty
Clare Fermont
Joel Geier
Lindsey German
Ian Gibson
Anna Gluckstein
Danny Gluckstein
Donny Gluckstein
Pete Green
Naomi Gunn
Steve Hammill
Chris Harman (†)
Nigel Harris
Tirril Harris
Dave Hayes
Simon Hester
Paul Holborow
Nick Howard
Roger Huddle
Richard Hyman
Richard Kirkwood
Roger Kline
Mark Krantz
Penny Krantz
Richard Kuper
Willie Lee (†)

George Leslie
Sheila Leslie
Fred Lindop
John Lindsay
Mickey Loeb
Ian Macdonald QC
Lord Macdonald of Tradeston
Paul Mackney
Zena Maddison
Ron Margulies
Sean Matgamna
Eamonn McCann
Sheila McGregor
Ian Mitchell
John Molyneux
Jakob Moneta
Sammy Morris
Volkhard Mosler
Stan Newens
Jim Nichol
Fergus Nicol
Mel Norris
George Paizis
John Palmer
Dave Peers
John Phillips
Mary Phillips
Eddie Prevost
Jack Robertson

Peter Robinson
John Rose
Chanie Rosenberg
Roger Rosewell
John Rees
Sabby Sagall
Rudi Segall (†)
Red Saunders
Ron Senchak
Dov Shas (†)
Ahmed Shawki
Dave Sherry
Tuvia Shlonsky
Martin Smith
Pat Stack
Andy Strouthous
Danny Tait (†)
Jean Tait
Bill Thomson
Martin Tomkinson
Sean Vernell
Julie Waterson
Alan Watts
Granville Williams
Andy Wilson
John Witzenfeld
Alan Woodward
James D Young

The following sent me written testimonies, provided documents or information, made helpful suggestions or assisted with translations and technical matters. Apologies to those who made comments when I wasn't taking notes, or who commented pseudonymously on websites. Apologies also to those whose material I have not used; I have acquired a wealth of information while working on this book, far more than could be contained in a single volume. Many testimonies not directly quoted have been taken into account.

Anne Alexander
Kieran Allen
Logie Barrow
Nimrod Ben-Cnaan
Danny Birchall
David Black
Christophe Bourseiller
Musa Budeiri
Sebastian Budgen
Paul Burnham
Pat Carmody
Glyn Carver
Joseph Choonara
Neil Cobbett
Candace Cohn
Werner Cohn
Geoff Collier
Richard Condon
Dave Crouch
Aleksa Djilas
Wilfried Dubois
Andy Durgan
Samuel Farber
Paul Flewers
Michael Foot (†)
Chris Ford
Daniel Gaido
Panos Garganas
Pete Gillard
Pete Glatter (†)
Paul Hampton
Dave Harker
Mike Haynes
Ron Heisler
Christian Hogsbjerg
Charlie Hore
Richard Horton
Sandy Irvine

Mike Jones
Ishay Landa
William Lefevre
Petra Lubitz
Wolfgang Lubitz
Dave Lyddon
Moshé Machover
Alasdair MacIntyre
Jimmy McCallum
John McIlroy
Owen Miller
James Monaghan
John Mullen
Annie Nehmad
Sandy Nicoll
Joanne Norbury
Einde O'Callaghan
Tom O'Lincoln
Akiva Orr
David Paenson
Mike Pearn
John Plant
Dragan Plavšić
Dave Renton
John Rudge
Tim Sanders
Susi Scheller
Richard Seymour
Mark Steel
Marion Tarbuck
Robert Taylor
Reiner Tosstorff
Noel Tracy
Air Vice-Marshal Andrew
   Vallance
Michel Warshawski
Leon Yudkin

Libraries

I have visited or consulted the following libraries, and thank the staff for their assistance:

Bibliothèque de documentation internationale contemporaine (Paris)

Bibliothèque Nationale (Paris)

British Library (including Colindale Newspaper Library and Sound Archive)

Centre d'Études et de Recherches sur les Mouvements Trotskyste et Révolutionnaires Internationaux (Paris)

International Institute of Social History (Amsterdam)

The Jewish National and University Library (Jerusalem)

Labour Party Archives, People's History Museum (Manchester)

London Library

Marx Memorial Library

Modern Records Centre, University of Warwick

National Archives

Special Collections, Senate House Library (London)

TUC Collections, London Metropolitan University

Wayne State University Archives of Labour and Urban Affairs (Detroit)

The Women's Library (London)

I am grateful to Stan Newens for allowing me to consult documents in his private archives.

Chris Bambery, Colin Barker, Alex Callinicos, John Charlton, Joseph Choonara, Donny Gluckstein, Gareth Jenkins and Chanie Rosenberg read the manuscript and made valuable comments. Thanks too to Sally Campbell and everyone at Bookmarks for their work on the production of the book.

Finally thanks to Danny Birchall for ensuring that my technical ineptitude did not have even more disastrous results.

Abbreviations

AEU	Amalgamated Engineering Union
ANL	Anti Nazi League
AO	Avanguardia Operaia
ASTMS	Association of Scientific, Technical and Managerial Staffs
AUEW	Amalgamated Union of Engineering Workers
BLSA	British Library Sound Archive
BNP	British National Party
BT	British Telecom
CAST	Cartoon Archetypical Slogan Theatre
CC	Central Committee
CCP	Chinese Communist Party
CID	Criminal Investigation Department
CLP	Constituency Labour Party
CND	Campaign for Nuclear Disarmament
CP	Communist Party
CPGB	Communist Party of Great Britain
CPSA	Civil and Public Services Association
DHSS	Department of Health and Social Security
DSS	Department of Social Security
EC	Executive Committee
EEC	European Economic Community
ENV	North-West London gearbox factory (from the French "En V", a reference to V-shaped cylinder layout)
GLC	Greater London Council
ICI	Imperial Chemical Industries
IEC	International Executive Committee
ILP	Independent Labour Party
IMG	International Marxist Group
IRA	Irish Republican Army
IS	International Socialists
ISL	Independent Socialist League (US)
ISO	International Socialist Organization (US)

ISUS	International Socialists of the United States
IWC	Institute for Workers' Control
JSSC	Joint Stop Stewards Committee
KAPD	Communist Workers Party of Germany
KGB	Committee for State Security (USSR)
KPO	Communist Party Opposition (Germany)
LCDTU	Liaison Committee for the Defence of Trade Unions
LSE	London School of Economics
MFA	Armed Forces Movement
MI5	Directorate of Military Intelligence, Section 5 (UK)
MK	Company making electrical accessories (from Multy Kontact spring grip socket)
MRC	Modern Records Centre (University of Warwick)
NA	National Archives
NALGO	National and Local Government Officers Association
NALSO	National Association of Labour Student Organisations
NATFHE	National Association of Teachers in Further and Higher Education
NC	National Committee
NCLC	National Council of Labour Colleges
NEC	National Executive Committee
NF	National Front
NGA	National Graphical Association
NLF	National Liberation Front (Vietnam)
NLR	*New Left Review*
NUM	National Union of Mineworkers
NUPE	National Union of Public Employees
NUT	National Union of Teachers
PAWS	Palestinian Arab Workers' Society
PCP	Palestine Communist Party
PD	People's Democracy (Ireland)
POEU	Post Office Engineering Union
POUM	Workers Party of Marxist Unity (Spain)
PRP	Proletarian Revolutionary Party – Revolutionary Brigades (Portugal)
R&F	Rank and File
RAR	Rock Against Racism
RCL	Revolutionary Communist League (Palestine)
RCP	Revolutionary Communist Party (Britain)

RILU	Red International of Labour Unions
RSDLP/ RSDRP	Russian Social-Democratic Labour Party
RSL	Revolutionary Socialist League
RUC	Royal Ulster Constabulary
SAG	Socialist Workers Group (Germany)
SAP	Socialist Workers Party (Germany)
SDP	Social Democratic Party (Germany)
SDS	Socialist German Student Union
SLL	Socialist Labour League
SLP	Socialist Labour Party
SOAS	School of Oriental and African Studies (London)
SPD	Social Democratic Party of Germany
SPG	Special Patrol Group
SPGB	Socialist Party of Great Britain
SRG	Socialist Review Group
SSDC	Shop Stewards Defence Committee
SWP	Socialist Workers Party (US from 1937, Britain from 1977)
TGWU	Transport and General Workers Union
TU	Trade Union
TUC	Trades Union Congress
ULR	*Universities and Left Review*
VSC	Vietnam Solidarity Campaign
WRP	Workers Revolutionary Party
YS	Young Socialists

Key dates

1917	March: Tsarism overthrown in Russia.
1917	20 May: Tony Cliff (Ygael Gluckstein) born.
1917	2 November: Balfour Declaration.
1917	7 November: Bolshevik Revolution in Russia.
1922	11 September: British Mandate proclaimed in Palestine.
1928	January: Trotsky exiled.
1933	30 January: Hitler takes power in Germany.
1933	Cliff joins Marxist Circles.
1934	February: Workers' rising against fascism in Vienna.
1936-39	Cliff student at Hebrew University of Jerusalem.
1936-39	Arab nationalist uprising in Palestine.
1938	Cliff's first contact with *New International* and US Trotskyists.
1938	3 September: Foundation of Fourth International.
1938	October-November: Cliff's first articles in *New International* under name "L Rock".
1939	3 September: Outbreak of Second World War.
1939	September: Cliff arrested and jailed.
1940-42	[?] Founding of RCL.
1945	February: Cliff marries Chanie Rosenberg.
1945	27 July: Formation of Attlee Labour government in UK.
1945	December: First part of "The Middle East at the Crossroads" (first use of name Cliff).
1946	25 September: Cliff arrives in Britain.
1947	September: Cliff expelled from Britain, moves to Ireland.
1948	February: Stalinists take power in Czechoslovakia.
1948	April: Second World Congress of Fourth International.
1948	14 May: Foundation of state of Israel.
1948	June: Cliff completes *The Nature of Stalinist Russia*.
1949	4-6 June: Dissolution of RCP.
1949	1 October: Mao comes to power in China.
1950	25 June: Outbreak of Korean War.
1950	30 September/1 October: First meeting of SRG.

1952	Cliff returns to London.
1952	*Stalin's Satellites in Europe.*
1953	5 March: Death of Stalin.
1954	January: Mike Kidron becomes active in SRG.
1955	*Stalinist Russia: A Marxist Analysis.*
1956	25 February: Khrushchev's "secret" speech.
1956	October-November: Hungarian Revolution and Anglo-French invasion of Egypt.
1957	*Mao's China.*
1958	4-7 April: First CND march – London to Aldermaston.
1959	January: Cuban Revolution.
1959	*Rosa Luxemburg.*
1960	February: Labour Party launches Young Socialists.
1960	April: Founding of journal *International Socialism.*
1960	3 October: Labour Party conference votes for unilateral nuclear disarmament.
1961	Launching of *Industrial Worker*, subsequently *Labour Worker*.
1962	22-28 October: Cuban missile crisis.
1962	December: SRG becomes IS group.
1963	January-June: Sino-Soviet dispute in the open.
1963	May: Paul Foot becomes editor of *Labour Worker*.
1964	15 October: Election of Wilson Labour government.
1965	January: *Labour Worker* appears twice monthly.
1966	16 January: Founding of London Industrial Shop Stewards Defence Committee.
1966	May: *Incomes Policy, Legislation and Shop Stewards* (with Colin Barker).
1966	16 May: Mao launches Cultural Revolution in China.
1966	May-July: National seafarers' strike.
1967	13 March: Student occupation starts at LSE.
1967	5 June: Start of Six-Day War in Middle East.
1968	30 January: Tet Offensive in Vietnam begins.
1968	20 April: Powell anti-immigrant speech.
1968	May-June: General strike in France.
1968	June: *Labour Worker* becomes *Socialist Worker*.
1968	August: *France: The Struggle Goes On* (with Ian Birchall).
1968	20 August: Russia invades Czechoslovakia.
1968	7 September: *Socialist Worker* becomes weekly.

1968	27 October: 100,000 on Vietnam demonstration in London.
1968	30 November: IS adopts democratic centralist constitution.
1969	August: British troops take responsibility for "law and order" in Northern Ireland.
1970	March: *The Employers' Offensive*.
1970	18 June: Tory government elected – Heath becomes prime minister.
1972	January-February: Miners' strike.
1972	21-26 July: Jailing of five dockers in Pentonville.
1973	September: Right-wing coup in Chile.
1973	October: Middle East war leads to oil crisis – end of post-war boom.
1973	March: IS begins to form factory branches.
1974	5 March: Labour government formed following miners' strike.
1974	30 March: First R&F conference.
1974	25 April: Portugal – army overthrows Caetano.
1975	January: *The Crisis: Social Contract or Socialism?*
1975-79	*Lenin* (4 volumes).
1975	1 July: Social Contract Phase Two – Labour government introduces wage controls.
1975	September: *Portugal at the Crossroads*.
1975	December: IS Opposition excluded.
1976	28 February-20 March: Right to Work march from Manchester to London.
1976	4 November: Walsall by-election.
1977	1 January: IS becomes SWP.
1977	13 August: Lewisham anti National Front demonstration.
1978	30 April: First ANL Carnival.
1978	19 August: Cliff becomes editor of *Socialist Worker*.
1979	23 April: Blair Peach killed by police at Southall.
1979	3 May: Tories win election – Thatcher becomes prime minister.
1979	10-14 November: SWP conference accepts "downturn" analysis.
1980	January-April: Steel strike.
1981	Tony Benn campaigns for deputy leadership of Labour Party.

1982	April-June: Falklands War.
1982	17 July: Closing of *Women's Voice*.
1984	*Class Struggle and Women's Liberation*.
1984-85	Miners' strike.
1986	*Marxism and Trade Union Struggle* (with Donny Gluckstein).
1988	*The Labour Party: A Marxist History* (with Donny Gluckstein).
1989-93	*Trotsky* (4 volumes).
1989	10 November: Fall of Berlin Wall.
1990	31 March: Poll tax riot.
1991	January-February: Gulf War.
1991	December: Dissolution of USSR.
1992	October: Large demonstrations against Tory pit closures.
1994	21 July: Blair becomes leader of Labour Party.
1995	April: Labour Party drops Clause Four.
1997	1 May: Election of Labour government under Blair.
1998	May: Suharto overthrown in Indonesia.
1998	September: "Revolution and Counter-Revolution: Lessons for Indonesia".
1999	*Trotskyism after Trotsky*.
1999	Cliff seriously ill – major heart operation.
1999	November: Seattle demonstrations mark start of anti-capitalist movement.
2000	9 April: Cliff dies.
2000	*Marxism at the Millennium*.

A note on sources

There is no single archive containing material from the SWP and its predecessors. The fullest relevant collections are in the Modern Records Centre at the University of Warwick (this contains Cliff's own papers and the papers of, among others, Ken Tarbuck and Steve Jefferys) and the Special Collections at Senate House Library in London, which include the Richardson Collection (incorporating the papers of Jim Higgins) and the Will Fancy Papers. Where internal documents have no archive reference, they are quoted from my own private collection. In due course I or my heirs will deposit these in a public archive. Internal documents are referred to by the titles on the documents themselves; numbering, dating and titling were totally inconsistent. In quoting, especially from typewritten material, I have corrected obvious misprints and added missing or illegible words in square brackets.

The most frequently mentioned archives are indicated as follows:

MRC   Modern Records Centre (University of Warwick)
Rich. Richardson Collection
Fancy Will Fancy Papers
NA   National Archives
BLSA British Library Sound Archive

Wherever possible I have given references to the first publication of items. Many of Cliff's writings were reissued several times, and full details will be found in the bibliography. I have given online references only in those cases where I was unable to trace a printed original.

However, a considerable amount of the material referred to is available online, and many archives are being constantly added to. I would refer readers in particular to the Marxist Internet Archive http://www.marxists.org/archive/index.htm which contains an extensive selection of Cliff's writings at http://www.marxists.org/

archive/cliff/index.htm. Much material from the first series of *International Socialism* is available at http://www.marxists.org/history/etol/newspape/isj/index.html, http://www.marxists.org/history/etol/newspape/isj/index2.html and http://www.marxists.org/history/etol/newspape/isj/index3.html, while material from the second series of *International Socialism* and from *Socialist Review* is at http://www.socialistreviewindex.org.uk/. Many other items cited can be found quite rapidly through Google.

In quoting from papers and magazines I have frequently not given page references, since the items can be easily located, and page references are not relevant to those consulting the material online.

There have been two series of *Socialist Review*: the first began in 1950 and terminated in 1962; the second runs from 1978 to the present. (For a while the second series was renamed *Socialist Worker Review*, but numbering was consecutive.) Likewise there have been two series of *International Socialism*, the first running (regularly) from 1960 to 1978, the second, in book format, from 1978 to the present. In both cases the two series can easily be distinguished by the year of publication.

A full list of those interviewed is given in the Acknowledgements. I hope these recordings can eventually be made available to other researchers. I refer to interviewees by their surnames throughout. Some of those interviewed have been known to me personally over 40 years and more; others I have met only in the context of researching this book. Since I did not want to create the impression of first- and second-class witnesses, I decided to standardise the form. The only exception is Chanie, who was always known as such to comrades, just as Cliff was almost always Cliff and not Tony.

IHB

About the Author

Ian Birchall is a longstanding member of the Socialist Workers Party.

The Socialist Workers Party is linked to an international network of organisations. For further information go to www.swp.org.uk/international.php

Contents

Introduction   i

Part One: The Making of a Revolutionary

1   1917-31: The Fateful Question   2
2   1931-46: From Palestine to Israel   18
3   1946-50: In a Strange Land   85
4   1950-60: The Loneliness of the Long Distance Perspective   128

Part Two: From Theory to Practice

5   1960-64: Second Youth   194
6   1964-67: Hard Labour   245
7   1968: Year of Wonders   282
8   1969-74: Years of Hope   306
9   1974-79: Moving On Up – With Complications   356

Part Three: Building for the Future

10   1979-84: Enforced Retreat   440
11   1984-89: Digging Deep   475
12   1989-97: Excited About the Future   508
13   1997-2000: Still Fighting   534
14   Conclusion   553

Bibliography of Cliff's works   560
Notes   604
Index   649

Introduction

Who was Tony Cliff, and why does he deserve such a long biography? In many ways Cliff falls outside established categories. He was a Marxist theoretician, but never held an academic post. He was a political activist, yet never even dreamt of trying to enter parliament. He was a professional revolutionary in the largely non-revolutionary years after 1945.

Yet it would be wrong to dismiss him as an obscure figure, marginal to the political mainstream. For those who are deeply unhappy about the way in which that mainstream is flowing, Cliff remains a pertinent and perceptive critic. He provides an important example of how Marxism can be developed to challenge and criticise modern society.

Perhaps Cliff's best-known contribution to Marxism was his theory of state capitalism applied to the so-called socialist regimes in Russia, China and Eastern Europe.[1] He also wrote substantial biographies of Lenin and Trotsky, a couple of handbooks for trade union activists that made some impact in their time, two volumes on the history of the British labour movement, and commentaries on the French general strike of 1968 and the Portuguese Revolution of 1975.

Cliff was always concerned to translate theory into practice. In 1950 he helped found the Socialist Review Group (SRG), which became the International Socialists (IS) and then the Socialist Workers Party (SWP). While originally minuscule, the organisation came to occupy a significant part of the space to the left of the Labour Party in British politics, and eventually to rival and then replace the Communist Party. Its role in building the Anti Nazi League (ANL) and later the Stop the War Coalition gave it a place in British political life. For 50 years until his death in 2000 Cliff gave day-by-day attention to the strategy and tactics of the organisation and the education of its members.

Beyond this, he was one of the unforgettable personalities of the British left. His sense of humour, his brilliant exploitation of imperfect English, his charm, warmth and generosity, his peculiar single-mindedness which could on occasion become ruthlessness (in the interests of the organisation, never to his personal advantage), all meant that he exerted a powerful influence on many who crossed his path. Time and again in preparing this book I have met people who still remember how Cliff encouraged and inspired them 30, 40 or 50 years earlier.

As a Marxist thinker Cliff was, he acknowledged, a "revisionist".[2] The term is often used as an insult, but unless Marxism is constantly revised to fit an ever-changing world, it becomes sterile. In the aftermath of the Second World War, Cliff became aware that the analyses provided by Marxism, not only in its distorted Stalinist version, but even in the highly perceptive writings of such anti-Stalinists as Trotsky, did not correspond to reality. As he used to say, the post-war Trotskyists were like people trying to find their way around the Paris Metro with a map of the London Tube. All Cliff's work reveals an effort to remain true to the fundamentals of Marxism while showing the willingness to look reality in the face and understand what has changed. His method provides a model for those trying to use Marxism as a tool of critical analysis.

Cliff was formed in the Trotskyist tradition and always identified with it, but he had nothing to do with that peculiar contradiction in terms known as "orthodox Trotskyism". The Trotsky who developed the theory of permanent revolution, who wrote on culture in post-revolutionary Russia and who elaborated strategies to fight fascism was not an "orthodox" thinker, but one who was striving to apply the essentials of Marxism to unforeseen realities. Cliff attempted to follow his example.

Cliff was not simply a theoretician. He had a remarkable ability to draw people around him and to win lifelong commitment. A great many people, from a range of social backgrounds, had their lives transformed by their encounter with Cliff. I have tried to trace a few examples of this in highly diverse individuals. When I have interviewed people about Cliff they have often made criticisms but they almost invariably expressed admiration and respect. Cliff had a remarkable ability to communicate with and influence those from a different generation and a totally different culture to his own. This cannot be explained simply by charisma, though Cliff was a remarkable, if unorthodox, public speaker. Nor was the loyalty he inspired in any way akin to that of a cult or sect. He made no concessions to the lifestyle of those he influenced. The only explanation lies in the content of the politics he put across.

I have therefore attempted not simply to trace the development of Cliff's political ideas, but to re-create at least some part of the impact he had on those around him. Yet in a sense this aspiration is doomed to failure. Words on paper can never re-create a living human being like Cliff.

In writing this book I have various audiences in mind. First and most important are the new generation of activists – some in the SWP, others active in various sections of the anti-capitalist movement. They are the people who will play a crucial role in the movement for social change over the coming half-century. They did not know Cliff, or only got a glimpse of him in his last few years. But Cliff's life and work has something to offer them, and I hope to give them a sense of what he was.

Secondly there are those who are, or were, active in or around the IS and the SWP. These are people who knew Cliff well, and value what he meant to them. Yet parts of Cliff's life would be unknown to them, as they were to me until I started to research this book. I hope to give a more fully rounded picture of a remarkable individual.

And thirdly there are readers not particularly sympathetic to Cliff or the SWP, but who are interested in the history of the socialist movement. The story of Cliff's life is also the story of the socialist left in the second half of the 20th century, and I hope this study may enhance the understanding of the troubled age he lived in.

At first sight biography seems alien to the socialist method. Socialist historians reject the "great leaders" approach in favour of mass action and social forces. Yet in the period since the Russian Revolution biography has made a surprising comeback. Trotsky wrote a powerful autobiography, Isaac Deutscher studied the Russian Revolution through biographies of Trotsky and Stalin which helped to form the understanding of a generation, Pierre Broué wrote a massive biography of Trotsky, and Jean-Jacques Marie has written major studies of Stalin, Lenin and Trotsky.[3]

The events of the Russian Revolution and its aftermath have raised for all socialists the difficult and complex problem of the role of the individual in history. The question of how individuals become socialist and how they remain such, is of great significance.

Cliff himself devoted several years to his biographies of Lenin and Trotsky because he wanted new generations to understand their experience and achievements, and apply them to the future tasks of the socialist movement. While Cliff lived in times that were less heroic, his life too holds important lessons.

What I have written is essentially a political biography. I have tried to trace the evolution of Cliff's thought and his responses to events. I have not concerned myself much with his "private life", if indeed that term can be used of someone as single-minded as Cliff. But I have tried to show Cliff as a human being, with human emotions and human failings. Cliff was not just a political thinker and activist, but a unique individual. Marx wrote, "Truth is general... My property is the *form*, which is my spiritual individuality. *Le style c'est l'homme* [Style is the man]".[4] I have tried to show not only what Cliff did, but how he did it.

There is little solid material on the first 18 or so years of his life. Those who knew him at that time are now gone, and Cliff himself rarely spoke of his early years – one feels that he regarded the time before he became a revolutionary as wasted. I have tried in the opening chapter to address the question of why a committed revolutionary emerged from such an unlikely background in the heart of middle class Zionism, but my account is necessarily speculative.

Cliff's life was bound up with the organisation he helped to build. I doubt if a single day passed over 50 years when he was not thinking of the problems of the organisation. Yet I have written a biography and not the history of the SWP and its predecessors.[*] The two overlap considerably but not completely. Where Cliff was not personally involved in an aspect of the organisation's activity, I have dealt with it lightly or not at all; this should not be taken to imply that I consider these activities insignificant.

Internal disputes in the organisation present a particular problem. Anyone who has been through such disputes knows that they can arouse strong feelings and are long remembered. For some readers the accounts of such disagreements will be the most controversial parts of the book. To those not involved the same disputes

---

[*] Many years ago I wrote a short pamphlet called "The Smallest Mass Party in the World" (London, 1981), which traced briefly the history of the SWP up to 1979. This has been much maligned, though Cliff was quite complimentary about it in his autobiography (T Cliff, *A World to Win*, London, 2000, p236). I stand by the positions expressed in it, though a full account would require much additional detail and documentation.

may appear obscure and trivial.

I have not dwelt on the detail of such disputes, though some reference is essential to show how Cliff operated. In particular I have tried to draw out the main issues in some of the arguments which may be of more general interest. For example the major debates in the 1970s were around such questions as what was the audience for revolutionary ideas at a particular time, or what a socialist newspaper ought to look like.

There is an additional complication. I personally was involved in several of these disputes. Sometimes I was on Cliff's side, sometimes I disagreed with him. More generally, I have to make clear my own place in the narrative. I knew Tony Cliff for 37 years, and I can say with certainty that he was the most remarkable person I ever met. I first encountered him when I was a postgraduate student in 1963. He changed my life utterly. In his novel *Birth of Our Power* Victor Serge describes Chernyshevsky's exile to Siberia. A voice comments, "Wouldn't he have lost a good deal more had he ended up an academician?"[5] Likewise, but for Cliff I might have ended up a pure academic – instead of writing this book I might be writing on the semiotics of La Fontaine's *Fables*.

I was enormously influenced by Cliff. I served on committees with him, was joint editor of *Labour Worker* with him for six months, and wrote a little book jointly with him. I was for a time one of his chauffeurs and got the kind of confidences that drivers get before and after meetings. During his final illness, when he was writing his autobiography, he would phone me at 8am to enquire if I had internal "byooletins" for 1973. (Despite over 50 years in the British Trotskyist movement, Cliff never mastered the pronunciation of one of the commonest words in Trotskyist discourse.) I remain committed to the overall politics of the SWP. However, since 1974 I have been a rank and file member of the organisation, and my perceptions of events and disputes sometimes differ from those of comrades who served on leading committees, several of whom have given me valuable interviews.

I am aware that Cliff would probably disapprove of the work I am doing. When I was working on his papers in his home after his death, I felt myself under the scrutiny of Chanie's wonderfully realistic sculpture of him, and I could imagine him saying, "Stop wasting your time and go to a picket line."

These factors might seem to be positive disqualifications. Am I too close to write such a book? For I have set out to write a serious biography, not a memoir. My admiration for Cliff and my 40-plus-year membership of the SWP are not matters that can be denied or concealed – readers have a right to know where I stand and to make their own judgements on the basis of the information I present. Any claim I make may legitimately be questioned on the grounds that "He would say that, wouldn't he?" But partisanship does not obviate the need for objectivity.

Anyone in my position has to take seriously the points made by Trotsky in his Preface to *The History of the Russian Revolution*. He argues that objectivity and partisanship are not incompatible, but that the historian must make a particular effort to ensure objectivity:

> This work will not rely in any degree upon personal recollections… The author speaks of himself, in so far as that is demanded by the course of events, in the third person… However, the fact that the author did participate in the struggle naturally makes easier his understanding, not only of the psychology of the forces in action, both individual and collective, but also of the inner connection of events. This advantage will give positive results only if one condition is observed: that he does not rely upon the testimony of his own memory either in trivial details or in important matters, either in questions of fact or questions of motive and mood.[6]

I hope I have achieved the balance of partisanship and objectivity required in an honest history. I have provided sources so that the reader may check the evidence independently. I have tried to present the positions of Cliff's opponents without distortion. There is no point producing a caricature of one's adversaries in order to claim an easy victory.

If I did not believe that Cliff's life and work had a considerable positive value, I would not have undertaken the substantial amount of work required to write this book. But I also have a respect for historical truth and for detailed accuracy. One of the last things Cliff said to me before he died was "Ian, you are a bloody pedantic bastard". He may not have meant it as a compliment, but I took it as one.

I shall not please everyone. I cannot present all the documents in full without making an already long book into an impossibly extended one. I am obliged to quote or summarise, but in so doing I lay myself open to charges of selectivity, misrepresentation and quoting out of context. All I can do is assure readers that I have written in good faith. Some will not believe me.

In one respect I have deliberately decided not to follow the approach laid down by Trotsky in the passage above. My own part in Cliff's story is a small one, and can be dealt with in two or three paragraphs. But I have a great many memories of him. I have drawn frequently on the written and oral recollections of others, and it would be absurd to cite other people's memories but refuse to rely on my own. I cite my own recollections where appropriate, confirming them by other people's memories where possible, but if not, clearly labelling them as author's recollections.

I have done this in particular in footnotes. (I have varied Trotsky's practice by referring to myself in the third person in the text, but in the first person in footnotes.) Such notes generally add colour and anecdotal detail to the narrative, rather than making substantive political points. At no point do I base a political defence of Cliff, or any significant claim about his political position, purely on my personal recollection.*

At a conference of the IS in the late 1960s it was resolved that since there were many new members, all speakers should introduce themselves by name and branch. Cliff was attached to a branch in the Angel Islington area, and when he came to give his report he proclaimed himself "Tony Cliff the Angel".

Cliff was not an angel; he could be dishonest and unscrupulous in argument, he sometimes badly misjudged situations, and he was on occasion a shockingly bad judge of character, making into stars comrades who would fade within a short space of time. But angels do not build revolutionary parties and it would be irresponsible to suggest that they do.

I have been repeatedly urged by those who knew Cliff to portray him "warts and all". Yet I have done so with misgivings. I am well aware that if I recount Cliff's errors they will be ripped out of context to discredit him and the organisation he built. This is Catch-22; if I made no criticisms I would be accused by the self-same

---

* In a very few cases I have omitted the source in order to protect the privacy of a third party. These all relate to minor points.

people of sycophancy and hagiography.

Yet I had to take that risk. I have written what I believe to be true. If history is not truthful, it will build nothing. I believe Cliff's merits far outweigh his defects – if I did not I would never have undertaken this task. But the defects also need to be understood. I am too old – and too cynical – to write hagiography. Cliff's real achievements were sufficiently great for there to be no need to attribute to him virtues he did not have.

In one of his finest lectures, a few years before he died, Cliff expressed his hatred of hagiography in the socialist tradition: "The worst thing in the world is hagiography. To come and say Engels knew everything, that he was always right – that makes me absolutely sick".[7] I hope I have written in that spirit.

I have attempted to draw on all available sources in writing this book. The first and most important is Cliff's own writings. I have compiled a (necessarily incomplete) bibliography of Cliff's work, including some 20 volumes and some hundreds of pamphlets, articles, reviews, letters and interviews. Some of his early writings from Palestine are probably lost for good, but more material may come to light.[*] If it does it will be added to the already excellent selection of his work on the Marxist Internet Archive.[†] There are tapes of some of his meetings.[‡]

I have followed Cliff's example in his studies of Lenin and Trotsky, and have allowed Cliff to speak in his own voice, with quite lengthy quotations from his writings, especially those that are not easily available.

Cliff did not take much care of his papers. After his death I sorted through the material that had been simply pushed into a cupboard at his home. I found the manuscript of a book that had been simply abandoned in the 1960s, but otherwise there were few revelations.[8] Cliff rarely wrote letters; the telephone was his main means of communication. If the recordings of his telephone calls made by British

---

[*] Certainly there is more to be said on Cliff's early years and the origins of Palestinian Trotskyism. I was hindered in pursuing the matter further by both the absence of documents and my own ignorance of Hebrew.
[†] All those interested in Cliff's work must be grateful to Einde O'Callaghan and others for the work they have done in building up this archive.
[‡] There are recordings of some of his meetings at http://www.resistancemp3.org.uk/. Cliff's Marxism meetings from 1992 onwards are in the BLSA, C 797.

security[9] survive, they may one day provide valuable material for historians.

In his last year, Cliff worked on an autobiography, *A World to Win*, published just after his death. It was a remarkable document, showing Cliff's own assessment of his achievements, and intended as a testament addressed to his organisation. As biography it was less than adequate. Cliff was seriously ill when he wrote it, and was unable to consult all the relevant documentation. Moreover, while he analysed his own role in the development of the organisation, he often underestimated the contributions of other comrades and, in particular, the significance of his own interaction with those comrades.

I have used the recollections of those who knew Cliff at various stages in his life. I have tracked down around ten people who knew Cliff in Palestine, and there are many more who knew him more recently. I have interviewed over a hundred people and have obtained many precious details and insights. This material is clearly labelled in the endnotes.

Yet this information has to be handled carefully. I am profoundly suspicious of the current fashion for oral history. It is my belief, based on both observation and introspection, that most people's presentation of their memories is selective and sometimes inaccurate.

Many of the generalisations I make in the course of the narrative are based on comments made by those I interviewed. However, I remain convinced that written evidence should always have priority. If Cliff published an article arguing X, while a comrade recalls that at the time he was arguing Y, then as far as I am concerned X is the position Cliff held (or at least is the position he wished the world to believe he held, which is perhaps as far as any historian can go). I may cite the comrade's testimony about Y, but it can never be used to challenge the validity of X. The basic line of argument about the coherence, consistency and development of Cliff's thought is based on published material.

The years I have spent on writing this book have been rewarding ones for me. I knew when I started that Cliff was a remarkable and fascinating individual, but only as I explored the subject in greater depth did I realise just how remarkable he was. I am not a historian by training, and have never previously written a biography. I have had to grapple with questions of method and I am grateful for the assistance of other historians, notably my good friends in the

London Socialist Historians Group and on the editorial board of *Revolutionary History*.

In my own work, this book follows two other studies, of Babeuf and Sartre.[10] They are an oddly assorted trio – the autodidact from Picardy, the Parisian intellectual and the professional revolutionary from Hackney. Yet socialism has a rich and varied history, and if it is to revive in the 21st century then it will draw on many different sources. In Cliff's words, "ideas are like a river and a river is formed from lots of streams".[11]

I could not have written this book without assistance from many, many people, inside and outside the SWP. I include a list of those who gave me interviews or sent written communications, but beyond that I have to thank many more who have given me information, suggested sources to be followed up, made illuminating comments or simply (and quite justifiably) told me to hurry up.

I have been struck by the fact that some of those I have contacted have been keen to help me, even though they had no particular sympathy for Cliff or the politics of the SWP. I can only attribute this to a recognition of Cliff's significance and a wish to see an adequate record of his life and work. I hope I have at least partly met their expectations.

I have spoken about Cliff at the SWP's annual Marxism event, to the London Socialist Historians Group, and at conferences organised by *Historical Materialism* and the British Sociological Association Theory Study Group. My thanks to all who participated in the discussions.

All errors are entirely my own responsibility. It is intended to set up a website which will contain a section devoted to Cliff's biography, where we will note any corrections and additional information brought to our attention. Details will be given at www.bookmarksbookshop.co.uk

Apologies to those who gave me information or suggested leads I might follow up, and who find I have not taken up their points. The book is probably already overlong, and I had to impose a limit somewhere.

Finally a few regrets and acknowledgements.

I first broached the idea of writing the book in a conversation with Paul Foot, and he sent me a wonderful letter of encouragement when I was still uncertain whether I could take on the job. I bitterly regret not having collected his memories of Cliff before his appalling sudden death.

Ross Pritchard, Duncan Hallas, Jim Higgins and Michael Kidron all died before I embarked on the book, and so I was unable to draw on their memories. Pete Glatter, who gave me great encouragement, died before it was finished. Al Richardson, who knew more about British Trotskyism than anyone else, offered me his help but died before I could tap his brains. I would have disagreed with him, but I would have learnt a great deal in so doing. I had an interview with Frank Henderson arranged for the day after the stroke that led to his death some months later.

Like all his friends, I was deeply shocked by the sudden death of Chris Harman in 2009. Chris had served with Cliff on leading committees of the IS/SWP over four decades, and I was looking forward to the critical comments on my biography which he was uniquely qualified to make.

My greatest debt, however, is to Chanie Rosenberg, Cliff's tireless companion for 54 years. Without her not only this book, but its subject matter, would have been utterly inconceivable. I dedicate it to her.

Ian Birchall
December 2010

PART ONE
THE MAKING OF A REVOLUTIONARY

1
1917-31
The Fateful Question*

May 1917. The First World War raged on. For nearly three years one soldier had died every 15 seconds. But in Britain the longest strike movement of the war, involving 200,000 engineering workers, was taking place. Throughout May the French army was shaken by a wave of mutinies. In Russia there was an uneasy balance – "dual power" – between the Provisional Government which had replaced the Tsar and the grassroots organisation of workers' soviets. Lenin worked tirelessly to convince the Bolshevik Party of the new possibilities open to it, and prepared to join forces with his old adversary Trotsky. General Sir Edmund Allenby was transferred from France to Egypt, and put in charge of British troops who later that year would capture Jerusalem. Chaim Weizmann and other Zionists vigorously pursued their demand that Palestine should become a Jewish national home; their efforts were rewarded later that year with the Balfour Declaration. An old world was dying; a new one was being born.

The war in Palestine meant constant movement for a Jewish couple of Russian origin, Akiva and Esther Gluckstein. In 1915 they were travelling northwards to Damascus when their third child, Chaim, was born. In 1917 they were moving south again, and came to the village of Zikhron Yaakov, in the vicinity of Haifa. Here lived Dr Hillel Yaffe, a leading Zionist and a medical man committed to the eradication of malaria. He was married to a relative of the Gluaksteins, who offered them accommodation in the village.[1] There, on 20 May 1917, Esther gave birth to her fourth and last child, Ygael,[2] later to be better known as Tony Cliff.

---

* I am most grateful to Moshé Machover for reading the first draft of the two chapters on Palestine and correcting a number of errors. Any remaining mistakes are entirely my responsibility.

Zikhron Yaakov had been founded in the later 19th century by Baron Edmond de Rothschild, of the French branch of the famous Jewish banking family. Rothschild was a pioneer Zionist, and the colony at Samarin was renamed Zikhron Yaakov in honour of his father, the Baron James de Rothschild ("Zikhron Yaakov" means Memory of James). Such colonies were meant to encourage Jewish settlement in Palestine with an ethos appropriate to the emergent Jewish society. The baron promoted an asceticism which anticipated that of the kibbutzim. At the same time he asserted his own control, wishing his officials to decide which colonists should be allowed to marry. The original purpose of the colony was vine-growing, producing high-quality wine for export. Soon, however, it expanded to include sheep and goat rearing, and arable crops.[3] The colony was thus the product of capitalist finance and of Zionism. But it would give birth to one of the most implacable opponents of both Zionism and capitalism.

Zikhron Yaakov was no more than a village, but it grew as a result of economic success. As Simon Schama describes it:

> Its population had gone over the 1,000 mark in 1898 but as the number of colonists' households was only 125, the majority of the residual 500 were employees, tradesmen, and swarms of hangers-on... The result was that what might be called the ancillary services boomed – cafés, taverns, boarding houses – with colonists subletting their own quarters to outsiders.[4]

A recent Israeli writer, Hillel Halkin, has tried to reconstruct Zikhron Yaakov on the eve of the First World War:

> It boasted three streets; nearly one hundred buildings (including a hospital, a bank, and a first sea-view villa, built by a wealthy Jewish couple from England); running water; a stagecoach service to Haifa and Jaffa; one automobile owner; two licensed bottlers of seltzer water; and one thousand inhabitants divided into six categories – colonists, ICA [Israelite Colonisation Association] officials, independent professionals and artisans, Second Aliyah laborers, Yemenites, and Arab help quartered in the farmyards. It was the second-largest Jewish village in Palestine and it took pride in being called by its sister colonies, with a mixture of mockery and envy, the "little Paris" of the East.[5]

The Glucksteins were a relatively prosperous family who had arrived in Palestine from Russia in 1902. Akiva Gluckstein was born in 1881 and his wife, Esther Voyseisky, in 1886.⁶ They had come at the very beginning of the wave of Russian settlers who arrived early in the 20th century. These immigrants, sometimes called "Muscovites", were in many ways different from the earlier generation of colonists encouraged by Rothschild. They often professed radical, even revolutionary ideas, yet were more committed to the creation of an all-Jewish economy. Whereas the earlier settlers had found Arab workers cheaper and more productive, the new settlers insisted that employing Jewish labour was a matter of principle.⁷

Akiva's elder brother was a banker of decidedly right-wing views. He himself was in the construction industry. His business partner at one time was Yehiel Mikhail Weizmann (known as "Chilik"), the youngest brother of the first president of Israel, Chaim Weizmann (not, as Cliff wrongly claims in his autobiography, Chaim Weizmann himself⁸). It is hard to establish when this partnership was formed, or how long it lasted. Weizmann settled in Palestine in 1914, after studying agriculture in Berlin. From 1920 to 1928 he was assistant director of the Palestine Government Department of Agriculture and Fisheries. So his partnership with Gluckstein must have belonged to the period of the world war or its immediate aftermath.⁹ In particular Gluckstein was involved in the construction of sections of the Hedjaz Railway, built to take Muslim pilgrims from Turkey to Mecca and Medina. The railways played a major strategic role in the First World War, and were an important contribution to the modernisation of Palestine.¹⁰ *

Gluckstein was a handsome, jovial man, greatly liked by those who knew him.¹¹ He was a born actor; he loved to tell jokes, and though he constantly told the same stories, he always varied them. In later life he joined a Yiddish theatre company and travelled around the country with it. He retained his curiosity and zest for life into old age. In the 1960s he travelled to Europe to see his son and grandchildren. He spoke no English, but had recently learnt French to prepare for the journey.¹² Certainly he belonged to a cosmopolitan tradition; many years later Cliff recalled, "My father used to say to me, 'I can sign my name in nine languages.' That was true. 'But the cheques always bounce'."¹³

---

* As Ygael wrote later, "The railways which were constructed for imperialist purposes, at the same time facilitate the development of Arab trade and commerce." *Middle East – drafts of book*, Tony Cliff Archive, Modern Records Centre (MRC), University of Warwick, MSS.459/box 6, p86.

Esther, his wife, was a bookish woman; she read Russian, Hebrew, French and German. Even in hospital during her final illness she was always reading.[14] She also had a lively sense of humour. Physically Ygael resembled his mother, a small woman. He was a sickly child, and for a long time had to be carried around in his mother's arms. He didn't start to talk until he was about four years old[15] – something he amply made up for in later years.* He acquired his mother's intellectual interests, while his father's humour and theatricality later appeared in his speaking style.

The new child had two brothers and a sister. His elder brother, Shimon, became a veterinary surgeon; the younger, Chaim, had more literary interests and was for a time a revolutionary. The sister, Alexandra (Alenka), was a talented musician; she went to Vienna to study music, but found the standards too exacting; in the 1940s she suffered acute depression and committed suicide.[16] Though in later life Ygael was surrounded by people with artistic gifts (including his wife and younger son), his own artistic side stayed underdeveloped.

As a well-respected prosperous commercial family, the Glucksteins were at the heart of the Jewish community. As well as the Weizmanns, David Ben-Gurion (later the first prime minister of Israel) was a family friend. The Jewish community was still small – at the time of Ygael's birth there were some 60,000 Jews in Palestine, and more than half a million Arabs. Many of the Jews were immigrants who had arrived since 1900. Ygael was one of the new generation of Palestine-born Jews – *sabras* as they were called after one of the native plants of Palestine, the edible cactus known as the "prickly pear".

How did the prickly pear embark on the hard road that would take him to revolutionary socialism? Why did one born at the heart of the Zionist project break with it so dramatically? One explanation that can be rejected is that his revolutionary ideas originated in family tensions. It has often been argued that revolutionary hostility to

---

* Cliff's later skills as a speaker may have been the result of overcompensation, just as Sartre showed that the great French novelist Flaubert was regarded as the "family idiot" because he couldn't read when he was seven.

capitalism results from a displacement of anger directed at the parents.* In Ygael's case, such analyses do not fit the facts. He was a well-loved, even spoilt child who stayed on good terms with his parents. They were not enthusiastic about his conversion to revolutionary socialism – he later recorded that when he was first arrested his father consoled his mother by predicting that he would soon grow out of it!17 But it never caused conflict or division in the family. When his father visited England many years later, it must have been a shock to find his son so deeply involved in revolutionary politics, but he showed no antagonism, simply evading any political discussion.18

Ygael's happy childhood was reflected in his later family life. Cliff was one of the most single-minded people it is possible to imagine – but if there was one thing to which he was devoted other than revolutionary socialism, it was his wife and four children. If Ygael grew to hate the capitalist system, that hatred was not a deflected hostility to his family. He hated the system because, as his life's work showed, there was good reason to hate it.

While the young Ygael struggled to walk and speak, monumental changes were taking place. In the Glucksteins' homeland Lenin and the Bolsheviks were establishing a new society based on working class rule. The Ottoman Empire had collapsed and Palestine had fallen into the hands of the British, who continued to occupy it under the terms of a League of Nations Mandate (1922). Seven thousand British troops plus civil servants, teachers and police were brought into the country to establish a colonial regime.

From the outset this was based on deception and duplicity. Contradictory promises were made to Jews and Arabs. There were many divisions in the British ruling class and in the British administration in Palestine. Among those responsible for British policy there were both pro-Zionists and anti-Semites (some, like Winston

---

* E.g. "Since the feelings are often extremely powerful and directed originally at quite inappropriate objects, such as mothers, fathers, and siblings, most individuals feel the need to displace these feelings, to direct them upon other and safer targets… The party offers a hostile person an attractive self-image of one who understands the cause of evils and the effective ways of combating them." (G Almond, *The Appeals of Communism*, Princeton NJ, 1965, p268) Cliff's comrade of the 1960s Jim Higgins provided a neat refutation of such theories: "Now, big though my father is, I have never considered him to be in the same class for violence as a capitalist state (not even a small one) and for a soft option I will take on my old Dad any day." (*International Socialism* 28, 1967, p30)

Churchill, were both).[19] But while British policy went through many turns and inconsistencies, it was clear that British imperialism would opt for Zionism.

Ygael was too young to be aware of any of this. But the adults who surrounded him must have followed the course of events with keen interest. Doubtless the words "revolution", "communism" and "empire", perhaps even the names of Lenin and Trotsky, reached his infant ears. Probably too he heard the name "London", a faraway city where decisions about the future of Palestine were being taken. No one in the family can have imagined that he would spend the last 50 years of his life in one of the poorer areas of the imperial capital.

Ygael's first educational experience was in a Montessori kindergarten. The Montessori method was at the height of its worldwide popularity, and was used in a number of Jewish kindergartens in the 1920s.[20] It was based on the premise that children are capable of self-directed learning and that they learn through discovery. It assumed that children will want to find out what they can, if they can be helped to do so. They learn through play and take a natural pleasure in learning to master their environment. Real learning involves the ability to do things for oneself, not the passive reception of a body of knowledge.

Hence the teacher was not the centre of the class, imposing passive obedience (which Montessori believed was not a good training for a democratic society), but rather allowed the children to get on with their activities while observing and intervening from the periphery.[21] The notion that real learning was learning through practice would stay with Ygael for the rest of his life. Many years later he paid tribute to the value of the Montessori approach.[22]

Not everything went smoothly at kindergarten. Once he was made to sing a Hebrew song. Everybody laughed at him, and he remembered this with resentment, insulted that he was being treated like a child when already he thought he was something more. He had already acquired a sense of self-belief.[23]

Then came elementary school. While the British authorities provided such education as was available for Arabs, the Jewish community financed its own schools. Education in the ethos of the hoped-for Jewish national home was an essential part of the Zionist project. The basic syllabus in the Jewish elementary schools stressed

Hebrew language and literature, biblical studies, Jewish history, the geography of the Middle East and the practical aspects of mathematics and nature study.[24]

Though Ygael's intellectual curiosity was being developed, his bodily health was less satisfactory. He suffered from rheumatism, and when he was around five years old he was taken to Vienna to see a specialist, who apparently provided successful advice.[25] For a child of his age, it must have been an enormous adventure. We do not know with whom he travelled, or how – whether by train through Turkey and Eastern Europe, or by boat across the Mediterranean and Black Sea and then up the Danube by steamer. At that time either route would have been a formidable journey. For one whose childhood had been spent in the area around Haifa, it meant discovering that the world was much vaster and more diverse than he could have imagined.

Vienna was a modern European city; its two million inhabitants made it the second largest city between Paris and Moscow. Arthur Koestler, who made the journey in the opposite direction, from Vienna to Haifa, at around the same time, described the culture shock he felt on arriving in Palestine:

> I walked through the Arab bazaars...amidst the gay, colourful and yet unhurried jostle of camels laden with durra flour, short-legged donkeys mounted by long-legged Biblical elders, and Arab urchins in garments resembling striped nightshirts.[26]

Ygael must have felt a similar shock. He spent his time in Vienna with members of the large Jewish community, which constituted over 10 percent of the city's population. His mother's sister lived in Vienna,[27] and he probably met various relatives. Eric Hobsbawm, an exact contemporary of Ygael who grew up in Vienna, writes that for Jews there was an assumption that "the family was a network stretching across countries and oceans, that shifting between countries was a normal part of life".[28] Ygael had relatives – uncles, aunts, cousins – in Russia, the US, Holland and Poland.

Austria was a rapidly changing society. The Austro-Hungarian Empire had collapsed at the end of the war; Vienna was now the capital of a modest republic rather than a large empire. Strikes and mutinies had led to the creation in Vienna and other cities of workers' councils, which lasted for some years and exercised considerable influence. The Social Democrats formed part of the first post-war coalition government; they were particularly strong in Vienna, often known as "red Vienna". Amid severe shortages and rapid inflation, there seemed a real possibility that Austria, like Hungary and Bavaria, could see revolutionary developments. There were violent working class demonstrations in 1921, and in June 1922, around the time of Ygael's visit, there was a three-day general strike "which cut off Vienna from the outside world, except by car or air".[29] Vienna was also a centre of Marxist theory and debate. It is not wholly fanciful to imagine that Ygael may have caught a glimpse of the Marxist philosopher Georg Lukács, exiled from the defeated Hungarian Soviet Republic,* or of Karl Popper, later one of the most prestigious enemies of Marxism.

Communism never took off in Austria, though it caused some anxiety in conservative circles. But Austria lived in the shadow of its larger neighbour Germany, a country on the brink of revolution. In 1922 or early 1923, the probable date of Ygael's visit to Vienna, many in the Communist International expected revolution in Germany within months. Victor Serge wrote in 1922, "What is certain is that the status quo in Germany – and in Austria, where the problem is exactly the same – *cannot last*".[30]

Such matters were undoubtedly much discussed by the adults with whom Ygael spent his time in Vienna. He could have grasped no more than a tiny part of the meaning of what he heard, but words like "revolution" and "communism" may have lodged in his brain. Years later, in February 1934, a general strike against Engelbert Dollfuss's attempt to crush the left led to fierce fighting in Vienna. Though unsuccessful, the Austrian workers showed an inspiring resistance to the rising tide of fascism. Ygael must have remembered the streets of Vienna and the people he had met there.[31]

The next turning point for Ygael came in the mid-1920s. In the wake of failed revolution in Europe, anti-Semitism grew, and many European Jews felt they would be safer in Palestine. The Jewish community grew rapidly and the building industry, which played a decisive role in the economy, experienced a considerable boom. Then boom gave way to slump and in 1926 a major economic crisis

---

* In the 1960s Cliff encouraged the translation of works from Lukács's Vienna period – *History and Class Consciousness* and *Lenin* – though he was ultimately thwarted by copyright problems.

affected the construction industry. Unemployment rose rapidly, building projects were halted and there were many bankruptcies.[32]

While the exact circumstances are not known, somewhere around this time the Gluckstein family firm went bankrupt. A hitherto prosperous family found itself in straitened circumstances. For Ygael, now aged about ten and beginning to have a grasp of how the world worked, this must have been a terrible shock. An orderly universe in which his own place seemed reasonably secure had become frighteningly chaotic. He later recalled that he was terribly upset when the bailiffs came to remove the family silverware; this was the "spark" which began the process that made him a revolutionary.[33] He did not become a socialist overnight, but the experience left him with questions; he would pursue the answers for years to come. Because he had enjoyed a comfortable childhood, Ygael now felt responsible and anxious not to be a burden on his parents in their misfortune.[34] Before he discovered politics there were moments of blind rebellion: he once systematically smashed all the windows of his school;[35] on another occasion he urinated down a flight of stairs.[36]

Another result of the economic problems of the mid-1920s was a crisis in the school system. Teachers' salaries fell into arrears and there were teachers' strikes, so Ygael may have observed industrial action at first hand.[37]

The family misfortunes did not disrupt Ygael's education. He was at school in Haifa; when he was aged around 11 the family moved to Jerusalem. His elder brother Chaim was left in Haifa at a boarding school, but Ygael, still a sickly child, was taken to Jerusalem, where he studied at the highly academic Gymnasium (comparable to an English grammar school), at the time the only prestigious high school in Jerusalem.

Ygael became a talented linguist. Elements of Russian (vital for his later work on state capitalism) were acquired at home, but the schools stressed Hebrew as part of the drive to make it the official language of the aspirant state. He became fairly fluent in English too, competent enough to translate books in the 1930s. Some French and German were acquired along the way, though of Arabic he had no more than a smattering. He had an impressive range of linguistic knowledge – he was once invited to be a translator for the Fourth International – yet in a sense he never had a native language. The content of what he had to say overspilled the limits of any particular language. Perhaps this explains why, although he spent the last 50 years of his life in England, he never totally mastered English – his speech was full of mispronounced words, ungrammatical structures and confused versions of common figures of speech. These, indeed, were part of his peculiar individual style as an orator, and he may have cultivated the effect, yet his discourse was that of a genuine internationalist, unwilling to be trapped within the bounds of a particular national language.

Ygael inherited from his mother a love of books which never left him; throughout his life he read voraciously. In adult life that reading was relentlessly focused on the political problems he faced. Only in his early years did he read widely. He tells in his autobiography that in his youth he read "literary classics unceasingly".[38] Occasionally traces of this reading surfaced in his later work, with passing references to Shakespeare, Goethe or Dickens. (John Rees, editor of the SWP's theoretical journal *International Socialism* in the 1990s, records that Cliff repeatedly quoted Mephistopheles' advice to the student in Goethe's *Faust*: "All theory is grey…but green is the tree of life"; however, Cliff may have taken the quotation from Lenin.[39]) More surprising were Cliff's occasional allusions to the delightful dialectical paradoxes of Lewis Carroll's Alice books.[40]

In 1994 Cliff responded to a questionnaire from the *New Statesman and Society* which asked him to name works of literature that he "would most like everyone to…read".[41] Since it is unlikely that Cliff had read much poetry or many novels in the preceding 60 years, these may give some clues to his youthful enthusiasms. It is no surprise to find him naming *Old Goriot* by Balzac, from whom Engels wrote that he had learnt more of French post-revolutionary society "than from all the professed historians, economists and statisticians of the period together".[42]

The poets he named were Pushkin and Heine. Pushkin, the great Russian Romantic poet and literary radical, had been admired by Lenin and Trotsky. But the writer closest in spirit to Ygael was Heine. Heine, friend of Karl Marx, had many qualities which must have appealed to him – a powerful sense of irony, based on the recognition of both the power and the limits of Romantic idealism, the ability to be funny and serious at the same time, and a keen sense of materialist analysis, shown in his comparison of Kant and Robespierre:

> Both, however, exhibit in the highest degree the typical features of the small-town philistine. Nature intended them to weigh out coffee and sugar, but fate meant them to weigh other things, and placed a king on one set of scales and a God on the other.[43]

Heine had given a voice to one of the first working class revolts, that of the Silesian weavers in 1844:

> The shuttle flies, the loom creaks loud,
> Night and day we weave your shroud –
> Old Germany, at your shroud we sit,
> We're weaving a threefold curse in it,
> We're weaving, we're weaving.[44]

Heine's deep scepticism towards revealed authority, whether Christian or Judaic, must have appealed to Ygael. Grappling with his own attachment to Zionism, Ygael would have appreciated Heine's ambivalence to his Jewishness:

> A hospital for sick and needy Jews,
> For those poor mortals who are trebly wretched,
> With three great evil maladies afflicted:
> With poverty and pain and Jewishness.[45] *

We should not overstate the importance of Ygael's early reading. His greatest admirer would scarcely claim that Cliff's work had literary merit. He pursued the argument in hand relentlessly, with no thought for literary embellishment. He did not share the cultural breadth of a Marx or a Trotsky. In his biography of Trotsky the chapter on Trotsky and culture was written by Chanie Rosenberg.[46]

Yet his early reading did leave him with a humanistic awareness that, however urgent the political tasks might be, the totality of human experience went beyond the limits of the purely political. As he put it in his scathing critique of the voluntarism of the Cultural Revolution, the Maoist view "demands a rejection of the validity of any artistic creation or tradition taken from the past, as these reflect the limitations of the individual. In "socialist realism" there are no

---

* In quoting Heine's verse I have used the translations made by Hal Draper, a leading US Marxist whose rejection of the "orthodoxies" of Trotskyism in many ways paralleled Cliff's.

Hamlets or Othellos – in the real world they are all too common".[47]

At the age of 13 Ygael decided to change his name – to Ygal. Since vowels are not normally written in Hebrew, this was not a major change. It was based on a grammatical point. Ygael means "he will be redeemed", whereas Ygal means "he will redeem"; it was a switch from passive to active,[48] an assertion that he was one who acted rather than being acted upon. There was also a well-known Zionist hero called Ygael in the time before the First World War, a member of an armed horseback Zionist self-defence organisation which defended kibbutzim against Arabs. It is possible that Ygael had been named after this rather violent character, but that he decided to dissociate himself.

In his autobiography Cliff claims that the decision related to a character from the Hebrew scriptures. Moses sent 12 men to spy out the promised land of Canaan. Ten of them (including one called Igal) were opposed to invading Canaan. These ten were punished and all died of the plague.[49] In retrospect, then, his choice of name might seem like an act of revolt by identification with one who had defied God, and even as a refusal of Zionism. His sister-in-law, Naomi Gunn, is sceptical. The Glucksteins were not particularly religious, though they respected traditions and celebrated Jewish holidays. The young Ygael, who probably did not attend the synagogue, might not even have known of this obscure figure, who gets just one mention in the Bible. Moreover, it was not really an act of rebellion – Ygal's parents were pleased and proud at the initiative their bright son had taken. Everyone accepted the change and in Palestine he was always known as Ygal.* He was thus a trend-setter – in Israel today the form Ygael is unknown, while Ygal is a common forename.

Ygal's character was formed by a mixture of conditioning, experience and ideas. But the most important question about his childhood is how he began to separate himself from the Zionist orthodoxy within which he was brought up. It was to be a journey of several years from being a loyal Zionist to being one of Zionism's sternest critics. That political evolution will be the subject of the

---

* In the 1950s Cliff published two books under the name Ygael Gluckstein. This was still his name on some official papers and this form is common in references to him after he came to Britain.

next chapter. But every evolution has a starting point.

Zionism itself was still evolving during this period. What had been the dream of exiles and settlers was forged into the ideology of a new nation-state. In the process the more progressive trends in Zionism were eradicated.

To begin with Zionism did not necessarily imply a hostility to the Arab population of Palestine. The current of thought represented by Zionists like Judah Magnes advocated a policy of cooperation with the Arabs. One such Zionist who had a considerable influence on the young Ygal was his uncle Chaim Kalvarisky. Kalvarisky was a land agent of the Israelite Colonisation Association, which took over the management of the colonies in Palestine established by Rothschild, including Zikhron Yaakov.

Kalvarisky was a contradictory figure. Simon Schama writes, "Kalvarisky was vain, headstrong, reckless and emotional. That he was a rogue no one, least of all Kalvarisky, seemed to contest." He was, moreover, a committed Zionist, who favoured unlimited Jewish immigration into Palestine; it was his job to acquire as much land as possible for Jewish settlement.

But unlike many Zionists Kalvarisky believed, in a way that may have seemed to have some plausibility in the 1920s, that the success of the Zionist project could be achieved through Arab-Jewish cooperation. In 1919 he drew up a manifesto which declared that Palestine was the homeland of Jews, Muslims and Christians, who should all be citizens with equal rights. He advocated associated development in health, economic and cultural activities and in education.[50] He established a school in which Jews and Arabs studied side by side. Though Kalvarisky's approach to the Arabs was often marked by manipulation and bribery,[51] the young Ygal saw his uncle as a man obsessed with Arab-Jewish cooperation.[52]

Zionism was a mass of contradictions. Human society is beset with contradictions, and through them history progresses. Most human beings learn to live with them, to get on with their lives and not ask too many difficult questions. But there have always been a few exceptional thinkers who refuse to accept the contradictions, and spend their entire lives pursuing a resolution to them.

The young Franz Kafka was so shocked by the fact that his father did not obey the rules of conduct which he tried to impose on his family that at the age of 36 he wrote an anguished letter of complaint to his parent:

> Bones mustn't be cracked with the teeth, but you could. Vinegar must not be sipped noisily, but you could...you, the man who was so tremendously the measure of all things for me, yourself did not keep the commandments you imposed on me.[53]

The eight-year-old Jean-Paul Sartre was appalled when his grandfather burst out laughing at the tears of his teacher, saying she was too ugly to get married; he saw the whole moral system he had been brought up to believe in as a sham, realising that "the order of the world concealed an intolerable disorder".[54]

Something similar happened with Ygal. Within the universe of Zionism there were three deep contradictions which he struggled to understand and overcome.

The first of these was inherent in the history of Judaism. Religious scholars see Judaism as the first great monotheist religion; the holy books are the story of how that religion developed from a tribal religion into a universal faith. Jehovah, originally the God of the Jews, became the God of all humanity. All nations were subject to the one God; at the same time the notion that the Jews were a "chosen people" was still deeply embedded in Judaism. Arthur Koestler, raised a Jew in Hungary, noted that the "traditionalist Jews...protested against racial discrimination, and affirmed in the same breath their racial superiority based on Jacob's covenant with God".[55]

Secondly, within the Jewish community, socialist ideas were widespread. Many of those who came to Palestine had previously been involved in socialist organisations. Leading Zionists often described themselves as socialists. Yet as the idea of a Jewish state became more tangible, the nationalist current within Zionism became dominant at the expense of socialist internationalism.

Finally, Zionism had been an ideology of the oppressed and persecuted. Founding Zionist Theodor Herzl had first formulated his ideas in the face of the wave of anti-Semitism which swept France at the time of the Dreyfus affair. As more Jews came to Palestine in the 1920s, Ygal must have heard many stories of the persecution and suffering undergone by Jews throughout Europe which had made them seek refuge in Palestine. Yet already the newly established Jewish community was taking on the role of persecutor, in particular denying employment to Arab workers.

So in Ygal's mind, Zionism became open to criticism precisely in the name of the best values he had learnt from the Jewish tradition. "If we believe in universal brotherhood," he must have wondered, "if we protest at persecution, then why do we not treat the Arabs as equals?" To Ygal this presented itself in the form of the simple question of why there were no Arab pupils in his school.[56]

As a child Ygal may well have played with Arab children. Haifa, where he lived some of the time, was a mixed town, and trust between the two communities had not completely broken down.* But though there may still have been contact on the streets, segregation in the schools was total. The languages of instruction were different; Hebrew for Jews and Arabic for Arabs.[57] To Ygal the segregated school system appeared an outrage against the principles of human equality. He acquired a deep hatred of racism which was to stay with him for the rest of his life.

To find an answer to that question of why there were no Arab pupils in his school would take Ygal on a long journey, both geographically and intellectually.

Ygal could not abandon his Jewishness in a world in which Jews remained the objects of persecution. Throughout his life Jewish mannerisms and above all Jewish humour were an essential part of his persona. Yet by renouncing Zionism he became part of a particular category of Jews, part of a tradition extending back to Spinoza, which Cliff's great contemporary and adversary Isaac Deutscher would call the "non-Jewish Jew":

> What then makes a Jew? Religion? I am an atheist. Jewish nationalism? I am an internationalist. In neither sense, therefore, am I a Jew. I am, however, a Jew by force of my unconditional solidarity with the persecuted and exterminated. I am a Jew because I feel the Jewish tragedy as my own tragedy; because I feel the pulse of Jewish history; because I should like to do all I can to assure the real, not spurious, security and self-respect of the Jews.[58]

Ygal's questions would take him far beyond Zionism into broader questions of the way human society is organised. One day he wrote a school essay in which he stated, "It is so sad there are no Arab kids

---

* As late as 1940 Jewish parents intervened to have Arab children excluded from an infants' playground financed by the Guggenheimer Foundation (T Segev, *One Palestine*, Complete, pp390-391).

in the school." His indignant teacher scrawled on it a word which Ygal must have heard, but which probably still had only a vague meaning for him – "Communist!" Many years later Cliff recorded his deep gratitude to that teacher who had pointed him towards his future.[59]

2

1931-46
From Palestine to Israel

Still an adolescent, Ygal had discovered the political commitment that was to shape his life. While his contemporaries were still grappling with their schoolwork and finding their first boyfriends and girlfriends, Ygal was already focusing on the problems that were to dominate his life – the question of what forces could change the world and how to organise to bring about that change.

This did not mean an instant break with Zionism. Loyalties to family, community and education would take a long time to erode. Many years later, when he wrote his study of Lenin, Cliff was scathing about the Stalinist historians who claimed that Lenin sprang to Marxist conclusions immediately after his brother's execution. Cliff dismissed this as an "insult" and "psychologically stupid", turning Lenin into "a freak – rigid, dry, dead, incapable of change".[1] He must have remembered his own youthful progress towards Marxism, the mistakes, hesitations and false starts, the bitter lessons of experience, the long days of study and the hours of passionate argument with comrades and opponents.

Arguably Lenin had an easier job than Ygal, who was now striving to understand the labyrinthine world of left politics in Palestine. Internationally the socialist movement had been split by the First World War and the Russian Revolution. On the one hand those who backed the Bolshevik Revolution were grouped in the Third, or Communist, International (or Comintern), while those who had refused to align with the Bolsheviks remained in the Second International, which contained various currents. As the Russian Revolution began to degenerate, a number of oppositional groups formed on the right and left fringes of the Comintern.

Jews active in left-wing politics were doubly threatened by Hitler's rise to power. Many took refuge in Palestine, ensuring that the debates and divisions of the European left were represented within the Jewish community. Some Jews had been active in organisations such as the Bund, which opposed Zionism. For many others there seemed no problem in combining Zionism and socialism, even Marxism. Zionism was not incompatible with support for post-revolutionary Russia – it was easy enough to believe that Russia was pursuing its road to socialism while the Jews of Palestine were following a different but parallel road through the creation of kibbutzim. Several radical socialist Zionist organisations existed, notably Hashomer Hatzair, which provided a first step towards revolutionary socialism for many radical young Jews in Europe and South Africa.

Ygal's teacher had marked him down as a "communist", but he did not join the Palestine Communist Party (PCP); "it was an underground party and I found no opportunity to join it".[2] In most parts of the world the pioneer Trotskyists of Ygal's generation emerged from splits and expulsions from the parties of the Comintern. In Palestine things were more complex.

The roots of communism in Palestine went back to the immediate aftermath of the Russian Revolution. In 1920 the Comintern convened the Congress of Eastern Peoples at Baku, on the borders of Europe and Asia, in order to encourage anti-imperialist movements in the Middle East and beyond.[3] Two of the three Comintern delegates, Zinoviev and Radek, were Jews,[4] and the Congress's manifesto implicitly called on Jews and Arabs to unite against British imperialism:

> What has England done to Palestine, where, at first, to please the Anglo-Jewish capitalists, she drove the Arabs from their lands in order to transfer these lands to the Jewish settlers, and then in order to provide an outlet for the discontent of the Arabs, she turned them against the very Jewish settlements she had established, sowing discord, hostility, and resentment among the various tribes, weakening both sides, in order to rule and govern herself?[5]

In 1920 the left wing of Poale Zion (the Socialist Labour Party of Palestine which had split into left and right sections in 1919), a Zionist socialist organisation, had sought affiliation to the Comintern. After extensive discussion of the conditions for affiliation, the Comintern ruled in 1922 that "the attempt to divert the Jewish working masses from the class struggle by propaganda in favour of large-scale Jewish settlement in Palestine is not only nationalist and petty-bourgeois, but counter-revolutionary in its effect", and declared "complete hostility" to Poale Zion. In January

1922 some of those who had broken with Left Poale Zion formed the PCP, with a membership of something over 100.[6]

Like other sections of the Comintern, the PCP went through the degeneration that accompanied the rise of Stalin and the pursuit of "socialism in one country". With the so-called "Third Period", initiated in 1928, the PCP made a sharp turn towards "Arabisation". The analysis was that Zionism was acting on behalf of British imperialism, while Arab nationalism was an anti-imperialist movement.[7]

In fact most of the PCP's cadres were Jewish. Not only were the Jewish members disconcerted by this turn; it was policy to replace them as soon as possible. In 1931 the Seventh Congress of the PCP resolved that in order to encourage peasant revolution in Palestine:

> The Communist Party must, in the first place, increase only those cadres of the revolutionary forces which could direct the peasant activities on the right road, the cadres of revolutionary Arab workers.[8]

Even if the young Ygal had found his way to the PCP, he would scarcely have been made welcome.

PCP policies were increasingly designed to alienate Jewish support. In accordance with "Third Period" doctrine the Jewish trade union was described as "the Nazi Histadrut".[9] When Hitler's accession to power in Germany increased the number of refugees coming to Palestine, the PCP backed the demands of the Arab national movement for a stop to immigration. On one occasion PCP members were involved with planting a bomb at a Histadrut-run workers' club. The PCP became increasingly isolated from the Jewish working class. In the late 1930s there is some evidence that it tried to remedy the situation by using different arguments in its Hebrew and Arabic publications.[10]

Many Jewish members resigned in protest at Arabisation,[11] in some cases doubtless reverting to Zionism. Of those who remained Communists, some, in particular recent immigrants, saw that the logic of their position was to leave Palestine as soon as possible, perhaps to fight in Spain, or to make their way to the "socialist motherland". In the words of one historian, the PCP became "a 'transit camp' on the way to the Soviet Union".[12] Many PCP leaders perished in Stalin's purges. Joseph Berger, the PCP's original secretary, spent more than 20 years as a political prisoner in Russia.[13]

Those Jews who remained were subject to increasingly heavy discipline; insubordinate branches were dissolved.[14] Originally the PCP had attempted to offer a more radical alternative to the Arab nationalist leaderships, but with the advent of the Popular Front in 1935 its strategy became to form a closer alliance with the leadership of the Arab national movement in Palestine.[15]

The PCP was scarcely a welcoming environment for an idealistic young *sabra*, and the young Ygal was fortunate that he never made contact with the party. How would he have ended up if he had become a Communist? Perhaps as a Stalinist *apparatchik* – nobody is born immune to corruption – more likely as a casualty of the Spanish war* or the Russian purges. Or perhaps he would have been excluded from the PCP as an alleged Trotskyist.

But in any case he would have spent a crucial period of his political development in the repressive structures of a Stalinist party, with little scope for independent thought. His adolescent exploration of ideas and activism would have enjoyed far less freedom. Ygal's path to revolution through left Zionism gave him a much greater opportunity to discover himself as an individual.

At the age of 14 Ygal joined Mapai (Mifleget Poalei Eretz Israel – The Party of the Workers of the Land of Israel). This was the successor of the right wing of Poale Zion; its leader was David Ben-Gurion, later to be the first prime minister of the state of Israel. This did not mean any break with the Zionist community – Mapai was a fervently Zionist party.

Already he was getting access to Marxist literature. The left wing of the Zionist socialist movement published works by Marx and Engels in Hebrew. Having no formal links with the Comintern it could be more eclectic in its approach to the communist tradition, publishing translations of Trotsky's *History of the Russian Revolution* and *My Life*.[16]

Ygal's voracious reading became ever more focused on political topics. At the age of 15, he read, in Hebrew, an abridged edition of Marx's *Capital* and Trotsky's *My Life*.[17] He later recalled how he had enjoyed the sections in Volume Three of *Capital* on the

---

* Some 500 Jews from Palestine fought in Spain – a large number from such a small population. See M Sugarman, *Against Fascism: Jews who Served in the Spanish Civil War*, London, 2000, pp2, 161-168.

"transformation problem" and differential rent, and how the mathematical aspect appealed to him.[18] As he began to discover Marxism, the reformist milieu of Mapai ceased to satisfy him. So, at the age of 16 he took the major step of joining the left-wing Zionist organisation called Mifleget Poale Zion Vehachugim Hamarksistim b'Eretz Israel (The Party of the Workers of Zion and the Marxist Circles of the Land of Israel),[19] the youth section of the left wing of Poale Zion.

He was recruited to the Marxist Circles in Haifa by Alon Talmi,* the son of Rabbi Binyamin of Brit Shalom (Peace League), who at that time was called Feldman.† The Marxist Circles were led by Abramovich and Yitzhaki, and the building worker Menahem Nadel, father of Baruch Nadel.[20]

The Israeli journalist Ygal Sarneh, who met Cliff in 1991, interviewed a few individuals who had known Ygal during his years in the Marxist Circles. While still a teenager he made an impression by his exceptional abilities. To Alon Talmi he was "a youth with an inner fire...a boy/old man who drew happiness not from the love life of youth but from complete dedication to the revolutionary cause. Intelligent girls were charmed by his sharpness."

He was already an impressive speaker. Yitzhak Moshaev recalled the meetings of the Marxist Circles: "In a small house in the backyard of the Ethiopian Church in Abyssinian Street, Ygal would come and speak and enchant everyone, a brilliant, riveting speaker – there in Jerusalem, where priests, black as coal, were coming and going".[21]

The Marxist Circles provided Ygal with an introduction to political activism. Here he became involved in forms of activity which would characterise the groups led by Cliff right up to the end of the century.

Firstly there was paper-selling. The Marxist Circles had a paper called *Bammifneh* (At the Turning Point). Ygal wrote for this, and was involved in its production and distribution. This was legal and sold openly on the streets. Hanna Ben Dov, one of Ygal's companions from this time, took part in such street sales.

Secondly there was strike support work. Cliff wrote his first strike

---

* Talmi dropped out of political activity and later pursued a successful career as a chemist.

† Binyamin advocated education for Arabs and Jewish-Arab intermarriage (T Segev, *One Palestine, Complete*, pp408-410).

leaflet in 1934.[22] At this time, despite the best efforts of the Zionists – and the Arab nationalists – there were frequent examples of Arab and Jewish workers coming together in mixed workplaces and even of attempts to build joint unions.[23] However, only in the relatively small public sector, such as the railways, was common workers' struggle possible. Left Poale Zion did have some success in organising Arab workers.[24]

Ygal's political understanding was developing rapidly. Because the Marxist Circles existed in the milieu of left Zionism rather than having an international affiliation to either Stalinism or social democracy, this development took place without clear organisational breaks.

Initially Ygal was drawn to a Stalinist position on international questions. Hitler's accession to power in 1933 must have been profoundly alarming to the Jewish population of Palestine, many of whom had friends and relatives in the territories ruled or threatened by Hitler. Ygal took a more optimistic position; he taunted members of the social democratic Mapai, saying, "Hitler finished you. Now it's the turn of us Communists".[25] This echoed the suicidal position of the German Communist Party which characterised social democrats as "social fascists". At least Ygal had the excuse of youth – he was still some months short of his sixteenth birthday – unlike the bureaucrats in Moscow and Berlin who initiated this insane line.

Soon Ygal understood how wrong he had been, and that realisation stayed with him for the rest of his life. If German Communists and Social Democrats had formed a united front, the Second World War and the Holocaust might have been averted. That experience does much to explain Cliff's lifelong hostility to Stalinism and his commitment to analysing the Stalinist phenomenon.

From his brief flirtation he learned that Stalinism was the product of defeat. Because workers elsewhere in the world had seen their own hopes and aspirations blocked, they transferred their allegiance to a supposed workers' paradise in Russia. "A defeated working class looked for a strong organisation to save it from the Nazi catastrophe. Stalinism became a religion".[26]

Cliff always scorned those who consoled themselves for their own weakness by glorifying victories in faraway countries. The enjoyment they took in the successes of others, he declared, was "vicarious". He never managed the pronunciation of the word, but his deployment of the concept was accurate.

In 1986, on the fiftieth anniversary of the Moscow Trials, Cliff contributed to a meeting addressed by the pioneer British Trotskyist Harry Wicks. He recalled the bleak days of the 1930s when, as fascism triumphed in Europe, the only hope seemed to lie in Russia; and how much more bleak things were for the tiny minority who saw that things had gone wrong in Russia too.[27]

Ygal's brief involvement with Stalinism had another important implication for his subsequent development. He soon realised the pernicious nature of Stalinism, but he did not believe that all followers of Stalinism were irredeemably corrupt. He had been there himself, and understood the grip Stalinism had on its followers. He never had any sympathy with the position sometimes found on the anti-Stalinist left that Stalinism was an alien force external to the workers' movement.

A crucial influence on Ygal's political development was news of resistance from around the world. The Vienna rising of February 1934 showed that workers could stand up to the challenge of fascism. After he learned of Mao Tse-tung's Long March of 1934-35, Ygal was for a time very enthusiastic about developments in China, believing it might lead a revival of the international revolutionary movement.[28]

In 1934 Ygal attended a Mapai meeting in Haifa in support of the Viennese workers. The speaker, Abba Khushi,* used a great deal of left rhetoric, invoking the memory of the Paris Commune, and ending with an appeal for "workers' unity". Ygal heckled him, shouting out the word "international". In the Palestinian context "international workers' unity" meant unity of Jewish and Arab workers, something which most Zionists could not accept. Khushi pointed at the heckler, and two stewards grabbed him while a third took hold of his finger and twisted it till it broke.†

Yet advocacy of Jewish-Arab unity, though a provocation to Zionists, was not yet in itself a break with Zionism. That would come only some years later, after considerable theoretical labour.

---

* In 1948 Khushi was the right-wing social democratic mayor of Haifa.

† Cliff himself later recounted various versions of this incident, but the account given here was confirmed by Alon Talmi in an interview with Ygal Sarneh. Talmi accompanied Ygal to the meeting, and had his coat torn by the Mapai stewards (Yarneh, "A Revolutionary Life", *International Socialism* 87 (Summer 2000), p142).

A less fruitful episode was Ygal's attempt actually to become one of the workers. In 1936 he worked for a year as a building worker, 12 hours a day, six days a week. He was permanently exhausted and had no time for political activity.[29] This was a formative experience for him. For the rest of his life Cliff never took full-time paid employment. He never achieved prosperity, but dedicated himself single-mindedly to life as a professional revolutionary.

Ygal's first girlfriend was a young woman called Beba. They came together when Ygal was 16, and the relationship lasted for six years. For Ygal romance could never be independent of politics – one of the first questions he asked her was, "Would you throw a bomb if necessary?"[30]

Activity in the Marxist Circles meant a new group of friends and comrades. One person who knew Ygal well in this period was Hanna Ben Dov, whom I interviewed in June 2005.* By 2005 she had moved a long way from her revolutionary youth, artistically and spiritually. Though her memory for political detail was often vague, there is no doubt of the impression that Ygal left on her.

Looking for adjectives to describe the young man, she found "passionate", "wilful", "fanatical", "extreme", and even "hysterical" and "violent" – though she hastened to add that the violence was not physical. What impressed her above all was his single-mindedness, his total commitment to the revolutionary cause. He was much admired by those who knew him – Hanna's sister used to call him "the Messiah". Others were a little frightened of his single-mindedness.

Yet this single-mindedness was balanced by Ygal's sense of humour. Hanna recalled the time when he lent her a book. When she returned it, he said so that all around could hear, "The amazing thing about this book is that not one page has been opened."

Ygal's determination in political matters was reflected in his personal relationships. He once arrived at Hanna's bedroom window at 3am and, finding her asleep, himself slept under a tree outside her house. When her parents remonstrated with him he

---

* I met her in her flat in the Latin Quarter of Paris, where she is now a well-known abstract painter. When I wrote to her asking for an interview, explaining that I was writing Cliff's biography because I considered him a remarkable man, I got a very moving note from her. She had not seen Cliff since 1946, and had not heard of his death, which had shocked her. She commented, "A remarkable man, a genius...and more."

responded that "this is between me and Hanna".

Yet in some ways Ygal met his match with Hanna. If he was single-minded in his political obsessions, she was at heart an artist, and although she was an active revolutionary for several years, her commitment to painting predominated. She remembered walking on the seashore with Ygal, while he made a long speech about some political question that was preoccupying him. She had caught sight of a fisherman in a light blue blouse silhouetted against the dark blue of the Mediterranean Sea, and she could think of nothing except what a picture could be made from these contrasting shades of blue. Later (doubtless to Ygal's extreme annoyance) she could not remember a single word he had said.

Ygal gave her little encouragement with her painting, dismissing it as a "petty-bourgeois occupation". But he was not a philistine. Although in later years Cliff took no interest in music, she remembered him listening to classical music. She recalled going to the theatre with him, and his comment that Shakespeare's strength was that he was always close to human instincts.

Ygal's main concern with Hanna, as later with so many of his followers, was to involve her in activity. He persuaded her to lecture to younger comrades. When she was still at school he got her to translate Lenin's *State and Revolution* from English into Hebrew. She was reluctant because English was one of her weakest school subjects due to her hostility to British imperialism. She was persuaded and spent a year on the task, greatly improving her English in the process.

Sixty years later Hanna believed that she and her comrades had been naive and credulous in a difficult and complex time, but at the same time she remembered the nice people she had known then. She had been sent to Egypt by the group to make contact with the Egyptian Trotskyists grouped around Georges Henein,[31] but had been struck by the "lightness" of the Egyptian group compared with the passion of the Palestinian comrades, and was "dumbfounded" at their superficiality in contrast with the comrades in Palestine who lived in danger and took things more seriously. For her it was a "beautiful, passionate period".[32]

Ygal got hold of some of Trotsky's writings on Germany, with their acute analysis of the need for the united front as the only way of stopping fascism. It is not known how he obtained these – perhaps from other supporters of Trotsky on the Palestinian left. The articles, showing Trotsky at his best in the application of a Marxist method to new phenomena, were an inspiration to Ygal. According to Hanna, he was the first among the members of the Marxist Circles to begin talking about Trotskyism, when many were beginning to have doubts about Russia.[33] A group of members of the Marxist Circles began to refer to themselves as Trotskyists, acting as an internal faction.[34]

Ygal had rid himself of Stalinism quite rapidly; the struggle to liberate himself from Zionism would take longer and be more painful. For members of the Marxist Circles and for the broader Zionist left, debates about events in Russia or Germany were abstract matters that could be considered reasonably dispassionately. Zionism affected the status and privileges of individuals as workers and as citizens; its adherents clung to it much more fiercely.

To develop as a Marxist in Palestine at this time was a more challenging task than that facing Marxists in Europe. A Marxist in Britain, France, Germany or Russia could look to a substantial native tradition of Marxism, with a wealth of analyses and debates; Marx, Engels, Kautsky, Plekhanov, Lenin and others had written at length about the history and development of their countries. Marxism in Palestine was largely the province of immigrants, who had learnt their Marxism elsewhere. For Marxists in the Middle East, there was no existing body of tradition and theoretical analysis. To develop a strategy for their own region they had to begin the task of theoretical analysis themselves.

This was no bad thing. Cliff's strength was that, while holding firm to the fundamentals of Marxism, he could develop new analyses of a changing reality. When the classical Marxists' work did not stand up to the test of reality, he criticised and discarded erroneous elements.

It is in this context that Ygal's earliest writings should be considered. What appears to be his first theoretical article was "The Present Agrarian Crisis in Egypt" (1935),[35] written for a Zionist journal concerned with the cooperative movement when he was just 18 years old. In his autobiography Cliff is rather deprecating about the article, claiming that it was written in a fortnight.[36] Perhaps so, and if it was, Ygal was already developing the powers of concentration and intellectual organisation he was to show in later life. Clearly it emerged from a process of thought extending over a much longer period.

The article contained only one passing reference to Palestine, and had nothing to say about Zionism, for or against. Ygal did not yet feel ready to take on that debate. Instead the whole article focused on Egypt, a country Ygal had never visited, but which, with some justification, he saw as the key to revolutionary prospects for the region.

Ygal began with a dense mass of statistical material and tables. He was anxious to show that his argument was not merely abstract Marxist assertion but founded in concrete, quantifiable reality. He placed Egyptian cotton production in the context of the current world economic crisis:

> Egyptian cotton, dearer than American, Indian or Chinese cotton, sustained itself for decades in the world market, despite its high price, thanks to its superior quality. Now, due to the fierce competition over shrunken world markets...Egyptian cotton has lost its comparative qualitative advantage, which used to give it inroads into the market.

This in turn had to be seen in terms of the strategy of British imperialism, which in Ygal's writings from this period consistently appears as the primary cause of the problems of the Middle East:

> A fundamental condition and means for freeing the Egyptian economy from the yoke of the crisis is a change in the crop structure of this economy. This trend, of diversifying crops and reducing the cotton-planted area, has met with fierce opposition on the part of the English government, which has managed by various means (financial, commercial, seizing control of transport, customs, etc.) to turn Egypt into a "hinterland" of the English textile industry, constituting an enormous cotton plantation. The English government is interested in a continual expansion of the planted area, because that keeps the price of cotton down, furthers the independence of the English textile industry of American cotton sources, and keeps the cotton stockpiles overfull for the eventuality of a world war.

He analysed the process of concentration of land ownership in the hands of the few, and the consequent exacerbation of class differentiation. While both large farms and very small farms were increasing in number, the intermediate classes of the Egyptian village were totally disintegrating.

He described the formation of a surplus rural population. In

Europe the process of industrialisation had meant that large parts of the surplus population were absorbed into the developing industry and trade; however:

> Egypt is a backward agrarian country, the industrialisation of which is very slow relative to the huge mass of people who are surplus and unneeded for agriculture, and so it cannot solve the problem of these inhabitants.

This led to the central point of his argument:

> The Egyptian bourgeoisie cannot assume any role of emancipation from feudal shackles because of the internal contradictions undermining the Egyptian capitalist regime itself. Abolition of Egypt's feudal class division would mean, given the decay of the Egyptian capitalist economy and the exacerbation of social conflicts within it, abolition of the class division of society as a whole. With the smashing of feudalism, the capitalist market would also be smashed; therefore the Egyptian bourgeoisie – notwithstanding its phraseology of liberation slogans – increasingly identifies its interests with feudalism and with the English government, and so would fight with all its might against any intensification of class conflicts, even within the feudal economy. Therefore, the central role in the liberation of the masses of peasantry in Egypt – a thorough agrarian reform along with the dissolution of the feudal economy – can only be performed by the proletariat, which, while struggling within the capitalist regime for its own liberation, liberates all the masses of oppressed toilers.

Here Ygal was using Trotsky's theory of permanent revolution. Trotsky had argued that in countries where capitalism developed later than it had done in Western Europe, the bourgeoisie would be unable to carry through a consistent revolution. Hence the working class, even if small, followed by the peasantry, would have to carry through the bourgeois revolution, and this would grow over into a socialist revolution. However, such a socialist revolution could not be completed within a single country, and could survive only if it spread internationally.

Ygal was now taking an analysis developed by Trotsky to explain the course of the Russian Revolution and applying it to the specific conditions of Egypt in the 1930s. His conclusions were overtly political, and while they were not particularly original, they stated themes which he would reiterate for over 60 years to come. First came the need for organisation, for a revolutionary leadership which could give direction to the spontaneous struggles of the masses:

> The appalling pauperisation of the masses of workers and peasants in Egypt and the exacerbation of class tensions are manifested very clearly in the spontaneous eruptions of the masses. The bitterness pent up in them erupts fruitlessly, as all these eruptions and insurrections are unplanned and are not guided by a proletarian leadership able to convert the destructive force of rebellion into the creative power of socialist construction.

Then came an affirmation of faith in the socialist future, the ultimate aim which gave meaning to all the struggles of the present:

> The agrarian crisis, born of the class crisis, has created the objective conditions for the abolition of classes [as well as] the famine and crisis they bring about.

The style of the article in the original Hebrew was rather inelegant, with overlong sentences and too many parenthetical clauses.[37] Cliff put content far above any demands of style.

The content, however, was impressive for one so young. Whether he received any guidance or assistance from more experienced comrades in the Marxist Circles can only be a matter of speculation. He grasped well the main features of Egyptian agriculture at the time – the growing inequality in land ownership, a deepening crisis as the increase in agriculturally productive land failed to match the increase in population, and chronic indebtedness among the fellahin. He was also right to point to the way the Egyptian bourgeoisie identified its interests with "feudalism". By the late 1930s and particularly during the 1940s the Wafd Party (the main nationalist organisation) came to be dominated by landowners. Since the Wafd was the main opposition to governments imposed by the king, this largely explains why several attempts at land reform failed.

What Ygal failed to predict was the impact that the coming war would have on the Egyptian economy. The economy did diversify, since local industrial production was stimulated by the demand to equip the British army. This may have soaked up some of the rural surplus population. The war also gave a boost to the Egyptianisation of industry, so by the mid-1940s the biggest and most modern textile mills were owned by Egyptians, not foreigners.[38]

Moreover, by describing Egypt as "a cotton-producing monoculture", Ygal raised the problem of monoculture in relation to imperialism and the world economy, a question that remains vital for many Third World countries to this day.[39]

On a much smaller scale, Ygal was following in the footsteps of Lenin's *The Development of Capitalism in Russia*, which stressed, not the numerical smallness of the Russian working class, but its developing historical potential. In seeing the Egyptian proletariat as the key to the revolutionary future, Ygal was right inasmuch as over the following half century the Egyptian working class would be the strongest and most militant in the Arab Middle East.

He was, however, wrong in his hopes for working class revolution in Egypt. Egypt was heading for revolution, but though strikes by workers played an important role in the process which led to the revolution of 1952, it was Nasser and the Free Officers, not the working class, who were the beneficiaries.[40] In 1935 Ygal was still striving to apply Trotsky's theory of permanent revolution; he had little inkling that permanent revolution could be "deflected" in as yet unimagined ways.

In the following year Ygal wrote an article in *Bammifneh* in which he argued that Zionism from a class standpoint brought blessings to the country and the Arab fellah. Ygal Sarneh reported that 30 years later this article was used by Professor Yehoshua Porat in debate with the by-then fiercely anti-Zionist Tony Cliff.[41]

Sarneh was right to claim that in 1936 Ygal was "still torn between Zionism and socialism". But he was also grappling with another problem, the Marxist analysis of the role of imperialism in undeveloped countries. There was no contradiction, for classical Marxism, between identifying the brutalities and crimes of imperialism, and seeing its role in modernising economies and creating a proletariat. Zionism might be the agent of imperialism, but it had helped bring modernisation to Palestine – for example, the railways built by Ygal's own father (although in Palestine, the Jewish and Arab economies were largely separate so the "positive" aspects of modernisation were less significant for the indigenous Arab sector).

The Marxist Circles gave the young Ygal far more scope to pursue his own ideas than he would have had within the confines of a Stalinist party. But as his political position became more coherent, he increasingly experienced difficulties with their politics.

The Marxist Circles were linked to the international organisation called the London Bureau (originally the International Labour Community), which had been initiated by the British Independent Labour Party (ILP) as a grouping of parties affiliated to neither the (social democratic) Labour and Socialist International nor the Communist International. Its main affiliates included the Workers Party of Marxist Unity (POUM) in Spain and the Socialist Workers Party (SAP) in Germany.

Trotskyists had to relate to the rather larger organisations of the London Bureau. In 1933 there were hopes of a fusion between the SAP and the German Trotskyists, although in the end this came to nothing.[42] As Stalin's regime in Russia became more blatantly counter-revolutionary, the ILP and other organisations of the London Bureau equivocated on the issue. The ILP was prepared neither to endorse the Moscow Trials* nor to support Trotsky's condemnation of them, preferring to call for "an impartial investigation".[43] When Mussolini invaded Abyssinia in 1935, the ILP leadership refused to support Abyssinia on the grounds that it was ruled by a "brutal Emperor".[44]

Organisations like those of the London Bureau are often described as "centrist". Frequently used as a term of abuse, the word does have a proper meaning. As Cliff argued many years later, such organisations are unstable:

> Centrism is always a political formation in motion – either to the left or the right, depending on the pressure of events. For a brief period (1932-33) events pushed the centrists to the left, and brought them into Trotsky's orbit. Subsequently the great weight of Stalinism, combined with the terrible defeats of the working class, drew them ineluctably back to the right.[45]

By the middle of the 1930s, the attitude of the Trotskyists towards the London Bureau was increasingly hostile. In July 1936 the International Conference for the Fourth International (part of the process of preparing what would become the Trotskyist Fourth International) issued a statement on the London Bureau which concluded:

---

* In the Moscow Trials (1936-38) Stalin's regime put many of the leading old Bolsheviks on trial on grotesquely implausible charges, found them guilty and executed them.

The direct duty of proletarian revolutionists is, therefore, the systematic and uncompromising exposure of the hesitations, equivocations, and hypocrisies of the London Bureau as the nearest and most immediate obstacle in the way of the further building of the Fourth International.[46]

The London Bureau proved unable to stand up to the pressure of events. In April 1939, shortly before the outbreak of the Second World War, it was disbanded. A Fourth International document of May 1940 dismissed it as "the international federation of centrist squeezed lemons".[47]

It is hard to know how far Ygal was aware of such arguments. But as he developed both as a theoretician and as an activist, the contradictions between Trotskyism and centrism must have become increasingly apparent. Events in Palestine served to clarify the situation further.

In 1936 Ygal became a student at the Hebrew University of Jerusalem. There is little record of his studies there, and it is reasonable to presume that he never allowed his academic commitments to interfere with his work as a revolutionary. In 1939 he was arrested just before his final examinations, and therefore never got a degree.[48]

In the year 1936 saw an Arab nationalist uprising against the extension of Jewish settlements in Palestine. A violent struggle continued until 1939. The leadership of the Arab revolt was extremely reactionary and attacked the Zionists in Palestine for their links with Communism. The Arab working class played little part in the revolt and the situation made unity between Arab and Jewish workers even more difficult. The revolt was crushed brutally by the British armed forces, which used executions, collective punishment, concentration camps and the chaining of prisoners. They were ably assisted by Zionist troops, notably the "Special Night Squads" (organised by a British intelligence officer, Orde Wingate) which were guilty of random killings and beatings in Arab villages.[49] Despite the protestations of the Arab leaders that their enemy was Zionism and that they were anxious to cooperate with British imperialism, the result of the revolt was to push the Zionists into closer alliance with the British occupiers.[50] The possibility of being both a revolutionary socialist and a Zionist, even a left, critical Zionist, became ever smaller. Ygal, indignant at the Zionist role, was being forced to choose sides.

By the spring of 1939 he was writing:

There is not today any internationalist force in Palestine: the Comintern people let themselves be taken in tow by the Arab feudal leaders, and the Socintern [Second International] and London Bureau people make up an integral part of the Zionist movement.[51]

This evolution of the London Bureau into the camp of Zionism was confirmed in early 1939 by a speech in the House of Commons by the ILP member of parliament John McGovern. He argued in pure imperialist terms that it was Britain's job to bring civilisation to the Arabs, and that the Jews had introduced the spirit of initiative into Palestine. He advocated unrestricted Jewish immigration into Palestine and the arming of the Jews to suppress the Arab revolt.[52]

For Ygal the crunch came in 1938. The ILP took a close interest in developments in Palestine, and two of the ILP's MPs, McGovern and Campbell Stephen, visited Palestine and addressed two public meetings. Stephen was a veteran of the ILP. He had formerly been a United Free Church minister; he "had a slow, dogmatic manner of speech that sorted well with his physical bulk. He scorned the social graces altogether".[53] He would cross Ygal's path again.

By now the lines were drawn between Ygal's Trotskyist grouping and the Marxist Circles. At the end of the first meeting, Ygal alone of those on the platform refused to stand for the Zionist anthem. At the following meeting a member of Ygal's group read out a statement opposing imperialism and Zionism. The leadership of the Marxist Circles avoided confrontation in the presence of the British MPs, but a few days later the group was expelled.[54] From now on Ygal, aged just 21, devoted himself to the task that would occupy the remaining 61 years of his life – the building of an openly revolutionary organisation.

It is impossible to say how big was the group that emerged from the Marxist Circles, but it can scarcely have reached double figures. In addition to Ygal there were Hanna Ben Dov, Gabriel Baer, Jacob Moshaev and Ygal's elder brother Chaim.[55] At around this time links were made with the Socialist Workers Party (SWP), the Trotskyist organisation in the US.

The initial contact was probably made with the monthly journal *New International*. This appeared spasmodically between 1934 and 1936, and was relaunched on a regular monthly basis at the beginning of 1938. While circulating primarily in the US, it was distributed abroad, especially in English-speaking countries such as Britain, Australia, Canada and South Africa. The back cover of the July 1938 issue carried an announcement that *New International* had "readers in 27 countries, in every continent of the world". Of the 27 listed, three were in the Middle East – Syria, Egypt and Palestine.

The next issue, in August, carried a feature called "At Home" giving details of the journal's circulation. This contained a letter from a "reader at the Hebrew University, Jerusalem":

> The people over here, workers and intelligentsia, have read THE NEW INTERNATIONAL with the greatest enthusiasm. The articles as well as the ideas, theoretical and tactical, have drawn the interest of many English-reading persons. Especially in these days, in which science and literature have become means in the hands of the bourgeoisie and their lackeys...in which Stalinism, the agent of Soviet bureaucracy and bourgeois cretinism, has become a yoke and a brake on revolutionary Marxist thought, it is most encouraging to see that there are yet in the international working class groups which boldly hold up the banner of revolutionary Marxist thought and struggle. We are especially glad that the problems of the colonies and the imperialist policy of the American and European bourgeoisie have found a considerable expression in THE NEW INTERNATIONAL.

It seems likely that Ygal was the author of this letter. He was at this time a student at the Hebrew University, and the date is close to that of his exclusion from the Marxist Circles. Moreover, Cliff later recounted that his first contact with the Fourth International had been with Martin Abern, business manager of *New International*.[56]

The September issue reported, "A group of Friends in Palestine have placed a bundle order for both THE NEW INTERNATIONAL and *Socialist Appeal* in Tel Aviv"* and the list of bookshops and other outlets where the *New International* could be obtained now included a Palestinian address for the first time – Pales. Press Co [presumably Palestine Press Company], 119 Allenby Street, Tel Aviv. By January 1939 there were three outlets in Palestine selling the *New International*, PO Boxes in Haifa and Jerusalem as well as the

---

* *Socialist Appeal* was the weekly paper of the American SWP from 1938 to 1941, when its name was changed to *The Militant*. The British paper of the same name was launched somewhat later. Though he was living in a British-ruled territory, Ygal's first contacts with the Fourth International were with the US and not Europe.

Tel Aviv address, and the business manager reported that the Haifa order had been increased by three. Ygal and his friends were working hard to increase their influence.

The group now began to receive Trotskyist literature and to be a part of the international movement.[57] Contact with the European International Secretariat was not made until after the end of the Second World War.[58] Whether the contacts with the Fourth International were made only after the exclusion from the Marxist Circles or whether they had been established earlier in anticipation of a split is impossible to say.

In September 1938 the Fourth International was founded. The exact status of the Palestinian group is unclear. In the minutes of the founding conference there is a membership report given by Pierre Naville. This stated that sections could be divided into three groups: (1) affiliated parties; (2) sympathetic parties and groups; (3) very small groups and contacts. It then listed groups in 18 countries, with memberships ranging from 2,500 in the US to 15 in Mexico. There followed a list of 15 other countries without figures attached; presumably none of them had memberships much higher than the Mexican 15. Palestine was not mentioned.

However, in the document "A Review of the Conference" published shortly after the founding conference, there is a list of "organisations affiliated to the Fourth International" which were "unable to send delegates because of conditions of distance, illegality and other adverse factors". This list includes four countries not named in the minute of Naville's report – French Morocco, New Zealand, Lithuania and Palestine. It is stated, "These organisations had already signified, in advance, their adherence to the new banner".[59] So there was a recognised section of the Fourth International, albeit a very small one, in Palestine.

Trotskyism in Palestine was marginal to the main political developments in the country, and it has not yet found its historian. A brief outline of the origins of Palestinian Trotskyism* shows the

---

* The document in question is entitled "On the development of Trotskyism in Palestine until the decade of the Sixties". It was written by Michel Warshawski (now a leading anti-Zionist activist in Israel). I am grateful to Wolfgang and Petra Lubitz for providing me with a copy. Warshawski's text is the main source for the account of Palestinian Trotskyism in RJ Alexander, *International Trotskyism*, Durham North Carolina and London, 1991, pp577-581. However, the fact that Ygal is never mentioned may reflect Warshawski's own political alignments.

various sources which contributed to the emergence of a Trotskyist grouping:

> Three factors contributed to the rise of the Trotskyist organisation in the second half of the decade of the 1930s:
>
> (1) During the '30s there took place the great Jewish immigration from Germany, which reflected almost the whole spectrum of political groupings. Included in this immigration were several comrades from the KPO (Brandler opposition), a majority of whom soon developed Trotskyist positions (1937-38). They were...relatively isolated politically from the mass of the population, and the comrades were active in economic struggles only individually...
>
> (2) The second factor was constituted by a group of youth, which was organised during the same period within the so-called "Chugim Marxistim" (Marxist Circles), the youth section of one of the two wings of the "Left Poale Zion". This wing was linked to the "London Bureau" of the time. There existed in it Trotskyist tendencies for a short time... The two groups soon found their common general positions and the way to political and organisational ties. The unity which arose considered itself as an integral part of the Trotskyist world movement and as the Palestinian section of the Fourth International...
>
> (3) Various other elements in the course of time were added to these groups, coming mainly from the "Hashomer Hatzair" (left-Zionist kibbutz movement). These elements united in the "Brit Kommunistim Mahapchanim" [Revolutionary Communists].

Independently of these organisations there developed a group of German immigrants who were of the conviction that Trotskyists should not be active in Palestine and should confine themselves to theoretical work.* This position was rejected by the RCL, which propagandised for active participation in events, in the social and political struggles of the working class and in anti-Zionist activity.

This shows the development of a united group from its various components was a protracted and complex process. It also points to a specific feature of Palestinian Trotskyism. In most countries Trotskyist organisations originated from splits from the

---

* See the obituary of Rudolf Segall in *Revolutionary History* 9/3 (2006), pp 233-236 for the history of these German exiles.

Moscow-oriented Communist parties.* The Palestinian group, where the main source of militants was exiles and left Zionists, was therefore unique to the particular circumstances.

The account does not name names and it is not clear exactly what role Ygal played in the process. Given what we know both about his single-minded commitment and his talent as a thinker and writer, we may suppose that his role was a significant one.

So a united Trotskyist organisation came into existence in Palestine. But what exactly did it mean to be a "Trotskyist"? The Fourth International at its foundation was overwhelmingly based in Europe and North America. Leaving aside the British dominions of Australia, New Zealand and South Africa, the only other significant sections were in Chile, Cuba and Indochina. A number of other Latin American countries had small groups, but as far as Africa and Asia were concerned, Palestine was the only country named between Morocco and China.[60] Palestinian Trotskyists were able to adopt the Fourth International's general analysis of the situation in Russia and in Western capitalism, but with regard to their native country, they were on their own. Moreover, much of the strategy of the new-born Fourth International was directed against the Comintern's Popular Front line. In Palestine, because of the weakness of the Communist Party, the Popular Front had little meaning beyond the tailing of the bourgeois Arab leaders.

So the body of Trotskyist writing on the Palestine question was somewhat limited. The 1936 conference for the Fourth International issued an address "To the Enslaved People of Morocco" which pointed to British imperialist interests:

> In order to guard this position, the English imperialist bandits incite race

---

* Warshawski records, "After the invasion of the USSR by the Nazis, the organisation came into contact with Dr Stein and his Democratic Front, which since the 20s had published the legal publication of the CP (in Hebrew and Arabic), without being officially a member of the party. During the murderous Moscow trials in the 30s, he took up the struggle against Stalinism, sympathised with the ideas of Trotsky, but still did not become a Trotskyist at any time." Dr Mordechai Stein was expelled from the PCP in 1935 for "Trotskyism" (A Greilsammer, *Les Communistes israéliens*, Paris, 1978, pp77, 93). It should be remembered that the Stalinists of the 1930s frequently used "Trotskyist" as a blanket term of abuse to cover any oppositionists; doubtless the PCP were delighted to be able to tell their Moscow masters they had unearthed and excluded a Trotskyist even though in fact he was not a Trotskyist but an independent socialist.

hatred between Jews and Arabs, constantly provoking bloody conflicts between the two. So long as the Jewish workers make themselves the accomplices of the capitalist agents of English imperialism; so long as the Arab workers do not seek the alliance of the Jewish workers and their brothers in India in order to beat their common enemy – English imperialism – the latter, posing as pacifier between them will not cease to coin profit from their blood while they kill each other.[61]

This was splendid rhetoric, but rather thin on analysis and strategy.

The Leon Trotsky of the 1930s was not usually hesitant when it came to expressing his views uncompromisingly. But on the relatively few occasions when he stated his position on the Palestine question, he showed a rather surprising agnosticism.[62] In a 1934 interview Trotsky was asked for his views on the 1929 Arab uprising. He responded:

> Unfortunately, I am not thoroughly familiar with the facts to venture a definite opinion. I am now studying the question.[63]

Three years later Trotsky was still disarmingly vague in his comments on Zionism:

> I have lived my whole life outside Jewish circles. I have always worked in the Russian workers' movement. My native tongue is Russian. Unfortunately, I have not even learned to read Jewish. The Jewish question has never occupied the centre of my attention.* But that does not mean that I have the right to be blind to the Jewish problem which exists and demands solution.

He then went on to discuss Birobidjan, the Jewish autonomous region within the USSR, and speculated on the possibility of a separate Jewish state in a socialist world:

> Are we not correct in saying that a world socialist federation would have to make possible the creation of a "Birobidjan" for those Jews who wish to have their own autonomous republic as the arena for their own culture?... The very same methods of solving the Jewish question which

---

* It is interesting to compare this with the supremely internationalist, non-Jewish Jew Rosa Luxemburg: "Why do you come with your special Jewish sorrows? I feel just as sorry for the wretched Indian victim in Puutamayo, the Negroes in Africa... I cannot find a special corner in my heart for the ghetto." ("To Mathilde Wurm", 1917, quoted in W Laqueur, *A History of Zionism*, London, 1972, p435)

under decaying capitalism have a utopian and reactionary character (Zionism), will, under the regime of a socialist federation, take on a real and salutary meaning.[64]

Earlier in 1934 Trotsky had envisaged the possibility of a Jewish state in Palestine, but insisted that such a thing could only happen democratically after world proletarian revolution:

> The establishment of a territorial base for Jewry in Palestine or any other country is conceivable only with the migrations of large human masses. Only a triumphant Socialism can take upon itself such tasks. It can be foreseen that it may take place either on the basis of a mutual understanding, or with the aid of a kind of international proletarian tribunal which should take up this question and solve it.[65]

The whole Palestinian situation presented a new set of problems which Trotsky and his small band of followers, faced with triumphant Stalinism, ascendant fascism and impending world war, had little time to study.

Marxists had traditionally been opposed to Zionism. Their grounds for opposition had been primarily that Zionism was a counsel of despair and a positive obstacle to the involvement of Jewish workers in class struggle in whichever country they happened to inhabit. But in the 1930s two radically new elements in the situation were emerging.

The first was the rise of Hitler. To begin with it appeared that his anti-Semitism was simply a continuation of the traditional pogroms. Soon it became apparent that something qualitatively more sinister was threatened. For Jews in central Europe emigration became an urgent practical matter, and many came to Palestine.

Secondly, the role of the Zionist community in Palestine was changing. Already they were increasingly playing the role of oppressors rather than of oppressed. The future was still unclear; while British imperialism never abandoned the Zionist option, this was not always obvious even to such a perceptive observer as Trotsky, who wrote in a posthumously published note dating from July 1940:

> Interested in winning the sympathies of the Arabs who are more numerous than the Jews, the British government has sharply altered its policy toward the Jews, and has actually renounced its promise to help them found their "own home" in a foreign land. The future development of

military events may well transform Palestine into a bloody trap for several hundred thousand Jews. Never was it so clear as it is today that the salvation of the Jewish people is bound up inseparably with the overthrow of the capitalist system.[66]

We do not know how much of Trotsky's writings were available to Ygal and his comrades. But there was no developed Trotskyist "line" on the problems of the Middle East. In both theory and practice they had to improvise. Ygal's entry into the world of international Trotskyist debate must be seen in this context.

In October and November 1938 the *New International* carried two articles signed "L Rock", Ygal's pseudonym.[*] They were published not as a statement of the Fourth International "line", but as an attempt to develop the Trotskyist position in an area which had previously had little analysis.[67][†]

Rock identified the three main factors in the situation as British imperialism, Arab nationalism and Zionism. The starting point was the real enemy, British imperialism. Ygal was just emerging from a long personal struggle with Zionism, but this was no "self-hating Jew" exorcising his own demons. For Rock, as for Cliff later, Zionism was always understood in the context of the imperialism whose interests it served.

He then moved straight on to what remains one of the most contentious points in his analysis, the role of Jewish immigration into Palestine. The argument reflected a deep-lying dilemma for the Jewish left in Palestine. Most left activists were themselves immigrants (Ygal was a rare exception), yet to support immigration as a right would have created a barrier to any cooperation with the Arab movement.

Noting that the British authorities had systematically encouraged antagonism between Jews and Arabs, Rock argued:

Jewish immigration represents a basic factor in the process of accelerating

---

[*] Several of Ygal's pseudonyms, including the most famous, Cliff, were based on words related to stone. This was based on his family name, Gluckstein, which is derived from a German word meaning "lucky stone" or birthstone.

[†] For an interesting analysis of the Rock articles and a comparison with other positions on the Palestinian left, see R Greenstein, "Zionism, Nationalism and Revolutionary Socialism: The Radical Left and the Colonial Model in Israel/Palestine", in I Pappe (ed), *Peoples Apart: Israel, South Africa and the Apartheid Question*, London, 2009.

capitalist development. The growth of a Jewish and Arab working class which, considered historically, represents a serious anti-imperialist force is bound up with Jewish immigration into the country. The British government is not interested in fostering any considerable working class population in Palestine. On the other hand if the Jewish population in the country were to become too strong its dependence on British policy could not be assured even by the threat of strong pogroms. It is therefore plain that the British are not interested in a broad Jewish mass immigration. At the same time the government does not desire to shut off Jewish immigration completely. The government's policy is therefore to open the door to a certain extent and for a limited time, and then to close it. In this way the government heightens the national tensions around the immigration question. The sharp changes in the tempo of immigration lead to sharp conflicts in the relations of Jews and Arabs.

Here Rock was not so much making concessions to Zionism as presenting a rather simplistic mechanical Marxist account of colonisation, claiming that colonisation was progressive, since it produced industrialisation and hence the working class which would be the gravedigger of capitalism.

He went on to accuse British imperialism of diverting Arab anti-imperialism into anti-Jewish sentiments:

The Arabs are made to see their national oppressors in the Jews, and the actions of the Arab masses are directed into chauvinist anti-Jewish channels, thus consolidating the role of the feudal leaders who are the real anti-Jewish element.

This argument required a class analysis of Arab nationalism. Rock juxtaposed the "feudal semi-bourgeois leadership" of the Arab nationalist movement to the desire for national liberation on the part of the "Arab masses". He believed the Arab leaders were afraid of the movement developing along independent anti-imperialist lines (again echoing the application of the theory of permanent revolution he had made in his earlier article on Egypt). This left the Arab movement prey to the influence of European fascism; it became "fertile soil for chauvinist, fascist and particularly anti-Jewish ideas".

As for Zionism, Rock showed his basic opposition:

Zionism is a nationalist reactionary conception because it builds its hopes not on the class struggle of the international working class but on the continuation of world reaction and its consolidation.

He illustrated this with the fact that in Palestine pickets were organised against Arab workers who held jobs in Jewish enterprises; these were supported even by so-called "left-wing" Zionists. He argued that it was necessary to understand the position of the Jews in Palestine in class terms, and not to fall into an oversimplified description. The Jews could neither be regarded "as an integral part of the imperialist camp" – the position taken not only by "the extreme Arab nationalists" but by the Communist Party ("their lackeys in the camp of the Stalinists") – nor as "an integral part of the Palestinian population and as such anti-imperialist". To reinforce his point he contrasted the Jewish workers in Palestine with white workers in South Africa:

> The South African whites are a thin "aristocratic" upper crust, who get about five times the pay of the natives. In Palestine the Jewish workers constitute not a thin crust, but a class.

Rock was making two central points: first, that the Palestine situation could be understood only by placing it in the context of imperialism; second, that both Arab and Jewish populations were divided by class. The logical conclusion, though not developed in the articles, was to assert – contrary to Zionists, Stalinists and Arab nationalists – that unity of Arab and Jewish workers was possible.

The *New International* was distributed in Australia, South Africa, Britain, India and Palestine as well as the US. Not surprisingly, since Rock had made an explicit comparison, it was from South Africa that the first response came. It was not a friendly one. The January 1939 issue of the journal carried a letter signed Paul Koston.* This described Rock's first article as a "*very bad article*", arguing that "it is not the time to speak of British Imperialism, but of those who are the agents of British Imperialism, and in this case it is the Jews in Palestine and particularly the leadership of the Jewish workers, the

---

* Paul Koston left South Africa in 1925 and joined the US Merchant Marine. His movements are not clear, but it seems that around 1930 he jumped ship in Cape Town and became an active socialist. He was secretary of the South African Labour Party, joined the Lenin Club and then the (Trotskyist) Workers Party of South Africa. He was one of the editors of the Trotskyist journal *The Spark*, and also owned and managed Modern Books, the main Cape Town outlet for Marxist books (B Hirson, "Profiles of Some South African Trotskyists", *Revolutionary History* 4/4 (1993), p93). He was still alive in 1991 when he attended a meeting on South Africa organised by *Revolutionary History*.

various Zionist 'socialists' of all kinds". After comparing the Jewish minority in Palestine to the Protestant minority in Ireland, he concluded, "If it comes to a question of who is a 'chauvinist', then the Arab peasant can be forgiven a hell of a lot more chauvinism than the Jewish worker. Why not? Whose country is it?"

The following month's issue of the *New International* carried a longer article on the question of "Zionism and the Arab Struggle",[68] taken from *The Spark*.* Like the Palestinian Trotskyists, the South Africans were a small, geographically isolated group striving to apply the Trotskyist view of the world to the concrete realities of their own situation. As Rock had pointed out in his article, there were interesting comparisons to be made between Palestine and South Africa.[69] These parallels were touched on only in passing in the *Spark* article (Rock was accused of echoing "the usual argument of imperialism concerning its beneficent work, an argument used by imperialism in China, India, South Africa and any colonial or semicolonial country"), but probably accounted for the passion with which the polemic was pursued.

The article argued that the Arab revolt and the subsequent report of the Woodhead Commission were "an end to the Zionist dream of a Jewish State in Palestine". It accused some Marxists (including Rock) of having "fallen victims to nationalism", and insisted that the fundamental issue was "the progressive revolutionary struggle of a colonial people against imperialism", although this could not be victorious under the leadership of the Arab bourgeoisie. While accepting that Zionism was "a servant of British imperialism", it argued:

> To blame British imperialism now for the present state of affairs in Palestine (as comrade Rock has done in a recent article in *The New International*), to accuse the British of sinister machinations and of the international sowing of hostility between Arab and Jew, is both futile and incorrect.

In particular it maintained that Arab opposition to Jewish immigration was a "just, defensive demand" and strongly dissented from Rock's support for Jewish immigration. The article concluded in apocalyptic terms which must have seemed all too plausible on the

---

* From 1935 till its closure on the eve of the Second World War *The Spark* was the organ of the Workers Party of South Africa. See B Hirson, "The Trotskyist Groups in South Africa", *Revolutionary History* 4/4 (1993), pp25-56.

eve of world war: "The sole form of rule for decaying capitalism is fascism… Only socialism can bring emancipation to the Jews."

Rock's final article, in the June 1939 issue of the *New International*, was largely devoted to a response to the *Spark* critique. He began by stressing the complexity of the Palestine situation; the job was not to defend a given line, nor to put forward abstract slogans, but to analyse the situation concretely in Marxist terms:

> The political situation in Palestine is highly complicated. Many factors are jumbled together in a large chequered knot.* Hence it is very hard to establish an internationalist class policy for the Palestine proletariat; hence also the great confusion in the circles of the revolutionary left with regard to the problems of this country.

Though Cliff would later move closer to *The Spark*'s positions, his recognition that there were still problems to be solved was in sharp contrast to the defence of orthodoxy which has so often characterised the Trotskyist tradition.

He went on to argue that any Marxist analysis must have the concept of class at its centre, while accepting that in the complex situation of Palestine, there were no easy answers:

> Palestine cannot emancipate itself from the imperialist yoke unless a unification of the Arab and Jewish masses takes place, for the latter represent a third of the population, the Jewish workers are half of the Palestine working class, and Jewish economy is decisive in many branches of industry. The Jewish toiling masses will not, however, support the anti-imperialist movement if no class differentiation takes place in the Arabian national movement. What is so terrible in the situation in Palestine is that, on the one hand, there is a strong national differentiation between Jews and Arabs and, on the other, the national unity in the Arab camp is very firm.

He rejected the Stalinist position that the Jewish population was an integral part of the imperialist camp, and denied parallels with South Africa, pointing out that Jewish workers in Palestine made up more than half the total working class, whereas in South Africa white workers were only one fifth of the working class. Still operating with an orthodox Leninist concept of the labour aristocracy,

---

* The phrase "chequered knot" looks like an early example of Cliff's lifelong taste for mixed metaphors. However, the articles were presumably written in Hebrew, and we do not know whether they were translated in Palestine or in the US.

Rock argued that "the white workers in South Africa represent a thin aristocratic layer. In Palestine the Jewish workers are not a layer, but a class in which, although there are aristocratic layers, there are still more simple workers."

Rock then showed the dual nature of the Jewish population in Palestine:

> The Jewish population in Palestine therefore has objectively a dual character. Corresponding to its class differentiation, it contains on the one hand a Jewish working class and accelerates the rise of an Arab working class,* that is, forces which are objectively anti-imperialist, and on the other hand, to the extent that it is permeated by Zionist exclusivist tendencies, that is, submitted to bourgeois influence, it strengthens the positions of imperialism and of reaction in the country.

He pointed out that the Comintern, until its change of line in 1927, had been in favour of unrestricted Jewish immigration. He concluded that unity of Arab and Jewish workers was possible only on the basis of winning Jewish support for national independence and Arab support for Jewish immigration:†

> The complete victory of the movement for independence in Palestine is, however, impossible without the support of the Jewish toilers, who hold important positions in Palestine's political and economic life. The liberation movement will not receive this support so long as the anti-Jewish terror exists and so long as the Arabian toiling masses will struggle against Jewish immigration. On the other hand, the existence of the Jewish population will not be assured, and there will be no immigration without terrible suffering for the Jewish masses, without the support of the Arabian toiling masses who are the majority of the country's population; and the Arabian masses will not give this support so long as the Jewish masses are against the independence of the country and remain a tool in the hands of England for the suppression of the Arab masses. Only an internationalist labour movement can be the leading force in the consistent anti-imperialist struggle.

---

* This fails to take into account the fact that the Jewish and Arab economies were largely separate (Communication from M Machover, June 2007).

† An idealistic but naive position. Moshé Machover argues that calling on Arab workers to support Jewish immigration was like asking sheep to support the admission of wolves into the meadow (communication from M Machover, June 2007).

The issue of the *New International* which carried the third Rock article had a brief editorial on the Palestine question, entitled "The End of an Illusion". The apparently dead illusion in question was the Zionist belief that the Jewish problem could be solved by the establishment of a Jewish homeland in Palestine. The editorial went on to state that the current issue was carrying two pieces on the Palestine question:

> Although they do not express the views of the editors – they are indeed in sharp conflict with them on many points – we feel justified in presenting them to our readers as contributions to the discussion of the problem that has reached an unheard-of stage of acuteness in recent times.[70]

Immediately following Rock's article was a piece signed "Haor (El Nour)". Among other things this argued, "There is no doubt that the best way to realise the independence of Jews and Arabs is the partition of the country, in one way or another, into two free parts, not depending on one another." [71]*

The editors promised that their own views on Palestine would appear in a future issue, but they did not. The outbreak of war and the internal dispute in the SWP must have prevented its appearance, but the range of material published in the *New International* confirms the view that there was no developed Fourth International line on Palestine at this time. Ygal and his comrades were acting on their own, striving to apply Marxist principles, rather than parroting a Trotskyist orthodoxy.

Rock did not convince his critics. The October issue of the *New International* carried a short piece entitled "Rebuttal on the Palestine Question" from the *Spark* group.[72]† The tone was even sharper than the earlier *Spark* polemic. Rock was accused of being "a man torn between the theory of Revolutionary Marxism and the practice of narrow Nationalism", and his article was actually said to have shown him to be "a Jewish Nationalist for whom the revolutionary aspects of the anti-imperialist struggle are completely overshadowed by the one single aspect of this struggle that affects the Jews". The main target of *The Spark's* fury was Rock's support for Jewish

---

* *Haor* was the publication of the group around the lawyer Mordechai Stein.

† This is dated 8 May 1939, but responds to the second and third Rock articles. Presumably they had received an advance copy of the third piece, which appeared in the June 1939 issue of the *New International*.

immigration, "which we maintain is not immigration but invasion under the protection of, and for the strengthening of Imperialism".

The Spark dismissed Rock's hopes for unity of Arab and Jewish workers, claiming rather optimistically that "the Arabs alone are conducting the struggle for independence in Palestine and have already achieved some success in this struggle without the support of the Jewish toilers", and concluding that "no rapprochement on class lines is possible between Arab workers and Jewish workers, so long as the latter...persist in their Zionist ideology of a Jewish State".

The question remains: had Ygal yet completed his break with Zionism? In his own eyes, undoubtedly – the Rock articles had labelled Zionism as inherently reactionary and as the tool of British imperialism. In the eyes of the Zionists also, who on more than one occasion used physical violence against him, he had done so.[73] But the contentious point which remained, as the debate with *The Spark* showed, was the question of Jewish immigration into Palestine.

The issue was a vital one at the time – the suspension of Jewish immigration was a major demand of the Arab national movement. The British authorities had imposed tight controls on Jewish immigration. For the Zionists the right of all Jews, anywhere in the world, to "return" to Palestine was a central plank of their programme.

But retrospectively it has acquired a weight of further meaning which it could not have had for Ygal. On the one hand, we now see the question in light of the Holocaust. Ygal knew leftists from central Europe who had come to Palestine to escape the threat of Nazism, but the scale of the Holocaust was as yet unimagined. It is scarcely reasonable to accuse those who then opposed Jewish immigration of wishing to condemn fugitives from Hitler to the extermination camps.

Moreover Ygal put his money where his mouth was. In the 1930s, at a time when the British authorities were imposing strict controls on Jewish immigration, boatloads of refugees would arrive in Palestine. Young men would stand on the quayside and make their selection from the women on deck; with the collaboration of the rabbis they were quickly married and circumvented the immigration controls.[74] Ygal was "married" after this fashion and saw no more of his bride. This caused some problems a decade later when he wanted to get married for real.[75] It would be a harsh anti-Zionist who would condemn Ygal for his personal contribution to Jewish immigration.

Jewish immigration is now perceived also in light of the creation of the Zionist state of Israel and its subsequent actions. Critics like *The Spark* argued that Jewish settlement in Palestine was not the free movement of peoples, which socialists have always defended, but rather colonisation. Rock argued in his articles that in 1938 British imperialism was still pursuing the traditional imperialist strategy of divide and rule, playing Jews and Arabs off against each other, though he probably overstated this point. (*The Spark* had claimed that the Arab revolt had made the establishment of a Zionist state impossible.)

Certainly there was no definitive Trotskyist line on the question. At the same time as Ygal was debating with *The Spark*, the French Trotskyist paper was declaring its "unconditional support" for the Arab demand for a halt to Jewish immigration.[76]

Ygal's views were to change radically over the coming decade, and he himself was later critical of the Rock articles.* But it was not only Ygal who changed; Zionism too was changing as it became the ideology of a dominant state. It is worthless to point to changes in Ygal's stance without setting them in the context of the changing nature of Zionism. As Cliff noted many years later Zionism (though it had always been a colonising ideology) had changed:

> I grew up a Zionist, but Zionism didn't have the ugly face we see today. However, there was always a fundamental crack between the Zionists and the Arabs. This same crack split Zionists from ordinary people in their countries of origin.[77]

The great strength of the Rock articles is the way they put class at the centre of the analysis. This enabled him, in a way that was impossible for both the left Zionists and the Stalinists, to advocate unity of Jewish and Arab workers. That this was possible can be shown by a number of disputes (though only in the public sector) in which Arabs and Jews fought side by side.[78] Whether that unity could have become powerful enough to offer an alternative political road after 1945 can now only be a matter of speculation. It is greatly

---

* "I used to argue that poor Jewish refugees should be allowed to come to Palestine, that they shouldn't be excluded. That was an unjustified compromise, when you look back at it." (T Cliff interview, "Fifty-Five Years a Revolutionary", *Socialist Review* 100 (July 1987), p14)

to Ygal's credit as a revolutionary that he attempted to point in this direction.

But the task of building a Trotskyist organisation in Palestine was scarcely begun before a new challenge appeared. The Second World War – and its aftermath – would put the whole Fourth International to the test.

Even before the outbreak of hostilities, the impending war raised political questions. The July 1939 issue of the *New International* carried an article entitled "A Step towards Social-Patriotism", published in the name of the Editorial Board of the *Bulletin of the Russian Opposition*, but written by Trotsky himself.[79] This was a response to a letter from Palestinian comrades, of which extracts are quoted (the full text does not appear to have been published).

Their main argument was that Lenin's position of "revolutionary defeatism" (the idea that revolutionaries should welcome the defeat of their own country in order to turn imperialist war into social revolution) was no longer relevant in the age of fascism. "Fascism has introduced a radical change. It so strangles the working class as hardly to make it possible to comply with Lenin's third condition for defeatist policy."

Trotsky's response was vigorous. It began by insisting on the continuing relevance of Lenin's positions from 1914-17: "All the fundamental rules of proletarian 'defeatist' policy in relation to imperialist war retain their full force today. This is our point of departure, and all the conclusions that follow are determined by it".* Basing himself on the perspective of the *Transitional Programme*, that capitalism was in its "death agony", Trotsky maintained, "A victory over the armies of Hitler and Mussolini implies in itself only the military defeat of Germany and Italy, and not at all the collapse of fascism. Our authors admit that fascism is the inevitable product of decaying capitalism, in so far as the proletariat does not replace bourgeois democracy in time. Just how is a military victory of decaying democracies over Germany and Italy capable of liquidating fascism, even if only for a limited period?"

What part Ygal took in this debate is not known. It appears more

---

* Trotsky was showing all the dogmatic zeal of the convert; during the First World War he had opposed Lenin's defeatist position. (See B Pearce, "Lenin and Trotsky on Pacifism and Defeatism", *Labour Review*, Vol 6, No 1 (Spring 1961)

likely that it would be the German exiles who questioned revolutionary defeatism in this way.* For Ygal, as for Karl Liebknecht, the German socialist opponent of the First World War, the main enemy was at home, and that enemy was British imperialism. The impact of the war cut any remaining links with Zionism.

Not surprisingly, the Jewish population of Palestine identified with the British side in the war. Many thousands volunteered to serve in the British armed forces or in civilian war services. The Hitler-Stalin Pact, signed a few days before the start of the war, led to a split in the Communist Party, with the Jewish Section unable to accept the Moscow line on Hitler.

In Haifa, Ygal's response to the war was to distribute or fly-post leaflets opposing the war. The message was clear: "Our enemy is not the aggressor of 1939. Our real enemy is the aggressor of 1917 that occupied the country".[80] For the British authorities there was no suggestion that Ygal had taken even the tiniest step towards social-patriotism. When the leaflet was carelessly left on a table, he and his brother Chaim were promptly arrested. The police tried to terrify them with threats, which greatly frightened Chaim, but Ygal reassured him that they were bluffing.[81] These arrests took place during a wave of repression based on Emergency Regulations whereby German citizens and others liable to oppose the war were interned without trial.[82] Ygal was never tried but, in effect, interned.

Conditions in the prison were harsh and repressive. For a while Jews and Arabs were held together, but then were segregated. Food was served in a large cauldron, and to get a piece of meat prisoners had to plunge their arm into the cauldron.[83] But Ygal was not to be deterred from continuing to pursue his dual task of developing a Marxist understanding and building an organisation. He had access to the prison library, and used to recount later that the British authorities were so inept that they did not know which books were dangerous; Marx's *Capital* was available, but Stendhal's *Scarlet and Black* was banned. Ygal spent his time learning French, and in developing a Marxist approach to biblical studies, something he never had the leisure to take further.[84]

The overcrowded conditions of prison life brought left-wing

---

* Though Jabra Nicola, not yet a member of Cliff's group, was opposed to revolutionary defeatism from the start of the war (communication from M Machover, June 2007).

militants together. One of the remarkable individuals who crossed Ygal's path at this time was Jakob Moneta. Born in 1914 into a Jewish family in what was to become Poland, Moneta grew up in Germany, becoming a young socialist during the years of Hitler's rise. In 1933 he emigrated to Palestine and went to live on a kibbutz, which strengthened his socialist conviction that people could live together uncompetitively. After the Arab rising of 1936 he began to question Zionism and was eventually excluded from the kibbutz. He also helped to organise a strike of orange-packers. Before the outbreak of war some of his anti-Zionist comrades had already made contact with the group around Ygal in Haifa.[85]

Two months before the outbreak of war, Moneta was arrested by the British authorities and flung into an overcrowded police cell in Haifa. He was never tried and never saw a judge. He was then transferred to the fortress at Akko (Acre). He later described the harsh conditions that British imperialism imposed on its colonial prisoners. Though disease was widespread in the jails, medical inspections were perfunctory: "We stood in a long row and were brought before a British military doctor, who asked 'Everything all right?' We replied 'Yes sir'. The medical inspection was completed." He was able to observe the methods used by the British CID on prisoners; they had pieces of wood forced under their fingernails, flames were put to the soles of their feet and they were hung up by the hands.[86]

It was in jail that Moneta first met Ygal. "We all brought something with us. I brought bugs and he brought lice." When everyone in the crowded cell was trying to sleep, Ygal would begin making speeches. The other prisoners swore at him and told him to shut up. This is testimony to Ygal's fighting spirit, but not to his sense of timing. Moneta remembers discussing Ygal's theories about the Bible, but has no recollection of any discussion of the Russian question; at this time Ygal still held to the Trotskyist orthodoxy. [87]*

Another person Ygal met in jail was Avraham Stern, an extreme right-wing Zionist. He had little sympathy for Stern's position, oriented as it was on the hope of a fascist victory in the Second World

---

* After his return to Germany Moneta was involved in solidarity work with the Algerian liberation struggle and later became editor of the journal of the metalworkers' union. He is the author of several books. I interviewed him in Frankfurt in March 2005, shortly after his ninetieth birthday. He was still a committed revolutionary and clearly remembered his encounters with Ygal.

War.[88] Later Cliff would write an article rejecting the "terrorist" politics of the Stern Gang and arguing that such organisations were opposed to the interests of Jews and Arabs alike.[89]

After a year Ygal was released from prison. He spent less time in jail than many of the other political prisoners. His release seems to have been the result of intervention by his parents, who were well placed in the Zionist establishment, and who had contacts with the British authorities. In particular Ygal's cousin was married to Norman Bentwich, who in the 1920s had been the first attorney-general in the mandatory government of Palestine. The exact circumstances of his release remain unclear, but there is no suggestion that Ygal himself sought to get special treatment. His family, despite disagreeing fundamentally with his political choices, remained well disposed towards him and, indeed, were very proud of him.

On release Ygal remained under surveillance, and for a time was under house arrest.* His activities had to be conducted in more or less clandestine conditions. His sister-in-law Naomi Gunn, married to Ygal's elder brother Chaim who had been a member of the group around Ygal, recalls that at one point he was hiding in an orange grove in the small citrus-growing town of Petach Tikva, living in the pump-house that provided water for the orange trees. She and Chaim would take him provisions, but what he wanted above all were books. Naomi was a student at the Hebrew University of Jerusalem, and every fortnight Ygal would give her lists of books on agrarian problems. These books had nothing to do with the course she was studying, and since her name was also Gluckstein, and Ygal had been a well-known figure in the small university, the librarian would ask pointedly whether the books were for her or for Ygal.[90]

He also had the problem of evading military service. In the early 1940s Cliff took a civil service examination in Palestine. He tried hard to get everything wrong, which was difficult as the questions were ridiculously easy. When he finally got the certificate explaining that Ygael Gluckstein was unsuitable for the British Civil Service, he carefully scraped off the words Civil Service (with a razor blade)

---

* A secret 15-page report sent by the High Commissioner for Palestine to the Colonial Office and Foreign Office in 1946 entitled "An outline of recent developments of Communism in Palestine" contains only vague references to Trotskyism and says nothing of the RCL (NA CO537/1735).

and typed the word Army. When stopped in the street he had papers to show that he was exempt from military service.[91]

Ygal had now apparently given up his biblical studies, and was working on the economics of the Middle East. He was more than ever isolated from the international Trotskyist movement. In May 1940 an "Emergency Conference of the Fourth International" was held in North America, but Palestine was listed as one of the countries where "the ravages of war and of ruthless internal suppression made it impossible for the affiliates of the Fourth International...to be contacted in time to obtain representation".[92]

This relative isolation continued for the duration of the war. Some Fourth International publications made their way to Palestine and there were contacts with British sailors.[93] But though comrades in Palestine might read Fourth International publications, they knew nothing of the internal discussions that gave a context to those publications.[94] Under normal circumstances an emerging group such as the one in Palestine would have received visits from representatives of the International and copious advice on how to develop their organisation. Ygal and his companions had to think on their feet and solve their problems for themselves, without the benefit of more experienced comrades to guide them. It was a tough school, but excellent training for the future.

Meanwhile the world was still changing, producing new problems for which there were no ready-made solutions. In June 1941 Hitler invaded Russia, transforming international alignments. The PCP took four months to adopt a line to meet the new circumstances.[95] Years later Cliff wrote an article documenting what he called "the unprincipled, dishonest twists and turns of the Kremlin agents".[96]

Although Ygal's main efforts were focused on an analysis of the Middle East, he was already looking to the broader problems of the post-war world. In 1943 he wrote a short review of James Burnham's *The Managerial Revolution* (1941).[97] Burnham had been a leading intellectual in the American SWP, and one of the editors of the *New International*, in which Ygal's 1938 articles had appeared. In 1939 Burnham and Max Shachtman developed the view that Russia was not a workers' state in any sense of the term. This led to a sharp faction fight inside the SWP ending with the departure of Shachtman and Burnham in April 1940. Burnham soon abandoned Shachtman and broke completely with Marxism. He published *The Managerial Revolution*, which created widespread interest. In it he argued that capitalism was giving way, not to socialism, but to a new form of society in which managers, rather than traditional capitalists, would constitute the ruling class. He saw Stalin's Russia, Nazi Germany and Roosevelt's New Deal as early forms of this new society.

Ygal must have been aware of the split, and was curious about its implications. He engaged in a vigorous demolition of Burnham's arguments. With extensive quotations from Volume Three of *Capital*, he showed that what Marx had written on managers and the "intermediate strata" already took up some of Burnham's points. Recent empirical material, notably from Corey's *The Decline of American Capitalism*, was also cited against Burnham.

Ygal thus showed that what Burnham called the "managerial society" was not a new mode of production but merely the development of capitalism. He responded to Burnham's claim that Nazi Germany was not a "profit economy" with the assertion that Nazism meant "the apogee of the rule of profit as the fundamental motive of the whole of economic and social life". He concluded that "instead of regarding state capitalism as the summit of [capitalism's] monopolistic development, Burnham regards the former as the negation of the latter".

Ygal used the term "state capitalism" repeatedly in the article. As he pointed out, "The increase in the state's share of the total national income does not prove that the economy is freed from the shackles of capitalism." Fascism was the "perfect form" of state capitalism, so that "the proletariat, therefore, regards state capitalism...as a class oppression system directed against it". As for Burnham's claim that it was no longer possible to believe, as Marx had, that workers could run production for themselves, Ygal responded, "Was the distance between a worker's education and that of the factory owner who managed the enterprises smaller in Marx's time than the present distance between the engineer and the 'manager'?"

Yet Ygal recognised that the apparent plausibility of Burnham's case rested on the fact that real changes had taken place in capitalism. It was necessary to understand those changes without believing that capitalism itself was disappearing. In particular he noted the way that "the mechanisation of office work, calculating machines, etc., have brought about the 'proletarianisation' of mental labour".

He rejected any mechanical view of automatic historical stages:

> If the conflict and contradictions within capitalism have reached a turning point and the critical revolutionary deed is not performed by the proletariat, then the proletariat is doomed to be torn apart by the tangle of contradictions in the system, and the decay begins to spread not only within the system, but even to the class hostile to it. The would-be gravedigger of the system will be buried under its ruins.

Burnham's three examples of the emerging managerial society were Nazi Germany, the New Deal in the US and Stalin's Russia. Ygal had no difficulty in seeing the first two as capitalist, but the question of Russia was left aside. A concluding editorial note (by Ygal himself?) pointed out that Burnham was a former socialist, and that "disappointment" at events in the Soviet Union had helped to lead him to his new position. Since this required separate treatment, the author would deal with the question in a future article. Whether that article was ever written or published, we do not know. But the logic of this piece backs up the recollections of Dov Shas and Tuvia Shlonsky that in 1945-46 Ygal was already expressing doubts about the validity of Trotsky's analysis of the society in the USSR.[98]

Some time after Ygal's release from jail a new organisation was founded – the Revolutionary Communist League (RCL). It was a tiny group, with a handful of members, including some of Ygal's old comrades from the Marxist Circles and a few political exiles, notably from Germany.

What exactly Ygal's role in the organisation was we do not know. He had already given proof of his outstanding abilities as a thinker and writer, and there is ample testimony to his single-minded commitment as a revolutionary activist. It is therefore more than likely that Ygal played a leading role in the building of the RCL.

So Ygal found himself working with some remarkable individuals whose abilities often complemented his own talents. The RCL was tiny and had little hope of making any impact on the course of events in Palestine, but it brought together a number of people who had a real contribution to make to the movement.

Gabriel Baer, born in 1919, came to Haifa in 1933 from Berlin with his parents. Gabriel Warburg notes that Baer "took an immediate and keen interest in his Arab neighbours living in this mixed city", and that this influenced his decision to study Islamic history and culture and Arabic language and literature at the Hebrew University of Jerusalem. Probably it was at the university that he first encountered Ygal. His studies of Arabic were of inestimable value to the RCL, since it aimed to produce publications in both Hebrew and Arabic, and Ygal did not have a knowledge of Arabic. Under the conditions of clandestine activity, Baer adopted the pseudonym "Munir". After the war he pursued an academic career and became a successful and highly regarded writer, author of numerous books and articles. His work focused on the history and sociology of the Middle East, especially the agrarian question and the emergence of the labour movement. These were subjects which must have first begun to interest him in his days as an RCL militant, and probably he discussed them with Ygal.

Baer became an influential teacher and for many years was head of the Institute of Asian and African Studies at the Hebrew University of Jerusalem, but he began to distance himself from revolutionary politics. Around 1960 he contributed regularly to the journal *New Outlook*, published in Israel, which declared itself committed to "the cause of the peaceful development of the Middle East" and "belief in the need and possibility of Jewish-Arab friendship and cooperation". His last book, *Fellah and Townsman in the Middle East*,[99] contains no references to Marxist thinkers, and draws on Barrington Moore and Mousnier. The academic tributes published after his death do not mention his youthful Trotskyism.[100]

In the early 1960s there were still frequent book reviews by "Munir" in *International Socialism*. The break came in 1964. Cliff wrote a review of Baer's *Population and Society in the Arab East*, which he described as "informative" but lacking in any analysis of the role of imperialism. "Has Dr Baer been muted by Zionist pressure in Israel where he lives?" enquired Cliff. In order to remind Baer of his revolutionary roots, he signed it "Y Sakhry", the name Ygal had used in the RCL's Arabic publications.[101]

Jabra Nicola was born in Haifa in 1912 to a poor Arab family. He left school at the age of 11, after only four years of formal education. For a time he drifted in the cities of Jaffa, Haifa and Beirut, and then joined the PCP before the age of 20. Despite his lack of educational qualifications, he was an impressive self-taught intellectual, and became one of the PCP's leading journalists, one of the editors of the PCP's main underground newspaper, *Al Ittihad* (Unity).[102] * In 1935 he became a member of the PCP's central committee. He was the author of a number of books, including works on trade unionism and the strike movement among Palestinian workers, as well as *In the Jewish World*, a study of Jewish history and an analysis of Zionism.[103]

At the beginning of the Second World War the PCP suffered a profound crisis. Not only was this the time of the Hitler-Stalin Pact, but the tensions over the Jewish-Arab conflict led the party to split into two sections, one Jewish and one Arab. Nicola refused to join either wing of the split, arguing that a communist could not have a national affiliation. Shortly after this he was imprisoned by the British authorities for two years until 1942, though he personally was opposed to defeatism.

Nicola continued to live in bitter poverty. He lived in one room "with his wife and one year old child, his widowed sister and her young child, and his mother who was dying from cancer".[104] Later he earned a modest living by translating detective stories, while his partner Aliza, a Jewish woman, worked as a cleaner.[105]

In his autobiography Cliff claimed to have recruited Nicola "at the beginning of 1940" by arguing with him for three or four hours every day for a month.[106] This may well be a lapse of memory, since it appears that Nicola joined the RCL in 1942, after his release from prison.[107] Moreover Jakob Moneta, who met Nicola in jail, claims that it was discussions with Jakob Taut which won Nicola over to Trotskyism and RCL membership.[108] Perhaps the truth lies somewhere between the different accounts. In any case, the recruitment of Nicola was an important acquisition for the RCL; although only a few years older than Ygal, he had far greater experience of the labour movement and made an important contribution to the political weight of the RCL. He was later to say that "the core of the Trotskyist group in Palestine were Cliff, Gabby Baer and myself".[109] Despite subsequent political differences, Cliff always spoke of him with respect and admiration. Ygal had won the argument about Trotskyism, but he must have learnt a great deal from the older man. They spent many hours together discussing and learning from

---

* In *A World to Win* (p23) Cliff claims Nicola was editor of *El Nour*. This must be a slip of memory.

each other.[110]

When the RCL collapsed after the founding of the state of Israel, Nicola returned to the Communist Party, and resumed work as editor of the Arabic newspaper, but was suspended from his post at the beginning of de-Stalinisation in 1956. He later left the PCP and in 1963 or 1964 joined the Matzpen (Compass) group, in which he became a leading figure. For a time he was a member of the international executive committee of the Fourth International; Ernest Mandel called him "the most impressive internationalist I ever met".[111] He moved to London in 1970, and died there in 1974. Cliff spoke at his memorial meeting in early 1975, saying:

> Jabra was an Arab. He detested Zionism, but he also hated anything to do with Arab nationalism. He was an internationalist to the core. He felt, as we should all feel, that the workers' struggle in all countries is as much to do with us as is the workers' struggle in our own country.[112]

Jakob or Jankel Taut was born to a Jewish family in Austrian Galicia in 1913. His family moved to Berlin and at the age of 14 he became an apprentice in an engineering factory where he became an active trade unionist and joined the Communist Youth. He opposed the German Communists' "Third Period" lunacy of rejecting a united front against Hitler and became a supporter of Heinrich Brandler.* After Hitler came to power, he moved to Denmark, but was not accepted as a political refugee because of his Polish nationality. Although he had no sympathies with Zionism, he was persuaded by Trotskyist émigrés in Denmark to go to Palestine, where he arrived in 1934.

Unlike many leftist immigrants from central Europe, who wished only to stay in Palestine until it was possible to return to their homelands, Taut was determined to establish roots in Palestine. He left the Brandlerite group because of its unwillingness to be sufficiently critical of the USSR, and he then became a Trotskyist and member of the RCL. He later described his position as follows:

> In principle we were against Zionism, against any Jewish *aliya* [immigration], for a congress of workers of the Arab East, for a socialist Arab East; our position was obviously a difficult one, inasmuch as we were a

---

* Heinrich Brandler (1881-1967), a former leader of the German Communist Party, was expelled in 1929 and formed the KPO (Communist Party Opposition), aligned with the International Right Opposition.

Jewish group without any organised contact with the Arab workers and also since we could not deny the fact that after 1933 a number of German Jews had come to Palestine because they had no alternative – I personally understood that situation. We were in contact, via British soldiers, with small Trotskyist groups existing in Cairo and Alexandria; by this means we had indirect contacts with the international Trotskyist movement.[113]

Ygal's first encounter with Taut was during an air raid. In a shelter he came upon someone reading Marx's *Capital* and immediately presumed the person must be a Trotskyist. This was typical of the chance opportunities which enabled a tiny group to grow in circumstances of clandestinity.

Later Taut's internationalism was put to a terrible test. He worked at the great oil refinery in Haifa, which employed nearly 2,000 workers, both Jews and Arabs. In December 1947, the Jewish terrorists of Etzel set off a bomb outside the refinery, killing several Arabs and wounding many more. Arab workers began to run through the refinery shouting, "Kill the Jews!" Some Arab workers he knew tried to help him escape, but he was beaten and left for dead. When the British police arrived it was noticed he was still moving beneath a pile of corpses and he was taken to hospital where he lay unconscious for five days.[114] His internationalism remained unshaken and later, still a worker in the refinery office, he too was an activist in Matzpen. He later wrote a book, *Judenfrage und Zionismus* (*The Jewish Question and Zionism*, 1986). He died in 2001.[115]

Susi Scheller and her husband Dov were also in exile from Nazi Germany. She remembers her first encounter with Ygal at what was probably the founding meeting of the RCL in around 1941. She remembers Gabriel Baer, Jakob Taut and then later Jabra Nicola. She became good friends with Ygal, although on one occasion he tried to remove her wedding ring because he found it "petty bourgeois" (*spiessig*). Whereas some of the German Trotskyists in Palestine were only interested in waiting for their return home, those in the RCL tried to be active in the politics of Palestine. But much of their discussion was necessarily concerned with the war and, in particular, the opening of a second front in Europe, which they awaited impatiently. When the war was over they had difficulty in getting out of Palestine and returning to Germany. Eventually in 1950 they returned to Germany and assisted with the rebuilding of German Trotskyism under the repressive Adenauer government.[116] Other RCL members were Moi Katz, Otto Weigler, Sigi Rothschild, Theodor and Hava Blauweiss and Ana Shohat.[117]

Towards the end of the war some new young recruits were made. Danny Tait's Jewish father had come to Palestine as a British soldier in the First World War. He married a Palestinian woman and stayed on, taking a post with the British Mandate. When the Second World War broke out his son Danny was evacuated to South Africa. Here he was radicalised by the experience of South African society and by meeting people sympathetic to Trotskyism such as Chanie Rosenberg and Baruch Hirson. On returning to Palestine in 1944 he became a member of the RCL at the age of 18. He remembered Ygal as the main animating figure in the RCL and recalled his self-assurance and his capacity to win any argument and to crush his opponents in debate. In particular when he met left Zionists from South Africa he was able to do a demolition job on Zionism. Ygal also took on the task of political education of younger comrades; he ran a study group on the French Revolution and persuaded Tait to read a book on the topic. Tait remembered him as "very genuine", though sometimes prone to exaggerate.

Danny's father was concerned at his son's involvement in far-left politics, and took him to England, where he continued in Trotskyist activity. In 1946, at the age of 19, he represented the Middle East at a Fourth International meeting in Paris.[118] He died in 2006.

Dov Shas was born in Romania and during the German occupation took part in the Communist underground resistance. At the end of the war he came to Palestine with Hashomer Hatzair, but rapidly broke with Zionism and joined the RCL. He was only 20 years old, considerably younger than other RCL members, and was regarded as an "apprentice member". He met Ygal and was very interested in a series of lectures he gave. Hopeful of cooperation between Jewish and Arab workers he went to work in the Haifa oil refinery. The creation of the Zionist state was an enormous setback for such hopes, but in the 1960s he too became a member of Matzpen, in which he was active for many years. He died in 2006.

The RCL was a tiny group.[119] While there are no records of membership figures, an estimate of somewhere around 20 is probably reasonable. The main groups were in Tel Aviv and Haifa, and for security reasons there was little contact between them. So there were no aggregate meetings and little opportunity for members to get a sense of the group as a whole. However, Dov Shas does recall that at one point Ygal did the cooking for other members of the group. He was not particularly gifted at this, and cooked lentils every day.

Circumstances required the group to act clandestinely. They had three sets of enemies – the British authorities, the Zionists and the Stalinists.[120] The Zionists were becoming increasingly violent and the Communist Party, though weak and divided, shared the loathing of Trotskyism that was common to all supporters of Moscow. The members used pseudonyms – Ygal was "Yosef", Jakob Taut "Michael" or "Fritz", Gabriel Baer "Munir", Dov Shas "Moishe" and Theodor Blauweiss "Aryeh".

The necessity of this clandestinity is questionable. Certainly the situation under British rule was less dangerous than it had been in Nazi-occupied Romania, where Dov Shas had first been active and where discovery meant immediate death. Danny Tait later believed that by 1944 the police were not interested in Trotskyists, and were far more concerned with the growing threat of Zionist terrorism. He thought Ygal's belief that the police were after him was probably exaggerated.

Tait was living in a little room on the first-floor landing of his grandfather's house. He had a duplicator and would print leaflets and papers at night. On one occasion the police saw the light on in his room late at night and raided it, but when they discovered he was a Trotskyist and not the Stern Gang, as they had imagined, they dropped the matter. Because he had a British passport, Tait used to take parcels of leaflets and papers by bus from Tel Aviv to Haifa. He insisted that this did not require any particular courage, although Chanie Rosenberg believes that what he did was quite hazardous.[121]

Yet Tait recalled that Palestine was a dangerous place to live in, and there was a general atmosphere of suspicion. When his father discovered that he was looking for some cans – to use to hold paint for daubing slogans – he immediately assumed his revolutionary son was engaged in manufacturing bombs.

Necessarily the main emphasis of the RCL was propaganda: the distribution of papers and leaflets. This could not be done openly in the streets; devices had to be used to get the leaflets into the hands of the public without exposing the distributors to arrest. Various mechanical means were employed in order to shower down leaflets from tall buildings alongside busy streets. A delayed action device involving a slow-burning candle or a can of water with a hole in the bottom meant that by the time the leaflets came fluttering down to the street the comrade responsible could be back at ground level watching the result of his or her actions.[122]

At other times the comrades used more risky methods. Danny Tait remembered himself and a young German going out on bicycles and throwing leaflets before cycling away to avoid capture. Such distribution was a hit-and-miss affair. It assumed that in any random selection of passers-by at least a few would be open to revolutionary ideas. This was based on the expectation that revolution was not far off. A combination of Trotsky's perspective and the memory of the revolutionary wave that had followed the First World War fed their optimism.

Sometimes, however, the leafleting was more targeted. Danny Tait recalled an occasion when they discovered the Young Communists were meeting in an empty shop. He and another comrade went to the shop, his friend pushed open the door, Danny hurled in a bundle of leaflets and then they both ran away.

In addition to leaflets the RCL produced a paper. Its very name was an assertion of anti-Stalinism. The paper of the PCP was called *Qol Haʿam* – Voice of the People. In a deliberate rejection of the Popular Front strategy implied by this title the Trotskyists proudly entitled their publication *Qol Hammaʿamad* – Voice of the Class.* In order to evade censorship, title was frequently changed.

Despite its proud title, the paper was a modest affair. It was not printed but produced on a flatbed copier. There was not even a handle to turn; each sheet had to be printed separately.[123] According to Hanna Ben Dov the printing machine had been stolen.[124] The circulation was extremely limited; at best a few hundred copies were produced. As with the leaflets, distribution had to be clandestine. Dov Shas remembers distributing copies around the workshops of Tel Aviv. Copies were simply left on the floor in the hope that

---

* I have not managed to locate any copies of *Qol Hammaʿamad*. It is listed in the catalogue of the Jewish National Library in Jerusalem, but when I visited in 2005 staff were unable to find it, and in 2010 I was informed that staff still could not locate it. Whether it has been mislaid or removed for political reasons I can only speculate. I have enquired of a number of other libraries, but none of them possess it. Hopefully copies will come to light at some point.

interested workers might pick them up. Chanie Rosenberg was given the job of taking copies to the university library in Jerusalem, where she left them on the tables and hastened to disappear.[125]

With such limited resources it was difficult for the paper to act as an organiser; it was simply a means whereby the RCL could advertise its existence and make known the possibility of an alternative to the prevailing ideas. Dov Shas believed the style of the publication was too theoretical and not sufficiently addressed to a working class readership. Nonetheless, the fact the paper appeared at all in such adverse conditions was testimony to the courage and dedication of the small band of comrades.

The RCL succeeded in making contact with the British army in Palestine. It may well have been through Trotskyists serving in the British army that some tenuous links with the Fourth International were maintained during the war years. Dov Shas remembered one instance in which a British soldier contacted the group. Chanie Rosenberg's first task for the RCL was to translate into English and then type a leaflet destined to be distributed to British troops.[126]

Despite the difficult circumstances and its meagre resources, the RCL had a firm orientation on the working class, and did what it could to encourage the unity of Arab and Jewish workers. As a brief history of Palestinian Trotskyism records, "During and after the world war, the League...frequently intervened with leaflets in the struggles in the British military camps, in the railway and oil companies – i.e. it concentrated on those enterprises where Jews and Arabs together were exploited by British capital".[127] In fact these were the only places where Jews and Arabs worked together.

The RCL had to stand up firmly against the Zionist trade unions and defend Arab workers. In a 1947 polemic with members of the American SWP Cliff pointed out:

> In the 1944 May Day meeting of the Jaffa Branch, the Histadrut was attacked for its Zionist policy directed towards turning Palestine into a Jewish State, and a resolution to this effect was passed unanimously. The Histadrut promptly reacted by bringing four of the Arab militants to the government court on charge of disturbing a meeting. We of the Revolutionary Communist League of course supported these militants, against the Histadrut.[128]

In particular, this meant an orientation on the organisations of the working class. Jakob Taut, who worked in the oil refinery in Haifa, worked inside the left-Zionist Mapam party, on whose platform he was elected to the factory committee.[129] Dov Shas, who later went to work in the same place, became a member of the PCP. In his activity for the RCL he concentrated on trade union work. This was difficult, because of the requirements of secrecy. Moreover there were no instructions from the organisation on how to work in the trade unions. The group itself had limited experience to draw on, and the writings on trade unionism from the Comintern and Trotskyist traditions had little to say that was relevant to the specific conditions of Palestine beyond the injunction that socialists should be inside the mass organisations of the working class. Shas also remembered Ygal's insistence that trade union activity was not enough, and that comrades must do political work.

Shas remembered that in the period just after the war there was real enthusiasm about the possibility of united action by Jewish and Arab workers. Looking back, after more than half a century of the sad history of the Zionist state, such hopes may seem mere illusion. But in the years immediately before the creation of the state of Israel there were real indications of the possibility of Arab-Jewish unity, above all in the general strike in the spring of 1946. Yossi Schwartz has described it:

> The largest and most dramatic episode of joint action between Arab and Jewish workers in the history of Palestine took place in April 1946. Postal, telephone, and telegraph workers were responsible for sparking off what became an unprecedentedly broad strike of white- and blue-collar government employees...
>
> On the appointed day the workers, including thirty or forty Arabs employed at the Tel Aviv post office, went on strike. The next day all the postal workers in Palestine had stopped work... Their militancy spread quickly and on April 14 both the Arab and the Jewish railway workers came out on strike...
>
> Thus the Arab and Jewish railway workers...through their joint struggle paralysed the country's railway system. There had never before been such a general strike of Palestine's railway and postal workers. What was even more striking was the fact that the middle and lower level white-collar government employees also took part in the strike.

By April 15, 1946, less than a week after the Tel Aviv postal workers had come out, around 23,000 government employees were on strike... However, both the Histadrut and the PAWS [Palestinian Arab Workers' Society] did everything to stop the strike from spreading by keeping the refinery and base workers at their jobs.[130]

The government sector was quite small and in the end the bureaucrats held the line, but the potential revealed in the events showed that the spectre of unity haunted both the British imperialists and the Zionists. With its tiny forces, the RCL did what it could to take the movement forward by distributing "a leaflet in Arabic and Hebrew among the strikers, pointing out that British imperialism feared that the strikes and demonstrations could have a resounding effect in neighboring countries, such as Egypt, where large-scale anti-British strikes were underway".[131]

As Schwartz points out, the Haifa oil refinery, where Jakob Taut and later Dov Shas went to work, was of strategic importance in terms of the potential unity of Arab and Jewish workers:

> In 1945 the Haifa refinery employed about a thousand workers, making it one of Haifa's (and Palestine's) largest workplaces. The PAWS had a strong base among the Arab refinery workers... Though Jews made up only about one-third of the refinery workforce, they held a much higher proportion of the skilled and clerical jobs; only half of the Jewish refinery workers were Histadrut members, possibly because of its racist line. The refinery and the petroleum industry were the most advanced sectors of the Palestinian economy.[132]

Towards the end of the war the RCL made its most significant recruit. The Rosenbergs, a prosperous Zionist couple from Cape Town, decided to emigrate to Palestine. One of their daughters, Chanie, had been active in the left-Zionist organisation Hashomer Hatzair, where Trotskyist ideas were current. Her friend and mentor, Baruch Hirson, was evolving towards Trotskyism.* When she left for Palestine Hirson urged her to get in touch with the Palestinian Trotskyists.[133]

On arrival in Palestine, Chanie joined a kibbutz. She greatly liked

---

* Years later Hirson was to contribute to *International Socialism* on behalf of the Socialist League of Africa – "South Africa: Ten Years of the Stay-at-Home", *International Socialism* 5 (1961), pp5-14, and "South Africa: Once Again on the Stay-at-Home", *International Socialism* 6 (1961), pp12-14.

the collective life of the institution, but was immediately confronted with experiences that challenged her attempt to reconcile Zionism and socialism. She later recalled:

> We were put into a kibbutz in the valley of Jezreel, which was on a strategically placed hill where there were four kibbutzim and four Arab villages. The Zionists wanted to get the whole hill. The Zionists had paid the Arabs for the land – or rather, the head man of the village, so the money didn't go to the peasants. The peasants said that they had got nothing for their land, so the kibbutzim (some of which, including ours, were considered extreme left), simply got out 1,500 people, picked up stones and threw them at the Arabs, who fled. I became an anti-Zionist from that moment.[134]

Ygal was invited to speak at Chanie's kibbutz. The meeting itself was not a great success: Ygal spoke for far too long (allegedly for 14 hours!), and his Hebrew was often incomprehensible to the audience of new immigrants.[135] But the meeting between Ygal and Chanie was to affect the whole of their subsequent lives. Soon they were living together and the following year they married. Partly the marriage was a matter of convenience. In British-ruled Palestine it was a distinct advantage to have a wife with a South African passport, and for travel abroad it was even more valuable.[136]

But there was much more to it than that. The term "soul mates" is a cliché, cheapened by misuse. But the alliance between Ygal and Chanie was to be a remarkable one, lasting more than half a century. Private emotion was paralleled by a public partnership. Chanie translated and typed Cliff's writings, shared in his intellectual development and played an active role as a militant in the organisation he built and led. Anyone who knew the couple would agree that without Chanie Cliff's achievements would have been quite simply inconceivable.

Chanie was a woman of phenomenal energy and had a very positive personality. Tuvia Shlonsky, who knew her in Palestine, remembers that despite the great difficulties she and Ygal underwent she was "always smiling".[137]

Chanie had come from a family where art, music and literature were highly valued (the Rosenbergs were related to the First World War poet and artist Isaac Rosenberg). One of her most cherished possessions was a set of Phaidon art books. Ygal persuaded her that as a revolutionary she did not need them; they were sold to Tuvia Shlonsky.[138] The young couple faced a life of deep poverty. They lived in one room, which was so small that when a bed was installed it was impossible to open the door and they had to enter through the window.[139] They lived on one meal a day.[140] At one point even the rats were obliged to eat Cliff's shaving-stick, because they could not find any food in the home.[141]

Civil marriage did not exist in Palestine, so a religious wedding took place in February 1945. Danny Tait borrowed hats from his uncle's home so that the comrades could attend in appropriate dress. The fact that Ygal had been married before caused some delay until his first wife could be traced and a divorce rapidly arranged.

Chanie's parents, together with her sister Mickey and her younger brother Mike, now arrived in Palestine. It may well be supposed that two such respectable families as the Glucksteins and the Rosenbergs scarcely approved of their children espousing fiercely anti-Zionist politics and operating on the fringes of legality and beyond. Yet both sets of parents were remarkably tolerant. The four became close and spent much time together, taking great pleasure in Ygal's father's jokes. Years later, when Ygal's mother and Chanie's father had died, Ygal's father was great friends with Chanie's widowed mother.[142]

Ygal was hired to give Hebrew lessons to Chanie's sister Mickey. Yet he was far too single-minded to make a language teacher. Mickey recounts that he would read a page of Hebrew with her and then give her a lecture on politics. He would then demand to know whether she agreed with him, following this with the knockdown argument that if she didn't disagree, she must agree, and should therefore join the RCL.[143] All this left Mickey somewhat confused, though later she moved to London, and became a stalwart of the SRG in the 1950s. Chanie's younger brother Mike was at school with Tuvia Shlonsky and they became firm friends.[144] Later Mike would move to England and be one of Cliff's closest collaborators.

Chanie, meanwhile, supplemented the couple's meagre income by teaching in a school. For a time she was employed as a governess, but was sacked for having revolutionary leaflets in her possession.[145] The establishment of the state of Israel in 1948, when many Arab workers were driven from their homes, put an end to the hopes nourished by the RCL. The group was never big enough to have an impact on events, and it largely disappeared from the historical record. While Ygal and his comrades were working so hard to build an organisation, they were faced with the fact that the world was changing rapidly. With only limited contact with international Trotskyism, they had to face the new realities of the post-war world, which was turning out to be rather different from what they had expected.

Firstly, on a global scale the pre-war predictions of Trotsky had been substantially mistaken. The war had not shattered the fragile equilibrium of the "degenerated workers' state"; on the contrary, the USSR, with Stalin firmly in the saddle, had emerged from the war greatly strengthened. Reformism, far from being exhausted, had taken on a new lease of life, as shown notably by the Attlee government in Britain.

Secondly, the relationship between Zionism and imperialism was changing. Until 1939 British imperialism's main concern was to preserve its influence in the Middle East and to do so it played off Arabs and Jews against each other (though generally it was more sympathetic to Jews than to Arabs). In the course of the war Britain, needing Arab support, became less sympathetic to Zionist goals. But the effect of the war was to weaken British imperialism. The Zionist movement turned to anti-British terrorism and looked to the newly dominant world powers for support – Russia and in particular the US. The prospect of a Zionist state was becoming ever more real.[146]

Thirdly, the true enormity of the Holocaust was just becoming known.* The Zionists exploited the Holocaust to legitimise their cause.[147] But even without such exploitation the impact of the Holocaust could only be to strengthen Zionism. As Cliff pointed out in an article written half a century later:

> Until the Second World War the overwhelming majority of Jews in the world, especially working class Jews, were not supporters of Zionism... Today the overwhelming majority of Jews are Zionists, and this is very understandable.[148]

It is possible to trace the new thinking of Ygal and the RCL through a series of articles published during and just after the war.

In December 1944 the British Trotskyist paper *Workers*

---

* Cliff and Chanie both lost relatives in the Holocaust. Cliff's aunt and cousin with their families died at the hands of the Nazis (Cliff, *A World to Win*, pp5-6).

International News published an article entitled "Zionism – An Outpost of Imperialism", described as an "Open Letter to Labour Party Conference by a Group of Palestine Socialists".[149] This is not specifically attributed to the RCL, but given its revolutionary content and its attacks on other sections of the left it could scarcely have had any other source. No names were attached, but since Ygal was one of the main thinkers and writers in the RCL, it seems likely that he had some part in drafting it; both style and content suggest quite strongly that he may have been the author.

The Labour Party conference was held in December 1944. It was due to debate a National Executive statement on the international post-war settlement. The section on Palestine committed the Labour Party to support for Zionism and for unrestricted immigration:

> There is surely neither hope nor meaning in a "Jewish National Home" unless we are prepared to let Jews, if they wish, enter this tiny land in such numbers as to become a majority... Let the Arabs be encouraged to move out as the Jews move in. Let them be compensated handsomely for their land and let their settlement elsewhere be carefully organised and generously financed. The Arabs have many wide territories of their own; they must not claim to exclude the Jews from this small area of Palestine, less than the size of Wales. Indeed, we should re-examine also the possibility of extending the present Palestinian boundaries, by agreement with Egypt, Syria or Transjordan.

The aim of the "open letter" was to dissuade delegates from supporting this policy. In fact the National Executive policy was carried overwhelmingly on a show of hands.[150]

The article began with a long account of the role of Zionism in Palestine and of the oppression of the Arab population. Among other things it was pointed out that "there is not a single Arab pupil in any of the numerous Jewish schools of the country" (perhaps a clue to Ygal's authorship, evoking the indignation he had felt in his childhood). But the question was not seen in national terms – class was brought to the fore:

> The strongest resistance against the Zionists comes from the lowest class of Arab society, which has suffered most from the impact of Zionism. The tale told by Zionists abroad – that the Fellahs are not in themselves anti-Zionist but that they are being influenced by agitators from the feudal classes – is a brazen lie. Gradually an Arab workers' movement is

growing and so is its resistance to Zionism.

The article then went on to deal with the question of immigration to Palestine, a matter in the direct control of the British government, and therefore a highly relevant topic for Labour Party members who were nourishing the hope that they would soon be in government:

> The question of a few hundred thousand refugees looms large in the headlines. Countless conferences are held – instead of opening the doors of the USA, England and her Dominions, with their vast spaces and great natural resources. You may ask: Open the doors of the United States and the British Empire – why not of Palestine? From all that we have said above it should have become clear that the immigration of Jews to Palestine is fundamentally so different from that to all other countries that it is every socialist's duty to oppose it.

This is perhaps the most striking point in the article. It marks a complete break with the position argued by "L Rock" in his 1938 articles, and shows just how far Ygal and his comrades had developed in the previous few years. At first sight the argument might appear callous, especially just at the time when the enormity of the Holocaust was being revealed to the world (Auschwitz was liberated in January 1945). Almost all the members of the RCL, apart from Ygal, were themselves immigrants who had taken refuge in Palestine to escape the Nazis. But the logic of further mass Jewish immigration could only be Zionist domination of Palestine and the creation of a Zionist state.

The article further pointed to the hypocrisy of the great powers who were on the verge of becoming victors in the world war, and who preferred to resolve the problem of Europe's Jewish population by shipping them off to Palestine rather than offering them refuge in their own ample territories.

Although in Palestine the RCL worked for the unity of Arab and Jewish workers, there was no triumphalist rhetoric about Arab-Jewish unity. On the contrary, the article noted the uncomfortable fact that "almost all the Jewish workers in Palestine are Zionists". This was explained by the higher wages enjoyed by Jewish workers, by the existence of a "closed Zionist economy and society", and by the "indifference of the allied governments towards the plight of the Jews in Europe" which made Jewish workers believe their sole salvation lay in Palestine.

It was also made clear that the Zionist project held enormous dangers for the Jewish population of Palestine, and that their future could be safeguarded only by the abandonment of Zionism:

> If the Jewish workers do not join the Arab struggle for liberation, the Jewish population will be used by Imperialism to strengthen its position in the Orient, and if necessary, the Jews will be sacrificed to the hatred of the Orient. Thus the fate of the Jewish State may become that of the Armenian State which was set up at the end of the last world war and was completely annihilated as soon as Imperialism ceased to bolster it up.

> The expansion of Zionism is therefore, ultimately, a disaster for the Jewish masses living in Palestine. Only the collapse of Zionism – the sooner the better – can save the Jewish population in Palestine from such a fate.

The article was written from the perspective that the end of the war would rapidly lead to a period of revolutionary upheavals comparable to those after 1918. The concluding appeal to British workers was based on the same premises:

> During this war, the British workers have been increasingly demanding their rights; their collisions with the bourgeoisie and government will multiply and become fiercer in character, as well as with the Labour Party leaders who are calling for national unity and the maintenance of the Empire. The great strikes that have lately taken place in Great Britain are the first signs of their awakening.*

> The colonial peoples will demand their freedom with increasing vigour; they no longer want to wait for the coming of the "new world" promised at the beginning of the war...

> The rising of the colonial peoples against all oppression and discrimination will help the revolutionary workers in the other countries. Britain's workers will support the colonies in their struggle for freedom, forging a new international solidarity for the building of a new society.

> Zionism will perish together with the rotten capitalist order.

The promised revolutionary wave did not arrive, except in stunted form in a few countries. The confident hope that British

---

* This indicates that the RCL was receiving some information about the situation in Britain. While there had been strikes in Britain, some led by Trotskyists, this seems to somewhat exaggerate the significance of the militancy.

workers and those in other imperialist countries would support the anti-colonial struggle was to be shown false on more than one occasion. Ygal was still indulging in the rhetoric of the early Communist International. A bitter road lay ahead of him.

A year later Ygal published a major study of the current situation in the Middle East, entitled "The Middle East at the Crossroads". The "crossroads" image was to stay with him; thirty years later he wrote *Portugal at the Crossroads*. It fitted his vision of history: not a series of mechanically determined stages, but a succession of historic choices.

The article, probably brought from Palestine to Europe by Danny Tait,[151] established Ygal as a figure of some significance in the Fourth International. It was serialised in *Fourth International*, journal of the American SWP, in *Workers International News* and subsequently as a pamphlet in Britain, and in French in *Quatrième Internationale*.[152] It was the first time Ygal had written under the name "T Cliff" (the stone theme continued – the erstwhile rock was now a cliff). Ygal had had many pseudonyms, and on occasion could hardly remember what his real name was.[153] He can scarcely have imagined that the name Cliff – Tony would be added a little later – would stay with him for over half a century. It was Chanie who gave him the name T Cliff; when asked what the T stood for, she initially said "Timothy", but later decided Tony was more appropriate.[154]

The article set out to explain developments in the Middle East after the end of the war, with Zionist terrorism in Palestine and strikes in Egypt, Syria and Iraq. As with the 1938 articles, Cliff's starting point was imperialism. In the first section he analysed the importance of the Middle East to imperialism in terms of air and sea communications. In particular he observed, ten years before the crisis of 1956, that the digging of the Suez Canal had "turned the Arab East into a large battlefield". With substantial statistical support he showed the role of foreign capital in the economies of Egypt and Palestine. He explained what this meant for the low living standards of rural and urban workers in the Middle East, and concluded, as he had done in earlier writings, that the Arab bourgeoisie could offer no way out. Consistent with his earlier analyses he saw Egypt and the Egyptian working class as the key to the situation: "Egypt is the weakest link in the imperialist chain of the Middle

East as social antagonisms are the deepest there."

In this context he set out to situate the complex role of Zionism in the Middle East. Zionist terrorists were making the headlines with anti-British outrages. But Cliff pointed out the double nature of Zionism:

> Zionism…plays a double role: first directly as an important pillar of imperialism, giving it active support and opposing the liberation struggle of the Arab nation, and second as a passive servant behind which imperialism can hide and towards which it can direct the ire of the Arab masses.

After describing the role of Zionism in Palestine and the oppression of the Arab population, Cliff went on to observe the paradox that, just as the horrors of the Holocaust were being made known, the Zionists in Palestine were playing the game of imperialism:

> It is a tragedy that the sons of the very people which has been persecuted and massacred in such a bestial fashion, and which today is the unprovoking victim of national hatred – of fascism, the highest form of imperialism – should itself be driven into a chauvinistic, militaristic fervour, and become the blind tool of imperialism in subjugating the Arab masses. In the same way that the existing social order is to be blamed for the calamity of the Jews, so is it to be blamed for the exploitation of their catastrophe for reactionary, oppressive aims.

The current Zionist terrorism did not undermine this argument, he claimed, because imperialism and Zionism had "both common and antagonistic interests":

> Zionism wants to build a strong Jewish capitalist state. Imperialism is indeed interested in the existence of a capitalist Jewish society enveloped by the hatred of colonial masses, but not in order that Zionism should become too strong a factor.

Cliff still held the orthodox Trotskyist position that the Second World War (which had come to an end only a few months earlier) would lead to a potentially revolutionary situation. Hence he considered that, however events turned out, Zionism did not have a bright future:

> The Zionists have come into a blind alley. The victory of the proletariat of the West and the masses of the East will put an end to Zionist dreams… If imperialism continues to rule over the world, then whatever the Jews do they are doomed. If the world revolutionary wave rises to the heights,

then all the weak peoples, including world Jewry, will be saved.

He considered the possibility, very real as it turned out, of "a Zionist switchover to America", but considered this could only mean a "short-lived postponement of Zionism's burial". The only solution for Jewish workers in Palestine lay in "renouncing Zionist dreams of domination". There was therefore a stark choice before the Middle East:

> Either the rise of a great revolutionary proletarian power which will lead the masses of peasants in the national liberation struggle, or the bloody victory of imperialist reaction and its allies in the upper classes... Either revolution or communal slaughter, pogroms, etc.

As a prophecy this was both false and terribly true; what Cliff had not fully grasped is that this time the Jews in Palestine would be the oppressors and not the victims.

In a final section he went on to examine the question of revolutionary leadership which could make the difference between a victorious and a tragic outcome. He studied in detail the role of the Communist parties of the Middle East, and the way they had abandoned socialism in favour of popular fronts and class alliances. Yet the overall perspective was too optimistic:

> There is a tremendous disproportion between the ripening of the objective conditions in the world and in the Middle East driving towards a revolutionary struggle, and between the building of the revolutionary party in the Middle East. If this disproportion is not overcome in time, a terrible catastrophe will threaten the masses in this region. But there is no place for pessimism or defeatism. The problem will be resolved not through one battle, but in a series of battles which can give even small revolutionary nuclei great possibilities of development.

So he argued that "the idea that strong organisations are a precondition for the class struggle is the product of a mechanistic, undialectical approach" and that sometimes revolutionary organisations could be "forged in the fire of the struggle". Even more optimistically he reported:

> The first nuclei of Fourth Internationalists exist in Egypt and Palestine. The primary task at the moment is to strengthen and unite them into one party of the Arab East.

It is hard not to see an element of bravado and wish-fulfilment in this claim. Cliff knew from bitter experience just how small and weak the RCL was, and the attempts to make contact with the Egyptian Trotskyists had not proved fruitful.

The article ended with an appeal for support to British workers, who were for Cliff still a distant abstraction, but with whom he would soon be making a much closer acquaintance.

"The Middle East at the Crossroads" was Ygal's best work so far. It was well-documented and contained many acute perceptions and observations. The last links with Zionism were well and truly broken, and from now on Ygal would be an implacable enemy of Zionism. But it contained some serious miscalculations. The possibility that Zionism could be successful and establish a state that would last 60 and more years had not crossed Ygal's mind at this time. His underestimation of Zionism was part of an underestimation of the ability of imperialism to survive and flourish in the post-war period. He was quite right that such survival would mean terrible human suffering, especially for those who were already the most deprived and oppressed. But the system did survive. There were many more questions for his enquiring mind to grapple with in the years ahead.

The article helped to establish Ygal's position as a recognised figure in the international Trotskyist movement. In the US the radical writer Scott Nearing commended it in *World Events*: "The article carries less heat and throws more light on the subject than anything I have read for many a day".[155] Subsequently it was reported that Nearing's review had led to a number of orders for the issues of *Fourth International* containing Cliff's article.[156] The veteran Albert Glotzer, despite reservations, described Cliff's work as "an excellent series of analytical articles".[157]

In a further article written in Jerusalem in July 1946,[158] Cliff traced the subsequent developments of the situation. He pointed out that in response to Zionist terrorism, British imperialism was directing at the Jews the same kind of repression it had used against the Arabs some years earlier. Though Britain wished to use Zionism, it had no interest in Zionism becoming "too strong a power". He stressed that neither the Zionists nor the Arab leaders such as the Mufti – who had supported the Nazis – and the "clerical-fascist" Muslim Brotherhood, could be consistent opponents of imperialism.

He pointed to the alternative, made concrete in the April 1946 strike in Palestine, "in which 26,000 Arab and 6,000 Jewish workers participated". This showed that the future lay with "the all-embracing unity of the trade unions in the Arab East countries irrespective of national or communal differences". The goal of the struggle must be:

> liberation of the Middle East, in which all the minorities – Jews, Kurds, etc. – will be given wide autonomy in the regions inhabited by them, within the all embracing framework of the Republic of Workers and Peasants of the Arab East.

Ygal's final contribution to the Fourth International debate on the Middle East came in 1947, shortly after his departure from Palestine. It was a polemic against some of the views held by members of the American SWP, and in particular a piece by Leo Lyons called "A Revolutionary Programme for the Jews".[159]

As history moved towards the creation of the Zionist state, Ygal's anti-Zionist passion grew ever stronger. He regarded the views expressed by Lyons as positively dangerous for the progress of Trotskyism in the Middle East:

> We are sure that acceptance by the SWP of the position expressed in all these items will do infinite harm to the cause of the Fourth International in all the Arab countries and may even bring about a cleavage between the colonial sections and the SWP.

The article was a little masterpiece of invective. Any deference Ygal might once have felt towards the larger and more established organisations of the Fourth International had now disappeared. He had full confidence in his views and in his superior grasp of the situation in the Middle East. He deployed cutting irony and launched a barrage of facts at the hapless Lyons:

> This article, bringing the superficial tourist approach to the Palestine question to its height, is no more than a mixture of ignorance as regards the situation in Palestine, an absolute lack of any understanding of the theory of the Permanent Revolution and the colonial question, and above all, an illustration of the proverb "Fools rush in where angels fear to tread". Its tendency is Zionist in all but words, and it is for this fact alone that it is important to analyse it.

In demolishing Lyons, Ygal set out his definitive critique of Zionism; it was his final and most complete statement on the question until 1967, when events opened up a new period.

To begin with, Ygal attacked Lyons's positions on both the role of the Histadrut and that of left-Zionist organisations such as Hashomer Hatzair, demonstrating their pernicious nature with a wealth of detail. He then took up the argument about immigration, arguing that "in the independent capitalist countries the struggle for free immigration is part and parcel of the struggle for socialism. This is not always the case in the colonies."

Moreover, he pointed out, the Jews in Palestine enjoyed a standard of living superior to that of the Arabs and privileges they would not have elsewhere:

> *In these conditions, to be against the Zionist policy of 100 percent Jewish labour means to be against Jewish immigration into Palestine.* He who is for Jewish immigration into a Palestine under imperialist rule *must*, by the logic of the objective conditions, be also for the Zionist policy of a closed economy, enmity towards the Arabs, etc.

As the state of Israel loomed ever nearer, he insisted that although in the past many Zionists had opposed the demand for a Jewish state, it was now "impossible to be a consistent Zionist without being for a Jewish State".

While he did not write off the Jewish working class, Ygal argued that the real hopes for the region lay with the working class in Egypt:

> The Jewish worker can on no account lead the struggle against foreign capital and imperialism, and against feudalism. The only thing he can do, if he renounces Zionism, is to follow the lead of the Arab proletariat, whose main centres are Cairo and Alexandria.

There was an interesting section on the "myth" of the kibbutzim, which, he pointed out, were financed by rich Jewish capitalists who had no interest in promoting communism.

He took on the argument that Zionism, and imperialism in general, played some sort of progressive historical role:

> Marx spoke most appropriately when he said that it was British penetration into India which, for the first time in history, built the basis for the unity of India. This it did by smashing the self-sufficient economy, by connecting all the fibres of the economy to the world market, by building railways, etc. At the same time imperialism did its best to preserve the

outworn feudal property relations, in this way preventing the economic, cultural and political unity of India from being really complete. To say, therefore, that imperialism suppresses the national movement, does not mean to say that it itself did not provide the impetus for its creation.

It is unquestionable that the Arab national movement would have come to life in Palestine in the same way that it came to life in Egypt, Syria, Lebanon and Iraq, without Zionist expansion. Zionist expansion served not as the generator of the Arab national movement, but only as its distorter.

With this passionate and devastating polemic Ygal finally settled his accounts with the Zionism of his youth.

Ygal had established himself as a revolutionary journalist. But he aspired to be more than a journalist, and was well aware that effective practice could not be developed without a parallel development of theory.

Throughout the difficult years of the war, despite the pressure of activity and the dangers of illegal work, Ygal was also working on a book. Its subject was to be no less than a Marxist account of the Middle East, something which neither the Comintern nor the Fourth International had managed to provide.[160] His stated aim was "to describe the Arab East as it is, stripped of all romantic camouflage".[161]

His concern was to give a concrete account of the specific features of the area, and for this he needed a historical approach. This immediately brought him up against a problem. Most Marxist accounts of the origins of capitalism dealt with the European experience. Breaking with this Eurocentric perspective, Ygal was confronted with the fact that from the 8th to the 13th century Arab civilisation had been at the "peak of world culture", but that it had not made the transition to capitalism,* so that it was European imperialism that had modernised the Middle East. To explain this, Ygal had to reject the view of history as a mechanical sequence of stages:

> History marches forward in the most crooked ways, ways rent with contradictions, jumps, sharp turns and lapses. European feudalism was backward, primitive, poor and unenlightened. Arab feudalism was progressive, developed, rich and enlightened. And it was just because of this

---

* His use of the term "feudalism" to describe the Arab world would now be rejected by most historians.

that it was easier for the third estate and capitalism to gain the day in Europe than it was in the Arab East. Cracks formed in the European economy through which the merchants and artisans could rise to form the powerful craft guilds and raise the militant towns which battled for their freedom from feudalism.[162]

He went on to trace the role of imperialism in Egypt from Napoleon to the British takeover. Behind the scholarly analysis, with abundant statistics, burned a fierce anger against the crimes of imperialism. He mocked the "civilising" role of British imperialism in Egypt, by noting that in the 28 years up to 1910, it had devoted no more than 1.4 percent of total expenditure to education and the same to health. He asked, "Is there any greater condemnation of imperialism?"[163]

After the historical introduction he proceeded to an economic and political analysis of the interconnected situations in Egypt, Palestine, Syria, Lebanon and Iraq (the states of the Arabian Peninsula were considered too "backward" to be of interest).[164] Looking at the situation of the Middle East at the end of the Second World War he noted that though it was currently the source of less than 6 percent of world oil production, oil was of growing importance for the area. He pointed to the increasing importance of US imperialism in the Arab East, and the consequent decline of British influence.[165]

Egypt got most space and was accorded the greatest importance. The Egyptian proletariat, he believed, was "the pioneer of the whole Arab East". Hence the Iraqi working class could not resolve its problems for itself, but would have to be part of "a revolutionary wave which will embrace all the countries of the Arab East and whose centres will be Cairo and Alexandria".[166]

Alex Callinicos has pointed out that he went beyond the Trotskyist orthodoxy according to which imperialism prevented industrial development in the colonial and semi-colonial countries. He showed that, in the specific conditions of the 1930s and the Second World War, Egypt could experience significant industrialisation. The analysis anticipated later discussions of the Newly Industrialising Countries of East Asia and Latin America.[167]

The underlying theme of the book was an attempt to apply the theory of permanent revolution to the Arab East. It was the emerging working class which would settle the future of the area:

> The proletariat of the Arab East must travel rapidly through a combined development. Young, raw, inexperienced and unlearned, it must march with seven league boots, skipping many stages which the proletariat of the developed countries passed through and passing through others very rapidly.[168]

The final chapters dealt with the trade unions and the Stalinist parties.

A separate section of the book dealt with Zionism, dismissed as "completely utopian and illusory" and an "attempt to run away from fascism and imperialism". Only if Jewish workers broke with Zionism would it be possible to achieve "true unity between Arab and Jewish workers".[169]

The analysis followed the standard Trotskyist view that the end of the war would lead to a revolutionary crisis. Ygal still accepted the Leninist theory of the "aristocracy of labour", but he believed its time had come to an end:

> Today English capitalism cannot throw crumbs to even the tiny layer of petty bourgeoisie, trade union bureaucrats and highly skilled workers, let alone the masses of the English proletariat. These latter are sentenced to mass unemployment and wars. Today capitalism-imperialism imprisons both the workers of the "mother" countries and the toilers of the colonial countries in the same train, even though in different carriages, a train which is rolling down into the abyss of crises, starvation, wars and barbarism.[170] *

In his conclusion he even speculated whether, in the probable event of a revolution in Britain coming before that in the Middle East, the "British Red Army" should liberate the area.[171] †

It was an ambitious enterprise; Ygal showed familiarity with the works of Marx, Lenin and Trotsky, and his bibliography contained works in English, French, German, Hebrew and Arabic (with the latter he was helped by Gabriel Baer, who as "S Munir"

---

* This insistence on the unity of the oppressed was to remain with Cliff. In 1983, on the occasion of the Marx centenary, he used the image that we are all in the same train but some have better seats (author's recollection).

† Cliff's optimism was not wholly unjustified. The late 1940s saw major struggles in the Middle East, notably strikes in Iraq. (See A Alexander, "Daring for Victory: Iraq in Revolution 1946-1959", *International Socialism* 99 (Summer 2003)).

is acknowledged in the preface).[172] The manuscript was one of the few things he brought with him when he moved to Europe, but it never found a publisher. Though the book was scholarly and scrupulously documented in detail, Ygal's revolutionary commitment shone through every page and it would scarcely have been a commercial proposition.

In order to earn a little money, he had translated two books.[173] One was by the German economist Fritz Sternberg, one of the main theoreticians of the SAP (the Socialist Workers Party of Germany, a centrist split from German Social Democratic Party in 1931), who wrote on contemporary developments in imperialism, drawing on the work of Rosa Luxemburg.

The other was *The Decline of American Capitalism* by Lewis Corey.* Though the translation was commissioned by Hashomer Hatzair, Corey refused to allow publication on the grounds that he had now abandoned Marxism. Corey's book, published in 1934, was an attempt to develop a critique of contemporary American capitalism and to reconcile the Keynesian view of overproduction and underconsumption with Marx's theory of the falling rate of profit. He concluded that the US faced a choice between communism and minimal economic recovery under fascism.[174] Corey had written a book that fitted neither the Stalinist nor the Trotskyist orthodoxy, and it must have given the young Ygal much food for thought.

The poverty in which Ygal lived was tolerable; he expected no reward for being a revolutionary. But he was becoming increasingly frustrated. The failure of the general strike of April 1946 was a major setback for any hopes of united action by Arab and Jewish workers. The establishment of a Zionist state was appearing ever more probable. Ygal was increasingly coming to believe, as he wrote later, that "the relation of forces between the Zionists and the Arab Palestinians means that the Arabs can never win on their own".[175] Among the European exiles who had been Trotskyists in Palestine there was a feeling that once the war was over they would do better to return to Europe. To Jakob Moneta "internationalist political work in Palestine seemed ever more hopeless".[176]

Ygal had thought of moving to Egypt, which he continued to see as the key to the region. But he was advised that it would be a

---

* Under the name Louis Fraina, Corey had played an important role in the founding of the Communist Party of the US.

difficult place to work politically.[177] Then the possibility of moving to Europe arose. Chanie, as a citizen of South Africa, had a passport which would gain her entry to Britain. Her father had a visa for Britain which he did not need and passed on to Ygal. All his political life Ygal had seen the British Empire as the enemy; now he had the possibility of moving to the heart of that empire.

Nicola, Baer and a few others kept the RCL going until the early 1950s, when Nicola went back to the Communist Party and Baer pursued his academic career. Even after the establishment of the Zionist state, the RCL published declarations motivated by an unshakable internationalism. Thus in 1948:

> Therefore, we say to the Palestinian people, in reply to the patriotic warmongers: *Make this war between Jews and Arabs, which serves the end of imperialism, the common war of both nations against imperialism!*...
>
> Jewish workers! Get rid of the Zionist provocateurs who tell you to sacrifice yourself on the altar of the state!
>
> Arab worker and fellah! Get rid of the chauvinist provocateurs who are getting you into a mess of blood for their own sake and pocket.
>
> *Workers of the two peoples, unite in a common front against imperialism and its agents!* [178]

Future historians will have little to say about the RCL. It was tiny in numbers, and quite unable to do anything to influence the course of events. Yet it was not entirely a futile enterprise. Anyone who looks at the bloodstained history of the first six decades of the Zionist state must ask whether there could have been an alternative. The dedicated few of the RCL at least bear witness to the fact that some people envisaged a society based on Jewish-Arab cooperation rather than conflict. When an independent socialist left re-emerged in Israel with Matzpen in the 1960s, a number of those who had been politically formed by the RCL – Nicola, Taut, Shas – were to be found in its ranks.

When Cliff came to write the history of the early years of the Trotskyist movement in his biography of Trotsky, he said nothing of Palestine, concentrating on France, Spain and Germany. But there is surely an echo of his own experience when he examined the failure of Trotskyism to achieve its goals:

> In no country did the Trotskyists achieve the minimum critical mass required to be effective in building a real mass organisation. There was a chasm between what the historical situation demanded and what was possible.[179]

In later years Cliff was often accused of being obsessed with the purely numerical growth of the party. But he was all too well aware that in Palestine the marginal nature of the organisation had made it unable to intervene. If, instead of 20 members, the RCL had had 2,000, it might have made a material difference to the course of events. It was a lesson that remained with him.

In the late summer of 1946, Ygal and Chanie took a boat for Europe. If their possessions were few, their hopes were great, yet so many of those hopes would be dashed. They could scarcely have imagined the hardships and disappointments they would face before their activity began to bear fruit. An unknown world awaited them. From now on Ygal was Cliff.

3
1946-50
In a Strange Land

The journey across the Mediterranean lasted about a week. Cliff and Chanie could not afford a cabin, so they travelled on the deck. The boat stopped in Italy, then continued to Marseille, where they disembarked. From here they took a packed train to Paris, where they stayed for about three weeks, living with relatives of Cliff's. It was just two years since the Liberation, and life was dominated by austerity and shortages. Their hosts were very poor, with a young child. They had no milk, no coffee, nothing but the barest necessities. The Communist Party was in government and putting a brake on all working class resistance.

Cliff and Chanie found Paris a beautiful city. Cliff's glasses had fallen into the sea during the journey, and he was unable to fully appreciate a visit to the Folies Bergères. In Palestine they had been told that there was an acute shortage of razor blades in France, so they had spent what little money they had on blades, hoping to sell them at a profit. Sadly razor blades were one of the few items not in short supply, and they were unable to supplement their meagre funds.[1]

The main reason for coming to Paris was to meet the leadership of the Fourth International. For ten hard years Cliff had been sustained by the ideas of Trotskyism, while maintaining only tenuous organisational contacts. Now at last he was setting foot in the family home.

Unfortunately the experience was to be something of a disappointment. Cliff and Chanie went to meet Sam Gordon, the representative of the American SWP in Europe, who was assisting with the post-Liberation reorganisation of the Fourth International.

The newcomers were immediately struck by an element of pretentiousness in Gordon's approach. When they arrived he was typing, and continued to do so for a couple of hours, ignoring his visitors. He was a busy man; perhaps he had a deadline to meet. But they could not help feeling that he was trying to create an impression. When he did find time to speak to them he talked about his intention to get equipment for simultaneous translation – something of an unnecessary luxury given the small size of the International.[2] As yet they had no idea of the political reasons behind these trivial symptoms. Cliff also had his first encounter with Ernest Mandel, with whom he would have a number of brushes in the future.

On 25 September 1946 Cliff and Chanie arrived at Dover. Cliff was permitted to enter Britain on condition that he did not remain more than three months.[3] They travelled to London, another city recovering from war. There were still numerous bomb sites throughout the capital. To add insult to injury the winter of 1946-47 would be one of the most severe on record, with power cuts and factories closed. For Cliff and Chanie, who had left behind the sunshine of Palestine, it was a terrible shock. Chanie had no suitable clothing for such harsh weather.[4]

This was the heart of the British Empire under which Cliff had suffered in Palestine. On many thousands of living-room walls throughout Britain there were still maps of the world, with the countries of the British Empire marked in red. That empire was now condemned to death. Over the coming decades British society would go through some startling changes, though scarcely those which revolutionary socialists hoped for.

Cliff was impressed by working class living standards in Britain. Partly this was simply the contrast between a colonial territory and the metropolitan country. But it was also a recognition that capitalism was not in total decay, that it was able to offer real reforms to workers. Cliff quickly observed that, unlike the Arab children he remembered from Palestine, in England even the poorest children had shoes. As he would soon have learnt, under the Labour government all children got free orange juice. Many years later he recalled:

> Another thing hit me between the eyes at the time. The standard of living for workers in Britain was high. When I first visited a worker's house – just an ordinary house – I asked his job and he was an engineer. My English wasn't very good so I thought he meant an engineer with a degree. But he was a semi-skilled engineering worker. It was a complete

shock. Children were better off than in the thirties. The only time I saw children without shoes in Europe was in Dublin. Children didn't get rickets any more. This helped me to realise that the final crisis wasn't around the corner.[5]

Cliff and Chanie were welcomed by the British Trotskyists. On arrival they were given temporary accommodation by Charles van Gelderen and his wife, accommodation which their hosts thought was somewhat cramped, but which they found luxurious,[6] though the bed was very small.[7] Van Gelderen was under close state surveillance, with his mail being opened, because of his activities in the army and his contacts with Italian Trotskyists.[8] When they got accommodation of their own, they were victims of the slum landlords of north east London in a dwelling infested with rats, lice and bugs.[9]*

Chanie soon found work as a teacher, a profession in which she was to stay for the rest of her life. Although her only qualification was a degree in Hebrew from a South African university, this sufficed to get her a job, although the school was in Kent, which meant an early morning start and a long journey. She was put in charge of teaching infants, for which she had no training or experience. But she soon mastered the required skills and became a very good infant teacher.[10] Still she found time to put Cliff's work into English and type it up.

Cliff's most pressing problem was the right to stay in Britain. With his papers and his South African wife he had got into the country – staying there was more difficult. For assistance he turned to the Independent Labour Party (ILP), with whom he had had contacts back in the days of the Marxist Circles. Sheila Leslie, a member of the Revolutionary Communist Party (RCP) who worked at the offices of the ILP weekly paper in Finchley, remembered Cliff and another Palestinian coming to ask for assistance. He seemed terribly clever but "liked a good gossip".[11] Cliff had a friendly manner, but he doubtless hoped to absorb as much information as possible about his new environment.

Although now in severe decline, the ILP still had Members of Parliament (though in 1948 they would rejoin the Labour Party).

---

* The claim by a *Daily Telegraph* journalist that "Tony Cliff is himself believed to have been wealthy on arrival in Britain" (B Baker, *The Far Left*, London, 1981, p109) seems to issue from the fantasy world inhabited by reporters when they write about the finances of the revolutionary left.

Cliff contacted Campbell Stephen, one of the two ILP MPs who had visited Palestine in 1938. Stephen, a former clergyman, gave Cliff a lecture on the historic mission of the Jewish people – but he did arrange for Cliff to stay in the country, at least temporarily. The requirement was that Cliff had to report once a month to Stephen.[12]

This was only a stopgap arrangement. Cliff was determined not to return to Palestine – as the foundation of the state of Israel came closer, the prospects of doing any political work there became minimal. He attempted to find a university place in Europe – France was his first preference, and he was accepted by 17 French universities. Chanie went to France, where she had a long telephone conversation with a French government official, but was subsequently told, "Your husband will never come to France".[13] He considered Denmark and even Spain.

For most people the problems of adapting to a new culture and getting right of residency would have been a full-time preoccupation. But for Cliff everything was subordinated to the political tasks. At last he would be able to participate in the Fourth International in the heartland of imperialism. Unfortunately the Fourth International was facing problems even more intractable than Cliff's domestic difficulties.

From the 1920s onwards Leon Trotsky had fought implacably against Stalin's corruption of the Russian Revolution. He had been hounded from one country to another and was murdered in 1940. His followers took up the struggle with enormous courage despite their tiny numbers. The Second World War was Trotskyism's finest hour. Almost alone the Trotskyists preserved the internationalist tradition while social democrats backed the war uncritically and Stalinists engaged in the most grotesque forms of nationalism. In France Trotskyists produced a publication in German in order to fraternise with German soldiers.

At the end of the war things were more complicated. Trotsky had bequeathed to his followers the basic socialist principles that had animated all that was best in the Russian Revolution. He had also bequeathed some false predictions.

Firstly, Trotsky had believed that the regime in Stalin's Russia – a "degenerated workers' state" as he called it – was fundamentally unstable and unlikely to survive long: "a sphere balanced on the point of a pyramid must invariably roll down on one side or the other".[14]

Secondly, he believed that capitalism was in such deep crisis that it had exhausted its capacity for reforms – and as a result reformist politics, in either a social democratic or a Stalinist form, had no further possibility of development, and would vanish. In July 1939 he specifically predicted the imminent disappearance of the British and French social democratic and Stalinist leaders: "Attlee and Pollitt, Blum and Thorez work in the same harness. In case of war the last remaining distinctions between them will vanish. All of them together with bourgeois society as a whole will be crushed under the wheel of history".[15]

By 1945 it was already clear that Stalinism had emerged from the war enormously strengthened, able to take most of Eastern Europe under its direct control and in a position to negotiate on equal terms with Britain and the US. In Western Europe reformism, far from having vanished, was very much alive; in almost every country Communists and social democrats formed the backbone of the postwar governments.

In his earlier years Trotsky, with the theory of permanent revolution, had been an important original thinker in the Marxist tradition. When Stalinism forced him into isolated opposition, he was pushed onto the defensive, obliged to stress his Leninist orthodoxy.[16] His beleaguered followers were forced into an even more defensive role. Stalinist parties with many times more members spread lies and slanders about them, accused them of being "Hitler's agents",* and used physical violence, even murder, against them.[17]

This defensiveness was all too understandable, but its consequences were nonetheless pernicious. Trotsky's analyses of a world in deep crisis, which had been realistic enough at the time they were made, did not fit the unexpected realities of the post-war situation.

There were two main problems. Firstly Trotskyists expected that the Second World War, like the First, would be followed by a major economic and social upheaval offering immense possibilities to revolutionaries. The end of the war did see brief revolutionary upsurges – for example in Italy, Greece and Vietnam – but these

---

* *Clear Out Hitler's Agents!* was the title of a pamphlet on Trotskyism by William Wainwright, published by the Communist Party of Great Britain in 1942.

were limited in scope, and the economic catastrophe did not take place. As time went by, revolutionaries had to ask whether it had merely been temporarily delayed, or whether the whole perspective on modern capitalism needed revision.

This was linked to what may be called the "Zimmerwald syndrome". In 1915 a group of fewer than 40 anti-war activists had gathered in the Swiss village of Zimmerwald, in total isolation from the European labour movement. Just over two years later two of the participants, Lenin and Trotsky, were in power in Russia. This episode provided a powerful inspiration for revolutionaries, reminding them of the possibilities waiting to be seized. But it also encouraged sectarianism, encouraging small groups to overestimate their own importance because they might soon be leading masses of workers.

But an even bigger dilemma was posed by events in Eastern Europe. Trotsky had insisted until the day of his death that Stalin's Russia, despite its monstrous bureaucratic perversion of socialist principles, retained the economic structures of a "workers' state". Following the post-war carve-up of the world into spheres of influence, Russia took over most of Eastern Europe, and soon new economies were being established that closely followed the Russian model. The initial response of the Fourth International was that since these new regimes did not owe their origin to the self-activity of workers, they could not be considered workers' states. But as time went on, the anomaly of states existing side by side, almost identical in their economic functioning, but one labelled a "workers' state" while the others remained capitalist, posed increasingly awkward questions.

Towards the end of his life Cliff revisited the debates of the 1940s in a little book called *Trotskyism after Trotsky*. It is striking that in describing the period he used the words "excruciatingly painful".[18] In retrospect it is easy to make fun of some of the intellectual contortions that Trotskyists went through at this time. But they were grappling with a profoundly difficult situation. This was a generation that had already faced up to the fact that, when reaction and fascism were sweeping the West, they could not look for salvation from the East. To recognise that Trotsky too might be an unreliable guide must have been an almost unbearable prospect. The leaders of the Fourth International were tough people who had lived through tough times. James P Cannon had been jailed for sedition during the

Second World War. Ernest Mandel had twice been imprisoned during the Nazi occupation of Belgium. Michel Pablo had organised the Fourth International clandestinely in Nazi-occupied France. Their revolutionary integrity was not in doubt. The problem was analysis.

The RCP, which Cliff joined immediately on arrival in Britain, was one of the best sections of the Fourth International, formed in March 1944 by a merger between two rival organisations. Trotskyists had played a very creditable role during the war, backing strikes opposed by the pro-war Communist Party. They faced government repression, and RCP members were put on trial and imprisoned.[19]

Its membership was small – falling from 363 in 1946 to 336 in 1947[20] – but dedicated, and largely working class.* The full-time general secretary was Jock Haston; as an organiser, public speaker and theoretician, he was the leading figure in the RCP. Two other important members were Ted Grant and Gerry Healy, both of whom would play a notable role in British Trotskyism over the coming decades.

The fact that the RCP did have some small base in the working class movement helps to explain the fact that it was largely in disagreement with the economic perspectives of the International. Whereas the Fourth International leadership denied the possibility of a post-war boom, the majority of the British section recognised that in the short term capitalism had been able to "gain a new breathing space", though nobody could yet imagine just how long the post-war boom would be. A minority headed by Healy argued that "British capitalism is on the edge of an abyss".[21]

The argument was not purely speculative. It concerned how the RCP should organise in the coming years. In the 1930s British Trotskyists had worked inside the ILP, then the Labour Party (a tactic often known as "entrism"). But during the war period entrism would have had little meaning, since Labour Party branches scarcely functioned.[22] So since its formation the RCP had operated more or less legally as an open party. In 1945 it had contested, not very successfully, a by-election in South Wales. In peacetime, with a Labour

---

* It is claimed that "nine out of ten members of the Revolutionary Communist Party in 1946 were blue-collar working class" (S Bornstein and A Richardson, *War and the International*, London, 1986, p238).

government in power and millions of workers looking to it with considerable hope, the situation was very different. The Healy minority advocated Labour Party entry, arguing that "the cadres of the future revolutionary party would be drawn from the most advanced political elements in the Labour movement".[23]

Cliff was already known by reputation to Haston and the other leaders of the RCP.[24] He was rapidly welcomed into the party and was promptly invited to attend meetings of the political bureau.[25] His pamphlet "The Middle East at the Crossroads" had been widely circulated in the International, and his reputation as a theoretician had preceded him. He was a studious and careful researcher, good with masses of empirical material, and (with the ever reliable assistance of Chanie) a prolific writer. He also, despite language difficulties, began to develop as a speaker. Ray Challinor heard him address a meeting in Staines in 1947 on the current situation in France. Despite his difficulties with English, he gave an exposition of the tactics of the French Communist Party since their ejection from government.[26] He also had experience of clandestine activity; he was shocked to discover that revolutionary literature was being posted to Czechoslovakia through the open mail, exposing its recipients to repression.[27] He enjoyed good relations with his comrades, and became particularly friendly with Haston.[28] Yet because he was an "outsider", he did not have ties of personal loyalty or friendship which might have inhibited him from engaging in vigorous disputes.

At the age of 30 Cliff was at the height of his powers. In Britain he was at the heart of the debates in the Trotskyist movement, and was able to develop his intellectual capacity far more rapidly than had been possible in the isolation of Palestine. Given the need to adapt to an unfamiliar environment and his problems in trying to remain in the country, his productivity during his first year in Britain was extraordinary.

Although sections of the ruling class still thought Britain could hang on to its traditional imperial role, it was becoming apparent that the British Empire was doomed. The independence of India in 1947 was a vital turning point, though the problems of postcolonialism, national liberation and the "Third World" were still in the future. As a recent citizen of a colonial territory Cliff had a particular interest in the question, and in 1947 he wrote three substantial articles on the development of imperialism.

The first two drew on the work he had done in the Middle East. "The World Struggle for Oil"[29] noted two important trends which would shape the world economy in coming years: the growing economic importance of the Middle East as a source of oil and the decline of British imperialism in relation to the US. While US imperialism faced serious problems, it had a strategy for overcoming them:

> The great development of American capitalism has deepened manyfold the contradictions within it, and the capitalists will try to overcome them by imperialist expansion on a terrific scale.

The article dealt with Russian ambitions in the Middle East, noting, "The Stalinist bureaucracy tries to get over its difficulties – the result of bureaucratic mismanagement, in a simple way: by gaining control of rich new fields." In his analysis, Cliff did not differentiate between the "great powers", maintaining that "the toilers of the Middle East cannot rely on any of the great powers. They can rely only on themselves, on their own strength, and on the help of the millions of fighters for national and social independence of the East and the working class of the West." In the struggle for oil he perceived "the seeds of a new world war".

Three months later came "Some Features of Capitalist Economy in the Colonies".[30] Here he focused on the Egyptian example, drawing heavily on his earlier research and including a good deal of statistical material. He drew out in particular the fact that the role of the state was changing in modern capitalism:

> The capitalist magnate of the Twentieth Century has no cause to fear the state bureaucracy. His strength is sufficient for him to negotiate with the ministers as the representative of a power on an equal footing with the state. And not only this; he even desires the state's increasing intervention in foreign affairs – by a policy of imperialist expansion, wars, etc. – and also in domestic affairs – having a "strong hand" against the proletariat.

The analysis was predicated on the view that this was a period of "decaying, agonising capitalism". Hence he argued:

> Not only is the world economy in its entirety ripe for socialism, but the most important colonies (e.g. Egypt, India, China) are ripe for the

socialist revolution *in themselves*.

All this provided "new confirmation of the theory of the permanent revolution". Within a few years Egypt would see a revolution of a very different type from what Cliff envisaged. There would be much rethinking ahead.

The most important article, published early in 1947, was "Conflict in India".[31] Cliff had never visited India nor had he studied the subject previously. But he was drawing on his Palestinian experience, and in particular his knowledge of Muslim organisations.

He remained sceptical about whether Britain was capable of giving full independence to India, a scepticism justified by the fact that the Attlee government had no clear strategy for India, and would be forced by circumstances into a botched and disastrous partition.

> And so, to the platitude of the Labour Government that they want to give independence, but the Indians are not capable of ruling themselves, and will cut one another's throats in communal clashes, we must answer that the occupation army has not yet left India, that the pillars of imperialist rule – the Princes, zamindars, etc. – are still in the saddle; and without their eradication the independence of India can only be a fiction.

As a result:

> The British workers must understand that Attlee's freedom for India is only a faked freedom. They must struggle for the evacuation of the British army from India; for an end to the economic control of British imperialism over the key industries of the country; for the liquidation of the British Civil Service; for an end to British Government support for the Princes and feudal leaders, and its opposition to universal franchise.

Cliff quite correctly applied the theory of permanent revolution to show that the role of the Indian Congress was limited: "that Congress will not lead any real struggle against the large landowners is evident from the capitalist social character of its leadership." But he was still too attached to orthodox Leninism to envisage the new directions in which imperialism was to develop.

The most interesting part of the article was his consideration, on the eve of partition, of the relation between Hindus and Muslims. He argued that the Stalinists were quite wrong to see Muslims as a nation. On the contrary, it was imperialism which had given rise to the conflicts between Muslims and Hindus:

> The power mainly responsible for communal clashes is British imperialism... The British rulers put Hindus to rule over Moslem peasants and vice versa, thus sowing the seeds of communal discord.

He gave various concrete examples of how communal conflict had class roots. In Punjab the usurers were mainly Hindus, while most poor peasants were Muslims. Competition among clerks took on a communal form because imperialism had denied Muslims education.

Hence he concluded, "Only the class struggle of the workers, Hindu and Moslem alike, can build real unity and overcome all communal differences." He pointed the way to a different future for the subcontinent.

Cliff was entrusted with the task of defending the economic perspectives of the RCP against the International Secretariat of the Fourth International. His article "All that glitters is not gold"[32] was published in the autumn of 1947. It was a reply to a document called "From the ABC to Current Reading: Boom, Revival or Crisis?" by E Germain. Germain was the pseudonym of Ernest Mandel who, as well as being a leading figure in the Fourth International, was later to become a distinguished professor of economics. He insisted that "in the period of capitalist decadence British Industry *can no longer* overgrow the state of revival and attain one of real boom...the situation of the British economy is *not that of a boom* if one wishes to give this term the significance that Marxists have always given to it".[33] *

In this article Cliff revealed a new talent, one which he might well have preferred not to discover: the art of internal polemic. In his earlier writings he had shown anger against the economic system, or against political enemies such as the Stalinists. Now his venom was directed against members of his own organisation. He was beginning to realise just how profound the crisis of Trotskyism was becoming.

Cliff was taking on a fairly easy target. An editorial in *Fourth International* had claimed that "the prospects in England are dimmer and dimmer for a return to the living levels of 1939, let

---

* At the time of writing this does not appear among Mandel's works on the Marxist Internet Archive.

alone the levels achieved before 1914".[34] Cliff needed merely to stroll through the streets of London and chat to a few older members of the RCP to know that this was false.

Likewise when Germain wrote that "Far from being a result of the boom the coal shortage is a factor limiting the revival and making its development towards a boom impossible", Cliff needed only to point out that the consumption of coal in British industry was higher than it had ever been.

Cliff was not particularly given to pedantry and academic point-scoring. Here, however, he took a certain malicious glee in pointing out Germain's "most elementary mistakes" and his "gross lack of knowledge of the Marxist theory of crises". He pointed out that Mandel had misquoted Marx's account of the economic cycle. Generously he attributed this to carelessness and not to conscious falsification. He concluded, "One could go on pulling the weeds out of Germain's garden. But I am afraid that were this to be done, nothing would remain at all."

By using extensive empirical material taken from *The Economist* and elsewhere (whereas Germain had given little factual evidence in support of his position), Cliff had no difficulty in demonstrating his conclusion: "The British Majority are right. There is a boom in Britain."

A number of interesting observations were made in the course of the argument. In response to a claim by Pablo that British production relative to before the war must have fallen because the level of imports of raw materials had fallen, Cliff pointed out that the shift from textiles to engineering had relatively decreased the dependence on foreign sources of raw material. The role of raw materials would be a significant point in the analysis of the changing nature of imperialism made by Cliff's comrade Mike Kidron a decade or more later.[35]

And secondly, when Germain wrote that "the number of active *men* has *declined* by 211,000 in relation to 1939", Cliff was able to respond that the number of active *women* had risen by 671,000. (As he also noted, about a million women had left employment after the end of the war.) At the time it was fairly normal for socialists to think of the working class as consisting of male workers (with wives and children); while Cliff's one remark does not make him a pioneer of feminism, it does show he was aware of significant changes in the nature of the labour force.*

But while Cliff had little difficulty in proving his point, the article was still a halfway house. He had no doubt that there was a boom in Britain in 1947, but he hastened to qualify this by saying that while there was a "possibility of certain reforms or semi-reforms being introduced...these reforms cannot be of a general and lasting nature".

Cliff still believed that crisis lay in the near future, even if temporarily postponed. In an article on the Marshall Plan in October 1947 he predicted that "the catastrophic outbreak of the contradictions between US productive capacity and the internal market" could be postponed "for but a few years at most". While he noted the impact of the massive military budget, he described it as "but a palliative", and argued that only the export of capital offered the US a means to "postpone the explosion of her inner contradictions".[36]

The idea of a boom that would last a full quarter of a century was well beyond his horizon. In the course of his argument Cliff cited Lenin's *Imperialism: The Highest Stage of Capitalism* to the effect that the decay of capitalism did not preclude the possibility of rapid growth. He also cited Trotsky's *Transitional Programme*, which argued that in the "epoch of decaying capitalism...there can be no discussion of systematic social reforms and the raising of the masses' living standards... Every serious demand of the proletariat...inevitably reaches beyond the limits of capitalist property relations and of the bourgeois state." He merely urged that this should not be interpreted "mechanically". Over the coming years events would force him to turn back to these two classic texts and make a much more radical criticism of them.[37]

The question which dominated Cliff's thinking in 1947, and which would become his major contribution to Marxist theory, was the class nature of Russia. The question was one of considerable importance. The consolidation of Stalinist rule in Eastern Europe and the beginning of the Cold War meant that a new world conflict was possible in the near future; the "defence of the Soviet Union" advocated

---

* The question of equal pay for women had been raised in the RCP in 1945 (S Bornstein and A Richardson, *War and the International*, London, 1986, pp166-167). Note also Cliff's comment in an article on "Women in the USSR" (*Socialist Appeal*, Mid-July 1947): "The degree of humanity's progress is measured by the condition of women."

by Trotsky might become a very practical question. In such a situation, the position that Russia was a workers' state, but that Poland and Hungary were not, would become utterly untenable.

Although Cliff had apparently given some thought to the Russian question while still in Palestine, on arrival in Britain he was firmly committed to the Trotskyist orthodoxy. Charles van Gelderen recalled him saying shortly after arrival in Britain: "The Old Man [Trotsky] is not yet cold in his grave and already they want to renege on his teachings... I will destroy them!"[38]

In August 1946, just before Cliff's arrival, Haston* had circulated an internal document in which he argued that Russia had "both capitalistic and socialistic features". While he claimed that this was merely a restatement of Trotskyist orthodoxy, his opponents, including Healy, accused him of heresy; in fact Haston did go so far as to argue that "out of the ranks of the bureaucracy there is being exuded a new possessing class" and that "there is no reason why a new capitalist class in Russia cannot arise and dominate the economic life of the country without destroying state property as such".[39] There was considerable discussion in the RCP, with some comrades following Shachtman's position that Russia was neither capitalist nor a workers' state,† while others denied that Russia was a workers' state without giving it "any final nomenclature". The argument extended beyond the "Russian question" to take in the whole problem of the Labour government, which was carrying through a programme of nationalisation far more radical than many had believed possible. As Haston moved further towards a "state capitalist" position, the International Executive of the Fourth International put up Cliff to defend the orthodox "workers' state" argument.[40] He had a number of discussions with Haston and Grant in which he defended the workers' state theory.[41]

He toiled hard at empirical work on the economic situation in Russia, producing a series of articles for the RCP press.[42] As he worked the realities of Russian society increasingly came into

---

* In 1935, between leaving the Communist Party and becoming a Trotskyist, Haston had been close to the Socialist Party of Great Britain, where he doubtless encountered the view that Russia was state capitalist.
† Bert Atkinson, a supporter of Shachtman, did not go along with Cliff, believing his position was "abstract" and did not appeal to workers (George Leslie interview, January 2004).

contradiction with the model he was trying to impose on them. For a while he struggled to resolve the contradiction, but eventually it was too much for him. One morning he awoke and informed Chanie that "Russia is not a workers' state but state capitalist".[43]* Chanie, who had a long journey to work ahead of her, may well have felt that this was not the most urgent piece of information he could have given her.

Many years later Cliff remembered the intellectual torment of that time, when he had to decide what was essential in Marxism and what had to be abandoned:

> The more convinced you are about basic Marxist ideas, the more you are ready to throw overboard things that are secondary to those basic ideas. If you are really convinced of your ideas you can face reality. But it was a very difficult period. For more than a month I hadn't slept in the transition from the old theory to the new.[44]

In reading Cliff's writings from the time, with their wealth of concrete examples and constant references to the Marxist classics, it is easy to drown in detail. Many years later he summed up what it was that had compelled him to change his mind:

> When I came to the theory of state capitalism, I didn't come to it by a long analysis of the law of value in Russia, the economic statistics in Russia. Nothing of the sort. I came to it by the simple statement that if the emancipation of the working class is the act of the working class, then you cannot have a workers' state without the workers having power to dictate what happens in society. So I had to choose between what Trotsky said – the heart of Trotsky is the self-activity of the workers – or the form of property. I decided to push away the form of property as determining the question.[45]

Cliff was far from the first to use the concept of state capitalism. The idea and the term had a long history in the socialist movement. To understand the significance and the originality of Cliff's work, it

---

* Bornstein and Richardson are misleading when they suggest that Cliff's document merely "took over and elaborated" Haston's theories (S Bornstein and A Richardson, *War and the International*, London, 1986, p223). Cliff's arguments about international competition, especially through the arms race, went far beyond Haston's position and raised the debate to a higher level.

may be useful to briefly trace the history of the theory.*

In *Anti-Dühring* Friedrich Engels had discussed the role of state ownership in a capitalist economy and had concluded that in itself state ownership had nothing to do with socialism:

> The modern state, no matter what its form, is essentially a capitalist machine, the state of the capitalists, the ideal personification of the total national capital. The more it proceeds to the taking over of productive forces, the more does it actually become the national capitalist, the more citizens does it exploit. The workers remain wage-workers – proletarians.[46]

Before 1917 the term "state capitalism" was sometimes used to indicate a traditional capitalist society in which the state made substantial interventions in the economy. One such account was given in William English Walling's *Socialism As It Is*,[47] with particular reference to the policies of the British Liberal government of 1906, supported by the Labour Party. This is of some significance because Walling was a major influence on Lewis Corey, whose *The Decline of American Capitalism* Cliff had translated into Hebrew.

When the Bolsheviks took power in 1917, there was immediately widespread debate among both their friends and their critics about the nature of the new regime that had been established. Many "orthodox" Marxists argued that the Bolshevik Revolution had been premature, that the material conditions for building socialism did not yet exist and that therefore the regime could not go beyond the limits of a new form of capitalism. This was the position held by Karl Kautsky (known before 1914 as the "Pope of Marxism"), who polemicised with both Lenin and Trotsky on the question. In his 1919 pamphlet *Terrorism and Communism* (to which Trotsky replied in a work of the same name) Kautsky argued that since post-revolutionary Russia would not be a highly developed industrial society, "industrial capitalism has been transformed from a private to a state capitalism".[48] The leading Austro-Marxist theoretician Otto Bauer likewise argued that the Russian Revolution could not go beyond bourgeois limits. (In the 1930s Bauer, working in the same mechanical framework, defended Stalinism as a historical

---

* The most complete account of the tangled debate among Marxists about the nature of the society existing in Russia after 1917 is provided by M van der Linden, *Western Marxism and the Soviet Union*. The bibliography (pp331-374) is comprehensive.

necessity.)⁴⁹ A similar position was held by some Mensheviks, although a variety of views developed in Menshevik circles.⁵⁰

All these positions could be said to represent a right-wing critique of Bolshevism, arguing that Lenin had tried to go too far too fast, and that a more gradualist approach would have been preferable. In the early 1920s similar positions emerged among "left" critics of the Bolsheviks.

This was particularly the case with a group of thinkers associated with the Communist Workers Party of Germany (KAPD), formed in 1920 by those expelled for ultra-leftism from the German Communist Party. Leading figures included Herman Gorter, Anton Pannekoek and Otto Rühle. Initially they had been enthusiastic about the Russian Revolution, but they soon developed reservations, believing that the objective conditions for socialist revolution did not yet exist in Russia. In an article of October 1920 Rühle argued that Bolshevik centralism belonged to the age of bourgeois revolution. Yet from this analysis of the differences between East and West they derived an ultra-left strategy for their own country. Pannekoek argued that the influence of bourgeois ideas on the working class was much stronger in Western Europe than in Russia, and therefore it was necessary to attack bourgeois institutions in which the workers still put their trust, such as parliament and trade unions.⁵¹

The Socialist Party of Great Britain, an organisation devoted entirely to propagandism, showed some initial sympathy for the Bolsheviks, but soon argued that the new regime could not be socialist and must therefore still be capitalist, although it occasionally expressed admiration for Lenin.⁵²

Hence the idea that the Russian Revolution had led to capitalism in a somewhat different form was associated from the beginning with critics of Leninism, whether from left or right. This explains why the argument was regarded with such hostility in Trotskyist circles.

Inside Russia the stakes were much higher. The nature of the new regime became a matter of life and death. In April 1918, just six months after the revolution, VV Osinsky, a revolutionary militant since 1907, warned that managerial authority and the use of bourgeois specialists could lead the revolution in the wrong direction: "Socialism and socialist organisation must be set up by the proletariat itself, or they will not be set up at all; something else will be set up – state capitalism".[53] In 1919 Osinsky, together with TV Sapronov and others, formed the Democratic Centralism faction.

In this period Lenin himself used the term "state capitalism" to refer to something which he believed could be reconciled with the dictatorship of the proletariat. He considered that, in a transitional period between capitalism and socialism, state capitalism could be understood as private capitalism under the control of a workers' state.[54] Lenin saw this simply as a temporary retreat in the process of development towards socialism, and not as some new form of society.[55] *

After Lenin's death, Stalin proclaimed his theory of "socialism in one country", and what remained of socialist democracy was slowly strangled by an emerging bureaucratic layer. Various oppositional groupings began to emerge, and the idea of state capitalism again appeared. In 1925 one of Zinoviev's supporters, Zalutsky, wrote a pamphlet denouncing the state capitalism of the regime. He was removed from his post on the Leningrad party committee, and at the 14th Congress in 1925 Stalin spent some time repudiating the use of the term "state capitalism".[56]

Initially the Democratic Centralists had worked with Trotsky, but in 1926 they broke with the United Opposition, arguing that it was necessary to form a new party. Trotsky and Zinoviev were both still convinced that it was possible to work for reform within the Communist Party. Karl Radek was briefly sympathetic to this group, but he found himself unable to accept the unthinkable conclusion that the whole revolution had been lost. When he contemplated the possibility and, as he put it, a precipice opened up before him, he decided to renounce the Opposition.[57] Sapronov, a militant since 1911, published a text denouncing the USSR as a state capitalist system where Asiatic despotism had destroyed proletarian democracy. There was no hope of reforming the party and the working class must prepare for a struggle to the death against the regime and in defence of the fundamentals of Leninism.[58]

The term "state capitalism" as used by the Democratic Centralists was not accompanied by much analysis. They were putting a negative

---

* Lenin thus used the term in a different way from another old Bolshevik, Nikolai Bukharin, for whom state capitalism was a stage in the development of imperialism, in which the state organised production as a collective capitalist.

label on a repressive regime rather than analysing the laws of motion of a social system. As Robert Daniels points out, "they could only describe the strange impending evil in terms of dangers already familiar to them".[59] Under Tsarism the enemy had been capitalism and they had fought it at the cost of great self-sacrifice; when a new enemy emerged, it was natural to give it the same name.

Trotsky had little sympathy with the Democratic Centralists, who had been his critics when he and Lenin were still in the leadership. He considered their tactic of forming a new party to be dangerously ultra-left and dismissed their position as "subjectivist" because they neglected the role of class relations and the workers' movement.[60]

In 1931 GT Miasnikov, a Bolshevik since 1906 who had moved to France in 1928, published a pamphlet in which he argued that Russian state capitalism involved exploitation and the production of surplus value. "The whole of the state economy of the USSR represents as it were one large factory, in which an ordered cooperation and division of labour between different workplaces is present". [61]*

After Trotsky's exile and the crushing of the Left Opposition, the debate about the nature of Stalin's regime continued. The question was argued vigorously in the jails and concentration camps, for Stalin's victims wanted to know exactly what force it was that had defeated them. Victor Serge, who experienced Stalin's repression, testifies to these debates in his novels. In *The Case of Comrade Tulayev* three men awaiting arrest and probable death disagree about whether their bodies will fertilise "Socialist soil" or "State Capitalism".[62]

In Britain the term was used quite widely by critics of the Stalinist regime, including George Orwell, Walter Citrine and Wyndham Lewis. A pamphlet by a follower of Oswald Mosley identified communism with "state capitalism" – while commending Stalin for executing Jews! But the phrase was simply an insult, an assertion that Russia did not represent any advance on Western society.[63]

A new element was introduced into the debate in the early 1930s in the work of Lucien Laurat, who argued that Russia was neither capitalist nor socialist, but a "new form of the exploitation of man by man". The surplus value received by the Soviet bureaucracy was

---

* This comparison of the Russian economy to a single factory was developed by Cliff.

described as an economic category which was "totally different from capitalist surplus value".[64] This position was taken up by Yvan Craipeau within the French Trotskyist movement, and won the support of a third of the French Section of the Fourth International.[65] Craipeau and Trotsky debated publicly on the question in 1938.[66] Later a similar position was adopted by Bruno Rizzi and subsequently by Shachtman and his associates in the US.[67]

The strength of the new analysis lay in the recognition that the society that had emerged in post-Leninist Russia was something new and unprecedented. However, whereas Marx had devoted many hundreds of pages to analysing the laws of motion of the capitalist system, the advocates of the view that Russia was a new form of society gave decidedly thinner accounts of how the new society functioned.

The theory of state capitalism was taken further forward in 1939 by the Australian Ryan Worrall. Worrall argued firstly that it was theoretically possible to have capitalism without private ownership of property, and secondly that the bureaucracy had the same function as the bourgeoisie in private capitalism, namely the accumulation of capital. Thirdly he insisted that Russia could not be a workers' state since the bureaucracy was not under the democratic control of the working class.[68]

One reason why state capitalism tended to meet disfavour in the Trotskyist movement was the fact that it was often associated with a range of ultra-left positions. Amadeo Bordiga, who had been one of the founders of the Italian Communist Party, was a lifelong ultra-leftist who opposed any participation in parliamentary elections, for which he was criticised in Lenin's *Left-Wing Communism*. He argued that the proletariat had played a major role in 1917, but with the failure of the revolution to spread, Russian society had become a form of capitalism.[69]

Grandizo Munis had organised the tiny group of Trotskyists in Spain during the civil war. In 1946, working in collaboration with the French surrealist poet Benjamin Péret, he developed a version of the state capitalist argument. He argued that in Marxist terms the regime was based on the extraction of surplus value. Planning had been effectively destroyed, and political repression was equivalent to that under fascism. From this he drew the conclusion that there could be no support for Stalinist parties outside Russia: "A party which adopts the slogan of 'Stalinism to power' is giving its own execution squad the order to fire".[70] Munis was politically close to Trotsky's widow Natalia Sedova, who broke with the Fourth International in 1951 over the Russian question.[71] Later he moved to even more extreme ultra-left positions, eventually arguing that the most urgent task for socialists was to destroy the trade unions.[72]

The most serious development of the state capitalist theory came from a small grouping – the Johnson-Forest tendency – within the Workers Party, the group led by Shachtman which split from the American SWP in 1940. Its main figures were CLR James and Raya Dunayevskaya. In 1941 Dunayevskaya published a short article with the uncompromising title "The Union of Soviet Socialist Republics is a Capitalist Society".[73] Here she attacked both the orthodox Trotskyist position that the "workers' state" was defined by state ownership, and Shachtman's analysis, arguing:

> Not even the most pious worker-statist would contend that the workers had any power in the present Soviet state. He would merely reiterate that so long as there was statified property, etc., etc. But I deny that the social conquests of October [1917] – the *conscious* and *active* political and practical participation of the masses in liberating themselves from the yoke of Tsarism, capitalism and landlordism – are to be narrowly translated into mere statified property, that is to say, the ownership of the means of production by a state which in no way resembles the Marxian concept of a workers' state, i.e., "the proletariat organized as the ruling class"... The Soviet Government occupies in relation to the whole economic system the position which a capitalist occupies in relation to a single enterprise.

Dunayevskaya, who knew Russian fluently, followed this up with a number of articles developing the analysis. In 1942 she made a devastating critique of the official Russian statistics to reveal the facts behind them, and argued that "the reality of the world market...would not permit Russia to tear itself out of the vortex of world economy and build 'socialism in one country'".[74] In 1944 she published a commentary on an official Russian text which argued that the law of value functioned in the USSR. She drew the conclusion that "the law of value entails the use of the concept of alienated or exploited labour and, as a consequence, the concept of surplus value".[75] A 1946 article saw Stakhanovism and the 1937 Moscow Trials as the culmination of the state capitalist counter-revolution. Russia was a society in a state of profound crisis: "Stalinist Russia is part of decadent world capitalism and is destined for no longer life span than world capitalism in its death agony".[76]

This theme was even more apparent in *State Capitalism and World Revolution*, written by CLR James in collaboration with Dunayevskaya and Grace Lee.[77] James later insisted that this document meant a complete break with the Trotskyist tradition.[78] While stressing the counter-revolutionary nature of Stalinism, the book argued that the "whole system is in mortal crisis" and that the proletariat had never been "so revolutionary as it is today".[79] The James-Dunayevskaya perspective was therefore very different from the one Cliff was slowly working his way towards.

Dunayevskaya visited London in July-August 1947, and wrote several letters describing meetings with the RCP leadership.[80] But, she recounted many years later, discussion of possible collaboration with Cliff did not get far.

Dunayevskaya had linked her theory to both her analysis of spontaneous workers' revolts and to her philosophical position. As a result, Cliff informed her that "he would rather have nothing to do with it until his own, strictly economic analysis was completed, and that would take another year".[81] *

She gave a fuller account in a letter to Sheila Rowbotham:

> Opposition to the concept of the "party to lead" was the very first topic I fought with Tony Cliff on in 1947 when I was in England on way to a congress of the Fourth International I had rejoined and given the right to present the theory of state capitalism. I would be the only one with that position even in that year and since Tony was working out the same thesis I had first projected in 1941, I asked for his help. He refused on the basis that my "giving up" the theory of vanguard party permitted no ground for our collaboration and, moreover, his thesis, which was not yet completed, would be quite different from mine, more "objective".[82]

As it turned out, they were to follow rather different paths. Dunayevskaya later wrote that "after the Russian admission, in

---

* Ray Challinor's later summary of this letter is rather misleading: "They agreed she would devote her time to study the philosophical implications and that Cliff would look at the economic issues." (R Challinor, "The Perspective of the Long Haul", *Workers' Liberty* No 21, May 1995)

1943, that the law of value operates in Russia, there was no further point to continue the detailed analysis of their State Plans";[83] her subsequent efforts went into the "philosophical" implications of the theory. Cliff, however, until at least the mid-1960s, continued to monitor closely political and economic developments in the Eastern Bloc countries.

In Cliff's 1948 bulletin, there was the promise of a further document which would deal with the Johnson-Forest tendency, whom he accused of "a simplification of the analysis of the industrial reserve army and the crisis". This does not appear to have ever been written.[84]

There were no further significant contacts between Cliff and the Johnson-Forest Tendency. In the 1950s Cliff reported to national meetings of the SRG on developments of state capitalist groupings around the world, and Johnson-Forest was mentioned.[85] But from the outset the SRG main fraternal contacts in the US were with the followers of Shachtman.*

Though Cliff never made any public criticism of Dunayevskaya, in private conversation he was disparaging, saying that her book, *Marxism and Freedom*,[86] had very little in it.[87] Dunayevskaya seems to have held Cliff in equally low esteem, and many years later commented acidly on the failure of any cooperation between them: "The six-year lapse between Dunayevskaya's study and Cliff's could tell quite a story about non-cooperation with state capitalists in the Trotskyist movement. Tony Cliff was quite adamant about making such an analysis 'purely economic'".[88] While a brilliant thinker, Dunayevskaya had, according to the testimony of her erstwhile collaborator Grace Lee Boggs, a strong sense of her own importance and a sectarian mentality.[89] Sheila Leslie, who met Dunayevskaya during her London visit, remembers her as rather high-handed, and thinks she probably put Cliff's back up.[90] It is hard to imagine any significant cooperation between her and Cliff; in terms of both personality and political perspective there was a huge gap between them.

---

* In the 1950s a number of members of the SRG were influenced by James's and Dunayevskaya's ideas. See J D Young, *Making Trouble*, Glasgow, 1987, p51, and R Challinor, "Tony Cliff's Early Years in Britain", *Revolutionary History* 7/4 (2000), p187.

Having decided that Russia was state capitalist, Cliff now faced a double task. On the one hand he had to convince the supporters of orthodox Trotskyism that state capitalism was not an ultra-left eccentricity but a valid theory compatible with the principles of the Trotskyist movement. At the same time he had to recognise the inadequacies of the theory as so far developed and give it a firmer grounding in Marxist theory and in the empirical study of Russian society.

While Cliff grappled with these problems, a new difficulty arose. He had lost contact with Campbell Stephen, the MP who had acted as his protector and with whose support he was able to stay in Britain. Cliff and Chanie tracked him down to a house in the country, where he was seriously ill.[91] In October 1947, just after rejoining the Labour Party, he died.[92] The British authorities were not prepared to allow Cliff to remain in the country. All attempts at finding a university elsewhere in Europe had fallen through. He looked at the possibility of going into hiding and staying in the country illegally. He briefly considered taking up the offer of an RCP member, Sam Bornstein, to let him take his identity papers.[93]

In the end this proved unnecessary. The Irish authorities agreed to admit him as a student. For once Cliff's Palestinian background worked in his favour. There was still a good deal of anti-British feeling in Ireland, dating back to the independence struggle of the 1920s. In 1949 Ireland (minus the British-ruled North) would withdraw from the Commonwealth and declare itself a republic. At this point, just before the founding of Israel, the Jews of Palestine were seen as fighting a struggle for national liberation from British colonial rule. So Cliff was welcomed to Ireland, where he arrived on 25 October 1947[94] to stay for four years. When he arrived in Ireland and the immigration official discovered he was from Palestine, he clapped him warmly on the shoulder.[95] Fortunately, when the authorities discovered that Cliff's politics were not quite what they had originally supposed, they did not revoke their decision.[96]

Chanie travelled to Ireland with Cliff. Wages were low there – as a teacher she could have earned only three pounds a week; in England she could get seven.* So she returned to London, where she

---

* In 1947 a British worker's average weekly earnings were £5 3s 6d (*Ministry of Labour Survey for British Workers*, April 1947, quoted in Cliff, *Marxist Theory After Trotsky: Selected Writings* vol 3, p132).

had a room in Stamford Hill, but she travelled frequently to visit him. School holidays provided an opportunity to visit, but from time to time she would conveniently "lose her voice" and take a fortnight off work in order to travel to Ireland.[97] Since Chanie's income had to support both of them, Cliff's lifestyle was frugal; his normal diet was bread, jam, a bar of chocolate and an egg each day.[98] In March of the following year he took up residence at 9 Grace Park Gardens, Drumcondra (a residential area in northern Dublin), where he was to remain for the rest of his time in Ireland. The British authorities were reasonably generous in allowing Cliff to visit England for quite long periods. He usually visited England for a period of four to eight weeks each year, and between 21 June and 25 October 1950 (the period of the formation of the SRG) he was in London for four months.[99]

The advantages of this arrangement were not only financial. Through Chanie Cliff was able to keep in touch with the movement in Britain, now entering a period of profound crisis. She was also able to inform him about other struggles in Britain. From the summer of 1947 fascist leader Oswald Mosley tried to make a comeback, holding meetings in Ridley Road, Dalston. The RCP were heavily involved in the demonstrations against Mosley, which mobilised up to 2,000 people. Every Saturday the Mosleyites and the anti-fascists would compete to be the first to set up a platform, which they would then have to guard until Sunday. The police protected the Mosleyites and there were violent clashes. On occasion the Mosleyites were pelted with stones and rubbish from the market. Chanie and Tommy Reilly, the RCP's anti-fascist organiser, toured Jewish-owned shops in Hackney and sweatshops in the East End, collecting money. This was the RCP's final involvement in mass struggle.[100]

Despite the hectic demands of political activity, the couple also started a family. In June 1949 Chanie gave birth to their first child, Elana. If there was one thing that Cliff allowed to distract him from his single-minded devotion to the revolutionary struggle, it was his deep commitment to his family, which must have been a powerful source of inspiration in the difficult days of political isolation.

On arrival in Dublin Cliff became a student at Trinity College. He did not take his studies seriously; he would sit at the back of the class, inwardly mocking the economics lecturer since his own knowledge was superior.[101] In one lecture he "burst laughing". The lecturer asked him why, and he said that all that had been explained with complicated diagrams and mathematics was the fact that when you go into a shop you have to buy things.[102] But he was serious about pursuing his knowledge of economics. In the autumn of 1948 he wrote to Cambridge economist and Communist Party member Maurice Dobb to enquire about work on the relationship of Marx and Keynes. Dobb replied with a short list of recommended articles.[103] Cliff would return later to work on Keynes.

His main concern was to complete his work on state capitalism in Russia, now growing to the size of a full-length book. When each chapter was completed, Cliff posted it to Chanie for typing. According to his account it was written in a mixture of English and Hebrew, and she was required to put it into comprehensible form.[104] On this basis Chanie qualifies as joint author of this seminal text.

In the summer of 1948 the text appeared as an internal document of the RCP. It is testimony to the high standard of internal democracy that still prevailed within the RCP that it agreed to circulate such a substantial oppositional statement.* The text was essentially the same as that published in book form in 1955 under the title *Stalinist Russia: A Marxist Analysis*, though the argument was restructured for a (slightly) broader audience. This was the book that established Cliff as a Marxist theoretician. It has been republished several times† and translated into a dozen or more foreign languages.‡

The opening chapter began by questioning the orthodox Trotskyist definition of a "workers' state". Cliff then went on to study the main features of Stalinist society, and its dynamic and contradictions. There were a number of features which made Cliff's work a more comprehensive and convincing version of the theory of

---

* The decline of the RCP led to an increasing concentration on internal debate though Haston was probably exaggerating when he claimed that "at one stage nine tenths of our activity was spent in producing Internal Bulletins (interview quoted in S Bornstein and A Richardson, *War and the International*, London, 1986, p199).

† T Cliff, *Stalinist Russia: A Marxist Analysis*, London, 1955; *Russia: A Marxist Analysis*, London, 1964; T Cliff, *State Capitalism in Russia*, London, 1974; T Cliff, *State Capitalism in Russia*, London, 1988. T Cliff, *Marxist Theory After Trotsky: Selected Writings* vol 3, London, 2003 contains the original document.

‡ Arabic, Bengali, Farsi, French, German, Greek, Italian, Japanese, Korean, Polish, Russian, Spanish, Turkish and possibly others.

state capitalism than anything that had gone before:

(1) Whereas many earlier theories of state capitalism had opened the door to ultra-left conclusions, Cliff remained firmly within the mainstream of anti-Stalinist Marxism and Leninism. Most proponents of the theory had seen the Russian Revolution as either a premature Utopian adventure, or as having been betrayed by its bureaucratic and authoritarian leaders. Cliff insisted that he was not breaking with the Trotskyist tradition, but simply taking it to its logical conclusion. In the introduction to his document Cliff stressed that his aim was the "reorientation and rearming of the Fourth International".[105] He later argued his innovation was possible "only by standing on the shoulders of the giant, Leon Trotsky".[106] He based himself on the achievements of the October Revolution, and criticised the Stalinist regime precisely from the standpoint of the principles of October.

(2) Some critics of Stalinism had been essentially moralistic – to call Russia "state capitalist" was simply a means of asserting that it was at least as brutal and oppressive as traditional capitalism had been. Cliff, however, was concerned to discover the dynamics of Russian society, to understand how it survived and how it might eventually perish. So he took fundamental Marxist categories – the law of value, exploitation, the falling rate of profit and the Marxist definition of class – and applied them in detail to the available empirical material on Russian economic and social life.

(3) In particular Cliff centred his account of Russian society on the Marxist theory of the state. Critics of socialism often argued that socialism could be defined simply in terms of state control of the economy – a centrally directed economy like that in Russia was by definition socialist. A mechanical adoption of Trotsky's criteria for a workers' state often made concessions to this analysis. In the tradition of Lenin's *State and Revolution* Cliff argued that the state was the weapon of one class against another, and that state-owned industry in Russia was a means of exploiting the workers. In the event of an authentic workers' revolution in Russia, the army and secret police could not be taken over and democratised: "The revolutionary party will have to smash the existing state and replace it by Soviets, people's militia, etc."[107]

(4) While Cliff drew heavily on the work of Marx, Engels, Lenin

and Trotsky, he also made use of the rich tradition of Marxist political economy. In particular he made several references to the work of Bukharin. Bukharin, executed after the Third Moscow Trial in 1938, had largely been written out of the Marxist tradition. For Stalinism he was a counter-revolutionary, but the Trotskyist tradition had not accommodated his work. However, Cliff drew heavily on his writings on the theoretical possibilities of state capitalism, citing from works published in German.[108] Cliff had probably first encountered his work in Palestine from German refugees he was in contact with.* He also drew on the work of Rudolf Hilferding, whose book *Finance Capital* Cliff described as "perhaps the most important book on Marxist economics since *Capital* itself".[109]

(5) While Cliff was concerned to understand the internal structures of Russian society, he gave fundamental importance to its place in the world system. As Marx had shown, capitalism was a global system, and Cliff's argument started from what he called "the spiritual unity of the world". Its essential dynamic derived from competition, and therefore any particular economy was conditioned by its place in the total world system. In Russia's case this took place partly through trade, but primarily through the arms race. The priorities of spending imposed by the international arms race exerted a determining pressure on the whole Russian economy.† Cliff argued, "Stalin decides on the division of labour inside Russia in the same way as the individual capitalist decides on the division of labour in his factory. But the decision itself is derived from powers over which he has no control

---

* This point was suggested to me by Chris Harman.

† In the conclusion to his comprehensive study of Marxist theories of post-revolutionary Russia, Marcel van der Linden writes:

"In fact, only two representatives of the state-capitalism theory took an approach compatible with an orthodox definition of capitalism: Cliff and Bettelheim. Both assumed the existence of a bourgeoisie in the Soviet Union, and both believed that competition existed. Bettelheim believed this competition existed in the domestic economy, while Cliff believed he could identify it at the international level.

"Cliff's approach forces him to reduce competition essentially to the arms race: a competition over military capacity. That, however, is still in conflict with orthodoxy. The arms race, after all, did not involve mainly commodities produced for an open market, and therefore cannot be considered as trade based on capitalist competition... Ultimately, we are forced to the conclusion that not a single theory of state capitalism succeeded in being both orthodox-Marxist as

whatsoever – it is derived from the autonomy of world economy, from world competition".[110]

(6) It is in this context that Russian "planning" had to be understood. Many advocates of the view that Russia was a workers' state argued this because of the "planned economy", while conceding that this planning was carried out in an undemocratic way. For Cliff such planning as existed in Russia was analogous to that which might exist within a single capitalist enterprise. For him socialist planning meant the "conscious direction of the economy", and this could be achieved only through workers' control, which was conspicuously absent in Russia. Indeed, it was precisely with the establishment of the first Five-Year Plan in 1928 that the bureaucracy became transformed into an exploiting class. Hence there was nothing progressive about Russian planning: "So long as the working class has no control over production, the workers are not the subject of planning but its object." Russian "planning" was not necessarily able to achieve even the same productivity of labour as Western capitalism.[111]

(7) By showing that Russia was, like Western capitalism, driven by the dynamic of international capitalism, Cliff was pointing to the essential similarities of the two social orders. Russian capitalism was doing exactly what British capitalism had done over several centuries – but much more rapidly and hence even more brutally: "Stalin accomplished in a few hundred days what it took Britain a few hundred years to do".[112] Thus the Russian development could illuminate the increasing role of the state in Western economies in the post-war period. Cliff noted, "The nationalisations in England carried out by the Labour government bring us sharply to realise that the form of property alone is not the fundamental determinant of the class character of an economy and a state".[113] From the

> well as consistent with the facts." (M van der Linden, *Western Marxism and the Soviet Unions*, London, 2007, pp312-13)

> This is less than fair to Cliff. To insist, as he did, that accumulation was driven by competition was retaining an essential theme in Marxism; to abandon that would mean departing from the very core of the Marxist analysis. But to observe that in the 20th century competition might take forms never envisaged by Marx was a simple recognition of the facts. The combination of the essential tenets of Marxism with an acceptance of the changing nature of reality was at the very heart of Cliff's method.

workers' point of view there was nothing to choose between the two regimes.

(8) There had been an important inconsistency in the orthodox Trotskyist view of Russia. On the one hand the Russian system was seen as unstable and in deep crisis (the ball balanced on the point of a sphere), yet at the same time Russia's economic achievements were hailed as proof of the superiority of the planned economy. Cliff was able to overcome this inconsistency by showing that the achievements of the Russian economy were indeed formidable: "The tempo of development of the productive forces in Stalinist Russia is greater than it has been in any other country at any time." (In 1957 Russia, with the Sputnik, would lead the world in the crucial field of satellite technology.) As Marx had shown, capitalism historically had "played a most revolutionary part".[114] But it was also a system with internal contradictions that would destroy it; Russia's rapid development derived in considerable part from the repressive regime's ability to depress workers' living standards.[115]

(9) Since the Russian economy was essentially driven by its place in the world economy, the production of armaments played a central role in its workings. Cliff devoted several pages of his document to analysing the place of armaments in the Russian economy, and the importance of the fact that such great resources were devoted to the means of destruction.[116] Cliff would later develop the argument to show how similar mechanisms operated in Western capitalism.

(10) Cliff recognised that the society existing in Russia was a new historical phenomenon, something which none of the classic Marxists, outside of brief hypothetical speculations, had ever envisaged. To define Russia as capitalist did not mean ignoring the profoundly original features in Stalinist society. Cliff resolved this problem by describing state capitalism as being a "partial negation" of traditional capitalism. Certain aspects of the system did not function in exactly the same way as in the West. Thus "the state as a regulator of economic functions, even if it is not yet the repository of the means of production, partially negates the law of value".[117]

(11) He even went so far as to describe state capitalism as "a transition to socialism". It is important to be clear what he meant by this. He argued, "Everything that centralises the means of production centralises the working class. State capitalism brings this concentration to the highest stage possible under the capitalist

system." There was nothing progressive about state capitalism, which "signifies the extreme subjugation of the working class by the capitalist class which controls the means of production".[118] Its only merit was to encourage the unity of its gravediggers.
(12) This led to the essence of Cliff's argument. The point was not to interpret state capitalism, but to destroy it. If the mechanisms of the Russian economy were essentially capitalist, then Russia had a massive working class with the potential to overthrow it. Russian workers were not slaves but proletarians, who posed a constant threat to the bureaucracy. Cliff recognised the difficulties in the way of working class organisation in a totalitarian state. But he also saw a fatal contradiction facing the bureaucracy. In order to raise the productivity of labour, working class living standards would have to be raised. "But workers, besides having hands, have heads. The raising of the standard of living and culture of the masses means to raise their self-confidence, increase their appetite, their impatience at the lack of democratic rights and personal security, and their impatience at the bureaucracy which preserves these burdens." He concluded with a hopeful scenario: "The final chapter can be written only by the masses – self-mobilised, conscious of socialist aims and the methods of their achievement, and led by a revolutionary Marxist party".[119]

Cliff may not have been original in all these points, but taken together they produced a synthesis which raised the argument for state capitalism to a higher level than anything written previously.

The document was circulated to the RCP membership, though unfortunately it was too late to be distributed to delegates to the Fourth International Congress.[120] Initially, however, it did not make a major impact. Ken Tarbuck, a young member of the Birmingham branch who would later join the state capitalist grouping, recalled:

> We had all seen his massive internal bulletin on the question of state capitalism in Russia...but none of us had been sufficiently convinced to become followers of Cliff. Given all the other matters that had been besetting us around that time it is hardly surprising that Cliff did not make much impression.[121]

Sheila Leslie was a young comrade who was very serious about reading all the internal documents. She had some doubts about the official theory, but found it hard to make a break; RCP members were reluctant to abandon defence of the USSR when the leadership were arguing that this underpinned all the other policies of the RCP. Yet she felt that while Cliff's contributions to the debate were somewhat academic, they did add to knowledge, unlike much of what was written.[122]

Though the initial circulation of Cliff's document was confined to the tiny RCP, over the coming years it was to exercise a certain influence on an international scale. Throughout the Fourth International questions were being asked about the nature of Stalinism, and an apparently obscure document like Cliff's rapidly got an international circulation.

After 1945 the Cuban Trotskyist organisation, the Partido Obrero Revolucionario, adopted a state capitalist position. They were clearly impressed when they received Cliff's document, for it confirmed their positions.[123] In 1949 they sent a letter to the French group Socialisme ou Barbarie (Socialism or Barbarism) urging them to study Cliff's 1948 internal document on Russia. It went on to state that Alfred Rosmer was translating Cliff's document into French, though nothing came of this.[124]

Socialisme ou Barbarie had split from the Fourth International in 1949 on the basis of an analysis which identified tendencies towards bureaucracy in both Western and Stalinist society. They rejected any notion that Russia was a "workers' state", though they did not see it as capitalist. Socialisme ou Barbarie did not take much further interest in Cliff's work (though there was correspondence in 1950[125]), but these references do show that Cliff's work was making a certain international impact on the declining and fragmenting Trotskyist movement.

There were also contacts with a publication called *La Lutte,* said to be the paper of the "independent French Communists". This group acknowledged receipt of Cliff's document on Russia and promised to translate it and publish it as a pamphlet,[126] although there is no indication that this actually happened.

Cliff and the SRG were in contact with the left wing of the Ukrainian Revolutionary Democratic Party, which published the paper *Vpered* (Forward).[127] These émigrés, former citizens of the USSR, had supporters in Britain, Germany, the US and elsewhere; their paper had a circulation of 3,000. They opposed both Stalinism and private capitalism, and some of their leading thinkers had developed the position, somewhat earlier than Cliff, that Russia was state capitalist: "the highest and final stage of development of the capitalist system because it brings the concentration of capital and the socialisation of labour to the highest possible point". In 1950 and 1951 *Vpered* published two chapters from Cliff's *The Nature of Stalinist Russia* on class struggle in Russia and the imperialist expansion of Russia.[128] An article by Vs. Felix (Vsevolod Holubnychy) on the social composition of the Supreme Council of the USSR appeared in the first issue of *Socialist Review*.[129] In the 1955 edition of his book on Russia, Cliff commended the UPA (Ukrainian Resurgent Army) for its opposition to both capitalism and "Stalinist pseudo-socialism".[130]

More surprisingly, Cliff's work succeeded in penetrating inside the Stalinist bloc. In 1956, at the time of Khrushchev's revelations about Stalin, the Russian KGB (secret police and intelligence organisation) commissioned a translation of Cliff's book. The introduction stated:

> The book...provokes understandable interest, especially in the light of the XXth Party Congress... The author's basic aim is to set out the Trotskyist thesis of the impossibility of socialism in one country. Analysing economic and socio-political aspects of the Soviet socialist system, Cliff arrives at the conclusion that the USSR is state capitalist. He argues that in the Soviet Union there has been a transformation of the workers' state and a bureaucratisation of the party and state apparatus, and that a new "class" of bureaucrats has arisen, which reduced to zero all the gains of the October revolution, usurping the rights and freedoms of the workers, and imposing on them the most cruel exploitation in the interests of capital accumulation. Cliff characterises the USSR as a reactionary social system in which there exist deep class contradictions.

The translation was not made openly available; it was kept in a special section of a library to which access was strictly controlled. But in the 1980s a student managed to photograph the book with a miniature camera. Copies of the translation were circulated by a group of anarchists; some people were jailed for being in possession of the translation.[131] It is proof of the significance of Cliff's work that it was taken so seriously in the heart of the enemy camp.

In 1957 the Yugoslav dissident Milovan Djilas was jailed for his influential book *The New Class*,[132] which argued that there was a new ruling class in Russia and Eastern Europe. In the 1960s there was a rumour, perhaps originating with the historian Vladimir Dedijer, who had been tried with Djilas in 1955 and who taught in Britain in the early 1960s, that at the time of his arrest in 1956 for supporting the Hungarian Revolution Djilas had been in possession of a copy of Cliff's book on Russia. Cliff used to recount the story with a certain degree of satisfaction.[133] Djilas's son believes that this is unlikely, though he cannot rule it out entirely.[134]

During the summer of 1968 Joel Geier, who was travelling in Europe, met Ivan Sviták, a well-known Czech dissident philosopher. Sviták told him that he had visited Yugoslavia in the 1960s and had got hold of a copy of Cliff's book on Russia. He asked Joel to thank Cliff for him.[135]

The official RCP reply to Cliff came from Ted Grant.[136] It was a serious but vigorous polemic, which initiated many of the arguments that would be used against Cliff over the coming 50 years. Grant defended Trotsky (often referred to as "the Old Man" to stress that Grant was a loyal disciple), and scornfully dismissed Cliff's claims to have found anomalies or contradictions in Trotsky's work. For Grant, Stalin's Russia was "a transitional society in which some of the laws peculiar to socialism apply and some peculiar to capitalism".[137] (This leaves the problem that, since transition implies movement, Russia would have to be moving closer to socialism, something for which Grant provided no evidence.)

Grant argued that if Cliff were right, "a new epoch, the epoch of state capitalism, opens up before us. This would shatter the entire theoretical basis of the Leninist-Trotskyist movement." And "if a new period of state capitalism looms ahead...then to talk of this being a period of the disintegration of world capitalism reduces itself to mere phrasemongering".[138] Grant had a point here: Cliff's position did challenge the perspective of revolutionary upheavals in the near future, though Cliff himself had not yet thought through all the implications. Grant seemed more concerned to defend the Trotskyist orthodoxy than to look at the realities of a changing world.

Grant contended that many of the features drawn out by Cliff would exist even in a healthy workers' state. This led him to accuse Cliff of drawing an "idealised and false picture of the state under Lenin and Trotsky", and to claim that "Cliff may argue, that unless the working class has direct control of the state, it cannot be a workers' state. In that case, he will have to reject the idea that there was a workers' state in Russia, except possibly in the first few months".[139]

Here Grant was on a slippery slope. By rejecting Cliff's insistence that a socialist revolution required conscious control by the workers, he was raising issues far more important than the precise chronology of the degeneration of the Russian Revolution. Grant revealed that he was prepared to accept some very odd criteria for a "workers' state". He argued that "a working class can be a ruling class when a great proportion of them are in jail in Siberia", and that "under certain conditions the dictatorship of the proletariat could also be realised through the dictatorship of one man".[140] The debate broadened from the "Russian question" in itself to a more general consideration of the nature of socialism and the process of transition to it.

There is no indication at this stage that Cliff envisaged that the argument about the nature of Russia was an issue which would lead to a split in the RCP. Nor, apparently, did the RCP leadership believe it was a question which should inevitably lead to a split. Trotsky himself, however hostile he had been to state capitalist analyses, had insisted in 1939 that the question in itself did not warrant a split in the movement.* The question that was causing much more immediate concern within the RCP was entry into the Labour Party. Intervention by the International Executive produced an ad hoc solution – the pro-entry minority would form a separate organisation and put their strategy into practice while the rest of the RCP would carry on as previously.[141] But now the crisis of Trotskyism was maturing rapidly.

In February 1948 the Czech Communist Party excluded other parties and took sole power. Despite a staged walk-on role for the working class, this was in effect a Stalinist coup.[142] Under the headline "Capitalists Routed in Czechoslovakia" Haston in *Socialist Appeal* described the events as "an important victory for the working class", while making some reservations about the way the Stalinists controlled the movement.[143] As the Cold War intensified,

---

* "It would therefore be a piece of monstrous nonsense to split with comrades who on the question of the sociological nature of the USSR have an opinion different from ours, insofar as they solidarize with us in regard to the political tasks." (L Trotsky, *In Defense of Marxism*, New York, 1965, p5)

the polarisation between East and West increased, and the pressure on anti-Stalinist revolutionaries to line up with one side or the other intensified.

In the summer of 1948 the Fourth International held its Second World Congress. A number of oppositional delegates formed a loose bloc at the Congress. These were Shachtman of the US Workers' Party (present with consultative status), Grace Lee on behalf of the James-Dunayevskaya group (which had now returned to the Fourth International), Cornelius Castoriadis from France who would soon form the Socialisme ou Barbarie grouping, Jacques Gallienne also from France, Munis from Spain, Bob Armstrong from Ireland and an observer from Indochina. Although they held a variety of positions on the Russian question, they argued that the Fourth International should drop its commitment to "defence of the Soviet Union".[144]

The "orthodox" leadership combined to crush them. The American SWP, Mandel, Pablo, and the leaders of the French section, Pierre Frank, Pierre Lambert and Michèle Mestre, all united to defend the majority line. The last hope of a Fourth International able to relate to the unexpected challenges of the post-war period had disappeared. Within a few years the dominant bloc would fly apart and they would be at each other's throats as split followed split.* At just about this time half the membership of the French section left in order to join the short-lived Rassemblement Démocratique Révolutionnaire headed by David Rousset and Jean-Paul Sartre, which took a line of opposition to both major power blocs in the world.

Shortly after the Congress an even bigger shock occurred. Tito's Yugoslavia broke publicly with Stalin. Within a short time Moscow was claiming that its former ally had degenerated into fascism. This split with Stalinism offered opportunities and posed problems for the Fourth International. The leadership, however, responded in a peculiar fashion. They sided enthusiastically with Tito, apparently forgetting that only weeks earlier Yugoslavia had been defined as a bourgeois state. They now saw Yugoslavia as a workers' state, and in order to avoid an intolerable inconsistency, they soon came to describe all Stalin's other satellites in Eastern Europe as

---

* Cliff did not generally make sectarian remarks in public speeches or writings. But I recall in around 1969 he told me with great glee, "There are now four Fourth Internationals" (Author's recollection).

workers' states also.[145] *

It was the end of the road for the RCP. Sheila Leslie recalls a terrible factional atmosphere, with squabbling and fighting all the time, though she thinks Cliff and Chanie were not really involved in the factional disputes.[146] In June 1949 the RCP was formally dissolved and replaced by a clandestine body with the innocuous title of "the Club". By now most of the RCP leadership had decided to follow the example of the minority and to support entry into the Labour Party; members of "the Club" joined the Labour Party as individuals.[147] As Rob Sewell, one of Grant's followers, has pointed out, at this stage "work inside the Labour Party was not based on a previously worked out strategy or tactic, but simply a matter of necessity".[148] Haston, the most able of the leadership, saw no future and resigned from "the Club", abandoning revolutionary politics in favour of open reformism.[149]

With the disappearance of Haston, and the failure of Grant to offer any political alternative, more influence came into the hands of Gerry Healy. Healy is now best known for his pathetic end in the 1980s, when he was expelled by his own organisation for violence and sexual abuse of female comrades. It is not necessary to project his later misdeeds back onto his younger self to recognise that while he was an organiser of some talent, he was both short on theory and very strong on authoritarian measures.†

The RCP annual congress had taken place in August 1947, just before Cliff's departure for Ireland. According to police reports on the events, classified "SECRET", but which may not be wholly reliable, Cliff "made a strong personal attack on HEALY and his record, saying that he merely wanted to collar the leadership of the party. The minority was, in his view, heading for expulsion". [150] ‡

Meanwhile Cliff, for the second time in two years, was adjusting

---

* To be technically accurate, these were "deformed" rather than "degenerated" workers' states, since, unlike Russia, they had never been healthy workers' states in the first place.

† For a full account of Healy's role, see B Pitt, *The Rise and Fall of Gerry Healy*, at http://www.whatnextjournal.co.uk/Pages/Healy/Contents.html

‡ The Special Branch officer who wrote the report, Sergeant W Jones, had observed the congress from the "vicinity", though he claimed to have heard "much of what transpired". That Jones did not know as much as he wanted his superiors to believe he did is shown by the bizarre claim that Cliffe (*sic*) "is now believed to be identical with Charles van GELDEREN"! (NA HO 45/25486)

to life in a new city. Dublin at this time was a conservative place. Divorce and contraception were both banned by the strongly Catholic regime. Cliff must have seen some parallels between the role of the Irish priesthood and the rabbis he remembered from Palestine. In the early years of the Cold War clerical reaction joined forces with pro-American anti-Communism. The mainstream of the labour movement was firmly in the grip of right-wing ideas, as Cliff himself could observe on the streets of Dublin:

> On 1 May 1949... an estimated 150,000 people, many of them workers following union banners, marched through Dublin against "the evils of Communism" in Eastern Europe... The platform was dominated by trade union speakers who threatened to suppress any communist party that reared its head in Catholic Ireland.[151]

In 1949 the Literary and Historical Society at University College Dublin invited Owen Sheehy-Skeffington to speak on the rather anodyne topic, "That the ideals of the *Communist Manifesto* are worthy of humanity". The meeting was promptly banned by the college authorities.[152]

In this situation there was not much of a left milieu. Trotskyism in Ireland had had a fairly tenuous existence.[153] At the beginning of the Second World War a number of British Trotskyists, including Healy and Haston, had moved to Dublin for a while, and groups were built in both Belfast and Dublin. In 1944 the Revolutionary Socialist Party was founded with some 20 members in Belfast and Dublin. But by the time Cliff arrived the organisation was in sharp decline. The leading Belfast comrades, Bob and Elsie Armstrong, had been forced to move to London. There were sharp internal differences over the Russian question, and the environment became more difficult to work in. The Stalinists persuaded the police to arrest Johnny Byrne, the leading militant in Dublin, for selling papers.

In August 1948, some months after Cliff's arrival, Byrne reported to the International Secretariat of the Fourth International. After describing the situation in Belfast as "rather hopeless", he went on to deal with Dublin:

> In Dublin we have lost one comrade. He is a Shachtmanite, and is almost completely demoralised. He has not met us for the past two months. He defends the position of the Belfast comrades with regard to disbanding the Irish Section. There are two comrades left, one in the Socialist Youth

(Stalinists) and the other, myself, active in the trade union movement. I am a member of the National Executive Committee of the Workers Union of Ireland (with a membership of 24,000), a member of Dublin Trades Council, was a delegate to the Irish Trade Union Congress for the last two Congresses, and am on the Branch Committee of my own union (Corporation Workers). I am in the Irish Labour Party, but it is very dead, and there is no prospect of quick returns.

The Socialist Youth (Stalinists) with a membership of about sixty is very active. I think this is our best field of recruitment, and as it is impossible for us, because of lack of forces, to work openly, we consider it best to work inside the Labour Party and the Socialist Youth.

We shall do our best to maintain and build the Irish Section of the Fourth International.[154]

Despite this brave conclusion, Irish Trotskyism was effectively dead. It would not revive until the different circumstances of the 1960s.

Byrne himself was a dedicated militant. Owen Sheehy-Skeffington's widow Andrée remembered him very favourably:

Another regular labourite, Johnny Byrne, was more down to earth... Honest and straight...he was very critical of the Labour Party and trade union leaders, but also of his fellow workers when he found them unreliable in their work, let alone in their union or Labour Party activities. He trusted Owen's judgement, although he knew that Owen, interested in every shade of left-wing thought, did not adhere to the Fourth International.[155]

Byrne and Cliff became good friends, and went to the cinema together every week, and sometimes to the theatre,[156] but there was little opportunity for any political activity.

One of the last publications of the Revolutionary Socialist Party before it disintegrated was a leaflet about the commemoration of the eightieth anniversary of James Connolly's birth. Entitled "Who Wears Connolly's Mantle?", it took a hard anti-Stalinist line, declaring that "the new social formation in Russia has absolutely nothing in common with the free Socialism envisaged by Lenin and Trotsky; nor does it bear any resemblance to the type of working class democracy envisaged by Connolly or any other true Socialist", and denouncing the "tyrannical, anti-Socialist, barbarous and totalitarian nature of Stalinism". It has been suggested that Cliff may have had a hand in drafting this, but there is no evidence of this (there were several others in the Revolutionary Socialist Party who rejected the "workers' state" analysis of Russia).[157]

Cliff made one other important friend during this period. Owen Sheehy-Skeffington had lived a turbulent life. His father had been shot by the British in 1916, and to escape from the country to America with his mother he had been obliged, as a child of only seven, to learn to give a false name to deceive the authorities.[158]

He later returned to Ireland and became a well-known academic and public figure. He was a man of the independent left, at times a member of the Labour Party, from which he was expelled in 1943. In her biography of him, his widow Andrée listed the issues on which he campaigned during his life:

> Housing, health, government's autocratic inclinations, education, partition, civil liberties, the profit motive, or simply smugness, hypocrisy and cant in high places.

In the Cold War context he showed equal distaste for Washington and Moscow, arguing that "McCarthyism and the thought-control sections of the Smith Act were the American counterpart of the Stalinist system, to be equally condemned". He commented wryly that "there is a tendency in this country for me to be considered a communist by virtually everybody, except the communists". When he spoke for the Labour Party against the government's Trade Union Bill, he was noted in police records as a member of the Fourth International. In fact he never had any organisational links with Trotskyism, though he was a good friend of such Trotskyists as Paddy Trench and Johnny Byrne.[159]

Every Friday evening he and his wife would open their home to foreign students and refugees in Dublin. Cliff was a regular attender; he enjoyed the intellectual company, but also, in view of his restricted diet, the cakes that were provided.[160] In her biography Andrée recalled, "Another type of dissident was the Israeli émigré Ygael Gluckstein, who entertained us with examples of dialectics from his upbringing as an orthodox Jew, and applied his nimble and well-trained mind to a critical examination of Soviet 'colonialism', on which he was writing a book".[161]

Cliff greatly liked Sheehy-Skeffington, who was most helpful to him and assisted with revising the style of *Stalin's Satellites in Europe*.[162] A decade later an SRG branch was briefly established in Dublin, and a school was organised at which Cliff, Alasdair MacIntyre and Sheehy-Skeffington spoke.[163] MacIntyre remembered that Cliff was delighted to be reunited with his old friend.[164]

On one occasion in 1949 or 1950 Cliff spoke to the Dublin Fabian Society on the basis of his research on Eastern Europe. A number of Stalinists were present – that they were active in the Fabian Society was a sign of the low level of left activity in Dublin.* Sheehy-Skeffington, who chaired the meeting, described the occasion in a letter to a friend:

> We had an excellent Fabian meeting at which a Jewish refugee from Israel (yes he had done gaol there for taking a proper Socialist line about Arabs!) attacked the Soviet persecution of the Jews (the "Doctors Plot", etc. – 11 Jews out of the 14 doctors)† and he was so well informed that the Stalinists present nearly lynched him! He was of Russian stock, Israel-born, and read Russian fluently and knew his facts – a good meeting![165]

There were few distractions for Cliff. His one great pleasure was the theatre.[166] Dublin had at least two theatres – the Abbey and the Gate – which staged serious drama, and they were often the subject of controversy because of the radical nature of the material performed there.[167] Here Cliff got an introduction to Irish drama, especially the work of Sean O'Casey; he probably saw such plays as the savage anti-war drama *The Silver Tassie*, or *The Plough and the Stars* (which dealt with the 1916 rising). The latter play had caused huge controversy when first performed in 1926 because it seemed to question how far the struggle for national independence was relevant to ordinary working people. Cliff would have appreciated the irony of the fact that the character in the play – The Covey – who most clearly sees the limits of the national struggle ("What's th'use o' freedom, if it's not economic freedom… There's only one war worth havin': th'war for th'economic emancipation of th'proletariat.") is presented

---

* In 1941 the Dublin branch of the Communist Party of Ireland, the only surviving branch in the South, had dissolved and its members had joined the Labour Party as individuals (M Milotte, *Communism in Modern Ireland*, Dublin, 1984, pp191-200).

† This was not the notorious "Jewish Doctors' Plot" denounced in 1953. From the late 1940s many Jewish doctors, intellectuals and other professionals were sacked or imprisoned.

as a boring abstract propagandist.[168] Many years later Cliff told the *New Statesman* that O'Casey was the playwright whose work he would like everyone to see.[169] He also had the opportunity of seeing some of the classics of modern theatre including Strindberg's *The Father* and Arthur Miller's *Death of a Salesman*.

Having finished his document on state capitalism, Cliff produced two more related texts. The first was a short consideration of the theory of "bureaucratic collectivism".[170] Cliff rejected the theory because it gave no account of the dynamic of the system, and because it denied Russian workers the status of being proletarians, and hence made them incapable of self-emancipation.*

The second was a much more substantial piece called "On the Class Nature of the 'People's Democracies'".[171] This was the basis for his first published book, *Stalin's Satellites in Europe*. It took up the argument about state capitalism from a different angle, dealing at length with the question of the Fourth International's change of tack over Yugoslavia. Cliff took on the whole question of the agency of socialist transformation. He pointed out:

> Members of the FI day in and day out repeat the basic Marxist conceptions: the liberation of the working class can be carried out only by the working class itself, class conscious and led by a revolutionary party, that it cannot lay hold of the bourgeois state machine but must smash it and establish in its place a state of a new type, a state of proletarian democracy (Soviets, etc.).

Yet if it was accepted that the satellite states in Europe were workers' states, these fundamentals of Marxism would have to be abandoned. If Stalinism could create new workers' states, then the whole role of the Fourth International was called into question.

One of the most important parts of the argument was the question of consciousness. Here Cliff distinguished between bourgeois and socialist revolutions. Bourgeois revolutions were often made without the conscious intentions of the bourgeoisie, and without the active involvement of the masses. In this respect the great French Revolution of 1789 was the exception rather than the rule.[172]

---

* Though hostile to the theory of bureaucratic collectivism, Cliff recognised Shachtman's strengths. When he heard of Shachtman's death in 1972, he expressed regret and liking for Shachtman (Edward Crawford interview, September 2008).

A socialist revolution, however, could only be made as the conscious act of the working class. Cliff insisted:

> Marx repeated hundreds of times that the proletarian revolution is the conscious act of the working class itself...Therefore, if we accept that the "People's Democracies" are workers' states, what Marx and Engels said about the socialist revolution being "history conscious of itself" is refuted. Refuted is Engels' statement: "It is only from this point [the socialist revolution – TC] that men, with full consciousness, will fashion their own history; it is only from this point that the social causes set in motion by men will have, predominantly and in constantly increasing measure, the effects willed by men. It is humanity's leap from the realm of necessity into the realm of freedom." (*Anti-Dühring*).[173]

This argument would remain at the centre of Cliff's conception of the revolutionary process and hence at the heart of his conception of socialism. The argument about state capitalism was not simply about how certain regimes were to be defined. It was about the essence of socialism. For Cliff no force, whether Labour politicians or Russian tanks, could substitute for the conscious self-activity of the working class.*

So Cliff continued his lonely studies in Dublin, longing to be reunited with his wife and new child, and perhaps hoping, against rational expectation, that the Fourth International would see the error of its ways and return to authentic revolutionary Marxism. But the whole situation would soon be transformed by events in a distant Asian country of which Cliff had probably scarcely heard.

---

* Doubtless Cliff was thinking of those in the Fourth International who were arguing that Tito was an "unconscious Trotskyist". In the discussion in the RCP that followed the publication of Cliff's 1948 document, David James had argued that "objectively it is Tito (and Gomulka, and perhaps tomorrow Mao Tse-tung) who expresses the programme of Trotskyism unconsciously, in a distorted form". (S Bornstein and A Richardson, *War and the International*, London, 1986, pp219, 223-234). It might be malicious to suggest that the only "unconscious Trotskyists" were those who had entered the Labour Party and fallen asleep at their ward meetings.

4
1950-60
The Loneliness of the Long Distance Perspective

On 25 June 1950 armed conflict began between North and South Korea. How exactly it started remains obscure – the historian Bruce Cumings, who devoted some 1,500 pages to the origins and course of the war, summed up his judgement: "Who started the Korean War? This question should not be asked".[1] Within a short space of time the war was taken over by the major powers. Possibly the US was surprised by the particular circumstances in which the war began. But as Cumings noted, "Washington committed to the war with lockstep efficiency and few if any doubts".[2] Under the aegis of the United Nations, troops from the US, Britain and other Western powers were sent to support South Korea. Russia avoided direct involvement, but provided North Korea with arms and political support; substantial numbers of Chinese troops fought for North Korea.

No decision about Korea had been taken at the Yalta and Potsdam conferences, which determined the post-war "spheres of influence" of the competing powers. In 1945 the country was occupied by Japanese forces, and when Japan surrendered following the bombing of Hiroshima and Nagasaki, it was the United States State-War-Navy Coordinating Committee which hurriedly drew a line at the 38th parallel, dividing Korea into zones to be occupied by American and Russian forces. Two satellite regimes came into existence side by side.*

---

* Cliff never wrote anything about the nature of North Korean society. There is an analysis of North Korean state capitalism, influenced by Cliff's work, in the book by the Korean Marxist scholar Kim Ha-yong, *The Korean Peninsula from an Internationalist Perspective*, Seoul, 2002. For a discussion of this, see O Miller, "North Korea's Hidden History", *International Socialism* 109 (Winter 2006).

What had started as a localised conflict rapidly turned into a proxy war between Washington and Moscow. In retrospect it is clear that neither side had any interest in turning the event into a global conflict (especially as from 1949 both sides had nuclear weapons), but at the time world war looked like a real possibility. The left was under greater pressure than ever to line up behind one side or the other in the Cold War. In Britain the Communist Party was firmly in Moscow's camp, but the parliamentary Labour left virtually disintegrated, with only two Labour MPs opposing government policy on the Korean War.

The situation posed problems for what was left of the Trotskyist movement. In the new analysis presented by the Fourth International, this was a conflict between a workers' state and imperialism.* In a democratic organisation there would have been a vigorous debate about the implications of the situation. But Healy, now the dominant figure in "the Club", was in no mood for debate. The situation offered an ideal opportunity for ridding himself of dissidents.

Cliff's supporters were not constituted in a formal faction, though according to Chanie Rosenberg they were already aware that the differences were so important that a split would have to come eventually.[3]

Now those who refused to accept the leadership's demands were summarily expelled. This included not only Cliff and those who supported his analyses, but everybody who would not accept Healy's edicts, including Ted Grant, who had been charged with responding to Cliff's advocacy of the state capitalist theory. Things came to a head at the conference of "the Club" held in July 1950. Ken Tarbuck, who attended as a delegate, described the atmosphere now prevailing in the organisation:

> As the discussions proceeded it soon became clear that the large majority of those present were supporters of Healy. Those few opposition delegates sat together in a small huddle at the back of the hall. There were two supporters of Cliff who protested at his exclusion from the conference on the dubious grounds that he was not a member of the British Section. His document had not been circulated because "it had arrived

---

* The Third World Congress of the Fourth International in 1950 redefined North Korea as a "workers' state" (P Shipley, *Revolutionaries in Modern Britain*, London, 1976, p66). It was the only "workers' state" to have been created by the US Navy, raising the argument about agency to a new level of absurdity.

too late". Ted Grant was present, but as far as I can recall had not submitted any counter-resolutions or documents. One of the most startling things was one of Gerry Healy's speeches when he shouted at Ted Grant that he "should get back to the dung heap of history where he belonged". I had never heard such abusive language used by anyone in the movement before, particularly to a comrade. Instead of protests this effluvia was met by wild applause from Healy's supporters. This was an indication of how degenerate the Club was already in 1950. The whole atmosphere which had been built up, secret names, clandestine venues, fear of police raids, etc., was hysterical. Any criticism of the leadership was met by boos, hisses or cat-calls.[4]

Healy's biographer Bob Pitt, who has no sympathy with Cliff's position, argues:

> The state capitalist position of Tony Cliff had won a growing number of adherents in the Club; but Healy, incapable of answering this faction theoretically, resorted to organisational suppression as a substitute for political argument, and the Cliffites were also expelled.[5]

Healy's position was that the confrontation between workers' states and capitalism was now the primary form of class struggle in the world, replacing that between classes within nation-states:

> The conflict between the Soviet Union and the United States is therefore fundamental and is the basic antagonism in the world today. Economic necessity compels the United States towards an armed showdown with the Soviet Union and the colonial revolution...
>
> A correct conclusion is that Imperialism is being forced to prepare for, and then embark upon, a world war *under extremely unfavourable conditions for world capitalism.*
>
> The future holds out the prospect of an *international civil war* in which the Fourth International will have every opportunity to lead the workers of the world to victory.[6] *

---

* This position was later taken to its logical conclusion by Michel Pablo, who argued that in the face of an impending world war between capitalist and socialist blocs, the Trotskyist organisations should engage in long-term entry work in the mass Communist parties in order to intervene in a new situation in which the class struggle would acquire the form of a conflict between blocs of states. Healy and his followers, who opposed this, used the term "Pabloite" as one of the most savage pieces of abuse in their vocabulary. Yet their politics were based on the same premises as Pablo's.

Cliff's response was that the struggle between workers and those who exploited them remained primary, whether in the East or in the West. This insistence would orient his politics over the coming decades.

In Birmingham a small oppositional group had developed before the outbreak of the Korean War. Ken Tarbuck, who was on of its members, described its development:

> We comrades of the old Majority now constituted ourselves into a sort of secret faction with those meetings held away from the branch. At that point we could not formulate what we were going to do, and what platform we should adopt. What we did feel however was a burning sense of being let down by Haston and all the other leaders of the old majority... We felt that we had been led to the slaughter, and had gone mainly because we had trusted our leaders. On the other hand we all felt repulsed by the politics and organisational methods of Healy and his clique. Our problem at that precise point was, what should we do?
>
> Having established our secret meetings on a regular basis we began to try to formulate some political criticisms of the political line of the Club. We also invited Tony Cliff to visit us for a discussion. Cliff came to Birmingham some time either in May or June of 1950, it was certainly before the Club's annual conference which was held in July. He attempted to persuade us to declare ourselves state capitalists, i.e. followers of his theory... The outbreak of the Korean War in June gave us a further impetus to wrestle with our problems. This time Cliff was more persuasive and argued along the following lines:
>
> "If you continue to see Stalinist Russia as a workers' state and admit that the Stalinists can carry through a revolution (Eastern Europe, China) then you end up adopting Stalinist policies (e.g. *Socialist Outlook*, the IEC line on Jugoslavia) and Stalinist organisational methods, e.g. Healy's purge. The only way out of this dilemma was to adopt a state capitalist line." (This is a paraphrase, not a direct quotation.)
>
> Although we were very sympathetic to Cliff's position, we did not feel that we had had sufficient time to consider all the implications at that point. We decided to postpone a decision until after the national conference due to be held in July. But it has to be said that we were more than half-convinced by Cliff at our meeting with him.[7]

Cliff was still domiciled in Ireland. That he was able to intervene so effectively in the situation and draw together the nucleus of a group was testimony to his remarkable tenacity and his ability to know when to seize an opportunity. Tarbuck's tribute to Cliff is all the more impressive since it was written many years later, when Tarbuck had become quite hostile to Cliff's ideas and organisation:

> He had not been able to obtain a residence permit for Britain, but was registered as a student in Ireland. This meant that he could only travel over to England on a visitor's permit for a few weeks at a time. Because of this he had to be cautious about appearing in public. However, despite all these problems he had been travelling up and down the country during 1950 meeting as many people as possible, trying to persuade them of the need to split from Healy and form another group. It was a remarkable achievement given his semi-legal status that so many people had turned up to the founding conference. By contrast we had heard nothing of Ted Grant since the Healy conference in July, he seemed to have withdrawn into his shell.[8]

The course that events then followed provides a striking illustration of the way that the Healy organisation had degenerated:

> It was against this background that we in Birmingham planned our tactics for exiting the Healy group. It was decided that Percy Downey should put a resolution down for discussion at the Birmingham Trades Council which would put a "third camp" position on Korea. This would place before workers an independent position on this conflict. This he did and it was duly discussed and rejected, the Healyites, Stalinists and right wing Labour all forming a bloc against the resolution. Harry Finch was livid at Percy's action and called a summoned branch meeting to take place within seven days… When we arrived at the meeting, in a pub near the Bull Ring, we found that Gerry Healy was present. The only item of the agenda was a resolution for the expulsion of Percy Downey for the breach of group discipline by laying the resolution at the Trades Council. When any of us attempted to raise the political issues involved Healy flew into a rage and insisted that the only issue before the meeting was "Did or did not Downey move the resolution at the Trades Council?" Percy was not asked to speak in his own defence; he was merely asked if he had moved the resolution. He attempted to elaborate his reasons, but Healy flew into his rage again. The resolution was put, but to Healy's chagrin the branch was split down [the] middle and there was no majority for the expulsion…

About two weeks later there was another summoned meeting called... The resolution for Percy's expulsion was again put. However, before the vote was taken Healy told us that if anyone voted against the resolution they would be suspended from membership. The vote was taken and this time, of course, there was a majority of one for the resolution... Immediately the vote was taken Healy ordered Percy to leave, which he did.

Healy then went round the room pointing his finger at each of us who had voted against Percy's expulsion and asked us to retract our vote. As each of us refused we were told that we were suspended from membership for one month. If after that date we wished to change our minds we would be readmitted to membership, otherwise we would be expelled. Of course none [of] us did retract our vote, and one by one we were told to leave. So nearly half of the Birmingham branch was expelled for voting against the expulsion of another comrade.[9]

Thus a Birmingham group came into existence, including Ken and Rhoda Tarbuck, Downey, Bill Ainsworth and Peter Morgan.

On the weekend of 30 September to 1 October 1950 an inaugural meeting of Cliff's supporters was held at 866a Camden Road, London NW1,[10] * the home of Jean and Danny Tait. Marmite sandwiches were served.[11] There were 21 people in attendance, representing a total membership of 33.† This small figure compared quite well with the 60 who, it was said, remained in the official Fourth International

---

* In today's Camden Road there is no number as high as 866. Either there has been renumbering since 1950, or a misleading address was given for security reasons.
† A record of the meeting gives initials of those attending, not all of which can be deciphered.
London
JCX (Jeff Carlsson?), RW (?), RC (Renée Carlsson), RG (?), RS (Ralph *or* Renée Shaberman), S (?), JT (Jean Tait), DT (Danny Tait), CD (C Dallas = Chanie), RT (Roger Tennant = Cliff)
Thames Valley
AK (Anil Kumarin = A Moonesinghe), JH (Jeanne Hoban), NW (?)
Crewe
RC (Ray Challinor), CQ (?)
Birmingham
PMX (Peter Morgan), PD (Percy Downey), KT (Ken Tarbuck), WA (William Ainsworth)
Sheffield
BC (?), T (?)
(Notes on Foundation Conference, Rich. MS 1117/box 211/file 3)

section.[12] This indicated the low ebb which Trotskyism had now reached in Britain. Over half of those who had been in the RCP just a couple of years earlier had abandoned the movement.

The meeting was a small success. A new organisation, the Socialist Review Group (SRG) was formed, and a national committee was established. Its first meeting was held in Birmingham on 9-10 December 1950. There were representatives from Birmingham, London and Thames Valley, Crewe and Manchester (Manchester comrades had been unable to attend the founding meeting).[13]

A letter was sent to the Fourth International seeking recognition as the British section. However, it was scarcely designed to obtain a favourable reply, since it described the existing leadership of the International as:

> bankrupt politically, capitulating to Stalinism and Titoism, lacking any consistent policy towards reformism, and showing all the signs of bureaucratic degeneration.[14]

A new journal, *Socialist Review*, saw the light of day. It was a modest enough publication. For its first year it appeared in duplicated form. Just 350 copies of the first issue were produced, but for the second this was raised to 375.[15] Six issues were produced between November 1950 and November 1951. It was presented with care – though it was produced with an ordinary typewriter the lines were justified to make it look more professional.* Despite the small circulation, stapling and collating each issue took five hours of the comrades' time.[16]

Money received for sales of *Socialist Review* between November 1950 and 1 September 1951 was as follows:

Thames Valley	£3	15s	6d
London	£11	1s	6d
Birmingham	£5	3s	6d
Manchester	£3	2s	0d
Crewe	£3	19s	0d [17]

Assuming this covers the first four issues average sales per issue

---

* For those used to justifying at the click of a mouse, it should be recalled that with a conventional typewriter justification could only be roughly achieved by counting the number of letters in each line before typing, and then adding an appropriate number of spaces. Clearly the typist (Rhoda Tarbuck assisted by the editor Bill Ainsworth) was a very dedicated comrade.

would be:

Thames Valley	38
London	111
Birmingham	52
Manchester	31
Crewe	40
Total	**272**

The first issue contained a major article by Cliff, written under the pseudonym Roger Tennant.* Under the title "The Struggle of the Powers",[18] this referred only briefly to the Korean conflict† as a starting point for an analysis of how the two major world imperialisms were increasingly symmetrical: "The war in Korea serves the great powers as a rehearsal for their intended struggle for the redivision of the globe. The fate of the Korean people is a grave warning to all humanity what sufferings the march of aggressive imperialist Powers will entail".‡

He began by arguing that after 1945 "only two imperialist powers remain to contend for world mastery – America and Russia". British imperialism was "weakened industrially and financially". Six years before Suez, and displaying his characteristic taste for mixed metaphor, Cliff argued, "The erstwhile proud western European imperialist powers are now standing, hat in hand, waiting for the dole of the young, sturdy American rival."

---

* It is surprising that when the volume of documents *The Fourth International, Stalinism, and the Origins of the International Socialists* (London, 1971) was published, this article was not included, whereas there was an inferior piece from a Sri Lankan Trotskyist (V Karalasingham, "The War in Korea", *The Fourth International...*, pp76-78, from *Socialist Review*, Vol 1, No 2 (January 1951). It appears that everyone, including Cliff, who was consulted about the volume, had simply forgotten the article (Richard Kuper interview, February 2009).

† In Labour League of Youth circles Cliff's position was characterised to the tune of a bawdy song called "The Ball of Kirriemuir":
  Tony Cliff, he was there,
  Talking about Korea,
  Don't give me your North or South
  They both give me diarrhoea.
  (John Palmer on Lenin's Tomb website, 7 December 2009)

‡ Some years later Cliff argued much more explicitly that "it is evident from North Korea's complete dependence on Soviet arms that her advance on the South on June 25, 1950, could not have taken place except by Moscow's dictate"(T Cliff, *Mao's China*, p411). This may understimate the extent to which Stalin reluctantly assented under Chinese and North Korean pressure.

Given his expected audience, he did not need to spend much time arguing that the US was imperialist. But although it would be some years before he did any serious work on the theme of the "war economy", he was already arguing that the US's "unprecedented superiority in world production and world politics is nourished by the war economy of the last war and the preparation for the future one".

To substantiate his claim that Russia was also imperialist, Cliff did not confine himself to observing military conquest or making moralistic denunciations. He showed that the economic mechanisms were the same East and West: "The traditional imperialist countries exploited their colonies in three ways: by buying the products of their colonies for low prices, by selling them the products of the 'mother' country for high prices, and by establishing enterprises owned by the capitalists of the 'mother' country and employing 'natives'. Russian state capitalism uses the same three methods to exploit its colonies."

Hence the ideological differences between the rival powers – the invocation of "peace" or "democracy" – were relatively unimportant: "The 'Peace' campaign of Stalin's Russia is not less hypocritical than Truman's 'Defence of Democracy'. Pax Stalin looks like this: an agreement with Hitler to divide Poland, a proposal to divide all Europe and the British Empire among Russia, Germany and Japan, an imperialist annexation of Poland, Czechoslovakia, Rumania, Hungary and Bulgaria, and impotent rage against Yugoslavia which 'threatens world peace'... No worker could desire the victory of Stalinist imperialism which unfurls the banner of 'Peace'."

The conclusion was clear – socialists must look to neither imperialist bloc, but only to independent working class action:

> In their mad rush for profit, for wealth, the two gigantic imperialist powers are threatening the existence of world civilisation, are threatening humanity with the terrible suffering of atomic war. The interests of the working class, of humanity, demand that neither of the imperialist world powers be supported, but that both be struggled against. The battle-cry of the real, genuine socialists today must be: Neither Washington nor Moscow, but International Socialism.*

---

* The slogan "Neither Washington nor Moscow" was borrowed from the Shachtman tendency. See "Capitalism, Stalinism, and the War", 1949 International Resolution of the Independent Socialist League, *New International*, April 1949, pp116, 117.

This was the first of a number of articles Cliff would write for *Socialist Review* over the coming decade. It was a modest and obscure publication, but for a small group of comrades in a period of almost total isolation it provided a forum for Marxist education and debate. From spring 1952 Ray Challinor secured a cheap printer in Preston,[19] and the paper appeared in printed form. There was now an editorial board consisting of William Ainsworth, Duncan Hallas and Ray Challinor. Later that year Cliff moved a resolution to the effect that "all members be written to asking them to contribute articles of a more popular nature and that an experiment be made with the printing of such articles".[20]

Cliff states in his autobiography that the initial membership was only eight.[21] This may be one of the rare cases in the history of the socialist movement where an organisation actually underestimated its membership. Some of the groups were at a considerable distance from London – in Birmingham, Crewe, Manchester and Sheffield – and in those days of austerity it may not have been easy for all members to travel. Certainly more then eight names crop up in accounts of activity in the first two or three years, and minutes show more than eight in attendance at some national committee meetings.[22] However, a number of the initial members had been burnt out by the collapse of the RCP and did not last long.[23]

A report of subscription income for the period from October 1950 to August 1951 showed a total of a little over a hundred pounds:*

Thames Valley	£5	0s	6d
London	£45	10s	7d
Birmingham	£51	10s	6d
Manchester	£5	10s	2½d
Crewe	£2	14s	0d[24]

The group had a formal structure suitable for a rather larger organisation. In addition to the National Committee from July 1951 Ken and Rhoda Tarbuck jointly assumed the function of general secretary.[25]

The early minutes show that the group stood very much in the organisational tradition of the Fourth International, making statements that sometimes appeared inappropriate for the group's tiny

---

* Weekly wages would often be between £5 and £10.

membership. The first national committee adopted a resolution on the building of the Marxist party in Britain:

> Our grouping, based on the conception of Russia as a State capitalist country, is the nucleus of that new Marxist party, and can be built firmly ONLY on the acceptance of party discipline in the tradition of bolshevism under Lenin's leadership.
>
> Acceptance of the political attitudes flowing from the State capitalist position on the Russian question, as and when these are defined by the Party, shall be a condition of membership, but no one shall be excluded from membership because of a different sociological estimate of the Russian society provided that Revolutionary defeatist conclusions are drawn from such an estimate. In discussion with close contacts, members must put the majority point of view. The party can decide to open up a particular discussion in public. The group must be satisfied that fresh applicants for membership are prepared to work loyally with the group, and accept its discipline before they are admitted to membership.[26]

However, Cliff was flexible in interpreting resolutions even when he had supported them, and in attempting to recruit Cyril Smith he assured him that disagreement with the state capitalist position was no barrier to joining the SRG. Unfortunately Smith regarded this as "unprincipled" and chose to join up with Healy.[27]

At a national committee meeting in November 1951, it was agreed that all new members should serve a period of three months probationary membership (something which in later years Cliff vigorously opposed). Cliff supported the resolution, and indeed backed an unsuccessful amendment to make the period six months rather than three.[28]

As in Palestine, Cliff, through his theoretical work and his committed enthusiasm, succeeded in drawing a number of able comrades around him. Whereas Healy seemed frightened to allow any potential rivals in his organisation, Cliff welcomed comrades who were able to take an initiative and who complemented his own abilities. With such a small organisation great attention had to be given to every member. So the minutes for the November 1952 national committee record that "RT [Cliff] gave a very long report on the state of London branch. They had six full members and three probationary members".[29] Cliff began the regular travels around the country which he would continue for the rest of his life. In March

1951 it was reported that he would be visiting Birmingham followed by a combined visit to Manchester and Crewe.[30]

Cliff took a particular interest in international contacts, and for a time hoped for some sort of international regroupment around the analysis of Russia. In 1951 he reported that "the basic document [presumably the 1948 internal document] was being printed in France, Bolivia, and probably Germany". He subsequently reported on developments in France, Israel and the US (the Johnson-Forest tendency of Dunayevskaya and James), and on attempts to make contacts in the Middle East, Indonesia, Italy and Germany, as well as with Ukrainian émigrés.[31] But little came of these contacts. The only international link that bore any fruit was with the Independent Socialist League (ISL) in the US. Ten copies of *Socialist Review* were exchanged for ten copies of the ISL's publications *New International* and *Labor Action*.[32] The ISL held the "bureaucratic collectivist" analysis of Russia, which Cliff had sharply criticised, yet he preferred cooperation with the ISL to closer contact with the state capitalists of the Johnson-Forest grouping. A letter was sent to Natalia Sedova inviting her to contribute to *Socialist Review*, but no reply was received.[33]

There were contacts with the Spanish POUM, whose paper *La Batalla* occasionally published pieces by Cliff on Russia and other questions. In May 1953 the POUM conference passed a resolution which stated that "the economic system of the USSR can and must be defined as one of state capitalism", though there was no specific reference to Cliff's work.[34]

It was Cliff's theoretical work which gave the group its coherence and its reason for existing. Chanie played a crucial role in the organisation, and while Cliff was still in Ireland she had to play a vital role in ensuring communications between Cliff and the rest of the group, as well as being a source of information for Cliff on grassroots activity. A number of other comrades played an important role in the early years of the SRG.

Duncan Hallas had joined the Trotskyist movement in 1940 at the age of 15 as an engineering apprentice. After serving in the armed forces, and taking part in a major mutiny in Egypt in 1946, he returned to Manchester where he worked in the Metro-Vickers engineering factory.[35]

Cliff and Chanie, with their young daughter, visited Hallas in

Manchester in the early 1950s. They were not easy times for those dedicated to the revolutionary movement:

> [We] stayed with Duncan in his tiny room, which contained a single bed and chest of drawers. Out went the contents of a drawer to accommodate the baby, the bed was given to us, and Duncan slept on the hard floor with a thin blanket. Whatever comforts there were – food, a hot water bottle – were piled on us. He was totally self-effacing. After giving us all he had he started on the politics and organisation we had come to discuss.[36]

Cliff encouraged[37] Hallas to write a reply to Ellis Hillman's claim that the Stalinist parties were embryonic ruling classes, which also involved a critique of Shachtman.[38] Hallas also wrote an important article called "The Significance of Nationalisation"[39] which explored the implications of the state capitalist theory for an understanding of nationalisation in Western capitalism.

Hallas dropped out of the group in 1954, and completed a degree in chemistry in Edinburgh gaining first class honours, then became a full-time organiser for the National Council of Labour Colleges, and subsequently a schoolteacher. He rejoined his old organisation in 1968 and was a leading figure for some 30 years. While not an original thinker in the style of Cliff, he was a man of enormous intellectual breadth. If Cliff resembled Lenin in his remorseless focus on the political, Hallas took after Engels in his vast range of interests in the natural and social worlds.

Ray Challinor had begun political life in the ILP, before becoming a member of the RCP. He had come to a state capitalist position independently of Cliff.[40] He soon became involved in the production and editing of *Socialist Review*. In later years he was a distinguished labour historian and author of several books.

Geoff Carlsson had been a member of the RCP and was in the Open Party Faction, which opposed Labour Party entry.[41] He worked at the ENV engineering factory in Willesden, north London, where he was a longstanding shop steward and at one time convenor.[42] Throughout the 1950s and early 1960s he was the leading industrial militant in the SRG.

Jean and Danny Tait also came from the RCP. Danny had been a comrade of Cliff's in Palestine while Jean came with Cliff despite a painful split in the family – her elder sister Mary, who had first brought her into the Trotskyist movement, was with the Healy group, but Jean found state capitalism a more satisfying theory and believed that Cliff offered a much more coherent political analysis. Asked if she was attracted by Cliff or repelled by Healy, she replied, "A bit of both." She remembered Healy as an effective organiser who attracted activists, but who was rather like a fundamentalist preacher. Cliff, on the other hand, had a tendency to overwhelm her with long arguments, leaving her feeling that she had objections but that he had not left her space to develop them. But his other qualities outweighed this tendency to hammer an argument. Danny soon dropped out, but Jean remained a stalwart of the organisation* well into the 1960s.[43]

Anil Moonesinghe, a student from Ceylon (Sri Lanka) then studying in London, was active for some time before returning home,[44] where in June 1964 he became Minister of Communications when the "Trotskyist" Lanka Sama Samaja Party entered the government of Mrs Bandaranaike.†

Syd Bidwell, a railway worker, had been a Trotskyist since 1937. He had drifted away when the RCP disintegrated, but in 1954 he joined the SRG and remained an active member for over ten years. In 1955 he became a full-time organiser for the National Council of Labour Colleges. From 1966 until 1992 he would be Labour MP for Southall in west London.‡

Stan Newens was a student at University College London, where he bought the first issue of *Socialist Review* from Anil Moonesinghe. Later he attended a debate on state capitalism at the college and met Chanie, who invited him to meet Cliff at their home, in an appallingly untidy room with an unshaded light bulb. Cliff harangued him for hours; if Stan ventured to disagree Cliff would say "Do me a favour" and carry on pacing up and down. After three such meetings Stan agreed to join. With Cliff's support – and despite Hallas's scepticism – Newens opted to work in the mines as an alternative to military service. He went to Stoke and stayed there four years, on

---

*   She wrote under the pseudonym Peter Mansell, a name which Cliff had suggested (Jean Tait interview, February 2004).
†   In the early 1960s Moonesinghe was still paying a subscription to the IS by banker's order, probably through failure to cancel rather than political support (author's recollection).
‡   For a fascinating account of Bidwell's entire political career see J McIlroy, "Adrift in the Rapids of Racism", *Revolutionary History* 7/1 (1998), pp134-165.

one occasion leading a strike. He was a leading member of the SRG until the late 1950s.[45] Subsequently he was a Labour MP and then a member of the European Parliament.

While Cliff doggedly pursued new recruits, he was not wholly free from some of the sexist prejudices then deeply embedded in the socialist movement. Sheila Leslie remembered that Cliff made great efforts to recruit her husband George, but seemed uninterested in her.[46]

The activity of the SRG was constrained by its small size. Minutes of the Birmingham branch[47] show regular discussion of intervention in the Trades Council, Labour Party and union branches. Like all the other fragments of the RCP its members joined the Labour Party. This was not done out of any hope of challenging the Labour leadership, nor of making any quick gains. It was simply recognised that, in the given circumstances, it was the best milieu in which to fight for revolutionary ideas and find such recruits as could be won. Comrades were expected to work hard at Labour Party activities so that they would be taken seriously by other people. When doing public paper sales they faced the opposition of Communist Party members, who would often jostle them out of the way, though there was no real violence.[48]

Despite its small size the SRG did not entirely escape the notice of the British state. In 1953 the Home Office produced a report – headed SECRET – on "Trotskyists in the United Kingdom". This contained a paragraph on the SRG, which was reasonably accurate on organisational matters, but had no grasp of the importance of Cliff's role, and was completely at sea when it came to the theory of state capitalism:

> The CLIFF Group. This group first came to our notice in December 1950, and is believed to number only about 50 persons. It has, however, formed a National Committee which meets every two months in Birmingham where its paper "Socialist Review" is produced by William Sylvester AINSWORTH. CLIFF is the cover name for Ygael GLUCKSTEIN, an Israeli who first came to notice in 1939 as an agitator and leader of a Trotsky group in Tel Aviv. He is at present attending a course at the London School of Economics and does not play a prominent part in the affairs of the group. He has written a book on "The Nature of Stalinist Russia" and it is on the views expressed in this book

that the CLIFF Group bases its beliefs. The chief theory is that a form of state capitalism such as exists in Russia is necessary before true Communism can be achieved and it is because of this theory that the members of this group are often referred to as the "State Caps".[49]

In April 1951 Aneurin Bevan and two other ministers resigned from the government in opposition to the imposition of health service charges. This led to a considerable revival of the Labour left. "Brains Trusts" organised by the Bevanite weekly *Tribune* attracted large audiences. This made it even more plain that the Labour Party was the main place for socialists to work, though the SRG had no illusions about the limitations of Bevanite policies. As an unsigned front-page article in *Socialist Review* put it:

> The first task of socialists is to defend Bevan and his colleagues against the Party bureaucracy... In the course of the struggle wide sections of the rank and file will develop far beyond the ideas of Bevanism, and will begin to forge a leadership really serious in its determination to achieve socialism.

Bevan himself was dismissed as "Attlee's left hand man", not to be trusted on account of his past support for the Labour leadership.[50]

Most of the SRG's members were young, and hence eligible for activity in the Labour League of Youth (19 out of the 33 members initially claimed were in it).[51] For a short time the SRG produced a youth paper, *Young Chartist*.*

In 1951 Ellis Hillman was expelled. He had written a document which, drawing heavily on work of the Johnson-Forest tendency, argued that Stalinist parties were not part of the working class movement. As a result, "The tactic of the united fronts with the CP which was considered a weapon to separate the rank and file from the bureaucratic leadership must be rejected *on principle*".[52] This was a disastrous conclusion which would have made any serious trade union activity impossible, since the Communist Party was still by far the most important left-wing force within the unions. Nonetheless it seems unlikely that his political position in itself was

---

* I have not found a file of this paper, but there is a copy of the second issue, dated June 1951 at Rich. MS 1117/box 50/file 2. There was an editorial board of four – three from London (including Geoff Carlsson) and one from Manchester.

the reason for his expulsion.* It was more likely that he been involved in personal acrimony with other comrades.⁵³ Hillman remained active in the labour movement and eventually became Mayor of Barnet. This was the only expulsion in the first 15 years of the group's existence.

On the question of the Korean War, members moved resolutions wherever they could. While refusing to line up behind either side in the conflict, they called for the withdrawal of British and all foreign troops.⁵⁴ An editorial in *Socialist Review* demanded, "The Labour movement must oppose the alliance with Truman, Adenauer, Syngman Rhee and the other representatives of 'Western Democracy'; they must fight for an alliance with the millions of toilers of Europe, Asia, Africa and the rest of the world".⁵⁵

In late 1951 there was a general election. The SRG issued a "Directive to All members" which stated that "it is most necessary that our comrades become known to the working class in their local areas as the most energetic and anti-Tory Labour Party workers".⁵⁶ But the Labour Party, despite obtaining more votes than at any other time, was defeated. In fact, given the continuing economic boom, the Tories did not need to attack the gains made by workers under Labour, and there was no major shift in political direction.

For Cliff personally, however, there was a change. The Tories were less paranoid than Labour about the threat posed by tiny groups of Trotskyists, and Cliff was allowed residency in the United Kingdom. In campaigning for the right to settle in Britain, Cliff had some support from the Labour politician Richard Crossman. Since Crossman was a well-known Zionist, Cliff's family in Israel were very proud that he was supporting "our boy".⁵⁷

There were stringent conditions on his right to remain. He was not allowed to engage in "politics", which meant that he had to keep his head down, not take part in public demonstrations, and use pseudonyms when writing political articles. Though the SRG worked in the Labour Party Cliff himself never joined. He was not allowed to "take any employment paid or unpaid"; this did not displease him too

---

* See the account in J Higgins, *More Years for the Locust*, London, 1997, pp42-44. The minutes of the national committee meeting of 17-18 November 1951 note the expulsion but do not give grounds (MRC MSS 75/1/1/1). See also Hillman's letter to the Secretariat, protesting that his position was the same as Natalia Sedova's (23 September 1951, Rich. MS 1117/box 209/file 6).

greatly. Ever since his unfortunate experience as a building worker, he had been convinced that full-time employment was incompatible with being a professional revolutionary. For some years he had permission only to remain for 12 months, though this was regularly extended for a further year. Only in December 1958 was the permission changed to "remain in UK until such date as may hereafter be specified by the Secretary of State".[58]

He did not have British nationality, and for the rest of his life he remained stateless. Since Chanie had a British passport and his child was British-born, it was unlikely he would be deported short of a major indiscretion, but he had to travel on an Israeli passport, and there was a danger that if he left the country he might not be readmitted. In the 1950s and 1960s he only rarely travelled abroad, and after 1968 not at all. In 1958 he visited Switzerland and Italy, in 1959 Belgium and the Netherlands, in 1962 Ireland and France, in 1963 Israel and in 1967 France.[59]

In 1952 Cliff's first book, *Stalin's Satellites in Europe*, was published. His success in finding a commercial publisher was an unintended consequence of Thor Heyerdahl's raft journey across the Pacific. George Allen and Unwin, having made large profits from Heyerdahl's *Kon Tiki* (1950), which sold 60 million copies worldwide, were willing to take a risk with unknown authors.

The book was a development of the document on the "People's Democracies" which had been circulated in 1950. Written as an academic study for a commercial publisher, it contained a great deal of empirical material, culled from a wide range of sources, about the establishment of the Stalinist regimes in Eastern Europe and the new social order created there; Cliff examined the problems of both agricultural and industrial development. While working on it he was in contact with the distinguished historian of Russia and Eastern Europe Hugh Seton-Watson.[60] There was no open polemic about the question of state capitalism, and references to Marxism were strictly limited.

Nonetheless, Cliff succeeded in making his position quite clear. He showed that the working class had not played an active role in the nationalisation of industry, and stressed that for the Stalinists "nationalisation is only a *means* to the end of the extraction of surplus value and the accumulation of capital".[61] He showed that state ownership did not necessarily mean people's ownership, and that Stalinism was carrying through at a highly accelerated rate the primitive accumulation of capital that had taken place in Britain and other capitalist countries. Democracy was essential to working class power: "A collective of people can only express its will by aggregating the wills of the different individuals who constitute it. Hence the form of rule of the working class must necessarily be democracy." He analysed the mechanisms of exploitation in Eastern Europe, notably the use of piece-work.[62] But he also emphasised the continuing resistance by workers which, when legal channels were denied them, took the form of absenteeism and poor-quality production. He made some unwise predictions, such as the claim that slave labour in the satellites was "bound to increase in importance as time goes on".[63] He could not yet foresee the impact of de-Stalinisation.

A number of other themes were developed in the book. At a time when anti-German attitudes were still widespread on the left, Cliff insisted that "the first victim of the Hitler terror was the German people itself". He gave a vivid account of the Warsaw rising of 1944 and its abandonment by Moscow. There was an interesting account of the persecution of religion in Russia and Eastern Europe, which "failed miserably" because the social roots of religion in the "real misery" of the people still survived.[64]

The final section of the book was devoted to the Tito-Stalin split. Cliff had earlier analysed the exploitative nature of Russian trade with its satellites; it bought below world market prices and sold above them. The dispute between Russia and Yugoslavia developed because Russia's interest in exploiting its satellites conflicted with the ambitions of the Yugoslav bureaucracy to industrialise their country.[65]

For Cliff, Titoism was not "a basic negation of Stalinism". The much-vaunted "workers' control" in Yugoslavia was illusory: "What autonomy can a workers' council have that is elected from a list of candidates put forward by the trade union, which is centralistic and controlled by the Party?" He showed that the bureaucracy functioned as a ruling class:* "The bureaucracy appears as...the

---

* However, Cliff distinguished himself sharply from the followers of Shachtman by stressing that Communist parties in the West, while being agencies of Moscow, were still part of the working class movement: "A big abyss has to be crossed before the Communist Parties will be transformed from working class parties, however subservient they may be to the state capitalist rulers of Moscow, into totalitarian ruling parties which are the open weapon of the state capitalist bureaucracy." (Cliff, *Stalin's Satellites*, p317)

incarnation of the accumulation of capital at the expense of the people and as the beneficiary from the accumulation".[66]

But while rejecting the pro-Tito positions which had developed in the Fourth International,* Cliff believed that Tito's emergence as a rival to Stalin would necessarily undermine the prestige of the Russian leader. He drew a number of historical parallels:

> The appearance side by side between 1378 and 1417 of numbers of Catholic Popes, each attached to a national monarchy, did great damage to Catholicism. When Henry VIII quarrelled with Rome and decided to cut the connection between the Church in England and the Pope without greatly modifying the religious rites and dogmas, he opened the door to non-conformism.[67]

Today nobody would argue about whether the popes of Rome or of Avignon deserved support. The task of socialists was not to take sides but to exploit the contradictions.

One reviewer found Cliff's work "diffuse", surprised that he could rise above a narrowly empirical account to discuss such topics as the Japanese industrialisation of Manchuria or Arab feudalism.[68] Some of Cliff's material, which described the conditions and way of life in the so-called "People's Democracies", could be harnessed for Cold War purposes. F Lee Benns of Indiana University, reviewing the book in *The Russian Review*,[69] commented approvingly:

> It would certainly help greatly in mobilising the people of the West in the struggle against Communism if all could in some way be made aware of the economic, political, social, and religious conditions now existing in the states of Eastern Europe, as set forth in *Stalin's Satellites in Europe*.

Nonetheless it is clear from a reading of the book that this was the work of a revolutionary independent of both Washington and Moscow. Cliff's account stressed that the People's Democracies were based on an exploited working class, and that this class was capable of resistance. It was this point which caught the attention of the veteran revolutionary Alfred Rosmer, when he discussed the book in

---

* For much of the Trotskyist movement the split between Stalin and Tito had provided an opportunity to line up behind Tito, often with the most outrageous claims being made about him. Thus, "The Russian Revolution was the springboard from which the Third International took its historic flight. The Yugoslav Revolution can become the historic spring-board from which the Fourth will launch itself on its conquest of the masses." (G Bloch, *Quatrième Internationale*, March-April 1950)

the French journal *Preuves*. He emphasised that Cliff saw the potential for struggle and resistance in the Eastern European working class:

> From all these patiently assembled facts, Gluckstein concludes that "Stalin's empire has no future". When the enslaved peoples of Africa and Asia are awakening and fighting for their liberation, it is impossible to imagine that the peoples of Europe will accept for long being subordinated to an imperialist power.[70]

Since the book was presented as an academic rather than a directly political contribution, Cliff used his real name – Ygael Gluckstein. This was a disadvantage, since it meant the book could not be used directly to win support for the SRG.[71] It was translated into French, and published by the Îles d'or publishing house, which specialised in critical studies of Communism.[72] More surprisingly, it was published in Franco's Spain.[73] (There is no evidence that Cliff was a party to this; presumably the deal was made by Allen and Unwin.)

Cliff had reached a turning point in his life. He was now 35 years old. He had been a revolutionary for 20 of those years, but had little to show for it. The SRG was no bigger than the group in Palestine had been, and was far smaller than the Bolshevik party had been even at its lowest ebb. There was much to be appalled at in the current state of the world, from poverty and exploitation to the threat of nuclear extinction. But the hoped-for revolution seemed further away than ever.

At the same time, with the publication of his book, Cliff had established himself as a commentator on Eastern European affairs. His residency in Britain now seemed more secure. If he had broken his explicit links with the revolutionary left, he could certainly have made a career for himself in journalism or the academic world. Yet it is hard to imagine that Cliff even considered the temptation. On the strength of *Stalin's Satellites* he was offered work writing for a right-wing American organisation, but he had no hesitation in refusing.[74] His commitment to revolutionary politics remained total.

It is interesting to compare Cliff's situation with that of another Jewish Trotskyist immigrant. Isaac Deutscher had arrived in Britain in 1939, scarcely able to speak English.[75] By the early 1950s Deutscher was receiving great critical acclaim for his books on

Stalin and Trotsky,[76] as well as his journalistic writings on Russia and Eastern Europe in *The Economist* and the *Observer*. Deutscher had become a formidable English stylist (sometimes compared to his fellow Pole Joseph Conrad), while Cliff never fully mastered English. It would be quite understandable if Cliff had felt a little jealous, although Deutscher, like Cliff, was never able to obtain a university post in Britain.

Cliff always showed a deep political hostility to Deutscher. He was enraged by the fact that Deutscher had withdrawn from active politics, advocating that the intellectual should "withdraw into a *watchtower*...to watch with detachment and alertness this heaving chaos of a world".[77] Such abstention from the day-to-day struggle was utterly alien to Cliff.

Worse, Deutscher had abandoned not only his own agency but that of the working class. Like Healy and Pablo, he believed the revolution was being carried forward, not by the struggle of the working class, but rather by the Russian bureaucracy, which was extending "socialist" economic organisation across the planet. This was not a price Cliff was willing to pay for greater success. He remained in the world of self-publication and small, scruffy, low-circulation papers.

Cliff combined his intellectual work with regular involvement in the activities of the tiny group. In August 1952 Cliff successfully moved at a national committee meeting that work on the production of *Socialist Review* should be moved to London.[78] He was probably concerned to involve himself more directly in the work now that he was permanently resident in Britain. Perhaps also he wanted to diminish the influence of the rather formalistic leadership based in Birmingham.

He wrote a string of articles for *Socialist Review*, mostly on Russia and Eastern Europe, a few on other international topics. He did not yet seem to feel confident to write about the British working class. He used a variety of pseudonyms – largely, it would appear, not for security reasons, but to give the impression that the paper had more contributors than it in fact had. He used the name "Turov" with, on different occasions, the initials L, M and N, as though there were some uncertainty about the matter.[79]

Not all his contributions were of equal value. In the early 1950s, following some actions by Puerto Rican terrorists which briefly made the headlines, Cliff (under the pseudonym L Miguel), wrote a short background piece. The main point he made was the undoubtedly correct one that most Puerto Ricans lived in considerable poverty, but the impact was somewhat marred by the fact that all but one of the sources named were from the 1930s. It had all the signs of having been knocked up in a library in a few hours in order to fill a hole in the paper.[80] Getting the paper out at all was an enormous burden for a tiny group; *Socialist Review* did not appear at all between May and October 1953.

Cliff now lived with Chanie and Elana in a small flat at 498 Seven Sisters Road, N15. In May 1954 a second child, Donny, was born. Chanie remained the sole breadwinner, and Cliff had to combine his writing and political activity with taking at least an equal share of the childcare burden.[81] In such a small group there were necessarily close personal contacts between members. Cliff used to baby-sit for the Taits. Jean Tait recalled a day at the seaside with Cliff and Chanie when both families had small children; Cliff just sat and read all day.[82]

There were, however, moments of encouragement. In the early 1950s Cliff received a visit from Alfred Rosmer, who had reviewed *Stalin's Satellites*. Rosmer, originally a revolutionary syndicalist, had been one of the tiny band of internationalists who had opposed the First World War from the first day. In 1920 he had gone to Moscow, and played an important role in the early years of the Communist International and the Red International of Labour Unions. He had known Lenin and had been a close personal friend of Trotsky, whom he visited in Mexico shortly before his assassination. Expelled from the French Communist Party in 1924, he had been active in the earliest days of the Trotskyist movement, and the Fourth International had been founded at his home near Paris.

Rosmer had been in correspondence with Stan Newens, who looked after international contacts for the SRG. He wrote explaining that while he had been working with the Révolution Prolétarienne grouping of revolutionary syndicalists, he had broken with them because they tended to favour the Western side in the Cold War.[83] He was therefore sympathetic to Cliff's slogan of "Neither Washington nor Moscow", and gave Cliff considerable encouragement by pointing out that although the SRG was tiny, the anti-war grouping in France in 1914 had initially been very small too.[84] Cliff also met Heinrich Brandler, one of the early leaders of the German Communist Party.[85] These encounters made a link with the early years of the Comintern, before it was dominated by Stalin.

In 1954 some new names appeared in *Socialist Review*. In January David Breen compared Labour and the Tories, concluding "Same ball, same team".[86] The following issue saw the beginning of a ten-part series by K Michaels called "On Our Programme", explaining the 12 points of *Socialist Review*'s "What We Stand For". In April there was a letter from Michael Kidron of Balliol College, Oxford, arguing against the view that Mao could be presented as a disciple of Trotsky. All three* were one and the same person, Chanie's younger brother, Mike Kidron, who had arrived in England in 1953.† He had still been a schoolboy when Cliff had known him in Palestine. Now he was a bright young economist who had come to Oxford to do his PhD.[87] After a short time he was persuaded to join the SRG.[88] He wrote prolifically for *Socialist Review*, became a member of the editorial board and subsequently editor. He made an energetic contribution to the SRG's activities. Chanie's sister Mickey was now in England, and Cliff estimates that the three Rosenberg siblings between them sold half the total circulation of the paper.[89]

Kidron was a very different personality to Cliff. Like his sister, he had broad cultural interests, appreciating poetry, painting and the theatre. He had a wry, ironic sense of humour; Cliff also made jokes, but usually in order to drive home a political point. Kidron had succeeded within the academic milieu, whereas Cliff, despite having been a nominal student at various institutions, had essentially developed as an intellectual within the revolutionary movement, and quite outside of academic structures. He liked the good life and in some ways lived in a different world to Cliff's.

Kidron was a committed revolutionary, but perhaps of a less orthodox nature than Cliff. The latter had nearly 20 years of small-group politics behind him, whereas Kidron did not have ties to any organisational tradition. Hence he was more eclectic and free-thinking in his relation to Marxism. He told an American

---

* Kidron continued to use the pseudonym "David Breen" in the 1960s; "K Michaels" is transparent.
† Not 1955, as stated in Richard Kuper's otherwise valuable obituary (*Guardian*, 27 March 2003).

interviewer that the organisation was "not Trotskyist but Trotskyist-derived", and that he welcomed all traditions of socialist thought that could be useful.[90]

He could be a savage polemicist. Condemning the Communist Party's practice of collecting signatures for peace petitions, he wrote, "Any petition to the manufacturers of H-bombs is as effective as asking brothel keepers to guard the virtue of the girls in their 'care'." Petitions, he argued, "lead to quietism and a useless salving of conscience".[91]

Perhaps for the first time since his friendship with Jabra Nicola in Palestine, Cliff had an intellectual equal with whom he could explore and develop new ideas. According to Chanie, they worked "like one person". In the late 1950s Cliff would have interminable phone conversations with Kidron, half an hour at a time at all hours of day and night.[92] For some ten years Cliff worked closely with Kidron. Over this period Cliff's work expanded from a narrow focus on defending and applying the theory of state capitalism to a broader concern to develop Marxist theory as a tool for understanding the contemporary world.

There were deep temperamental differences between Cliff and Kidron, and there was of necessity a certain friction between them. But it was, in the early years at least, a creative friction. As Cliff put it, "I have had many rows with Mike, because he is worth it".[93] Richard Kirkwood recalled observing them together at SRG events in the early 1960s; when they disagreed it was good-humoured, and the differences between them were questions of emphasis. They sparked off each other.[94]

Despite its tiny size, the SRG managed to irritate the Communist Party. At a meeting in Slough in 1955 the party's national organiser was asked about its support for the use of nuclear weapons against Japan in 1945. He told his audience to disregard the question, since it was based on an article in *Socialist Review*, which represented "the extreme right wing inside the Labour Party".[95]

After completing *Stalin's Satellites*, Cliff continued with his work on applying the theory of state capitalism to two areas – Russia after Stalin, and China. Stalin had died in March 1953, with the party leadership already preparing to fight for the succession. For over 20 years his position had been so unchallenged that mostcommentators, Cliff included, used his name to define the social system he ruled over. "Stalinism without Stalin" presented a new problem for all points on the political spectrum.

Most analyses ranged between two extremes. On the one hand there were those who believed that now the old butcher was dead, democracy would rapidly re-emerge in Russia and the country would embark on a course of healthy development towards socialism. At the opposite extreme were those who saw Russian society as totalitarian and therefore unchanging, and who dismissed any so-called reforms as merely cosmetic.

Cliff's first attempt to confront the problems came in a short article entitled "What Lies Behind Malenkov's Moves?", published in May 1953 under the name L Turov. He observed that, for the moment, the regime was offering various reforms – amnesties and price cuts, the abandonment of purges – and playing down the cult of Stalin, who had been "the arbiter between different sections of the bureaucracy in a system which is torn by great stresses and contradictions". With Stalin gone, no section of the bureaucracy was ready to accept complete subordination, hence there was a cessation of purges (which Cliff, wrongly, thought was merely temporary). However, the system had not changed in essence:

> A regime of bureaucratic state capitalism, with the terrific social strain it involves, needs the blood of a purge to make the wheels go round. The present set-up at the top is therefore temporary but, as long as it exists, it works against any mass purges.

He observed the growing economic tension between Russia and China, and argued that China's demands for steel to assist in industrialisation meant that Stalin's disappearance had not eliminated the drive to war in the system. Cliff overestimated the expansionism of the cautious Russian bureaucracy, but he was quite right to see that war preparations would remain central to the Russian economy till the very end:

> There is no doubt however that this international factor can exert only a temporary influence in Russia towards pacifism. The Russian bureaucracy are, after all, not philanthropists, and they will not build China up into a giant overshadowing Russia. They will not reduce the war preparations indefinitely. For, even now Western Europe produces far more steel than Russia does after a whole generation of tremendous industrial effort, accomplished by great sacrifices. The Russian bureaucracy,

exploiting its own people, cannot but see in the possibilities of looting Western Europe an attractive, if risky, proposition.[96]

In 1955 Cliff's original document on state capitalism appeared in book form under the title *Stalinist Russia: A Marxist Analysis*. Cliff had revised the text quite substantially, with a number of cuts and additions. The main changes reflected the fact that the book had a different target audience. The 1948 document had been directed at a specifically Trotskyist milieu; the 1955 book was aimed at people in the labour movement who read *Socialist Review*. This was still a tiny readership, but not one that had a Trotskyist culture. So the original first chapter, which dealt with Trotsky's varying definitions of a workers' state, became an appendix and was replaced by a new first chapter entitled "Socio-Economic Relations in Stalinist Russia", containing empirical material on the position of workers in Russia. A good deal of this was taken from the original document, without much updating, but there were new sections, for example on female labour.

The book remained, however, a much more overtly political text than *Stalin's Satellites*, and it was published by the organisation, in the name of Michael Kidron, rather than by a commercial publisher. Sales were modest – 450 copies by January 1957 – but apparently better than expected, for Newens wrote to Hallas asking to buy back any unsold copies: "We are down on our last legs as far as our supplies go and are kicking ourselves that more were not printed".[97]

The book did not make much of an impact, but it did receive an interesting review by Hal Draper, an American supporter of the "bureaucratic collectivist" analysis. Draper argued that Cliff ended up by analysing Russia as "so basically different from 'private' capitalism that it tends to take on the characteristics of a new social system, which is not the same as any other existing system, and which is labelled a hyphenated-capitalism only as a matter of terminological taste". Nonetheless, he concluded that "Cliff's political standpoint is that of the Third Camp and makes no compromise with any illusions about Stalinism... Without any doubt, the book belongs in every socialist's library".[98]

In *Socialist Review* Peter Morgan (a member of the SRG) brought out the value of the book for arguments with Communist Party members, but also drew out the more general significance of Cliff's work:

> For so long, socialists and capitalists alike have identified private ownership with capitalism that they have, consciously or unconsciously, accepted the converse that state ownership equals socialism (or something very like it). But this book gives very convincing arguments to disprove this easy assumption.[99]

On 25 February 1956 Khrushchev made his so-called "secret speech". His aim was to consolidate his own position in the power struggle, but in so doing he denounced many of the crimes of Stalin, crimes already well known within the Trotskyist movement over the previous 20 years. Reports of the speech began to spread and by June the Western press published the complete text.

In this situation many looked to the USSR with renewed hope, believing that there might be a renewal of soviet democracy. In a little pamphlet published in the spring of 1956, before the publication of the Khrushchev speech,[100] Cliff, his eyes firmly on the base rather than the shifting sands of the superstructure, argued that "the much-lauded 'changes' have changed very little since Stalin died... Russia is still the Stalinist Russia of old".[101] The 1955 Budget had actually *raised* heavy industry's share of resources and *cut* the allocation to light industry. Military expenditure had not changed significantly since Stalin's death. There was still a serious lack of consumer goods. In the factories workers still lacked any vestige of control. Stalin's successors were urging the strengthening of "one-man management". The apparent measures of liberalisation did not extend to the fundamental antagonism in the process of production: "Though Stalin has left the scene, the power of the factory managers has not diminished. On the contrary, it has gone from strength to strength... Stalin's departure has left the subordination of man to property, the oppression and exploitation, untouched".[102]

De-Stalinisation was merely a facade: "But the present leaders want to start with a clean slate... Even the most sordid gangsters aim to achieve respectability." The amnesty for inmates of slave camps was to be explained in economic terms, not as the result of good intentions on the part of Stalin's heirs: "Slave labour is not very productive, and when labour becomes short, as in Russia today (because of the expanding industrial economy and the stagnation of agriculture which still keeps two-thirds of the population in the countryside) it becomes uneconomical".[103]

He concluded, "Stalin is dead, Stalinism lives." Only the working class could be the agency of social transformation: "The dictator's death will not break the Bureaucratic State Capitalist regime. Its overthrow, whether under Stalin or under Khrushchev, is a historical task to be accomplished not by bureaucrats, but by the working people of Russia".[104] The pamphlet was sufficiently successful to require a second printing.

Cliff's hopes of a working class rising in Russia itself were to be disappointed, but his focus on the role of working class agency was entirely correct. In the summer and autumn of 1956 workers and intellectuals in Poland and Hungary, taking seriously the apparent promise of change, took to the streets in pursuit of their demands for reform. In Poland the bureaucracy managed to head off confrontation, but in Hungary the movement grew out of control. A new government took over, more sympathetic to the popular demands, but most important of all workers' councils were formed. Peter Fryer, the *Daily Worker* correspondent in Hungary, whose reports were mutilated and suppressed, pointed out that these councils showed a "striking resemblance...to the soviets or workers', peasants' and soldiers' councils which sprang up in Russia in the 1905 revolution and again in February 1917".[105]

For Cliff this was a moment of great excitement; revolution was back on the agenda: "During the first week of the Hungarian Revolution, I could hardly close my eyes. I stayed up practically throughout the night, every night, listening to the radio".[106]

For Khrushchev, despite all the rhetoric about de-Stalinisation, it was intolerable that authentic soviets should challenge the power of a regime that had stolen the name "soviet". Russian tanks were sent to Hungary to crush the rising at the cost of thousands of lives. The Russian intervention coincided, almost to the day, with the Anglo-French invasion of Egypt – Britain's last desperate bid to prove itself as a major imperial power.

The news of the Russian invasion came through just as a large demonstration was assembling in Trafalgar Square to oppose the invasion of Egypt. Newens later recalled the SRG's intervention:

Using the Epping CLP duplicator, I copied 6,000 leaflets drafted by myself and my *Socialist Review* colleagues, calling on workers to strike against the Suez intervention.

The Trafalgar Square rally turned out to be a seminal event in British Labour history. My 6,000 leaflets, which a crowd of dockers helped us to distribute, disappeared in a flash.[107]

The leaflet was brief, but it summed up the SRG's politics beautifully. On the one side it expressed support for the Hungarian workers:

> PROTEST AGAINST THIS MASSACRE!
> RUSSIAN TANKS are crushing the heroic Hungarian struggle for national liberation and democracy.
> YESTERDAY "the Soviet Government...declared that it had instructed its military command to withdraw Soviet units from Budapest as soon as the Hungarian Government finds it necessary".
> (*Daily Worker*, November 1)
> TODAY, despite frantic appeals by the Hungarian Government to withdraw, Russian troops are battering and blasting Budapest.
> YESTERDAY the Nagy Government was one that "listened to the voice of the people". (*Daily Worker*, October 29)
> TODAY, Nagy is gone and his government one of "counter-revolutionaries" and "Fascists". (*Daily Worker*, Nov. 5)
> The Issue is Clear:
> The demands of the Hungarian workers and peasants are:
> THE WITHDRAWAL OF RUSSIAN TROOPS
> THE RIGHT OF NATIONAL SELF-DETERMINATION
> We Must Support Them
> THE RUSSIAN EMBASSY MUST HEAR OUR PROTEST

On the other side the leaflet opposed British imperialism's role in Egypt, and called for industrial action against the war:*

---

* There were calls for industrial action against the war among dockers, firefighters, miners, engineers and others, but they were held in check by the union bureaucracy, all the more easily because the Communist Party, which could have been the main mobilising force, was in disarray because of the Hungarian events. In the end the only industrial action was a brief stoppage in Crawley. (See I Birchall, "Striking against Suez", *Socialist Review*, November 1986.)

STOP THIS DIRTY WAR!
The British attack on Egypt is naked slaughter in the interests of oil profits
The Choice is Simple
WE MUST STOP THE SLAUGHTER
OR
WE ARE PART OF IT
Our Weapons Are Ready
INDUSTRIAL ACTION – STRIKES – DEMONSTRATIONS
Parliamentary action is not enough. Appeal to U.N.O. is futile; we can expect nothing from the American butchers of Korea or the Russian butchers of Hungary.
The murder of Egyptians and the sacrifice of our soldiers can be halted if the Dockers, Railwaymen and Factory Workers use their strength.
WILL WE USE THIS STRENGTH?[108]

The Hungarian rising was crushed, while the Suez invasion ended in a debacle. The Hungarian events caused considerable confusion on the left: while the Communist Party was divided, Trotsky's biographer, Isaac Deutscher, saw the Hungarian events as a "struggle between communism and anti-communism" in which "the people of Hungary in a heroic frenzy tried unwittingly to put the clock back".[109]

By the end of the year Cliff had written a major article on the context of the Hungarian events, entitled "The Future of the Russian Empire: Reform or Revolution?"[110] This was published by *Labor Action* (organ of the ISL in the USA) in collaboration with *Socialist Review*;[*] the pages containing Cliff's article were printed in New York. But Cliff made no compromise on his politics. He saw in the Hungarian events confirmation of the position he had been arguing for some years.[†]

Firstly, he saw a refutation of the Deutscherite perspective. Dismissively, he compared Deutscher to the 19th century Russian

---

[*] In the 1950s and early 1960s the ISL and the SRG considered themselves to be comrades, despite differences on the Russian question and certain other tensions. Cliff's articles were published in the *New International*, and Kidron, who frequently visited the US, was a popular figure. ISL members who came to Britain automatically became SRG/IS members, and the same applied to British comrades who went to the US. (Joel Geier interview, March 2009).

[†] A version of the article was also published in French, in the paper launched by Marceau Pivert, veteran leader of the Socialist Party left (*Correspondance Socialiste*, No 69 (December 1956), pp9-11).

radical Alexander Herzen, who "continued to believe in the reforming zeal of the tsar". The post-Stalin reforms were of value, not in themselves, but because "any concession from the top, instead of averting the revolution from below, kindles the flame of liberty; and in the final analysis armed autocracy has to face the armed insurgent people".

He stressed that the workers of Eastern Europe and of Russia itself were not slaves and were indeed capable of standing up against the system that oppressed them:

> The mighty working class of all nationalities oppressed by the Russian autocracy (and above all the Russian working class) is a waking giant which is bursting asunder the chains of social and national oppression.

He concluded:

> Whether the fighters of Warsaw and Budapest win their present battle or not, the international working class will remember them as the glorious harbingers of the new world, the world of revolutionary democratic socialism.

Now the map of the British left was being redrawn. Until 1956 the area to the left of the Labour Party was dominated by the Communist Party (CP), which exercised significant political influence over the Labour left. The CP was a disciplined Stalinist party, which followed the Moscow line unquestioningly; it had a well-organised presence in the trade unions and in workplaces. The various surviving fragments of the RCP had little influence and numbered less than a couple of hundred in total.*

The Khrushchev speech and the Hungarian events produced a massive crisis in the ranks of the CP. A vigorous internal debate took place, covering not only Hungary but the question of inner-party democracy. There was a stormy congress in April 1957, and by early 1958 the party had lost over a quarter of the membership it had had two years earlier.

It was often claimed by the CP leadership, a claim believed by many right-wing commentators,† that most of those who left were

---

* The Healy organisation, which was larger than either the SRG or the Grant group, had fewer than 50 members in 1955 (B Pitt, *The Rise and Fall of Gerry Healy*, chapter 4).

† Thus historian Henry Pelling entitled the chapter on Hungary in his history of the Communist Party "After Stalin: Exit of the Intellectuals" (H Pelling, *The British Communist Party*, London, 1958, p164).

intellectuals. Some of the party's leading intellectuals, notably the historians Edward Thompson and Christopher Hill, were indeed among those who left. But many losses came from the party's industrial base, which was considerably weakened.[111] The claim that workers were not interested in international issues such as Hungary was repeated avidly by both Stalinists and right-wingers; it was patently untrue.

In the short term the SRG made few gains from the post-Hungary situation. There were at most two or three new recruits. Probably the most significant contact was with a group of ex-CP members in Nottingham, who had discovered Trotsky through the work of Deutscher. One of them, Pat Jordan, set out to visit representatives of the various Trotskyist currents, including Ted Grant, Sam Bornstein and Cliff; he was taken to Cliff's home by Stan Newens.[112] Subsequently Cliff wrote a pamphlet entitled *Why We Left the Communist Party*,[113] and persuaded the Nottingham Marxist Group to publish it in their name. There were no individual names on the pamphlet, which stated that it was prepared by 12 former members of the CP. The argument centred on the lack of democracy and open discussion in the CP; the question of the class nature of Russia was not touched on. The pamphlet was sold by the SRG.[114] Though no recruits ensued, useful contacts were made, especially with Ken Coates, who contributed to *Socialist Review* and *International Socialism* over the next few years.

The year 1957 saw the publication of Cliff's next book, *Mao's China*.[115] Published again by Allen and Unwin, this was a substantial piece of work, over 400 pages in length, and had been some years in preparation. Cliff had been enrolled as a student of Chinese at the School of Oriental and African Studies, where he had acquired what he called a "scant acquaintance with the Chinese language". Mike Kidron used to allege that Cliff would not know the Chinese for pig if he were asked, but this may have been a slander.[116] He was assisted by the distinguished theoretician of oriental despotism Professor Karl Wittfogel.[117]

Though it was difficult to find reliable sources, Cliff provided a remorselessly detailed account of economic and social life in post-revolutionary China, showing the real achievements of the new regime, but also the enormous difficulties it faced. He began by showing the terrible economic backwardness that Mao's revolution had inherited, and the enormous problems it faced in trying to "jump from medieval times to the supersonic age".[118] In particular, rapid industrialisation would be impossible without the collectivisation of agriculture, but that would inevitably provoke resistance from the peasantry.

Cliff was particularly concerned with the situation of the Chinese working class. He set out not simply to show that it was exploited, but to examine the means whereby it was exploited. This involved both repression and incentives – "the carrot must accompany the knout".[119] He described labour discipline, piece-work, differentials and "labour emulation" (the Chinese version of Stakhanovism). Beyond this he looked at housing, female labour and the way in which the state intervened in family relations. He pointed to the most Stalinist aspects of Chinese society, the millions of slave labourers and the purges and scapegoating of alleged "counter-revolutionaries".

Cliff drew many parallels between China and Russia. He also had to deal with the fundamental difference between China and the other state capitalist regimes. Unlike Stalin's Russia, Mao's China was not built on the ruins of a defeated workers' revolution. Nor had the Communist state been established under the military and political hegemony of Russia, as had happened in Eastern Europe. In coming to power, Mao had little to thank Stalin for.

Rather the Chinese Revolution was the first in a series of revolutions in the Third World during the 1950s and 1960s, notably in Egypt, Cuba and Algeria. The political rhetoric differed, but the basic processes were similar. From his earliest writings Cliff had drawn heavily on the theory of permanent revolution as it applied to various parts of the colonial and underdeveloped world. Now, in the 1950s, it was clear the theory needed to be revised; revolutions were taking place in the Third World, but they were not being led by the working class.

Cliff showed that the urban working class played no role in the Chinese Revolution, and that the Communists encouraged it to remain inert.[120] The Chinese Communist Party (CCP) was certainly not a workers' party, but "it was never a peasant party – that is, a party made up of peasants and representing their interests on the usual pattern – but an élite made up of ex-peasant army professionals and officials". The CCP was "certainly a movement of peasants, but it was not a peasant movement. It behaved like an élite, now moderate and mild, now baring its teeth and exhibiting its power".[121] Cliff later generalised from this in developing the theory of what he would call "deflected permanent revolution", an account of how, when neither the bourgeoisie nor the proletariat could play the leading role in revolution, the vacuum was filled by the revolutionary intelligentsia.[122]

Cliff's perspective for China's future was expressed with great caution. He showed how the regime aimed to prevent workers making demands that could endanger the progress of modernisation, while at the same time avoiding any direct confrontation with the working class. Since the working class was still small and undeveloped, the prospects for working class revolution were far less favourable than in Russia or Eastern Europe: "In all probability, if revolutionary events elsewhere do not cause China's course to be steered along a different path, she will have to pass through a generation, perhaps two, before the rule of the bureaucracy is threatened".[123]

Cliff gave particular attention to the relations between Russia and China. He rejected both the Stalinist myth that economic relations were based on socialist fraternity, and the anti-Communist myth that world Communism was a monolithic bloc. On the contrary he showed that Russia had a strong bargaining position in trade between the two nations, since China needed Russian imports much more than Russia needed Chinese imports. Hence Russia was buying from China below world market prices and selling to China above world market prices.

Cliff was cautious in his predictions, but recognised that there were serious tensions between the two major Communist powers:

> The Moscow-Peking axis will have to face great trials. It is clear that if the alliance were ever to break, Mao's China would be a much greater menace to Moscow than Kuomintang China could ever have been... Mao has united China and is turning her into an economic and military power far surpassing anything her past has seen, while Moscow is helpless to intervene in her internal affairs.[124]

Inasmuch as Cliff had attempted to show that the theory of state capitalism applied to China, he had made a plausible case. As an account of Chinese society the book had serious limitations. In some ways it became outdated almost as soon as it was written. There were big changes ahead in China in the coming decade – the Great Leap Forward (agricultural communes and rapid industrialisation) and then the Cultural Revolution – which required major developments in the analysis, something Cliff attempted to provide in a number of articles.[125] His prediction that "the day of major famines has gone"[126] was sadly far too optimistic; the famine of 1958-61, in which millions died, was still ahead.

The strength of the book was the way he drew the contrast between the desperate poverty of China and the needs of accumulation. The mass of detail on the conditions of both workers and peasants showed that both were objects of accumulation, without any control over the process.[127]

Mao's China stands up reasonably well in comparison to the more naive pro-Chinese accounts of the period. Shortly after it appeared came the English publication of Simone de Beauvoir's *The Long March*, based on a six-week visit to China in 1955. [128] De Beauvoir was far from being a hard-line Stalinist, and admitted that China suffered from both poverty and lack of freedom. Nonetheless she concluded optimistically that Maoist China embodied a historical moment "in which man, so long reduced to dreaming of what humanity might be, is setting out to become it". She dismissed the possibility of a split between Russia and China as "pure poppycock", since "Russia's interests are identical with those of the Chinese".[129] In comparison with this analysis, which doubtless sold rather more extensively, *Mao's China* has stood the test of time better.

Mao's China was not widely read. It appeared in a small hardback edition and was never reprinted. With its accumulation of statistical detail it was hard going. By the early 1960s copies were difficult to come by, and it was Cliff's book on Russia that was promoted among a new generation of recruits. But the analysis, revised and developed by Cliff himself and by Nigel Harris, served to immunise Cliff's followers against the lures of Maoism, which swept like a tide over the international left in the 1960s, and then receded equally rapidly in the 1970s, leaving behind a host of demoralised renegades such as France's "New Philosophers".

The book was reviewed by Joseph R Fiszman of Michigan State College in the journal *Problems of Communism*.[130] Fiszman commended Gluckstein's analysis of the economic aspects of Chinese Communism, which was "well supported with facts, figures, and almost over-abundant documentation". In contrast to authors whose main concern was with political aspects, Gluckstein tended to "explain everything in terms of economic causes". He noted favourably Gluckstein's recognition of the "real competition" between Russia and China. George E Taylor, Professor of Chinese History at the University of Washington, despite some reservations, judged that "few writers on Chinese Communist economics have made Communist statistics reveal so much that they were intended to conceal".[131]

1957 showed a significant broadening of Cliff's concerns. For the last ten years he had written almost exclusively on the question of state capitalism. He had established himself as a significant Marxist theorist in this area. But there was a danger in the SRG being identified too much with its position on the Russian question. Its members were referred to by other sections of the left as "state capitalists". No revolutionary organisation could hope to make any real impact solely on the basis of having a negative analysis of a group of foreign countries.

Moreover, there were now other problems. At the time of the crisis in the RCP Cliff had been at pains to stress that he was an "orthodox" Trotskyist who simply had differences on the Russian question. He aimed to show that his position actually stood in the tradition of classical Marxism, Leninism and Trotskyism. As time went on, and the world changed around him, it became clear that broader revisions of the Marxist tradition were required.

In particular, in the late 1940s and early 1950s Cliff had recognised that the expected post-war crisis of capitalism had been delayed, but this had been seen as essentially a matter of a few years. By 1957 it was clear that the boom was real, and that it was long-lasting. Some on the left, notably the CP, remained trapped within a dogma that had no relation to reality. CP economist Maurice Dobb wrote in 1958 of a "new slump" beginning to spread from the US to Europe.[132] More dramatically, Peter Fryer of the SLL claimed that capitalism was in its "death agony" with "no more possibilities for development", and that the current "state of stagnation…could be the prelude to still steeper economic decline".[133]

Meanwhile far more influential currents were claiming that capitalism had changed its nature. Anthony Crosland, a leading member of the Labour Party right wing, wrote an influential book called *The Future of Socialism*,[134] in which he assumed that large-scale unemployment and capitalist crisis had disappeared for ever.* Karl Popper, one of the most prestigious critics of Marxism, asserted that the problem of mass unemployment had largely been solved and that racial discrimination was disappearing.[135]

Cliff began to confront the new set of problems in two linked articles published in the summer of 1957. The first was entitled "Perspectives of the Permanent War Economy".[136] This began by tracing historically the massive increase in armaments expenditure, even during peacetime, in 20th century capitalism, and linking this to changes in the economy:

> For more than a century capitalism has gone through a rhythmical cycle of prosperity and slump. Slumps occurred more or less regularly every ten years. But since the advent of a permanent war economy the cycle has somehow been broken.

He argued, "The basic cause of capitalist crises of overproduction is the relatively low purchasing power of the masses compared with the production capacity of industry".† He then went on to show that arms production was a form of "'Public Works' undertaken by the state", and set out a number of conditions which showed that arms, and arms alone, could play this particular role in the economy.

However, in contrast to claims by the likes of Crosland that capitalism had been permanently transformed, Cliff stressed that the war economy had sharp internal contradictions of its own, which would eventually bring the period of capitalist boom to an end:

---

*   Crosland was far to the left of the modern Labour Party; he still believed in promoting equality through the redistribution of wealth.
†   This sometimes laid him open to the charge of being an "underconsumptionist". (See P Goode, "Over-production of Under-consumption", IS Bulletin, February 1972.) A more sympathetic critic believes that "for the most part the gist of the piece was Keynesian" and that Cliff's position required to be "updated and reformulated" by Kidron and Chris Harman (G Pozo, "Reassessing the Permanent Arms Economy", *International Socialism* 127 (Summer 2010)). Kidron himself later claimed that Cliff had taken over Vance's Keynesianism "more or less intact" (M Kidron, "Two Insights Don't Make a Theory", *International Socialism* 100 (July 1977)).

Then the United States may learn...how to cut the defence budget in order to circumvent defeat on the world market. The war economy may thus less and less serve as a cure for overproduction, a stabiliser of capitalist prosperity. When the war economy becomes expendable, the knell of the capitalist boom will surely toll.

Cliff's prediction was borne out at the end of the 1960s when the US arms budget was cut quite substantially. Cliff's arguments here were taken up and developed by Mike Kidron* in articles[137] and a book, *Western Capitalism since the War*.[138] Kidron tended to give more importance than Cliff to the impact of arms spending on the rate of profit.

It is often claimed[139] that, although this was not acknowledged by Cliff, the origins of the permanent war economy theory lie in a series of articles published in 1951 in the Shachtmanite journal *New International* by TN Vance[140] (also known as Walter J Oakes, Frank Demby and Ed Sard). Cliff would certainly have known the articles, which made some important points about peacetime war expenditure, state intervention in the economy and the falling rate of profit, though he had already developed his own ideas on the role of arms in the capitalist economy in his 1948 document on state capitalism.

But there were major differences between Vance's position and that developed by Cliff.[141] Vance believed the war economy could reduce unemployment, but he insisted that it could not raise working class living standards: "As the Permanent War Economy becomes more thoroughly entrenched, it is goodbye...to all significant attempts to raise average living standards." This is the exact opposite of Cliff's position on the war economy and reformism.†

Secondly Vance recognised that the war economy could not offer a definitive solution to the problems of capitalism but only a "temporary respite". However, he seems to have believed that there would be "all-out shooting war" between the US and Russia within a few years. (Unlike Cliff he had apparently not grasped that nuclear war would be qualitatively different from all previous wars.)

---

* Kidron generally used the term "permanent arms economy" rather than "permanent war economy".

† However, it took Cliff some time to come to his position. In 1952 Hallas wrote an article which took a position similar to Vance's in which he implied that the peak of the post-war boom had already passed. There is no evidence that Cliff disagreed with this position in 1952 (D Hallas, "The Permanent Crisis", *Socialist Review*, June-July 1952).

He had only a very vague idea of the economic factors which would limit the lifespan of the war economy, whereas Cliff confidently predicted its eventual demise.[142] Cliff himself wrote little more on the question, other than to reiterate the fundamentals. In the 1970s Kidron, earlier known as the leading proponent of the theory, came to see it as inadequate.[143] Chris Harman, however, later wrote a book, *Explaining the Crisis*, which defended and developed the theory. [144]

However, it was not so much the technical details of the theory as its general thrust which had practical implications. It had two strengths which gave it great importance over the coming years. Firstly it established that the boom was real and likely to last for a decade or more. Political strategy had to be adapted to this. To imagine that economic crisis was around the corner in the late 1950s and early 1960s could lead only to wrong tactics and the demoralisation of comrades. At the same time Cliff rejected the reformist myth that the boom was permanent – capitalism was still a contradictory system prone to crisis. On both points he was proven right.

Secondly, the theory linked arms – and in particular nuclear arms – to the dynamics of the world economy. A movement in opposition to nuclear weapons was beginning to take off (the first Aldermaston march would be at Easter 1958). Many of those involved saw nuclear weapons as a single issue, or as a purely moral question. The arms economy theory showed that the anti-nuclear struggle was inextricably linked to the struggle for socialism.

The sequel, published the following month, was "Economic roots of reformism".[145] Cliff began by asking why, when the 20th century was facing the horrors of fascism, nuclear war and colonialism, reformism still maintained its grip on workers. "Why the general political apathy and rejection of revolutionary changes in society, when humanity as a whole is in the grip of life and death struggles?"

Cliff began with Lenin's theory of the labour aristocracy, which argued that the "super-profits" obtained by imperialism allowed capitalism to bribe a small section of the working class who became the "agents of the bourgeoisie in the labour movement". However, the logic of this analysis was that:

a small thin crust of conservatism hides the revolutionary urges of the mass of the workers. Any break through this crust would reveal a surging revolutionary lava. The role of the revolutionary party is simply to show the mass of the workers that their interests are betrayed by the "infinitesimal minority" of "aristocracy of labour".

This, however, did not fit the facts. Cliff had no difficulty in showing that over the last hundred years and more "the whole of the working class benefited from increasing living standards", and that rising living standards tended to diminish differences between skilled and unskilled workers.

It was this ability of capitalism to grant reforms in the form of improved living standards that made reformism possible; as a result, a reformist bureaucracy came into existence, which saw its aim as mediating between workers and bosses, not overthrowing the system. If reforms ceased to be available, then reformism would soon collapse.

Referring back to the article on the war economy, Cliff argued that eventually there would be a crisis which would lead "to a big deterioration of workers' conditions, and thus to a withering away of the roots of Reformism". However, he pointed out that such a deterioration need not be in absolute standards, but rather in workers' expectations:

> For this to happen it is not necessary, of course, that the standard of living of workers should be cut to the bone. An American worker would react very strongly to a threat to his car and television set,* even if workers elsewhere look at these things as undreamt-of luxuries. To the extent that past reforms are accepted as necessities, a series of new reforms becomes the expected course of events. With the eating comes the appetite. When capitalism, however, decays to the extent that any serious demands of the working class reach beyond its limits, the bell will toll for Reformism.

In concluding, Cliff tried to draw the lessons of the analysis for political organisation. He pointed to the combination of subjective and objective factors – not only a crisis in the system was required, but also conscious political organisation of the working class. It would be in the course of day-to-day struggle that the grip of reformism would be undermined:

---

* In the 1950s cars and televisions were still unavailable luxuries for many British workers.

Of course, even when the economic roots of Reformism wither away, Reformism will not die by itself. Many an idea lingers on long after the disappearance of the material conditions which brought it forth. The overthrow of Reformism will be brought about by conscious revolutionary action, by the propaganda and agitation of consistent Socialists. Their job will be facilitated by a future sharpening of the contradictions in capitalism.

Every struggle of the working class, however limited it may be, by increasing its self-confidence and education, undermines Reformism. "In every strike one sees the hydra head of the Revolution." The main task of real, consistent Socialists is to unite and generalise the lessons drawn from the day-to-day struggles. Thus can it fight Reformism.

In the course of his argument, Cliff took a highly critical attitude to Lenin's theory of the labour aristocracy, and argued that the reality of the experience of British imperialism "invalidates the whole of Lenin's analysis of Reformism". He likewise argued that "Trotsky's prognosis [in *The Death Agony of Capitalism*] was belied by life". This showed a much more critical attitude to the whole Trotskyist tradition than he had shown a few years earlier, and helped to pave the way for the work he and Kidron would do in the coming years on the nature of modern capitalism and modern imperialism.

In challenging the theory of the labour aristocracy Cliff was going up against a view which had wide acceptance in all branches of the Marxist left. In Britain Eric Hobsbawm had developed the theory in a number of articles in the 1940s and 1950s, even though some of his own research had served to undermine the thesis. Only much later, in the 1970s, did he adopt a more critical attitude to the idea of a labour aristocracy.[146] Cliff's critique stressed two themes that would recur in his work over the coming years: the deep roots of reformism and the essential unity of interests of all sections of the working class.

The implications were that there would be no quick gains. In discussion at an aggregate meeting in January 1957 Cliff had pointed to the disintegration of the Bevanites, and predicted that "development and growth of our ideas would be very slow".[147] It remained important to cultivate every individual. Cliff and Newens paid a week-long visit to the North, going to Leeds, Sheffield, Newcastle, Edinburgh and Glasgow. There were no striking results, but useful discussions with a number of contacts.[148]

In the course of 1957 there were discussions about possible unity between the SRG and both the Revolutionary Socialist League (RSL – supporters of Ted Grant), of which Duncan Hallas was "becoming a member", and the Nottingham Group of ex-CP members. In 1958 the SRG took part in a Revolutionary Socialist Unity Committee involving the Independent Labour Party, the RSL, the Nottingham Unity Group, Vanguard Pamphlets and the Socialist Workers' Federation (which included Eric Heffer).[149] But nothing much came of these ventures; the SRG remained small and isolated.

Before the growth of the Young Socialists, the SRG was far too small to be a threat to the Labour Party bureaucracy, and so it was generally untroubled. However, Peter Morgan was expelled from the Labour Party in Birmingham for, among other things, advocating free public transport for old age pensioners. Later Mike and Zena Maddison were excluded from the particularly right-wing East Islington Labour Party. When Stan Newens was selected as a Labour parliamentary candidate, he was summoned before the party bureaucrat Ray Gunter, who had a file of *Socialist Review* in front of him.[150]

But slowly the left milieu was offering more opportunities. Of those who had left the CP some, exhausted by years of hard work in support of an unworthy cause, dropped out of politics. Others, like the future leaders of the Electrical Trade Union, moved rapidly to the right. Many joined the Labour Party, a logical move since for some years a major part of the CP's strategy had been to try to move the Labour Party to the left. A substantial number, however, remained on the left, rejecting Stalinism but remaining Marxists.

Conferences and debates were held, notably one at Wortley Hall near Sheffield in April 1957, attended by Ray Challinor from the SRG.[151] New publications emerged – the *New Reasoner* and *Universities and Left Review*, which in 1960 merged to form *New Left Review* (*NLR*). In London the Partisan coffee bar in Carlisle Street, with skiffle and folk music, became a meeting place for the left,[152] and a little later a network of New Left Clubs – a loose, decentralised form of organisation – was set up. By the end of 1960 over 40 clubs were listed, but few if any survived more than a couple of years. For a brief time, however, the New Left provided a milieu in which socialists could be active, discuss and argue for their ideas. The SRG comrades did their best to relate to this new milieu. Many years later John Palmer remembered:

> the role played by IS in the New Left clubs and movement of the early 1960s. That was decisive in bringing part of my generation to IS. Mike K, Nigel H and MacIntyre (as well as Peter [Sedgwick], Ray Challinor and later Duncan Hallas) were influential; in making IS appear more than just another Trotskyoid faction. The debate about Williams' "Long Revolution" helped win some of the YS [Young Socialists] in my area. [153]

Nick Howard, a former seaman who became a student at the London School of Economics (LSE), used to attend New Left meetings[154] in London of up to 600 people. At one of them he met Mike Kidron, who recruited him to the SRG. He soon got to know Cliff and helped with the production of *Rosa Luxemburg*.[155]

The main gains after Hungary had been made by the Healy grouping. It was somewhat larger than the SRG and through links with the American SWP had access to copies of Trotsky's *The Revolution Betrayed*[156] (Trotsky's writings were hard to come by at this time). The argument that Russia was a "degenerated workers' state" was probably easier to accept for those who had spent years defending Stalinism.

One working class CP member who joined Healy (and later became a leading member of Cliff's organisation) was Jim Higgins, who explained the initial attraction of Trotskyism: "For those who had for years struggled through Stalin's clotted prose, to read Trotsky was akin to finding a clear mountain spring after a lifetime of drinking from a puddle in a livery stable".[157]

Certainly the Healy organisation looked like an attractive proposition. In the short term Healy managed to conceal his more sectarian and authoritarian characteristics. A weekly paper, the *Newsletter,* was launched and a new organisation, in which ex-CP members were in the majority,[158] emerged, and in 1959 acquired a public face as the Socialist Labour League (SLL). Among the new recruits were Peter Fryer, the *Daily Worker's* correspondent in Hungary, Brian Behan, a building worker and the only member of the CP's National Executive to leave over Hungary, and a number of able intellectuals including Brian Pearce, Cliff Slaughter and Tom Kemp.

The Healy group produced a lively theoretical journal, *Labour Review*, the early issues of which reached a high standard. Brian Behan was in the leadership of a major building workers' strike on the South Bank in 1958. In November 1958 it called a rank and file conference attended by over 500, mainly shop-floor workers.[159]

Members of the SRG were impressed by this. A number of members had not experienced Healy back in 1950, and others were prepared to believe that the leopard had changed its spots. In May 1958 the SRG received a letter signed Burns (the pseudonym of Healy) proposing the establishment of a joint committee to examine the possibilities of fusion. There was considerable debate on this and initially Cliff was in a minority in opposing possible unity. However, opinions changed when *Labour Review* refused to publish an article by Cliff on state capitalism.[160] According to Newens, it was clear that Healy would not make any concessions, while Cliff was not going to sacrifice his ideas.[161] In June the SRG replied, noting that the two organisations had different attitudes to Stalinism and that the *Newsletter* refused open discussion of differences; as a result "complete fusion" was impossible.[162]

Cliff continued to maintain contacts with other people on the left, sending carbon copies of long letters to several people. The letters would later appear as articles in *Socialist Review*. One of the recipients was Ken Coates, who learned quite a lot from Cliff about the Asiatic mode of production at the time Cliff was working on *Mao's China*.[163]

However, the SRG was making slow progress. Around 1956 there were meetings in Hampstead of the entire London membership, and there would be six to 12 people present, on occasion as many as 20. These meetings were in a house apparently loaned to the group by a sympathiser; meetings on a Saturday would be followed by a party. Apart from meetings the main activity was distributing the paper. Zena Maddison remembered delivering papers in blocks of council flats in Pimlico, to regular readers acquired through the Labour Party or other activity. Despite the small membership she had good memories of comradeship and saw them as "happy days".[164]

Recruits were being made one by one, but a number of able individuals were drawn to the group. For a time Seymour Papert was a great asset. He wrote an important article on the shop stewards movement, orienting the group to changing patterns of industrial struggle.[165] However, he left by 1960. Later he became well known as a pioneer of the study of artificial intelligence and a contributor to educational theory.

James D Young had a more negative experience of the group. During his membership – 1956-60 – the group contained a number of "talented socialists", and it gave him "a first-rate education in socialist theory and socialist history".[*] Nonetheless he was harsh in his judgement of the group: "With an acquired and cultivated rather than inborn Leninist puritanism, essentially middle class elitism towards the 'backward' workers and an offensive utilitarian contempt for people, this sect crushed the potential socialist *individuality* of many working class men and women".[166] He complained that when Cliff visited his home in Grangemouth in 1955 he did not exchange a word with Young's father, a docker and militant trade unionist.[167] [†]

Recruitment was often on the basis of personal contact. Journalist Mike Maddison met Mike Kidron and was drawn into the organisation. He then took Zena, who was to become his wife, to meetings. In 1958 her brother, John Witzenfeld, had just completed his national service and she took out a subscription to the *New Statesman* for him to get him interested in politics. Then she took him to meet Cliff and Kidron. Witzenfeld found Cliff likeable, with a fine intellect and a good sense of humour. Cliff encouraged him to sell *Socialist Review* and to join the Labour Party in Sidcup. Witzenfeld remains an SWP member to this day.[168]

In 1958 Mary Phillips was a young graduate who belonged to a pacifist anarchist group. She was rather dissatisfied with this and an Australian friend suggested she contact the SRG. She rang up the contact number and was invited to meet "Tony Cliff and Honey [Chanie]" – from the names she expected a couple of upper class twits. She went to their home in the Seven Sisters Road and found herself almost immediately being drawn into the family, doing baby-

---

[*] Young reiterated to me that despite his criticisms he acknowledged that Cliff was a great teacher and very good with young people (JD Young, telephone interview, February 2004).

[†] The explanation is perhaps that Cliff was, basically, a rather shy person. When political requirements made it necessary, he overcame his shyness, but he was not good at simply making conversation.

sitting, teaching Elana German and having huge political rows with Cliff. When she had been attending meetings for some months, Cliff told her she should pay subs; since she was not well off, she paid sixpence a month (the price of half a pint of beer). Initially she was not sure that this made her a member. She found the meetings "unbelievably boring". Cliff was comprehensible, but the other members were not.

Suddenly she found herself being given typing to do, and drawn into many other activities. She discovered later that Cliff had said, "That woman is bored out of her head. If we don't give her something to do we'll lose her." Phillips still had some pacifist ideas and she had many rows with Cliff about the question of violence. Also she opposed canvassing for the Labour Party in 1959. Cliff would get angry and shout "Stupid woman" at her, but despite this she developed a loyalty to the tiny organisation (there were just 36 members when she joined) and on occasion she later recognised that Cliff had been right. But sometimes she stood up to Cliff and she learned a great deal from that too.

She was sent by Cliff with two other comrades to do a street meeting and paper sale in Chelsea. Phillips had to stand on a box to speak. It was a complete disaster – not a single paper was sold. But 50 years later two of the three – Phillips and Roger Cox – were still active members of the SWP. This was an indication of Cliff's ability to inspire long-term political loyalties, not simply through his personality, although he was regarded with great affection, but because he provided a political analysis that made sense of the world. She stayed in the group, despite her rows with Cliff, because he explained things and always had an eye to activity; the group as a whole was friendly and made jokes.[169]

Roger Cox was active in the Labour Party youth section, and was drawn into the SRG by Mike Kidron and Reuben Fior. He heard Cliff lecture on Marxist economics and got to meet him. It was the ideas which made an impact on him; Cliff offered an interpretation of the way things were in the world at that time. The theory of state capitalism explained things in a way that the CP and the Healyites could not.

Cliff took a particular interest in Cox because he was an industrial worker. He would telephone him twice a week, and would constantly ask him questions, for example about strategies for fighting redundancy. Cliff would ask Cox and other workers question after question about life in the factory – for example about tea-breaks – so that he acquired an understanding without having been inside the factory. Cox and Carlsson would tell Cliff stories about the robust anti-authoritarianism of the post-war working class. Cliff was particularly interested in hearing from Cox about the extent to which workers exercised control on the shop-floor.

But if Cliff was focused on the workplace as the main locus of class struggle, he could be quite naive about other aspects of working class life. On one occasion Cox and Carlsson took him to a football match – Spurs versus Arsenal. Cliff took little interest in the game, but was fascinated by the crowd, enquiring whether they were all workers.[170]

John Phillips joined the Labour Party at the time of Suez and became involved in the Shoreditch youth section. About a year later Roger Cox, Malcolm Tallantire and Harold Freedman persuaded him to go to a meeting at Cliff's home in the Seven Sisters Road. He remembers Cliff as a "hugely charismatic figure" who produced a "whirlwind of words and ideas". By his own account Phillips was very "bureaucratic" – good at taking minutes, organising things, etc. Cliff quickly recognised his talents and gave him jobs, and persuaded him to write for *Socialist Review*. Nearly 50 years on Phillips is not involved in any kind of politics, but still thinks Cliff was a "fantastic bloke" who was always totally principled and never showed any interest in spending money on himself.[171]

Another talented recruit was Peter Sedgwick, who left the CP after Hungary, and had joined the SRG by 1958. Sedgwick was a gifted scholar, who translated works by Victor Serge, and a fine writer, with the rare talent of being extremely funny and serious at the same time.[172] His organisational skills did not match his political insight. On one occasion Cliff went to Liverpool to speak at a meeting organised by Sedgwick; when nobody turned up, Cliff discovered that the leaflet had a time but no date. The meeting was rearranged, but now Sedgwick's leaflet had a date but no time. Sedgwick was an independent-minded individual, an unpredictable maverick. Many years later Cliff commented, "Every organisation should have one Peter Sedgwick, but no organisation could survive with two of them".[173]

The SRG remained tiny and was only able to maintain its activity by means of a high level of commitment from those involved. On occasion Stan Newens and his wife would sit up until 3am packing copies of *Socialist Review*.[174]

The Labour Party and its youth sections continued to be one of the SRG's main areas of activity. Cliff took a personal interest in monitoring this. He would telephone comrades the day before Labour Party meetings to discuss with them the intervention they should make; he always knew the dates of meetings.[175] This despite the fact that he was still somewhat nervous of the authorities, and often preferred to telephone from a public call-box rather than from his home because he thought the phone might be tapped.[176] The telephone was then a relative novelty, as there had been no telephones in Palestine until the 1940s;[177] later Cliff would make extensive use of the telephone.

The SRG continued to work within the Labour Party. For Cliff this was a tactical question and a necessity imposed by the group's small size. Other members did not always see things in the same way. Late in 1957 the Greenwich branch (including Bernard Dix, who later became assistant general secretary of NUPE, and who wrote for *Socialist Review* under the pseudonym Owen Roberts[178]) produced a document arguing that "it is possible to transform a conservative workers' party into a genuine Socialist party". In line with this perspective of reforming the Labour Party, it insisted that "participation in the affairs of the SR Group must be confined to Labour Party members".

For Cliff this was a break with revolutionary politics. A reply to Greenwich was issued in the form of a document entitled "On Social Democratic Illusions". This bore the name of the secretaries of the SRG branches in West London, North London, Hackney and Hendon. According to Newens it was inspired by and probably written by Cliff himself.[179]

Cliff began by dismissing the possibility of transforming the Labour Party: "All the experience of the world working class movement contradicts these assertions." He was sharply critical of claims about the Labour Party's record in government:

> The nationalisation that has been undertaken, however, with its vast burden of compensation, concerning itself mainly with deficit industries, and allowing private industry to benefit from it (by getting cheap coal,

electricity, etc.) has nothing to do with Socialism. Without workers' control it is state capitalist nationalisation.

He insisted on the limitations of parliamentary democracy:

> Workers' representatives in Parliament can use this body for wresting reforms from capitalism, but they cannot make it the weapon of the transition to Socialism. The workers themselves will achieve Socialism, self-mobilised and self-organised in the factories, railways, etc.

Cliff set out his perspective on the relation between Labour Party work and the building of an open revolutionary party:

> While it is obvious that a revolutionary party will have to be formed sooner or later, as long as it is still possible for Marxists to work in the Labour Party without abandoning their principles, they must do so and not leave the mass of its members in the hands of the right-wing leadership. The only other alternative under such conditions is the creation of a new party (which could not, in present circumstances, be more than a sect).

He was scathing about the suggestion that only Labour Party members should be admitted to the SRG:

> Do the writers of the Greenwich letter really believe that the class struggle is limited to the Labour Party Ward? Do they believe that all, or most, or even a large number of industrial militants, attend Labour Party wards?

He concluded by drawing a line between Marxism and reformism:

> The SR [*Socialist Review*] is a Marxist paper. It is a paper of revolutionary, international and democratic Socialism, and not a Social Democratic paper. And so it should continue to be.[180]

Dix did not remain long in the SRG. Stan Newens did not agree with all the Greenwich positions,[181] but he too had a number of disagreements about the Labour left, and Cliff accused him of being a revisionist. By 1959 Newens had become involved in the Labour left grouping Victory for Socialism and drifted out of the SRG.[182]

The Labour Party youth sections allowed Cliff to broaden his range as a speaker. A report in *Socialist Review* in 1958 showed Cliff tackling a topic on which he had not previously professed expertise:

> I went to the second of Shoreditch Youth Section's day schools on June 1,

and found it most worthwhile. In the morning Tony Cliff lectured on "Sex and Socialism", showing how the social and economic structure of society is reflected in human relationships; that morals are an instrument used by the ruling class to maintain its position, and pointed out that a socialist morality is concerned with human values rather than price tags. All this was obviously new to some of the Youth Section members who came from various parts of the London area to the school.[183]

Another important area of work was in the National Council of Labour Colleges (NCLC), an independent labour movement educational body which was taken over by the TUC in 1964. Sid Bidwell was NCLC organiser for North London from 1955 to 1964, and he arranged for many SRG members to give lectures and address trade union meetings. Mike Kidron was particularly active, addressing meetings ranging from Leatherhead AEU to TGWU cabmen, and Chanie Rosenberg addressed many meetings; Seymour Papert, James D Young, Reuben Fior, Geoff Carlsson and others also lectured. Jock Haston was South London organiser, and was sufficiently friendly to arrange for Kidron and later Cliff to speak in his area. Up to 1961 Cliff was not conspicuous as a speaker, perhaps because he was cautious about his legal status. In May 1957, using the name Y Gluckstein, he spoke on "Mao's China" to the Paddington Monthly Forum at the Prince of Wales Hotel.[184] At the ENV factory where Geoff Carlsson was a shop steward, Cliff ran a class for shop stewards, explaining how to read a company balance sheet. Cliff used the opportunity to analyse the ENV balance sheet, and to show that company profits were much higher than the management claimed. This provoked an open controversy between the stewards and the management.[185]

Another sign of the reshaping of the left came with the growth of the nuclear disarmament movement. The Campaign for Nuclear Disarmament (CND) was launched in February 1958. It was a response to a world which had become increasingly dangerous as the two rival superpowers developed ever more deadly weapons and ever more effective ways of delivering them. International crises and confrontations, which through accident or miscalculation might easily have led to nuclear war, had occurred at regular intervals ever since the Berlin blockade of 1948. CND represented a coming together of Christian pacifists, longstanding anti-war activists, Labour leftists and members of the New Left.

At Easter 1958 a nuclear disarmament march from London to Aldermaston took place. *Socialist Review* supported the campaign from its inception, launching the slogan "BLACK THE BOMB! BLACK THE BASES!" and urging the movement "to march on, beyond Aldermaston, into the factories and the building sites".[186] *Socialist Review* members were among those who took part.* As the paper reported, "those of us who marched to Aldermaston – slogged more than 50 miles – we marched into a corner of history".[187] Zena Maddison looked after young Donny while his parents went on the march.[188] As Ray Challinor, one of the SRG marchers, reported, the comrades put a distinctive political line:

> Being opposed to socialist ideas, the Nuclear Disarmament Committee sought to confine the protest march to purely bourgeois limits. Speakers advocating trade union action were not allowed. Banners, such as the *Socialist Review*'s and the *Newsletter*'s "BLACK THE BOMB! BLACK THE BASES!" were discouraged. Indeed, an attempt was even made, at the behest of the Chief Marshal, to take our banner down by force. So much for pacifist consistency![189]

The following year's march, from Aldermaston to London, was much larger, and the third march, in 1960, had up to 100,000 participants. The campaign had a major impact on British political life. Aneurin Bevan, the major leader of the Labour left in the early 1950s, had turned his back on nuclear disarmament in 1957, arguing that a British foreign secretary could not go "naked into the conference chamber". But the demand for unilateral nuclear disarmament by Britain was taken up widely by the Labour Party left and by left-wing trade unionists. By 1960 the campaign was a genuine mass movement, with branches and local activities throughout the country. A new generation of students and young people, for whom Korea and even Hungary were only a childhood memory, flocked into the movement.

By the end of the decade some slow progress was being made. In January 1958 *Socialist Review* announced it was moving to twice-monthly production. An editorial statement recognised this was a

---

* James D Young claims that Cliff and Kidron were initially opposed to participation (JD Young, "*Socialist Review* and libertarian Marxism", *Workers' Liberty* 19, March 1995) but others involved at this time do not remember this.

"risk", but considered that in the current circumstances the risk was "necessary and justified":

> The Tories are hammering home the need for class politics; British workers are learning that bosses are dangerous as well as nasty; that the struggle between labour and capital is the inescapable crux of our lives; that, in this age of nuclear weapons and intercontinental ballistic missiles, our very existence depends on the outcome of this struggle; that our sharpest weapon is a socialist programme and leadership.[190]

In 1959 the editor described the past year as "reasonably successful", but noted that "twice this year we have had to skip an issue when sales promised to show a seasonal fall. Each issue has been an excruciating search for funds".[191] After June 1959 the paper reverted to monthly appearance.

For a time John Phillips was appointed as a full-timer. He met Cliff daily to discuss what needed to be done, such as contacting people in the provinces. He also worked closely with Kidron on the production of *Socialist Review*.[192]

The minuscule group did not pass unnoticed in the mainstream press. In 1958 the *News Chronicle* published two articles entitled "The New Revolutionaries" by one W Roy Nash. While mainly concerned with the SLL, he referred to "a further Trotskyist sect, headed by a man using the pen-name of Tony Cliff".[193] *Socialist Review*'s comment on the allegations of widespread influence was "if only it were true".[194]

Trade union influence was growing very slowly. By the early 1960s there was a small group of experienced trade unionists, including Geoff Carlsson and Les Bennett at ENV, railway worker Stan Mills and dockers Jimmy Jewers and George Green. In 1959 Carlsson ran for the presidency of the AEU. The incumbent was William Carron, who stood on the far right of the labour movement. (He once called militants in the car industry "werewolves who are rushing madly towards industrial ruin and howling delightedly at the foam on their muzzles".[195]) The main left candidate was Reg Birch, a longstanding CP member who had taken particular responsibility for defending the line on Hungary.[196] Carlsson had no organisation to support him, just a few individual members of the AEU in the SRG. But he had the right to circulate an election address which took up both trade union and political questions, and tried to offer an alternative to both right-wing Labour and the CP. While recognising the "militant activities" of CP members, he also referred to the "anti working class measures" taken by Russia in Hungary and elsewhere. He ended up with the respectable vote of 5,615 votes out of a total of 91,400, against 57,127 for Carron and 19,799 for Birch.[197] Communist Party activists were more worried by the vote for Carlsson than by the large right-wing vote for Carron.[198]

Given the growing ferment of ideas and the growth of a Marxist milieu outside the CP, it was felt desirable to launch a theoretical journal. In September 1958 the first issue of *International Socialism* appeared in duplicated form. The two main articles were by Cliff and Kidron. Cliff's article "Changes in Stalinist Russia" examined changes in industrial management in the Khrushchev period, and the attempts to deal with lagging labour productivity. Despite changes since Stalin's death, Russia remained a repressive, irrational society. Kidron's "The Economic Background of the Recent Strikes" took up two themes that would be developed in his later contributions to the journal: the decline in Britain's imperial role and the significance of the arms budget. But apparently the venture was too much of a strain for the meagre resources of the organisation, and no further issues appeared until the project was revived in somewhat different form two years later.*

In 1959 Cliff published another short book, *Rosa Luxemburg*.[199] This took up some of his existing interests, but also showed a developing concern with new questions, in particular the problem of revolutionary organisation.

It is important to stress the originality of the book. In 1959 Luxemburg was not a well-known figure. She had stood up to Lenin and argued with him on equal terms on more than one occasion. Stalin had denounced her as a Menshevik,[200] and the Stalinist tradition did little or nothing to encourage discussion of her ideas. In 1950 the CP historian Eric Hobsbawm managed to write an extensive review of a book on the history of the German Social Democratic Party from 1914 to 1921 without ever mentioning her name.[201] Sometimes, too, her criticisms of Lenin were torn out of context by those wishing to belittle the Bolshevik leader. Even in the orthodox

---

* Technically Cliff's book on Rosa Luxemburg constituted numbers two and three.

Trotskyist current, with its insistence on loyalty to Lenin, Luxemburg was not much cited.* The one rather limited milieu where Luxemburg was discussed was the ILP, whose paper *The Socialist Leader* carried articles by Ken Eaton, FA Ridley and Walter Kendall commending Luxemburg.[202]

There was little by or about Luxemburg available in English.† It was only with JP Nettl's biography in 1966[203] that a detailed study of Luxemburg's life and politics became available; after 1968 there was a revival of interest in Luxemburg, and Daniel Guérin's study of spontaneity in her thought helped to make her better known.[204] With his knowledge of German, Cliff was able to translate key passages from her writings unavailable to English readers.

It is sometimes said that in 1959 Cliff was a "Luxemburgist", or that he was passing through a "Luxemburgist" phase. In fact it is far from certain whether a coherent doctrine that could be described as "Luxemburgism" actually exists. When the book was reissued in 1969 Cliff revised a few sentences, but what is most striking is how many themes initiated in this short study remained with Cliff for the next 40 years.

Cliff began by noting that the work was written in a "spirit of admiration and criticism of its subject".[205] While the book was unambiguously partisan, he was concerned to make a critical assessment of Luxemburg, drawing out her relevance to the present-day struggle. In the conclusion he praised her attitude to Marxism, saying that "as a real disciple of Marx she was able to think and act

---

* In 14 bulky volumes of the *Writings of Leon Trotsky* (New York, 1969-79) there are only a handful (27) of references to Luxemburg. There are two short articles, one defending Luxemburg against Stalinist calumnies (*Writings 1932* (New York 1973), pp131-142), and another dealing with the misuse of Luxemburg's theory of spontaneity (*Writings 1935-36* (New York, 1970), pp29-32). Apart from these there are merely passing references to Luxemburg as an opponent of war and reformism, and as the victim of murder.

† *The Accumulation of Capital, Reform or Revolution* and *The Russian Revolution* had appeared in English in book form. Other articles had been translated, often in fairly obscure places, and were not easily available. A list of English translations and their dates can be checked at http://www.marxists.org/archive/luxemburg/index.htm. *Socialist Review* had published her pamphlet on *Socialism and the Churches* in 1951. The only major study of Luxemburg in English was Paul Frölich's *Rosa Luxemburg*, which had been published in 1940 (by the Left Book Club just after Gollancz's break with Stalinism). For a full bibliography, see JP Nettl, *Rosa Luxemburg*, vol 2, pp863-934.

independently of her master".[206] Such was the attitude to the Marxist tradition he wished to encourage.

Cliff began his account of Luxemburg with a biographical sketch, drawing out her theoretical contributions and her active involvement in the German labour movement. The unity of theory and practice was his central concern. While his account was careful and scholarly, he missed no opportunity to draw lessons for activity in the present. After quoting a long passage on the dynamics of the mass strike in Russia in 1905, he simply commented, "Budapest, 1956!"[207] He cited Luxemburg's famous statement of the alternatives facing humanity – "either a transition to Socialism, or a return to barbarism..." – and added the comment, "And we who live in the shadow of the H-bomb..."[208]

The short chapters of the book covered different aspects of Luxemburg's contribution to socialist thought. Her debate with Eduard Bernstein (the advocate of "evolutionary socialism") on reformism was summarised. Cliff noted that Luxemburg recognised the necessity for revolutionary violence, yet at the same time insisted that any unnecessary bloodshed was a crime.[209] He also observed that she rejected the idea that workers are driven to revolution only by starvation. Developing his own reflections on the impact of the post-war boom, he added that "empty stomachs, besides encouraging rebellion, lead also to submission".[210]

Her anti-war campaigning before and after 1914 was described, and Cliff drew the simple lesson (again highly relevant as the nuclear disarmament movement began to gather strength) that "the fight against war is inseparable from the fight for Socialism".[211]

He discussed her argument that under capitalism the slogan of national independence for Poland had no progressive value, showing that it had to be understood in the context of the debates within the Polish labour movement. He concluded that Luxemburg had been gravely mistaken because, unlike Lenin, she had failed to give sufficient importance to the difference between "the positions of oppressed and oppressor nations".[212] This distinction between the nationalism of the oppressor and that of the oppressed would help define Cliff's position on many issues in the coming years, from the Vietnam War to black nationalism.

Cliff analysed in some detail the criticisms that Luxemburg had made of the Bolsheviks in power. At the same time, he stressed that her criticisms were entirely subordinated to her total commitment to the general aims and principles of the Russian Revolution; as she wrote, "the future everywhere belongs to 'Bolshevism'".[213]

The most difficult chapter was the one dealing with *The Accumulation of Capital* (1915), in which Luxemburg had developed a controversial critique of Marx's reproduction schemes in Volume Two of *Capital*. The mathematical analysis was probably skipped by many readers. The main theme which Cliff drew out was that of the relationship between capitalism and the non-capitalist societies existing on its frontiers. Cliff used this to develop some of his own concerns about the nature of imperialism and the role of the war economy.[214]

The central theme of *Rosa Luxemburg* was the question of socialist organisation and how it related to mass struggle. Cliff had previously had little to say about the question of the revolutionary party, other than to note that the Fourth International's position on Eastern Europe would logically make revolutionary parties – and the Fourth International itself – unnecessary. The distance between the tiny cluster of people around Cliff and a revolutionary party big enough to make any significant intervention in the class struggle was so great as to make the question hardly worth discussing. If the SRG was a rather looser and less disciplined organisation than the RCP, this was attributable to its small size and the low level of class struggle, rather than to any debate about the principles of organisation.

Now the question was acquiring new relevance. Many of those who had left the CP were throwing the baby out with the bathwater by rejecting all forms of centralised organisation because of the hideous parody that Stalinism had been. Meanwhile, in the name of "Leninism", the SLL was reviving some of the worst forms of sectarianism and vanguardism.*

Cliff defended the basic principle of the necessity for a revolutionary party, because of the uneven consciousness of the working class:

> While the working class as a class must be conscious of the aims of Socialism and the methods of achieving it, it still needs a revolutionary

---

* Cliff Slaughter's article "What is Revolutionary Leadership?" (*Labour Review*, Vol 5 No 3, October-November 1960) provided an intelligent defence of Leninism, drawing on Lukács and Gramsci. Unfortunately the SLL did not put these precepts into practice. Slaughter's reference in the article to "Rosa Luxemburg, whose shabby 'friends' emphasise her weakest point, and are incapable of learning from her strength", was doubtless aimed at Cliff.

party to lead it. In every factory, on every dock and on every building site, there are more advanced workers – that is, workers more experienced in the class struggle, more independent of the influence of the capitalist class – and less advanced workers. It is up to the former to organise into a revolutionary party, and try to influence and lead the latter. As Rosa Luxemburg said, "This mass movement of the proletariat needs the lead of an organised principled force".[215]

The question was, what form should such a party take? Cliff was resolutely opposed to formalism – for him content preceded and determined form. In the argument about Russia, he had insisted that the actual content of relations between classes was more important than the form of property ownership.* In comparing the views on organisation of Lenin and Luxemburg, Cliff ridiculed those (Stalinists but also Trotskyists) who tried to use Lenin's 1902 book *What Is To Be Done?* as though it fitted all times and places. He pointed out that Lenin himself had "emphasised that his organisational views were not universally applicable".[216]

Cliff argued therefore that forms of organisation must be understood in their historical and social context. Lenin's views, which varied radically from one phase of the struggle to another, had to be placed in the context of the "concrete historical conditions of the Labour Movement in Russia".[217] The comparison between Lenin and Luxemburg, which he developed at some length, had to be made in relation to "the special environment in which each worked".[218]

Because of the repressive conditions of Tsarist Russia there was no mass trade unionism, and hence no milieu in which a bureaucracy could develop. Luxemburg, on the other hand, had to face a highly developed trade union bureaucracy, whom she enraged by defining trade unionism as "a labour of Sisyphus",† and insisting that trade union struggle was "not a substitute for the liberation of the working class".[219] As a result of this different experience, and not because of any innate superiority, Cliff judged that "Rosa

---

* Likewise in discussing Luxemburg's account of revolutionary crisis, he argued, "The form of expression of the fundamental contradiction is not as important as its content." (Cliff, *Rosa Luxemburg*, p21)

† Sisyphus was a figure in Greek mythology who was punished by being eternally condemned to roll a huge rock up a steep hill, only to have to begin again when it rolled back to the bottom.

Luxemburg had a much earlier and clearer view of the role of the labour bureaucracy than Lenin or Trotsky".[220]

For Cliff, grappling with the problem of revolutionary strategy in 1950s Britain, the question of reformism was crucial. He argued that Luxemburg's writings were invaluable on this question because they urged that "a principled fight against reformism...does not degenerate into flight from it. She taught that a revolutionary should not swim with the stream of reformism, nor sit outside it and look in the opposite direction, but swim against it".[221] Although he did not make the point explicit, this formulation justified the SRG's position of remaining inside the Labour Party while fighting for its own ideas.*

It was on this basis that Cliff came to the conclusion that "For Marxists, in advanced industrial countries, Lenin's original position can serve much less as a guide than Rosa Luxemburg's, notwithstanding her overstatements on the question of spontaneity".[222]

Cliff was also concerned with the relation between the revolutionary party and the mass struggle of the working class. This must be a two-way relationship – the party must lead the class, but also learn from it: "The party, in consequence, should not invent tactics out of thin air, but put it as its first duty to *learn* from the experience of the mass movement and then generalise from it." He gave as examples the way in which Marx had learnt from the Paris Commune and Lenin had been suspicious of the first soviets.[223]

He cited Luxemburg's now famous formulation: "Mistakes committed by a genuine revolutionary labour movement are much more fruitful and worthwhile historically than the infallibility of the very best Central Committee".[224] He quoted this from a journal article in German, so it may have been a new quotation for most English readers. Certainly it was a phrase that stuck in the memory of many of his audience, who may have recalled it at a later time when Cliff himself was a central committee member.

Luxemburg had recognised the importance of both organisation

---

* At around this time the SLL was pursuing a policy of open confrontation with the Labour Party bureaucracy, in such a way as to ensure that it became a proscribed organisation and the maximum number of its members were expelled. See B Pitt, *The Rise and Fall of Gerry Healy*, chapter 5. The SLL was proscribed by the Labour Party early in 1959; *Socialist Review* (mid-April 1959) condemned the ban as "an authoritarian and unprincipled act".

and spontaneity, and Cliff did not attempt to make any false dichotomy between them. On the contrary, he showed that it was only in the context of a spontaneous mass struggle that the revolutionary organisation had a vital role to play. Nonetheless he concluded that Luxemburg had made an "overestimation of the role of spontaneity".[225] He showed that this was understandable in the context of the debates she was engaged in, in opposition to the elitist German Social Democratic leadership.

He concluded that "in doing so she may have bent the stick a little too far".[226] Cliff was to become very fond of this particular metaphor, borrowed from Lenin,[227] with the sense of overstating a position in reaction to an overstatement in the opposite direction. It was an idea he was to use frequently over the coming years.

Cliff touched on some more general philosophical issues in the book. Although he never became obsessed with philosophy in the fashion of Dunayevskaya, he was concerned to establish the basic principles underlying his view of history and of socialism. So he quoted Luxemburg to emphasise the centrality of human agency in the socialist revolution:

> Rosa Luxemburg has been accused of mechanical materialism, a conception of historical development in which objective economic forces are independent of human will. This accusation is totally unfounded. Hardly any of the great Marxists has laid greater stress on human activity as the determinant of human destiny.[228]

In particular he took up the argument about the role of consciousness in the socialist revolution that he had set out some ten years earlier in his document on the "People's Democracies":[229] "Rosa Luxemburg believed that consciousness of the aims of socialism on the part of the mass of workers is a *necessary prerequisite* for achieving socialism".[230]

Yet he pointed out that Luxemburg had been quite right to reject Bernstein's claim that capitalism was not necessarily condemned to crisis, and that therefore socialism was simply a matter of human will independent of material circumstances: "Abstracted from the contradictions of capitalism, the urge towards socialism becomes merely an idealistic chimera".[231] The problem of agency and of voluntarism was one with which Cliff would wrestle over the years.

Cliff used Luxemburg to reaffirm the essentially moral nature of socialism. It was all too easy for revolutionaries to become absorbed in the detailed means of organisation and to forget the nature of their goal. Luxemburg offered a powerful reminder of the ultimate reasons for being a socialist:

> During a period when so many who consider themselves Marxists sap Marxism of its deep humanistic content, no one can do more to release us from the chains of lifeless mechanistic materialism than Rosa Luxemburg. For Marx communism (or socialism) was "real humanism", "a society in which the full and free development of every individual is the ruling principle".[232] Rosa Luxemburg was the embodiment of these humanistic passions. Sympathy with the lowly and oppressed was a central motive of her life. Her deep emotion and feeling for the suffering of people and all living things expressed themselves in everything she did or wrote, whether in her letters from prison or in the deepest writings of her theoretical research.[233]

Such a passage gives us a rare example of Cliff exposing the feelings that had led him to become a socialist. In discussing Luxemburg's work on the mass strike, he cited the sentence "The most precious thing, because it is the most enduring, in the sharp ebb and flow of the revolutionary wave, is the proletariat's spiritual growth".[234] Cliff himself used the term "spiritual" from time to time. It seems an odd word for one who was a committed materialist. In this particular quotation it rendered the German *geistig*, which might be better translated as "intellectual" or "of the mind". But Cliff's use of the term indicated a recognition that workers are not motivated solely by economic factors, and that the ideas in their heads and the values they hold are of immense importance.

Of necessity sales of the book were not extensive, but it was reported that 97 copies had been taken by London bookshops, and that 36 had been sold in the ENV factory – though it is said that some workers believed it to be a detective story because of the opening lines about Luxemburg's murder.[235]

It was now over nine years since Cliff had been ejected from "the Club". As a writer and thinker he had completed a substantial body of work in that time, but in terms of building an organisation he had made little progress. The SRG was probably less than a tenth of the size of the RCP, and that had been tiny enough. It was Healy, and not Cliff, who had made substantial gains from the crisis in the CP, and already he was beginning to squander those gains. But in the next couple of years the tide would turn quite sharply.

In the 1959 general election the Tories, trying to capitalise on the general rise in living standards produced by the long boom, launched the slogan "Life is better with the Conservatives". *Socialist Review* responded with a front-page headline "Life is bitter with the Tories".[236] The article quite rightly pointed to the poverty and exploitation that still existed in Britain: "bitter rents, bitter pensions, bitter victimisation of shop stewards and militant workers". But it also looked at the political consequences of the long boom, factors which would help to explain the Tory landslide victory:

> Capitalism's present prosperity puts a premium on a non-political labour movement, on a movement whose energies are devoted primarily to the industrial struggle. In this atmosphere the Labour Party's empire tends to shrink, and has been doing so. Every defeat will lop off yet another section of the movement: youth don't want to know, militant workers couldn't be bothered, intellectuals aren't stimulated.

In November 1959, after Chanie had inherited some money,[237] the family moved to 52 Chatterton Road, N4 in Finsbury Park.[238] This was a modest terrace house, but was larger than their previous accommodation, so hospitality could be offered to more comrades. The front and back rooms on the ground floor were separated by a removable partition, so that quite large meetings could be held there, and for a time national meetings of the SRG took place in Cliff's home.

Cliff's recognition of the modest but real possibilities that were emerging was expressed in two perspectives documents he wrote as the new decade was opening. The first explored the current state of class consciousness and took a pragmatic view of the Labour Party:

> While conditions of full employment over a long period make for the general limitation of the workers' struggle to a struggle for reforms, they at the same time instil a self-confidence which time and again inspires the workers to make excursions beyond the confines of reforms, and encroach on the precincts of private property. The main expression of this has been opposition to sackings (i.e. the raising of the question of workers' control over hiring and firing)...

But while the Labour Party *as an organisation* is quite weak, the loyalty of the mass of the workers to the Labour Party *as their political representation*, is in no way diminished...

Quite a lot of the political ideological discussion takes place outside the framework of the CLPs [Constituency Labour Parties] – in ULR [*Universities and Left Review*] clubs, in new magazines like that of ULR, New Reasoner, etc.

Practical conclusions from the above were:

(a) Marxists should, as individuals and as a body, try to take part in *all* campaigns against *all* kinds of oppression, whether against low wages, the bomb, fascists...

(b) They should do all they can to orientate all the above campaigns towards the Labour movement...

(c) In the fight for reforms Marxists should point to the need for a transitional programme, and the central point in all our industrial agitation should be the demand for workers' control...

(d) Marxists should take part in all leftward-moving organisations whether officially part of the Labour Party or not, which have power of appeal to any serious section of the people...

(e) Special attention should be devoted to students, who, while quite sensitive to the horrors of capitalism, are at the same time not yet attracted to the CLPs – like the membership of ULR, CND, etc.[239]

The second document dealt with the question of left regroupment. Cliff noted that the isolation of Marxists had led to sectarianism, and that there was now a mood for Marxist unity. The Marxist movement must be "not a church but...a fighting organisation", and he proposed unity around a number of basic points: nationalisation under workers' control, troops out of the colonies, working class action against the Bomb and British withdrawal from NATO.

He then looked at the concrete problems of Marxist unity in the present world situation:

The question of the attitude to Russia in case of a third world war, which has bedevilled the Marxists for a long time, is today scholastic and lifeless. If a third world war breaks out it will mean the end of humanity, and therefore any discussion on possible policies *during* or after such a war is at best a useless scholastic argument, and at worst a numbing of the fear and hence antagonism to the threatening war. For us the aim is not, as it was for Lenin before the H-bomb, to turn an imperialist war into a civil war, but to prevent the imperialist war, the annihilation of civilisation. (Because of this, although I have a certain conception of Stalinist Russia – believing it to be State Capitalist – I feel sure I would not have any *practical* differences with Marxists who have a different conception)...

The question of inner democracy is absolutely central to the Marxist movement. The crisis in the SLL, reflecting the crisis of inner-Party democracy, following upon a similar crisis in the CP, makes it abundantly clear that a decisive, uncompromising stand on this issue must be taken: To guarantee democracy in any organisation the Constitution or Statutes of the organisation are far from enough. Unity in action combined with freedom in discussion can be assured only if discussions on *general* problems of policy are conducted in the open press...

The *Socialist Review* and *International Socialism* can play an important role in the regroupment of Marxists by (1) showing in practice what a non-dogmatic Marxist attitude means, (2) demonstrating the strength of democracy in the development of ideas and the building of a trend in the labour movement.[240]

These two documents show Cliff grappling with the new emerging situation. Though some points would have to be rethought over the coming few years, they showed a realistic assessment of the challenges ahead.

PART TWO
FROM THEORY TO PRACTICE

5
1960-64
Second Youth

In October 1960 the Labour Party conference in Scarborough carried two resolutions pledging the party to a policy of unilateral nuclear disarmament. The right-wing leader of the party, Hugh Gaitskell, promised to "fight and fight and fight again to save the party we love" and refused to be bound by the resolutions. The Labour Party was split from top to bottom and a vigorous and often savage debate erupted.

The new milieu created by CND was much more favourable to the ideas of the SRG than the post-1956 audience had been. For the new generation the idea that the two great powers were symmetrical fitted their experience. Until the spring of 1960 the CP had stood aside from the movement, arguing that summit conferences rather than unilateral disarmament would unite the broadest number of people.

At the 1961 conference Gaitskell and his allies succeeded in reversing the 1960 decision. For those who had believed that the Labour Party could be taken over by the left, this was a demoralising setback. Cliff had a more realistic perspective of integrating the disarmament movement into the class struggle. At an SRG meeting in October 1961:

> T Cliff said that at the Conference the Left felt much less defeated than the press made out... The role of Marxists is to concentrate on the section of the movement which is simultaneously within the spheres of the Labour Party, anti-nuclear and industrial activity. It is necessary to avoid falling into either error, of building political organisations (e.g. Ward Labour Parties) and neglecting the industrial struggle, or of struggling in industry against the bomb and neglecting to build an enduring political organisation. The Left in the LP [Labour Party] tends to hamstring itself by arguing only about the Bomb and neglecting all other fields of struggle – strikes, tenants' struggles, etc.[1]

Alongside CND had grown a movement for direct action against nuclear weapons, in particular the Committee of 100, which organised sit-downs and provoked large numbers of arrests. As publicity stunts – a number of well-known intellectuals and writers (Bertrand Russell, John Osborne, Arnold Wesker) were involved – these made a positive impact. But some of those involved, including members of the SRG periphery like Peter Cadogan and Chris Pallis (Martin Grainger), considered that direct action had a potential for more than publicity.* At an SRG meeting in early 1962 Cliff set out a perspective for work in the nuclear disarmament movement. The minutes record:

> There had been a danger during the late period of enthusiasm of forgetting certain basic facts, e.g. that politics are concentrated economics, that foreign and home policies cannot be divorced, and that, in particular, we cannot expect to have the working class united on foreign policy issues until it is united on British economic questions. We must distinguish between mass action (e.g. the civil disobedience movements against the bomb in Britain and against racial discrimination in the USA), which might draw in enormous numbers but could never involve a majority of the people, and class action. A majority of the US demonstrators were students and a majority of the Committee of 100 supporters were not workers.
>
> Workers are not united on home economic issues because they do not yet face a united capitalist class. The technical revolution in production, the permanent war economy, expansion into underdeveloped countries and, potentially, the European Common Market have allowed the trade union movement as a whole to gain regular wage rises over the last 15 years.
>
> The Committee of 100 etc. do not always realise that they are a minority. Thus Cadogan and Grainger supported the idea of a quarter of an hour strike against the bomb. Industrial workers showed this was unrealistic. If anything a strike against the budget was more likely to bring out large numbers than one against the bomb. This talk of strikes, running candidates on purely CND platforms – ignoring the numerous issues which workers consider important – and the Committee of 100's consideration of going underground were all indicative of the middle-class composition

---

* Reuben Fior of the SRG was a member of the Committee of 100. For an expression of critical support for the Committee see P Sedgwick, "The Direction of Action", *Socialist Review*, May 1961.

of CND and the Committee. Going underground could be justified by (a) suppression (b) the Committee being on the verge of achieving state power. Neither of these conditions prevailed...

Conclusions: (a) the battle against the bomb must be used mainly for propaganda and education at present; (b) generally economic issues must be the main ones to concentrate on; these will lead on to the battles on political and military issues; (c) supporters of CND and Committee of 100 should be encouraged to make contact with the working class organisations, through the Labour Party, NCLC, white collar delegations to trade councils and support for CND/Committee-TU organisations; (d) these trade union groups must be autonomous. In them CND and Committee of 100 should be encouraged to collaborate. Their propaganda aims were similar and there was also a need to prevent the small Committee of 100 splitting into numerous utopian groups, for which it had a tendency; (e) efforts should be made to draw CP members into these TU anti-bomb activities, as it was the only political group able to organise the semblance of working class action.[2]

The milieu opened up by CND and the New Left allowed the SRG to make some very small but significant progress. New recruits were made, including Jim Higgins, an important addition to the leadership team. Higgins had joined the CP as a teenager, and left over Hungary. He joined the SLL, but soon tired of the Healyite leadership, and became a member of the Stamford faction, which opposed Healy's ultra-left strategy and authoritarian methods.[3] He joined the SRG in 1959. He was a well-established member of his union, and a genuine worker intellectual; he had left school at the age of 15, and all his subsequent education had been obtained through voracious reading and experience in left-wing organisations. Yet he had a breadth of knowledge that contrasted sharply with the narrow specialisation often encountered in the academic world. (Such worker intellectuals were even then a rarity; a generation later it is inconceivable that someone like Higgins would not have gone to university.)

The other striking thing about him was his monumental irreverence. Nobody, in his own organisation or in the socialist pantheon, was immune from criticism and indeed mockery. His irreverence fitted well with the style of the group at this time. It was a tiny, marginal group and it knew it – in contrast to the SLL, a tiny marginal group which thought it was the vanguard of the proletariat. Whereas Cliff's humour had a direct political purpose, Higgins's was often straightforwardly vulgar, and sometimes cruel. Tact was not his strongest point, and he quite often offended people.

Higgins soon became secretary of the IS group and worked closely with Cliff, and throughout the 1960s there was genuine warmth between the two men. Higgins was intelligent and well read, but not himself an original thinker, and he had great admiration for Cliff as a theoretician. He looked upon Cliff rather protectively, and usually referred to Cliff as "Glixon" – this was Chanie's pet name for Cliff. There was an element of irony to this, but it was also indicative of Higgins's real feelings of affection for Cliff.* He was deeply committed to the organisation; on one occasion he apparently took out a second mortgage on his house to raise money.[4]

Another significant recruit at this time, Alasdair MacIntyre, was a quite different character. He was a successful young academic who in 1961 obtained a fellowship at Oxford University. He had briefly been a member of the CP before 1956, and had written a book on Marxism for the Student Christian Movement.[5] He had been for a time a member of the SLL, and was (for one issue) "Literary Editor" of its theoretical journal *Labour Review*. He left the SLL in 1960, somewhat later than the Stamford faction. He was also a member of the original editorial board of *New Left Review*. However, he was removed after the first issue, apparently because he reported back on activities to the SLL.[6]

He joined the SRG, and then the editorial board of *International Socialism* in 1961. To begin with he was very active, writing copiously for *Socialist Review* (of which he became editor in November 1961) in the period just before it was wound up.[7] Later he became one of the best-known philosophers in the English-speaking world, renowned in particular for his book *After Virtue*.[8]

MacIntyre was an impressive individual. He was a fine speaker – his clear, measured Irish accent made him appear like a synthesis between a true scholar and a Celtic romantic revolutionary. He was phenomenally well read: he could talk about philosophy, sociology, literature and Marxism with equal authority. In this respect he was

---

* This account is based on the author's own recollections of the relationship between the two men.

superficially more impressive than Cliff, whose knowledge was also phenomenal, but much more concentrated in the Bolshevik-Trotskyist tradition.

Cliff was never close to MacIntyre in the way that he was close to Kidron and Higgins, but felt a certain distrust towards him. He was suspicious of MacIntyre's academic philosophical work, which he believed had little to do with Marxism. He was also opposed to MacIntyre writing in *Encounter** (this was before the revelation in 1967 of the covert CIA funding of the magazine, but *Encounter*'s reputation as an anti-Communist journal was well known). The group was fairly loose in terms of discipline and intellectual cohesion, and these disagreements were never raised as a formal disciplinary question, or indeed discussed much in the leading committees. In Cliff's words, "At that time we were glad of anyone we could get".[9]

There was also a philosophical disagreement between them. In 1963 MacIntyre wrote a piece in *International Socialism* entitled "Prediction and Politics".[10] This concluded, "The fall of capitalism is in no way inevitable; but nor is its survival. The condition of its fall is a long-term mass change in consciousness; and there are no conditions which can make such a change either inevitable or impossible."

Cliff rejected this position. In reply *International Socialism* reprinted an article by Hal Draper, "The 'Inevitability of Socialism'".[11] This was a sophisticated discussion of the question, which distinguished clearly between determinism and fatalism, though it concluded by invoking "the historic inevitability of man's ascent to humanity". Cliff claimed that this represented his own position. [12] †

Cliff distrusted voluntarism because he thought it led to substitutionist and elitist politics. In a four-page typescript entitled "The

---

* For example his review article of Deutscher's *The Prophet Outcast*: "Trotsky in Exile", *Encounter*, 21(6) (December 1963), pp73-78.
† One practical expression of the disagreement was at a national meeting where MacIntyre wanted the group to make an intervention in the London docks, but Cliff responded that the group was too small and could not do anything (Colin Barker interview, May 2008).

Crisis of Society is the Crisis of the Leadership" (undated, but probably late 1950s or early 1960s)[13] he wrote:

> The wider, the more massive, the missing revolutionary link, the less is it possible to explain the lack by fortuitous or accidental factors. The lack of a Lenin can be explained by an accident; the lack of 100,000 revolutionaries cannot be explained by accidental circumstances. An "accident" that occurs 100,000 times proves by this fact alone that it is not an accident, but the product of general objective factors.

Trotsky's formulation that "the crisis of society is the crisis of leadership" can therefore be misused as a general blanket to encompass the whole problem of the revolutionary party and its leadership, thus leading to the most absurd and "substitutionist" conclusions, to completely idealist voluntarism. We, the few dozen Marxists, can decide history!

In the original version of his document on bureaucratic collectivism he attacked Shachtman's denial of the inevitability of socialism, though making quite clear that determinism did not lead to fatalism; action was always at the heart of Cliff's concerns. This passage disappeared in the revised 1968 version:

> The consciousness of the inevitability of socialism can on no account lead to quietism, as in the same way as the fight of the proletariat for socialism is inevitable, so also is the struggle of the oppressors in defence of capitalism inevitable. It will use ever more brutal and bureaucratic measures for the oppression of the working class. Capitalist barbarism, however, expressed in wars, crises, fascism, Stalinism, etc., does not signify the total negation of capitalism, but the price the proletariat and humanity are paying for the belatedness of the socialist revolution.[14]

There was little public debate on the issues, though on one occasion in the autumn of 1961 Cliff debated with MacIntyre on Marxism and philosophy at a London branch meeting. Not surprisingly Cliff, who generally had little interest in philosophy, was "trounced".[15] Many members found MacIntyre's position more convincing. However, MacIntyre, who still stands by the position argued in "Prediction and Politics", considers that this disagreement with Cliff helped to persuade him that he was not a Marxist.[16] Cliff, meanwhile, used to joke that Cliff the determinist worked all the time, but that the voluntarist MacIntyre did nothing.[17] When MacIntyre drifted away from the leadership, it was fair comment.

Cliff's determinism* must be understood in context. For Cliff, a voluntarist position could easily lead to the SLL's obsession with leadership. The agency of the working class was central to his analysis, and the action of the working class would be determined by economic and social factors quite outside the control of tiny revolutionary groups. But he was no fatalist, and in 1968 he would shift his emphasis.

The growth of the group and new forms of activity led to a number of changes in organisation and publications. *International Socialism* was launched as a quarterly in 1960. It appeared just after the first issues of *New Left Review*, and was conceived as a more explicitly Marxist alternative to *NLR*. It aspired to be a journal of analysis and debate, where rational argument might rise above sectarianism.

In 1960 a volume of essays by *NLR* contributors was published, entitled *Out of Apathy*.[18] Mike Kidron wrote a fraternal but rigorously critical review of this.[19] In an article in *NLR* Edward Thompson devoted a substantial amount of space to responding to Kidron. Thompson was scathing about Kidron's insistence on the centrality of class – "a 'working class idea' is an idea of which Michael Kidron approves" – but went out of his way to add that, unlike the more dogmatic and abrasive SLL, "*International Socialism*...seems to me the most constructive journal with a Trotskyist tendency in this country, most of the editorial board of which are active (and very welcome) members of the Left Club movement". [20]

Originally its editorial board was not limited to the SRG, but drew from almost all the Trotskyist-derived currents except the SLL. Nick Howard, who was on the editorial board from the first issue, recalls that Kidron wanted a forum journal and was more adventurous than Cliff, who was uncomfortable with involving people from outside the SRG. In particular, Cliff was impatient with the debate on left reformism[21] which ran over several issues of the journal.[22]

This attempt at a broad journal of the Marxist left failed. There were various resignations: Ken Coates left when an editorial statement was published without the board being consulted.[23] By 1963

---

* Cliff did not spend much time on philosophy and thus was not wholly consistent. His account of "deflected permanent revolution" (see below) was very much a theory of historical alternatives.

International Socialism was to become simply the theoretical journal of the International Socialism group. For the first five years Mike Kidron was the editor. Theoretical articles by Alasdair MacIntyre, Peter Sedgwick, Nigel Harris as well as by Cliff and Kidron provided vital support for the heated debates in the Young Socialists. It was serious but not solemn, had glorious covers designed by Reuben Fior, and contained such delights as poems by the 28 year old Adrian Mitchell. Cliff, however, showed no interest in the aesthetic aspects of the journal. It had a beautiful layout designed by Fior with blank spaces and broad margins, but Cliff could see no point in blank paper and wanted it filled with political material.[24] He also proposed there be a standard cover "to avoid unnecessary expense".[25] Happily he was overruled by his less philistine comrades.

International Socialism was the political focus of the group at this stage and its main success story. In December 1962 the SRG was renamed the International Socialism group (or the International Socialists, IS). Its structure remained loose and lacking in formalism. Quarterly meetings open to all members were held under the rather misleading title of "Executive Committees", and the day-to-day running of the organisation was left to a London-based body called the "Working Committee". (Jim Higgins, the secretary, had a notoriously scatological sense of humour and notification of the meetings would consist of a postcard reading simply "WC Saturday 2pm".)

But the most important factor in the situation, and the one which made possible the recruitment of a number of new members, was the founding of the Young Socialists (YS). The 1959 general election had given the Tories an increased majority. There was a widespread recognition that the Labour Party had to move somewhat to the left, in order to revitalise its activists and regain its traditional vote.* CND showed that there was a new audience of young people who could be attracted towards the Labour Party. At the Labour Party conference in 1959 it was agreed that a new national youth movement should be set up, and at Easter 1961 the first national

---

* Dick Marsh MP told the 1959 Labour Party conference with undisguised cynicism, "A youth movement will not be polite and respectful but will pass resolutions of no confidence in everybody on the platform and inform us how we can have the socialist revolution in the next 24 hours. If they did not do these things they would not be any good to this movement anyway." (Quoted in M Coggins, *The Young Socialists*, p4)

conference of the YS was held; by this time there were more than 600 YS branches.[26]

This was a gamble for the Labour bureaucrats. The Labour Party had set up youth movements before, but in 1939 and again in 1955 they had been closed down because the left had become too influential. Although the risk was recognised, and a number of bureaucratic safeguards were set in place,* the Labour Party accepted that this was the only way to ensure a supply of recruits from the younger generation.

The SRG had not escaped the notice of the Labour Party bureaucracy. In June 1960 John Phillips reported a meeting with Bill Jones, the London Region Youth Officer. Jones had enquired about *Socialist Review* and "announced that there was going to be some trouble about the *Review* soon, because it wasn't exactly a Social Democratic paper, was it?"[27] But given Labour's need to pull the left behind it, no action was taken at this stage.

The Trotskyist left was still tiny, but it recognised a unique opportunity that could not be ignored. The Healy group was the best placed. A youth paper sponsored by Healy supporters, *Keep Left*, had been in continuous existence since 1950.[28] The Healy group was the biggest and the best organised; its main problem was the fact that the SLL had been proscribed by the Labour Party in 1959, and so *Keep Left* was particularly vulnerable to witch-hunting because of alleged association with a banned organisation. The supporters of Ted Grant also had a youth paper called *Rally*, based mainly in Liverpool.

The SRG now launched a new youth paper under the name *Rebel*. Initially about 200 copies were produced on a hand-printing press, and they were dried on the radiators in Cliff's front room. On one occasion they ended up illegible, whereupon Cliff put the blame on John and Mary Phillips because they had been away on holiday.[29] *Rebel* involved some of the younger recruits, including Mary Phillips, Roger Cox and Mike Heym. Cliff urged on this activity and was always directing from behind the scenes.[30] New recruits were soon made.

---

* As the SRG youth paper *Rebel* put it, "What a bloody farce! If the Young Socialists is to be a separate wing of the party, as it is claimed, then why do our resolutions have to be examined by local general management committees and party officers?" (February 1961, quoted in M Coggins, *The Young Socialists*, p9)

John Palmer had been active with Irish far-left groups in the London area since 1956 and had read *Socialist Review*. He was advised by one of his Irish comrades to contact the SRG which, he was told, was "run by a clever bunch of Jews". He met Cliff, who made an intense effort to recruit him, telephoning him every night and meeting him regularly. Palmer soon joined and became a leading activist in *Rebel*. He was impressed by Cliff's infectious enthusiasm and by the fact that, unlike other Trotskyists of the older generation, he had a sense of humour. The ideas – state capitalism and the permanent arms economy – came later but were very important. Palmer found Cliff and those around him – Kidron, Sedgwick, MacIntyre – to have a more rational and less dogmatic approach than other Marxists.[31]

Chris Davison had joined the SRG in Ramsgate in 1959, and shortly afterwards heard Cliff speak. He was a former member of the Young Communist League and was impressed by Cliff, feeling that he could relate to his politics.[32]

Cliff was anxious to expand the scale of the activity and to cooperate with other groups in order to establish a national youth paper. In particular he pushed for a merger with *Rally*.[33] In 1961 *Rebel* and *Rally* agreed to join forces. They drew in a group of YS apprentices from Glasgow, and supporters of *NLR* and *Labour's Northern Voice*. The new, printed, paper, called *Young Guard*, first appeared in September 1961. It took its name from the youth section of the Belgian Socialist Party, the Jeunes Gardes Socialistes, who had played a significant role in the Belgian General Strike of 1960-61.[*] The first editor was Chris Davison. Circulation soon reached 3,000, in comparison to only 4,000 for the official Labour Party *New Advance*.

Young Guard was run by a quarterly National Editorial Board to which delegates were elected, in proportion to area sales, by open readers' meetings. In practice the IS had editorial control. However, the paper featured a range of articles and there was vigorous debate about the new regimes in Cuba and Algeria.[34]

The YS gave many hundreds of young people their first initiation into socialist politics. But the original hopes of the organisation,

---

[*] A statement from the Jeunes Gardes Socialistes appeared in *Young Guard* in October 1961.

which had reflected the optimism and idealism of those who had marched from Aldermaston, were quite rapidly soured. The Labour Party bureaucracy, fighting hard to reverse the Scarborough decision on nuclear disarmament and to make Labour a respectable contender for the next election, was determined not to let the rebelliousness of youth go beyond modest boundaries.

The main opposition came from the *Keep Left* grouping. This reflected a genuine radical opposition to the rightward-moving leadership of the Labour Party, but it embodied some of the worst features of the Healy tendency as it had developed since 1950. It had a dangerously unbalanced political perspective, believing there was an imminent threat of fascism in 1961.[35] This led to a sectarianism in which its own importance was grossly exaggerated and political opponents were vilified.* It saw its rivals in the IS as a real threat; in 1962 most of a whole issue of the SLL theoretical journal was devoted to attacks on "state capitalism" in general and Alasdair MacIntyre in particular.[36]

The atmosphere in the YS soon became poisonous. At the first conference in 1961 Roger Protz, the appointed editor of the official YS paper *New Advance*, distributed a statement condemning the Labour Party bureaucracy for the way it had tried to control the paper. He was promptly sacked and became editor of *Keep Left*. *Keep Left* was proscribed in May 1962 and could only be sold clandestinely.

Young Guard was the third horse in the race. This explained both its strength and weakness. It was able to appeal to a wide constituency in the YS, those who supported nuclear disarmament and public ownership against the Gaitskellite leadership, but who at the same time were repelled by the sectarian style of *Keep Left*. But it found itself squeezed between the two main protagonists. It was denounced as treacherous and an ally of the right wing if it failed to follow every twist and turn of *Keep Left* policy. John Robertson told critics at a *Keep Left* meeting during the 1964 YS conference, "If you are not 100 percent with us, you are 100 percent against us. Get out of our way or we will go over your bodies".[37]

---

* In 1959 some *Keep Left* supporters were expelled from the Labour Party in south London. At roughly the same time some activists from 1956 were executed in Hungary. *Keep Left* linked the issues: "Youth such as these in Streatham, Norwood and Hungary, who fight, and face expulsion or death, for their principles." (*Keep Left*, August-September 1959)

At the same time the Labour Party was well aware of the revolutionary socialist influences on *Young Guard*. Members of the editorial board, including Chris Davison and Gus Macdonald, attended a meeting with the disciplinary subcommittee of the Labour Party National Executive Committee in July 1962.[38] While *Young Guard* was not proscribed, certain constraints were placed on its activity. In 1963 it was reported that Chanie Rosenberg was being investigated by Islington Labour Party.[39] In December of that year James Callaghan sent the general secretary of the Labour Party, Len Williams, a copy of Jim Higgins's article "Ten Years for the Locust".[40] Williams replied rather bitterly:

> The Tony Cliff Group is bitterly opposed to Gerry Healy's Socialist Labour League, but they are an equal nuisance because of their *Young Guard* activities. Let us hope that the warring Trotskyist factions will destroy each other before long.[41]

The atmosphere in the YS became ever more embittered. In 1964 supporters of *Keep Left* won a majority of positions on the YS national committee, but the Labour Party responded by stepping up the witch-hunt against *Keep Left* supporters. The IS was committed to defending *Keep Left*'s democratic rights; at a Working Committee meeting "TC stressed the need to oppose the persecution of KL, since otherwise those floating leftwards will float on to join KL [*Keep Left*]".[42] *Keep Left* had now embarked on a policy of open confrontation, courting expulsions in order to walk out of the Labour Party and form an open organisation,* which it did in late 1964 (making it unable to profit from disillusion with the Labour government). YS meetings turned into bear gardens, with any possibility of fraternal debate eliminated,† as shown by the following

---

* As Healy himself put it the following years, "It is *we* who have *chosen* the moment of split because we now believe it is possible to recruit large numbers of working class youth." For the evolution of the SLL/*Keep Left* from entrism to "the need to build independent Marxist parties in order to provide alternative leadership", see B Pitt, *The Rise and Fall of Gerry Healy*, chapter 6.

† A low point of factionalism was reached when the SLL sent a member into the IS group, where he worked as an undercover "entrist" for some months before denouncing *Young Guard* in a tense public meeting. Cliff said that he had "stabbed us in the back when our backs were to the wall". In keeping with the relaxed disciplinary style of the time, the infiltrator was not expelled but merely suspended (author's recollection and Working Committee minutes, Rich. MS 1117/box 209/ file 6).

account by Jim Higgins* of a weekend school held by the West London YS Federation:

> Sheila Torrance...immediately set the tone for the discussion by indicating her intention of proving the right wing connections of *Young Guard*, and their gross betrayal of working class youth. This she attempted to do on the basis that YG [*Young Guard*] is willing to print articles by such well known agents of reaction as Ben Sawbridge and Willie Lomax... YG had compounded this felony by putting the YS before John Robertson at the Easter YS conference, thus justifying the epithet, political scabs... After this badly delivered diatribe, a number of Sheila Torrance's supporters stood up and, referring to carefully prepared notes, detailed a number of instances where alleged YG supporters had behaved in an anti-KL fashion in YS branches.[43]

Chris Davison now thinks that Cliff was mistaken in pushing for the merger with *Rally*. What had originally attracted Davison to *Rebel* was a fresh concept of politics compared to the tired old politics of orthodox Trotskyism. But *Young Guard* was pulled back into sectarian infighting.[44]

Yet there was real debate and discussion in the YS. In particular, the debate about Russia came alive. Many Young Socialists had first been radicalised by involvement in CND, yet *Keep Left* defended Russia's right to have nuclear weapons. A satirical song popular in *Young Guard* circles showed just how grotesque this position was (to the tune of "The Red Flag"):

> While Western arms we strive to end,
> The Russian bomb we will defend.
> Degenerated though it be,
> It is the People's property.
> Then raise the Workers' Bomb on high:
> Beneath its cloud we'll gladly die;
> And though our critics all shout "BALLS"
> We'll stand beneath it when it falls.[45]

It was through activity in the YS that the IS began to recruit a small but significant membership. The group was still tiny – in February 1963 the total funds in the bank amounted to £80.[46] But

---

* The article appeared in *Young Guard* under the signature of Mike Caffoor. However, the style is unmistakably Higgins's – and I was present when Higgins, who was over-age for the YS, asked Caffoor to sign it.

now, after ten years in which the membership had never reached three figures, a significant number of new recruits were being won. While some of those who had gone through the 1950s began to fade with the more activist turn of the 1960s, many of the new generation would be central to building the organisation over the coming decades.

John Charlton was involved in the YS in Newcastle.* He had been on the fringes of the SLL, who initially moved much quicker than the SRG at following up contacts. But he disliked the SLL's style. He first met Cliff in the summer of 1962 when he came to speak. Charlton found him generous and cheerful and became involved in building a branch. Cliff now visited frequently to speak at meetings and day-schools. At one point he came to Newcastle every fortnight to give his series of 12 lectures on Marxism.[47]

Also in Newcastle Jim Nichol first heard Cliff speak on Russia at a New Left meeting when he was 15. He was impressed by Cliff's enthusiasm and his willingness to take an interest in Nichol's questions. Cliff got together five supporters – of these, three (Nichol, Charlton and Jim Hutchinson, who recruited Charlton and who is still an active SWP member in Tyneside) remain in the SWP and another was a member until his death a few years ago. Some time after this Nichol decided to hitch-hike to London for a national IS meeting. He arrived at Chatterton Road just as the meeting was ending. Chanie gave him a bath and a bed, and the next day took him to Victoria Coach Station and bought him a ticket home.[48]

Jim Cronin, a young watchmaker, was active in the YS in Islington, north London. After hearing Cliff speak at a YS meeting, he and a couple of other Young Socialists were invited back to Cliff's home where they sat up right through the night discussing a range of issues. Cronin at the time had a poor view of adults, but to him Cliff seemed totally different. After that he followed Cliff around, listening to his lectures on Marxism in various places. He lived close to Cliff and spent a lot of time at Cliff's house, where he was allowed to borrow any of Cliff's books. Cliff encouraged him, for example getting him to chair meetings in order to gain experience, but didn't allow encouragement to go to Cronin's head. He had a

---

* For more on the left milieu in Newcastle during this period, see J Charlton, *Don't You Hear the H-Bomb's Thunder?*, Newcastle and Pontypool, 2009.

Lenin-style beard and Cliff would say, "Jim, you look very like Lenin but that's as far as it goes." Forty-five years on Cronin is still an SWP member.[49]

Alan Woodward completed his national service in 1959 and started a teacher training course. Through a friend he became involved in the Labour Party and CND, and started to attend meetings of a *Socialist Review* readers' group in west London. It was here he first encountered Cliff, whom he invited to speak at a very small meeting (around four people) of a socialist society he had set up in his college. Later he moved to Islington, then Tottenham, where he became more deeply involved in the organisation. Nearly 50 years on he remains an active socialist. Though he now has many criticisms of Cliff, he acknowledges that Cliff's capacity for building an organisation was magnificent.[50]

Mel Norris first heard Cliff's course of lectures at Tottenham Young Socialists in 1962. He found the lectures impressive. In a way Cliff was like a schoolteacher, asking questions of his audience, but his lectures were full of jokes and mixed metaphors – for example "a rolling stone gathers no needles". His jokes always made a political point and kept his listeners waiting for the next one.

Alan Watts was a young engineering worker when he became involved in Tottenham Young Socialists through Mel Norris. Cliff was a frequent speaker and Watts heard his series of lectures on basic Marxism. He had no previous engagement with political ideas and although he found some things impossible to understand, he could not help being moved by Cliff's passion. At the same time Cliff made sense of things like Russia and arms expenditure. Watts remembers going to work the next morning, drilling holes in a piece of metal, with his head spinning with ideas from the previous night's meeting. For a while, Cliff became a "sort of father" to him. In the 1970s Watts was a militant at MK Electric in north London; he helped to organise a factory branch of the SWP and sold 45 copies of *Socialist Worker* a week. He believes the activity in the 1970s was based on the motivation acquired in the 1960s. Almost 50 years later he remains an active SWP member.[51]

Fergus Nicol had been involved in CND and the YS while a student. He joined the IS and became secretary of the IS branch in Hornsey, north London. During this time Cliff would telephone him regularly, at least once a week, to stress the importance of activity in the YS. In 1965-66 Nicol went to Ghana, despite opposition from Cliff, who wanted him to stay and help build the organisation. When he returned the first person who telephoned him (to his mother's horror) was Cliff. Nicol remembered that what he learned from Cliff was not just theory but the attitude that nobody should be allowed to slip through the net – people should not be dismissed or allowed to drift away. He is still an active member.[52]

Noel Tracy was drawn into the IS by Kidron and Nigel Harris, and only met Cliff later. Tracy was less impressed with him than he had been with Harris and Kidron. Cliff seemed rooted in the struggles of the past to him and to view things from an entirely economistic perspective. Tracy thinks Paul Foot, Gus Macdonald and John Palmer were more influential in recruiting young activists into the group. However, Tracy believes the theory of state capitalism was important since the other propositions on offer were nonsense.[53]

Dave Peers had joined the SRG after contact with Peter Sedgwick in his home town of Liverpool, but first met Cliff as an Oxford student in 1961. He then visited Cliff in London. Cliff used his charm shamelessly and Peers "sort of fell in love" with him. He soon became part of the inner circle, took pleasure in learning about Marxism and had a sense that the 1960s offered the possibility of social change.[54]

Roger Rosewell first heard Cliff speak at a YS meeting in Esher, to the south west of London, in 1962 or 1963. He was struck by Cliff's inspirational qualities and his quirky use of the English language. He found him personally likeable and recognised him as having "star quality".[55]

In September 1966 Roger Huddle, an apprentice compositor, went on a YS coach to lobby the TUC in Blackpool. A "rather odd individual" asked him to hold a placard, saying "otherwise I'll be deported". Huddle talked to Cliff on the coach and joined the IS on the return journey. Huddle had been at a secondary modern school and felt Cliff gave him the education he had not had at school.[56]

Another important area was Glasgow. A number of young workers were politicised by the 1960 apprentices' strike and decided to join the YS. Govan and Gorbals YS was the biggest in the country and attracted the attention of many on the left – meetings were visited by Ted Knight (an SLL supporter, later to be leader of Lambeth council), Ralph Schoenman (a leading activist in the Committee of 100) and others. Some young socialists were influenced by Harry McShane, a veteran activist who had been a founder member of the CP and one of the leading organisers of the hunger marches in the 1930s. He had broken with the CP in the early 1950s and was associated with Raya Dunayevskaya's grouping in the US. The IS were invited to send a speaker and Cliff visited Glasgow.[57] This enabled the IS to draw in a number of recruits, some of whom would play an important role in the development of the organisation.

Among those who first heard Cliff at this time was Jimmy McCallum. He is now strongly anti-Leninist and thinks he and his friends got it "spectacularly wrong", but still remembers Cliff as a "marvellously humorous, theatrical, magical and electric performer".[58]

A number of the Glasgow recruits decided to move to London and initially sought accommodation at Cliff and Chanie's home in Chatterton Road. The couple's third child, Danny, was born there in August 1961, but they always found room for comrades. The large ground-floor room could accommodate twenty-odd people sleeping on the floor. Cliff has given a vivid description of the arrival of the young Scottish comrades.[59] They included Ross Pritchard, Bill Thomson and Gus Macdonald.

To Gus Macdonald Cliff seemed preferable to the other Trotskyist currents, being more open-minded and humorous. Macdonald stayed with Cliff and Chanie for about nine months. He found the household chaotic but warm, and got on well with Cliff. In turn Cliff had great hopes of Macdonald's potential, telling him on one occasion that he could sell the New Testament to rabbis. But at the same time Macdonald began to develop reservations about Cliff. He felt he had a messianic element similar to Gerry Healy, and disliked the feel of a group built around a guru figure. He also felt Cliff's attitude to people was instrumental – if people were not useful they were ostracised. In 1964 Macdonald left the IS and went to work for *Tribune*.[60]

Other members, including Peter Bain and Ian Mooney, remained in Glasgow. This was a solidly working class group, and in many ways the most successful branch of the organisation. By 1963 it had 76 members and one shop steward was selling a hundred copies of *Labour Worker* in the Singer factory.[61]

But there was one recruit from a quite different background. Paul Foot was son of Sir Hugh Foot, who had been an Assistant District Commissioner in Palestine in the 1930s. Foot had just graduated from Oxford University, where he had come under the influence of a very talented member of the SLL, Colwyn Williamson. In Glasgow he became active in the YS and encountered Cliff. Many years later he wrote a vivid description of their first meeting:

> The first I heard of Tony Cliff...was from Gus Macdonald... Forty years ago, Gus was a charismatic leader of the Govan and Gorbals Young Socialists and had an awesome reputation from a Clydeside apprentices' strike. In late 1961, he reckoned it was time the Young Socialists took some serious lessons in Marxist theory and arranged a weekend school to be addressed by two leaders of an obscure Trotskyist sect called the International Socialists.
>
> Gus and I met the couple in an airport lounge. I can still see them coming in: Michael Kidron, smart, suave, urbane, and Tony Cliff, short and scruffy, looking and sounding like a rag doll. As we mumbled through the niceties of introductions, the rag doll looked irritated and shy. We climbed into a taxi.
>
> As we did so, I saw a newspaper poster about events in the Congo, and remarked, partly to break the silence, that I'd never really understood the Congo. Quick as a flash, the rag doll came to life, and started jabbering with amazing speed and energy. I can't remember exactly what he said, but I do remember my clouds of doubt and misunderstanding suddenly disappearing and the role of the contestants in the Congo, including the United Nations, becoming brutally clear.[62]

CND and the rise of the New Left had a major impact on the student milieu. A number of student activists were recruited.

Nigel Harris had first encountered Cliff when chairman of the National Association of Labour Student Organisations. When he moved to London he and his wife Tirril visited Cliff's home and were bombarded with demands to join the SRG. He found Cliff a "great guy", humorous and ebullient. But it was Kidron rather than Cliff who really impressed him and was the decisive factor in persuading him to join the SRG. Tirril found Chanie warm and welcoming; she thought Cliff and Chanie were uncorrupted, unlike many on the left.[63]

From 1962 onwards there was a vigorous IS student grouping in Oxford. Richard Kirkwood first heard Cliff when he spoke to the Socialist Group of the University Labour Club in the autumn of 1961. He was impressed by Cliff, and attended an SRG aggregate meeting in early 1962. He was struck by the democracy of the group; Cliff was on the losing side of a vote. The combination of libertarianism and Trotskyism in the SRG appealed to him. In 1965 when he moved to London he stayed at Cliff's for two or three weeks while he looked for somewhere to live. Cliff and Chanie would open their home to any comrade moving to London; they were generous and hospitable, though their lifestyle was truly chaotic, with cups, babies' bottles, papers and books strewn everywhere.[64]

Ian Birchall was a postgraduate student who had been active in CND. He supported the *Tribune* left but found it intellectually inadequate. So when he heard first Kidron, then Cliff, he discovered a coherent way of looking at modern capitalism. Cliff was always enthusiastic to involve and develop new comrades; when he found out that Birchall knew some Western European languages he promptly ensured that he was given responsibilities for international contacts that went far beyond his limited political experience.

Fred Lindop heard Cliff and Kidron speak in Oxford. Kidron was an impressive academic, but Cliff was much more immediate and involved in experience.[65] Richard Hyman first heard Cliff speak in Oxford in around 1963. He was impressed by Cliff's passion and rhetoric, and also by the remarkable range of intellectuals in the tiny IS group, which he decided to join.[66]

Colin Barker joined the SRG in Oxford in 1962 and attended a national meeting at Cliff's home later that year. Initially, like a number of others, he was more impressed by Kidron than by Cliff. In 1963 he moved to Manchester, and in 1964 he persuaded the student Labour Club to set up a debate between the Labour Party, the CP, the SLL and Cliff. Nobody had heard of the IS, but Cliff made a very good impression. He also spoke to a small meeting in Barker's student room – four people sat on the bed and Cliff had the one chair. At the end all four joined, creating the first Manchester branch.[67]

Chris Harman was involved in an independent youth group while still at school in Watford in 1961. He went to the Partisan and also took part in the Aldermaston march, where he bought a copy of *International Socialism*, assuming from the high standard of production that this must be a large organisation. Through Nigel Harris he got Cliff to come and speak in Watford. Cliff offered the choice: Marx and Engels (overthrow capitalism) or Marks and Spencer (accept capitalist competition). In the autumn of 1961 Harman went to Leeds University, where he and Mike Heym tried to build a branch in face of tough competition from the CP and the SLL. Cliff would visit about twice a year and speak to meetings of between 12 and 20.[68]

Richard Kuper first heard Cliff when he spoke to the Labour Club in Cambridge in January 1964. He was "entranced". He was part of a group in the university who were interested in Marxism, but found Russia a stumbling-block. Cliff overcame this with the brilliance of his analysis and there was soon an IS group in Cambridge with 16 members. Kuper was also struck by the fact that Cliff was a classical Jewish figure with a Jewish sense of humour; this resonated with his own background. When Kuper moved to London later that year Cliff soon discovered he had a van and gave him the job of collecting from the typesetter the lead with which the paper was printed. Kuper found that IS meetings made sense of the world, whereas little of what he was studying at the LSE helped him to understand the world.[69]

Not all recruits came through the YS and student politics. Ewa Widowson, in her first teaching job, found herself talking to Chanie Rosenberg in the staff room, and was soon invited to meetings where she met Cliff. Having grown up a Polish nationalist she was initially bewildered by Cliff, but eventually came to see how the state capitalist theory explained what was happening in Poland.[70]

In December 1962 the membership was, for the first time, just over 100.[71] By 1964 it was more than 200. More important, it was this new influx which provided the central core of the organisation for the next two decades. There were losses, and some would achieve advancement in the labour movement or in the academic world through retreat from their revolutionary principles, but a good many remained for 20 years and more; quite a few are still members at the time of writing. The experience of this period built up a powerful sense of loyalty.

Cliff's part in all this was extremely important. In the 1950s he had functioned mainly as a writer, while at the same time his constant enthusiasm had served to hold together a tiny, marginal organisation. Now his role widened. For the new members, he functioned as both a theoretician and a day-to-day leader. He inspired both political agreement and personal affection.

On the face of it there was a great gap between Cliff and the new membership. They were young, mostly born during or just after the Second World War. Though many came from working class families and would have heard tell of the hardships and struggles of the 1930s, they had grown up during the post-war boom; they had not experienced mass unemployment or deep poverty. Most of them were young and single – and in some cases highly promiscuous. The culture around *Young Guard* was one of beer-drinking and folk-singing.

Cliff was 43 in 1960, a married man and father of three. He did not pretend to share or even to sympathise with the lifestyle of his younger followers. He was generally abstemious and rarely went to the pub after meetings. He regarded folk song with the same blank indifference as all other forms of music. On the other hand, although his own life had been much tougher than that of the younger generation, he rarely moralised. On the contrary, he recognised the fact that having not experienced defeat made the new generation all the more likely to set their sights higher.

So what was it that drew young people towards Cliff? Certainly there was an element of charisma. Though he spoke relatively little of his Palestinian years, it was generally known that he had been a revolutionary and had been imprisoned. His foreign accent and imperfect grasp of the structures of spoken English gave him an exotic air, enhanced by his total lack of interest in clothes or personal appearance. There was certainly something of the legendary professional revolutionary about him.

But it was 5 percent charisma and 95 percent politics. What really attracted his young supporters was his political understanding. His breadth of knowledge of the Marxist classics, of the Russian revolutionary movement and of current developments throughout the world, was combined with an ability to explain things simply, to sum up a complex problem in an image, a joke or an anecdote.

Cliff at this time seemed to have inexhaustible patience. His home was always open to young comrades, and he found time to discuss things with them and to pass on his experience and knowledge. He knew that only the masses would make history, but that individuals were necessary to build an organisation. He took his share of household duties, looking after his young children while Chanie was at work. He was a devoted parent; when one of his children was suffering from tinnitus, he was "like a wild animal" because his child was in pain.[72] But his domestic skills were limited. Chris Davison recalls visiting Chatterton Road when Cliff was decorating; he was putting up wallpaper, but had not removed the furniture, simply putting the wallpaper round the sides of the wardrobe.[73] There was little luxury; any spare money went into the organisation. When Jim Nichol was staying at Chatterton Road he once had to help hunt down the back of the sofa to find change to pay for domestic necessities.[74]

It was at this time that Cliff really began to blossom as a speaker. He had been, according to accounts,[75] an impressive speaker even while in Palestine. But in the 1950s he had relatively few opportunities to develop. Now he was being drawn into a routine which would last for the rest of his life. From 1961 he began to speak widely for the National Council of Labour colleges (NCLC), addressing Finsbury Park AEU on the 1962 pay pause, and giving classes on socialist theory in Plaistow, Croydon, Tottenham and Loughton. (There is a bizarre reference to someone called "Cliff Rosenberg" speaking to Shoreditch French Polishers on immigration – one or other of the indefatigable couple.[76]) In addition there were YS branches and student groups inviting him to speak. Cliff's role as a speaker was undoubtedly one of the main factors in spreading the influence of the IS.

In addition to ordinary meetings, Cliff gave a series of 12 lectures on basic Marxism to YS branches and NCLC groups.* These covered historical materialism, the economic analysis of capitalism and the nature of the state, and set out the case for revolutionary socialism against reformism, stressing the centrality of the self-emancipation of the working class. They made a great impact

---

* The version of these lectures as reproduced in *Marxist Theory After Trotsky: Selected Writings vol 3*, pp295-310, is not the original version, and contains a number of points updated to the early 1970s. There is a copy of the original version, priced at one shilling and published by the NCLC, at Rich. MS 1117/box 209/file 2.

on many young socialists who heard them, as is shown by an organisation report from June 1963:

> Over the last few months cde. TC has given seven separate series of lectures on Marxist theory. Despite uneven results the completed series resulted in approximately 40 new members.

Given that the total membership was just 197 the impact of the lectures had been extremely significant.[77] Cliff justifiably complained at the burden of so much lecturing and it was agreed to prepare a list of 12 lecturers to share the work;[78] unfortunately none of them was likely to make anything like the impact Cliff did.

A speech by Cliff was a performance as much as a lecture, in which Cliff certainly drew on his love of the theatrical. Yet content always prevailed over form. Cliff had rejected the formalism which he believed underlay the orthodox Trotskyist theory of Russian society. He was contemptuous of formalism and appeals to constitutional correctness in political organisation. In his public speaking he ignored formal conventions. Most speakers begin by thanking the chair and the body which has invited them. Cliff spurned any such courtesies. He often began with the terse formula "I'll start by saying", which enabled him to move directly to his first point.

Though Cliff had been in Britain for well over a decade, he still had (and retained until his death) a distinctive foreign accent. He had never troubled to study the niceties of English sentence construction. When his sister-in-law heard him speaking in England, she recalled, "He spoke in English, but I heard Hebrew".[79] He had a gift for mixed metaphors. Often he only managed approximations to well-known expressions and exclamations – "My bloody good God!", "I wouldn't touch it with a barge".[80] Pronunciation of English words was often random. On one occasion when talking about racism he intrigued his audience by noting that in the 1930s workers had been prejudiced against Italian immigrants whom they had referred to as "yetis" (he was later informed that the term was "Eyeties"). These details combined to produce a remarkably idiosyncratic speaking style which was generally able to hold its audience far better than many more conventional speakers. In particular it made his speaking more accessible to those whose knowledge of English was less than perfect. Turkish comrades, for example, noted that they understood Cliff more easily than conventional English speakers.[81]

He also had the gift of summing up a complex argument in a simple concrete phrase. After 1968 he would sum up the case against working inside the Labour Party by saying, "You don't move a wheelbarrow by jumping inside it".[82] The centrality of profit to capitalism was summed up by, "If you are allergic to petrol, for heaven's sake buy a camel." The very oddness of his metaphors could make them more vivid: "When people are dead, there is nothing interesting about it – it is only when there are convulsions".[83]

A speech by Cliff was notable for the jokes and anecdotes it contained. Unlike speakers who thought that they could only prove their seriousness by solemnity and humourlessness, Cliff had learnt (perhaps from his early love, the poet Heine) that there was no contradiction between being profoundly serious and being funny at the same time. He aimed simultaneously to entertain, to educate and to enthuse his audience.

Cliff's jokes were sometimes in bad taste, or, to use modern terminology, "politically incorrect". When asked a question which he could not answer, he would often comment, "The most beautiful woman in Paris can only give what she has got." There were many ironic allusions to his own Jewishness.

The anecdotes and stories he told were generally aimed at putting across a political point in a brief and memorable form. Often the stories were not original. He would tell of the flea which spent all day buzzing around the head of an ox who was ploughing, and at the end of the day said proudly, "My, haven't we ploughed a lot today." This may have come from Aesop's fable "The Gnat and the Bull", or La Fontaine's tale of the fly which claimed credit for getting a coach up a steep hill.* Doubtless it had a general moral sense. But for Cliff it was specifically a criticism of those individuals and political grouplets who claimed the credit when much larger social forces had been responsible.

Many of the jokes came from traditional Jewish humour. One of his favourite stories was that of the rabbi and the goat. A man went to the rabbi in deep distress, complaining that his living conditions were intolerable. He, his wife and children, as well as his grandparents, all

---

* Gramsci also frequently used the image of the fly who believes he has pulled the coach to the top of the hill. So it is possible that Gramsci was Cliff's source (communication from Joseph Choonara, September 2010).

lived in two rooms. The rabbi listened sympathetically, then told him that the whole family should move into just one of the rooms. A few days later the man came back, pleading that things had now become absolutely impossible. The overcrowding was bringing him to total despair. Again the rabbi listened, and told the man that he should bring his goat into the room with the family. They man obeyed, but a few days later, on the brink of losing his reason, he went back to the rabbi. The rabbi told him to take the goat outside. The next day the man returned, overflowing with thanks. "Things are so much better now," he told the rabbi.

This was a traditional Jewish story,[84] and originally satirised human folly. But in Cliff's hands it acquired a far more concrete meaning, the way in which our rulers and employers can manipulate our expectations to make us think we have gained an improvement when we have not. It fitted perfectly the scenario of the employer who announces several hundred redundancies and then, when workers resist, cuts the number to a mere hundred, leaving the workers believing that they have won a victory.

Another story was set against the sombre background of the rise of Hitler, but gave a vivid illustration of the way in which a situation can look radically different according to the standpoint of the observer. Two Jews were sitting in a park in Berlin in around 1930. One was reading a Zionist newspaper, the other a Nazi newspaper. The one with the Zionist paper remonstrated fiercely, "Why are you reading that disgusting Nazi paper?" The other responded, "Your paper is so depressing. Look – Jews beaten, Jews arrested, Jews killed. Look at my paper – we Jews rule the world."

Cliff spoke without notes, apart from press cuttings or quotations from a book. He would have been amazed at professional politicians who were unable to speak without notes or autocue. But two things distinguished him from most professional politicians: he knew what he was talking about and he said what he believed. All the information was marshalled in his head, and he was able to present a topic without preparation.* In later years his son Donny recalled that if he had to speak on a particular topic, he could phone his father who

---

* I recall meeting Cliff in the early 1970s and taking him up one flight of stairs to the room where an audience was waiting for him. Halfway up the stairs he enquired, "Tell me, Ian, what am I speaking about?" He spoke for 40 minutes, backing up his argument with detailed factual support.

within two minutes would summarise what needed to be said.[85]

In the early 1960s he must have addressed hundreds of meetings. There is a vivid account of a meeting in Oxford (attended by some 60 students[86]) published in the student paper *Isis*. It will serve to represent the many, many similar meetings he addressed at this time:

> Although his train from London…was almost an hour late, Tony Cliff, from the magazine *International Socialism*, finally arrived last Friday evening to address the Labour Club on "The Limits of De-Stalinisation". His colourful mixture of Slavonic accent, wry jokes about Stalin and his successors on the Kremlin throne, and hard facts about the impasse in all aspects of Soviet society has to be heard to be believed.
>
> The fact that the agricultural statistics published in Russia now are lower than those issued for the greater glory of Stalin does not mean that production has fallen off; in fact, it is no higher now than it was in 1916, and never had been. Khrushchev is no more successful than his political mentor was. He has handed over the machinery from the tractor stations to the peasants themselves; he has cut down the size of the tiny plots of land owned by each peasant. Yet the peasant relies on this plot for HALF his income and the collective farms continue to fail.
>
> The secret of Stalin's industrial success was that he allowed Russian agriculture to stagnate, and siphoned off the manpower into the towns. But the miserable output of the collectives goes far deeper. The only Communist countries with successful agriculture are Poland and Yugoslavia, where the vast majority of farmland remains in private hands. A peasant is not like a factory worker – if he has no will to work for his boss (which can mean either a capitalist or a member of the Russian ruling bureaucracy) then he does not work. Who can lay the blame on him rather than someone else. Nature, the weather…?
>
> But is even Russian industry so very spectacular? Russian machinery and technique is in advance of the USA, and the labour force is larger, yet production is only one half as large. The distortions in the Russian price mechanism have grown so huge in the past thirty years that no one knows the real prices any more. When the Russians trade abroad they have to rely on world market prices, and it is a Polish joke that when they have world Communism they will have to preserve one capitalist country to give them an idea of prices!
>
> The bureaucracy has grown larger and larger in a tragic-comic caricature

of Parkinson's Law. Especially under the influence of Stalin's purges, every official has come to need someone to tell him what to do, someone else to tell him what to think, someone else to watch him, someone else to denounce him... They too are demoralised and inefficient.

People tend to speak in abstract terms of the bureaucracy. Otto Bauer said in 1936 that Russia must become democratic, because advanced industrial society demands it. Two years later came the Zinoviev and Kamenev trials – the need is for realistic analysis, not abstract theory. The realistic observer will see that the theorist's argument that the bureaucracy only receives a tiny proportion of the national income is irrelevant when a Deputy of the Supreme Soviet earns 1,200 roubles for a four-day session and a charwoman earns 14 roubles 85 kopecks in the same period. Isaac Deutscher may write of the great advance in Soviet education, but only 2 percent of the population are reaching the top of the educational pyramid.

The crisis in the Soviet economy is a permanent one, which Khrushchev cannot overcome. Nor does he dare publish the true figures about production for the workers of the "workers' state" to read. In Russia, any criticism is a criticism of the state. What Khrushchev can do is patch up the crisis. It is generally thought that the Sino-Soviet split is ideological in content, but Marx, whom the Russians claim to follow, believed in looking for economic causes. Every time Khrushchev shouts "peaceful co-existence" he means "cut off aid to China"...

The conflict between Khrushchev and Mao must be seen in concrete form, and not merely in terms of mutual accusations of "Trotskyism". Russia is in a state of transition not to democracy, but to a revolution of rising expectations. Reforms are instituted by a ruling class in order to mitigate discontent, but mitigation is fatal. The French Revolution began not among the poorest members of the community, but among the more prosperous ones. The workers' revolution in Hungary in 1956 followed the beginning of de-Stalinisation and liberalism. Tsar Nikolai I died in his bed in 1855. His son, Alexander II, saw that the advance of the Russian economy depended on reforms; in his reign the serfs were liberated, local government was set up, the jury system was instituted, censorship was lifted, and so on.

But reforms, by which the ruling class attempts to remain a ruling class, cannot go beyond a certain point unless the social system is to be changed. Alexander II, unlike his despotic father, was assassinated, and opened the door to the Revolution of 1917. If Nikita Sergeyevitch were not so bald, he might be turning grey at the thought of the future of Russia.[87]

In 1961 a new monthly paper was launched aimed specifically at trade union activists. It was originally entitled *Industrial Worker*, but soon was renamed *Labour Worker*, and was edited from London by Karl Dunbar. It was not a great success; a meeting in December 1962 was informed that members took "no interest" in it and that "the financial situation is the worst ever".[88] In May 1963 the paper was transferred to Glasgow where Paul Foot became editor. The editorial board included Harry McShane, although he was not a member of the IS group. While industrial reports continued to form a major part of the paper, it became increasingly oriented to entry work in the Labour Party. *Socialist Review* had ceased publication in 1962.

Despite his heavy commitment to public speaking and to building the organisation, Cliff continued to write extensively. The new theoretical journal provided him with an opportunity to develop arguments at greater length and in more depth than had been possible in *Socialist Review*. He contributed many book reviews, several under the pseudonym M Turov, often on Russia and Eastern Europe. He continued to observe developments in China, and the first issue of *International Socialism* contained a piece on the Chinese communes under his academic name Ygael Gluckstein.[89]

Now he was spreading his theoretical interests more widely. It was no longer adequate to define himself, and his group, by a mere negation – the denial that Russia was a manifestation of working class power. Those involved in the heated and often bitter debates in the YS required an analysis that went beyond mere sloganising, and they looked to Cliff, Kidron and MacIntyre to provide it for them. The early 1960s saw the publication of a number of Cliff's most influential articles.

"Trotsky on Substitutionism" appeared in 1960.[90] The editorial note accompanying the article said that Cliff was "currently engaged on a political assessment of Trotsky". Among Cliff's papers are four typewritten sheets headed "A very rough draft of a synopsis of a book on Trotsky".[91] This was conceived as a series of critical studies after the fashion of *Rosa Luxemburg*, rather than the more extensive biography which Cliff was to write later. There were to be ten chapters:

> The Man
>
> The "Permanent Revolution"
>
> "Socialism in One Country"
>
> Trotsky on Economic Planning
>
> Trotsky on the Workers' Party
>
> Trotsky on the "Transition a Programme"
>
> The Colonial Revolution
>
> Nationalism and Internationalism
>
> Trotsky on Fascism
>
> Trotsky on Literature, Art and Science

The articles on substitutionism and deflected permanent revolution originated here. If more was written it did not survive.

The section on the *Transitional Programme* contained an interesting reflection on consciousness:

> Socialist thinking usually falls between two stools: either emphasis on the need to change the environment as a precondition to a change in consciousness or to change consciousness as a precondition to a change in social environment. The struggle to change both is integrated by the "Transitional Programme". This is extremely important to anaemic socialism wilting in an affluent society.

The section on the workers' party was divided into three parts: (1) Trotsky's critique of substitutionism before 1917; (2) his position from 1917 to 1923 – "The party is always right"; (3) after 1923 a position similar to, yet different from, the one he held before 1917.

It was on some of these arguments that "Trotsky on Substitutionism" was based. In the article Cliff followed on from *Rosa Luxemburg* and took on the basic arguments about the role and structure of a revolutionary party. In doing so he was polemicising against the supporters of the SLL/*Keep Left* tendency, but also against the British followers of the French group Socialisme ou Barbarie, who would shortly form the *Solidarity* group.*

It should be remembered that when Cliff wrote this article he had never – apart from a brief period in the RCP – been in a revolutionary organisation of more than 100 members. It was thus based on historical study rather than practical experience. Critics might counterpose some of its formulations to Cliff's later practice in the leadership of a revolutionary organisation. Certainly life threw up many problems which Cliff had not envisaged when writing this article. But he encouraged the reprinting of the article after 1968,[92] and it remained in print for a good part of his lifetime. It therefore stands as a statement of how he conceived of revolutionary organisation.

Cliff began with Trotsky's 1904 pamphlet *Our Political Tasks*. This was unavailable in English at the time, and was known to English readers only through the discussion in Deutscher's *The Prophet Armed*.[93] Cliff quoted from the Russian original.

Trotsky had warned that Lenin's conception would lead to a situation in which "the organisation of the party substitutes itself for the party as a whole; then the Central Committee substitutes itself for the organisation; and finally the 'dictator' substitutes himself for the Central Committee". Cliff praised this insight as showing Trotsky's "prophetic genius", but went on to argue that it must be understood in historical context. He rejected the idea that Bolshevism had led directly to Stalinism.

Cliff argued that "the Bolshevik Party had never been a monolithic or totalitarian party... Internal democracy had always been of the utmost importance in party life," and he illustrated this with a number of examples. It was not the Bolshevik concept of organisation that caused the problems, but rather the nature of the Russian Revolution, which had been a combination of a working class and a peasant revolution. The working class had been a small minority, and under the impact of post-revolutionary conditions, even that minority had begun to disintegrate. This produced a decline in inner-party democracy: "It was as if they were in a small rickety boat in the midst of rapids. The atmosphere of free

---

* The leading figure in *Solidarity*, Chris Pallis, was a member of the editorial board of *International Socialism* under the name Martin Grainger.

discussion necessarily died."

He showed that the rise of Stalinism was the product of objective circumstances. However, this did not mean a fatalistic approach to the failure of the Russian Revolution; its fate was sealed by the failure of the international revolution, and that was not determined in advance: "Only the expansion of the revolution could have spared Bolshevism from this tragic fate... Only abstentionists and cowards could advise the Bolsheviks not to go to the limit of the revolutionary potentialities of the Russian proletariat for fear of finding themselves at the end of the cul-de-sac."

Cliff then went on to make some more general considerations about the nature of the revolutionary party. He explained the necessity for a revolutionary party from the uneven consciousness of the working class:

> The fact that a revolutionary party is at all needed for the socialist revolution shows that there is an unevenness in the level of culture and consciousness of different sections and groups of workers. If the working class were ideologically a homogeneous class there would not have been any need for leadership.

This argument was absolutely central to Cliff's account of the revolutionary party. If the working class were homogeneously progressive, then no party would be needed; if it were homogeneously reactionary than revolutionaries might as well pack up and go home. For Cliff it was the contradictions and conflicts *within* the class that produced the need for the party, which represented the most developed and militant sections of the class.

This led logically to another point which was central to Cliff's concept of the party – that it must be a mass party, drawing in considerable numbers of militant workers. He was contemptuous of the pretensions of small groups to claim to be the vanguard of the class: "From this it is clear that little groups cannot in any way substitute for the mass revolutionary party, not to say for the mass of the working class".*

He went on to consider the nature of revolutionary leadership,

---

* At around this time Cliff used to tell the story of how Gerry Healy had claimed that the SLL had already got the cadres for the revolution. Cliff had responded, "You don't have the cadres for a sanitary inspection of Tottenham." (author's recollection)

and identified three different forms which it could take:

> One can visualise three kinds of leadership that for lack of better names we shall call those of the teacher, the foreman and the companion in struggle. The first kind of leadership shown by small sects is "blackboard socialism" (in Britain an extreme example of this sort is the SPGB) in which didactic methods take the place of participation in struggle. The second kind, with foreman-worker or officer-soldier relations, characterises all bureaucratic reformist and Stalinist parties: the leadership sits in a caucus and decides what they will tell the workers to do, without the workers actively participating. What characterises both these kinds of leadership is the fact that directives go only one way: the leaders conduct a monologue with the masses.
>
> The third kind of leadership is analogous to that between a strike committee and the workers on strike, or a shop steward and his mates. The revolutionary party must conduct a dialogue with the workers outside it. The party, in consequence, should not invent tactics out of thin air, but put as its first duty to learn from the experience of the mass movement and then generalise from it.

From this he concluded:

> The revolutionary party that seeks to overthrow capitalism cannot accept the notion of a discussion on policies inside the party without the participation of the mass of the workers – policies which are then brought "unanimously" ready-made to the class. Since the revolutionary party cannot have interests apart from the class, all the party's issues of policy are those of the class, and they should therefore be thrashed out in the open, in its presence.

In December 1960 a general strike broke out in Belgium. The government, faced with general economic difficulties aggravated by the particular problems caused by the rapid end to colonial rule in the Congo, attempted to make the working class pay with a series of attacks on living standards and the welfare state. The strike lasted four weeks and brought the country to a standstill. The situation was contained and Belgian capitalism survived intact.

Nonetheless it was an event of some significance. For the first time since the upheavals immediately following the Second World War there had been a mass militant struggle by a Western European working class. The idea, advanced by some social theorists, that the working class was now totally integrated into capitalism and no longer a threat, had suffered something of a blow. And all this in a country close to Britain and not so different from it.

Cliff devoted a substantial article to the struggle.* It was the first time he had devoted a major study to the class struggle in Western Europe. He began with a survey of the economic problems of Belgium in the post-war period. He argued that the impact of the Congo debacle should not be overestimated; it did not refute the general view of modern imperialism that he and Kidron were developing.† He then looked at the specific traditions of the Belgian labour movement, and the experience of previous general strikes in that country, and noted the particular circumstances of the linguistic divide between Walloons and Flemings. All this showed a relatively cautious approach to the events; there was no indication that such events were likely to recur, nor that Western capitalism faced any immediate threat.

Yet for Cliff what was central was the question of working class self-activity and self-organisation. The strike was proof that the working class was still ready to play its historic role:

> Years of full employment and "affluence" may put a gloss of conformism on the working class, but they also strengthen its self-confidence and combativeness. The "apathy" is transitory at worst. If workers who face deterioration on the present scale in their conditions show such militancy and revolutionary fervour, what heights of heroism and initiative will workers scale when the contradictions in world capitalism reach really tremendous dimensions, as they are sure to in the future?

---

* There are two versions of this article, one in *Socialist Review* (February 1961) and one in *International Socialism* 4 (Spring 1961). They are largely identical but the *Socialist Review* version contains a section on the role of Mandel and *La Gauche* which is missing in *International Socialism*. It is possible that the *International Socialism* version was cut because the journal was still conceived as a "broad" publication, and some members of the editorial board were very hostile to Mandel.

† Arguing that Lenin's theory of imperialism needed radical updating, Kidron wrote, "Taking Lenin's 'last stage' literally, colonial independence and the continuation of capitalism are incompatible. And yet we have both – in increasing quantities. Moreover, opposition to colonial independence, although evident enough in the metropolitan countries and brutal enough overseas, has had in most cases little of the spirit of the 'last ditch stand' one would expect from a society fighting for its existence." (M Kidron, "Imperialism – Highest Stage but One", *International Socialism* 9 (Summer 1962))

In particular he stressed the way in which the strike had broken down the division between politics and economics which was so deeply rooted in conventional labour movement attitudes, not through abstract propaganda, but through the concrete experience of the real movement:

> All reformists see a Chinese wall between political struggle for economic reforms and the political struggle for revolution. The mass strike exposes the hollowness of reformism. The police and army – the political weapons of the ruling class – are there for all to see as decisive factors in the struggle. The mass strike is the best demonstration for Lenin's saying that politics is nothing but concentrated economics.

Hence he pointed out that a general strike alone could never overthrow capitalism, and that to achieve complete victory armed insurrection was required. He noted with approval the fact that "already at the beginning of the Belgian strike efforts were made to draw the soldiers to the side of the workers". He pointed out that the logic of a general strike raises, in the most concrete fashion possible, the question of workers' control, and hence the creation of "embryonic forms of dual power":

> When, in the Belgian strike, coal merchants go to the strike committee to get a permit to take a certain amount of coal from stock and deliver it to authorised persons – old people, hospitals, etc., who is the master in the country?
>
> When workers, coming to repair a damaged sewer, carry placards "We are on strike; we work by permission of the strike committee and for humanitarian reasons", who is the sovereign power?

Such an analysis raised the question of political leadership. He showed the inadequacies of both the Belgian Socialist Party and the Communist Party. Despite his previous brushes with Mandel, he identified the role of Mandel's grouping within the Socialist Party as the most positive element in the situation:

> To the present writer it seems that the only revolutionary and realistic lead was given by one national paper – *La Gauche*. This is a weekly of the extreme Left of the Socialist Party including a number of Trotskyists which has quite considerable influence, especially among the young Socialists.

Cliff did not agree with some of Mandel's left critics, who believed that *La Gauche* was too uncritical of the left trade union leader André Renard, who opposed the widespread demand for a march on Brussels.* Cliff believed that since it was not a revolutionary situation Mandel had been right.[94]

Cliff's next major article, "The Labour Party in Perspective",[95] broke new ground for him. He had now lived in Britain for around 15 years, but this was the first article he had devoted to the British labour movement. The question of the Labour Party was now of central importance to the organisation. Cliff had played little part in the debate on Labour Party entry which had divided the RCP in its last days. The SRG, at its foundation, had decided to operate inside the Labour Party, but this was entrism for want of anything better rather than with any clear perspective.

After the unilateralist victory in 1960 the tensions in the Labour Party had become much deeper. Many of those radicalised by CND had joined the Labour Party and especially the YS. But now there were various views about the way forward. The SLL, with its provocative and confrontational behaviour, was moving towards an open break with Labour. Those around Pallis and the new *Solidarity* grouping were opposed to work in the Labour Party.

Elsewhere in the Trotskyist left entrism was being elevated from a tactic to a principle. The Selby group in Glasgow argued that revolutionary publications should be sold only to known Labour Party members.[96] Within Cliff's own group there was the danger of members being totally sucked into Labour Party activity. Some members had been elected councillors, and there was a discussion of the value of such work in *International Socialism*.[97] Two members of the group, John Palmer and Syd Bidwell, were parliamentary candidates in the 1964 election.

Cliff began with an account of the Labour Party from its origins, in which he drew heavily on the recent book by Ralph Miliband,

---

* See S Simon, "The Belgian General Strike", *Revolutionary History*, Vol 7, No 1 (1998), in particular pp13-33. The IS distributed the original pamphlet by Simon, published in Paris in 1961. The article by Xavier Mourre, "Belgium: Success Beyond our Grasp", which appeared alongside Cliff's piece in *International Socialism* 4, was very critical of *La Gauche* over the question of the March on Brussels. The Agitator/New Generation Pamphlet *Belgium: The General Strike* by Maurice Brinton (Chris Pallis, 1961) was also critical of Mandel. For an account more sympathetic to Mandel, showing his reservations about Renard, see JW Stutje, *Ernest Mandel*, London, 2009, pp76-77.

Parliamentary Socialism.[98] [*] His main point was to show that the Labour Party had never been a militantly socialist party:

> The traditional picture of the Labour Party drawn by many on the left is that of a socialist party with a glorious socialist record, betrayed only now and again by a MacDonald or a Gaitskell – a couple of aberrations in an immaculate story.

Then he came on to the real problem for socialists in the 1960s – the apparent passivity of the labour movement, not only in Britain, but throughout Western capitalism. Why did British workers show "a stubborn adherence to reformism, a belief in the possibility of major improvement in conditions under capitalism, and a rejection of the revolutionary overthrow of capitalism"?

To explain this Cliff had to challenge some of the main dogmas of orthodox Trotskyism. Using the arguments of his 1957 article, he rejected Lenin's notion that merely a tiny conservative minority was holding back the "the revolutionary urges of the mass of the workers". He also rejected the political perspective of Trotsky's *Transitional Programme*. While acknowledging that he had himself accepted Trotsky's analysis in the 1930s, he scorned those who simply repeated Trotsky's formulations in a different world; as he observed sourly, "Parrots have never made a revolution." Reformism maintained its grip because it fitted the daily experience of most workers in a period of prolonged boom:

> So long as capitalism is expanding and the conditions of the workers are improving, and are seen to be able to be ameliorated within the framework of the present social system, reformism has stronger roots than revolutionary socialism.

Here Cliff's determinism was in the ascendant. Basically he was arguing that while capitalism was able to permit a certain number of reforms, there was little that revolutionaries could do to counter it, other than on the level of propaganda. Yet this did not mean a capitulation to reformism. For Cliff the class struggle was paramount, and this continued even in the conditions of the boom. He was able to identify various tendencies in the present situation which showed a positive development in working-class consciousness:

---

[*] Cliff respected Miliband's historical work, but was critical of his political practice. As he used to say, "He wrote a very good book – but he never read it" (communication from Sabby Sagall, November 2010)

The vulgar "Marxist" view sees in poverty only a cause for rebellion, and in reforms only a numbing of fighting ardour. Actually empty stomachs may lead not to rebellion but, especially if it is the stomachs of workers' wives and children, to submission. On the other hand, a full stomach may lead not to contentment, but to self-confidence and assertiveness...

Workers today are far more self-confident. They will not allow themselves to be pushed around. They go so far [as] to resist the sacking of their mates, invading the prerogative of management regarding hiring and firing, fighting for an element of workers' control in the midst of capitalism...

Even the assertion of many workers that they are no different from the middle class is not only a negative, damaging element from the standpoint of socialism. No, workers declare thereby that they are not inferior to other people. The idea of "the deserving poor" is gone – no more "the rich man in his castle and the poor man at his gate", the idea that our "betters" are born to rule.

With self-reliance comes also a much greater generosity of spirit, so clearly shown in the sympathy strikes of thousands of lorry drivers, dockers and engineers in support of the nurses' pay claim this May.

Here Cliff identified a number of features of working class struggle that would become more prominent with the rise in militancy of the late 1960s and early 1970s.

Cliff rejected two scenarios that were commonly discussed on the left. On the one hand he argued that it was improbable that the Labour Party would split, creating a new left-wing party. On the other hand, he argued that there was no likelihood of the left capturing the leadership of the Labour Party. Therefore, revolutionaries should continue to be active in the Labour Party:

> Marxists should not set themselves up as a party or embryo of a party of their own. They should remember that the working class looks to the Labour Party as the political organisation of the class (and no doubt when a new wave of political activity spreads among the working class millions of new voters will flock to its banner and hundreds of thousands will join it actively).

These were issues that Cliff would have to seriously rethink over the coming two or three years.

"Deflected Permanent Revolution"[99] was the second of Cliff's two major reappraisals of Trotsky's thought. This went to the heart of the argument: for "orthodox Trotskyists" the theory of permanent revolution had been the essence of Trotsky's originality as a Marxist thinker. The theory had been of great importance for Cliff himself; his earliest writings were an attempt to apply the theory to the Middle East.

But an understanding of the post-war world, and especially of what was now often called the "Third World", required a critical examination of Trotsky's theory. Cliff began by setting out for younger readers the central points of the theory.[*] He showed how the theory had given an accurate account of the development of the Russian Revolution of 1917, and had been superior to the earlier positions adopted by Lenin.

However, two more recent revolutions in the Third World, which had created great interest among Western socialists, seemed to throw the theory into question. These were the Chinese Revolution of 1949 and the Cuban Revolution of 1959. Drawing mainly on material he had already used in *Mao's China*, Cliff showed that "the industrial working class played no role whatsoever in the victory of Mao". As for Castro's revolution, it was "a case in which neither the working class nor the peasantry played a serious role, but where middle class intellectuals filled the whole arena of struggle".

Cliff then attempted to explain why the theory needed to be amended. Here he showed that his determinism was by no means total. As he pointed out, Trotsky had argued that it was possible for the working class to play a revolutionary role when the bourgeoisie was conservative and cowardly, but the "revolutionary character of the young working class...is neither absolute nor inevitable". Cliff gave various reasons why the working class failed to play its revolutionary role, including the counter-revolutionary nature of the Stalinist parties.

Consequently permanent revolution was "deflected" – the role that might have been played by the working class was instead taken over by the intelligentsia, which played a much more central part

---

[*] The book had been unavailable in English for some time until it was republished by New Park (London) in 1962. In the article Cliff referred to the Russian originals of some of Trotsky's writings and to the 1947 Calcutta edition of *Permanent Revolution*.

than it had done in the Russian Revolution:

> The revolutionary intelligentsia has proved itself a much more cohesive factor in the emergent nations of today than in Tsarist Russia. Quite understandably bourgeois private property is bankrupt; imperialism is intolerable; state capitalism – through the weakening of imperialism, the growing importance of state planning, plus the example of Russia, and the organised, disciplined work of the Communist Parties – gives them a new sense of cohesion. As the only non-specialised section of society, the intelligentsia is the obvious source of a "professional revolutionary elite" which appears to represent the interests of the "nation" as against conflicting sectional and class interests. In addition, it is the section of society most imbued with the national culture, the peasants and workers having neither the leisure nor education for it.

As a result of its social and ideological situation, the intelligentsia found "totalitarian state capitalism a very attractive goal".

In concluding Cliff argued that "deflected permanent revolution" could explain developments of the colonial revolution in such countries as Ghana, India, Egypt, Indonesia, and Algeria, although it took a different form there. He did not deal with the implications of the theory for revolution in the advanced countries. But the argument was complementary to that developed by Kidron in his article "Imperialism – Highest Stage but One", where he pointed out that in modern international capitalism, "Capital does not flow overwhelmingly from mature to developing capitalist countries. On the contrary, foreign investments are increasingly made as between developed countries themselves".[100]

The deflection was not inevitable. The working class had missed one chance, but it was still there, and still exploited, though by a new set of bosses. For revolutionaries the struggle continued:

> The central theme of Trotsky's theory remains as valid as ever: the proletariat must continue its revolutionary struggle until it is triumphant the world over. Short of this target it cannot achieve freedom.

Cliff himself wrote little more on deflected permanent revolution other than to restate the basic points of the argument. But it had a significant and lasting influence on a number of his followers. In 1964 Nigel Harris drew on Cliff's work in his analysis of India,[101] and nearly 50 years later Leo Zeilig was using it to analyse modern Africa.[102] Mike Gonzalez, who has written extensively on Latin

America, states:

> On Latin America, the framework of everything I have written has been shaped by Cliff's early analysis, of Cuba but most importantly State Capitalism...his writings on Eastern Europe and Cuba were critically important for me. Because my academic milieu was very hostile to my critical take on Cuba and Chile, it was Cliff's authoritative work that gave me the confidence to take all that on.[103]

Cliff's analysis of the Cuban Revolution provoked a debate with some of his own comrades. *International Socialism* had carried two pieces on Cuba, one by Ken Coates taking a pro-Castro position,[104] and one critical of Castro by "Sergio Junco".[105] * Junco was the pseudonym of Samuel Farber, a Cuban student living in London, who had been encouraged to get in touch with Cliff and the SRG by a number of Shachtmanites in the US. [106] †

Cliff wrote a piece in the Internal Bulletin which was in effect a first draft of the section on Cuba in his "Permanent Revolution" article. Here he stressed the absence of working class activity and the middle class nature of Castro's leadership.[107]

Junco replied by accusing Cliff of fatalism and of underestimating the importance of political leadership in favour of a purely sociological analysis of the situation:

> This, unfortunately, sounds to me very like our old friend "inevitable"... Since the political will of this leadership was irrelevant to the situation and since ideological and political processes were also irrelevant, then the whole process is reduced to a twentieth century Cuban version of Greek tragedy.

Junco insisted that there were many "political and ideological facts" in the Cuban situation which did not "automatically follow from a certain *structural* framework of underdevelopment and imperialism".[108]

While Cliff was still developing his article on deflected permanent revolution, developments in Cuba threw all the major elements of

---

* Nick Howard had spent the summer of 1961 in Cuba and had written an article on his experience. Cliff was unhappy at its pro-Castro sympathies and introduced Howard to Sam Farber, who took over the article (Nick Howard interview, December 2008).

† Farber later became well known as the author of *Before Stalinism* (Oxford, 1990) and *The Origins of the Cuban Revolution Reconsidered* (Chapel Hill, 2006).

Cliff's analysis of the world situation into dramatic relief. Cuba, isolated economically and attacked militarily by the US, was obliged to develop closer economic and political links with Khrushchev's Russia. Russia then decided to build nuclear missile sites in Cuba. In October 1962 the US imposed a blockade on Cuba which brought the world to the brink of nuclear war. Though in retrospect it has been customary to applaud the skill of US president Kennedy in handling the crisis, it was clear that both of the world's superpowers were prepared to risk total destruction in pursuit of their interests. Never had "Neither Washington nor Moscow" been a more relevant slogan.

Sam Farber remembered Cliff's response to the crisis:

> When the missile crisis of October 1962 broke out I went over to Cliff's (and, of course, Chanie Rosenberg's) house near the Arsenal tube station to discuss the situation. Initially Cliff supported the slogan put forward by the orthodox Trotskyists demanding "US missiles out of Cuba". I, on the other hand, agreed with the slogan put forward by the anti-nuclear, direct action Committee of 100 for "All missiles out of Cuba". As a number of comrades active in the Young Socialist newspaper *Young Guard* began to drop by the house, it became evident that they agreed with the Committee of 100's slogan and not with Cliff's. By the end of the day, Cliff dropped the matter and the group ended up supporting the slogan "All missiles out of Cuba".[109]

While most members of the IS, quite legitimately and understandably, were profoundly frightened by the episode, Cliff took a more sanguine view. He told two young American comrades – Gavin McFadyen and Sam Farber – that the missile crisis of October 1962 would not lead to war because the rate of profit was too high.[110] Perhaps his analysis of the logic of class positions was too mechanical, and he discounted the dangers that pure accident could play in such a situation.

The Cuba crisis was a major factor in provoking, early in 1963, an open split between the leaderships of Russia and China. Cliff's major article "China-Russia: The Monolith Cracks"[111] analysed the causes and implications of the split.

Since *Mao's China* Cliff had written several articles tracing developments in China.[112] Now he explained the split, not as a disagreement about Marxist principles and strategy, but essentially in terms of the economic conflicts of interest between Russia and China. Russia was more interested in giving economic aid to uncommitted countries than to its Chinese ally. Trade between Russia and China worked to the advantage of the Russians, since "world market prices entail the exploitation of backward countries by advanced countries". This was an aspect of Russian imperialism that Cliff had already studied in *Stalin's Satellites*.

Although the Chinese rhetoric seemed more revolutionary than that of the Russians, Cliff insisted that mere words should not be taken too seriously, and that the Chinese were not authentic revolutionaries. He was caustic about the Chinese indifference to the dangers of nuclear war: "Nuclear weapons cannot be used in civil wars: popular control of nuclear weapons is a contradiction in terms." He stressed that the Indonesian Communist Party, despite its alignment with Peking, was "in no way revolutionary". (His judgement was proved right in 1965, when the Indonesian party suffered a catastrophic defeat.) He observed the "equivocation" of Fidel Castro: "While his heart is in Peking, his stomach is in Moscow."

But Cliff still saw progressive potential in the dispute. Just as the splits in the Catholic Church at the end of the Middle Ages had opened the way for radical social movements, so too the crisis of international Communism offered hope for the future.

The first manifestation of Maoism in Britain – the Committee to Defeat Revisionism, for Communist Unity, led by old Etonian Michael McCreery – was farce rather than tragedy, but within a few years Communist trade unionist militants would start moving towards Maoism.

In 1963, on the occasion of the publication of the final volume of Isaac Deutscher's biographical trilogy on Trotsky, Cliff published an essay entitled "The End of the Road: Deutscher's Capitulation to Stalinism".[113] The title was deliberately provocative, and may have seemed shocking to many on the left. At a time when Stalinist slanders against Trotsky were still widespread and Trotsky's writings were not easily available, Deutscher's books were the best introduction to Trotsky's life and thought for the generation coming into revolutionary politics in the early 1960s. Cliff did not deny the positive value of Deutscher's writings, but he was anxious to prevent Deutscher's overall political values being absorbed uncritically by his readers.

Cliff's study ranged over the whole of Deutscher's work, his extensive journalism as well as his major biographies of Stalin and Trotsky. He began by challenging Deutscher's claim that as Russia developed into a modern industrial society, there would be an inevitable move towards greater democracy and equality. Whereas Deutscher extolled the virtues of the "planned economy" in the Eastern Bloc, Cliff showed that in reality there was "economic irrationality" rather than authentic planning:

> Unable to rely on the self-activity of the people, prohibiting any working class democracy, the Kremlin has to rely on bureaucrats to control other bureaucrats. The hydra of bureaucratic anarchy and its concomitant, bureaucratic control, flourishes in the sea of workers' alienation from the means of production and their exploitation.

What particularly provoked Cliff's anger was Deutscher's claim that "Stalinism not only protects the achievements of the revolution, but also deepens and enlarges them". Deutscher believed the revolution was being carried forward not by the struggle of the working class, but rather by the Russian bureaucracy, which was extending "socialist" economic organisation across the planet.

> Deutscher draws the conclusion that in the international arena also Stalinism plays a revolutionary role... Accepting the international revolutionary role of the Russian state makes it an easy step to the conclusion that the struggle of the Powers in the Cold War is the main, or perhaps only, arena of struggle between socialism and capitalism. Deutscher informs us that from now on "...the class struggle, suppressed at the level on which it had been traditionally waged, would be fought at a different level and in different forms, as rivalry between power blocs and as cold war".[114]

Savagely, Cliff enquired, "What role in *this* class struggle can the workers play? How many H-bombs or sputniks have they?" He juxtaposed to Deutscher Marx's statement in the *Communist Manifesto*: "The proletarian movement is the self-conscious independent movement of the immense majority, in the interest of the immense majority."

For Deutscher, then, there could be no question of refusing to take sides in the Cold War; despite what he himself had written about Stalin's role, he was unequivocally on the side of the "socialist" bloc. As Cliff pointed out, Deutscher went so far as to support the Russian bureaucracy against workers' self-activity: "Deutscher opposed all the popular uprisings in Eastern Europe, from June 1953 in East Germany, to October 1956 in Poland and Hungary. He declared the latter to be counter-revolutions trying 'unwittingly to put the clock back'.[115] He cheered the Russian tanks which smashed the workers' uprisings."

Deutscher was right that changes were taking place in Russia; as Cliff observed, it was quite wrong to believe that "totalitarianism is and can only be a rigid, unchanging system of government". But those changes were merely from one form of exploitation to another: "The change from the rough, shouting foreman to the soft-spoken personnel officer does not abolish alienation nor exploitation, and the subordination of the workers to capital accumulation continues unabated."

Scathingly Cliff pointed out the appeal of Deutscher in the period of the New Left – and, as it was to transpire, for decades to come afterwards:

> Deutscherism is attractive to tired socialists whose belief that the working class could emancipate itself was destroyed by the defeats of the movement in the 1930s and then by the general political apathy of the fifties and sixties.

As well as writing these articles, Cliff was working on no fewer than three books.* The first was a full-length manuscript of 292 typescript pages – around 100,000 words – on the collectivisation of agriculture. It was a finished work, though there were many handwritten amendments and deletions; from the sources cited it appears to have been written in about 1962.[116] The manuscript was simply put into a cupboard in Cliff's home when his political priorities changed. It was discovered there after his death and is now at Warwick. Although Chanie had typed the entire manuscript, she

---

* The quantity and quality of theoretical work emanating from the tiny IS group seems all the more remarkable if one contrasts it to the lack of such activity among the orthodox Trotskyist groups. As Peter Sedgwick noted in 1970, "Except for Peter Fryer's fairly staid *The Battle for Socialism* and Tom Kemp's monograph *Theories of Imperialism* (1967), not a single book, or even any original and lengthy pamphlet, has been produced by any member of a British Trotskyist section since the thirties." (P Sedgwick, "Varieties of Socialist Thought", in B Crick and WA Robson (eds), *Protest and Discontent*, Harmondsworth, 1970, pp66-67)

had no recollection of its existence.

The book contained seven sections:

I. Collectivisation of Agriculture (General Analysis)
II. Russian Collectivisation
III. The Chinese People's Communes
IV. Communist Regime Upholds Individual Farming (Yugoslavia and V. Poland)
V. Castro's Transformation of Agriculture
VI. The Israeli Communal Farm (Kibbutz)
VII. Communism and the Peasantry

The main argument, set out in the opening section, was as follows:

> The essence of workers' rule, according to Marx – consistent democracy prevailing in the working class – cannot co-exist with coercion practised against a large mass of toiling peasants...
>
> All that has happened in the Communist countries – the revolution in backward agrarian countries, the predominance of small farming, the scarcity of capital resources, forced industrialisation, etc. etc. – has been in complete contradiction to everything Marx said about the path of the cooperative organisation of agriculture. This is partly a result of defects in Marx's understanding of the countryside – his underestimation of the difference in development of agriculture and industry – but above all it was the result of objective factors, of the "primitive capital accumulation" carried out by a State Capitalist bureaucracy. This is the theme of the rest of the present study.

A good deal of the material was published in various forms – for example, the articles on the Chinese communes, and the discussion of Cuba in the article on deflected permanent revolution. On Cuba Cliff concluded that, just as Russia had proved the impossibility of socialism in one country, "Castro's Cuba will prove the impossibility of building 'socialism in one island'."

The chapter on Israel was Cliff's first proper consideration of his native land since he had come to Britain. Given the passions which Zionism aroused, it was a strikingly balanced piece. He recognised the egalitarianism of the kibbutz – "The only inequality between members results from inequality of needs" – and acknowledged that "the agricultural achievements of the kibbutz are truly magnificent". But he also noted its military role – "the Zionist movement found the kibbutz to be an admirable weapon"- and he showed how the division of labour in the kibbutz discriminated against women.

The basic arguments of the book were condensed into an article entitled "Marxism and the collectivisation of agriculture".[117] Cliff began by pointing out that this was a "revisionist" article, that is, it was sharply critical of some basic Marxist theories of the position of agriculture in a socialist revolution. Marx had assumed that under capitalism, large-scale social production in agriculture would triumph. In fact historical experience had shown that small-scale production continues to predominate in agriculture. This posed serious problems for the role of the peasantry in a socialist revolution.

Cliff went on to examine the views of various leading Marxists on the question – Kautsky and Lenin, Bukharin and Trotsky. In conclusion he looked at the implications for a post-revolutionary society. Marx had believed that the superiority of large-scale production would mean that peasants would voluntarily abandon small individual farms in favour of large cooperative estates. On the contrary, Cliff argued, the private farm would get "a new lease of life under the socialist regime". While the socialist revolution in the long run would undermine the private farm, this would take a long time, "even decades":

> The organisation of agriculture in cooperative farms is bound to be an extremely slow process, impeded by some factors that are brought into play by the new socialist regime, not gaining much stimulation from the assumed decline of small farming under the technical superiority of the large ones.

The second book was on Keynes. A manuscript was completed, but he does not seem to have taken any steps towards getting it published.*

In 1964 Cliff published *Russia: A Marxist Analysis*.[118] Although Cliff's position defined his political following – his supporters in the YS were often described as the "state caps" – his 1955 book was almost completely unavailable. The new volume contained the whole

---

* I found some scattered sheets of this while sorting Cliff's papers after his death, but unfortunately I have been unable to locate them in the material deposited at Warwick.

of *Stalinist Russia: A Marxist Analysis* (with some changes), but had a second part devoted to "Russia after Stalin". It was financed by getting all members to buy two copies each in advance.[119]

Cliff recognised that there were important changes taking place in Russia, some of them bringing real benefits to working people, but that the system was still an exploitative one which suffered from deep contradictions.

He began by recognising the continuing crises in the main sectors of the economy. Agriculture was "bogged down in a slough of stagnation that has lasted over a quarter of a century".[120] The legacy of Stalin's policies was that Russia was compelled to import grain. Stalin's methods had led to rapid industrialisation and enabled Russia to catch up with the West. But "Stalin's siege economy with its command methods, irrationality and waste, became a greater fetter on industrial advance".[121] Khrushchev had been forced to abandon "Stalin's policy of squeezing the last ounce out of the East European satellites", but he had been unable to establish an effective "economic division of labour in the Bloc as a whole".[122]

In one of the most interesting sections of the book Cliff examined the state of the class struggle in Russia. After Stalin's death many of those in labour camps had been freed, and repressive measures against other workers had been relaxed. There were good reasons for this; as the economy developed, purely repressive policies became less effective:

> The more complicated production is, the less effective is a penalty. The latter can prevent a worker from committing a certain misdemeanour, but it cannot make him do what he does not want. If the threat of penalty stops him from loafing or absenting himself, it cannot prevent him from pretending to be busy while not really working, or from damaging equipment, stealing supplies, etc.[123]

But the use of the carrot instead of the stick was producing a new set of problems, because working class creativity and ingenuity had not been crushed:

> Increasing workers' resistance in production reveals itself in many ways. The failure of Stakhanovism and other methods of "socialist emulation" is one. The authorities decree that the norm of production shall be such and such, and bonus will be earned only after this quota. The workers declare that the norm is too high and demonstrate the fact before the

time and motion study men. Management must needs lower it, after which the workers promptly step up production and far surpass the norm – in engineering by as much as 60-80 percent![124]

He concluded a detailed study of workers' resistance in Russia with an optimistic prediction that could be more generally applied:

> The more skilled and integrated the working class the more will it not only resist alienation and exploitation, but also show an increasing contempt for its exploiters and oppressors. The workers have lost respect for the bureaucracy as technical administrators. No ruling class can continue for long to maintain itself in face of popular contempt.[125]

(Many of Cliff's insights into the problems of labour discipline would be developed further when he moved from the Russian working class to a study of British workers.)

Closely linked to the changes in labour discipline were the general relaxation of terror, although Soviet law remained far harsher than law in bourgeois-democratic states, and the retreat from Stalin's repressive nationalities policy – although the main lines of the nationalities policies did not change radically under Khrushchev.

Cliff then examined the changes in the international Communist movement following the Sino-Soviet split. He argued that in an age of defeat Russia had been "the opiate of the international labour movement". With the post-war boom the working class had acquired a new self-confidence and "such a working class, even if its horizon does not go beyond reforms, does not seek vicarious pleasure".[126] Moreover, the existence of nuclear weapons meant that the Communist parties were less important to Russian international strategy. Russia was quite happy to make deals with countries like Egypt, where Communists were jailed. China got far less aid than countries Russia was trying to win over. "It seems a country gets much more aid from Russia if it puts Communists in prison than if they are in power".[127]

The final chapter was entitled, with Cliff's characteristic optimism, "The coming Russian revolution". Most on the left, Trotskyists as well as Stalinists, believed that Russia had made the transition to a demonstrably superior post-capitalist form of society. Thus Ernest Mandel wrote in 1956:

> Growth rates averaging around 10 percent over a half-century will

provide definitive, irrefutable proof of the historical superiority of the socialised mode of production by comparison with every social form of production that humanity has known until now.[128]

Cliff, however, pointed to the fragility of the Russian order:

> Capitalist state ownership raises the ire of the masses. From the beginning of the bureaucracy's formation as a class, therefore, the sword of Damocles has hung ominously above its head. Whereas the capitalist of the sixteenth to nineteenth centuries could visualise a glorious future with himself as the representative of the whole of humanity, the Stalinist bureaucracy, today fulfilling the historical function of this capitalist, cannot but feel that its roots are in a temporary and transient concatenation of national and international circumstances. Hence its totalitarianism.[129]

For Cliff the bureaucracy was creating its own gravedigger in the form of a working class which was growing ever larger and more difficult to discipline. He saw the Hungarian rising of 1956, in which "workers spontaneously created a system of workers' councils which became the leaders of the entire people in revolt", as a model for the revolution that would eventually overthrow the state capitalist regime.[130]

Cliff did not envisage the possibility of a restoration of private capitalism in Russia. As he argued:

> From a state-owned and planned economy there can be no retracing of steps to an anarchic, private-ownership economy. And this not only, or even mainly, because there are no individuals to claim legal or historical right to ownership of the major part of the wealth. The replacement of large-scale state industry with private industry would be a technical-economic regression.[131]

He can therefore be legitimately criticised for not foreseeing the events of 1989 and after, which took place in a totally different world conjuncture. Nonetheless his work had the enormous merit of pointing to the fragility and crisis-ridden nature of Russian society at a time when most of its friends and enemies tended to see it as permanent and irreversible.

The book got a brief review in the academic journal *Soviet Studies*.[132] The reviewer, "R.S." (perhaps former Communist and pioneer of Soviet Studies Rudolf Schlesinger), had little sympathy for Cliff's project of defining the class nature of Russia, which he dismissed as a dispute about "allegedly Marxist pigeonholes".

In one way the 1964 edition of *Russia* was unique among Cliff's works in that he not only wrote it, he also printed it. In 1963 it was decided that, faced with the difficulty of finding a publisher for Cliff's book and the need to produce a regular monthly paper, the IS should establish its own printshop, and a printing machine was purchased for £375.[133] A ground floor and basement in Landseer Road (off the Holloway Road in London N19) were rented for £13 a month,[134] and a small printing press was bought. Bill Thomson, one of the Glasgow Young Socialists who had come to London, took a week's course in printing and became a full-time worker there. Cliff worked alongside him in the printshop, and in the summer of 1964 he could be seen stripped to the waist working the printing machine.[135] Thomson remembers that Cliff worked hard, but was very impatient. On one occasion he picked up a forme and threw it on the floor, scattering lead all over the place because he was in a hurry.[136] On another occasion *Labour Worker* published a short report on a strike in Scotland. The strikers were so pleased they ordered a few hundred extra copies. By now the lead had been broken up for return to the typesetters, so Cliff spent two days and nights reassembling the lead so that the paper could be reprinted.[137]

The venture did not last long. The quality of work produced was not high.* Moreover, Cliff had little time left for writing and the other political work which he was actually good at. Two professional printers took over the printshop in return for free printing of *Labour Worker* and *Young Guard*,[138] an arrangement which Cliff described as not capitalist but feudal.[139] This lasted till the summer of 1965 when the machine was sold and *Labour Worker* was again printed commercially.[140]

In the summer of 1963 Cliff, having received a sum of money in damages for the plagiarising of one of his books, decided to revisit his native land and to see his family again; he took Chanie and their three children with him. When they were in Haifa about to get the boat home, Cliff was informed that he would be detained because he had not done his military service; the alternative was to leave his son behind (Donny was then nine). Chanie threatened to telephone

---

* See *International Socialism* 17 (Summer 1964) for an example.

her brother Reggie, who was an Israeli ambassador. The authorities backed off. But by now the boat had sailed, and the family had to be sent out in a speedboat to catch it up.[141]

Eighteen years after his first arrival in Britain, Cliff sought to regularise his situation by applying for naturalisation. He was sponsored by Michael Foot MP (doubtless enlisted by his nephew Paul). But on 8 May 1964 he was sent a cursory rejection. The official who signed (illegibly) the brief letter declared himself "Your obedient servant", but informed Cliff, "I am directed by the Secretary of State to say that, after full consideration, he has decided not to grant you such a certificate".[142]

No grounds were given for the refusal. A Freedom of Information request by Cliff's son Donny produced the response that no documentation could be found relating to the grounds for refusal.[143] In 1950 there had been some discussion among senior officials in the Home Office about the question of naturalisation for former members of the RCP. MI5 recommended that "members of the RCP should not in general be permitted to acquire the citizenship of a state whose Government and political system they hope to overthrow by force". The Home Office seems to have agreed the slightly more nuanced position that "applications from existing members of these parties or groups [RCP, Jehovah's Witnesses, etc.!] and from persons whose present or past associations with these parties or groups were such as to cast doubt on their loyalty, should be refused", while allowing the possibility of naturalisation for those who had "disavowed their previous connections".[144] If these principles were still in force, they would explain the rejection of Cliff's application.

The five years from 1960 to 1964 were a period of considerable advance for Cliff. He was writing prolifically and getting far more opportunities to exercise his ability as a speaker. The organisation was growing, modestly enough, but moving in the right direction. For those who had recently joined it was a time of intellectual exhilaration. *International Socialism*, under Kidron's editorship, was a stimulating journal, with regular contributions from Cliff, Kidron and MacIntyre helping to forge a perspective on the world which was genuinely radical without being dogmatic.

But the world was moving on and events were taking place, in both Britain and the Far East, which would lead to another radical shift in Cliff's development.

6

1964-67
Hard Labour

By the end of 1962 the right wing had regained its ascendancy in the Labour Party. The Campaign for Nuclear Disarmament was still flourishing, but its hopes of winning a second victory inside the Labour Party were slender. Then early in 1963 Hugh Gaitskell, who had staked his career on crushing unilateralism, fell suddenly ill and died.

The new leader, Harold Wilson, was a very different figure. He had resigned from the Attlee government in 1951 along with Aneurin Bevan, in protest at the imposition of health service charges. He had soon detached himself from the Bevanites, but was still perceived as more left-wing than Gaitskell.[1] While Gaitskell had sought head-on confrontation with the advocates of nuclear disarmament, Wilson tried to defeat them by offering conciliation. He was elected, not because of any shift to the left by the parliamentary Labour Party (who at that time elected the leader), but because his main right-wing rival, George Brown, was a notorious drunkard. (He was the man for whom the press coined the phrase "tired and emotional".)

Within months the political landscape began to change quite dramatically. The Tory war minister, John Profumo, was forced to resign because he had been caught out lying to the House of Commons. His fall brought to light a succession of scandals, involving sex and possible breaches of security. The situation was ripe for what became the boom in "satire", typified by the television programme *That Was The Week That Was*, and the magazine *Private Eye*, with which IS member Paul Foot was centrally involved. As Foot later noted, it seemed that "satirists and sectarians" provided the only voice to the left of Wilson.[2]

The Tories slumped in popularity. Prime Minister Harold Macmillan resigned, ostensibly on grounds of illness. The leadership contest became an undignified scramble, and the new leader was Alec Douglas-Home, a minor nobleman who renounced his title in order to become an MP. Douglas-Home was an inept buffoon, who admitted using matchsticks to understand economic problems.

Anticipating victory, the Labour left collapsed, putting electoral success ahead of any reservations about policy. Former Bevanite firebrand Michael Foot wrote a sycophantic book stating that Wilson "by his abilities, training and character, has high qualifications for the role of leadership at such a time".[3] Even the austere *New Left Review*, which had been promising to bring more rigorous theory to the British left, invested great hopes in a Labour victory.* In October 1964 Labour was elected with a majority of just five seats.

Cliff personally had written little on the prospects for a Labour government. But the position developed by *International Socialism*, in which Cliff had certainly played a part, was clear. (Editorials for the journal were circulated to all members of the editorial board for collective comment.) A Labour government would act in the interests of British capitalism, and inasmuch as that would necessarily mean taking measures against the interests of the working class, it would not hesitate to do so. Alasdair MacIntyre argued that a Labour government would be the agency of capitalist planning.[4] The IS analysis was confirmed when *The Economist*, a journal wholly committed to the interests of British capitalism, declared that "the riskier choice of Labour...will be the better choice for voters to make".[5]

Labour was committed to imposing some sort of incomes policy. For some years there had been debate on the left about the appropriate attitude to incomes policy. The New Left had published a pamphlet called *A Socialist Wages Plan*,[6] and there had been a polemic in the columns of *Socialist Review*, with the authors John Hughes and Ken Alexander defending a "socialist" incomes policy, and Mike Kidron and Eric Heffer (later a Labour MP) opposing it.[7] Subsequently there was a polemic with the journal *The Week*, produced by Trotskyists in association with Labour left-wingers.[8]

This positioned the IS on the far left of Labour's internal critics. *Labour Worker*, while headlining "OUT WITH THE TORIES",

---

* "The Labour Party has at last, after 50 years of failing, produced a dynamic and capable leader" (Perry Anderson, "Critique of Wilsonism", *New Left Review* 27 (September-October 1964) p22).

insisted that "electoral support to Labour must not blind us to the total inadequacy of Labour's present programme".[9] *International Socialism* warned that "rather than ask a future Labour Government to act in ways we know to be unrealistic, socialists should be directing their energies to the point of production where the real and ascribed interests of workers are bound to collide".[10] Most of the active membership of the IS had joined through the YS, and they took an active part in canvassing for Labour. On election night Wilson's narrow victory was greeted with a greater degree of euphoria than a strict interpretation of the IS line would have warranted.

While it was still unclear exactly how the Wilson government would develop, there was a recognition that the IS were entering a new phase of their existence. At a Working Committee meeting in the summer before the election, "TC said there were two traps: 1 – LP cretinism – the idea that resolutions represent working class consciousness. 2 – the Open Party. He remarked that the main recruiting ground for the group, the YS, was going to be buried".[11]

At a national meeting on 19 September 1964, just before the election, a resolution was put forward by a group of younger comrades – including Chris Harman, Fred Lindop and Roger Rosewell – making various proposals in response to the changed situation, in particular a more effective Working Committee and a fortnightly *Labour Worker*.[12]

Cliff was sceptical about the proposals, believing that a reorientation to industry was much more important than internal organisation. The minutes record:

> Cde TC was against reorganisation at this stage. The YS is no longer a horizon of growth and we must be prepared for much slower growth in the future. The struggle in the industrial front was much tougher than in the YS but it must be faced. Organisational resolutions will not help the group to grow when conditions are against dramatic increases in membership.[13]

When Jim Higgins drafted a new, more formal constitution, Cliff objected to its "bureaucratic spirit".[14]

The most important change agreed by the meeting was that *Labour Worker* should, as from January 1965, appear twice a month instead of monthly. At the same time Paul Foot, who had been invited by Penguin to write a book on immigration, asked for six months leave of absence. It was therefore agreed that Cliff and Ian Birchall should edit the paper jointly for the first six months.*

In retrospect, the decision was almost certainly a mistake. It was undoubtedly desirable to have a publication able to intervene in what was at times a rapidly changing situation. But the material prerequisites for a fortnightly paper simply did not exist.

There were no full-time staff, apart from Cliff. And not only did Cliff have all his other responsibilities as a speaker and a writer, but in November 1964 Chanie had given birth to their fourth and last child, Anna.

These were the days before fax and email. Articles were submitted from around the country, generally in handwritten form, and were sent by post. They then had to be typed up and taken to the typesetter in Fulham in west London. When the articles were set up in lead, they had to be collected by car. The layout was done on the table in Cliff's living room, on large pieces of cardboard:. Headlines and pictures were added, and the whole thing taken with the lead to a printshop in Finsbury Park. The folding and distribution was done by the Cliff family.[15]

There were no new pictures. Cliff had bought a collection of lead picture blocks from the left Labour weekly *Tribune* when that went over to a more modern form of illustration. These blocks were labelled and stored in a cupboard in Cliff's living room (where they were occasionally disturbed by his younger children). The cataloguing (done, I believe, by Cliff himself) was somewhat eccentric. A picture of two Arabs wearing robes in the desert, always used to accompany articles on the Middle East, was labelled "Sad Arabs", and catalogued under the letter "S".

With good luck the production cycle took a week; often it was ten days or more. So the ability to respond to events was limited. Occasionally there were mishaps. In 1966 the paper responded to a forthcoming railway strike with the commendably militant headline "NOT A TRAIN MUST RUN ON FEBRUARY 14". Unfortunately the strike had already been called off.[16] The cheapest typesetters and printers were found; often their cheapness was explained by their inadequate grasp of English. During the seafarers' strike of 1966 it was decided in the process of production to improve the look of the

---

* Most of what follows is based on the author's own recollections.

headline "INJURY TO ALL IF SEAMEN LOSE" by adding the word THE. The printer misunderstood the instruction, and the paper appeared with the headline "INJURY TO ALL IF SEAMEN THE LOSE".[17]

Cliff's role in the detailed process of production was relatively limited, and he wrote comparatively little for the paper, although on occasion he helped to fill gaps, for instance cobbling up at short notice an obituary of Winston Churchill which totally rejected the adulation of the mainstream press.[18] But his role in overseeing the political direction of the paper and suggesting topics to be covered was very important.* He could be a stern critic when mistakes were made, for example when a sharp attack on the finances of the Catholic Church drew a highly critical response from three workers at the ENV factory in north west London.[19]

The IS perspective on the forthcoming Labour government had centred mainly on the predicted clash between government and unions. But the 1964 election brought to the fore an issue which would be central to British politics over the coming decades – racism. During the years of full employment there had been substantial immigration into Britain from Commonwealth countries. Originally any Commonwealth citizen was entitled to residence in the United Kingdom, although this had been restricted by the Tory government in the early 1960s.

In the 1964 election a Tory candidate in Smethwick, in the West Midlands, Peter Griffiths, fought his campaign on an openly racist platform. He refused to condemn the slogan "If you want a nigger neighbour, vote Labour", saying it was "a manifestation of popular feeling".[20] He won the seat, reversing the national swing to Labour and defeating a leading Labour figure, Patrick Gordon Walker. Gordon Walker subsequently fought, and lost, a by-election in Leyton in east London, after a campaign in which the question of racism was also prominent.

The Labour government did introduce some mildly progressive measures like the Race Relations Act of 1965, which, among other things, prohibited discrimination in public places. But it further tightened immigration controls. This merely encouraged the far

---

* When I threatened to resign, overwhelmed by the responsibility of a job for which I had neither the experience nor the self-confidence, it was Cliff's kindly but firm encouragement which persuaded me not to.

right to demand more, and various far-right groupings became increasingly visible on the streets.

From the beginning the IS took a firm line of opposition, not only to racism,* but to immigration controls. *Labour Worker* argued the case against "the artificial division of the world into national blocs", and for "the right of free movement between nations of workers of all nationalities".[21] The group became involved in the rather respectable Campaign Against Racial Discrimination (CARD) and argued for an orientation to the working class.[22] At the YS conference in 1965 Mike Caffoor, one of the very few black IS members, received a standing ovation for a scathing attack on the Labour government's immigration policy.[23] When the far right began to make its presence felt in the 1966 general election campaign, IS members helped to organise counter-demonstrations. In Southall† there was "a remarkably heated evening...when hecklers made a thorough job of disrupting a British National Party meeting", and there was fighting at Finsbury Town Hall where Oswald Mosley was speaking.[24]

In general the enthusiastic anti-racism cut with the grain among the IS membership, but there was one casualty. Syd Bidwell, a veteran of the RCP who, as a full-time organiser of the National Council of Labour Colleges, had done much to get speaking engagements for Cliff, stood as Labour candidate in Southall in 1966. During his successful campaign he made quite unacceptable concessions to racism:

> Mr Sydney Bidwell favours restricting immigration on the lines of the Labour government, but he would like a few trimmings too, like more control of housing to stop coloured immigrants living in the same streets.[25]

He was expelled from the IS a few weeks after his election.[26]

One thing which raised the profile of the IS as an anti-racist organisation was Paul Foot's book *Immigration and Race in British Politics*, which gave a careful analysis of the roots of racism in class society. Foot was a talented young journalist with many possibilities

---

* Even in 1959, when the SRG had only a handful of members, each London branch was asked to send "a nucleus of 3 hecklers" to Oswald Mosley's meetings in North Kensington (Minutes of SR EC 17 September 1959, Fancy MS 1171/box 24/SR).

† Working Committee minutes for 19 March 1966 record that "all London comrades are urged to show their muscle" (Rich. MS 1117/box 209/file 6).

open to him. If he had only broken his organisational links with the revolutionary left, he could have had an immensely successful career as a licensed radical critic of the establishment.*
Cliff's role was crucial. He acted as Foot's "conscience", reinforcing his links to the revolutionary left. He would guilt-trip Foot quite shamelessly, reminding him of his father's role in the British administration in Palestine, and rebuking him for not "pulling his socks". It was done with a genial good humour which appealed to Foot.†

The anti-racist struggle was not always straightforward. In 1965 a strike broke out at the Courtauld factory in Preston. The strikers were Asians and West Indians, who were faced with deteriorating conditions in a department almost entirely staffed by black workers because of the discriminatory policies of the employers. They got no support from their union, which had a vested interest in preserving the privileges of white workers. White racism bred its opposite, black nationalism, and there were efforts to set up a separate black union, a development which could have been disastrous for working class unity.

For a small group, the IS made a significant intervention. Ray Challinor was an executive member of Westhoughton Labour Party, and he joined the strike committee and used his labour movement contacts to raise money. This was extremely important in establishing that it was possible to win support from white workers and that black separatism was a dead-end.[27]

Cliff took a keen interest in the strike, which was defeated after three weeks. He described it as representing "in a compact form everything we stand for",[28] and ensured that it got full coverage in *Labour Worker*.[29] He was particularly keen that secondary issues should not stand in the way of working class unity. Since there were various religions among the strikers, strike committee meetings began with a prayer from each religion, and Ray Challinor was asked to say the Lord's Prayer. Cliff was insistent that he had been right to do so.[30]

---

* See Richard Ingrams's affectionate and moving portrait *My Friend Footy* (London, 2005) which plays down the overtly revolutionary component of Foot's career.

† I recall being told that Foot was originally in favour of some immigration controls, but was persuaded by Cliff to adopt the position of opposition to all immigration controls argued so effectively in the conclusion of the book. However, I can't substantiate this.

One response to racism was the black power movement which began to appear in the 1960s, inspired by the Black Panthers in the US. Many sections of the left either became cheer-leaders for black nationalism, or dismissed black nationalism as reactionary. From the outset Cliff had a more balanced formulation: as far as the Panthers were concerned he stressed that self-confidence was good, but that self-sufficiency was bad.[31]

The Labour government had opened up a new phase for the IS group, although it took time for the changes to become apparent. In the summer of 1965 a national meeting carried a resolution, moved by Mike Kidron, defining the group's relation to the Labour Party:

> The IS Group rejects the Labour Party as an instrument for social change; rejects it as a milieu for *mass* conversion to socialist consciousness; and sees in it primarily an arena for ideological conflict, a link to a living working class audience and a source of individual recruitment to a revolutionary programme.[32]

At a northern weekend school Cliff argued that this was a time for experiment:

> Comrades should try to learn from other groups. We should *experiment* in our activities, and tell other branches.

He told the Durham branch:

> They should get out into the mining area, selling papers, then people would join.[33]

There were important shifts in the leadership team around Cliff. In the late 1950s and early 1960s Mike Kidron had played a key leadership role, and had often appeared to be of equal stature to Cliff. In 1964 he stepped down as editor of *International Socialism* after five years in which he had established a journal of very high quality. He remained active, contributing a regular column to *Labour Worker* under the name "Frat Cain", but became rather more detached from the leadership, though there were no obvious political differences. In 1965 he moved to take up an academic post in Hull.

Alasdair MacIntyre had been an active member of the group, especially on the editorial board of *International Socialism*, until 1964. Cliff had disapproved of his contributions to *Encounter*, but there had never been a confrontation. Now MacIntyre too began to take his distance. On 5 June 1965 the magazine *Solidarity* held a meeting in a pub room in London, where MacIntyre and Paul Cardan (Cornelius Castoriadis), the leading theoretician of the French group Socialisme ou Barbarie, discussed Cardan's recent book *Modern Capitalism and Revolution*. Many of those who turned up were IS members in London who expected that MacIntyre would be defending IS politics. Instead MacIntyre largely agreed with what Castoriadis said. An ill-tempered debate ensued. Kidron, with cutting irony, referred to the speakers as "Cardan 1" and "Cardan 2".[34]

Cliff was furious and launched a long attack on Cardan, as is recorded in the following account.*

Cardan's "whole book was a plagiarism of Marx pure and simple, a distortion of Marx pure and simple and a kick at Marx pure and simple"... Cliff sought to "refute" what Cardan was imputing to Marx by pointing out that "Marx had supported the 10-hours bill, had been involved in a debate in 1864 about higher wages and had been a member of the General Council of the First International which, as was well known, had fought for higher wages"...

Cliff saw another "filthy distortion" in the allegation that there was some kind of connection between Marx's economic theories and bureaucratic politics ... "It is simply not true", said Cliff, "that Marx proclaimed 'we are the General Staff and we will use the rest of them as cannon fodder'."...

In relation to alienation, there was "not one comma in Cardan's book that Marx had not written much better before". Cliff instanced the "Philosophical Manuscripts"... And when it came to "moving forward from Marx" all we get in Cardan was "description of what everybody knows". Cardan's analysis lacked laws, rules and perspective. "There was the present status and one fine day a revolution would come...one fine morning everything would be marvellous". This reminded Cliff of the Stalinists and of their conception of the dictatorship of the proletariat...

As for the final chapter of Cardan's book, Cliff thought it "quite

---

* *Solidarity*, Vol 3, No 10 (August 1965). The article (probably written by Chris Pallis) was hostile to Cliff and interpolated critical comments into the account of his contribution. But the report was based on a recording, so the *verbatim* quotes are authentic. I was present at the meeting and the account does not contradict my memories.

fantastic" and "stinking elitist of the first order". It dared propose an organisation of a new type. Summing up Cliff stated that Cardan himself had once been in a traditional organisation. The book was therefore only "spitting into the well from which one drank".

MacIntyre responded sourly that the contributions by Cliff and Kidron were "translated from the Russian, about the year 1905".

Despite this bad-tempered exchange Cliff did not want to lose MacIntyre. There was clearly some contact, direct or indirect, with MacIntyre after the debate, for Cliff, who had already defended MacIntyre for non-attendance at meetings,[35] reported to the next Working Committee meeting that MacIntyre still intended to remain in the group and was in fact more enthusiastic than ever. "His only troubles were that he had no roots and was against supporting the Labour Party".[36]

It was in fact this question of the Labour Party that apparently produced the final break some months later, when MacIntyre wrote that he did not want any more copies of *Labour Worker*, since he disapproved of the attack on Richard Gott's independent candidacy in the Hull by-election (see below).[37] Although MacIntyre remained on the editorial board of *International Socialism* until 1968, he played no further role in the group's activities.

The responsibility for orienting the politics and activities of the group fell more and more on Cliff's shoulders. The Working Committee (this was effectively the executive of the organisation, which also functioned as the editorial board of *Labour Worker*) now consisted mainly of relatively recent recruits who had come into politics through the YS. The most experienced members were Jim Higgins, who had been in the labour movement since the Second World War, and John Palmer, who tended to be more oriented to Labour Party work than Cliff.* Chris Harman, who had moved to the LSE in 1964, was developing as a writer and speaker and became one of Cliff's closest allies. Nigel Harris, who had returned from travelling in the Far East, became editor of *International Socialism* and played an increasingly important role as a theoretician.

---

* Palmer was selected as Labour candidate for North West Croydon in the 1966 election. The Labour Party NEC removed him and instructed the constituency party to reselect; they again selected Palmer, and the NEC had to impose a candidate. Labour lost the seat by only 2,696 votes; if Palmer had been candidate, with an enthusiastic local party behind him, he might have won.

Around this time Cliff and his family moved house, to Allerton Road in Stoke Newington, just over half a mile from their previous residence. It was a modest terrace house, which would remain his home for the next 35 years.

In the autumn of 1965 Cliff made two tours of northern branches and produced detailed reports on his experiences. Manchester was having some success at breaking out of the student milieu, Hull and Leeds less so. In particular the turn to industry was beginning to show some results. In Glasgow there was "an important meeting at the Rootes Linwood factory, which included six shop stewards", while in Newcastle there were "fortnightly mid-day meetings at Parsons (turbine factory)".[38] A second tour later the same year noted significant progress in York, Hull and Manchester.[39]

A major strategic shift was now taking place. Over the previous five years the group's activity had centred on the YS. Without that work the IS would have remained the tiny, marginal propaganda group it had been in 1959. But the YS was now in serious decline. The atmosphere had been so poisoned by factional competition, and especially by the sectarianism of the *Keep Left* tendency, that it had become uninhabitable for new members. After *Keep Left*'s departure, the Labour Party imposed new tighter limits on the activity of the YS. A "Save the YS campaign" was launched but achieved little. The followers of Ted Grant had withdrawn from *Young Guard* in September 1963, and the following year launched a new publication, *The Militant*. *Young Guard* was now simply the organ of the IS and those politically close to it, and it ceased publication in 1966. A new youth paper, *Rebel*, was launched in 1966; it was lively and well designed, but it had no new audience to appeal to, and tended to rely on in-group references and jokes, notably in the "Supertrot" strip cartoon. It did not last beyond the following year.

However, one important recruit was made. Early in 1964 Roger Protz resigned as editor of *Keep Left*. After a brief period with *Militant*, he turned to the IS group and became a member. Given the amateurish way in which *Labour Worker* was produced, an experienced professional journalist was an enormous acquisition. Protz became production editor in December 1965. The experiment with the fortnightly *Labour Worker* was finally ended in late 1966, and the paper became a monthly again. Protz became editor, and a much

1964-67: HARD LABOUR 255

improved publication appeared.

But the main development was, as Cliff had predicted, in the industrial field. Wilson's Labour government did introduce some reforms and increased, although modestly, expenditure on housing, welfare, education and health, but there was no significant redistribution of wealth. Wilson also aimed, through his links with the trade union bureaucracy and his credibility among workers, to discipline workers more effectively and above all to control wages. Throughout its six years in office the Wilson government was preoccupied with the attempt to impose various forms of incomes policy. In 1966 a Prices and Incomes Bill became law and a six-month standstill on wages and prices was imposed. Even the title contained a deception, for while it is relatively easy to impose legal restraints on wages, prices are far more difficult to control effectively.

Another important shift was taking place. Since the Second World War the main organised political manifestation of the left in the trade union movement had been the Communist Party. The re-emergence of a shop stewards' movement in the 1950s had given considerable influence to CP militants; workers who would not have dreamt of voting Communist in a parliamentary election were happy to entrust representation in their workplace to a Communist activist.

The CP had lost some of its membership and influence in the aftermath of the Hungarian Revolution, but by the early 1960s, largely because of its activity in CND, it was gaining in numbers again. As the first phase of the Cold War drew to a close, its politics were undergoing a significant change. More and more attention was devoted to electoral politics. In 1964 it was decided that National Congresses of the party, which had been held at Easter, should henceforth take place in the autumn in order not to interfere with campaigning in the municipal elections. In the unions, too, electoralism became more important, as the party attempted to win full-time positions in the union machine. Often this involved closer relations with left Labour members of the union bureaucracy. The factory branches which had been an important part of the party's structure were in decline.

To some members this looked like a shift to the right. At the same time the Sino-Soviet split was becoming public, with vehement Maoist denunciations of the "revisionist" line of pro-Moscow parties. Some of those who looked back to the more militant episodes of the party's history were attracted by the Maoist rhetoric. The CP found it ever harder to impose a centralised discipline, and opportunities for those to the left of the CP were growing.

The IS group's roots in the labour movement were, however, rather limited. It had a membership of between 200 and 300, the great majority of whom were aged under 30. Of the handful of older industrial militants in the group, some were becoming less active. Of the more recent recruits from the YS, quite a few were employed in industrial or manual jobs, but for the most part they still had relatively little trade union experience or credibility among their fellow workers.

The group's only real industrial base was the ENV gear-box factory in north west London. Geoff Carlsson was a veteran of the RCP and a founder member of the SRG. He had worked at ENV for many years and was a well-known activist. Although politically isolated (many of the stewards were CP members) he had a long record as a steward and had been convenor for a time in the 1950s. He had twice stood for the presidency of the AEU on the basis of an overtly socialist, anti-Stalinist statement of position. ENV was an exceptionally well organised factory, where the stewards' organisation had an excellent record of defending their members' interests and organising solidarity for other workers in struggle.[40]

Carlsson's record had not, in the conditions of the post-war boom, led to any significant recruitment. Only one other militant from the factory, Les Bennett, had been recruited to the IS before 1964. Cliff used to contrast the successful recruitment through the YS to the failure to recruit in ENV.[41]

In the new atmosphere things began to change. Carlsson was able to build a small group of stewards and activists around him, and by 1966 an ENV workplace branch was set up, the first such branch in the history of the organisation.

In 1965 Geoff Mitchell, AEU convenor of the ENV Joint Stop Stewards Committee (JSSC), was successfully sued for libel after writing a letter on behalf of the JSSC pointing out that a Labour councillor had failed to take part in a strike at ENV. A Defence Committee was set up to raise the £500 damages awarded against him.[42] Mitchell had now become a member of the IS, and since it appeared that similar attacks against stewards, individually and collectively, were likely in the coming period, a meeting was held on 16 January 1966 to establish a London Industrial Shop Stewards Defence Committee.

The committee was an attempt at a united front and contained some IS stalwarts alongside one member of *Militant* and other non-aligned trade unionists. The achievements of the committee were relatively limited. There were a few more meetings, a bulletin called *Resistance* which made little impact, and a pamphlet about the strike at Woolf's rubber factory in Southall, where 700 workers, mainly Indian immigrants, came out for six weeks over the suspension of one worker.[43] But it must have irritated the AEU bureaucracy; in September 1966 it was reported:

> The AEU executive had issued instructions for Geoff Carlsson to withdraw from the committee and to stop AEU branches in London from affiliating.[44]

Events were now moving more quickly. In March 1966 there had been another general election, in which Labour increased its overall majority from three to 97, and gained its highest vote since 1951. The Labour government no longer had any excuses for failing to carry through radical measures. But in May a major industrial dispute erupted, with a national strike by seafarers for higher wages and shorter hours. This lasted almost seven weeks and had a serious impact on the economy; it became a head-on confrontation with the government. Wilson attempted to blame the strike on the CP, which he described as a "tightly knit group of politically motivated men".[45] (In fact the CP's role had been somewhat ambiguous, and was sometimes to the right of the most militant seafarers.[46]) The IS had no seafarers among its membership, but argued for solidarity action and financial support in the labour movement.[47]

Then in the autumn of 1966 the incomes policy strategy was taken one stage further and a total freeze on wages was imposed for six months. The freeze was vigorously opposed by *Labour Worker* and the Shop Stewards Defence Committee (SSDC), but December 1966 saw the first meeting of the CP-dominated Liaison Committee for the Defence of Trade Unions (LCDTU), which was able to mobilise much larger rallies and demonstrations. Hence the SSDC never really took off. A Working Committee discussion in May 1967 noted that the SSDC "pretends to be something that it isn't" and resolved to retain it merely "as a 'shell' that can serve as a means of contact with militants".[48]

The SSDC had one significant achievement. In May 1966 it published a short book* by Cliff and Colin Barker entitled *Incomes Policy, Legislation and Shop Stewards*.[49] This was a major turning point for Cliff. The book helped to change the organisation, but it also changed Cliff himself. He was now just short of 50 years old, and his reputation was based almost entirely on his books on state capitalism. He had written little on the British labour movement. Now he perceived a rising level of struggle and the possibility of more direct political intervention. His previous work on state capitalism had been, in a sense, negative; it was devoted to the vital but unfulfilling task of defining what socialism was *not*. Now there was the possibility of building a movement which could fight actively for socialism. The two books on which Cliff was working, on Keynes and on communism and the peasantry, were thrust unceremoniously to the back of a cupboard in his home, where they lay undisturbed until his death.

Instead Cliff devoted himself to a detailed study of the current state of industrial struggle. His partner in writing the book was Colin Barker, a postgraduate student of industrial sociology in Manchester. Cliff wrote the earlier chapters, drawing on the work of Mike Kidron and Andrew Shonfield's *Modern Capitalism*,[50] and Barker revised the style. As Cliff grew more confident in Barker, he sent him sketchy versions of the later chapters and left him to write them up. For chapter six, "Dead Weight of Bureaucracy", he merely sent Barker some press cuttings and told him to write the chapter. Barker wrote the conclusion. Barker did not have a telephone, and if necessary Cliff would communicate by telegram.[51]

The main theme was set out in the first paragraph of the book:

It is doubtful whether any of the problems facing the labour movement of Britain in the 1960s is of greater importance than the two related questions of Incomes Policy and Trade union Legislation.[52]

In their analysis of modern British capitalism Cliff and Barker

---

* Dave Peers had originally proposed that Cliff write this as an IS pamphlet (IS Working Committee Minutes, 22 May 1965 [Rich. MS 1117/box 209/file 6]). By the time it was written it seemed more appropriate for it to be published by the SSDC.

drew on important themes from Cliff's earlier work. They began with the place of planning in modern capitalism and especially in the strategy of the Wilson government, which had made the idea of a "National Plan" central to its policies. Technology and competition meant that modern capitalists needed to plan their investments years in advance. Hence, they noted, "the state has already become a central factor in the economy of the capitalist countries". But, they stressed, such planning "has nothing to do with socialism at all".[53] It was the same logic which had led Cliff to deny that state ownership and five-year plans in Russia had anything to do with socialism.

Secondly, they examined the effects of the post-war boom. In particular this had removed the threat of unemployment as a means of disciplining workers; indeed there was a labour shortage. Consequently workers' bargaining power had increased considerably.

But if capitalism had changed, it remained capitalism. A Labour government could try to control wages, but it would not control profits, for profit was the lifeblood of the capitalist system: "If you are allergic to profit then you just can't run a capitalist economy".[54] British capitalism could not act independently of the Swiss bankers, whom Harold Wilson had famously called the "gnomes of Zurich". And with one of the concrete images which Cliff loved, he concluded that modern capitalism might appear less brutal, but it was the same old system:

> There are many farmers who warm their cowsheds to get more milk, but we are still waiting to hear of the farmer who gives over control of his shed to the cows.[55]

Cliff and Barker then went on to examine the changing patterns of the wages struggle. They observed the important phenomenon of "wage drift", whereby national wage rates were substantially increased by local agreements. They also challenged the allegedly "socialist" rationale for incomes policy, namely that if better-paid workers moderated their demands, this would benefit the low-paid. On the contrary, they argued, the best-organised workers prepared the way for other workers to make gains: "If the strongest and best-organised workers hold back, the whole working class will be held back with them".[56]

Meanwhile the trade union bureaucracy was increasingly drawn into the machinery of the state. Consequently ever fewer workers were actively involved in the trade union branch except where this was directly based on the workplace. One aspect of this was the "apathy" widely discussed by political commentators in the 1960s.* As Cliff and Barker pointed out, "apathy is the reverse of the coin of centralisation".[57]

Apathy, they showed, was two-sided. The official trade union machinery was ever less able to deliver real gains to workers: "Any strategy of opposition to incomes policy that looks to trade union officials, of the left or of the right, to play an important role in this opposition is fundamentally misconceived." But on the other hand, local organisation – especially that of shop stewards – revealed the self-confidence of workers who "for a whole generation...have known not one serious defeat".[58]

In particular it was argued that unofficial strikes were symptoms of an aspiration for workers' control. As Cliff and Barker showed, an increasing number of strikes were concerned, not with wages, but with issues of control and a challenge to managerial authority. The book did not idealise shop stewards, showing that their actions were generally fragmented and often had narrow horizons. Nonetheless Cliff and Barker predicted:

> Out of the shop stewards' organisations will rise a new socialist movement, much mightier than ever before. Its roots will be in the class struggle at the point of production, and it will lead the fight against all forms of oppression – economic, national, cultural or political.
>
> To defend and extend the shop stewards' organisation of today is to build the socialist movement of tomorrow. To fight for the socialist movement of tomorrow is to strengthen the shop stewards of today.[59]

After a discussion of proposals for anti-union legislation, the final chapter of *Incomes Policy, Legislation and Shop Stewards* dealt with political prospects. This began with the decline of "reformism from above", that is, the reliance on parliament and trade union leaders to bring in reforms. Now the struggle for reforms had shifted to the shop-floor, to what the authors called "do-it-yourself"

---

* In a collection of essays by contributors to *New Left Review*, Edward Thompson had defined apathy as a situation where "people have, increasingly, looked to *private* solutions to *public* evils" (EP Thompson et al, *Out of Apathy*, p5).

reforms. Less and less could be expected of MPs and trade union leaders; of them it was true, in a phrase Cliff used repeatedly in public meetings, that "power corrupts, but lack of power corrupts absolutely".[60] At the same time the growing role of the state made the traditional distinction between political and economic struggle less and less meaningful.

The authors noted as a positive feature the growing unionisation of white collar workers. At the time (as so frequently in later years), there was much discussion of the argument that the traditional working class was disappearing. Cliff and Barker concluded that it was not a case of workers becoming "middle class", but rather "that a good section of the people who used to call themselves 'middle class' are now beginning to recognise that they are workers too".[61]

Not everything was progressive in working class consciousness – in particular the racism widespread among workers – but Cliff and Barker believed the decline of traditional reformism opened the way for "the rebirth of a revolutionary working class movement". While stressing that "no one can win socialism for the workers – they must do it themselves", they called for "a political as well as an industrial response", and concluded by advocating:

> a national shop stewards' movement – an idea which, since the First World War, has existed almost solely in the minds of some of those whom Harold Wilson calls "wreckers", and whom we see as the potential builders of the mightiest socialist movement yet in the history of Britain.[62]

The pamphlet was one of the most important things Cliff had written and it reoriented the whole strategy of the IS group for the coming years. The opening assertion that the questions of incomes policy and trade union legislation would be central for the working class movement was proved absolutely correct. Three prime ministers – Wilson, Heath and Thatcher – would confront the working class movement with repressive laws – the first two unsuccessfully. Incomes policy would be central to the political scene of the 1960s and 1970s. Shop stewards' organisation, battered but not destroyed, has remained at the heart of working class resistance until the present day.

The whole analysis was predicated on the fact of full employment. Cliff and Barker did not consider what would happen when full employment came to an end, as it was to do in the 1970s. Certainly in their optimistic account of the rising movement they did not foresee just how brutal a defeat would be inflicted by Thatcher in the 1980s. But considered as strategists rather than prophets, they deserve substantial credit for their analysis.

One weakness of the book which appears clearly in retrospect is the way in which it depicted the working class as exclusively male. The terminology ("brothers" etc.) reflected a predominantly male movement. The only female worker mentioned in the book was a young woman who had achieved press notoriety after being disciplined for spending too much time in the lavatory.[63]

The growth of white-collar unionism was quite rightly given importance, but the book tended to concentrate on white-collar workers in industry. Though Cliff himself was married to a teacher who was highly active in her union, there was no mention of teachers' trade unionism in a decade which would end with a wave of teachers' strikes. The authors praised the "generosity of spirit" of dockers and engineers who took strike action in support of a nurses' pay claim. But nurses were listed along with old age pensioners as "people who cannot defend themselves very well".[64]

The most problematic point was the way in which it related trade unionism to the political struggle. The introduction to the book was written by Reg Birch. This was something of a coup. Birch was a longstanding and well-respected militant of the AEU, who had three times been the left candidate for the union's presidency. He was becoming increasingly critical of the CP, of which he had been a member since 1939, and was hence willing to collaborate with forces to the left of the CP.* He was no innocent, and undoubtedly knew of Cliff's Trotskyist connections.†

Birch praised the book as "timely" and "a great service to all workers", but expressed an important reservation:

I do not accept that the extension of shop stewards' organisations, their increase in number, will automatically lead to the development

---

* He was to be expelled from the CP a little later, and in 1968 helped to found a Maoist grouping (the Communist Party of Britain Marxist-Leninist).

† Birch's biographer claims Birch was "strongly opposed" to Trotskyism, and cites the critical paragraphs from his introduction to the book. This is dishonest, since it fails to mention Birch's warm commendation of Cliff and Barker. Moreover, by allowing his name to be used on the book's cover, he was clearly endorsing it and encouraging its sale (W Podmore, *Reg Birch*, pp64-65).

of a Socialist movement. There needs to be politics – working class politics.[65]

The problem was a real one. Cliff and Barker made no secret of their commitment to socialist politics. The socialist goal was present throughout the argument. But they were noticeably vague about how the shop stewards' struggle would develop into a socialist movement. The formulation which would be almost a cliché in Cliff's post-1968 writings – the need for a revolutionary party – was absent from the argument.

There were tactical reasons for this. The London SSDC was a united front body, with members from a variety of political groupings. To have posed the problem of a political strategy too specifically could have caused divisions. More generally, Cliff rejected the position, based on a misunderstood caricature of Leninism, that it was the job of small groups of revolutionaries to bring "politics" to the working class. He was well aware that the politicisation of the struggle would result from the intervention of the state in trade union struggles, as was to be seen in dramatic form in the big struggles of the early 1970s.

Cliff was now rethinking his 1962 position that revolutionaries would remain inside the Labour Party for the foreseeable future. But what form of organisation would be required was still unclear. The course of events would throw up some answers over the next few years.

In terms of presentation the book was an undoubted success. It was written in a popular and accessible style, with no reliance on Marxist jargon or academic terminology. Yet it did not patronise or talk down to its readers, and presented a wealth of statistics and references designed to arm militants who would have to argue with their fellow workers.

Given the IS group's tiny resources, the pamphlet made a certain impact. After two and a half weeks 4,300 out of 4,950 copies printed had been distributed, and money had already been received for 1,282 copies. Arrangements for a reprint were in hand.[66] By July sales had reached 7,500 – though not all the money had come in.[67] The book was well received and was Cliff's best seller so far.

It marked an important shift in the activities of the IS group. Comrades who a year earlier had been discussing the finer points of

Trotskyism with other factions in the YS had to reach out to a new audience. Members were sent off to visit shop stewards in their area and persuade them to buy a copy of the *Incomes Policy* book or, better, half a dozen for their union branch or stewards' committee. The IS had around 300 members; 10,000 copies were sold – around 30 per member.

To Roger Cox the book represented a major breakthrough for a small group. It filled an intellectual vacuum for left-wing militants and enabled the IS to tap into the CP network. Some of the best industrial militants were turning to Maoism, but they welcomed Cliff's book. The book was taken to stewards, who were asked if they knew of other people who might want it. In Cox's own factory he worked on a line of 21 men; 15 of them bought copies. On 23 May 1966 Cliff and Reg Birch addressed a meeting of 400 industrial militants at the Anson Hall in Cricklewood.[68] As a means of publicity, IS comrades were urged to get shop stewards' committees to submit copies of the book to the Royal Commission on Trade Unions which was currently taking evidence.[69]

In particular the book was a bridge to CP members. Colin Barker went to London for a lobby against incomes policy on a coach organised by the CP He sold 60 books on the coach and demonstration – Reg Birch's name was very important. A CP member then gave him a list of everyone on the two buses from Manchester. Six comrades in Manchester spent the next months visiting everyone on the list; people bought two or half a dozen copies. Six comrades in Manchester sold 500 books. The Manchester branch grew, eventually reaching 60 members.[70]

Mel Norris's father was working in a large factory in Tottenham, where the CP was strong. He put Mel in touch with the convenor, who bought a copy, then ordered a dozen copies for the senior stewards, and finally a number more so that all the stewards could have copies.[71]

The *Incomes Policy* book explored the strengths and weaknesses of shop steward organisation. All too soon some of those weaknesses would be exposed by the course of struggle. It had been the organisation at the ENV factory which had made the London SSDC possible. Cliff's close links with Geoff Carlsson had enabled him to draw on that experience in developing his analysis of the shop stewards' movement.

But organisation within a single workplace, however effective, had its limits. In 1962 ENV had been taken over by an American firm that was determined to break the power of the stewards. For some time they resisted successfully, but in the summer of 1966 management announced that the factory was to be closed. Carlsson, chairman of the stewards' committee, and other leading militants believed this was a bluff, but were unable to convince the majority of workers and get united opposition to the management. There were redundancies, including many known militants, and early in 1967 Carlsson and Geoff Mitchell, the two leading IS members, were sacked. Then it was announced that the factory would stay open – with a reduced labour force and without the experienced stewards.[72] Not much later the factory was, in fact, closed.[73] It was an important setback, and one that must have weighed heavily on Cliff's thinking about how to redefine the strategy of the group.

Quite rightly Cliff was always looking to new possibilities. Sometimes this meant he could appear callous to old comrades. Carlsson, a founder member of the SRG, had for some years been invited to Cliff's home for Christmas. After the ENV defeat he was no longer invited. With his remorseless political focus, Cliff sometimes seemed not to realise how much people were affected by his actions.[74]

Another important area of activity was around the docks. Cliff, who already in the 1964-65 period was occasionally visiting the LSE, asked Nigel Coward, an LSE student, to make contacts in the docks. Coward contacted Terry Barrett and they worked together closely during the dock strike in the autumn of 1967 against the Devlin proposals for reduced manning and greater mobility of labour, trying to organise a national response. Briefly a rank and file paper was produced, with some 3,000 copies printed. Coward became a full-time organiser for about a year and a half. Given the informal nature of the group's structure, he was effectively appointed by Cliff, who dealt with finance on a hand-to-mouth basis.[75]

The IS took part in the Nottingham Workers' Control Conference in June 1966 which laid the basis for what was to become the Institute for Workers' Control. But Cliff was in many ways critical of the approach to workers' control being developed, and he and Chris Harman wrote a document setting out the distinctive IS position:

Complete workers' control is impossible unless political power is in the [hands] of the working class. Partial workers' control is an encroachment on capital, the extent of which depends entirely upon the relationship of class forces. From this it follows that any discussion on workers' control must be linked [to] the movement as it is and based upon its present direction rather than upon abstract blueprints.

It is a contradiction in terms to talk about control given from above. Workers' control cannot be legislated into existence by Act of Parliament. It must be taken by the actions of workers themselves.

The comments on transport were prescient and are even more valid 40 years on:

Even partial workers' control cannot work unless decisive inroads are made into the capitalist principles and values determining the relationship with the wider economy. E.g. workers' control on buses in London would not alleviate the situation of the busmen at all if it [did] not challenge the role given to public transport in a capitalist society. The ten percent of the public who travel by private car would still produce congestion etc. If workers' control was really to mean workers controlling their own conditions of work it would have to mean a struggle for the abolition of fares, an end to the petrol tax for public transport, and an end to interest [payments].[76]

If workplace struggle was the main priority in this period, the IS group was also involved in other forms of working class resistance. In particular the mid-1960s saw a wave of tenants' struggles. By the end of 1966 local authorities, many of them Labour, were making large increases in the rents charged for council housing. There was widespread opposition to this. IS members were able to play a significant role in a number of campaigns. In some cases Labour Party membership provided a good starting point for intervention. In the London borough of Haringey a group of IS members in the Labour Party declared public opposition to the Labour council's decision to raise rents, and used this as a base to begin organising tenants' associations across the borough.

Cliff was not personally involved in this work and did not write about it. But he regarded involvement in such grassroots campaigning as highly positive. In Cliff's own area, Islington, there was a major campaign against a particularly exploitative private landlord, a campaign which highlighted racism in the area.[77] Cliff was enthusiastic about the possibilities this offered to develop a new audience. Though of necessity he had little direct experience of work in a broad movement, and hence sometimes misunderstood situations, he compensated using his ability to listen to the experience of comrades involved in various campaigns.[78]

One of the leading activists in this field was a young lawyer called Ian Macdonald. He had been active in the Islington Tenants Association where he met Chanie, who introduced him to Cliff. He found Cliff charismatic, fluent and possessed of enormous emotional energy. It seemed to him that Cliff's politics came right out of his belly; he enjoyed what he was doing and was not at all what the Scots call "crabbit".

Macdonald was also in touch with CLR James and was greatly influenced by him, but James had no objection to him joining the IS.* Macdonald and a few of his friends set up the GLC Action Committee against rent rises imposed by the Greater London Council. They produced *Not a Penny on the Rent*, which sold 30,000 copies every fortnight. At one point 100,000 people were on rent strike. Macdonald recalls this as being significant because it represented a shift towards community-based activity similar to that of the US civil rights movement.[79]

Cliff was impressed by Macdonald and frequently cited him as a model of the kind of activity that IS members should be engaged in. This was a frequent practice with Cliff; he would adopt younger comrades and for a shorter or longer period they would become one of his favourites. The aim was to encourage both the comrade in question and the rest of the membership by providing a positive example. It also indicated a willingness by Cliff to show that he could learn from comrades who were much younger and less experienced than himself. But sometimes it had a negative effect on comrades who found themselves being excessively lionised. Ian Macdonald and his friends left the IS in 1968, partly because they were unhappy with the turn to democratic centralism. However, Macdonald saw Cliff from time to time afterwards and always found him very friendly.[80]

---

* In this period James contributed a book review to *International Socialism* 18 (1964), and permitted the reprint of his "Trotsky's *Revolution Betrayed*" in *International Socialism* 16 (1964).

Dave Peers, who worked closely with Cliff over a number of years, now has a more negative view. He believes that Cliff had a very personal style of leadership and that people were either "in" or "out". Comrades became stars on the basis of information that was often dubious. The stars became like members of the family and Cliff's enthusiasms clouded discussion.[81]

If shop stewards and tenants were one side of the new orientation, the Labour Party was the other side. In 1967 most IS members were still members of the Labour Party, but generally their activity had declined sharply. Partly this was a question of priorities; new forms of activity meant there was much less time left for electoral activities like canvassing. Partly, too, it was a reflection of the general unpopularity of the Labour Party. Just one year on from Wilson's landslide general election victory, Labour suffered heavy losses in the 1967 county council elections, retaining control of only three out of 59 English and Welsh counties. In practice the IS was following a middle course between the SLL, who had noisily walked out of the Labour Party, and those revolutionaries who still regarded Labour Party entry work as a matter of fundamental principle.[82]

At the end of 1966 and early in 1967 Cliff published three long articles on the Labour Party in *Labour Worker*. The first, "Palest Pink in Word and Deed",[83] dealt with the Labour Party up to 1931, aiming to demolish the myth that Labour had "a glorious socialist record" marred only by "a couple of aberrations in an otherwise immaculate history".

The second was called "Labour's addiction to the 'rubber stamp'".[84] The main argument was that, because of changes in modern capitalism, parliament had "ceased to be a central locus of reform". Hence workers looked less and less towards parliamentary action:

> A Gallup poll showed that many people do not know who [Foreign Secretary] George Brown is – some think he is a band leader, others that he is an escaped train robber! Everyone, of course, knows the Beatles. The explanation is probably quite simple – one gets more pleasure from the Beatles than from Brown.

Cliff had probably never listened to a Beatles track in his life, but he was keenly aware of shifts in class consciousness. As he pointed out, parliament's main function was now to "rubber-stamp decisions made elsewhere". As a result:

> Suspended between state monopoly capitalism above and an indifferent mass of people below, Labour MPs are completely powerless and more and more irrelevant.

Labour, he concluded, was not even a reformist party in the traditional sense. He did not call on comrades to leave the Labour Party and in his conclusion he noted that "the overwhelming majority of organised workers still by tradition see in the Labour Party their political organisation". But the message was clear. No strategy oriented on the Labour Party, aiming to change the leadership or to benefit from a split, was now viable for revolutionaries.

A third article – "The sad saga of the soggies'* decline"[85] – examined the decline of the Labour left from George Lansbury to Michael Foot. The former, though a "soft reformist", had real links with the industrial struggle, whereas the "powerless, irrelevant Foots" of the 1960s had hardly any connection with workers in struggle.

Cliff was also maintaining a punishing schedule of public speaking. In the autumn of 1966 his engagements were listed as follows: "TC will be visiting the following places to speak: Newcastle Oct 7: Glasgow Oct 8/9: Manchester Oct 10: Leeds Oct 11: Sheffield Oct 12".[86]

All this activity did not pass unnoticed by the left's enemies. In winter 1965-66 *Common Cause Bulletin* (mainly devoted to anti-Communist campaigning) published a piece by Arthur Duncan on "Trotskyist Groupings and associates". This was poorly researched, claiming that the "Cliff group" originated from a "breakaway from the American Trotskyists led by *Mr Max Schachtman*", but it did publish Cliff's real name and address.[87]

In April 1967 there was an IS aggregate meeting at Wortley Hall in Sheffield. Cliff took advantage of the occasion to develop his thoughts on perspectives for the organisation.[88] He began with the unity of theory and practice. On most occasions when Cliff referred to the unity of theory and practice it was in order to stress the centrality of practice, to polemicise against the kind of academic Marxism that played with ideas for their own sake rather than seeing them as a guide to action.

---

* The term "soggy" was in common currency among IS members to refer to the soft, or Tribunite, left of the Labour Party.

Now, however, he recognised a danger in the opposite direction. The IS were attracting new members by their activity around industrial and tenants' struggles, often people who had little knowledge of earlier discussions around such issues as state capitalism. As Cliff argued:

> we moved into much more activism and there'll be a danger that we'll become mindless militants. It's true that theory without action is sterile, but activity without theory is blind.

He went on to state his view of Marxism, its need both to hold firm to the fundamentals inherited from the past and to adapt to a constantly changing reality:

> The truth is always concrete and because Marxism therefore has always to be bloomin' concrete, always practical, has to change all of the time. Unless it changes it's bloomin' dead, and that's why on the one hand you have to stick to tradition but on the other hand you have to stick to growth. This dialectical relation is central to the whole thing.*

He then went over the theory of state capitalism, and the relation of his own thinking to Trotsky's ideas. In particular he returned to a theme which ran through his entire work, his deep hatred of formalism:

> If it was true that the working class was the agent of the socialist revolution then the form of property is a bloody stupid criterion for deciding whether a state is a workers' state or not, because the worker as an active element in society doesn't give a damn about the form of property. What the worker as an active agent cares about is the relations in production, in other words what place the worker is in the process of production; whether the worker comes to a state enterprise like the railways or private enterprise like ICI it [sic] doesn't come in relation to it as regards the form of property.

Here again we can sense Cliff's recognition that the organisation was in a transitional phase. What it was in transition to was not yet apparent. Events were beginning to move quickly and Cliff's mind was fully occupied in grappling with the implications.

Recruitment was still on the basis of ones and twos, and Cliff found time to help members all over the country. In 1967 John

---

* This is transcribed from a spoken presentation; in Cliff's use of the vernacular, and especially of mild expletives, it is a good representation of his speaking style.

Charlton became a student at York University and began building a branch in Doncaster. Cliff would visit frequently and sometimes Charlton would spend all day with Cliff, asking questions. He found Cliff attentive and patient despite his other commitments.[89]

When Nick Howard moved to Sheffield in 1965 Cliff kept demanding that he should set up a branch. In 1966 Howard set up a meeting for Cliff; six people attended, three from the Labour Party, and three from the SLL (two of whom later joined the IS). Despite competition from the CP and the SLL, the branch grew to a membership of 20 and played a significant role in a rent strike.[90]

Volkhard Mosler was a German student in London, who first came across some of Cliff's writings, notably his article on Deutscher, in copies of *International Socialism* at the home of Chris Pallis. He was favourably impressed and translated some of Cliff's articles for the publications of the German SDS (Socialist German Student Union). He got to know Cliff and when he returned to Germany helped to found the Sozialistische Arbeitergruppe (SAG) in 1969. Mosler maintained contact with Cliff, through meetings and correspondence, over the next 30 years.[91]

Cliff and Chanie also found time to help consolidate the organisation by dabbling in matchmaking. Colin Barker and Ewa Widowson, who had just got to know each other, came to stay at Cliff's home for two nights. On the first night they were provided with a couch and a camp bed, but when they returned for the second night the camp bed had disappeared. Forty years later they are still together.[92]

Amid all this frenetic activity Cliff and Chanie were raising a family. There was no attempt to manipulate the children. Donny Gluckstein remembers making tea for Tariq Ali and Robin Blackburn, and being paid ten shillings (50 pence) for inserting the centre pages of *Labour Worker*, but there was never any pressure on him to join the organisation, and when he did join – at the age of 15 – he was left to get on with it without parental guidance.[93]

Cliff and Chanie's home life was totally dominated by their commitment to the organisation. Nigel Coward remembers returning from the docks to Cliff's house one day around lunchtime. Chanie was in the process of feeding the four children. Without a word she took some of the peas from each of the children's plates to give him a portion.[94]

Cliff had an amazing capacity for concentration amid the pressures of domestic life. Sometimes he and Chanie would go to visit Nigel and Tirril Harris in their cottage in Suffolk. Nigel remembers finding Cliff at 6am surrounded by half a dozen screaming children (the young Glucksteins, Kidrons and Harrises), reading Brailsford's *The Levellers and the English Revolution*, quite oblivious to what was going on around him. But he did not shirk his duties. Tirril was struck by the fact that "he didn't mind shit" – he did a lot of nappy-changing and volunteered to empty the Elsan chemical toilet.[95]

International events were now having an effect on the IS group's evolution. The US military build-up in South Vietnam had begun in the early 1960s, but it was in February 1965, with the bombing of North Vietnam, that it became clear that this was escalating into a full-scale war. Although no British troops were sent to Vietnam, the Wilson government gave slavish support to the US war effort.

IS members were present at the first small demonstration against the war on 14 February 1965,[96] called after Malcolm X had visited the LSE. *Labour Worker* published some well-informed articles on the situation by Nigel Harris.[97] IS members (including Ian Birchall and Roger Rosewell) were present at the founding conference of the British Council for Peace in Vietnam in 1965. This body, dominated by left Labour MPs and the CP, confined its demands to peace and a negotiated withdrawal of US troops. As a result, in the spring of 1966 the Vietnam Solidarity Campaign (VSC), which took an unequivocal position of support for the Vietnamese National Liberation Front, was launched on the initiative of the Fourth International and Ralph Schoenman, Bertrand Russell's secretary. Again IS members were involved in the founding, and two members, John Palmer and Jim Scott, were elected to its National Council.[*]

The IS had no difficulty in accepting the VSC line. The Vietnam War was quite different from the Korean War 15 years earlier. The former, as Cliff had argued, had been a "struggle of the powers", a limited trial of strength between Washington and Moscow. In Vietnam there was an autonomous struggle by a genuine national liberation movement, based on a peasant struggle for land. Indeed

---

[*] The fullest history of the VSC is Celia Hughes, "The History of the Vietnam Solidarity Campaign: the substructure of far left activism in Britain, 1966-1969", History MA, University of Warwick, September 2008.

the war was, if anything, something of an embarrassment to Moscow.

Nonetheless, until 1967, the IS's response to Vietnam was relatively muted. Partly this was simply a question of priorities. For a small group, activity around shop stewards and tenants left little time for campaigning on Vietnam. Moreover the war did not quite fit with the analysis of imperialism developed by Kidron. He* had warned quite explicitly that "to believe nowadays that the short route to revolution in London, New York or Paris lies through Calcutta, Havana or Algiers, is to pass the buck to where it has no currency".[98] Cliff was hostile to the "Third Worldism" prevalent in many sections of the left, believing that it meant taking "vicarious pleasure" in distant events rather than engaging in more mundane struggles at home. On one occasion he told a meeting that Vietnam was "a long way away"[99] – a statement which, in geographical terms, was unquestionably true, but politically was less than the whole picture. When in early 1966 Richard Gott stood as an independent candidate in a by-election in Hull to protest at British support for the US in Vietnam, *Labour Worker* was highly critical, calling him a "scab" and accusing him of "radical masturbation"[100] – though Cliff was less indignant than some of the leadership, like John Palmer, who were more strongly oriented to the Labour Party.[101]

By 1967 widespread opposition to the Vietnam War was developing, especially among a generation of students and young people not old enough to have been through the experience of CND and the YS. It was Chris Harman, in touch with the mood among students at the LSE (increasingly a centre of student militancy – see below), who helped to reorient the IS towards a greater involvement

---

* In around 1964 I recall suggesting to Kidron that *International Socialism* might carry an editorial on Vietnam. He looked at me with withering scorn and said, "You mean that little war! That silly...little...war!" By 1970 Kidron was writing of the "US decision to withdraw from Vietnam", and describing the Vietnam War as "a distraction from the essential American interest" (M Kidron, *Western Capitalism Since the War*, revised edition, Harmondsworth, 1970, pp153-154). The prediction was correct, but the analysis ignored the five years of political struggle before the final withdrawal. Cliff shared Kidron's overall perspective, but was more alive to the need to oppose imperialism, whatever its motivations. This was shown by his later strong support for campaigns against British imperialism in the Falkland Islands, the 1991 Gulf War and Kosovo.

with the Vietnam question. In July 1967 IS members in the VSC (Harman, Ian Birchall, Norah Carlin) argued for the building of a large demonstration; Harman in particular argued that the demonstration should "aim to immobilise the American embassy for a token period".[102] On 22 October the VSC called a march to the US Embassy in London. Despite lack of enthusiasm from the CP (which preferred rival demonstrations the previous day[103]) this attracted several thousand marchers, and led to violent clashes with mounted police in Grosvenor Square. Described as an "anti-war riot" and a "pitched battle",[104] the event raised the political profile of the VSC considerably.

Cliff himself said and wrote very little about Vietnam, but was adamant in insisting that the IS should become involved in the VSC.[105] Some years later he was to admit that if it had not been for the movement against the Vietnam War, the IS might never have moved beyond being a tiny propaganda group.[106]

Another international event touched Cliff more closely. In June 1967 war broke out between Israel and Egypt, Jordan and Syria. Israel won a rapid victory in the so-called Six Days War, and took the opportunity to extend its frontiers considerably. But Israel's short-term victory produced a Palestinian movement which would continue to struggle for the next 40 years and more.

Cliff had given little attention to the Middle East during the 20 years he had been in Britain; the enemy was at home, and he immersed himself in struggle in the land where he lived. On one occasion in the early 1960s he had been asked about Israel and simply responded, "What's done is done" – the state of Israel existed and history could not be rolled back.[107] There had been little or no discussion of the Middle East in the IS group, and many members were initially confused by the turn of events. However, Tariq Ali has a distinct memory of hearing Cliff speak about Palestine in Oxford before the Six Days War. He was greatly impressed because, despite his background in Pakistan, he knew little about the Middle East. He was struck by Cliff calling Israel a "racist country" and by his vivid description of the treatment of Arabs in Israel.[108]

Now within weeks Cliff had written a short pamphlet on the situation. *The Struggle in the Middle East*[109] was four pages long in newspaper format, and analysed the situation produced by the war. Cliff traced the many changes that had taken place since he had last made a serious analysis of the Middle East 20 years earlier.

He began, as ever, with imperialism and the centrality of oil – he commented in a typical mixed metaphor that "Middle East oil is really a gold mine". By now US imperialism had largely taken over Britain's role. He then gave a brief history of Zionism and defined Israel as "a settler's citadel, a launching-pad of imperialism". Since imperialism was the main enemy, Jews could be seen as in some sense victims:

> Zionism does not redeem Jewry from suffering. On the contrary, it imperils them with a new danger, that of being a buffer between imperialism and the national and social liberatory struggle of the Arab masses.

But while there were real class divisions in the Jewish population of Israel, the Israelis remained "the privileged and oppressors, the allies of imperialism". Like white South Africans or Algerian settlers, they were unlikely to unite with those they oppressed.

He then turned to the Arab national movement. The Arab states were divided between those ruled by feudal kings and sheihks and the more progressive regimes in Egypt, Syria, Algeria and Iraq. He noted that Nasser had "inconsistently, haltingly" carried through certain measures of nationalisation and redistribution of wealth. But he saw Nasser's Egypt and the Ba'ath regime in Syria in terms of his analysis of "deflected permanent revolution" and stressed their "middle class social base". Hence he believed Nasserism was incapable of "successful anti-imperialist revolutionary struggle". The Communist parties merely tailed the Arab nationalists.

Cliff located the recent war in the context of threats to imperialism in the Middle East, notably a dispute between Syria and the Iraq Petroleum Company. It was Western imperialism which benefited from the Israeli victory. But Nasser was incapable of mobilising a Vietnam-style mass struggle. Cliff concluded that the only solution lay in the establishment of a Middle Eastern "socialist republic, with full rights for Jews, Kurds and all national minorities".

One of Cliff's sharpest critics, Werner Cohn, has argued that the pamphlet marked a qualitative shift from Cliff's writings of the 1940s, especially with the dropping of references to Arab violence against Jews; Cohn sees this as a "rewriting of history" comparable to that of which Stalinism had been guilty.[110] Certainly there was a shift here, and one which would stay with Cliff for the rest of his life. But the real shift in 1967 was not inside Cliff's head; it was in the real world. With the Six Days War Israel confirmed that it was a client state of the US, an expansionist power and a major force of reaction in the Middle East. Cliff's merit lay simply in being one of the first to recognise and analyse this.

The pamphlet was certainly against the stream as far as the British left was concerned. Labour movement sympathies were largely pro-Israel; the Palestinian case was still little articulated. Out of about 360 Labour MPs, 222 – almost two-thirds – were paid-up members of the Labour Friends of Israel.[111] Leading figures of the Labour left such as Ian Mikardo and Sidney Silverman fiercely defended Israel.[112] But the pamphlet, of which 3,600 were distributed by 1 July,[113] made some impact. Fred Lindop recalls that it was useful for arguing in a largely Jewish Labour Party in London, where there was a bitter debate over the whole question of Israel.[114]

Cliff was also taking an interest in the re-emerging Irish left. A number of IS members were active in the short-lived Irish Workers Group, which was riven by constant internal conflicts. Gery Lawless set up a series of classes on Marxist economics led by Cliff in his flat near the Arsenal in London. Lawless was a supporter of the United Secretariat of the Fourth International, but was friendly with Cliff.[115] One of those attending was Eamonn McCann, who found that he was able to grasp Marxist economics like a sudden revelation. He remembers Cliff as a good teacher and very entertaining.[116] Another member of the Irish Workers Group was Michael Farrell, who was to become a leader of People's Democracy, and whom Cliff would try to convince of the need for a revolutionary party oriented towards class politics.[117]

The 1960s saw important cultural changes in British life. The contraceptive pill changed patterns of sexual behaviour, and abortion and homosexuality were legalised. The decade saw the emergence of the phenomenon of hippies. New drugs, notably the hallucinogenic LSD, came into widespread use, and there were important innovations in popular music.

There is evidence that Cliff had heard of the Beatles, but beyond this he had little interest in the counterculture. On one occasion he conflated advocates of "flower power" and pot-smokers with the term "flower-pot men" (the name of a popular children's television programme).[118] As with the YS a few years earlier, Cliff made no concessions to lifestyle; he knew that if he was to win supporters it would be through his politics and nothing else. But he was sensitive to the spirit of revolt, whatever form it might take.

In particular, there were important shifts going on in the student milieu. The IS group had always recruited a number of students. But until the mid-1960s student politics had meant essentially campaigning for a political party or tendency within the universities. In the early 1960s IS member Nigel Harris had been president of the Labour Party's National Association of Labour Student Organisations (NALSO) and many other comrades had been active in student Labour Party bodies.

In the spring of 1967 everything changed. Students at the LSE had launched a campaign against the appointment of a director who had collaborated with the racist regime in Rhodesia. Following disciplinary measures by the LSE authorities against student activists, there was an eight-day occupation of the college, which led to the overturning of the victimisations.[119] This struggle transformed the face of student politics; student activists now began to centre their concerns on democratic rights for students within their universities, and on the whole content of higher education and its role in capitalist society. (Internationally, the modern student movement could be traced back to the Free Speech Movement at the University of California in 1964.)

Cliff responded quickly, whereas both the SLL and the *Militant* grouping showed much less interest in student struggles.[120] He had already taken an interest in the LSE, since Chris Harman, Richard Kuper and others were students there, and around the time of the occupation he gave a series of weekly lectures to the LSE Socialist Society.[121] In the period after the occupation Cliff began turning up once or twice a week in the LSE refectory where he would sit and talk. The people closest to him at this point were Laurie Flynn, John Rose and Ted Parker; Chris Harman was around, but he was already integrated into the organisation. Cliff thus developed an influence on members of the LSE Socialist Society and began to draw people into the IS.[122]

The IS students at the LSE played an important role in organising the occupation. Rapidly they drew around them a number of other student militants – John Rose, Steve Jefferys, Laurie Flynn, Sabby Sagall, George Paizis, Basker Vashee, Phillip Hall, Mike McKenna and others. A number were won to the IS, and were to become key figures in the growth of the organisation over the coming decade. Several who went through that experience remain members of the SWP 40 years later.*

Sabby Sagall first heard Cliff speak at the LSE in 1966 when he was a postgraduate student who had just left the Labour Party over Vietnam. Cliff spoke on Mao, and Sabby was impressed with his rigorous intellectual clarity. After a second talk, on state capitalism, "everything fell into place". Sagall joined the IS just after the occupation, following a three-hour discussion with Cliff which convinced him to break with the last vestiges of Zionism. He was swept along by Cliff's overpowering optimism at a time when the world seemed to be on fire.[123]

Martin Tomkinson, who had been a "rabble rouser" at the LSE, found himself drawn into the IS circle and soon got to know Cliff. He was struck by his warmth and humanity, especially the warmth of his relationship to Chanie and their children; at the same time he seemed to have the aura of a link to the old Bolsheviks, while being immune to any kind of hero worship.[124]

A range of issues proved important in this situation. In particular Cliff was able to have an important influence on Jewish students who were concerned at the impact of the Six Days War. John Rose – later editor of *Socialist Worker* – has recalled how he, an idealistic young Zionist who admired Sartre and Deutscher, was won over by Cliff's ideas. He was an LSE student who had taken part in the occupation and was sympathetic to the IS, but was still a Zionist. During the Six Days War there was a teach-in at the LSE, lasting from lunchtime until well into the night.

> Two of the main speakers were Tony Cliff and Ronnie Kasrils. Kasrils, a mature LSE student, was Jewish and an exiled member of the outlawed South African Communist Party...
>
> Cliff and Kasrils both agreed that socialists had to support Gamal Abdel

---

* Among those who moved out of the organisation at various stages were people who have made a contribution to the cause of the left in one way or another: Steve Jefferys is Director of the Working Lives Research Institute at London Metropolitan University, Laurie Flynn is a well-known investigative journalist, Phillip Hall wrote the book (*Royal Fortune*, London, 1992) that forced the Queen to pay income tax, and Basker Vashee became director of the Transnational Institute in Amsterdam.

Nasser's Egypt in the war. For over 100 years the Arab people had been subjected to Western domination, plunder, racism and contempt…

But Cliff and Kasrils disagreed about how effectively he would prosecute the war. They also disagreed about Nasser's vision of Arab socialism for the Middle East.

This teach-in, for me, operated at two levels. There was the open political argument about Nasser's revolutionary credentials. They were thrown into doubt by Cliff's view that Nasser would not mobilise Arab workers and peasants across the Middle East for a mass-based revolutionary war against Israel.

This would have meant taking on the pro-US regimes like Saudi Arabia. Nasser was also far too dependent on the Soviet Union. Cliff had an unerring insight that this would lose Nasser the war…

Important though this argument was, I was hearing and seeing something in addition. I saw two fearless revolutionaries, both of Jewish origin, who felt completely at ease with their Jewish identities…

Cliff and Kasrils…represented a wider Jewish tradition, believers and non-believers, which, in every generation, has poured thousands of Jewish men and women into the socialist and communist movements, and other progressive causes.

It is a Jewish humanism, deeply offended by oppression and exploitation, that takes internationalism for granted.

During those six days I learned that Zionism and this Jewish humanism were incompatible. I have never looked back.[125]

On 6 November 1967 Cliff was one of the speakers at a rally at the Mahatma Gandhi Hall in London to commemorate the fiftieth anniversary of the Russian Revolution. The other speakers were Harry Wicks, a member of the British Communist Party from the early 1920s and a pioneer Trotskyist, CLR James, also a Trotskyist veteran from the 1930s, and Gery Lawless. The platform represented a convergence of various currents of a far left which was beginning to move out of the marginal position it had occupied for the last two decades.

Earlier that year, in April, Cliff had found time for what was to be his last opportunity to travel abroad.[126] With Colin Barker he went to Paris to meet with Pouvoir Ouvrier, an organisation which had emerged from a split in Socialisme ou Barbarie, with which the IS had loose contacts in the early 1960s. There were discussions of the permanent arms economy, on which Cliff gave a presentation, and the working class movement in Britain and France, and an exchange of views on practical activity. The Pouvoir Ouvrier comrades recorded with interest the discussions that had taken place. In particular they noted Cliff's view of revolutionary organisation:

> On the question of revolutionary organisation, Trotskyists have made a virtue of necessity. The form of organisation advocated by the Bolsheviks was in fact forced on them by the conditions of activity in Tsarist Russia (as was that advocated by Rosa Luxemburg in Poland). Necessity imposed on the Bolsheviks a highly centralised and clandestine organisation; such a form of organisation can in no way be valid in the present situation in Western Europe. The bureaucratisation of the unions and the labour movement requires us to give vigorous support to the spontaneous outbursts of the proletariat against the restraining role constantly played by the bureaucracy. [127]

It was a position Cliff would rethink radically in the coming years.

On the return journey Cliff was nervous about passport control, saying to Barker, "If there's any trouble don't wait for me." But there were no problems.[128] Cliff can scarcely have imagined how important the French connection would prove in the coming year.

7

1968
Year of Wonders

In January 1968 the Vietnamese National Liberation Front (NLF) launched the Tet offensive. NLF fighters penetrated to the heart of Saigon and took over the city of Hue. For a time the US forces seemed to have lost control of the situation. Eventually the offensive was repulsed, but the events, televised around the world, communicated a powerful message. The world's greatest economic and military power had been humiliated by a Third World peasant army. The US government decided to open peace negotiations. In Sartre's words, the "field of the possible" was now seen to be immense.[1]

This gave an enormous boost to the confidence of groups engaged in struggle all around the world. As Cliff sometimes put it, workers were often held back not by consciousness (the belief that the existing order was legitimate), but by lack of confidence (the sense that they were not strong enough to win).[*]

Tet opened what was to be the most remarkable year of the second half of the 20th century, a year which transformed the expectations of revolutionary socialists around the globe. With his political instinct, Cliff was aware of new possibilities; he remarked early in the year that he could smell a change in the air.[2] The events of the year confirmed the beliefs he had stood by through two decades of terrible isolation; they also confronted him with a range of new problems which he had not hitherto had to deal with.

IS had begun the year with 447 members.[3] It was small enough – though bigger than the RCP had been in 1947, and so the biggest organisation Cliff had been in during his life so far. Because of the activities of the preceding years the membership was geared to making interventions, albeit fairly low-level ones. Without the base

---

[*] For example, "Class consciousness cannot exist independent of class confidence." T Cliff, "The Balance of Class Forces in Recent Years", *International Socialism* 6 (Autumn 1979).

and the orientation established before 1968, the breakthrough of 1968 could not have taken place. If the IS had begun the year with only 200, it might have ended up with little more.

So Cliff devoted great attention to the small growing-points of the organisation. He had encouraged Sabby Sagall to get involved with activity around Ford in Dagenham, and when Sagall organised a small group around him, Cliff travelled to Dagenham every week to speak to them. Sagall was struck by the fact that he didn't hector workers but listened to them. He used to say, "We learn from the class and we teach the class".[4]

Cliff was also eager to draw in individuals, perhaps excessively so. In April 1968 he called a meeting of the *International Socialism* editorial board at Akiva Orr's home. When Orr protested that he was not a member, Cliff merely responded that the board would meet and make him a member. In fact Orr was politically closer to *Solidarity*, which he then joined.[5]

On 17 March the VSC had called another London demonstration, this time supported, somewhat half-heartedly, by the Communist Party. The action in Grosvenor Square was at least as vigorous as the previous October, and up to 20,000 people took part. IS members, joined by new recruits and sympathisers, especially in the universities, played a major part in building the demonstration, during which "the embassy was virtually under siege for two hours".[6] A CND demonstration the following week attracted only around 3,000; the initiative in the anti-war movement was passing into the hands of the far left.[7]

Within the movement, the IS strove to recruit on the basis of linking the anti-war activity to the struggle at home. A leaflet distributed on the March demonstration stated:

> the battle against wage freeze; against social service cuts; against bad housing and rent increases; against bad hospitals and schools; against unemployment; against the government's racialist policies; is the *same battle* against the Vietnam War... In the factories workers *are* fighting against the wage freeze and unemployment. On the housing estates tenants *are* resisting rent increases. If we are to help the Vietnamese we must go on from Grosvenor Square to fight these struggles.

A blow against the boss is a blow against the Vietnam War.[8]

If the left was able to feel some satisfaction at progress being made around Vietnam, it soon got a savage shock. In April 1968 Enoch Powell, a former Tory cabinet minister and still a leading figure in his party, made a viciously racist speech predicting violence – a river "foaming with much blood" – as a result of immigration, already tightly restricted by the Labour government. Tory leader Edward Heath promptly sacked Powell from his shadow cabinet, creating a backlash in Powell's support.

Powell was not a fascist; he was an old-style right-wing Tory racist with a full set of obnoxious opinions.* But for a mainstream politician to take up the question of immigration so aggressively was an open encouragement to the activists of the far right. There was an even more alarming consequence: various groups of trade unionists decided to take strike action to demonstrate their support for Powell. On May Day London dockers struck in support of him.

This revealed the bankruptcy of the traditional left. The Labour Party had made so many concessions over immigration that when racism began to get out of control it had no response. For a fortnight after the Powell speech Wilson and the other Labour leaders remained silent, offering no answer. The only comments came from David Ennals, a junior minister at the Home Office. One of Wilson's ministers, Bob Mellish, found this an appropriate time to call for the deportation to Pakistan of revolutionary socialist activist Tariq Ali. When one left MP, Ian Mikardo, spoke out against racism, he was physically assaulted.

The CP, which had some influence in the docks, failed to use it to fight Powell. There had been no experience of fighting racism in the docks before 1968, and so there was virtually no input from the CP. "Most militants, including CP members, simply took the line of least resistance, avoided the meeting and kept their heads down." One CP member who did speak out faced a "lynch-mob situation".[9] Danny Lyons, a leading CP militant, brought along two clergymen, one Catholic and one Protestant, to try to dissuade dockers from striking.[10] This intervention was counterproductive. Fred Lindop has summed up the CP's limitations in these circumstances:

Their socialist politics, though important in contributing to their ability

---

* In his youth, Powell, later to be Minister of Health, had written a poem beginning "I hate the ugly, hate the old, I hate the lame and weak"(E Powell, *Collected Poems*, London, 1990 p5). For a full analysis of Powell's politics, see P Foot, *The Rise of Enoch Powell*, Harmondsworth, 1969.

to lead their fellow workers, were not connected in any direct way with the daily conflicts through which the traditions of solidarity were created and maintained, and consequently gave them no confidence in their ability to fight for an unpopular political standpoint.[11]

The situation highlighted what an editorial in *International Socialism* described as "the vacuum on the left",[12] a term used widely in discussions within the organisation. The political decline of the CP and the Labour left meant that there was no organised force able to give the necessary lead in such situations. The IS was far too small to fill the gap, but it was now clear that its political aim must be to create an alternative organisation of the left. It is no surprise that Cliff, with his deep loathing of racism, grasped the gravity of the situation.

The immediate problem was the dockers' strike. The IS, which had been active in the 1967 dock strike, had just one docker, Terry Barrett, in membership, but he made every effort to argue the point in class terms. Cliff discussed with Barrett late into the night about the best way to respond to the situation,[13] and persuaded him not to cross the picket line.[14] Barrett was almost completely isolated, and other dockers threw pennies at him.[15]

Barrett, together with some IS members and other revolutionaries, signed and distributed to dockers a leaflet, written by Paul Foot, putting the class case against Powell:

> Who is Enoch Powell? He is a right-wing Tory opportunist who will stop at nothing to help his Party and his class. He is a director of the vast National Discount Company (assets £224m) which pays him a salary bigger than the £3,500 a year he gets as an MP.
>
> He lives in fashionable Belgravia and writes Greek verse.
>
> What does he believe in? *Higher Unemployment.* He has consistently advocated a national average of 3 percent unemployed. *Cuts in the Social Services.* He wants higher health charges, less council houses, charges for state education and lower unemployment pay. *Mass Sackings in the Docks.* Again and again he has argued that the docks are "grossly overmanned".[16]

Powell's speech initiated a series of new initiatives on the part of the IS. The first was an appeal for left unity. A leaflet distributed with the May issue of *Labour Worker* was headed "The Urgent

Challenge of Fascism". It was written by Chris Harman; the title was added by Nigel Coward, with Cliff's approval, when he was taking it to the printer.[17] (Despite the title, the leaflet referred mainly to the rise of racism, and contained only one mention of "long-term fascist development".) This called for the establishment of a united organisation on the basis of four fundamental points of principle:

(1) Opposition to imperialism; for the victory of all genuine national liberation movements.

(2) Opposition to racism in all its forms and to controls on immigration.

(3) Opposition to state control of trade unions – support for all progressive strikes.

(4) Workers' control of society and industry as the only alternative to fascism.

The appeal fitted the mood of the time. With the decline of the Labour Party, which was losing members rapidly,* Vietnam and the Powell speech, there was a significant number of young people looking for a political alternative, to whom the debates which had divided the Trotskyist movement over the previous 20 years seemed unimportant. A united revolutionary organisation could have drawn them together and created a body capable of effective intervention.

The initiative was doomed to failure. What had been until 1968 (when the IS overtook it) the largest of the British Trotskyist groupings, the SLL, was an inherently sectarian organisation.† Several other organisations, including the CP, were approached, but no response was received. The International Marxist Group (IMG), British section of the Fourth International, which had played a leading role in building the VSC, had already had unity discussions with IS the previous year.[18] It responded by proposing additions to the four points, and discussions continued for a while[19] but did not

---

* Official figures, which were substantial overestimates, showed that Labour Party membership fell from 830,000 in 1964 to 680,000 in 1970, a fall of over 18 percent (A Thorpe, *A History of the British Labour Party*, Basingstoke, 2008, p183).

† In October 1968, when 100,000 people marched against the Vietnam War, SLL members turned up to give out a leaflet headed "Why the Socialist Labour League is Not Marching" (D Widgery, *The Left in Britain 1956-1968*, Harmondsworth, 1976, p349).

produce a result.*

Cliff was keen to recruit Tariq Ali, who had acquired a high public profile as one of the new generation of revolutionaries. According to Tariq, Cliff in 1968 made "non-stop" efforts to recruit him. Once when Tariq visited him at his home, Cliff locked the kitchen door and said he would not let Tariq leave till he joined the IS, and was cross to learn that Tariq had decided to join the IMG.[20] Chris Harman believed that if Tariq had agreed to join, it might have been possible to build an organisation of several thousands.[21]

Three years later Duncan Hallas wrote an assessment of what the unity proposals might have achieved:

> The situation in 1968 was that there was a big movement of youth, especially student youth, towards socialist politics and this was given organisational form by the Vietnam Solidarity Campaign (VSC). There was a reasonable possibility that if a united revolutionary socialist organisation could be established it would be possible to draw in some thousands of anti-Vietnam War demonstrators. In particular, it was hoped that the IMG (then only two years old) would agree to unite with IS. These two organisations had between them the dominant position in the VSC and, if united, could probably have converted it into a revolutionary socialist organisation of some substance. There were also prospects that, given the impetus generated by such a unification, various New Left May Day Manifesto elements and unaffiliated left wingers could be drawn in.
>
> Such a unified organisation, overwhelmingly student in composition and "libertarian" and voluntaristic in sentiment, would have had powerful ultra-left tendencies. The perspective was of a long, hard fight inside it for Marxist politics and a working class orientation. Splits would have

---

* A document entitled "International Marxist Group Statement on Unity" (probably May 1968) sums up the IMG's position: "The four points suggested by the International Socialism Group, while being the basis for a united front type committee, are clearly inadequate for the formation of a new revolutionary organisation, which requires a more rounded out programme which has a theoretical basis. Should the four points be accepted as providing the basis for coordination and collaboration among socialists, we propose that they be re-drafted to make them *offensive* rather than *defensive* slogans. They need relating to the upsurge of the world revolution as evidenced by Vietnam, France, Germany, the United States, etc. Before we could participate in such a process we would have to see a fifth point added: solidarity with revolutionary Cuba." (Newens archive)

been inevitable. These costs were considered acceptable in the circumstances, given the opportunity and the urgent need to break out of small group politics".[22]

The Powell speech was rapidly followed by even more dramatic events which changed the whole context in which the IS operated.

After several weeks of student demonstrations in Paris, the authorities closed down the Sorbonne. There were further confrontations between students and police; on the night of 10 May students tore up the cobbles from the streets in the Latin Quarter and built barricades. Despite vicious police attacks with CS gas, they held their ground all night. Police brutality was rapidly made known to the population at large through radio broadcasts.

By their action the students had shown it was possible to resist General de Gaulle's authoritarian French government. They thereby gave confidence to the working class that it was possible to fight. On Monday 13 May the trade unions called a one-day strike in protest at police brutality. For the bureaucracy it was a token protest designed to let off steam. A million people marched through Paris. On 14 May workers in Nantes voted to occupy their factory. Within days occupations spread across the whole of France, and by the following week there were some ten million workers on strike, most of them involved in workplace occupations. It was the biggest general strike in human history.

Within the student milieu there were a number of revolutionary groupings – Maoists, Trotskyists and anarchists. They were small in size (what the CP dismissively called *groupuscules*), with a total membership of at best a few thousand. In a situation of rising struggle they set sectarian differences aside, and were sufficiently strong to arouse the wrath of the CP; in June the government banned the main revolutionary groups.

The events in France surprised everyone, on right and left alike. In the first week of May *The Economist* had published a special supplement predicting a rosy future for French capitalism, concluding that "a French swing to industrial expansion and modernisation and intelligent economic liberalism after de Gaulle could yet astonish the world".[23] A little earlier André Gorz, one of France's best-known left intellectuals, had predicted that "in the foreseeable future there will be no crisis of European capitalism so dramatic as to drive the mass of workers to revolutionary general strikes."[24]

Cliff was as surprised as anyone else, but he responded with delight. This display of working class power confirmed what he had been arguing for the last 30 years – that capitalism remained an exploitative and unstable system, that the working class remained the potential agency of social change, and that revolution was possible. He wrote a few weeks later:

> None of the capitalist powers of our era is stable enough to be immune from proletarian revolution... France has shown, more clearly even than Hungary or the Belgian general strike, that the working class of the advanced countries has not been bribed or integrated into complacency, but retains enormous revolutionary potential.[25]

The coming together of the Powell speech and the French strike provided a dramatic image of the possibilities and dangers of the situation. Meanwhile a wave of occupations and demonstrations swept through Britain's universities; a new layer of radicalised young people were open to revolutionary ideas. Cliff realised that opportunities had to be grasped, and grasped very quickly.

He travelled tirelessly, speaking at meeting after meeting, trying to convey to his audiences the urgency of the situation. Bob Clay heard him at a public meeting in Teesside. He was "gobsmacked"; everything came from a carefully structured world-view, yet it was not academic but related to everyday life. One new member who joined after hearing Cliff immediately donated £20 (more than a week's wages for many workers) to the organisation.[26]

At some meetings Cliff spoke together with Chris Pallis, the leading figure in *Solidarity*, who had published a remarkable eye-witness account of the events in Paris.[27] For a moment it appeared that old divisions were breaking down, though this state of affairs would not last.

In the heat of the moment, he could overstate the situation. At a meeting in Hornsey in north London on 29 May (the day after the start of a six-week occupation at Hornsey College of Art) Cliff told a large audience that capitalism and trade unions could no longer coexist. Perhaps it would be five years, perhaps it would be seven before the final confrontation. He concluded, "If I am wrong, I see you in the concentration camps".[28]

A number of new recruits were made that evening, but the

perspective was exaggerated. Over the next weeks, as the French CP and the trade union leaders succeeded in bringing the strike movement to an end, he modified the analysis somewhat.* Yet it was not wholly unrealistic. Concentration camps were not on the agenda for Hornsey, but just three years later internment would be introduced in Northern Ireland. In five years time the Chilean coup would show how ruthless a threatened capitalism could be.

Cliff seems to have gone through some sort of philosophical development at this point, though he did not make it explicit. In earlier years he had tended to emphasise the deterministic nature of Marxism, for example in the disagreements with Alasdair MacIntyre in the early 1960s. Now there was a distinct shift towards voluntarism; as he put it, "History, that old horse, does nothing"; change depended on our actions.[29] He wrote a little later, "If the study of history – even the most recent – were enough by itself to solve political questions, Social Democracy would have died a long time ago, and so would Stalinism. Alas, this is not how history works. And there is nothing more foreign to socialism than fatalism".[30]

One manifestation of this shift was the fact that, after decades in which he had taken a close interest in economic developments, he was now less concerned with purely economic factors. Instead, over the next three decades, his interest was focused on the subjective factor as he constantly looked for signs of working class resistance.

There were now two significant changes in the way the organisation operated. From June 1968 *Labour Worker* changed its name to *Socialist Worker*. This signalled that the entry tactic in the Labour Party had come to an end, and that the IS would be an openly revolutionary organisation. There was some opposition to this turn, notably from John Palmer, who thought the old name had built a certain reputation,[31] but in general there was widespread disillusion with the Labour Party and a strong desire on the part of IS members to dissociate themselves from the Labour government.

More controversially, Cliff proposed that the organisation should adopt a democratic centralist structure. He argued the point in a three-page document entitled "Notes on Democratic Centralism" circulated in June 1968.[32]

---

* Though he continued for some years to stress the sense of urgency required by the new period, and in the early 1970s would occasionally still evoke the threat of the concentration camps. (Communication from Alex Callinicos, August 2010).

He began with the observation that the IS had moved in recent years from being a purely propaganda organisation, which sought to win a small audience for its ideas, to becoming an agitational organisation, which was able to intervene in the class struggle. "This demands a different kind of organisational structure. A revolutionary combat organisation – especially if it becomes a party – needs a democratic centralist structure."

Cliff justified this with reference to two historical precedents, the First International and the Bolshevik party. In the First International the followers of Proudhon and Bakunin had argued that only workers should participate, and that the organisation should have a federal structure. In response:

> Marx argued that as the prevailing ideology under capitalism is the ideology of the ruling class, revolutionary politics *does not* reflect the current ideas of the class. As there cannot be a revolutionary movement without a revolutionary theory, the leadership of the International would not necessarily be workers, and could not be delegates on a federative principle.

A federal structure, he argued, was undemocratic – it could not provide adequate representation for minorities, nor allow the vital "inner-organisation struggle of ideas". It was also "unstable and inefficient", since "a revolutionary combat organisation faces the need for tactical decisions – daily and hourly – hence the need for great centralisation". Here the example of the Bolshevik party was particularly relevant.

The actual organisational proposals were not particularly radical – as Cliff pointed out, they were a transition between federalism and democratic centralism, and would probably, in a rapidly changing situation, last only a few months. The most controversial element was the insistence that the new organisational form would require much tighter discipline. "All decisions of Conferences and between Conferences of the Executive are binding on all members of the organisation."

The IS group had traditionally been fairly lax organisationally. In the 18 years since the founding of the SRG there had been just three expulsions. A propaganda group did not need tight discipline. Where there was little intervention, and hence no experience to be evaluated, there was little value in a centralised structure. As Cliff put it, "if you have a bunch of idiots, they will elect an idiot to lead them".[33] There was a quite legitimate reaction against the vanguardism of the SLL, the IS's main rival on the far left.

The document was short – just over 1,000 words. Jim Higgins – then one of Cliff's closest allies – later argued that it was inadequate for its purpose in introducing such a radical change.[34] Likewise Nigel Harris, one of Cliff's allies at this time, thinks that what was impressive about Cliff was his "nose", his ability to realise the significance of a situation, rather than his ability to argue a case. He operated on instinct and often took a long time to find out why he was doing what he was doing.[35] * Some of the more longstanding members – a very relative term at this time – felt that though Cliff had quickly understood what was happening, he had simply made up his mind without bothering to explain why and was not taking the membership seriously.[36]

There is some truth in this. Cliff had a justifiable faith in his own ability to convince the organisation, but he underestimated the difficulties. Among the older membership libertarian ideas were deeply implanted, and most of the new membership – the organisation doubled in size during the year – had come from the anti-authoritarian milieu of student struggles.

Cliff was indeed impatient. He was quite right to be so, for the opportunities offered by the unfolding situation were immense and there was no time to waste. Yet as Cliff himself later noted, even amid the dramatic events of 1917, Lenin stressed the need for patient explanation.[37]

One manifestation of this impatience came from the only positive response to the unity proposals, from a small grouping called Workers' Fight, a split from the *Militant* based mainly in the Manchester area. Its politics were "orthodox Trotskyist", similar to those of the Fourth International, but with many agreements with the IS.† Initial discussions had been held with Colin Barker, and with Noel Tracy and Constance Lever. After some fairly hurried negotiations – conducted

---

* This was also true of his approach to the "downturn" a decade later, where he recognised the problem, but took some time to elaborate a strategy. (see chapters 9 and 10 below).

† The *Labour Worker* front-page lead in June 1967 – "Wilson: Puppet on the Oil Bosses' String" – was written by Sean Matgamna under the pseudonym Anthony Mahony, reprinted from the journal *Workers' Republic*.

by Cliff personally – the Workers' Fight grouping joined the IS. Joel Geier, who was staying with Cliff at the time, observed Cliff conducting the negotiations single-handedly. Cliff was certain that the merger would work because once Sean Matgamna, the leading figure in Workers' Fight, joined the IS he would never want to go back to a group of 20.[38] Matgamna assumed that Cliff was not acting as a freelance and that he was reporting back to the IS leadership.[39] How much reporting back actually took place in the frenzied atmosphere of 1968 is not clear.

In retrospect it appears that Matgamna entered the IS in order to build his own organisation. Jim Higgins, closely involved in the IS leadership at this time, has argued that Cliff should take responsibility for the fusion, and that he let it happen without adequate discussion because he wanted Matgamna's support in the internal debates.[40]

But Cliff's main contribution to the understanding of 1968 and the reorientation of the organisation came in the pamphlet he wrote jointly with Ian Birchall during the summer of 1968, *France: The Struggle Goes On*.[41] * Like Marx's work on the Paris Commune, it was written from afar; in the heated atmosphere of 1968, Cliff was not prepared to travel outside Britain for fear that he might not be permitted to return.† He had long discussions with various French activists who visited London, including two leading members of Lutte Ouvrière (the successor to Voix Ouvrière, which had been banned in June).

The pamphlet gave a narrative account of the events in France,

---

* Since I am named as joint author I should clarify my role in the pamphlet. I wrote most of the material in the three chapters on the CP and the non-Communist left, and provided some of the material on the strikes and occupations. All the theoretical analysis was Cliff's. I was originally asked to provide Cliff with "background" research notes. When I next saw my notes, Cliff had cut up the typescript and stapled pieces of it onto sheets of paper, interspersed with his own handwritten commentary. Not so much scissors and paste as scissors and staples. It should also be said that the appearance of my name on the cover was not simply a recognition of my research ability. The pamphlet contained some rather inflammatory formulations, for example, "In our epoch not a single serious issue can be decided by ballot. In the decisive class battles bullets will decide." (p65) Since Cliff did not have British citizenship, he was concerned about possible reprisals, and it was agreed that I would take responsibility for such passages, saying that Cliff had contributed only historical material – the exact opposite of the truth.

† I visited France in July, conducted interviews and collected published material.

drawing out the centrality of the working class struggle and the development of the factory occupations. It thus contrasted with other early analyses in English. Chris Pallis's eye-witness account (published under the pseudonym Maurice Brinton)[42] gave a vivid account of the rising movement, but ended too soon to show how the bureaucrats had brought it under control again. The Penguin publication, *French Revolution 1968*, by Patrick Seale and Maureen McConville, focused largely on the student movement.[43]*

Cliff examined the history of working class grievances before 1968, the "dry tinder" before the conflagration. He showed the important role of young workers, more immune than others to the control of the bureaucracy. He noted "the relative isolation of the immigrant workers" as a sign of weakness in the strike. Above all he stressed the need for "strike committees democratically elected by all workers, union or non-union". In a situation where perhaps only a quarter of the ten million strikers were unionised, fetishising the union structure could only be a brake on the movement. If such committees had existed, "they would have been basically the same as the soviets of 1917 or the Workers' Councils of Hungary in 1956".[44] He showed the difficulties the union bureaucracy had in bringing the strike to an end, and the various ways in which they manipulated the ballots. The strike had broken down the barriers between economic and political struggle, and he judged that the situation in May had been "prerevolutionary, potentially revolutionary".[45]

Beyond this Cliff set out to confront a number of more general issues raised by the French events. First there was the question of the new student movement, something that was not merely important for understanding the French events, but of great strategic importance for building a revolutionary organisation in Britain. In France the students had acted as the "detonator" for a mass working class struggle. On the one hand there were those who failed to see the changing position of students in society, who saw them as still the small privileged minority who had, for example, scabbed on the General Strike of 1926 in Britain. On the other there were those who saw students as a replacement for the traditional role of the

---

* The excellent analysis of the factory occupations by Andrée Hoyles, *Imagination in Power* (Nottingham, 1973), first appeared somewhat later as an article in K Coates, T Topham and M Barratt Brown (eds), *Trade Union Register 1969*, London, 1969.

working class. The new radical newspaper *Black Dwarf* had just appeared with a front page reading "STUDENTS – THE NEW REVOLUTIONARY VANGUARD".[46] *

Avoiding both extremes, Cliff argued that, traditionally, students had identified with bourgeois values. But over recent years student numbers in Britain and throughout the world had increased massively: "The majority of students are not being trained any more as future members of the ruling class...but as white-collar employees of state and industry, and thus are destined to be part and parcel of the proletariat".[47]

Cliff located the upheaval in higher education in the contradictions within capitalism:

> The central contradiction of capitalism is that between the production of what Marx called use-values, and the production of value. The first are natural. The second are specific to the capitalist order of society. In the university this is reflected as a contradiction between the ideal of unlimited intellectual development, free from social, political and ideological restraint, and the tight intellectual reins imposed by capitalism. The liberal mystique of education clashes with its social content.[48]

Increasing international competition would mean pressure to cut expenses and hence resistance to students' demands.

Cliff argued that whereas workers' militancy began from trade union consciousness, students tended to think in abstracts: "Behind the complaint about the tangible reality of low grants, bad food, strict rules and overcrowded amenities, the student feels the intangible manipulation of his mind." Consequently "students at present rebel more readily than workers because they are less shackled mentally by the traditional...organisations... The rootlessness of the student acts as oil to the wheels of revolt".[49] Whatever else had changed, Cliff had not lost his taste for mixed metaphor.

Cliff's observations here were a first approximation. Much more would be said about the political role of students in the coming years.[50] Cliff's analysis at least provided the base for the argument that student struggles were of immense importance, but that they could only succeed if linked to the working class movement.

Second, Cliff attempted to assess the perspective ahead. Here he

---

* Some of those involved claimed that a question mark had been inadvertently omitted (D Widgery, *The Left in Britain*, p313).

was still cautious: "No economic collapse of Western capitalism – in the form of a slump and mass unemployment – is on the agenda for the coming few years." In fact the crisis of 1973, though it would be quite different from 1929, was just a few years in the future. He rightly predicted that in the coming decade "we can expect creeping unemployment, inflation and pressure on wages".

Hence he warned that "we must expect many zigzags in the struggle, from economic strikes to political battles and vice versa". As a counter to the optimism of those who believed that the French struggle would revive in the autumn, he stressed, "The long haul ahead will be the work of years, rather than of months".[51]

In political terms he predicted the decline of the French Communist Party, which would find it increasingly difficult "to retain custody of the working class", since "Moscow has lost its magical influence in the world".[52]* In the short term he was proved wrong – the French CP grew considerably in the 1970s. In the longer term his prediction was correct.

Comparing the British movement to the French, Cliff argued that Britain had certain advantages – the Labour Party was less able to hold back struggle than the French CP, and the British shop stewards' organisation made the class much stronger. His conclusion was undogmatic but optimistic:

> France today, Britain tomorrow!
>
> We cannot be sure of the rhythm of events, but there can be no doubt that there will be an acceleration… We cannot gauge the timing, duration and sweep of the coming revolutionary crisis in British capitalism, but it is not far off.[53]

Within less than six years industrial action would bring down a Tory government.

This perspective was merely background to Cliff's main aim in *France: The Struggle Goes On* – to argue for an immediate strategy of building a revolutionary party, a sharp shift in the orientation of the organisation. The need for such a party was argued concretely from the actual experience of the French struggle. Describing the way the

---

* In a public meeting he put it more dramatically: "For many years I have argued against the danger of capitulating to Stalinism. Now that danger does not exist. They are moving to the right so fast you cannot catch them." (Author's recollection)

bureaucracy manipulated the return to work, Cliff commented, "What a difference would have been made by a revolutionary party with a daily newspaper and possibly even a radio transmitter!" In the absence of such a party, French students and workers had built Action Committees to fill the gap: "As a substitute Soviet that did not exist and a substitute revolutionary party that did not exist, arose the Action Committees! What a magnificent improvisation!"[54]

Without a "credible revolutionary alternative", he warned, the betrayals of the bureaucracies could be repeated. Looking at the experience of the French and Russian Revolutions, he argued, "All revolutions in history have begun spontaneously, none have ended so." He concluded with the classic arguments for the revolutionary party:

> The revolutionary party is, so to say, the memory of the class, the store of experience of the class struggle internationally, the university of the class. Facing the strictly centralised and disciplined power of the capitalists there must be no less centralised and disciplined a combat organisation of the proletariat.[55]

Production of the pamphlet strained the resources of a tiny group already preparing to produce a weekly paper.* Nonetheless it created a certain amount of interest in left circles, and it received a recommendation in the austere pages of *New Left Review*.[56] It was rapidly translated and published in Japanese.[57]

Not all reviewers were complimentary. A polemic from the *Solidarity* group, doubtless written by Chris Pallis, declared, "Comrades Cliff and Birchall fail to recognise the specific, new features of the May events in France. They fail to explain why the students succeeded in inspiring 10 million workers".[58] Even in *International Socialism* Peter Sedgwick expressed reservations. While commending the pamphlet for containing "a mass of data and a deal of hard-headed argument", he was highly sceptical of Cliff's organisational conclusions: "The 'responsible central and local bodies, stable in their composition' (i.e., the same people get elected) 'and in their attitude to their political line' (i.e., they pretend not to change their minds) belong to the traditions of a religious

---

*   I read the proofs in what was reputed to be the cheapest printshop in London, sitting on the edge of the printing press under a naked light bulb. The printer, whose command of English was limited, responded to my proposed corrections by waving a dictionary at me.

order (the Comintern) breathing the stench of an era of defeat and recession within the international proletariat. That era is not ours".⁵⁹

Even while the pamphlet was being printed, Russian tanks invaded Czechoslovakia, to Cliff's surprise,* to put a stop to the reforms of Alexander Dubcek. All round the world Communist parties criticised the Russian action, confirming Cliff's claim that "Moscow has lost its magical influence in the world". The IS analysis enabled comrades to respond promptly to the events. In Hull comrades produced a leaflet on the invasion in Russian and English and through contacts in the docks and fishing industry got copies distributed on Russian cargo ships and trawlers.⁶⁰

Events continued to unfold at a hectic pace. In October another Vietnam demonstration was planned. There was a degree of press hysteria, with claims that violence was being planned. Some groups, notably Maoists, wanted the march to go to Grosvenor Square, where there would undoubtedly have been a major confrontation and many arrests; IS comrades supported the majority proposal for a march to Hyde Park. One hundred thousand people marched. According to one poll, two-thirds of them were opposed to "capitalism in general", not just the war in Vietnam.⁶¹ Given the volatile atmosphere, Cliff decided to leave London for the day of the march. When he returned home he found the police were watching his house.⁶²

By now the talks between the IS and the IMG had broken down. Before the demonstration Cliff approached Tariq Ali and proposed that the IS and the IMG should issue a joint call at the end of the demonstration to set up a united non-sectarian revolutionary youth organisation, which would offer thousands of those marching something to join. Cliff added, realistically, that even if they were to split in a few years time, there would be more revolutionaries in Britain. Tariq supported the argument and took the proposal to the IMG Political Committee, but did not get a single vote in favour.⁶³ †

In the same month the emergent Northern Ireland civil rights

---

* I was due to visit Prague in August, and asked Cliff if he thought the Russians would invade (the possibility was being widely discussed). He told me that he thought not.

† There is a discussion of this in C Hughes, "The History of the Vietnam Solidarity Campaign". See also T Ali, *Street Fighting Years*, London, 2005, p307, where he describes the failure to implement this proposal as a "big tragedy".

movement clashed with police, and in October a threatened national engineering strike was called off at the last minute.

Cliff continued to travel and speak to meetings, doing his best to encourage recruitment. By the end of the year the membership was approximately 1,000. He was also involved in raising money for the organisation's expanded activities. Yet he never forgot the importance of individuals. John Molyneux had joined Camden IS in the summer of 1968 and had rather rashly offered to lead a discussion on bureaucracy, based on a reading of Weber. For some reason Cliff was present at the meeting; he listened carefully and refrained from saying anything to embarrass the young comrade.[64]

Of necessity Cliff now had to devote a considerable amount of attention to the internal development of the organisation. In *France: The Struggle Goes On* and in his "Notes on Democratic Centralism" he had argued the case for the IS becoming an open revolutionary organisation, committed to turning itself into a party. Convincing the membership and carrying through all the necessary organisational changes was a quite different matter.

Central to the IS's new orientation was the weekly *Socialist Worker*, produced from a tiny printshop in Paxton Road, N17, near the Tottenham Hotspur football ground. There was a staff of three: Roger Protz, now the full-time editor, Mike Heym, a former Leeds student who had worked as a building worker, and Ross Pritchard, one of the Glasgow Young Socialists who had moved to London. Pritchard was a skilled printer who made a considerable sacrifice to work for *Socialist Worker*:

> At the time he had, I think, one child and another on the way... I saw his wage slips from his previous job, and he was earning something like £50 or £60 a week, which in 1968 was an enormous sum; and we eventually took him on at something like £20 a week... The cut in wages was phenomenal, and his family suffered financially, from that day until the day he died, because of it.[65]

The new paper aimed to relate the international mood to the industrial struggle at home. The first issue dated 7 September led with an article by engineering worker Roger Cox – "NO RETREAT! ENGINEERS CAN SMASH PAY FREEZE" – next to a picture of Czech students climbing onto a Russian tank.

Many years later Jim Nichol, the paper's first business manager, recalled, "We needed a paper that workers would engage with. It couldn't afford to be filled with worthy tracts that militants never read. And it had to be sold by workers, not just IS members. We needed shop stewards and other militants to see it as their paper".[66]

The paper was rather scruffy, had just four pages – and was very cheap, costing two pence.* From the second issue it bore the slogan "The 2d paper that fights for YOU". The initial print run was 8,000. It was sold at factory gates and on high streets, whereas the old monthly paper had mainly been sold at Labour Party and trade union meetings. By the end of the year the average total paid sale was just over 8,000.[67] The first issue contained contact details for the IS's 47 branches, under the heading "Join International Socialism – for a real alternative to capitalism and stalinism". Although Cliff did not contribute to the early issues of the paper (he was busy elsewhere), he took a keen interest in its progress.

The new orientation was effectively an end to work inside the Labour Party. There was no public decision to withdraw from Labour Party work, but by the end of 1968 most IS members had left the Labour Party; many of the new members had never been in it. In a few areas, for example Haringey in north London, there was a formal resignation. Elsewhere comrades simply let their membership lapse. In some places comrades stayed in the Labour Party, but since they were not engaging in any activity, there was no need for the Labour bureaucracy to take any measures against them.†

The biggest challenge was the debate on internal organisation. Cliff seriously underestimated the difficulties of persuading the membership to accept a new constitution based on democratic centralist principles. He later wrote, "I myself was panicked by the situation".[68]

A stormy conference on 28-29 September proved unable to resolve the situation; it was agreed that there would be a recall conference later that year. This led to the most heated internal discussion the organisation had ever seen. A number of factions and platforms were formed. A group based mainly on LSE students

---

* This was two pence in old money – equivalent to 0.83 of a modern penny. One could buy 12 *Socialist Workers* for the price of a pint of beer.

† I believe it was the case that Jim Higgins remained a Labour Party member even when he was national secretary of the IS.

known as the "microfaction" (named after an oppositional grouping in Cuba) argued that the IS did not have "an adequate historical analysis...of working class consciousness".[69] The Democratic Centralist faction argued that it was necessary to develop a consistently democratic centralist form of organisation and that the IS leadership was "combining a formally correct theory with a purely empirical practice".[70] Platform Four, centred on Manchester, argued that failure to pose the question of building the revolutionary party had inflicted a possibly fatal wound on the organisation.[71]

The 30 November conference agreed a new constitution. A national committee (NC) of 40 was elected by conference, which in turn elected a London-based executive committee (EC). In fact the NC, meeting monthly with a mainly non-full-time membership, was never able to effectively control the executive, but that was a problem for the future.

The changes were reflected in the leadership team. Cliff remained the central figure. Indeed the responsibility for the group's direction now weighed even more heavily on him. Mike Kidron, his long-term ally in the organisation, had reservations about Cliff's position on democratic centralism, believing there should be a balance between a centrally elected political committee and a delegate executive. He wrote a document arguing this entitled "We are not peasants".[72] Alasdair MacIntyre had chosen the time of the rising student struggle to finally sever his connections with the organisation.[73]

The most important new recruit to the leadership was Duncan Hallas, a member of the original SRG, who had dropped out in 1954, but who had re-established contact with the IS through work in the National Union of Teachers. He was a powerful speaker and prolific writer, with a prodigious range of knowledge. He played an important part in the internal discussions, often engaging in the patient persuasion for which Cliff sometimes did not have time or inclination. However, Cliff failed to recruit Roy Tearse, another RCP veteran, despite offering him various leadership positions if he joined.[74] Cliff believed that a new period was opening in which old differences could be forgotten.

Among the veterans from the late 1950s Jim Higgins and John Palmer were closely allied with Cliff. A number of the members recruited in the early 1960s now took on leading roles. Chris Harman became the leading theoretical writer alongside Cliff and Nigel Harris, and took over as editor of *International Socialism*. Jim Nichol, a former Young Socialist from the North East, was responsible for the group's finances. Roger Rosewell, an engineering apprentice who had become a full-time union official in Birmingham, was particularly concerned with the group's industrial intervention.

The year 1968 marked an important period of transition for the IS, the year it became an independent revolutionary organisation committed to the building of a revolutionary party. It moved ahead of its rivals on the far left, the sectarian Socialist Labour League and the International Marxist Group (which accommodated to the student vanguard approach).*

Cliff's role in all this was central. It was one of the major turning points in his life. But it is important to understand exactly what had changed. It is often alleged that in 1968 he switched from Luxemburgism to Leninism. This is a misleading oversimplification.

There is no such precisely defined doctrine as "Luxemburgism". While Rosa Luxemburg did indeed give great importance to spontaneity, she spent most of her life in an organisation which claimed to be a revolutionary Marxist party. "Leninism" is also a rather slippery concept, and Cliff's own interpretation of Lenin, to be developed in his four-volume biography, was far from a conventional one.

In fact, Cliff had always been a great admirer of Lenin. His 1947 document on state capitalism had been Leninist (unlike some versions of state capitalism), because it regarded Stalinism as a negation of what Bolshevism had stood for in 1917. In his 1959 book on Rosa Luxemburg, many of the references to Lenin were positive. New recruits from the 1960s who had reservations about aspects of the Russian Revolution such as Kronstadt remember Cliff consistently arguing a Leninist position.[75]

In 1968 he turned back to Lenin because he thought there were new things to be learnt. In the summer of 1968, while working on the French pamphlet, he was rereading his way through the complete works of Lenin, which he had piled up on the floor of the front room of his home in Allerton Road.[76]

The shifts in his position were a response to the changes in the

---

* The *Militant* did not begin to take off until the 1970s.

real world rather than a radical reconsideration of his political philosophy. Work in the Labour Party was abandoned because of the new possibilities offered by the political situation. In his 1960 article "Trotsky on Substitutionism" Cliff had given a rather idealised picture of internal democracy in a revolutionary party; the problems and challenges of real life meant that this ideal could not always be achieved in practice.*

In particular Cliff did not make a dichotomy between spontaneity and organisation. Like Luxemburg he attributed great value to spontaneous working class action, and he insisted that revolutionaries had to learn from the working class. He gave enormous importance to conscious organisation, but believed that the form of organisation must be flexible according to circumstances. In real life spontaneity and organisation are closely intertwined.

The myth of a Luxemburgism-Leninism transition has been greatly encouraged by the story of the new edition of *Rosa Luxemburg*, which was produced early in 1969. This story has been much used and misused by Cliff's opponents.

The new edition contained two alterations. These amounted to no more than a few lines out of 80 pages of text; Cliff saw no reason to amend the vast majority of what he had written ten years earlier. In 1959 he had stated:

> Rosa Luxemburg's reluctance to form an independent revolutionary party is quite often cited by Stalinists as a grave error and an important cause for the defeat of the German Revolution in 1918. They argue that Lenin was opposed to the revolutionary Left's adherence to the SPD [Social Democratic Party] and continuing association with Kautsky.
>
> There is no truth at all in this legend. Actually, Rosa Luxemburg made a clearer assessment of Kautsky and Co, and broke with them long before Lenin did.

In 1969 this became:

> Rosa Luxemburg's reluctance to form an independent revolutionary party followed her slowness to react to changed circumstances. It was a

---

* Chris Harman's article "Party and Class" (*International Socialism* 35 (Winter 1969)), which drew on Gramsci as well as Lenin and Luxemburg, raised the debate to a new level. It contained a couple of footnotes criticising Cliff's inconsistencies, and may possibly have influenced Cliff to make revisions to the new edition of *Rosa Luxemburg*.

central factor in the belatedness of building a revolutionary party in Germany. In this, however, she was not alone. Lenin was no quicker to break with Kautsky than Rosa. There is no ground to the Stalinist story according to which Lenin was opposed to the revolutionary Left's adherence to the SPD and continuing association with Kautsky. Actually, Rosa Luxemburg made a clearer assessment of Kautsky and Co, and broke with them long before Lenin did.

And later, a single sentence:

> For Marxists, in advanced industrial countries, Lenin's original position can serve much less as a guide than Rosa Luxemburg's, notwithstanding her overstatements on the question of spontaneity.

was in the revised edition replaced by:

> However, whatever the historical circumstances moulding Rosa's thought regarding organisation, these thoughts showed a great weakness in the German Revolution of 1918-19.

These changes were significant, and reflected the way Cliff had rethought his position in the light of the events of 1968 (it would be a strange revolutionary who did not engage in some rethinking in the light of the biggest general strike in human history). But they did not show any deviation in his concern, in 1969 as in 1959, to assess the contributions of two great revolutionaries and show how their thought could be applied in the present.*

There was no intention to deceive or to suggest that Cliff had always held the same view. The new edition was printed from photocopies of the original text, and the changes were inserted in a different typeface so that they were visible at a glance. Unfortunately, in a meeting Cliff was asked about the changes and denied that he had made any alterations. Perhaps he was flustered in the middle of a polemical exchange; perhaps he was too impatient to be bothered explaining why he had changed his mind. It was a foolish action which caused more trouble than it was worth, and was symptomatic of one of Cliff's weaknesses. He was flexible enough to change

---

* A few years later Cliff wrote an introduction for the classic study by Paul Frölich, *Rosa Luxemburg* (London, 1972). Here he argued that since reformism had only very weak roots in Russia, Luxemburg's critique of the labour bureaucracy was more relevant to Western Europe: "Her scalpel was a much more powerful weapon than Lenin's sledgehammer" (px). No mention was made of her limitations on the party question.

his mind when reality required him to do so. But often he was reluctant to acknowledge the change and to account for it.[77]

But this was the least of Cliff's worries. The constitution had been changed, but as Cliff, always opposed to formalism, well knew, the formal constitution was the least important thing. It merely opened the way for the real task, transforming and building the organisation. This would have to be done in a situation where the pace of events was accelerating, and there would be little time for reflection.

8

1969-74
Years of Hope

Early in 1969 Cliff wrote a document with the mundane title "On Perspectives".[1] It was one of his most thoughtful and perceptive articles. He attempted to assess the situation after the monumental events of 1968, and to set out the tasks for the organisation in the coming years.

While noting that 1968 would be a point of reference for the coming years, just as, in the past, 1848 or 1871 had been, he stressed that what was now needed was "not a euphoric generalisation... but a sober analysis". If the French pamphlet had aimed to show the scale of possibilities, now he was concerned to show the harsh realities of the period ahead. The outcome of the French strike had been at best stalemate, and it was necessary to recognise both the weakness of the revolutionary left and the resilience of the Communist Party.

This led on to a discussion of class consciousness. The long postwar boom had seen an increasing alienation of workers from their traditional organisations. The Labour Party, which had once had two daily papers, now did not even have a weekly. "It is true that the Labour Party has six million members, but it is doubtful if ten percent of these know they are members." Whereas the Russian Revolution had sprung from a growing politicisation of the working class, the French events had "followed years of depoliticisation". At one time class consciousness could be deduced from "institutional barometers" like party membership, newspaper readership, etc. Now "the deep alienation of workers from traditional organisations smashed all such barometers to pieces".

Consequently, the class struggle became much more unpredictable: "When the path of individual reforms is being narrowed, or closed – apathy can transform into its opposite, swift mass action." In the circumstances of the boom, Lenin's claim that reforms are the by-products of revolutionary struggle was no longer valid. The consequences were not necessarily progressive: "A declining interest in the traditional reformist organisations...does not mean the *overcoming* of reformist ideology." He went on to examine the current economic perspectives. The permanent arms economy had not reached its end, but it was past its peak:

> The stability of Western capitalism is beginning to falter. This does not mean that Western capitalism is faced with collapse, as in the thirties. In the coming years we can expect an unevenness in the rate of economic growth, and intermittent expansions.

In this he was to be proved fundamentally right. The 1973 oil crisis would mark the end of the boom, with a rapid rise in unemployment, but it was not a collapse on the 1929 scale, and it did not put an end to working class resistance. What was in prospect was increasing instability and a situation in which independent shopfloor organisation would be less tolerated.

The next section had the title "Beyond the fragment". The overall situation was uneven and contradictory: "the picture is a mosaic, patchy and inelegant". It was necessary to find ways of overcoming fragmentation. "We cannot follow the syndicalists in idolising fragmented militancy".* Sectional militancy did not automatically produce an understanding of the general situation; hence the same workers could be militant industrially but still be racist.

He pointed to various ways in which the fragmentation of resistance could be overcome. A government incomes policy meant that workers had to confront the state as well as their own employer. The new trend towards productivity deals (in which workers negotiated on working conditions and traditional working practices in addition to wages) would raise the question of workers' control.

Cliff drew attention to the way the French events had highlighted the division between young workers and older workers. Young workers were more self-confident and less bound by trade union traditions than their older workmates. However, they could not sustain their

---

* Cliff tended to use the term syndicalism to mean unpolitical trade union militancy. Whether this was what syndicalism had meant in working class history is debatable. See R Darlington, *Syndicalism and the Transition to Communism*, Aldershot, 2008.

struggle except in unity with older workers in their workplace.

He therefore argued that "transitional programmes of demands connecting the particular with the general are needed". This was not a revival of Trotsky's abstract and outdated *Transitional Programme* of 1938, but programmes geared to "the specific conditions of different industries, different plants, etc.".

Cliff observed that shop-floor organisation was under ever-increasing threat and that the trade union bureaucracy was "both reformist and cowardly". As a result the struggle for trade union democracy, for "workers' control of the trade unions", would become important.

As he wrote, "the old forest of reformism is withering away". In particular the CP was becoming increasingly irrelevant and divided. In 1969 the CP still had a much larger organisation and much deeper roots in the working class than all the revolutionary groups combined. But Cliff was right to foresee that the next two decades would be a time of bitter splits and remorseless decline for the CP (it finally liquidated itself in 1991).* Though he did not make the point explicitly here, Cliff foresaw the real possibility that IS could replace the CP as the main militant force in the trade union movement.

In concluding, Cliff made a point he would repeat again and again throughout his life, that change in consciousness comes only through struggle:

> Reformism can never be defeated by programmes. It can only be defeated by deeds... Only struggle discloses to the workers the magnitude of the struggle, widens their horizons, and clarifies their mind.

Revolutionaries had to be always ready to learn and to experiment, if necessary making mistakes and correcting them. They must not retreat into purely theoretical activity; on the contrary, in a phrase Cliff was to use again and again throughout his life, it was necessary to "raise theory to the level of practice". The "do-it-yourself reformism" of recent years had meant increased self-confidence, but at the price of a decline in more general class consciousness. Cliff rarely resorted to dialectical terminology, but here he made a cogent summary of the new possibilities:

---

* The CP enjoyed a slight recovery in the 1970s, but mainly as the organisation of the moderate, non-revolutionary currents in the National Union of Students. This influx of members actually aggravated the divisions with the party.

The third stage the British working class has entered is a "negation of the negation" – synthesising elements of the first stage (the 20s and 30s) – class identification – and of the second stage (1945-1965) – self-confidence. The synthesis is higher than the individual elements joined in it and pregnant of great revolutionary possibilities.

Such was the perspective; the point was to implement it. The organisation was small and ramshackle. New premises for the printshop and a national organising centre were acquired in a rather dingy warehouse building in Cottons Gardens, Shoreditch. The membership was largely young and inexperienced, and rather less working class in composition than it had been in the early 1960s. Numbers had actually declined to around 800-850 in January 1970, as some of the more transient recruits of 1968 disappeared.[2]

Cliff continued to devote phenomenal energy to building the party. He had made friends with Sabby Sagall (Sagall's mother had come from the same town in Russia as Cliff's parents) and he was invited to join Cliff and his family on holiday in Cornwall in the summer of 1969. For Cliff it was no holiday – he sat on the beach ploughing his way through the text of productivity deals.[3]

The main priority was what became known as the "turn to the class". Initially this meant *Socialist Worker* sales outside factories, strike support work and the attempt to recruit working class members. The hope was that eventually a worker leadership would be developed. By 1969 the weekly sale of *Socialist Worker* had risen to over 10,000 a week.[4]

To build the IS's industrial influence it was necessary to develop a critique of the Communist Party while at the same time forming fraternal relations with CP members wherever possible.[*] In October 1969 Cliff published an article under the implausible pseudonym of "Harry Jones"[†] in which he made a sharp critique of CP industrial policy, pointing in particular to the role of CP members in

---

[*] Betty Reid's CP pamphlet *Ultra Leftism in Britain* (London, 1969?) showed that the CP could not ignore the IS and the other far-left groups. It was, however, both ignorant – arguing that the theory of state capitalism had originated with Shachtman (pp31-32) – and dishonest, claiming that – the IS wished to establish a rank and file movement "in opposition to the trade unions" (p33).

[†] I attribute the article to Cliff on the basis of style as well as personal recollection. He presumably adopted the pseudonym because he was preparing to publish his book on productivity deals which he hoped would be sold widely to CP militants.

negotiating the pioneering productivity agreement at Esso's Fawley plant, and the failure of the CP to mobilise solidarity among dockers during the 1966 seafarers' strike. He concluded:

> The party is tired and old... And more and more of the excellent militants in and around the party feel neglected and let down.[5]

On 18 January 1970 Cliff debated in public with the CP industrial organiser Bert Ramelson on the topic "Which way for the unions?" before an audience of over 300 people. The fact that the CP were prepared to engage in such a debate showed the way that the relation of forces on the left was shifting.

The focus of the debate was productivity bargaining. Ramelson took a position of formal opposition to productivity deals, which had been introduced in order to smash collective bargaining.* Cliff stressed that such formal opposition was not enough. Trade unionists had to prepare a massive campaign against productivity deals. The main difference was the attitude to the left wing of the trade union bureaucracy:†

> He attacked the Communist Party for not criticising "left" union leaders like Hugh Scanlon and Jack Jones who had signed productivity deals, often against the wishes of their own members. When would we see such criticism in the *Morning Star*, he asked?[6]

Cliff's main contribution was his book on productivity deals, *The Employers' Offensive: Productivity Deals and How to Fight Them*,[7] which appeared in March 1970. Originally conceived as "a major pamphlet on anti-TU legislation, productivity deals etc.",[8] Cliff found the logic of his argument leading him to focus on the specific question of productivity deals. In many ways this was one of his most remarkable books. Cliff applied to his subject the same scrupulous attention to detail, and in particular the ability to

---

* Ramelson's pamphlet *Productivity Agreements* (London, 1970) appeared at roughly the same time as *The Employers' Offensive*. The contrast is striking. Ramelson's work is slight (24 pages) with little documentation and no reference to concrete workers' experience. There is formal opposition to productivity deals – "greatest swindle on the wages front" – but the style is abstract with no strategy for negotiation, while the whole question of the trade union bureaucracy is ducked.

† This theme was developed in a sharp exchange of letters between Jim Higgins and Monty Johnstone of the CP (*Socialist Worker*, 4, 11, 18 December 1969, 1, 15, 22 January 1970).

marshal large amounts of statistical data, that he had shown in his works on state capitalism. His account was based on a detailed examination of over 100 productivity deals, and dealt in some detail with the specific problems of Post Office engineers, bus workers, miners, dockers, firefighters, steel workers, lorry drivers, car workers, printers and electricity supply workers, also noting that white-collar workers were increasingly being covered by productivity deals. He never failed to see the wood for the trees; the specific struggles were located within the general problems of modern capitalism in the latter stage of the post-war boom.

It was a book written for the organisation. Every IS branch was urged to sell it, to use the book to recruit members and to make trade union contacts. But beyond that it was a book written by the organisation. Though the IS was still small Cliff had gathered around him a group of experienced trade unionists – Jim Higgins, Roger Cox, Terry Barrett and others – as well as talented academics like Richard Hyman and Colin Barker. Altogether, in preparing the book, Cliff spoke to around 200 workers.[9] Two of the three people acknowledged as particularly helpful, Steve Jefferys and Hyman, later became professors in the area of industrial relations. Hence he could draw on collective experience.* As Hyman put it, he was "very good at exploiting people". Hyman (under the pseudonym Bernard Ross) would get letters from Cliff asking him to write something on a particular topic and to comment on a particular question. He would sometimes respond in note form and Cliff would incorporate the notes *verbatim* into his text. Several sections of the book were written by Hyman.[10]

The basic thesis of *The Employers' Offensive* was simple: productivity deals had proved to be a bad bargain for workers because:

> The relatively large wage increases have soon been eaten away by inflation, but the conditions [workers] sold and the changes in work practice they accepted have become a serious threat to job security, earnings and,

---

* Some passages in the book were taken from a mimeographed bulletin of the Institute for Workers Control (IWC). Ken Coates complained about this, since at the same time the IS was being highly critical of the IWC. Cliff was distressed by the accusation, saying the material had been lifted by one of his collaborators without his knowledge. He travelled to Nottingham to discuss the matter with Coates, and promised to make amends Ken Coates interview, October 2008).

above all, trade union organisation within the factory.[11]

The employers' aim was to get rid of piece-work, because it gave too much power to locally based trade unionism. In essence "all productivity deals aim to undermine the power of the shop steward". This in turn was a challenge to management power; strong factory-floor organisation was "creeping workers' control".[12] As Cliff put it:

> The "bloodymindedness" of workers, and the thousand and one ways in which they express their demand, implicitly and explicitly, for control over their own lives, is the embryo of workers' power, of socialism.[13]

The book ended with a set of detailed demands to be made in negotiating a productivity deal.[14] For, Cliff pointed out, such deals were not a simple "yes and no" question: "Any fool can denounce a Productivity Deal and say we should have nothing to do with it".[15] * In reality militants had to fight for the best solution possible when management tried to impose a productivity deal.

The Employers' Offensive was designed to be a practical manual for trade unionists, giving "facts and figures that socialists and militants in the unions will be able to use in discussions with fellow workers". As well as statistics, Cliff had "drawn directly on the experience of workers".[16] It was this that gave the book its unique quality, its ability to see the class struggle from both sides. Cliff tried to unveil the employers' intentions, but at the same time he presented workers' own experience of resistance.

Early in the book Cliff quoted from a "a secret circular from the headquarters of ICI to the senior management of its local factories, which has come into our hands". (How he had obtained this 1965 document was, naturally, not explained.) This dealt frankly with the problems posed by militant trade unionists, and the difficulty of disciplining them without provoking confrontation. The hope was expressed that "in time the trade union side will itself remove this resistance", but it was stressed that "attempts must be made to isolate the militants from their membership before any sanctions are applied".[17]

Later Cliff quoted extensively from a 1968 document published

---

* This was precisely the attitude of the SLL, which accused Cliff of "supporting" productivity deals (see R Protz, "Productivity deals: grotesque distortion of IS line", *Socialist Worker*, 29 January 1970).

by the Coventry and District Engineers' Employers' Association known as the "Coventry Blue Book" (its full title was "Working Party Report on Wage Drift, Work Measurement and Systems of Payment"). Here workers could see themselves depicted as the objects of management strategy.[18]*

But Cliff also showed workers as the subjects of their own resistance, something that was still relatively rare at a time before the development of "oral history" and "history from below".† He published a letter from a car worker describing the experience of assembly line work:

> I work on an overhead section of the track. For the first few weeks you go home and dream about these monsters always coming at you over your head. Then you accept it so much that you can't even dream about it any more. While you're working, if you look away, at something that isn't moving – you feel giddy, like when the train at the other platform moves away and you adjust yourself as if your train was going.
>
> Most of the day you just hope that the line will stop – that there'll be a breakdown. And you'll always find the men on the track ready to walk out on strike when the men working on sub-assembly would rather stay in.[19]

A Doncaster miner described the decline in workplace organisation since the National Power Loading Agreement:

> The miners' lodge has been impotent, union officials being trusted even less. If you go in with a union official you have got less chance of a favourable settlement than if you go in yourself.
>
> The one remaining rank and file power lies on the safety question, the authority of the worker-appointed inspectorate being very strong.[20]

A steward at the Linwood car factory near Paisley described what the much vaunted "flexibility" meant in practice:

---

* Richard Hyman had obtained this through academic channels and the employers complained to his boss, Professor Hugh Clegg. Hyman was able to respond that the document was in the public domain, and that he had already cited it in a 1968 pamphlet *Know Your Enemy*, written under the name Bernard Ross (Richard Hyman interview, September 2008).

† Between 1965 and 1969 *New Left Review* had published a remarkable series overseen by Ronald Fraser entitled "Work", in which people engaged in a wide variety of jobs described their own alienation. However, these were not linked to any strategy for fighting back.

I'll tell you what flexibility means... If you work with a group of men for some time, then maybe you'll form a militant block – begin to make demands which are taken up by other groups and so on.

"Flexibility" means that on the advice of a so-called expert, the management can move men all over the shop and the factory. Very quickly the most militant sections get broken up. It's happening already, every day.[21]

As for "bloodymindedness", a (not surprisingly) anonymous steward in a glass factory described resistance to speed-up:

> I stand over the conveyor belt with a stop watch in my hand. Whenever management dares to speed it up beyond what is reasonable, I, being responsible for quality control, do the following: I pick up a bottle, newly produced, raise it up towards the light, turn it this way, turn it the other way, for a time, until I'm sure that it is up to the required standard...in the meantime, the conveyor belt goes on...and tens of bottles are smashed to pieces. Then slowly I put the bottle down and pick another one up for a check of quality. In no time at all the supervisor rushes up to me and asks for an explanation and then the speed of the conveyor belt is reduced.[22]

It was passages like this that gave the book its power, that made it not just a book *for* workers but a book *by* workers.

While much of *The Employers' Offensive* dealt with minutiae like tea breaks, the overall political perspective was always present. Cliff pointed to the role of the state – it was the nationalised industries which had the grimmest productivity deals. He also showed the great difficulties surrounding any attempt to make strike action illegal, citing the case of the Australian militant Clarrie O'Shea, jailed under anti-union laws; when a million workers struck in his support, an anonymous donor paid his fine and got him out of prison.[23] This prefigured what would happen in Britain in 1972 when five dockers were jailed.

Cliff examined the position of full-time officials, and how they became estranged from the interests of those they were supposed to represent. This was particularly relevant to one of the main underlying themes of the book – the role of the CP. There were only a few brief mentions of the CP in the text (mainly side-swipes in footnotes), since it was hoped to sell the book to CP militants. But Cliff was well aware that the trade union bureaucracy was deeply involved in selling productivity deals, and the CP's relations with the left bureaucracy thus meant it could not make an all-out attack on productivity deals, though many CP stewards were fighting them.

The Employers' Offensive was a book of its time, and to reread it in the 21st century is to observe just how much the world has changed. Today, for example, bus conductors are almost unknown. As Cliff reminds us, the 1968 productivity deal gave London bus workers £1 a week in return for accepting one-man operated buses.[24] * Today that increase has long been swallowed up by inflation, but the driver still does two jobs. Cliff's analysis has been proved right.

The book was still mainly oriented to a male working class, though Cliff did note the importance of the 1968 Ford sewing machinists' strike against sex discrimination, which first sparked off the women's movement in Britain, and he pointed out that "Job Evaluation" confirmed "the most extreme forms of discrimination against women".[25] But when he made comments such as "any steward has to remember the first rule of negotiation: the girl who starts by saying No gets a higher price for her virtue than the girl who talks money at the outset",[26] he was appealing to the all-male culture of traditional trade unionism, and was legitimately criticised by women readers.

The language of the book was clear and unpretentious, with many colloquialisms – money was called "lolly". Cliff added a neat twist to Rosa Luxemburg's description of trade union struggle as a "labour of Sisyphus", by remarking, "Sisyphus did develop strong muscles as a result of all his labours".[27] It was a point he would frequently make in meetings over the next 30 years. But his gift for mixed metaphor survived: referring to workers' disillusion with the gains from productivity deals, he wrote that "the ginger on the cake starts peeling off".[28] †

---

* This was always the term used at the time. There were then few women bus drivers. Younger readers may be unaware that once there were two workers on a bus – a driver and a conductor to collect fares.

† When I asked Cliff what this meant, he replied, "Tell me, Ian, what is ginger?" He must have found out later, since he once told a members' meeting that we needed "some ginger up our bums".

The Employers' Offensive was published by Pluto Press.* It was priced at six shillings (30 pence) – cheap for a 234-page book – and intended for mass sale. Unfortunately the standard of production was not high, though this does not seem to have affected the book's popularity; two pages were transposed because the paste-up was done by amateurs.[29] Twenty thousand were printed and money received for about 15,000. There was an expensive hardback edition for libraries and for the few requests received from managements.[30]

Chanie took a term's leave of absence from her job as a teacher to promote the book around factories in north west London. Most factories had CP stewards, but they generally took two, six or 12 copies of the book. She recalls a union meeting where railway workers were discussing a strike. Many workers turned up carrying *The Employers' Offensive*, and it became a major item of discussion at the meeting.[31]

Most sales took place through the local IS branches. Frank Henderson was a veteran Trotskyist from the 1940s and a trade union activist at the Longbridge car factory in Birmingham. He bought *Socialist Worker* at the factory gates, but had no contact with the IS organisation. He saw *The Employers' Offensive* advertised and decided to get a copy:

> So I wrote my name and address on a bit of paper. The following Thursday night as I was going into work I gave the paper seller this strip of paper with my name and address, plus the six bob [shillings] for the *Employers' Offensive*. I thought that might be a bit of a test for them. If I didn't hear any more, somebody had walloped my six bob and they were a bunch of thieving bastards. They might send the book to me, in which case they're not really serious. Or, if they are serious, the heavy mob would bring the book in person and talk the hind legs off me.
>
> The following Sunday afternoon Paul Holborow and Dave Hughes came to see me and we spent several hours arguing the toss, mainly on the class nature of Russia.[32] †

---

* Pluto Press had been established by IS member Richard Kuper in 1969, and was originally conceived as a publishing-house closely linked to the IS; he was later joined by Mike Kidron. However, its priorities were different from those of the organisation, and it published books which, while not hostile to IS politics, did not relate to the organisation's activities. There were a number of disagreements, and by 1977 Kuper and Kidron had both left the party (Richard Kuper interview, February 2009).

† Henderson remained an SWP member till his death in 2009.

Sammy Morris was a young print worker in Glasgow. There was Measured Day Work in his factory, and he found the detailed discussion of bonus schemes in Cliff's book very helpful in his trade union activity. He himself sold three or four dozen copies of the book, and 50 copies were sold at John Brown's shipyards.[33]

Alan Watts, a north London engineering worker, sold 80 copies. He remembers going out night after night, visiting trade union contacts, who would take one or two copies, and in one case ten. Productivity deals were a major issue at the time. For him, the book was important in establishing the credibility of the IS and in making contacts.[34]

Politically the book did much to establish the credibility of the IS within the established labour movement. In particular it altered the balance of forces in relation to the CP. The trade union bureaucracy, including the "left" bureaucrats supported by the CP, were heavily implicated in productivity deals. The CP, despite its much greater industrial influence, could not have produced the book.

Cliff followed up the book with meetings around the country. In one week at the end of April he spoke on productivity deals in Aberdeen, Edinburgh, East Kilbride, Glasgow and Paisley, finding time for a Lenin centenary meeting in Clydebank. In following weeks he spoke in Manchester, Birmingham and various parts of London. In north London he shared a platform with Mike Cooley, vice-president of the Draughtsmen's and Allied Technicians' Association.[35] In Devon he addressed a meeting of 150 to 200 workers from a power station threatened with closure.[36] He addressed the founding meeting of the Wolverhampton branch on productivity deals; there were about 45 people in attendance, including the AUEW district secretary and some 15 shop stewards. Cliff spoke well, combining the concrete and the general. Comrades took *The Employers' Offensive* round all the factories in Wolverhampton.[37]

For the first time in his life Cliff found his arguments being taken seriously far beyond the sphere of the far left. In the weekly *New Society* Jeremy Bugler praised Cliff's "impressive research", and argued that since many companies had used productivity deals to deceive and attack workers "by and large, this book is the one our managements have deserved". He commented that "if Lord Stokes [chief executive of British Leyland] wants a hernia, I recommend him to read it".[38]

In the *Times*, economics editor Peter Jay was less sympathetic. He began by recommending the book to "any business executive who expects to be engaged in negotiating productivity deals" on the basis of the maxim "Know your enemy". But he found Cliff's data "inaccurate or misapplied" and his theoretical material "lamentably threadbare". But just who had the better "economic model" was shown in Jay's conclusion. He cited Cliff's comments that if a company laid off 20 percent of its workers and maintained the same level of output, then the company would benefit but "for the 20 percent who get the sack and for the community as a whole there is nothing gained at all".[39] Jay responded, "This is drivel. The 20 percent can, and most of them do, take other jobs (cyclical fluctuations in unemployment notwithstanding), thereby increasing total output and the real standard of living." Jay apparently believed in the permanence of more or less full employment; within five years he would be proved sadly mistaken.[40]

In *Management Today* Christopher Mansell also recommended the book on the grounds that "it is best to know your enemy", and while rejecting Cliff's class struggle framework noted that "the book illuminates the fears of the militants who find the productivity format substantially weakening their hold on their own informal organisations".[41] For the *Birmingham Post* it was simply "the troublemakers' bible".[42]

Looking back nearly four decades later, Richard Hyman, now a professor at the LSE, believed that in the context of the time it was a very good book, which provided a synthesis of a lot of people's knowledge and experience.[43]

Slowly the organisation began to draw around it more industrial militants and other activists. Willie Lee was working at Linwood in Glasgow when he joined the IS in 1970. When he first heard the name "Tony Cliff" he was expecting someone like Rock Hudson, so he was rather surprised when they met. But he was impressed by the way Cliff could make militant shop stewards think about politics. Lee found Cliff had the ability to break down ideas to make them understood by workers: he could talk to young workers with no political experience as well as to more experienced comrades.[44]

Arthur Affleck, a legendary militant in the Teesside steel industry

Above: The village of Zikhron Yaakov circa 1917, the year Cliff was born.

Below: Cliff and Chanie (standing, centre) in 1954 with, from left, Cliff's parents Akiva and Esther, Chanie's parents Jane and Solomon, and in front eldest daughter Elana and baby Donny.

A family photo-shoot circa 1959, with Akiva (seated), Elana and Donny.

Above: Cliff takes some time to think during the 1980s.

Left: IS 2 contained Cliff's key early article on the role of the revolutionary party, "Trotsky on Substitutionism".

Below: IS 12 carried his major reappraisal of Trotsky's thought, "Deflected Permanent Revolution".

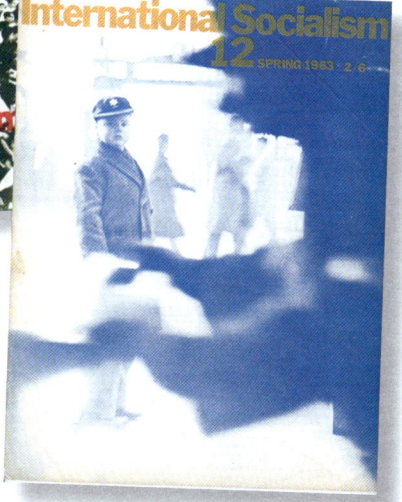

Socialist Wor
BUY IT...
LENIN
50
YEARS LATER
1924-74
LENIN
50
YEARS LATER
1924-74
50
YEARS LATER
1924-74

LENIN
50 YEARS LATER
1924-74

Previous page: Cliff speaks at a rally on the 50th anniversary of Lenin's death, Manchester, February 1974.

Above: Speaking at Marxism 86.

Below: Speaking at Marxism 92.

Opposite: At a march for pensions, central London, 1997.

Socialist Worker
Our message to Tony Blair...
END
POVERTY
PENSIONS
Restore the link
No privatisation
Tax the rich

Some 3,000 people attended Cliff's funeral on 19 April 2000, marching with SWP flags from Golders Green station to the crematorium.

who had left the Communist Party in 1956, joined the IS the first time he heard Cliff speak. Within quite a short time the Teesside district of the IS had 27 stewards in the steel industry.[45]

Dave Sherry had joined the IS in Glasgow in 1973 and some time after this first heard Cliff at a public meeting. He had never seen such a public speaker and was stunned. Within a couple of years he was a full-time organiser.[46]

One comrade in Exeter was very impressed at seeing Cliff with Granville Williams's young child, saying he was clearly not the sort of person who would send millions to Siberia.[47]

Shaun Doherty was a young teacher and new recruit to the IS in Liverpool when he first heard Cliff. He had heard his name and was surprised to find that Cliff was not as he had imagined, but wild-haired, partly bald, five-foot-nothing* with a strong East European Jewish accent. But he found Cliff's arguments very interesting.[48]

Cliff continued to speak all over the country. His range was phenomenal; a speakers' list circulated in early 1970 listed the topics in which various comrades specialised and concluded "TONY CLIFF SPEAKS ON PRACTICALLY EVERYTHING".[49] Besides workers, he drew in a new layer of students, some of whom would play key roles in the organisation over the coming decade. By now he had a reputation among students and could attract large audiences.

Sheila McGregor had been an IS member in York, but was thinking of leaving when she first heard Cliff speak at a meeting in Scarborough. He made a profound impact on her and convinced her to stay in the organisation. Within two years she had become a full-time organiser.[50]

In 1969 Paul Holborow, a former Labour Party supporter, had attended an IS day-school at the University of St Andrews where he was a student. Cliff spoke on the industrial struggle and Joan Smith on the Middle East. He was impressed by both speakers. Cliff captivated his interest and imagination. He was struck by the combination of passion and understandable analysis.[51] He joined the IS and soon became a full-timer.

Pete Clark had just joined the IS in Oxford. He went to a meeting in a horrible smelly pub, which the branch had chosen because they

---

* Actually Cliff was 170 centimetres (5 feet 7 inches) tall (Passport: MRC MSS 459/6/1).

believed it to be "proletarian". He had seen *The Employers' Offensive* and believed Cliff was a shop steward. On seeing Cliff he thought he looked old and out of place. But as soon as Cliff spoke he was captivated. The next time he heard Cliff was at a debate with Sean Matgamna where Cliff merely shouted that one of Matgamna's supporters had not paid subs. This, he felt, reflected Cliff's great strengths – and weaknesses.[52]

Peter Alexander first heard Cliff at the School of Oriental and African Studies (SOAS) in London in 1973. He was impressed by Cliff's use of references to popular television, which showed his ability to relate to ordinary people.[53]

Though Cliff was adept at dealing with the details of productivity deals, he also had a gift of being able to draw out the absurdities of international capitalism through simple images. Thus he explained how gold was mined in South Africa in difficult and dangerous circumstances but could not be used to make anything and so was shipped across the world to the US – where it was buried underground.[54]

The central focus of the IS at this time was on the working class, but the organisation did not become narrowly workerist. Meetings by Cliff, Hallas and others were sometimes prefaced by a half-hour show by the Cartoon Archetypical Slogan Theatre (CAST), which in effect became the IS theatre group (although the group also performed with Pink Floyd). Red Saunders first met Cliff as a CAST member. He found Cliff slightly remote and clichéd "mad professor", with his unruly hair, glasses and hands flying about. But he was greatly impressed by Cliff as a fount of wisdom and by the clarity of his arguments.[55]

Cliff had grasped the significance of students in 1968, but in the aftermath he commented that the student movement had gone up like a rocket and come down like a stick. In a typical piece of stick-bending he urged students to leave their books and go to the factory gates. A number of ex-students played a key role in factory gate paper sales, recruiting workers and eventually the creation of factory branches.[56] Yet Cliff could also bend the stick the other way, pointing to the need for political education:

> We do need worker-intellectuals. Workers and intellectuals face different situations and therefore have different view of the world – the big thing

for workers is immediacy, concreteness; intellectuals face lack of roots, abstractness; the key problem is the will to fight. On theory, Marx rooted the question of class for example in historical, concrete terms. You can't create cadres in the abstract, away from struggle, you have to start with the concrete. You have to give the cadres traditions. We must have cadre schools in every area.[57]

While the industrial struggle was Cliff's major priority, he could not devote himself to it exclusively. The leadership core was still small, and there were few full-time workers. Over the next couple of years Chris Harman and Duncan Hallas were to become full-timers. Under pressure from Cliff, Hallas was persuaded to leave his teaching job without proper notice to take up full-time duties, though he was somewhat reluctant to do so.[58]

Cliff had to involve himself directly in building the organisation. Roger Rosewell, who became full-time organiser in Birmingham in 1970, would talk to Cliff on the telephone every day. Cliff and Rosewell were interested in sharing experience, in learning that a new approach had been tried, say, in Exeter, and passing this on to other activists around the country.[59]

He also had to devote some efforts to raising the money necessary to maintain a printshop and a weekly paper. Sabby Sagall was fortunate enough to have a trust fund and Cliff persuaded him to make a substantial financial contribution. Sagall was convinced because he found Cliff such an inspirational figure. Cliff never treated him differently in any way because of his financial support.[60]

On top of this Cliff had to involve himself in the various political problems that arose for the organisation. Of these by far the most important was the situation in Ireland. The growth of the civil rights movement in Northern Ireland had led to increasingly violent clashes with Loyalists and police. In August 1969 fighting between police and Catholic residents erupted in Derry, and British troops were sent in, ostensibly to preserve the peace. This presented the IS with a serious problem of tactics.

In the immediate situation, the Catholic population welcomed the arrival of the troops and there were reports of local people bringing cups of tea to the soldiers. Some members of the leadership, including Duncan Hallas, Andreas Nagliatti and Fred Lindop, argued that as a British organisation, the IS had a duty to demand the withdrawal of the troops. Cliff was initially sympathetic to this position, but after discussion with John Palmer, he spoke passionately against it, saying it was untenable for comrades in the North of Ireland.[61] As he pointed out, if socialists were outnumbered by fascists, then they might quite legitimately seek protection from the police.

It was decided not to make "Withdraw the troops now" an agitational slogan. However, the main emphasis in *Socialist Worker* was on the need for Catholic self-defence and on the potential role of the troops. The week that the troops went in, *Socialist Worker* was headlined:

THE BARRICADES MUST STAY UNTIL
B-Specials disbanded
RUC disarmed
Special Powers Act abolished
Political prisoners released

The lead article expanded on this, arguing:

> Certainly the mass of Catholics, after three days of bitter fighting, were relieved to see the RUC [Royal Ulster Constabulary] and the Specials withdraw, and to this extent were glad to see the British troops…

> The role of the British troops is not to bring any real solution to the problems of the people of Northern Ireland, but to freeze a situation that looked like getting out of hand and damaging the interests of the British ruling class in Ireland.

It predicted that the current role of the troops would be temporary:

> The British armed presence may prevent the worst excesses of the Specials in the short term, but in the long term the troops are there to protect the regime.

A National Committee resolution made this even more explicit:

> Although British imperialism wants to prevent a mass pogrom, this doesn't mean that troops won't be used against civil rights comrades agitating for socialist demands.[62]

This reflected Cliff's position. He defended this at a lively conference at Easter 1970. In 1971, in a polemic against the Workers' Fight faction, he argued:

> We continually stressed that *only armed self-defence* could protect the

Catholic workers against renewed pogroms, and, in the long term, against the British troops as well... Workers' Fight accuse the NC majority of capitulating to the pressure of public opinion in 1969... If we were sensitive to public opinion it was to the opinions of the Republicans and Socialists in Northern Ireland. Neither the IRA nor PD [People's Democracy] nor any other socialist organisation in Northern Ireland raised the slogan of Withdrawal of British Troops as an *immediate* slogan in 1969. The only place where slogans like "Army Go Home" were written on walls was in Paisley [i.e. militant Loyalist] territory at the time. As revolutionaries in an imperialist country we are proud to plead guilty of being sensitive to the cries of the colonial underdog, sensitive to the heartbeats of Republicans and Socialists in Northern Ireland.[63]

By 1970 the repressive role of the British troops was becoming ever clearer and *Socialist Worker* began to campaign for the withdrawal of British troops. However, the line Cliff and the executive had argued was often evoked by political opponents, often with no recognition of the difficult circumstances in which the original line had been determined.*

The Irish situation continued to be a major preoccupation for the IS. When Bernadette Devlin was elected a member of parliament for People's Democracy in 1970 she worked closely with the IS. (There were negotiations for her to become an IS member, but these fell through.) In the first half of 1971 she spoke at a number of IS public meetings on "How to Fight the Tories", sometimes sharing the platform with leading IS members such as Duncan Hallas and Roger Rosewell.

As the IRA took up the armed struggle there was continuing debate about how far the IS should support the Republican movement. The formulation endorsed by Cliff was that such support should be unconditional but critical. In January 1972 British

---

* In 2008 the *Guardian* published an obituary of former IRA commander Brendan Hughes. This noted, "Hughes could also recall the time before the IRA and Britain became enemies, when British troops were first deployed in Northern Ireland in the late 1960s, and were seen as being present to protect Roman Catholic houses against Protestant fire bombers. Hughes, who was only in his early 20s then, used to chat to the soldiers, teenagers who came from working class backgrounds just like his own." (Anne McHardy, "Brendan Hughes", *The Guardian*, 19 February 2008) Those who malign Cliff for the line he took in 1969 should be reminded that the issues were complex.

paratroopers killed 13 people in Derry. *Socialist Worker* denounced this as "Murder", and carried a message from Bernadette Devlin who declared that "if you continue to do nothing after these 13 murders, then they will remain on the memory of an idle and indolent working class movement".[64] Three weeks later an IRA bomb at Aldershot barracks killed six civilians and an army chaplain; *Socialist Worker* criticised this as "senseless retaliation" which had achieved nothing, but put the blame on the Tory government and demanded withdrawal of British troops from Northern Ireland.[65] On 15 March Special Branch raided the homes of 60 people, including seven IS members, among them John Palmer and Frank Campbell of the Executive Committee; documents were examined and confiscated.[66] The IS's involvement in Irish solidarity work had not gone unnoticed.

At the IS conference in spring 1972 Cliff defended the IS position: "Unconditional but critical support for the IRA meant we had to be critical when we thought they were wrong. We could not leave the criticism until the struggle was over".[67]

Beyond the debate about the IRA Cliff stressed the need to build a separate socialist organisation in Ireland, even if initially only in embryonic form. Therefore he constantly urged comrades such as Eamonn McCann and others to go back to Ireland to take part in this task.[68]

The Irish question raised the more general question of terrorism. As the euphoria of 1968 subsided, there was a temptation for some leftists to turn to terrorism. This was most visible in continental Europe with the disastrous dead-ends of the Red Brigades in Italy and the Baader-Meinhof gang in Germany. When the Angry Brigade planted a bomb at the home of Tory minister Robert Carr in January 1971, the action was condemned by *Socialist Worker*, with Cliff's strong approval, as "a menace" to the building of a mass movement.[69] It can be argued that the fact that no serious leftist terrorist current developed in Britain in this period, while such currents did develop in many parts of Europe, can be explained in part by the IS's firm rejection of terrorism and its insistence on the self-emancipation of the working class.

Cliff was also involved in a variety of internal debates, and in debates with other sections of the left. Although most of the factions from the 1968 dispute dissolved after the December conference, the

Workers' Fight grouping remained as a permanent faction, as did the Democratic Centralist faction. The latter advocated a more centralised and disciplined organisation, and gave great importance to internal matters – an approach Cliff characterised as "inward-looking". While he saw no hope of winning over the Workers' Fight group, Cliff put considerable effort into the Democratic Centralists.* When comrades from the faction complained of Cliff's salami tactics, he rejoined, "You call yourself steel-hard Bolsheviks. You can't slice steel like salami".[70]

Noel Tracy, who left the IS around this time, believes that Cliff's greatest weakness was that he could never envisage the IS without himself as the leader and he would engage in any manoeuvring to ensure he remained in control. Tracy considers that he drove many competent people out of the IS when they found there was no way IS could develop a collective leadership which marginalised him or reduced his power.[71]

Certainly Cliff did not submit meekly when he was in a minority. In 1969 there was disagreement over the war then raging in Nigeria. While some supported the demand for independence for the breakaway region of Biafra, others opposed taking sides. The National Committee carried, by the narrow majority of 13 to 11, a resolution supporting "the right of the Biafrans' struggle for self-determination".[72] Cliff, who had voted against this, immediately wrote a piece for *Socialist Worker* putting the opposite point of view. He argued that the differences between Biafra and Nigeria were basically tribal, and that Biafra could not become a nation since "there is no possibility of a viable capitalist development and hence authentic national development in any part of Africa under imperialist rule". The job of British socialists was not to take sides but to expose "the role of British imperialism". It was not one of his best articles, being largely based on Frederick Forsyth's Penguin Special on the war.[73]

Despite other commitments, Cliff found time for polemic with other currents of the revolutionary left. On 10 February 1969 he

---

* The Democratic Centralist faction included Fred Lindop, Constance Lever, Tom Hillier and myself. I recall one day in the autumn of 1969 being summoned to Cliff's home – a car was sent for me – where he spent three hours haranguing me and unsuccessfully urging me to dissolve the faction. Although the argument was vigorous, there was no personal unpleasantness, and it did not affect my future working relationship with Cliff.

debated with his old enemy Gerry Healy at the University of London Union. As might be expected, little positive emerged from what was largely a dialogue of the deaf. Healy was in aggressive mood and had no time for the IS unity proposals. "When we talk of unity with an opponent organisation, it is to get rid of that organisation. We are in arms against you." In face of this, Cliff was able to taunt the SLL for having failed to make any developments of theory to meet the needs of a new historical period; as he put it, "Their theory and heritage is religious, kept in a box".[74]

On 30 October 1970 a debate was arranged in London between Cliff and Ernest Mandel. Here Cliff came off less well. He was an impressive if unorthodox speaker, but he lacked Mandel's skill as a debater. According to one (admittedly hostile) observer his speech contained "hysterical ranting accusations that the Fourth International had capitulated to Stalinism and that *The Red Mole* [the IMG paper] did not 'smell of the factory'."[75] Cliff's own supporters were not impressed. A resolution from Southampton expressing "disappointment at the overall sectarian attitude of IS" shown at the debate was endorsed by the executive (in Cliff's absence).[76]

In September 1970 Cliff took part in a small international conference held in London. This was jointly sponsored by the IS, the International Socialists of the United States and Lutte Ouvrière. It was attended by delegates from Spain (Acción Comunista), Italy (Avanguardia Operaia and Potere Operaio), Ireland (People's Democracy) and the US (National Caucus of Labor Committees), and by individuals from the French West Indies, Denmark and the US.[77] Cliff took a lively interest in the discussion and contributed to debates on British industrial struggle and on state capitalism in the Eastern Bloc. Confronting Hardy (Robert Barcia) of Lutte Ouvrière – who still argued, as many Trotskyists had done back in the 1940s, that Russia was a workers' state but the Eastern European satellites were "bourgeois states" – Cliff commented, "I understand your position on Russia but I don't agree with it; I agree with your position on Eastern Europe, but I don't understand it".[78] There was no intention to create an international organisation: the sponsors agreed that the time was not ripe for such a body. The conference was merely an attempt to re-establish a dialogue between different groups on the anti-Stalinist revolutionary left.*

In 1970 the Wilson government, which had undermined its own support, was defeated in the general election, and Tory Edward Heath became prime minister. The IS gave highly critical support to Labour in the election. The fact that democratic centralism had not yet been fully established is shown by the fact that an IS member, Jim Murray, stood as a Labour candidate (against Jeffrey Archer in Louth), though apparently without the approval of the organisation.[79]

In 1971 the Tory government under Edward Heath was preparing to enter the Common Market (as the European Union was then known). The IS position, dating back to the early 1960s, had been to reject the Labour left's opposition to the Common Market. As an editorial in *International Socialism* (almost certainly written by Mike Kidron) had argued, "to hark back to an independent capitalist Britain is illusory... For us the move to Europe extends the scope of class struggle in which we are directly involved; it worsens its conditions for the present. But it makes ultimate victory more secure".[80]

At a time when a heated debate was raging in the trade union movement, Cliff recognised that there was a danger of the IS being condemned to ultra-left isolation if it took an abstentionist line in the votes on the issue. He and Chris Harman produced a set of theses which concluded:

> We oppose the process of capitalist rationalisation, but...merely keeping British capitalism out of the Common Market will in no way improve the conditions of British workers... Our aim in union conferences and the like should be to fight for resolutions to this effect, thus making clear both our opposition to the Common Market and our separation from the confused chauvinism of the Tribunites, CP, etc. However, if we are defeated on such a stand, we should then vote with the Tribune-Stalinists in opposition to entry.[81]

This was carried by the June 1971 National Committee, but there was vigorous opposition from within the NC, and among the membership. There were heated arguments in the branches and an attempt was made to call a special conference to reverse the NC decision.

This debate brought to a head the conflict between the IS

---

* A second conference was held in 1971 in France, which Cliff was unable to attend due to his lack of a passport. Some subsequent conferences were organised by Lutte Ouvrière alone.

leadership and the Workers' Fight group. Workers' Fight (or the Trotskyist Tendency, as they called themselves) had fused with the IS in 1968; in fact they had preserved their own organisation, their own membership subscriptions, their own internal discipline and even probationary membership. There had been a number of internal disputes in areas where they had some influence, and in Manchester and Teesside branches had been divided to avoid the damage caused by constant internal conflict.

For quite a while Cliff was against driving Workers' Fight out. He told the NC, "We should not expel Workers' Fight but use them to educate our members".[82] But in 1971 Workers' Fight raised the stakes by circulating an internal document which characterised the IS as "centrist", that is, not a revolutionary organisation. Cliff and others decided that enough was enough. In the autumn of 1971 the NC voted to hold a special conference to end the fusion with Workers' Fight. There was a period of internal discussion, with numerous documents and debates in branches.

The special conference was held in Birmingham in December 1971. Cliff did not open the debate on behalf of the executive, as it was felt his polemical style might be too abrasive, though he did contribute to the debate. The executive position was introduced by Nigel Harris, whose suave academic manner was intended to lower the temperature. Workers' Fight representatives claimed that Harris was playing "soft cop" to Cliff's "hard cop". At the end of the day the executive won by 205 votes to 120.[83] About 50 members left to form a new organisation, while a few more were lost, but the organisation emerged largely unscathed.

Amid all this frenetic activity Cliff was working on his study of Lenin, which would be published later in the decade. On 18 April 1970, on the occasion of the centenary of Lenin's birth, he spoke at a rally in Conway Hall in London about Lenin's life and work. He drew out the central themes in Lenin's work: the central role of the working class and the interaction between party and class – the party learns from the class and talks to the class. Hence the importance of inner-party democracy, since different party members will hear different voices from the class. But the basic principles had to be related to changing concrete situations; hence Lenin made "fantastic zigzags". The growth of the IS meant that the meeting attracted a range of political opponents, from the SPGB to pro-Stalin Maoists. Cliff responded to their questions with typical vigour and a display of his vast historical knowledge.[84]

As Cliff had been arguing for several years, if a working class party was to be built, then the industrial struggle would have to be at the centre of the perspective. Events now showed that he had been right. The Tory government of Edward Heath adopted from the outset an aggressive policy towards the working class movement. The Industrial Relations Bill set out to seriously limit the rights of trade unions and of workers in struggle by outlawing the closed shop, enforcing secret ballots and establishing an industrial court. The trade union movement launched a major campaign against this with demonstrations and strike action. Half a million workers struck on 8 December 1970 and 1.5 million engineering workers stopped work on 1 March 1971. In some parts of the movement the demand for a general strike was raised, and an edition of *Socialist Worker* was headlined "GENERAL STRIKE" (preceded in much smaller type by the words "action to force TUC leaders to call").[85] Cliff argued that the demand must be raised carefully and with due recognition of the IS's place in the movement:

> Some attention must be paid to the slogan "General Strike". It is in the struggle and we cannot ignore it. It is important though that the slogan is not raised in an ultra-left way. The headline in SW [*Socialist Worker*] was bad because it looked as if we were calling for a General Strike. The slogan is the centre of our propaganda but shouldn't be in the headline. We have to expose the TUC by calling upon them to call a General Strike.[86]

In early 1971 a 44-day strike by postal workers ended in defeat. An atmosphere of confrontation continued, and with it the real possibility of making the IS into a larger and more proletarian organisation. At the end of his life Cliff recalled that the years 1970 to 1974 had been the "best years of my life".[87]

The growth of the IS and the intensifying class struggle meant that the organisation achieved more public prominence, though much comment was misinformed. Early in 1971 the *Times* published a series of four articles on "The revolutionaries", in which the IS featured prominently. But despite employing three journalists the investigation managed to misspell the name of "leader Tony Cliffe" and Paul Routledge claimed that the IS was still, in 1971, following a "strategy of 'entrism'".[88] The *Times Literary Supplement*, however, gave a highly favourable review to *World Crisis*, a volume of essays by IS members including Cliff,[89] describing it as "more cogent in its arguments and analysis than any social project of the recent past".[90]

Early in 1972 the balance of forces shifted sharply. A national miners' strike began – the first since 1926. The miners adopted a strategy towards winning the support of other workers, with the widespread use of flying pickets travelling throughout the country. Power stations were picketed; the miners received support from students who raised money and occupied colleges to accommodate pickets.

Cliff flung himself into support for the miners. He travelled around the coalfields speaking at meetings and was well received, though there was a problem when enthusiastic miners bought him drinks.* John Palmer remembers a meeting in the Durham coalfield where he spoke together with Cliff. Afterwards they retired to the miners' club where miners began buying Cliff pints which he didn't like to refuse; Palmer had to dispose of them into an aspidistra plant.[91]

One issue of *Socialist Worker* reported:

> Four hundred people packed a lively and spirited International Socialists' meeting in support of the miners in Grimethorpe, Yorkshire last week. Main speakers were Tony Cliff of IS and Tony Kinder. 16 people applied to join IS at the end of the meeting.
>
> Birmingham: 250 people attended an IS meeting on the miners' strike on Sunday. Speakers were Tony Cliff and three miners from the Rugeley pits in Staffordshire.

The same issue announced that Cliff would be speaking at an IS regional rally in Bristol on 19 February, at a Teesside rally on "The Struggle for Socialism" on 25 February – and for good measure at a London meeting "Is China Socialist?" on 23 February.[92]

Pete Green first heard Cliff speak at Ruskin College in Oxford during the strike. Green was inclined towards anarchism and had previously been repelled by Oxford IS members such as Christopher

---

* Cliff never drank alcohol. While it was the custom for comrades at local and national gatherings to go to the pub at the end of meetings, it was relatively rare for Cliff to accompany them.

Hitchens. He was impressed by Cliff and joined IS a few months later.[93]

The IS intervention in the strike was highly successful, notably in the Yorkshire area. A large number of students had been recruited, especially in York, and they helped to start winning workers to the organisation. On Saturdays during the 1972 miners' strike a bus would take 30 or 40 students to the coalfields. The bus would go to Barnsley and other towns and villages in the mining area, dropping off up to six sellers in each place. These would sell more than 100 papers and collect contact addresses; then during the week cars would go round to visit the contacts. This laid the basis for the subsequent establishment of the *Collier* newspaper. There was recruitment of engineers and bus workers as well as miners.

At this time, Cliff was in Yorkshire almost every week and would attend the Yorkshire committee about once a month. At one meeting in Ossett he recruited between 12 and 20 workers in a single evening, several of whom remained in the organisation for some years. In addition, Cliff was on the phone to John Charlton every day, asking for detailed breakdowns of every meeting.[94] On the other hand Granville Williams, an experienced organiser, had little telephone contact with Cliff, presumably because Cliff trusted him to get on with the job.[95]

The strike came to a head with the Saltley picket in February. Yorkshire miners led by Arthur Scargill came to Birmingham to picket a coke depot. There were discussions with local engineering unions, and 10,000 or more engineering workers stopped work and marched to join the miners' picket. The sheer size of the crowd was such that the police simply surrendered: the chief constable closed the depot "in the interests of public safety". The government, unwilling to risk further such confrontations, backed down and the miners won a substantial wage increase.

Saltley was another demonstration, this time on British soil, of the power of the working class. But it also showed the weakness of the IS. IS members supported the action but were not the initiators. Their overall role was marginal; the IS had some stewards but the CP were still the key movers.[96] However, Arthur Harper, a convenor who had played an important part, joined the IS shortly afterwards.

The victory was not complete. Cliff noted in an article at the end of the year that one of the defects in the settlement was that future agreements would end in February, meaning that if strike action were required in future, it would begin in early summer rather than in winter. As he put it, "Ice-cream workers should have agreements from May to May, miners from November to November".[97]

He continued to be involved with rank and file organisation among miners. Years later he recalled, "In June 1972 I spoke in Barnsley to a meeting of over 100 miners including a member of the National Executive of the NUM, Tate, and a member of the Yorkshire executive, Arthur Scargill. We launched the *Collier* newspaper".[98]

The miners' victory was just the beginning of what was to be a remarkable year of working class militancy. There were strikes by engineers, railway workers and building workers,[99] with a total of around 30 million days "lost"* in strikes, the highest figure (excluding miners' strikes) since 1919.[100] For Cliff this translated into great optimism about the organisation: during the Manchester factory occupations, Cliff discussed the possibility of recruiting 200 engineering workers.[101]

In July the struggle rose to a still higher level. Five dockers picketing a container port – where dockers were being replaced by workers who did not have the wages and conditions the dockers had fought to win – were arrested under the terms of the Tory anti-union laws and jailed in Pentonville prison. Dockers immediately launched a campaign of aggressive picketing. IS members were involved in the pickets that went to Fleet Street and secured strike action which prevented national newspapers appearing. A special issue of *Socialist Worker* called for (illegal) industrial action: "Strikes and demonstrations should be called in every area in support of our brothers behind bars".[102]

The rather primitive IS centre at Cotton's Gardens, with only a handful of telephones, received calls from all over the country telling of groups of workers who had stopped work in protest at the jailings. It was a directly political confrontation, since the strikers were taking on not their own employers but government policy and the state machine. Even the TUC General Council was moved to threaten to call a general strike for the first time since 1926. Within

---

* As Cliff often pointed out, while official reports used to refer to days "lost" in strikes, workers should consider them as *gained*.

a couple of days the authorities had discovered a legal loophole and an obscure legal figure called the Official Solicitor (who normally acted for young children and the mentally handicapped) spoke on behalf of the five dockers who were refusing to recognise the legitimacy of the court. They were promptly freed. It was one of the most dramatically visible victories in working class history and millions of workers could see the immediate results of their action. The government's legislation and its strategy were in ruins.

In an article published a few days later Cliff assessed the results of the confrontation: "This has been the greatest victory for the British working class for more than half a century. The battle has been won, but the war against capitalism is still going on." Quoting Lenin, he noted that "there is no crisis of capitalism the capitalists cannot find a way out of if the workers are ready to pay the price". The workers had shown their strength, and British capitalism was facing real problems. This was not an economic crisis as such, but a situation in which the ruling class was having great difficulty maintaining its power to exploit:

> The capitalist machine does not work the way the bosses want. The driver steers and the machine doesn't turn. He presses the accelerator and it doesn't speed up. He puts on the brake and it doesn't stop.*
>
> What, in heaven's name, is affecting the engine? The answer is the workers' will and ability to resist.

The most important part of Cliff's article set out his proposals for the way ahead. While continuing to stress the importance of building a revolutionary party, Cliff now underlined the importance of a rank and file strategy. The IS had for some time been involved in the development of rank and file groupings within various unions and industries.

Cliff's analysis was based on a simple concrete image of cog wheels:

> *Three cog wheels*: The trade union movement, with 11 million members and 250,000 shop stewards, is a powerful cog, with by far the strongest shop organisation of the working class anywhere in the world.

---

* This is the tidied up version. In meetings Cliff, for whom the internal combustion engine always remained a mystery, would say, "It is like a car. You pull the gear lever and it does not start."

Let's assume that we had in this country a revolutionary socialist party, a combat organisation, steeled in struggle and schooled in the art of strategy and tactics for the overthrow of capitalism. Let's assume that we, the International Socialists, who are building such an organisation, had 50,000 members.

There is no question that this would indeed be a powerful cog wheel. However, one cog wheel of this size could not have moved the cog wheel of 11 million. If it tried it would only break its cogs. A connecting cog wheel is necessary between the two.*

This is the organisation of militants in different unions and industries who work together round specific issues, issues wider than those affecting a small group of workers in one place of work and not going as far as to aim at a complete emancipation of the working class by the overthrow of the capitalist system.

IS members participate in building such a cog wheel in the form of rank and file organisations round papers like the *Carworker*, the *Collier* and *Rank and File Teacher*. The aim of these is to influence the policies of the trade unions.[103]

From now on the building of rank and file organisations would be central to the IS perspective.

The model was provided by the work carried out since 1967 in the National Union of Teachers. A small group of IS teachers (including Chanie Rosenberg and Duncan Hallas) had come together with some CP members who were disillusioned by their party's increasingly conservative role. The paper *Rank and File* was set up, and rapidly became the focus for the militant left in the union, attracting support way beyond the IS and IS sympathisers.†

The role of the trade union bureaucracy as the main obstacle to shop-floor militancy became ever more obvious in the early 1970s, and IS members were able to participate in, and in some cases initiate, the creation of similar papers in a number of unions and

---

* The image of the cog wheels was borrowed from Trotsky; see T Cliff, *Trotsky* vol 1 (London, 1989), p283 (referring to L Trotsky, *The History of the Russian Revolution*, London, 1997, p1130). See also T Cliff, *Lenin*, vol 2, London, 1976, p369.

† Initially Cliff had not taken this work in the NUT very seriously (Ewa Barker interview, May 2008). But it was to prove an important influence on his strategic thinking.

industries – the *Collier*, the *Carworker*, the *Hospital Worker* and several others.

An additional factor in the situation was the role of the Liaison Committee for the Defence of Trade Unions (LCDTU). This had been set up by CP militants in the 1960s to oppose the anti-union policies of the Labour government. In the early 1970s it had held large conferences and even called strike action against the Industrial Relations Act.[104] On 10 June 1972 it had called a conference attended by almost 1,300 delegates to discuss resistance to the Industrial act. The conference was strong on rhetoric but weak on practical proposals. No resolutions were accepted. IS member Alan Woodward argued, "If the Liaison Committee was going to develop as a new rank and file movement in the years ahead then it had to do more than hold occasional conferences. In the localities it should encourage the development of a network of liaison committees".[105]

But when the dockers were jailed the LCDTU was largely invisible. As a letter from four docks shop stewards in *Socialist Worker* put it some time later:

> If the average docker who took part in this struggle was asked what the LCDTU did, they would not even know who they were.
>
> Many individuals involved with the LCDTU gave the dockers vital assistance in getting support but the movement itself, was in our opinion, lacking.[106] *

Certainly many CP members played an important role in pushing for industrial action, but the role of the LCDTU as a potential rank and file leadership was far from what was required. The dissatisfaction of dockers with the CP's intervention was shown by the fact that in the aftermath of the dispute the CP branch in the London docks collapsed. Some leading activists like Michael Fenn and Eddie Prevost joined the IS.[107]

Prevost had been on the CP's London District Committee but by 1972 was drifting away from the CP. During the strike he had been in contact with IS members. Towards the end of 1972 there was an IS public meeting (probably organised by Bob Light) at which Cliff spoke on the strike, putting it in historical perspective. Prevost was

---

* The LCDTU issued a press statement calling for industrial action and circulated a letter to affiliated branches, few of which can have received it in time to take any effective action. See R Darlington and D Lyddon, *Glorious Summer*, pp165, 226.

impressed by Cliff, whom he saw as a cross between James Cagney and Edward G Robinson, a "little big man", up front and telling it how it was. Cliff urged his audience to join the IS – but said that if in a few years it wasn't doing its job, they would have to scrap it and start again. Prevost joined and has remained a member.[108]

The building workers' strike in the summer of 1972 led Cliff to turn his attention to the problem of workers in the construction industry. For an IS building workers' conference in Birmingham in September 1972 he wrote a four-page document as a basis for discussion. He dealt concisely but concretely with the patterns of ownership in the industry, pay and work conditions, the role of the unions and the CP, and concluded with the strategy for IS building workers:

> It is not enough for IS members, however tiny in numbers, to concentrate on being the best militants, as we are prone to do. We have to anticipate the really crucial issues, like the forthcoming press tirade against the building workers and we have to push for building workers' leaflets to be put out in massive numbers to really tackle this forthcoming press attack, and to undermine the whole "one man's pay rise is another man's price rise" philosophy.[109]

With *The Employers' Offensive* and his public speaking, Cliff was becoming a well-known figure in the labour movement. On 22 November 1972 work stopped at the huge Anchor Steelworks construction site in Scunthorpe and 2,000 workers marched to the local football ground. They were not striking for their own wages or conditions but in support of the demand for higher old age pensions. They were joined by delegations of trade unionists from all over Yorkshire.

Nick Howard suggested Cliff as a speaker to one of his contacts[110] and he was invited to speak from the platform, alongside trade union militants Geoff Garbett (national president of the construction section of the AUEW), Wally Preston (secretary of the Manchester Power Workers' Shop Stewards Combine Committee) and Gwynn Reed (of Rotherham Trades Council and the Doncaster area of the NUM). Cliff regarded this as extremely important, since it showed workers were generalising, using their industrial strength to fight on issues that went beyond wages and working conditions.

Tony Cliff…said he was proud to be present at "a day in the history of the working class movement".

"The tears of Jack Jones break my heart," he said. "But they will not give higher pensions. The only way to help the pensioners is to fight through strike action."

Cliff went on to say, amid loud cheers, "We are the army of the working class. I believe that the rank and file is strong enough by industrial power to raise pensions now. I believe that the rank and file, by industrial power, can smash this Tory government".[111]

Small meetings were often as significant as the larger ones. Whenever Cliff visited Manchester to speak at a public meeting, he would also go and talk to a small *Socialist Worker* discussion group in Trafford Park where engineering workers met after work. A number of people with standing in their workplaces were drawn towards the IS.[112] Two or three times a year he would go to Glasgow, and speak at several branch and college meetings in two or three days.[113]

There were no major strikes in 1973. The year saw a number of public sector disputes. The defeat of various sections of workers who had fought against the Tory wage controls meant that more workers were realising the need for revolutionary politics. The atmosphere was still one of impending confrontation and this was highly favourable for the IS. At the spring conference Cliff told delegates, "History is knocking on our door. We must open that door. 1973 will be the most important year in our organisation's history".[114] The tasks ahead were rapid recruitment,* turning the IS into a workers' organisation and building the rank and file organisations. In a series of *Socialist Worker* articles[115] and in meetings all over the country, Cliff urged that time was short and that it was necessary to build rapidly. The growth of the party was also reflected in the fact that in the early months of 1973 £30,000 was raised to enable the purchase of a new and larger printshop in Corbridge Crescent, Hackney.

---

* Phil Piratin, later elected Communist MP for Mile End in 1945, was impressed by the Communist Party Hunger Marches in 1932: "I would have joined the Communist Party had someone asked me. Some of my best friends were Communists, but no one asked me to join. I didn't join." (P Piratin, *Our Flag Stays Red*, London, 1948, p5) Piratin only joined the CP in 1934. It was an error that Cliff was determined the IS should not repeat.

Occasionally, Cliff's focus on building the organisation could have a sectarian downside. The Teesside branch was concerned to reach out to the local Pakistani community and organised a public meeting at which Tariq Ali (then in the IMG) was invited to speak. Two hundred people attended and useful contacts were made, but Cliff was appalled and angry that the IS had given a platform to a rival organisation.[116]

By June the recruitment drive was showing real results. A report to the June National Committee registered a net gain of 456 new members since the conference.[117] As Cliff wrote a little later, the organisation was changing, not only numerically, but in class composition:

> In the first eight weeks following our conference we recruited 211 members and in the last four weeks we have recruited another 281. 49 percent of the new recruits are manual workers.
>
> For the first time we are recruiting more TGWU and AUEW members than members of the National Union of Teachers. Since the conference, in 12 weeks, 56 members of the TGWU and 51 members of the AUEW joined us, as against 29 in the NUT.[118]

However, Cliff was impatient, recognising that the favourable conditions would not last long. He wrote a short article jointly with John Charlton, a leading figure in the Yorkshire region, which Cliff held in particularly high esteem.

This emphasised the importance of the "subjective element...in determining the speed of recruitment", and showed Cliff's concern for the practical details of organisation and his willingness to learn from Charlton's experience. New recruits had to be followed up as rapidly as possible: "If you leave seeing them for a week after you have recruited them it can go wrong – you want to get back to them as soon as possible... The next evening is best."

In particular "batch recruitment" was to be encouraged: "When you recruit a worker do not give him only one membership card for himself, but at least another two for his friends he has to recruit immediately."

Public meetings had to be carefully planned: "The dynamics of the meeting are important. Maximum length of time for the formal part of the meeting is one hour so there is a good hour left for talking to the contacts – it's no good ending the meeting at 10.30 and then finding the contacts who have come along can't stay for a beer but have to rush off to get a bus... One of the most disturbing pictures in IS public meetings is quite often after the end of the meeting the IS members collect together in a clique, leaving visitors as pariahs".[119] For a time Cliff took on the role of membership secretary. He distributed regularly to the executive lists of new recruits from around the country.* In particular he was concerned that the best branches in the country – the so-called "leading areas" – should be encouraged and should set the pace for the rest of the organisation. In the four months from April to July 1,260 new members were recruited.[120]

Cliff believed in easy recruitment because he thought that those outside the party were better than those already in it. When there was a debate on probationary membership at one conference, Cliff argued that anyone who had been a member for more than three years should be put on probation until they proved they were still revolutionaries; new members should be admitted straight away.[121] He would certainly have agreed with Peter Sedgwick's dismissal of probationary membership: "We don't put the working class on probation; we are on probation to the working class".[122]

For Cliff, now in his fifties, the rapid growth of the organisation was an exhilarating experience. To be surrounded by admiring young men and women must have been flattering and a source of temptation. Yet in the end his life changed little; it was the same intensive routine of speaking, writing and keeping a close eye on the organisation, and behind that, enjoying the security of his home and family.

An important development at this stage was the decision to build factory branches. To Cliff's great indignation the 1972 conference had voted against forming factory branches – although the majority was formed of an alliance of those who opposed factory branches in principle (because they separated workers from intellectuals) and those who simply thought it premature to establish them.[123] The argument for factory branches stressed that members had to be organised for action, not discussion, and that factory branches would enable a great increase in the recruitment of workers.

---

* Few if any copies of these survive, as they had to be destroyed a few months later for security reasons.

The conference held in March 1973 resolved to go ahead with factory branches. Within months about 40 were established. Cliff took a close interest in their progress. Sabby Sagall was involved in setting up a branch at Ford Dagenham with 12 members. Cliff followed the situation and gave considerable assistance. Sagall went to Cliff's home two or three times a week for "revolutionary tutorials".[124]

Success produced a new set of problems. In September 1973 a conference of factory branch members was held. In preparation for this Cliff discussed with many of those involved and wrote a short pamphlet on the problems of factory branches.[125]

This remains a remarkable document which provides much information on the state of the organisation and Cliff's role within it. As with *The Employers' Offensive*, but on a smaller scale, he drew on the contributions of many comrades, members of factory branches and local organisers, who were quoted *verbatim* and extensively in the course of the argument. Cliff again showed his gift for accumulating information, fitting it into a broader framework and generalising from it.

Apart from the ENV branch in the 1960s, factory branches were a new experience for the IS and, indeed, for the entire revolutionary left since the 1920s. With gentle mockery, Cliff recalled the days, only a few years previously, when IS activity had consisted mainly of students standing at factory gates with bundles of papers:

> One remembers the virtuous glow one used to get after standing in the rain outside the factory handing out sodden sheets of paper or failing to sell *Socialist Worker* to tolerant but indifferent workers.

The CP had wound up most of its factory branches,* and those that remained were concerned mainly with electoral politics – either parliamentary and municipal elections or the election of "left" trade union officials. So the IS was entering uncharted waters and it was necessary to analyse the experience carefully.

The atmosphere of the time was somewhat frenetic, and Cliff himself often revealed impatience. But here, in a document

---

* The number of CP workplace branches declined from 265 in 1964 to 126 in 1979 (J McIlroy, "Notes on the Communist Party and Industrial Politics", in J McIlroy, N Fishman and A Campbell, *British Trade Unions and Industrial Politics II: The High Tide of Trade Unionism 1964-79*, Aldershot, 1999, p222).

addressed to the industrial militants of the organisation and to the key party activists, he stressed the need for honesty and sobriety: "We need to face up to the problems as realistically as possible, without flannelling and without evasion." It was important to be flexible, and not sacrifice the necessity for self-criticism to the personal pride of individuals:

> The one thing that simply cannot be afforded is a situation in which for fear of "losing face" comrades will not be prepared to reverse a decision made at a previous meeting.

While encouraging rapid recruitment, he warned, "Think 'small', don't overreach and risk demoralisation."

The pamphlet was concerned with the concrete question of how a branch was to operate in the workplace, and how revolutionaries related to their fellow workers. It raised the argument about party and class to a new level:

> If there are 1,000 workers in a factory, in all probability there will be a tiny minority of scabs at one extreme and a tiny group of militant socialists at the other. Between them stands the big majority – not right wing but simply an uninformed conservative mass.

This meant careful application of the united front tactic: "We have to agree to differ from many militants on some important questions in order to unite with these same militants for some immediate aims." It also meant building a rank and file organisation. He recognised that there were real difficulties, real problems of balance between party-building and a rank and file strategy:

> Comrades sometimes see a contradiction between pushing, for example, the *Carworker* or the *Dockworker*, and pushing *Socialist Worker*, or between pulling people into supporting a rank and file organisation and pulling people into IS. The contradiction does exist. Sometimes the rank and file movement can be a substitute for building the party. Sometimes building the party can be used as an excuse for not developing the rank and file movement. But both are needed.

The central question was consciousness; the value of the branch was raising socialist consciousness among the workforce as a whole. This was far more important than passing particular resolutions or winning particular elections. The main principle was:

> to increase the participation of workers in determining their activities – for

mass meetings and shop meetings to decide policy, and to mandate shop stewards and delegates. Obviously we would prefer to be in a minority getting, say, 100 votes among 500 workers at a meeting, to an IS majority of seven among ten workers coming to a meeting.*

In a useful and practical section on victimisation, Cliff pointed out the need for reasonable precautions, but cautioned against excessive secrecy since that would impair the relation of trust needed between militants and their fellow workers:

> Secrecy may at times be necessary. As a rule, however, one should attempt to operate as openly as possible. The greater risk for our members is the possible suspicion on the part of their workmates that we have not been honest. The "reds under the bed" scare can be devastatingly effective if one has kept one's politics carefully hidden. The best defence is honesty, and being able to say it was all above board. In the last analysis the best defence is the support one gets from one's mates. This will not be forthcoming if they can be convinced that they have been taken for a ride.

Throughout the pamphlet Cliff attempted to deal with concrete problems rather than laying down abstract principles. Factory branches varied greatly: in some the IS members were young and inexperienced, in others they formed the established leadership in the factory. Then there was the problem of "industrial branches", a sort of halfway-house, where, for example, hospital workers from several workplaces came together in the same branch.

Cliff showed considerable attention to detail, for example in the discussion of the timing of meetings – a real problem when there was a complex pattern of shift-working. The importance of systematic work in trade union branches and trades councils was emphasised. There was detailed discussion of the production and distribution of factory bulletins.

Cliff demanded the active involvement of all members. In words

---

* Cliff's insistence on consciousness gives the lie (if it were necessary to do so) to the claims later made by former IS industrial organiser Roger Rosewell (on the claimed basis of "first-hand experience of how Marxists organise") that SWP shop stewards were "drilled in the knack" of organising meetings: "Thus trade union branch meetings might be held in small, cold and dismal rooms with long agendas and crucial matters left to the last item of any other business...these tactics are designed to discourage ordinary members from attending meetings" (R Rosewell, *Dealing with the Marxist Threat to Industry*, London, 1983, pp1, 3).

he would often repeat during the years to come, "In a revolutionary party there is no rank and file. Every member must be a leader." Recruitment was central; Cliff was aware of the urgency and fragility of the situation. Opportunities that were not seized immediately could disappear in a short space of time:

> Methods of establishing personal contacts include striking up an acquaintance with workers in the factory during the meal break or when leaving work, or in the buses, the pubs and clubs, or in the trade union branch or trades council.

Cliff was aware of the danger that factory branches could become confined to a discussion of matters within the workplace; it was vital to develop members as revolutionaries and not simply as trade union militants:

> There is no Chinese wall separating the factory from the world outside it – factory workers do not live in a world cut off from life in the surrounding area. Local issues such as rents, fares, social services, etc. affect them, being in fact disguised wage cuts. Hence the factory branch has to relate to all these and similar issues. Above all, racism as a weapon in the hands of the employers must be combated inside the factory and in its neighbourhood.

Hence political education was vital, but had to be geared to the needs of the members, not simply imposed through a predetermined syllabus: "Workers who had a tough and nasty relation with school authorities in childhood certainly don't enjoy the word 'education'."

The pamphlet showed Cliff at his best, exercising the role of leadership within the organisation and grappling with new problems. Yet in some respects it now appears very dated. It is mainly oriented to manual, productive workers in large workplaces. There is little sense of how radically that workforce was to change over the coming decades. Although there are several references to the importance of involving workers' wives, there is no reference to women workers, no awareness that some workers might have husbands rather than wives.

Cliff was the driving force in the building of the factory branches, above all because of his remarkable ability to talk to workers. On one occasion he attended a meeting of strikers in Peterborough. There were about 200 workers there who were expecting a detailed discussion of the strike, not a political meeting. Nonetheless he captured the audience, showing his capacity for connecting with ordinary workers.[126]

In some cases the factory branches were able to exercise real power. In one factory in Ossett there were ten members out of a workforce of 180; fifty papers were sold. Workers learned that in a local school pupils on free school meals had to stand in a separate queue and were served last. They demanded that the factory management should put pressure on the local council to change this policy, threatening strike action. They won.[127]

Cliff was careful to recognise that in some circumstances growth might be slow, but the underlying assumption was a continuation of the current rapid expansion of the organisation and the transformation of the IS into a party dominated by workers and based in the workplaces. A general mood of optimism characterised the IS in the summer of 1973. In Glasgow Cliff told students that the priority was to organise workers: "Don't waste your time reading books".[128]

There seemed to be little time for theoretical work. When Alex Callinicos told Cliff he was going to do a PhD on Marx's *Capital*, Cliff explained how he had worked on Marx and some of the writers he drew on and criticised, such as Locke and Petty, and therefore Callinicos did not need to work on the material. Fortunately Callinicos's response was to think, "Fuck you!"; he became more determined than ever to study these writings.[129]

Yet as Cliff's hopes of a development towards a larger, more worker-based organisation were being realised, problems arose inside the organisation. The leadership team that had been constituted at the time of the move to democratic centralism was now under considerable strain. Serious tensions were appearing between Cliff, the effective political leader of the organisation, and Jim Higgins, the national secretary.

Higgins had been a well-established militant in the Post Office Engineering Union and on its national executive; it was possible he might have become its general secretary.[130] In January 1972 the IS National Committee appointed him full-time national secretary, to replace Duncan Hallas, who was one of the finest socialist propagandists of his generation, but not a particularly good organiser. The IS was growing rapidly, but the structures were still rather chaotic. Hallas had spearheaded the faction fight against Workers' Fight at the end of 1971, and the executive was anxious to heal any wounds left from that dispute.

This was a major step for Higgins, who was now in his 1940s. He lost his union base and possible future, withdrew from the pension scheme and took a salary cut in order to work in a rather squalid office. Cliff played a major role in persuading him to take the job and campaigned vigorously for his appointment. When a few members of the NC opposed the appointment, saying that a well-established trade unionist should not be withdrawn from a position of influence in the labour movement, Cliff was scathing: "Who do you want as national secretary?" he enquired. "My son?"[131] (Donny was 18 at the time.)

Higgins's brief was to introduce some order and to complement Cliff's leadership. Cliff's talent was to grasp new tendencies, to focus attention on the priorities of the organisation. He needed someone to preserve balance, maintain an organisational routine and pick up the tasks which were not priorities but still essential.

Things did not work out as Cliff had intended. Higgins ran the organisation as he would have run a trade union office. He seemed to be a secretary, more interested in his files, than a leader.[132] He was hard-working and dedicated, and issued a stream of branch circulars, all carefully numbered for reference. But he treated it as an office job, travelling out of London far less than Cliff did. Cliff began to become annoyed by the sheer quantity of paper issuing from the centre. Penny Krantz, then a very new comrade doing secretarial work at the centre, was shocked when Cliff said to her, "I wish I could throw that typewriter out of the window".[133] Cliff, meanwhile, toured the country tirelessly, enthused comrades, argued with them, and spent hundreds of hours on the telephone, persuading – and listening.

There was a certain amount of friction, but at the spring 1973 conference largely the same leadership team was re-elected to the NC and the executive. *Socialist Worker* carried a picture of Cliff and Higgins side by side and smiling.[134]

But within weeks serious divisions within the leadership began to emerge. Firstly there was the question of age. Cliff had noted the difference between the younger, more radical workers and the older, more conservative elements in France in 1968. There seemed to be a similar pattern within the party. Higgins and Hallas were men in their forties, who had developed politically (as had Cliff) in the Trotskyist movement of the 1950s, a world of marginal groups and bitter sectarianism. John Palmer, though younger, also went back to the 1950s. Cliff was anxious not to return to that world of small-group politics and wanted to see the leadership in the hands of younger comrades who had emerged in the 1960s and were more outward-looking.

More generally, Cliff believed that when members had been in the organisation for a few years they tended to become more conservative. Therefore whenever there was a new turn it had to be led from behind, with the most active part of the membership going over the heads of the existing leadership. Cliff's strategy was for the minority to lead the majority.[135]

Secondly there was a geographical division. The most rapid growth of the IS had taken place in the provinces, especially in the North. Cliff was much influenced by John Charlton, a college lecturer who was the driving force behind the organisation in Yorkshire, and by Roger Rosewell, a former industrial organiser who had moved to Liverpool and become the organiser there.

Paradoxically, Cliff's first attempt at restructuring the leadership involved a look backward. *International Socialism* had moved to monthly publication in January 1973, in an attempt to make it more relevant to the organisation. Under Hallas's editorship there was a maximum of 2,000 words set on all articles in the interests of accessibility. It was not a great success, being an uneasy compromise between a current affairs magazine and a theoretical journal.

Cliff now proposed that Mike Kidron should be brought back as editor. Kidron's role in the group had declined sharply since 1968. His academic career had taken him abroad for considerable spells of time, and he had become increasingly involved with Pluto Press. Cliff campaigned vigorously for Kidron's appointment.* Kidron was elected, but at a meeting between Kidron and the executive committee about the future of the journal Cliff was quite critical of Kidron, suggesting he was out of touch with the current membership.[136] Subsequently Kidron imposed conditions about absolute editorial

---

* I was summoned to Cliff's home and harangued for half an hour as to why I should vote for Kidron.

independence which made it impossible for him to take up the position.[137]

The second move was more drastic and provoked what became the most serious internal crisis in the organisation's history. Following a report from Cliff on problems caused by recent growth, the July NC set up an organisation commission consisting of Cliff, Andreas Nagliatti, Rosewell, Higgins, Charlton and Roger Kline.[138] This commission came up with the proposal that the executive committee should be sacked and replaced by the six members of the organisation commission, plus Roger Protz, with Harman, Harris and Nichol as observers.[139] (The London-based executive was a subcommittee of the NC of 40, which was elected annually by conference.) This was confirmed by the following NC though technically it may have been unconstitutional – one member of the new executive committee, Roger Kline, the Coventry organiser, had never been elected to the NC. Higgins remained in post as national secretary, but others of the "old guard" were removed – Hallas, Palmer and Birchall.

For a few weeks Higgins worked in harness with the new EC, but such a division of power could not last long. At the September NC he offered his resignation, recounting how he had discussed his doubts about originally taking the job with Cliff, who, in the biblical style he sometimes adopted, had responded, "You must measure your cloth three times." "And so I did," he said, "but I forgot to measure the fucking tailor".[140]

Higgins was understandably bitter. He had worked closely with Cliff since the early 1960s, and had been personally fond of him. He was given a job on the staff of *Socialist Worker*, where Roger Protz shared some of the criticisms of Cliff.

At this stage the differences between Cliff and Higgins were primarily organisational; disagreements on political perspective were not yet apparent. It was Higgins's formalism which Cliff saw as an obstacle to building the organisation. At every level, from the theory of state capitalism to the administration of the organisation, Cliff detested any approach which gave too much importance to form; for him form had always to be subordinated to content.

Roger Rosewell, one of Cliff's closest allies at this point, saw the dispute as a clash between the older comrades like Higgins and Hallas and the younger members of the leadership. Higgins and to some extent Hallas, were sceptical to the point of cynicism. They didn't encourage activity, and didn't believe the new recruits would stay. Higgins relied too much on imitating models provided by the CP and the Minority Movement* in the 1920s. Meanwhile the provincial organisers were building the organisation.[141] To Roger Kline, who was new to the leadership and did not quite understand what was going on, it was a case of "young Turks" against "old lags"; Higgins appeared bureaucratic and cautious.[142] Jim Nichol, who worked closely with Cliff throughout the 1970s, believes that Cliff generally aimed to avoid conflict, and that he would have avoided confrontation with Higgins if possible, but that he was pushed by Nichol and others to the conclusion that Higgins was an impediment to growth.[143]

The national secretary's job was given to Dave Peers, who moved from Newcastle to London. Peers now feels he was shoved into the job as a manoeuvre to get someone not aligned with either group. His role was to help to hold the organisation together, which meant saying things he did not believe.[144] There were other changes in personnel as Cliff tried to develop a new leadership.

The new executive was not a great success. The new set-up was rather messy; the atmosphere was not good and comrades were not friendly. The idea of having EC members from outside London was that they should draw on the experience of the strongest and most active areas, but in practice the out-of-town members did not attend regularly.[145] Charlton, who was combining his EC role with a full-time teaching job and travelling from Leeds, found himself psychologically exhausted by the following spring.[146] To Roger Kline, Cliff seemed the dominant figure; Rosewell, Charlton and Steve Jefferys (who had moved to London) spoke a lot.[147] Granville Williams, who had been added to the EC after he had made some critical comments about the changes, felt the new committee lacked a sense of direction.[148] With the increasing tempo of events, the internal disputes faded into the background, but they would return to haunt Cliff. However, Paul Holborow, who was for a time on the new EC, recalls the exchange of information between Cliff and the local organisers on a basis of equality, and Cliff's complete tolerance

---

* The Minority Movement, built by the CP in the 1920s, attempted to develop militant currents working inside the trade unions.

of those less experienced than himself, showing Cliff's ability to encourage comrades.[149]

In September 1973 came news of the right-wing coup in Chile, a perfect illustration of the IS argument about the inadequacy of the parliamentary road and the need for revolutionary politics (indeed, in the immediate aftermath of the coup the IS tended to stress these lessons rather than the need for solidarity with the workers of Chile). In a situation of impending confrontation between the government and the labour movement, it served to convince everyone that the stakes in the current situation might be very high.

The following month came the war between Israel and Egypt. This forced the questions of Zionism and the rights of the Palestinians to international attention, but more importantly, it produced an international oil crisis. In Britain the price of petrol rose sharply, with an inflationary impact on the rest of the economy. An oil crisis increased the strategic importance of coal at a time when the miners were again threatening industrial action. This marked the end of the long post-war boom, meaning that a very new situation now lay ahead. Cliff's 1968 prediction that rising unemployment would be accompanied by inflation was borne out by events.

The central question remained the looming industrial confrontation. The question was how to take the rank and file movement forward, how to move beyond the various scattered rank and file groupings to a more generalised organisation. From the spring onwards there was a discussion of the possibility of holding a national rank and file conference, based on trade union delegations after the fashion of the Liaison Committee for the Defence of Trade Unions.

This meant moving into new territory, beyond the experience of anyone in the organisation. There were serious questions about the viability of a delegate conference. Would the trade union bureaucracy be able to obstruct the efforts to build such a conference? Would the CP try to block it? Could the IS trade union members, who, with a few exceptions, were young and inexperienced, carry through the job of building such a conference? There was also an argument about recruitment. The organisation was growing rapidly. Would the building of a rank and file conference, involving united front work with non-members, contradict the aim of recruiting as widely as possible while favourable circumstances lasted?

There were long and heated arguments about this in the leading committees. Some of those involved remember that Cliff had been initially sceptical about the possibilities for a genuine delegate conference, but found himself in the minority.[150] By the end of May he was arguing that there was no contradiction: "We have a two-pronged perspective – membership and work towards rank and file conference go hand in hand, and reinforce each other".[151]

At the June NC Rosewell and Charlton argued strongly against a rank and file conference, believing that the organisation was not yet ready and that it would be an obstacle to recruitment. Cliff remained sceptical – he was quoted as saying that "we would be doing well to get 200 bona fide TU delegacies". But he argued, against Rosewell, that "this is what united front work is all about, a political fight against the CP. We cannot any longer attempt to put the LCDTU on the spot unless we can offer a positive alternative."

A resolution was carried calling for a conference which would have genuine trade union delegates, but which would also admit other militants "on discretion of [the] organising committee" to make up the numbers. Cliff abstained – something he rarely did.[152]

After further discussion a new formulation was produced. There would be a large rally in November, open to all, which would essentially be a party-building operation and a full rank and file conference early the following year.

At the October NC Cliff argued that it was impossible to predict how the union bureaucracy would react in the coming months. He foresaw problems for the organisation: "Our growth...will not continue as in the past period and we will have to protect our members from disappointment...we will have to improve our *quality*, not so much our quantity".[153]

The rally was planned for November at Belle Vue in Manchester. A few weeks earlier the Heath government announced Phase Three of its incomes policy with a below-inflation limit of 7 percent on wage increases. This meant a direct confrontation with the trade union movement, and especially with the miners, who were again preparing for industrial action.

In *Socialist Worker* (3 November) Cliff wrote a call to action, urging supporters to prepare to resist the Heath government, and to build the rally:

The crying need is for rank and file organisations. The need to cement the militants throughout a whole industry, through a rank and file organisation assisted by its own paper, will become more and more vital...

To create a rank and file organisation, let us say, between miners in hundreds of pits, isolated geographically from one another, is not an easy task.

Without the inspiration of a socialist world outlook, without the clear conviction that the struggle is greater than the immediate issue of wages and conditions, however important they are, one could not build a viable rank and file movement.[154]

At the November NC, Cliff stressed the gravity of the crisis:

I am not trying to say capitalism is collapsing but I believe they cannot solve the problem by direct confrontation, they cannot use the police to smash, the incomes policy is not working, I believe they will find themselves in a massive crisis, one form of which will be massive unemployment if [the] oil crisis bites, miners etc. Bitterness will rise to a high level, then perhaps big business will throw their money on the Labour Party? Everything they are doing is stupid.[155]

On both rising unemployment and the Labour Party, he was to be proven right.

The rally itself was a considerable success, with 2,800 present. The speakers included miners, a firefighter, a print worker, a docker, a building worker and many others. Cliff gave a keynote address; his call was to build both the party and the rank and file movement. *Socialist Worker* reported his words:

To mobilise millions we need strong rank and file movements – plus a central cog to bind them together...

We need a socialist outlook, so that militants think, "I'm a socialist first, a miner second, a socialist first, a docker second," and so on.

The rank and file papers created in recent years could not survive without IS politics – even though our members are in a minority on their editorial boards.

We are fighting a political battle. We need a workers' party.[156]

Just before Christmas the first trial ended of militants accused of violent picketing in the building workers' strike of 1972, three receiving jail sentences (three more were jailed in February). This was a direct confrontation between working class organisation and the state, and a challenge to the right to picket. But a call for strike action[157] was largely swallowed up in the general opposition to the Heath government. There was a widespread solidarity movement with the pickets, and IS members played a leading role despite the sometimes uncooperative attitude of the CP when it tried to marginalise the IS.[158]

Cliff participated in a number of activities in support of the Shrewsbury pickets, as they were known. On 17 December more than 900 activists came to a *Socialist Worker* rally in London in support of the pickets. "Gerry Kelly, Tony Cliff and Laurie Flynn spoke, Jake Thackray sang. Sandra Kerr and John Faulkner – 'The Combine' – performed 'tough and funny sketches' and 'pilloried the "law and order" gibberish of the building bosses'. The event raised £940".[159]

In the New Year a major campaign was organised, with Cliff as one of the speakers:

> SW [*Socialist Worker*] announced that from the 11th January there would be "Socialist Worker Free the Shrewsbury Three!" public meetings in Coventry, Manchester, Liverpool, Wolverhampton, Nottingham, North West London, Birmingham, Glasgow, Edinburgh, Leeds, Sheffield, Hull, Teesside and Tyneside to offer "major rallying points in the working class movement for the demand to free the three jailed pickets". The halls held up to 500, thousands of leaflets had been distributed and the meetings would be "a central part of the IS effort to build stronger socialist organisation at the heart of the working class movement". IS speakers, including Tony Cliff, Roger Rosewell, Glyn Carver (... Manchester organiser), Bob Light and George Kelly, would "draw the political lessons of the trial" and "link it with the overall attack on workers' liberties and living standards". John Carpenter or John Llywarch would speak. Both would appear with Paul Foot in Birmingham. "Special canvass squads have been touring two of the city's biggest council estates, introducing people to *Socialist Worker* and telling them about the rally".[160]

Cliff spoke at rallies in north west London, Sheffield, Teesside and Tyneside, together with John Carpenter or John Llywarch, two of the pickets who had been tried but not jailed.[161]

The pace of events had quickened further. The miners persisted with their pay claim in direct contravention of the government's policy. Heath responded by announcing that, because of the fuel crisis, industry would be put on a three-day week. For hourly-paid workers this amounted to a 40 percent pay cut. It was a direct attempt to isolate the miners and coerce them into calling off their action. When they did not do so, Heath called a general election, in effect on the question of who was running the country: the elected government or the trade unions.

In January a new executive was formed, consisting entirely of London-based full-timers, an indication that the previous EC had not worked. Only four names were published: Peers, Nichol, Nagliatti and Protz. Cliff's name was presumably omitted for security reasons.[162] It is inconceivable that he did not play a full part.

In two important articles in *Socialist Worker* Cliff set out his analysis of the situation. In the first he argued:

> There is only one way for British capitalism to overcome its crisis. To slash workers' real wages radically. And as Lenin put it, capitalism always has a way out of every crisis if the workers are ready to pay the price.

The aim of the three-day week was to weaken and divide workers. Otherwise it made no economic sense; it was "like a doctor ordering a bloodletting for a person suffering from severe anaemia".[163]

Two weeks later he argues, "The employers' offensive *must* become harsher and harsher." The choice ahead would be decisive:

> In the final analysis a capitalism that suffers from permanent and deepening crisis is incompatible with trade unionism...
>
> For a time the ruling class can use two different weapons – the trade union bureaucracy on the one hand, and the police, army and courts on the other. But with the deepening crisis they will more and more use the second.
>
> After a few years of deepening crisis the stark alternative will be either the employers will break the back of the workers' organisations in the factories or the workers will get rid of the employers.[164]

Cliff carried this message at public meetings around the country. In the first two months of 1974 he addressed meetings on the current crisis in Southampton, Tower Hamlets, West Middlesex, Glasgow and York. He found time to speak to meetings on the fiftieth anniversary of Lenin's death at the LSE in London, and in Manchester and Merseyside.[165]

He visited Cwm Colliery in South Wales, where the IS had a pit branch. He listened carefully to a discussion about how the action could be stepped up; the miners were still working to rule, but were considering going on to a three-day week. After hearing all the arguments, Cliff insisted that they should support an all-out strike. Subsequently IS comrades from Cwm were in the forefront of the demand for all-out strike action.[166]

In February, after an 81 percent vote in a ballot, miners went into a national all-out strike. There was a general recognition of what was at stake. There were rumours that if Heath were re-elected on his anti trade union platform, internment would be introduced for industrial militants and revolutionary activists. Members of the executive were required to adopt pseudonyms.[167] However, though the atmosphere was undoubtedly tense, Cliff expected much greater working class resistance to the three-day week.[168]

At the end of February the election took place, and by the narrowest of margins Labour was able to form a minority government. Heath had asked the question "Who runs the country?", and the electorate had responded that it was not Heath.

Cliff rarely attended demonstrations, but just after the election a group of activists gathered outside Downing Street, and George Paizis recalls that Cliff was there. He was somewhat nervous, asking Paizis to stay with him in case he was attacked, but at the same time he had a sense that for the moment the ruling class was off balance.[169]

A month later the Rank and File Conference in Birmingham was attended by more than 500 delegates from over 300 trade union organisations, including 40 shop stewards' and combine committees, and 239 trade union branches [170] – rather better than had been hoped for.

There was little press coverage of the event, apart from a brief and predictable piece in the *Morning Star* complaining that "the intention was to establish a rival body to the Liaison Committee for the Defence of Trade Unions".[171] However, the *New Statesman* carried a perceptive analysis by "George Bishop" (pseudonym of well-known labour correspondent Robert Taylor). While remaining legitimately agnostic about the rank and file movement's future, he recognised its potential:

> The Rank and File movement...does pose a major and immediate threat to the Communist hold on shop-floor militancy. Rank and File has no need for open compromise and equivocation with the union establishment. It does not have to keep a cautious eye on the attitude of leftist union bosses as the Communists must do if they wish to retain their broad left strategy.
>
> At the moment Rank and File remains tiny, but its influence is undoubtedly growing in a number of unions, most notably among the teachers, local government officers and clerical civil servants. In the past year Rank and File has made some impact on blue-collar unions and in particular in the Engineering Workers, the Transport and General Workers and the Building Workers, where they have managed to push the union into a fairly tough line over the six imprisoned Shrewsbury workers.

Bishop noted that "the whole affair was...devised and orchestrated by the International Socialists", who had "become a formidable force on the far left".[172]

The IS had indeed moved a long way since 1968, and Cliff had played a key role in transforming the organisation. But success bred new problems, and it was soon to become apparent that these were much bigger than Cliff had expected.

9
1974-79
Moving On Up – With Complications

For the only time in British history, working class action had brought down a government. The miners had resisted Labour Party pressure to call off their strike for the duration of the election campaign and this may well have tipped the balance in a close-run election. Labour had been brought to power not by the positive virtues of its programme or its leaders, but by the success of the working class opposition to the Heath government. Labour received a smaller share of the vote than at any election since 1945, but an anti-Tory vote going to the Liberals and others put Wilson into power.

Labour now had to pick up the pieces. The 1974 election marked an important turning point. Heath had pursued confrontation with the trade union movement; Wilson's strategy was to co-opt it. Trade union leaders were invited to cooperate in formulating a policy which was given the title of the "Social Contract". Prominent Labour leftists Michael Foot and Tony Benn joined the cabinet.

Workers had not been defeated, but had just won a remarkable victory (although the Shrewsbury pickets remained in jail). The balance of forces was confirmed a couple of months later when an "anonymous" donor paid a large sum of compensation awarded against the engineering union under the Tory laws in order to avert a major strike.

The meetings that Cliff did around the country in the first months of the Labour government reflected a sense of confidence. Whenever a new branch was set up, Cliff would come to address the first meeting.[1]

Steve Hammill, a young South Yorkshire miner, heard Cliff shortly after the end of the strike. When Cliff arrived, his first reaction was "Who the bloody hell's this?" Cliff looked like a tramp in his trenchcoat, with his hair all over the place and mumbling to himself. But when he spoke he was "absolutely wonderful" – he spoke of revolution, of socialism, of the way forward for the working class and for the miners in particular.[2] For Hammill it was the start of a commitment that would last through the 1984-85 strike and continues today.

Dave Hayes heard Cliff at a public meeting in Sunderland in 1974, when he was a young postal worker. He had never heard anything like the mix of inspiration and explanation; it articulated a critique of the Labour government. Hayes joined the IS a few months later, a membership that would last till the present day.[3]

Andy Strouthous, a clerical officer in the DHSS and a trade union activist, heard Cliff at a public meeting in Tottenham. He had never heard anything like it and was fantastically impressed by Cliff's dynamism, honesty and freshness, by the way he got ideas across in a way that could be understood. The experience persuaded him to join the IS; he has remained a member over four decades.[4]

It seemed reasonable to assume the class struggle would continue at the same level as under Heath, and that the possibilities of building the party and the rank and file movement remained unchanged. But as Cliff had written five years earlier, "a declining interest in the traditional reformist organisations…does not mean the *overcoming* of reformist ideology".[5] The grip of reformism was going to prove rather stronger than Cliff suspected, and it would take some time for all the implications to be absorbed into the organisation's practice.

Initially the perspective was that the Labour government would merely offer a brief respite before massive struggles of the 1972 type would break out again. Cliff told the March NC that the "honeymoon" period of the Labour government would be much shorter than in 1964-66. While most workers would want to give Labour a chance, there would be a larger group of militants more critical of Labour than ever before:

> For the first time we stand alone in championing these militants. When it was a fight against the Tories, we were ranged alongside all sorts of other groups. But with the Labour government in office, the Communist Party will be more cringing than ever before. We have to be patient, but hard in our criticism of the government.

There was a divergence between Cliff and the group around Jim

Higgins, but only over the relatively trivial question about how long the "honeymoon" would last. Higgins argued that "the honeymoon period might be longer rather than shorter – six or seven months rather than three or four", but he agreed that when the honeymoon was over there would be "real opportunities for an IS breakthrough".[6] What had originally been a dispute about routinism and organisational approaches was now becoming a political divergence. Both sides were catastrophically wrong; the honeymoon was prelude to a marriage, though certainly a stormy one, and the divorce courts were nowhere in sight.

During the hectic months from the Belle Vue rally to the Rank and File Conference the internal dispute vanished. Everyone pulled together in face of the urgent tasks confronting the organisation. Higgins co-authored with Paul Foot a glowing report of the Rank and File Conference,[7] and seemed happy with the progress the organisation had made.

But immediately after the election Cliff returned to the attack. He believed major changes were required not only in the internal working of the organisation but in the whole strategy required in the immediate future. The consequent dispute led to a major split in the organisation and the loss of a number of longstanding members. Whether Cliff had intended, or even foreseen, that this would happen is unclear. Higgins at this time wrote to some of his supporters, "Of course the last thing we want is a split".[8]

A document produced by the oppositional grouping round Higgins in the autumn of 1974 accused Cliff of impatience – "an unwillingness to accept any pace but his own. Those of us, less gifted perhaps, or with a dissenting opinion, are ignored, circumvented and finally dispensed with".[9] Another critic believes that in the 1970s Cliff could see his chance of fame slipping away and tried to hurry things up. As a result the IS lost the sense of reality which had been its great virtue in the 1960s. He also believes the leadership were guilty of keeping the argument from the membership, of adopting an attitude of "not in front of the children".[10]

There is some truth in these charges. Cliff was justifiably impatient for the organisation to grow and to transform itself. The mass confrontations he had foreseen back in 1968 were offering enormous opportunities. Even if he did not yet realise that the tide was beginning to ebb, he knew that there was no time to waste, that chances would not wait around to be seized.

Such impatience was healthy. Cliff was always keen to encourage new comrades, to take initiatives – virtues which Higgins and those around him often lacked. Higgins in particular often found it easier to sneer than to encourage.

But Cliff's impatience had a negative side. Just as he had a tendency to "fall in love" with young comrades, to make favourites of those he saw as having a positive role, so too he tended to "fall out of love" and to be unduly harsh to those he saw as an obstacle to the progress of the organisation.

Often when Cliff had convinced himself, after discussion with a small group of comrades, of the correctness of a particular course of action, he lacked the patience to argue the point with everyone else. In this respect Hallas was an important complement to Cliff's leadership. Cliff often "bent the stick" (overstated his point in order to convince comrades of the importance of a new strategy); on occasion Hallas would gently but firmly bend it back again. Hallas rarely initiated new forms of activity, but had enormous patience in argument. He had a long practical acquaintance with the British trade union movement and understood its peculiar strengths and weaknesses. But since the "coup" of 1973 Cliff had fallen out with Hallas, who had been removed from the executive.

Cliff, like most human beings, had the vices of his virtues, and in Cliff's case the virtues were considerable. Would it have made any difference if he had shown a little more tact, a little more patience? Perhaps individual losses could have been avoided, but the disputes of the 1973-75 period were not trivial squabbles or a petty fight for power; they were about real issues of party-building.

Initially Cliff attacked on the question of *Socialist Worker*. The paper was one of the IS's strongest assets. It had improved immeasurably since 1968, having moved from a rather scruffy four-page paper to a well-designed 16 pages. Industrial coverage was well balanced with political analysis. Its full-time staff included Paul Foot, already a nationally known journalist who had been named journalist of the year in the *What The Papers Say* Awards in 1972, and Laurie Flynn, who had a distinguished career in journalism ahead of him. Members took a legitimate pride in the paper. In the week of the election the print order of *Socialist Worker* had risen to over 50,000, with a paid sale of around 35,000.[11]

Now Cliff was saying that it was good, but not good enough. In the March issue of *International Socialism* he published an extract from his forthcoming biography of Lenin, dealing with the daily *Pravda* of 1912-14, with a good deal of colourful detail about the production and distribution of *Pravda* in semi-legal conditions, which for Cliff must have been reminiscent of his own years in Palestine.

The central thrust was clear: "*Pravda* was not a paper for workers; it was a workers' paper." So, by implication, should *Socialist Worker* be. What is striking is that Cliff was here using Lenin precisely to attack the common caricature of "Leninism". Both Stalinists and anti-Communists had stressed the alleged central message of Lenin's *What Is To Be Done?*, that socialism had to be brought to the working class from outside. Cliff was insisting that a workers' paper had to be produced by workers themselves.

He rammed the point home by repetition. In *Pravda* "over 11,000 letters and items of correspondence from workers were published in one year". Lenin had argued that the paper must present "a chronicle of workers' life", since "he believed that workers themselves must build a picture of their particular struggles for the whole movement".

He argued that a socialist paper must be accessible to workers without any developed political traditions:

> It is far more difficult to write in Marxist terms for the masses than it is to write for Party cadres. For the latter the argument can be developed as a theoretical Marxist analysis. For the former it has to be based on the workers' own experience without using arguments that demand a knowledge of Marxism.

The point was not simply to produce a readable and enlightening paper. For Lenin the paper was above all "an organiser"; he gave great importance to the "formation of workers' groups to collect money for it".

Cliff concluded with some explicit parallels with *Socialist Worker*: "Workers who are not yet in IS should be asked to sell the paper to their workmates, to their neighbours on the estates, at trade union meetings, in the local pub." This was summed up in the slogan "buyers into sellers", which acquired considerable currency in the organisation in the coming months.

The indirect attack via Lenin was followed up by a much more direct onslaught. In the Internal Bulletin[12] he wrote a piece entitled "The use of *Socialist Worker* as an organiser" in which he developed the arguments explicitly. Noting that "nearly half the IS membership are manual workers" he argued that "the paper must become a workers' diary". He quoted Trotsky's criticisms of the American *Socialist Appeal*: "You do not hear at all how the workers live, fight, clash with the police or drink whiskey".[13]

This would mean a new way of working for the paper's staff: "This will mean of course a fantastic burden on our journalists. It is much easier for Paul Foot, for instance, to write a whole page on his own than to edit five or six stories written by workers that will also fill a page."

He spelt out the significance of the "buyers into sellers" strategy:

> A worker that buys one copy of the paper has a very different attitude to it than the one who sells a couple of copies. If he buys he doesn't have to read the paper, he doesn't have to take a position on the different ideas in the paper. If he sells the paper he can't avoid doing both because always he faces the possibility of one of the buyers arguing with him about the paper. In reality people never grasp ideas clearly unless they have to fight for those ideas and therefore if one paper is sold it doesn't create a conflict of ideas – if five are sold in the same place, it does.

The argument was not just about the paper; it was about transforming the organisation: "Above all it will make it possible for workers to come to the front in the running of our organisation."

This was a direct attack on Roger Protz, the editor of *Socialist Worker*. The same issue of the Internal Bulletin contained a reply to Cliff.[14] This was signed by 13 members of the NC, but the style suggests it was drafted by Protz and Higgins. It began by summarising the argument Cliff had apparently put at various internal meetings:

> The nub of the argument as presented by Cliff...is that *Socialist Worker* is not a "workers' paper", that its style is too "intimidating", that it contains too many long articles, too few pictures and, in any case, is aimed at the wrong audience. We are told that the paper must be transformed with shorter articles, more exposures of the "ugly face of capitalism". That done, we are assured, we can look forward to a substantial increase in circulation up to the 70,000-80,000 mark with sales directed in the main towards workers with little political experience and

tradition. The paper must be written mainly by workers, helped by an enlarged staff of the paper whose chief function, according to Cliff, is to "correct the workers' English".

To this Protz and his allies responded sharply:

> But while the paper must and will improve in quality, we feel that any attempt to make it more "popular" – i.e. less political through the use of even more pictures and over-simplified text could fracture the paper's relationship with our most important readership – the experienced, politically aware militant with real roots in the labour movement. The task of a revolutionary socialist paper is to seek to raise the level of political consciousness, not pander to the prevailing level. The EC's prescription for chasing the will o' the wisp of a "mass audience" is a prescription for disaster given the current level of struggle in our best worker readers find [sic] patronising and over-simplified we could end up with the worst of all worlds, a declining circulation. Cliff used to argue correctly, that the most important people were the sellers, not the buyers. They would only sell the paper enthusiastically if they liked its politics, style and content.

Protz had edited *Socialist Worker*, and *Labour Worker* before that, since 1967. He could take a good deal of the credit for the massive improvements in the paper. But he was very much the professional journalist. He appeared to resent anyone else trying to intervene in the production of the paper, while he tended to remain somewhat aloof from other aspects of the organisation's work (with good reason, since he was working hard on the paper). Towards the end of his editorship the level of distrust was so great that the front page had to be taken to Cliff's home for approval before the paper was printed.[15]

There was a vigorous argument at the April NC, and Cliff's position was carried by 26 votes to eight with four abstentions. Protz was supported by Duncan Hallas and John Palmer and by some of the leading industrial militants on the NC.[16] The next day national secretary Dave Peers and Jim Nichol visited Protz at home and told him that he would have to resign. Protz agreed[17] and his job was taken by Paul Foot.* Higgins was also sacked.

---

* Protz's account of his departure is to be found in the document "A Funny Way To Go", part of which is reproduced in J Higgins, *More Years for the Locust*, London, 1997, pp149-150.

Cliff was determined to pursue the changes he believed were necessary, whatever the cost. He would not allow personal friendships or loyalties to stand in the way of building the organisation. The next stage of the conflict came at the May NC. In view of the seriousness of the issues, this was a special two-day meeting with a substantial number of observers. It was a dramatic and at times alarming affair. A group of workers from Liverpool standing at the back kept switching the lights off and on in a threatening manner because they claimed they should have speaking rights.

Cliff's presentation on organisational perspectives argued that the IS's audience consisted "largely of younger workers without established political traditions". Here he was taking up a point he had first discussed in *France: The Struggle Goes On*, though it had apparently not been absorbed by all members of the leadership. He called for an organisation commission to "look into the whole working of the organisation – the centre, fractions and districts".[18]

His position was spelled out in a document entitled "The way ahead for IS".[19] He began with the assertion that "The central issue we face is that of defining the workers' audience to which IS relates and has to relate." The argument about the readership of *Socialist Worker* was broadened to the question of the target audience for recruitment. He looked back to the debates of the 1960s, and the arguments developed by himself and Kidron that "the locus of reform had moved since the Second World War to the factory floor…that a wide and deep fragmentation of the labour movement had taken place, that there had been a depoliticisation of the mass of the workers".

Consequently "our audience is largely made up of young workers with very little political tradition, and quite often even with very little trade union experience… The big majority of the members of the factory branches are young workers with very few shop stewards among them."

This in turn affected the approach to recruitment:

> If the workers we related to were mainly those with political tradition, even if ex-CP or left Labour, the membership campaign would have been quite irrelevant if not damaging. People with long political tradition could not be recruited today in a campaign of a few months duration.

He concluded by reiterating that "our main task is to transform IS into an organisation led by workers". He stressed the close interaction between leadership inside the organisation and leadership in the workplaces and trade unions:

> A worker who has no influence in his place of work and/or trade union, cannot fulfil the role of a workers' leader in IS. On the other hand, a worker who has influence, but does not relate to any constituency in IS – whether a district, a fraction, etc. – cannot really play a leading role either.

When criticised by Peter Bain from Glasgow for not having a strategy for the new conditions of the Labour government, Cliff responded that he agreed with much of what Bain had said "but I like gut reaction – it is what brings people to revolutionary politics".[20]

It was a brave contribution, brave perhaps to the point of foolhardiness. Cliff was putting his leadership on the line, convinced that he could win over the organisation even at the cost of antagonising some of his oldest and closest allies. And antagonise them he did.

Protz and Roger Rosewell (see below) were both suspended for two months for applying for trade union jobs without permission; it was Cliff who argued for suspension and not expulsion on the grounds that "we are still a soft group and we have to convince our people and learn the lessons".[21] Jim Nichol called Higgins a "parasite and a leech" (for which he subsequently apologised)[22] and Higgins had to be dissuaded from thumping him.[23]

There were some 67 resolutions from districts and branches expressing varying degrees of concern at the handling of the dispute about *Socialist Worker* and the lack of adequate internal discussion.[24] Cliff defended the dismissal of Higgins and Protz:

> I would resign if I was against factory branches. It is not the same as printing or typesetting where personal relations are not terribly important. But to edit the paper you must believe in what you are saying and what you want – it is not mechanical. If we reinstate them what will happen? These same 5 weeks will happen again because relations will have deteriorated even more.[25]

There was a genuine disquiet in the organisation that a lot was going on without any consultation, as the IS conference, which should have taken place in the spring, had been postponed because of the pressure of activity. Cliff seems to have recognised at this point that some sort of tactical retreat was required. A resolution criticising the executive for neglecting the internal life of the organisation was carried by 30 votes to five, with Cliff voting for it.[26] The executive which had emerged from the previous year's "coup" now looked very tattered, and it was replaced by a new executive charged with holding things together until the conference, now planned for September. Designed to restore the confidence of the membership, it contained some "old timers" – Ross Pritchard and, significantly, Duncan Hallas.

However, the argument had only just begun and continued up to the conference in September. One of the most coherent replies to Cliff came from Ruth Nelson, a close ally of Jim Higgins, in an article entitled "Who Is Our Audience?"[27] She denounced Cliff's position as "a radical departure" from the IS's traditional analysis, claiming that in the past the IS had argued "we must relate to the thin layer of politically experienced and class-conscious militants, primarily shop stewards and convenors, who can in turn relate our politics to broader layers of workers".

She conceded that "younger workers act as an important pressure on their elected representatives", but insisted that "we cannot see the recruitment of these young workers as the *main task*", and stressed that "we must take very seriously the length of time it takes to become an experienced, credible leader of workers".

There had been an ambiguity in Cliff's thinking. The *Incomes Policy* pamphlet had certainly analysed the decline of traditional reformism, but it had also pointed to the central importance of shop stewards in the struggle for working class democracy. Like Christians who argue by exchanging quotes from the Bible, Cliff and his opponents were both able to draw on what had been the IS tradition over the previous two decades.

The contradiction, as Cliff was wont to point out, was in "life itself". The working class depicted in *Incomes Policy* and *The Employers' Offensive* was in a process of rapid change. It was indeed true that for a militant like Jim Higgins in the POEU it had taken 20 years or more to become a "militant of some standing". Now increased labour turnover, deskilling and the decline of traditional manufacturing industries were changing that situation rapidly.

The debate caused a considerable furore in the organisation. Cliff was accused of saying that experienced shop stewards were "bent".[28] To the best of my knowledge, such a statement was never made in any of his written contributions. If it was said, it was in the heat of one particular discussion. But it was widely believed that he had said it, and a lot of shop stewards were, not surprisingly, rather annoyed. What Cliff was concerned with was the fact that the layer of "experienced trade unionists" was being increasingly incorporated into the bargaining machinery, especially with the growing number of full-time convenors. In the debate at the May NC he argued:

> Quite often convenors are in the machine. There has been very little *plant* struggle in the engineering industry in the last two years. Why? Of necessity in our factory branches we recruit new workers without experience – they have of course to fight for shop stewardships and we have to recognise that if capitalism were to expand, 90% of the convenors *would be* bent [my emphasis, IB].[29]

As in all factional disputes, things were said that would have been better not said. Cliff told Sean Hallahan, a militant in the print industry and an IS member since the early 1960s, "You have always been a miserable little sectarian, and you will always be a miserable little sectarian." Hallahan was deeply offended and left the organisation shortly afterwards.[30] Perhaps because of his imperfect command of English Cliff sometimes did not realise the full force of language that he used.

Yet with the benefit of hindsight, it appears that Cliff was more in the right than the opposition. If the IS had continued to orient, as Higgins wanted, on the layer of experienced workers, it would have been condemned to disaster. The characteristic strikes of the later 1970s – Trico, Grunwick, Garners – were not led by "experienced militants". That layer of the class was seriously weakened by changing patterns of employment, and later by Thatcherism, and it took the CP with it. Moreover, since Higgins was narrowly orientated on the trade union movement, he might well have missed the opportunities offered by such developments as the Anti Nazi League.

Indeed, it is arguable that the changes in the working class at this time were so substantial that Cliff did not go far enough in his attempt to develop a new strategy.* In particular, Cliff was still very

---

* This point is argued by Nigel Harris in his obituary "Duncan Hallas: Death of a Trotskyist" (*Revolutionary History* 8/4 (2004)).

much orientated on the traditional manual working class, though in reality the rank and file strategy had most success among non-manual workers. Ian Gibson, a leading militant in the ASTMS technicians' union in the 1970s, recalls sharp disagreements with Cliff about the role of white-collar workers. He feels Cliff was too negative about white-collar struggles, arguing that white-collar workers would not change the world.[31]

Cliff was right to focus on the importance of *Socialist Worker*. Events were to show that in a sharpened political atmosphere the paper was making a real challenge to the existing order. In the pre-election period there had been many reports of police harassment of paper-sellers and flyposters. In June a Warwick student, Kevin Gately, was killed by police on an anti National Front demonstration. The next week 2,000 IS members marched through London with placards reading "Murdered by Police". *Socialist Worker* then faced a threat of action for criminal libel.[32] In October *Socialist Worker* was fined £500 with £5,000 costs for naming wealthy witnesses in the Janie Jones blackmail case.[33] * Attacks from both the state and the trade union bureaucracy continued throughout the 1970s making it much more uncomfortable to be a revolutionary socialist.

The "buyers into sellers" slogan was less successful and was soon dropped. Cliff's argument that a seller felt a deeper political commitment than a buyer was correct, but although it was not yet apparent, the growth in the IS's periphery was coming to an end. The tide was turning and the supply of new readers was not inexhaustible.

By the 1970s MI5, which had previously concentrated its attention on the threat from the CP, began to devote more attention to the "Ultra Left", namely the IS, IMG and WRP (Workers Revolutionary Party). One security service officer later remembered the "relentless tedium" of surveillance of the CP and noted that his contemporaries "had no doubt that the Trotskyists were a far more interesting target". Most attention was devoted to *Militant*, since MI5 were under pressure from Labour ministers who were

---

*   Janie Jones was jailed for "controlling prostitutes" and tried for blackmail while her wealthy clients preserved their anonymity (*Socialist* Worker, 13 April 1974). She yelled "Thank God for Paul Foot" as she was taken from the dock (*Evening Standard*, 17 April 1974). She was immortalised by the Clash song named after her.

concerned at *Militant*'s influence within the Labour Party.[34]

The trade union bureaucracy were also irritated. In 1974 Ian Gibson was barred from holding office in ASTMS for three years[35] for having written an article in *Socialist Worker* critical of the union leadership.[36] In the 1970s Clive Jenkins, the ASTMS leader, saw the IS as being a dangerous force in the union.[37]

The leadership which had steered the organisation since 1968 had now flown apart. Protz and Palmer had joined up with Higgins. There were also defections among those who had been closest to Cliff.

Roger Rosewell was the most notable of these. Rosewell had joined the IS in the early 1960s as an engineering apprentice, and later became a full-time union official. He was a competent if dry public speaker and a prolific if sometimes shallow writer. His two pamphlets, *The Struggle for Socialism* and *The Struggle for Workers' Power*[38] were highly regarded as giving a good elementary introduction to IS politics.

He had become full-time industrial organiser and played a valuable role around the occupation at Upper Clyde Shipbuilders in 1971. He had a good knowledge of the trade union movement, and had written some informed commentaries in *Socialist Worker* and *International Socialism*. He was respected by industrial militants in the organisation, as was shown by a letter to the executive committee from two prominent industrial militants, Roger Cox and Gerry Jones, which stated that he "understands more than most the individual situation of our leading workers and is seen by these workers as someone who they can turn to for advice".[39]

Rosewell had moved to Liverpool as part of the "leading areas" strategy and at the Belle Vue rally in November 1973 he had made a rousing speech urging support for the rank and file conference, denouncing the "rotten" elements in the labour movement "whose sole ambition in life is to rise above their class and get a seat on a board".[40] But by the beginning of 1974 he believed the national mood was changing. The 1974 miners' strike was passive compared to that of 1972. The anger and optimism that had characterised 1972-73 was disappearing quickly. Rosewell's analysis, that the wave of struggle was now subsiding, differed sharply from Cliff's. They discussed the situation, but could reach no agreement. Rosewell therefore decided to return to being a union official.[41] He was an ambitious man, and when there had seemed to be a real possibility that the IS would replace the CP as the main militant force in industry, he may have imagined himself as the successor to the CP's Bert Ramelson, negotiating deals in smoke-filled rooms. Now, sooner than others, he sensed that the tide was ebbing.

Cliff had a high opinion of Rosewell and had worked with him closely. When he learned that he had defected, Cliff's epitaph was short and sharp: "Roger was a talented boy, but he had no guts".[42] Rosewell went on to become a leader writer for the *Daily Mail* and political adviser to Lady Shirley Porter, formerly Tory leader of Westminster City Council.[43]

However, Cliff had one important success. After the coup Duncan Hallas had lined up with Jim Higgins, and indeed it had been Hallas who had pushed hardest for resistance to Cliff and had initiated the opposition grouping.[44] The two of them combined made a formidable team, with an impressive knowledge of Marxist theory and the labour movement. Both were popular figures in the group, though Higgins must have regretted the number of enemies he had made with his rather abrasive style. Hallas had fewer enemies; if he had stayed with the opposition, Cliff might still have won, but the split would have been deeper and more damaging.

In the middle of 1974 Hallas broke with the opposition grouping. He still felt the opposition was correct on the question of perspectives, and that Cliff was on a voluntarist binge. But Cliff had taken Hallas on a long walk to discuss things, and Hallas felt that he had shifted Cliff's position to some extent, and that Cliff was beginning to listen. He recognised that Cliff was willing to push things to the point of a split, and he knew that the organisation could not survive without Cliff.* He then turned up at an early meeting of the opposition grouping to announce that he was breaking with them "because we can't beat Cliff".[45]

When the executive was reconstituted, Hallas returned to the leadership and he remained an ally of Cliff, though sometimes a critical one, until his retirement in the 1990s. (While Hallas had great respect for Cliff as a Marxist intellectual, he could also be very critical, accusing him of having obsessions and of lacking a sense of

---

* This account is based on Hallas's own recollections as told to Pete Green (Pete Green interview, August 2008)

proportion.[46]) Pat Stack, who knew both men well, believes that despite their long collaboration, there was no real closeness between them. Cliff was disappointed in Hallas; although he understood alienation in the abstract, he found it hard to grasp how someone with Hallas's abilities could waste his talents in heavy drinking.[47]

Hallas's decision was a serious blow to the prospects of the opposition group. As John Palmer wrote many years later:

> In order to win we would have had to fight full-time for months – perhaps a year. Neither Jim Higgins nor myself were prepared to do that – and perhaps that puts a question mark over our own leadership. We thought Duncan Hallas would fulfil that role, and when Cliff won Hallas over, that was a big blow.[48] *

Winning back Hallas meant that Cliff had to restrain some of those he had earlier encouraged. At one point Andreas Nagliatti demanded Hallas's expulsion. Cliff responded that if that happened the IS would end up with 500 members. When Nagliatti said that he didn't care, Cliff rejoined that Nagliatti wouldn't be one of them.[49] Nagliatti resigned from the executive because he thought the leadership was failing to carry through the programme of changes required.[50] When Nagliatti moved reference back of Steve Jefferys' industrial report, Cliff opposed him, warning of dangers in the organisation:

> There is a problem of demoralisation in IS at the moment, of expecting more than we can get, e.g. factory branches. I don't complain about the mistakes, on the contrary, but what is true at the moment is that there *is* this demoralisation and people should know the real size of factory branches, and it is therefore important to spell this out. If you put a target you can't possibly achieve, you have either vicarious pleasure or demoralisation.[51]

Nagliatti had replaced Rosewell as industrial organiser. He had been recruited from the student movement in 1966, and had for two years been a factory worker. But he had come increasingly under the influence of the Italian organisation Avanguardia Operaia (AO). The original core leadership of AO had emerged from a split in the Italian Trotskyist movement; it had developed activity around the rank and file "base committees" (CUBs) of the early 1970s,[52] but

---

* More recently Palmer has said that if Hallas had stayed with the opposition, it might well have won the majority (John Palmer interview, June 2008)

had an undogmatic Maoist analysis of the world. Some of its positions seemed ultra-left, although in the crisis of 1976 it was to reveal rightist tendencies. Increasingly Nagliatti was acting as a conduit for AO's ideas into the IS, though at the May 1974 NC he protested against accusations that he was a Maoist.[53] He then moved to Liverpool in an attempt to build on the base that Rosewell had abandoned, but in 1975 dropped out of political activity and later became a factory owner.

Dave Peers, who found himself in the middle of the dispute, thinks Higgins had been very good when the IS group was still small; he recognised limits and was against trying to go too quickly. Cliff believed in will-power, and a slightly hysterical atmosphere developed as the difference became more than one of emphasis. Cliff could never take a "steady as she goes" attitude, while Higgins did, sometimes to the point of somnolence.[54]

At the same time Cliff had to involve himself in other arguments about building the organisation. Cliff was committed to the rank and file perspective and welcomed the success of the Rank and File Conference. But he saw a danger of rank and file organisation becoming an end in itself. For Cliff, politics was paramount and he argued that a rank and file organisation could only develop with a hard core of political ideas and political organisation, as is shown by his contribution to a discussion with IS members on the Rank and File organising committee:

> Tony Cliff raised the question of the "stages theory" of some hospital worker comrades – which is that nurses should initially be approached with the *Hospital Worker* [rank and file paper] whilst the struggle is rising – in the rising struggle we build rank and file organisations, then consolidate, *then* perhaps get people into IS. The trouble is that when the struggle rises it rises quickly and then disintegrates quicker than it rises. If you don't recruit the people into IS you don't keep the rank and file organisation. Don't let's have any illusions about it. There is *not* an independent rank and file movement in which we as IS are fishing. The close periphery of IS is the same as that of the rank and file movement. Politicos carry rank and file organisation. Otherwise what happens is [the] movement comes and goes and what you get at the end is demoralisation. IS is the motor. We cheated ourselves by the conference on 30 March. IS were less than half the delegates, that is true. But it was a one-day thing. This R&F

Organising Committee *will* be 90 percent IS members. You don't work day in day out getting small results without being inspired politically. I am worried about the present nurses campaign that our members will become demoralised. If they can say "at least we doubled our membership in terms of nurses" they won't be. If, on the other hand, we say we built a big *Hospital Worker* base, we won't have really built it because the struggle will go down and a lot of them will be lost. We therefore have to have:

(1) Direct recruitment of nurses to IS

(2) Direct selling of *Socialist Worker* and *Hospital Worker*

(3) Non-hospital workers should intervene

Of course we make mistakes, but the worst mistake is being so careful that at the end of the day you find you have no results at all.[55]

Cliff took an active part in the new organisation commission, although the minutes show that his role was often to ask questions rather than to push for particular solutions.[56]

At the end of September the postponed IS conference was held. Cliff's introductory address was powerfully optimistic. The ruling class was in deep crisis: "Everything they try won't work." He dismissed with scorn the Labour Party's claim that inflation was worse in other countries: "When your house is burning, don't worry. Your competitor's house is burning faster." But the workers' movement was also in crisis, beset by divisions between different groups of workers. The IS had the task of linking individual struggles to the overall offensive against capitalism. The situation offered "fantastic opportunities". He concluded, "The revolutionary party is made of leaders. There is no rank and file in the revolutionary party. We must all give a lead, intervene wherever the struggle is taking place around us. We don't have a formula. We have a general line, and we have to keep our eyes and options open for the specifics".[57]

Most of Cliff's positions were carried, though his organisation commission report was rejected.[58] Despite the real problems, the organisation had made some substantial progress in intervening in the continuing industrial conflict, as shown by the report to conference from the industrial organiser Steve Jefferys.[59] Membership was up to 3,310, of whom about 1,200 were manual workers; half the members were under 25, and a third were women.[60]

Higgins was not re-elected to the NC, though John Palmer was. Dave Peers also failed to be elected, and lost his post as national secretary, being replaced by Jim Nichol. Peers, who had worked closely with Cliff for more than ten years, felt abandoned and thought Cliff had failed to support him. Peers stayed in the organisation for another ten years, but he was never close to Cliff after 1974. Though Cliff was always friendly he made it clear he considered Peers was finished.[61]

In October a second general election was held. Labour made small gains, just enough to establish an overall majority of three. The central plank of Labour's policy was the "Social Contract", to be based on cooperation between government and trade unions. (Within the IS it was generally known as the "social con-trick".) Initially the Social Contract was simply a voluntary agreement between the government and the union bureaucracy that wages should not rise faster than prices. The formulation was kept deliberately vague in order to avoid anything that might again politicise the wages struggle as Heath's policies had done.

The aim was to bring the leaders of the left in the TUC, Jack Jones and Hugh Scanlon, into ever closer association with the government. One indication of success had come when at the 1974 TUC, Ken Gill, the first CP member on the TUC General Council for many years, withdrew his union's resolution against the Social Contract "in the interests of the broadest unity". (He was criticised by the *Morning Star*.)

The defeat of Heath had increased workers' confidence and industrial struggle continued at quite a high level, with wages a major issue because of the high level of inflation: between August 1974 and August 1975 the retail price index increased by 26.9 percent. In Scotland in the autumn of 1974 so many disputes came together there was almost a general strike. But whereas in 1971 and 1972 three-quarters of all strike days were official, in the ten months of Labour rule in 1974 almost 90 percent of strike days were unofficial.

The IS continued to involve itself in such disputes, attempting to raise the political level wherever possible. In March 1975 the Labour government, alleging a "health hazard", sent troops to break a strike by dustcart drivers in Glasgow. Trade union bureaucrats and left MPs spoke scarcely a word of protest. When the Glasgow IS issued a leaflet to troops asking, "Would you have to act like this if you had your own trade union?", the CP secretary of Glasgow Trades Council told the press that the IS were "fleas in a bed who turn up at other people's picketing".[62]

The IS continued to attract the attention of its enemies. A pamphlet by the Economic League blacklisting organisation noted ruefully that "wherever and whenever an industrial dispute was in progress IS members were quickly on the spot".[63] In the *Daily Telegraph* one Gerard Kemp warned his anxious readers that "Left-Wing Extremists Plot Take-Over of Industry", and published a full list of IS national committee members.[64] On 26 February 1975 Lord Chalfont opened a debate in the House of Lords on "subversive and extremist elements in our society". He gave particular attention to the IS and informed his noble colleagues:

> In a pamphlet about the violent events in France in 1968, Mr. Cliff and another leading member of the IS Group, Mr. Ian Birchall, describe the attacks on the police by student demonstrators and say, "...when the means of communication and the machinery of State are in the hands of a hostile ruling class, one cannot expect parliamentary elections to do anything other than play into the hands of this class...in our epoch not a single serious issue can be decided by ballot...in the decisive class battles, bullets will decide".

Lord Gisborough believed that the IS disposed of "massive resources...from places like Libya and Cuba", while Lord Clifford of Chudleigh described the IS and other organisations (including the Nalgo Action Group) as "bloodthirsty, class-hate groups".[65]

In January 1975 Cliff published a short book of 192 pages entitled *The Crisis: Social Contract or Socialism*.[66] The book was promoted through IS branches and public meetings with a range of speakers. Cliff himself embarked on a gruelling schedule of meetings around the country. On 27 January he was in East Kilbride, on the next day in Paisley and the next in Edinburgh. During February he spoke in Keighley, Hull, Tower Hamlets, Newham, Coventry, Birmingham, Sheffield, Wakefield, Pontefract, Sunderland and Liverpool. In early March he was in Oxford, Leeds and Leicester.[67]

In the book Cliff set out to make a critique of the whole ideology of the Social Contract, using arguments he had developed over the previous ten years. After showing that the world economic crisis derived from a decline in the rate of profit, he moved on to the fundamental flaw in all reformist strategies, in all strategies that purported to achieve greater fairness without challenging the capitalist framework, namely that profit was central to the capitalist system and reformism could not challenge it.[68]

He scoffed at the widely touted notion that incomes policy should be supported because it helped the low-paid:

> If ICI workers were to hold back on a claim for another £1 a week, would the management of ICI transfer the money they have saved to, say, the nurses, or would they transfer it to ICI's bank account? To ask the question is to see the answer.[69]

If the best-organised workers held back their demands, the whole working class would be held back with them.

With the sharp eye for concrete detail that characterised his best work, Cliff pointed to the obscene contrasts of modern capitalism, the contrast between "velvet 'Marie Antoinette' kennels for £148, and small doggy winter coats – in mink – for £400 at Harrods" on the one hand, and on the other the fact that "long queues of pensioners form each morning outside Greggs' bakery shop in Westgate Road, Newcastle. The reason? Stale cakes and bread returned from the firm's other shops are sold to the pensioners for half price".[70]

But if Cliff's analysis was acute, his predictions were less so. Looking back at the failure of Wilson's incomes policy in the 1960s, Cliff was confident that this time round the policy would be "doomed even faster": "This time the breakthrough will come much more quickly, and through the activity of workers on a much wider front, from relatively well-paid car workers to ancillary workers in hospitals".[71]

Yet the final conclusion was realistic:

> We are entering a long period of instability. International capitalism will be rent by economic, social and political crises. Big class battles are ahead of us. Their outcome will decide the future of humanity for a long time to come.[72]

The economic crisis was indeed the most serious since the 1930s. The coming decade would see major upheavals in Portugal, Spain, Italy, Iran and Poland. In Britain the ups and downs of industrial struggle would culminate in the defeat of the miners in 1985.

The Crisis was envisaged as a successor to *Incomes Policy* and

The Employers' Offensive. In fact the book in no way emulated the achievement of its predecessors. The earlier books had been genuine workers' handbooks; they had included masses of practical information that could be used in negotiations and in organising struggle. They also contained accounts of workers' experience, told in workers' own words. *The Crisis* contained a good deal of solid information, collected with Cliff's usual gift for detailed research, but it was based largely on journalistic sources, both the mainstream press and socialist and rank and file publications. One of the very few sections based on workers' direct experience of wasteful mismanagement was taken word for word from *The Employers' Offensive*.[73] While it made a sharp and justified indictment of the Labour government's policies, it aspired to a level of generalisation which did not correspond to the actual state of class consciousness. It was not one of Cliff's best works.

However, it was a symptom of the fact that the revolutionary left could still provoke a degree of nervousness that it received a substantial eight-column review in the *Financial Times*.[74] Not surprisingly, the reviewer was sceptical about Cliff's arguments, while admitting that many of his points would strike a chord with "people who genuinely and sincerely believe that there are unfairnesses in our society", and that the IS had "some very bright young people, full of idealistic verve".

At the IS conference in the summer of 1975 there was a partial recognition that the previous year's perspective had been overoptimistic. As one of the conference documents, approved by Cliff, put it:

> We predicted, in our perspectives for last September's IS conference, that the rising level of unemployment and the acceleration of prices would put the Social Contract under pressure from two opposed directions – from workers inspired by the success of the miners in breaking the Tories' Phase Three, and from the ruling class intent on pushing down workers' living standards.
>
> Our economic perspective in general was correct. But it was mistaken in one important respect.
>
> *We overestimated the speed with which the economic crisis would drive workers to draw revolutionary political conclusions.*[75]

Before Wilson could have a head-on confrontation with the trade unions, he had to deal with the tricky question of the European Economic Community (EEC) (or Common Market as it was often then called – now the enlarged European Union). Divisions on the question cut across party lines and Wilson decided to get the result he wanted by calling a referendum. Cabinet ministers were given freedom from discipline on the issue since Michael Foot and Tony Benn, who were vital for maintaining the Social Contract, were opposed to the Common Market.

The IS took the position of calling for a "no" vote, not only out of opposition to the EEC as such, but because a defeat in the referendum would make the imposition of the Social Contract so much more difficult for the Wilson government. As *Socialist Worker* pointed out, "The main campaigners for the Common Market are also the main campaigners for workers' 'restraint' to pay for the crisis".[76] However, the IS was totally opposed to any unity on the question with right-wing Tories who were campaigning for a "no" vote.

Compared with 1971, there was relatively little dissent in the organisation, although there was a lively debate on the letters page of *Socialist Worker*. Among those who opposed the line was Mike Kidron, who argued that the choice for Britain was simply between being a partner of US capitalism or a partner in European capitalism. He urged, "Don't vote. Boycott the referendum".[77] The relationship between Cliff and his old ally was wearing extremely thin.

Just before the referendum Cliff addressed a rally at the Conway Hall in central London. He laid into the national illusions which had characterised the campaign run by much of the left, being much harder than most IS speakers had been, and asserted basic internationalist principles.[78] Having bent the stick one way, he now bent it back a little.

Cliff also spoke in Edinburgh at the time of the referendum. In the audience was a young IMG member called Chris Bambery, who had recently heard a speech by Fourth International leader Ernest Mandel. The contrast was quite shocking. Mandel was a good speaker, but was basically scholarly. Cliff had an utterly different style and was able to communicate to an audience of young workers. Later, in 1979, Bambery joined the IS.[79]

Around this time Cliff spoke in Winchester at a meeting to set up a new branch. One of those attending was a new recruit from Portsmouth, Pat Stack. His image of what a revolutionary leader would look like was based on Che Guevara, so he was initially shocked and disappointed at seeing a "little old man". But when Cliff began to speak he was soon caught up. Cliff was challenged by an old Stalinist; Cliff responded with a devastating list of facts from Russian history, ending, "My friend, there is nothing you can tell me about Russia." Stack would go on to be a full-timer and work closely with Cliff.[80]

With the referendum out of the way Wilson was able to move to Phase Two of the Social Contract. The government now announced, in agreement with most of the trade union bureaucracy, that there would be a maximum limit of £6 a week on all wage increases during the coming year. The fact of a flat-rate increase gave a veneer of egalitarianism to what was in fact a massive defeat for the working class. Shares rose by £2 billion on the Tuesday afternoon that Chancellor of the Exchequer Denis Healey announced the new deal.[81] Wilson already had the approval of the class-conscious *Economist*: "This government of Labour men and consensus measures could prove to be the least bad government Britain could have for this bad year of 1975".[82]

The 1975 conference completed the process of restructuring the IS. The old NC was abolished and the conference directly elected a central committee (CC), which was to be the leading body of the organisation between conferences. Critics naturally saw this as a move by Cliff to concentrate more power in his own hands. As Jim Higgins wrote, "a system that had only fitfully been able to restrain the full time apparat was being replaced by a system of absolutely no control at all".[83] The reality was more complex.

The national committee's control over the executive in the old constitution had always been a fiction. A lay NC, meeting once a month, could not conceivably control an executive of full-timers. Political decisions had to be expressed in the weekly *Socialist Worker*; by the time the NC met, the political line was an accomplished fact which had been made known to the world at large. On administrative matters the NC could generally manipulate the EC or sell its agreed position to it.

The new arrangement at least had the merit of straightforwardness. It was clear where the political leadership of the organisation lay, and any criticisms could be directed to it.

It has been argued that the new arrangement flowed directly from the coup of 1973. Thus Martin Shaw has written:

> The "coup" of July 1973 was only the first step in remodeling the leadership of IS so that it would step up the pace of change in the organisation.[84]

In fact things were far from being so simple. The new CC consisted of six people: Cliff, Hallas, Harman, Nichol, Jefferys and John Deason. Hallas had been one of those purged by the coup, while Deason and Jefferys had played no role in it and Jefferys in particular had reservations. Only Harman and Nichol had been Cliff's allies throughout. If Cliff had a master plan, it was one which had been revised several times in the face of events.

Two things, however, are clear about the new organisational structure. Firstly, after all the conflicts of the previous two years, Cliff had succeeded in reconstructing a new leadership team which would be able to take the organisation into new developments and new initiatives. There were more stormy days ahead.

Secondly, this team of full-timers was a long way from the "worker leadership" of which Cliff had been talking only a year earlier. This was not a change of principle, but rather a tacit admission that circumstances were now different. The level of class struggle had not risen and become more political, the factory branches and rank and file groups had not blossomed as expected. In this situation the kind of workers' leadership that Cliff had aspired to was simply not possible.

Another question was increasingly claiming Cliff's attention. In April 1974 the authoritarian regime in Portugal, dating back to the 1930s, was overthrown by a section of the army which promised to establish democracy. This opened up a wave of working class struggle, strikes and factory occupations, which passed completely out of the control of the original instigators. For some 18 months the future of Portugal seemed to hang in the balance between an advance to workers' power and right-wing reaction. IS docker Bob Light visited Portugal and reported that "the country is like sweating gelignite. The question is whose face it blows up in".[85]

In a *Socialist Worker* article[86] at the end of June, Cliff argued that

Portugal was "in a pre-revolutionary situation", with "the possibility of a revolutionary situation within a matter of months". He stressed the need to "to win the rank and file soldiers to the revolution" and warned that in the past, when workers failed to seize the time, the working class had been "broken to pieces".

As the situation developed, Cliff became ever more convinced that "Portugal, the weakest link in the capitalist chain in Europe, can become the launching pad for the socialist revolution in the whole of the continent".[87] In this Cliff was wholly correct. The large number of IS members who visited Portugal in this period came back enormously enthused at witnessing a mass uprising which in some ways was unparalleled since 1917.[88]

In the summer of 1975 Cliff wrote a short book which appeared as a special double issue of *International Socialism* under the title "Portugal at the Crossroads", echoing his "The Middle East at the Crossroads" of 30 years earlier. Here he showed his usual ability for detailed research combined with a grasp of the total picture. He gave a vivid narrative account of the remarkable sequence of events which had shaken Portuguese society over the preceding 18 months.

Cliff showed the origins of the crisis in Portugal's disastrous wars in Africa resulting from its inability to withdraw from direct colonial rule as other European powers had done.* He analysed the impasse of the Portuguese economy and showed the role of the multinationals, which owned much of Portugal's industry, in sabotaging the economy. He drew a striking parallel between the Portuguese events and Marx's account of the French revolution of 1848.

But the central theme was the growth and development of the working class movement. He emphasised the "tremendous creative abilities" of the workers and the spontaneous nature of the initial wave of struggle: "The mass of the workers did not wait for the Government or for the labour leaders to tell them what to do, but immediately and effectively entered upon the historical arena".[89] He drew out the central role of the workers' committees that were elected to lead rank and file struggles, and showed how the movement had gone beyond mere strikes to factory occupations. He

---

* Back in the 1960s Mike Kidron had argued that Portugal was still "ferociously old-model imperialist" in the Leninist sense ("International Capitalism", *International Socialism* 20 (Spring 1965)).

pointed to the close interaction between economic and political struggle.

As in *The Employers' Offensive* Cliff wanted to let workers speak in their own words. Cliff could not visit Portugal, but a great many IS members went there in the course of 1975. He drew on 54 reports written by IS members who visited Portugal during August, some of which recorded stories told by workers or interviews with activists. He had a sharp eye for the telling detail which could sum up what the revolutionary process meant for an individual life. He told of how the authorities tried to evict shanty-town dwellers who had been rehoused in empty buildings:

> An old widow...had just moved with her six sons to a two-bedroom flat with electricity, water and toilet. She replied, "You better shoot me right here. All my life I have had the earth for a floor. At least I will die on a proper floor".[90]

The army backed off.

It was army officers in the Armed Forces Movement (MFA) who had initiated the process of change. Cliff was concerned to stress that the army was not monolithic, but deeply divided by class: "The leaders of the MFA are middle class through and through".[91] Hence it was important to raise demands that would give greater strength to common soldiers rather than the privileged officers – election of officers by the rank and file, equality of pay between officers and men, abolition of separate messes.

The merits of Cliff's account become clear if it is compared with the most widely available account in English, *Insight on Portugal*, published at almost exactly the same time by the Insight Team of the *Sunday Times*.[92] This was honest enough, based on serious research and without overt bias. But it was an almost entirely top-down account. The main focus was on the army and it gave considerable detail about the April 1974 coup, but it dealt mainly with senior military personnel with little sense of class divisions in the army. The authors were willing to take the "declared aims" of the MFA "at face value". There were only a few pages on the working class, which was seen from the outside as a problem rather than the solution – it referred to "the threat of labour unrest" and "the sudden localised strikes which had afflicted industry since April". The authors interviewed "leading participants" in the events, but did not take the trouble to talk to rank and file workers.[93]

There were, however, serious problems with *Portugal at the Crossroads*. Whereas *France: The Struggle Goes On* had been written after the end of the strike, and was able to view the events as a completed whole, *Portugal at the Crossroads* was written while the situation was still in flux. In *France: The Struggle Goes On*, the absent revolutionary party was noted, as a lesson for the future. In *Portugal at the Crossroads*, Cliff was aiming at intervention not commentary; he was not writing history, but aspiring to play a part in making it. This was its strength, but also its weakness.

Cliff stressed, rightly, that revolutionary change was on the agenda, and that revolutionary situations do not last long: either the working class or the forces of reaction would come out on top. The situation was still in the balance. Repeatedly Cliff argued that the choice was between revolution or "extreme reaction". The strength of the working class meant that there could be no half measures:

> The working class is far too strong, too assertive, to be put in its place except through very extreme measures… For the capitalists to re-establish their order – with the high aspirations of the awakened, assertive proletariat – a bloodbath will be necessary.[94]

He recalled the events in Chile just two years earlier, when a military coup had smashed all working class organisations at the cost of thousands of lives.

In pointing to this danger Cliff was not exaggerating or being alarmist. Whatever may be argued in retrospect, at the time a Chilean solution looked all too plausible.[95] The CIA was active in Portugal as it had been in Chile; there were many supporters of the former regime and frightened property-owners who would happily have backed a Chilean-style "solution". The fact that such a solution was not adopted certainly did not spring from any moral compunction on the part of the enemies of the working class.

But Cliff's focus on the far-right danger apparently blinded him to the potential of the Socialist Party, and he seriously underestimated the strength of its support:

> So long as the masses hesitate between revolution and reaction, they continue to support the Socialist Party. But this situation of hesitation cannot last long…it is clear that a general election now must lead to a landslide electoral victory for the right.[96]

In fact after the election of April 1976 Soares, the Socialist Party leader, became prime minister. It was Soares who, over the next two years, was able to roll back, slowly but ruthlessly, the gains of the revolutionary period.*

That Cliff made a wrong prediction is not important; so did most other commentators in this volatile period. But it does reveal a certain underestimation of the power of reformism in Cliff's analysis. Certainly he was right to see the long-term decline in the traditional mass reformist organisations of the working class. And he had no truck with the post-1968 ultra-leftism which thought reformism could be simply bypassed. But he failed to see that, in some circumstances, reformism was still capable of holding back mass struggle. This was to affect his judgement, not only of Portugal, but of Britain.

Cliff rightly argued that there could be no successful outcome to the struggle without a revolutionary party. He pointed to the dangers of *apartidarismo* (non-partyism), the attitude of many militants who distrusted the involvement of political groups in the mass workers' organisations. He had no illusions that effective leadership could be provided by left officers, even the most radical such as Otelo Saraiva de Carvalho.

He spelt out the kind of party that was needed: not a self-appointed vanguard substituting itself for the class, but an organisation in constant dialogue with the workers' struggle:

> In short they have to learn from their fellow workers as much as – or more than – they have to teach. To repeat, the job is to *lead*, and to lead you have to thoroughly understand those you are leading. Leadership

---

* Peter Robinson, who was IS representative in Portugal from October 1975 to June 1976, has written that, in retrospect, he considers the "socialism or fascism" line to have been seriously mistaken: "It failed to prepare workers to resist the consolidation of bourgeois democracy. The neo-fascists were not real contenders for power. The Portuguese ruling class itself had suffered the inconvenience of [a] right-wing authoritarian regime. Nor was the example of Chile as inspiring to big business and the CIA as the left liked to imagine. Since the coup of September 1973 the Chilean economy had faced continuing crises. Both the NATO powers and the Portuguese ruling class now preferred the option of building a 'stable' bourgeois parliamentary system, if at all possible. Progressive sections of Portuguese capitalism wanted to join the EEC, which demanded democratic credentials." (P Robinson, *Portugal 1974-75: The Forgotten Dream*, London, 1999, p25) See also I Birchall, "Social Democracy and the Portuguese 'Revolution'", *International Socialism* 6 (Autumn 1979).

is a two-way process…

The job of party leadership is to generalise the experience of the party militants and to lead them as they lead their fellow workers. It is the same two-way relationship *inside* the party.

Many on the left see the party as a substitute for the class, or primarily as the teacher of the class. Equally, many see the party leadership as the repository of doctrine, of theory, of organisational skill and knowledge. Of course it has to be all these things to some degree. But mainly it has to be the most apt *learner*, the most sensitive ear and the firmest will.[97]

These words were not addressed into a vacuum. The question of the revolutionary party in Portugal was a concrete one. In 1974 the IS had established contacts with the Proletarian Revolutionary Party – Revolutionary Brigades (PRP). This had been formed in 1969 from a split with the Communist Party, and under the dictatorship it had functioned as a clandestine guerrilla organisation. It differed from the CP and the various Maoist groups in that it rejected a stages theory of revolution – the idea that there must first be a national democratic revolution, followed, at some ill-defined point in the future, by a socialist revolution. It argued that "the task of the Portuguese Revolution was the establishment of the dictatorship of the proletariat". Cliff saw the PRP as "an authentic revolutionary Marxist organisation" making a real effort to transform itself into a workers' party, which was playing a positive role in the various workers' struggles. But he argued:

> The healthy emphasis on self-activity by the proletariat, however, is accompanied by a certain lack of clarity about the relations between the revolutionary party and the proletariat.[98]

Parts of *Portugal at the Crossroads* can therefore be seen as a fraternal polemic with the PRP and an attempt to persuade it to develop along certain lines. The attempt was doomed to failure. Several members of the IS leadership visited Portugal and PRP leaders met Cliff in London. The PRP leaders respected Cliff and there was a proposal to enable Cliff – despite his not having a British passport – to travel to Portugal. After consideration he decided not to,[99] though he would have dearly loved to visit a country on the brink of revolution.[100]

The PRP's traditions were those of a clandestine guerrilla group, preoccupied with military technique. Cliff's insistence that the PRP was the key to the situation was understandable, given the short timescale of the situation, but the close links with the PRP became a barrier to developing contacts with others on the Portuguese left. Peter Robinson, who stayed in Portugal for seven months and was regularly on the phone to Cliff, had a number of arguments with him about the PRP.[101] In order to keep abreast with the developing situation, Cliff wrote a number of follow-up pieces, designed to have some influence on the PRP and the Portuguese left. In October *Socialist Worker* published "Portugal: An open letter to the revolution". This consisted of extracts from the Portuguese pamphlet *Portugal – O Caminho a Frente* (Portugal – the Way Ahead), of which 2,500 copies had already been sent to Portugal, having been written, translated and printed in two days. This stressed the need for workers' councils and a mass revolutionary party, and warned the PRP that time was short: "Every member has to understand that unless the organisation is built, the revolution will be destroyed".[102] There followed "Portugal: The Great Danger". This lamented that the PRP, "by far the best revolutionary organisation in Portugal, is speaking only to the soldiers and to a very narrow section of the working class". Cliff urged the need for a daily paper and a united front strategy towards the CP.[103]

On 25 November right-wing officers disarmed the left-wing soldiers in and around Lisbon. Effectively the tide had turned, and though the working class was not crushed, its strength was now much diminished. In December a short pamphlet translated into Portuguese, entitled "The lessons of the 25th November", by Cliff and Chris Harman was issued. Translated within days by Annie Nehmad, it offered an analysis at a time when the Portuguese left was in complete disarray. It sold "like hot cakes"; on one occasion Peter Robinson sold 60 copies in an hour at a station.[104]

It recognised that the left had suffered a "major defeat", but that "the revolution can still be saved". The prime responsibility for the defeat lay with the CP, which had initiated the rebellion and then abandoned it to its fate. However, it was "necessary to know why the revolutionary left could not counteract that treachery". The real problem was "the weakness of the revolutionary left. When it came to the decisive test, the reformists were shown to have incomparably more weight within the working class than the revolutionaries."

The pamphlet was thus a polemic against some of the ideas of organisation current in the PRP:

> Even with the best elements of the revolutionary left there is a failure to understand the need to organise politically those workers who are breaking with reformism. The notion is widespread that the job of the party is to deal with technical questions, like the organisation of the insurrection, while the functioning of organs of workers' power can be left to the "non-party" bodies themselves. In practice this means that the Party is seen as being made up of small, highly trained (in military terms) cadres, which does not need to permeate every single section of the class.
>
> This aversion to a stress on building up the organisation of the Party and its periphery is perhaps a natural reaction to the crude, Stalinist notion of the Party peddled both by the Communist Party and the Maoist sects (which leads the Maoists to counterpose building the Party to the tasks of the mass movement). But it is extremely dangerous at present.

Cliff continued to take a keen interest in developments in Portugal, and in the spring of 1976 spent a whole day discussing them with Peter Robinson.[105] In March 1976 Cliff published "Portugal: The Last Three Months", written jointly with Robin Peterson.[106] * This was quite clear about the way in which reactionary forces were reviving in Portugal and about the role of the Socialist Party in assisting them:

> Many of the hundreds of bosses kicked out of their factories last year and others who deserted the factories, are now trying to get them back with a little help from their friends – the so-called Socialists in the government.

Yet this role was seen as temporary – in the coming elections a landslide for the extreme right was to be expected. The Socialists would only have any power until the generals were ready to "take on the unions and workers commissions frontally". The threat of Portugal becoming the "Chile of Europe" still seemed very real.

Criticism of the role of the PRP was now explicit. Over recent months the PRP had "changed: it moved to the wider recruitment of workers, it publishes its paper more regularly and so on. But the

---

* Robin Peterson was the rather transparent pseudonym of Peter Robinson. Robinson recalls that Cliff spent a lot of time on this, and that he cut and pasted material written by Robinson (Peter Robinson interview, June 2008).

changes were too slow for the needs of the time." The defeat had meant a need for defensive struggles, and that required above all trade union organisation.

Alas, over the last three months, the revolutionary left in Portugal, and its best section the PRP, did not show any clear radical change of direction towards the industrial struggles, towards active participation in trade union affairs, and towards fighting for the leadership of the workers' commissions… The PRP is paying a very high price indeed for its failure to understand the central role of trade union activity, and its avoidance, in the name of "anti-Partyism", of the struggles for the leadership of the workers' commissions.

Cliff emphasised the need for revolutionaries to participate actively in the election campaign. But though it was written in the form of encouragement to action, in fact the article was an epitaph. The revolutionary opportunity had passed. Cliff returned to the subject of Portugal just once more, in February 1977. He noted that more than a year after November 1975 the working class had not been defeated; though its advance had been reversed, its organisations were intact. But the revolutionary left, and especially the PRP, was in disarray and unable to give a lead. So he concluded, rather agnostically, that the future might see a "a new period of struggle, from the left or the right".[107] After this Cliff never wrote about Portugal again.

Portugal at the Crossroads was rapidly translated into a number of languages during the autumn of 1975. The IS International Department produced translations into Portuguese, French, Italian and Spanish. The Spanish translation was published under the misleading and apparently innocuous title *Primavera* ("Springtime") with a cover showing trees in bloom and without the author's name for clandestine distribution in fascist Spain.* A German translation was produced by the Sozialistische Arbeitergruppe in Germany, and a Greek version by Greek and Greek Cypriot comrades.[108] There were also Japanese and Danish editions.[109] A shortened version appeared in the American journal *Radical America*.[110]

The versions produced in London were done on the basis of very limited resources. Translations were made hurriedly by teams of

---

* I handed over copies at a clandestine conference of the POUM held in France at Christmas 1975.

comrades, and did not reach high literary standards. The typesetting for all four translations was done on a single electric typewriter in the IS headquarters at Cotton's Gardens under the supervision of Joanna Rollo, the IS international organiser. The typewriter had different golf balls for the accents required in the various languages, and small pieces of sticky paper had to be put on the keys to indicate which golf ball was in use.[111]

Distribution was arranged through individuals and small groups sympathetic to the IS in the various countries concerned. It was therefore spasmodic and the print runs for some of the translations were overoptimistic, so that a number remained undistributed.[112] Nonetheless it did ensure that Cliff made a contribution to the debate taking place on the European left, and it helped to raise the international profile of the IS. In Portugal the book was sold on the streets and through bookshops, and on demonstrations, including a mass demonstration shortly before 25 November. But there was not an adequate infrastructure for distribution and many copies were left over.[113]

Cliff was enthusiastic about the translations. He believed, with some justice, that Portugal presented a major test for the European left and that it might lead to a regroupment. In the early years of the Comintern Marxists had united with militants from a revolutionary syndicalist background.* Similarly, he thought the current period might see a convergence between groups like the IS emerging from the Trotskyist tradition and some of the non-dogmatic Maoist or semi-Maoist organisations like Avanguardia Operaia in Italy and Révolution! in France.[114]

Portugal led to a dispute with the IS's fraternal organisation in America, the International Socialists of the United States (ISUS). Initially the two organisations had been in agreement on Portugal and Joel Geier, a leading figure in the ISUS, spent some time there. While Cliff became increasingly critical of the PRP for not building a party, Geier thought they were building better than anyone else. Geier still thinks the PRP were the most supple and innovative group he has ever seen. Visiting London in the summer of 1976, Geier attended a meeting in Cliff's front room, where for eight hours

---

* Cliff had a high regard for Alfred Rosmer's *Lenin's Moscow* (London, 1987), which described this process in some detail.

uninterruptedly he had to argue with Cliff, Duncan Hallas, Chris Harman and Ian Birchall.* Geier found the meeting extremely depressing and thought the two sides were speaking different languages.[115] The differences were not resolved and the following year there was a split in the ISUS, in which Portugal was one of several issues in dispute.

Cliff's political work left him little time for anything else. In his autobiography he recalled that his younger daughter Anna had asked, "Why didn't I have a daddy between my fourth and tenth birthdays [1968-74]?"[116]

Political activity took over his home in Allerton Road. His son Danny remembers a house constantly full of people, "like an international hotel". During the miners' strike there were visiting pickets and the whole place stank of socks. Party members and others were always visiting. Danny remembers Bernadette Devlin and, more bizarrely, on one occasion the serial killer Dennis Nilsen.

Yet Cliff was very fond of his family, and deeply protective. The only time he ever hit Danny was when he was upset because the child had run out in front of a car. Once he bravely stood in front of Danny and Anna when they were threatened by an Alsatian dog in the park. However, young Danny once asked his father how he would choose between the revolution and saving his children from dying. Cliff, honestly enough though perhaps insensitively, replied that he would choose revolution, leaving his son quite upset.[117]

The level of activity maintained by Cliff – and Chanie – must have put strains on the family. The environment was very different from a "normal" family. When the youngest child, Anna, was around seven or eight, she was asked at school what her dad did for a living. She didn't want to say that he was a professional revolutionary, so she said he was a writer – writing children's books about a wizard called Lenin.

Anna remembered that her father was grumpy – but very loving. Although there was political discussion going on all the time at home no pressure was put on the children to join the party – Anna didn't join till she was 21. Likewise she was under no pressure to succeed academically; Cliff hated academic elitism and once offered

---

* Unlike many in the Trotskyist tradition, Cliff tried to keep personal animosity out of political disputes. At the end of this intense meeting, he told me to take Geier to the pub and be nice to him.

Anna £5 for every examination she failed.

Anna remembered his obsessive concern to see every television news bulletin – and to demand that the children be quiet while he watched. He would carefully note the changes from one bulletin to the next. Anna learned not to trust authority by the way her father shouted at the television and laughed scornfully when someone was presented as an "expert".[118]

Her brother Danny also remembered that Cliff took little interest in his schoolwork, and that there was no pressure on him to join the party. His main interest in his life was music, not politics, but Cliff was quite happy that he should do what he wanted to do.

Certainly Cliff had little time left to look after himself. During the 1974 miners' strike he and Chanie visited Bob Clay in Teesside. Chanie noticed that there were holes in the soles of Cliff's shoes and insisted they must find a shoe shop. Cliff protested that he had more important things to do and that the holes kept his feet cool, but for once he was overruled.[119]

In 1975 Cliff published the first volume of his biography of Lenin. He had been working on this since 1968. Whenever he turned up for a meeting, he would have a different part of Lenin's *Works* with him; he devoted his train journeys to reading them.[120] Three more volumes on Lenin were to appear in 1976, 1978 and 1979.* Running to almost 1,300 pages, the complete biography was Cliff's most substantial work so far.

Cliff's *Lenin* has been pilloried by some of his critics. It has been described as resembling "a biography of John the Baptist written by Jesus Christ".[121] Jim Higgins has alleged that Cliff's method was first to "dredge up" an idea from his subconscious and then to "seek out buttressing quotes from Lenin".[122]

Such criticisms were unfair, but they did have a point. It is important to define what Cliff's project was. He had not the remotest interest in writing dispassionate, "objective" history. He was an

---

* In the second edition (London, 1986) volumes three and four were combined in a single volume. Cliff had always wanted them to appear as a single volume, and was very annoyed that Pluto, for commercial reasons, decided to publish the two volumes separately (Donny Gluckstein interview, February 2009). Shaun Doherty went with Cliff to take the manuscript to Mike Kidron; Cliff seemed very nervous, presumably concerned that there might be a confrontation over the form of publication (Shaun Doherty interview, November 2008).

"activist historian".* For him the whole point of studying history was to learn lessons from the past in order to better understand how to shape the future. He would have had nothing but contempt for such philosophers of history as Quentin Skinner, who argues that statements and texts from the past are trapped in the situation in which they were produced and "cannot be concerned with our questions and answers, but only with their own".[123]

Such activist history has honourable credentials, especially as far as the history of revolutionary movements is concerned. Some of the finest histories of the French Revolution came not from professional historians, but from writers like Jean Jaurès, who wrote parts of his history of the French Revolution during dull debates in the French National Assembly, where he was a deputy, or Peter Kropotkin, who was unable to consult French archives because he was liable to arrest on French territory as a result of his anarchist activity.

Activist historians can bring to their subject insights and illuminations not available to those who have spent their lives in the archives. Few who have written about Lenin can have had firsthand experience of a clandestine revolutionary organisation, as Cliff had done in Palestine. Cliff had a grasp of the dynamics of leadership, of the conflicts and compromises and shifting alliances within a central committee, because he had spent many hours serving on such a committee.

Duncan Hallas wryly observed that the first volume of *Lenin* might have been better called "Building the Party – Illustrated from the Life of Lenin". But he recognised that "a manual for revolutionaries – and that is what we have here – is needed more urgently than a fully rounded biography".[124]

Cliff had a deep disdain for the methods of academic scholarship. "If you copy from one book it is plagiarism," he used to say. "If you copy from several books it is research".[125] He was always willing to make use of others' detailed research. "I do not collect straw for my own bricks".[126] †

He relied heavily on *verbatim* quotations from Lenin's writings, to the extent of sometimes making the narrative difficult to read. At

---

* I take the term from an unpublished manuscript by Dave Renton.
† This was a reference to *Exodus*, chapter 5, verses 6-19, where the children of Israel in Egypt were required to gather their own straw for brick-making without loss of production. This was perhaps the first productivity deal in history.

the same time he sought to set Lenin in context by drawing on the recollections of his contemporaries and showing the realities to which Lenin's various polemics referred.

He specifically recognised the danger of using quotations from Lenin to prove a point. Referring to Lenin's habit of "stick-bending", he wrote:

> He always made the task of the day quite clear, repeating what was necessary *ad infinitum* in the plainest, heaviest, most single-minded hammer-blow pronouncements. Afterwards, he would regain his balance, straighten the stick, then bend it again in another direction. If this method has advantages in overcoming current obstacles, it also contains hazards for anyone wanting to use Lenin's writing on tactical and organisational questions as a source for quotation. Authority by quotation is nowhere less justified than in the case of Lenin. If he is cited on any tactical or organisational question, the concrete issues that the movement was facing at the time must be made absolutely clear.[127]

Whether Cliff always avoided this danger in his own writings is less certain.

Cliff's basic aim was to rescue Lenin from his friends as well as from his foes. Lenin's enemies, often motivated by Cold War politics, sought to demonise him; Stefan T Possony, while acknowledging his "political genius", condemned the "immorality and even criminality" of this "compulsive destroyer".[128] Stalinist writers turned him into some sort of mythological hero who could do no wrong.[129] The distinguished historian Christopher Hill took time off from his work on the 17th century to produce a simplified account of Lenin in which many of the problems, hesitations and conflicts were omitted in order to stress Lenin's consistency and correctness, and to contrast him to the "Westernising émigré" Trotsky.[130] Even within the Trotskyist tradition, there was a tendency to produce an idealised caricature of "Leninism" rather than examine the complex reality.

The first volume of *Lenin* dealt with Lenin's evolution up to 1914. To trace, year by year, sometimes month by month, the factional disputes in the Russian socialist movement, with ample quotation from polemics, seemed laborious. But Cliff was concerned to use the account to put across certain central themes. One of the key premises of Cliff's method was set out early in the volume:

Another of Lenin's characteristics already apparent at this early stage of his development is an attitude to organisational forms as always historically determined. He never adopted abstract, dogmatic schemes of organisation, and was ready to change the organisational structure of the party at every new development of the class struggle. Organisation, he was convinced, should be subordinated to politics.[131]

It is important to draw out just how radical this argument was. Right-wing anti-Communists, Stalinists and "orthodox" Trotskyists have all argued that there is such a thing as the "Leninist party" which had a distinct form of organisation. Cliff repudiated this myth.*

Cliff's hatred of formalism was obvious here. He noted with approval that Lenin's draft rules for the RSDLP were "extremely simple and few in number", and that the Bolshevik apparatus was "very modest". He deflated the notion that Bolshevism meant a highly disciplined and ultra-efficient organisation: "There was a total cleavage between the ideal of a coherent, efficient party structure as visualised in Lenin's writings, and the ramshackle party organisation that existed".[132]

Hence Cliff took a critical attitude to Lenin's *What Is To Be Done?*, generally seen by friends and foes alike as the definitive recipe book for the revolutionary party.† While drawing out some of the important arguments in the book about the need for stable organisation and the role of the revolutionary newspaper, he was

---

* A few others in the Trotskyist tradition have also done so. See P Broué, *Le Parti bolchevique*, Paris, 1972, pp44-49, and H Draper, "The Myth of Lenin's 'Concept of the Party'", at http://www.marxists.org/archive/draper/1990/myth/index.htm

† Thus as late as 1970 Georges Cogniot of the French Communist Party argued that "the denigration of *What Is To Be Done?* is a constant feature of opportunism" (G Cogniot, *Présence de Lénine*, Paris 1970, II 86, 92). On the other side of the fence, to take one academic example among many, Geoffrey Swain has argued that Bolshevik strategy towards the Red International of Labour Unions in the 1920s can be explained by the simple fact that "As every student of *What Is To Be Done?* knows, Lenin did not think much of trade unions." (G Swain, "Was the Profintern Really Necessary?", *European History Quarterly*, Vol 17, No 1, 1987, p58) In mitigation it should be said that *What Is To Be Done?* is not an easy read; any researcher who has ploughed her way through it may well feel she has the right to attribute great explanatory significance to it. In fact, as Lars T Lih has demonstrated, *What Is To Be Done?* "was written to score off some very specific opponents and to advocate some very specific policies that were relevant only for a fleeting moment" (LT Lih, *Lenin Rediscovered*, Leiden/Boston, 2006, p5).

critical of some of Lenin's positions. Thus he argued that the juxtaposition between consciousness and spontaneity* was a false polarisation. "Pure spontaneity does not exist in life... The smallest strike has at least a rudimentary leadership".[133] He showed that *What Is To Be Done?* did not exalt intellectuals above workers:

> Unlike the workers, who are accustomed to discipline by factory life, the intellectuals have to be disciplined with an iron rod by the party. Above all, their role in the party is transitory. "The role of the intelligentsia is to make special leaders from among the intelligentsia unnecessary".[134]

There is no doubt that Cliff made a sharp break from orthodox "Leninism" in his account of *What Is To Be Done?* But a recent study of Lenin by Lars T Lih has argued that Cliff's interpretation still had a great deal in common with the standard academic account. In particular he claims that the view that Lenin wanted an all-powerful central committee derives not from Lenin's writings, but from Luxemburg's criticisms of him.[135] Lih displays formidable erudition in his knowledge of the debates in the Russian socialist movement, and he is doubtless correct in pointing to errors in Cliff's account.[136] He concludes that though Cliff is a "great admirer" of Lenin, his picture of the 1895-1905 period is "not an attractive one", making Lenin seem "a rather incompetent and incoherent leader", whereas Lih's own account stresses the "fundamental continuity" of Lenin's views.[137]

However, Lih's stress on continuity tends to downplay one of Lenin's supreme virtues, his ability to respond to unpredicted and unpredictable actions of the working class, such as the originality and perceptiveness of his thought in 1905. Cliff, on the other hand, was much less interested in *What Is To Be Done?* than in the more heroic moments of Bolshevik history, and especially in 1905, when Lenin urged rapid recruitment to the party, and 1912, when the daily *Pravda* was launched. It was such phases of Bolshevik development that appeared most relevant for party-building in the present. In particular he pointed to the democratic and anti-authoritarian nature of Bolshevism, referring to the "contempt which Lenin was to retain throughout his life towards any pecking

---

* As Lars T Lih has shown, the Russian word generally translated as "spontaneous" – *stikhiinyi* – has a range of connotations and is virtually untranslatable (Lih, *Lenin Rediscovered*, pp616-618).

order in the movement, and overbearing attitudes in its leaders, any dishonest covering-up of the leaders' own past mistakes".[138]

Cliff defended Lenin's habit of "stick-bending":

> In principle Lenin was right when he insisted on "bending the stick", one day in one direction, another in the opposite. If all aspects of the workers' movement had been equally developed, if balanced growth had been the rule, then "stick bending" would have a deleterious effect on the movement. But in real life the law of uneven development dominates. One aspect of the movement is decisive at any particular time. The key obstacle to advance may be a lack of party cadres, or, on the contrary, the conservatism of the party cadres may cause them to lag behind the advanced section of the class. Perfect synchronisation of all elements would obviate the need for "bending sticks", but would also render a revolutionary party or a revolutionary leadership superfluous.[139]

Cliff's critics have often derided his stick-bending.[140] It could be seen as a justification for inconsistency, for flitting from one enthusiasm to another. It could also be seen a manifestation of an elitist and manipulative approach, a belief that the leader, or the leading committee, is the source of all wisdom, which it has to impose on the membership by overstatement.[141]

There is some validity in such criticisms. But Cliff was well aware that in a small organisation prioritisation is essential; a group of a few hundred that attempts to do everything will end up doing nothing. So it was necessary to argue for a central emphasis in a given context. Moreover Cliff had a proven ability to spot significant changes in the objective circumstances, and to recognise the shifts of emphasis required. For Cliff "bending the stick" meant a struggle to persuade, to convince a substantial section of the organisation of the need for a new priority, since if they were not convinced nothing would actually be achieved.

John Molyneux has made an acute defence of Cliff:

> Cliff had learned from experience that shifting an organisation of several thousand members (as opposed to winning an academic or historical debate) from one strategic orientation and one way of working to another to meet the challenge of changed circumstances, required an almighty great tug on the relevant levers and, sometimes, a certain exaggeration. For Cliff achieving the desired end was more important than terminological exactitude or consistency and he rather thought...

that Lenin felt the same way.[142]

Often Cliff revealed a deep empathy with Lenin, finding in him aspects of his own style and personality. There were dangers in such an approach, but it gave him insights into the psychology of a professional revolutionary that were absent in the frigid dissections of academic historians. When he noted that "there has probably never been a revolutionary more single-minded, purposeful and persistent than Lenin",[143] Cliff could see a reflection of his own personality.*

He observed, "If Lenin had one weakness, it was that he fell in love with people too easily... But these enthusiasms did not continue for long. While on first acquaintance Lenin was always ready to 'fall in love' with a new collaborator, after a longer acquaintance he would nearly always discern elements of weakness in him".[144] In writing these lines he must have been all too well aware that he was describing one of his own foibles.†

Occasionally Cliff let hero-worship carry him away. In dealing with Lenin's role during 1905 he argued that "almost from the outset, Lenin's appreciation of the future historical role of the soviets was much more advanced than that of the participants".[145] There is a good deal of truth in this, but Cliff rather glosses over the fact he himself remarks on elsewhere,‡ namely that Lenin too was somewhat slow in recognising the importance of the soviets, which were a product of working class creativity.

Cliff rightly observed that Lenin was wrong in seeing the coming Russian revolution as a bourgeois revolution and that Trotsky's theory of permanent revolution had provided a far better account of coming events. But he was reluctant to point to the inadequacy of Lenin's theory of the "democratic dictatorship of workers and peasants", insisting that "even in his mistakes regarding perspectives, there was a central core of strategy and tactics that led directly

---

* In 1973 Cliff reviewed Tamara Deutscher (ed), *Not by Politics Alone: The Other Lenin* (London, 1973). Cliff described this as "a valiant effort to describe the other traits and activities of Lenin besides his political ones", but judged that it was "bound to fail", because the political so completely dominated all other aspects of Lenin's life (*International Socialism* 63 (Mid-October 1973)).

† Cliff cites as his source Nadezhda Krupskaya's *Memories of Lenin* (London, 1970), p76. But while Krupskaya does record Lenin's "periods of enthusiasm", the subsequent disillusion seems to be a projection of Cliff's own experience.

‡ For example, *Marxism at the Millennium*, London, 2000, p12, though I recall him making the point in lectures in the 1960s.

to just such a victory of the proletarian revolution".[146] This came a little too close for comfort to "he was right to be wrong". Cliff defended Lenin by citing the phrase "*On s'engage, et puis... on voit* [You join battle and then...you see]". The formula is attributed to Napoleon, who undoubtedly knew something about battles. Nonetheless it did make concessions to blind activism. But in a very interesting chapter on "Strategy and Tactics"[147] Cliff explored the relationship between theory and practice in Lenin's politics. He argued that Marxism was an art as well as a science, and stressed the need for intuition and imagination. The party had to be able to learn from the class, and for this party democracy was essential.

The second volume of *Lenin* dealt briefly with Lenin during the First World War, before moving on to the revolution of 1917. Cliff omitted to mention that at the outbreak of the war Lenin spent several months studying Hegel; perhaps he was afraid that comrades would imitate him and retreat to libraries at a time of deep social crisis.* He also pointed to the limitations of Lenin's *Imperialism*, a work given "almost canonical authority" by many of Lenin's followers, but which Cliff showed to be much narrower in scope than comparable writings by Luxemburg, Hilferding and Bukharin; in particular he stressed Lenin's debt to Bukharin.[148]

Cliff's main concern was with the events of 1917. Not surprisingly he focused on the role of the party; as he argued, the one defect of Trotsky's otherwise masterly *History of the Russian Revolution* was that it neglected the part played by the party.

Cliff set out to demythologise Bolshevism, to undermine the idea of a highly efficient, highly centralised and infallible party. In February 1917, 200,000 workers struck before the Bolsheviks called for a general strike. He stressed the informality of the central committee, which "again and again reached decisions which its members forgot all about immediately afterwards". Sverdlov was commended for his "great lack of concern about pedantic exactness" in reporting wildly inaccurate membership figures![149]

The party was far from monolithic and Lenin was often isolated, obliged to fight for his position. Cliff's main concern was to show that most of the time Lenin was right, and to draw a wealth of

---

* In the first volume Cliff had contrasted the "magnificent, dialectically terse and lively" *Philosophical Notebooks* (Lenin, *Collected Works* XXXVIII) with the Stalinist-endorsed *Materialism and Empirio-Criticism* (Lenin, vol 1, p291).

lessons from his capacity for analysis and his methods of leadership. The book was a powerful defence of the revolutionary tradition.

His account was far removed from the Stalinist myth of Lenin's unfailingly correct leadership. While showing the real strengths of the Bolshevik party, he noted the element of conservatism in Bolshevik organisation: "Every party, including the most revolutionary, inevitably produces its own organisational conservatism – without routine there is no stability".[150]

He was sharply critical of Lenin's tactical judgements about the insurrection – the proposal to start in Moscow rather than Petrograd, and above all the idea of carrying out the insurrection in the name of the party rather than of the soviets – on which he was opposed, successfully and correctly, by Trotsky:

> Having been out of touch with the practicalities of the situation, he could not judge it correctly. It is also possible that his emphasis on the strategic decision – his accustomed stick-bending – made it difficult for him to grasp the particulars. Concentrating on the key link, on the strategic choice, and absent from the scene of the struggle, Lenin was almost bound to make serious tactical miscalculations.[151]

There was perhaps an element of self-criticism here.

Cliff was right to show that behind Lenin's politics lay a deep moral sense: "He hated with the oppressed, loved with the oppressed, and hoped and fought with the oppressed." He was on shakier ground when he commended Lenin's "uncanny intuition", arguing that "in a period of great changes, the number of unknown factors...is so great that sober analysis alone will not suffice. An unsurpassed ability to detect the mood of the masses was Lenin's most important gift".[152] A reliance on intuition can all too easily lead away from scientific and democratic politics.

The third volume of *Lenin* dealt with Russia after the revolution. Cliff resisted all temptations to romanticise; the revolution was beset by terrible difficulties from the outset. The new regime lacked skilled personnel. There were no shorthand writers or even typists. As for anyone with the experience to run the economy, the Commissar of Finance had once been a clerk in a French bank. Less than 10 percent of party members had membership dating back before February 1917.[153]

Unlike the dishonest authors of such works as the *Black Book of*

Communism, who depict Lenin as bloodthirsty by abstracting his actions from the context of counter-revolution,[154] Cliff was quite clear that revolutionary violence was necessary to defend the revolution. He pointed out, "Compared with the White terror... the Red terror was mild".[155] He did not conceal the "indescribable" suffering of the post-revolutionary period – food and fuel shortages, disease and even cannibalism.[156]

In honestly depicting the weaknesses of the revolution, Cliff never forgot what was central to it – the self-emancipation of the working class.* Lenin repeatedly invoked creativity – the "creative faculties of the masses", "creative activity at the grass roots", "living, creative socialism".[157] Having stressed the importance of the party in his first two volumes, Cliff now pointed out its limits:

> The revolutionary party is indispensable, but it is not sufficient for revolutionary advance... In the final analysis the party remained always subordinated to and dependent on the working class. The party can affect the class only to the extent that its words, its propaganda, produce the desired activity by the class; without working class action the party is impotent.[158]

Cliff carefully examined the decline in working class democracy produced by the growing fusion between party and state. He cited at length Rosa Luxemburg's criticisms precisely because she was an enthusiastic supporter of the revolution. The Bolsheviks faced enormous difficulties, but "to explain the reasons for the Bolsheviks' circumscribing of workers' democracy is not to justify it". As Luxemburg pointed out, the Bolsheviks were inclined to "make a virtue of necessity" and Cliff conceded that Lenin was not entirely innocent in this respect; indeed his celebrated "stick-bending" was partly to blame: "Although he would deal with a particular situation very *concretely*, he always inclined to generalise too far from the immediate task in hand".[159]

The third volume of *Lenin* received an enthusiastic review from David Widgery, one of the SWP's most talented writers, who inhabited a cultural universe of surrealism, punk rock and sexual politics that was alien to Cliff's preoccupations. Widgery's response

---

* Compare Jean-Jacques Marie's *Lénine* (Paris, 2004) which, while scrupulously honest about the failings of the revolution, is sometimes so immersed in gloom that the author loses sight of the hope that inspired the whole enterprise.

is a recognition of the fact that Cliff was able to communicate a vision of Lenin to a generation and a milieu far removed from the orthodoxies of traditional Leninism:

> The Russian Revolution was both overwhelmingly and genuinely a mass social revolution and yet...it began to lose its authentic socialist character within months of the workers' seizure of power.

> Yet it is exactly this agonising and contradictory process which Cliff studies in *The Revolution Besieged* with commendable honesty and clarity. The skill with which the author co-mingles the heroic and the tragic makes this the most moving volume in what was in danger of becoming a worthy but somewhat tedious biography.

Widgery, quite rightly, grasped that Cliff's essential message was not the revival of some mythical "Leninism", but the rebirth of Lenin's revolutionary spirit in a form appropriate to the modern world:

> We have a responsibility to select the aspects we now need to emphasise rather than attempt to imitate a "pure" Leninism to order, which would be both impossible and irrelevant.[160]

In the final volume of *Lenin* Cliff dealt with the Comintern. Since the defeat of the Russian Revolution derived essentially from the failure of the revolution to spread, especially to Germany, this was a key question. In his treatment Cliff was at his most innovative.

Most Trotskyist historiography of the Comintern has been defensive, trying to show that while Lenin and Trotsky held key leadership positions everything was splendid, but that after their departures things went rapidly bad. Often such defensiveness reflected a political attitude which tried to lift recipes for the present mechanically from an account of the past.* The best Trotskyist histories – James's *World Revolution 1917-1936*[161] or more recently Duncan Hallas's *The Comintern*[162] – are valuable in that they defend what was best in the early years of the Comintern (and there was much worth defending) while sharply contrasting that early period to the later Stalinist horrors. Yet they remain essentially defensive.

Cliff drew on a different tradition, the work of Alfred Rosmer and Victor Serge,[163] which combined a total commitment to the

---

* The Workers' Fight group in 1968-71 had made the first four congresses of the Comintern part of their platform. Cliff was contemptuous of this, since many of their members did not know when the congresses took place.

basic aims and ideals of the Comintern with a recognition of its limitations in practice. In particular he pointed to the way in which the Bolsheviks dominated the Comintern:

> Even when the Russian leaders spoke complete nonsense, they were not criticised by other communist leaders... This uncritical attitude towards the Russian party was dangerous. The latter took charge of the whole policy of the Comintern, being given the credit for successes, and completely exonerated for the failures, which were always someone else's fault.[164]

Cliff pointed to "the cleavage between the strategic and tactical decisions of its congresses – especially the second and third – and the actual policies of its national sections".[165]

Even Lenin himself had serious weaknesses. Cliff points out:

> The fact that until the outbreak of the 1914 war Lenin had *never* criticised Karl Kautsky or the German Social Democratic Party shows that he did not appreciate the strength of the hold of reformism and opportunism over the labour movement in western and central Europe. The same unawareness is shown by Lenin's overoptimistic expectation in 1918 and 1919 of victory for the proletarian revolution in Europe, even though there were no mass communist parties, and certainly no experienced ones, in existence.[166]

The low political level of the Comintern meant that democratic centralism could not function effectively. Bureaucratic organisation filled the gap left by the absence of consciousness:

> The successful working of democratic centralism on a national or international scale requires a high level of homogeneity in the party, a high level of consciousness, training and also trust between leaders, as well as between all members and the leadership. If "staff" and "troops" are well integrated, discipline follows 99 percent from conviction and only 1 percent from mechanical obedience.[167]

Consequently a number of unhealthy aspects developed in the earliest years of the Comintern. Moscow distributed large financial subsidies – a "financial bonanza" – to national sections, but this was often unhelpful when, as happened in Germany, the party acquired 27 daily papers, but did not have the experienced militants to write for them. Comintern agents, acting on behalf of the executive, were "actually more powerful than the national leaderships". At the top Zinoviev, the president, relied on authority to cover up for his political inadequacies; in Cliff's view he "lacked theoretical depth and strength of character, being cowardly, erratic and prone to duplicity and intrigue".[168]

Cliff argued that Zinoviev's attitude to leadership in the Comintern was responsible for the defeat of the German Revolution in 1923:

> A process of natural selection of the unfittest was encouraged by Zinoviev. It is true that Paul Levi was not a Lenin, but neither was he a Zinoviev or a Bela Kun. Zinoviev preferred lieutenants who would be overawed by the mantle of October that he wore. The clearest result of the Zinoviev leadership was the 1923 catastrophe in Germany.[169]

Drawing on Pierre Broué's history of the German Revolution,[170] Cliff stressed that the real problem was not simply incorrect guidance from Moscow, but the fact that the German leadership, after the debacle of the adventurist March Action in 1921, had become dependent on Moscow. "Throughout 1923 the KPD leadership lacked independence and was totally subservient to the orders of the Comintern in Moscow".[171] The best Leninists were not those who waited for orders from Lenin. Although neither man might have welcomed the comparison, Cliff's work was in some respects parallel to Broué's supremely non-defensive history of the Comintern.[172] Cliff had no compunction in writing of "the degeneration of the Comintern leadership while Lenin was still alive".[173]

Cliff's concluding picture of Lenin was a sad one. He could see the growth of bureaucracy, yet was unable to turn to the proletarian element in the party because it was now a small minority:

> He was groping for a direction. After every spell of illness, when he returned from his sickbed to watch over the movements of the state and party machines, his alarm grew, and with pathetic determination he struggled to grasp the helm in his faltering hands.[174]

There was no hero worship here, just an honest recognition of the defeat of the great hopes of 1917.

Cliff's *Lenin* was rich in lessons and many of the work's themes guided his approach to particular organisational questions in the SWP. Yet much of Cliff's organisational thought came from direct experience and observation rather than from applying the classic texts. So if the SWP was a "Leninist" organisation, it was one of a highly original form. Some of Cliff's contemporaries, like James and Dunayevskaya, were more vocal than Cliff in their denunciation of "Leninism". Yet in practice Cliff may have gone further than they did in organisational innovation.

In the autumn of 1975 the longstanding internal dispute revived. It finally came to a head over the question of strategy towards the Broad Left in the AUEW. Members of the AUEW fraction had decided that they should support a rank and file candidate for the post of AUEW national organiser. A number of IS members in the Birmingham area AUEW, already committed to supporting a Broad Left candidate, refused to accept this perspective, broke discipline and were expelled.[175]

The expulsions were implemented by Steve Jefferys, who, even among his colleagues on the central committee, acquired the nickname "hanging judge Jefferys", but there is no evidence that Cliff in any way disapproved of what was done.* Jefferys has subsequently claimed that in fact he went along with the policy in order to try to moderate it by holding on to some of the Birmingham engineers, though he plainly failed to do so.[176] Jim Nichol believes Cliff was reluctant to expel, but that he preferred expulsions to disintegration and permanent disputes.[177]

A faction calling itself the "IS Opposition" was now established, including many of those who had opposed the 1973 coup and Cliff's line on *Socialist Worker* and the orientation to younger workers. This refused a requirement from the December 1975 party council that the faction be dissolved, arguing that "we are concerned that the present lurch to ultra-leftism will destroy any working class base, while it may generate the sort of self-perpetuating irrelevant work that we associate with the WRP".[178] Faced with the choice of dissolving their faction or being excluded from the IS, about 150 members, including former executive members Jim Higgins, John Palmer, Granville Williams and Roger Protz, were expelled and formed the Workers League. A considerable number more were demoralised by the internal dispute and dropped out.

---

* Cliff often opposed expulsion as a means of resolving disputes. When there was a clash in Manchester between young workers and some older, experienced trade unionists, Cliff was strongly opposed to expulsions (Peter Robinson interview, June 2008).

It was the biggest split in the history of the organisation and a very serious setback. The losses included a number of experienced comrades and, in particular, a number of established trade union militants. As is usual in such disputes, a great deal of ill-feeling and personal bitterness was engendered and friendships were destroyed. Over 30 years later opinion was still divided among those involved in the dispute. Paul Mackney, one of those expelled who had briefly been in the SLL, felt that the IS was coming closer to Healyism, especially with a switch away from shop stewards towards youth.[179] John Rose, who at the time loyally supported Cliff, now thinks that Cliff had misunderstood the nature of the period and that the expulsions were a serious mistake, while Pete Clark, who was involved with the rank-and-file paper *Carworker*, thinks the expulsions were terribly damaging to the organisation.[180] Paul Holborow, however, thinks Cliff was broadly right in this period: the organisation had to be pushed to seize opportunities, and the opposition group could not relate to the current momentum of the working class.[181] Cliff himself in his autobiography justified the expulsions.[182]

Certainly Cliff must take a considerable degree of responsibility for the split. It was he who initiated the changes which led to the dispute and who persevered with them even when some of his original allies had faded. He was impatient in campaigning for his goals, and he did not always appreciate the kind of long-term work necessary to build credibility within the trade unions.[183] His impatience can be explained, if not justified, by his recognition of the possibilities in the state of affairs then current and the awareness that they would not last long. It is also true that he, and the rest of the leadership, had little experience of running an organisation of more than a few hundred.[184] But the losses were substantial and could probably have been much smaller if the situation had been handled more skilfully.

Cliff was not a personally vindictive individual, but if he was convinced that a particular course of action was necessary for the good of the organisation, then he could be ruthless in pursuing his ends and did not allow personal sentiment or longstanding friendship to stand in his way. In particular his relationship with Jim Higgins – which had been very close in the 1960s – was totally destroyed, and it is unlikely that they ever spoke again. John Palmer remembers that in 1978 he was invited to Cliff's home and asked if he would support the Anti Nazi League, then about to be launched.

When Palmer suggested that Higgins be approached, Cliff broke into a tirade against him.[185] But Richard Kirkwood, another of those expelled, recalls that when he met Cliff on occasion in later years, Cliff was always amiable and enquired after his current activity.[186] Sometimes, if he met a former member whom he had not seen for some time, he would say, "I thought you were dead," or, "I didn't believe in life after death till I saw you," suggesting that there was no life outside the party.*

Jim Higgins has written that the split marked the end of the high hopes for the IS in the early 1970s, and concludes, "Do I blame Cliff for most of this? Well actually I do".[187] This is too harsh. The hopes of the IS in the early 1970s were not realised because the Labour government succeeded in enforcing its Social Contract and large-scale industrial conflict virtually came to an end. As in Portugal, reformism proved rather more resilient than had been expected. Nothing that Cliff, Higgins or anyone else in a small revolutionary organisation could have done would have affected the main course of events.

In the mid-1970s the post-1968 revolutionary left throughout the world was affected by a deep crisis, essentially because of the discovery that reformism was a lot more resilient than had been supposed. The Italian revolutionary left, with three daily papers and six MPs, was much bigger than the IS, but it crumbled in the two or three years following the 1976 elections. Cliff preferred the expulsion of a rightward-moving section of the organisation to allowing the whole organisation to be drawn to the right. Doubtless things could have been handled better, but Cliff must also take some of the credit for the fact that the organisation survived.

The new organisation, the Workers League, was liberated from the constraints of the IS membership, free from Cliff's manipulations, able to pursue its own perspective with a number of "experienced militants" at its disposal. Yet it disappeared without

---

* Richard Kuper compares this to the Jewish practice of mourning for children who had married out (Richard Kuper interview, February 2009).

trace within three years.* The IS leadership around Cliff held the organisation together at a time when many revolutionary organisations in Europe were going into serious crisis.

Cliff continued to be impatient, aware that the favourable circumstances of the mid-1970s would not last long. Willie Lee, a leading activist at Chrysler Linwood, recalled a dispute with Cliff; there had been a management threat to close the factory and Cliff wanted the IS members to be adventurist and launch an occupation. He called one of the leading IS members a "conservative influence". Lee remembered that Cliff would travel 500 miles to have an argument with you: "He didn't hold grudges, but if you argued with him you felt you had blotted your copybook".[188]

There were other losses around this time. John Phillips, a longstanding member and twice a full-timer, was critical of the shift to a small central committee. He became involved in the Faction for Revolutionary Democracy.† He took part in two debates with Cliff, in west London and Newcastle, which he found difficult since he knew he would be crushed. But Cliff was never personally antagonistic. Shortly afterwards Phillips drifted out of the organisation.[189]

It was not only factional disputes that engaged Cliff. He took a close interest in the printshop and talked politically to the workers there. On one occasion when printshop workers were complaining about their working conditions, Cliff held a meeting with them and talked about the conditions under which Bolsheviks had worked in pre-revolutionary Russia. When printshop workers had to take a wage cut, Cliff took the wage cut too.[190] ‡ Roger Huddle, who

---

* The fact that Cliff's IS/SWP survived, while the Workers League was short-lived, seems to confirm the choice of those who, like myself, opted to stay with Cliff. But Cliff was quite wrong to claim that "hardly any" of those expelled remained "active politically" (*A World to Win*, p135). In the course of writing this book I interviewed several of those who were expelled at this point – Richard Kirkwood, Paul Mackney, John Palmer, Granville Williams, Edward Crawford – and who remain activists over 30 years later. Many others remained active as trade unionists. Cliff's relentless focus on party-building could sometimes blind him to the significance of activity outside the ranks of the party.

† See *Faction for Revolutionary Democracy* (April 1976) at Rich. Ms 1117/box 117/file 4. This argued for changes in the "group's internal democratic procedures" in order to "provide a democratic structure that retains the unity and fighting capacity of the organisation".

‡ After many years as an unpaid full-timer Cliff received the modest sum of £27 a week (Finance Report, January 1979, MRC MSS 244/2/1/2).

worked in the printshop for 12 years, recalled that Cliff would come on the annual printshop outing, but that he did so because he wanted to hold the printshop together, not because he wanted to go on a works outing.[191] He continued to speak around the country, still making a powerful impression on young workers and students. On one occasion he was being driven to a meeting in Coventry when the van broke down; he hitch-hiked in order not to let the comrades down.[192] John Rees heard him as a student in Portsmouth and was impressed that someone so old was still a revolutionary (Cliff would have been some years short of 60 at the time); he reflected that it could not be true that people became more right-wing as they got older.[193]

Cliff also found time for international contacts. In 1976 a group of members of the German SAG came to London and spent the weekend at Cliff's home discussing the problems of their organisation. Cliff quizzed them in detail about their activities and then gave them some advice. He was appalled at the large number of mainly internal meetings, and argued that a worker with two children should be able to feel at home in the organisation.

He stressed the importance of political arguments. When a German comrade told how they had set up a regular informal meeting for contacts from a factory, Cliff "jumped up as though bitten by an ant, tore his grey hair" and shouted that most people were attracted by revolutionary ideas, not by discussion about the workplace. He argued that a mass organisation would spend 80 percent of its time campaigning on bread and butter issues, but a small group should devote only 20 percent to bread and butter and 80 percent to politics.[194]

The political situation was now shifting rapidly. The perspectives document for the 1976 conference recognised that the movement was on the defensive, though it looked to a renewal of industrial struggle in the near future.[195] The fact that the Social Contract was holding meant that the large industrial confrontations of the early 1970s were giving way to much smaller disputes. In 1976, there was a strike for equal pay at the Trico-Folberth windscreen wiper factory at Brentford Middlesex; the women were out for 21 weeks. The strike at Grunwick Film Processing Laboratories in Willesden, north London for trade union recognition began in 1976 and lasted almost two years. The strike begun in 1978 at the Garners Steak Houses in central London was also for union recognition. These were the characteristic strikes of the next couple of years. They did not involve "experienced militants", but in the cases of Trico and Grunwick mainly women, at Grunwick and Garners largely workers from ethnic minorities. IS comrades were active in picketing and support work for all these disputes.

In this changing situation the IS had two major new initiatives. The first was the Right to Work Campaign. Unemployment had officially topped one million (in reality it was considerably higher), with women, black people and the young especially badly affected. The Right to Work Campaign was launched in October 1975 as an initiative from the Rank and File Organising Committee. For the next couple of years, the Right to Work Campaign largely overshadowed the Rank and File Movement.

The Right to Work Campaign in practice depended largely on the initiatives of IS members and was, not surprisingly, smeared as an IS front although a significant number of non-IS members were involved. Politically it was based on the principle that the unemployed had to have a voice in the struggle. The argument that everything must be done through the "official channels" left the unemployed simply as the recipients of fine words. In the spring of 1976 an Assembly on Unemployment (a Broad Left initiative called by the London Co-op Political Committee and the London District Committee of the Confederation of Shipbuilding and Engineering Unions) attracted 3,000 trade union delegates. There were many speakers on the evils of unemployment, but the only unemployed worker who got to the microphone was John Deason of the Right to Work Campaign.

In particular unemployed school-leavers, a significant section of the jobless, could not fight through the unions because they had never belonged to one. Local Right to Work Committees and Right to Work marches provided a possibility for self-activity by the unemployed.

But the unemployed alone could not fight unemployment. It was necessary to fight for the unity of employed and unemployed, to confront employed workers with their responsibilities. This meant taking the struggle for sponsorship of the Right to Work Campaign into the workplaces and union branches.

The first Right to Work march, from Manchester to London in

March 1976, was sponsored by over 400 trade union bodies, including 70 shop stewards' committees. This was possible despite the ambiguous attitude of the CP. In some areas CP members opposed the march in a grossly sectarian manner, but in other places they recognised that the IS was now taking initiatives of the sort the CP had made in the 1930s, and gave constructive support.

The march was significant, not just for the support it obtained, but for the style it adopted. Marchers joined picket lines and even entered factories where sackings were being threatened in order to encourage workers to fight. This was a big step forward from the "hunger marches" of the 1920s and 1930s organised by the National Unemployed Workers' Movement, which in other respects provided a model to be imitated; the hunger marchers had found great difficulty in making contact with employed trade unionists and scarcely ever entered workplaces.

The success of the first march was shown by the fact the final rally in the Albert Hall was attended by some 5,500 people. It was the first time an IS initiative had filled such a large venue. Cliff took great delight in attending and during the applause could be seen "punching the air and screaming 'Black and white unite and fight!'".[196]

As the march entered London it had been attacked by police and 44 arrests were made. Cliff took a personal interest in those arrested. Seven of those facing the most serious charges and likely to be jailed were invited to Cliff and Chanie's home for dinner before the trial for a "Last Supper".[197] A number of marchers were sentenced to imprisonment, but the campaign against the repression provided an important focus for the Right to Work in the coming months. The most serious charges, against campaign secretary John Deason, were dropped on the second day of the trial because of inadequate police evidence. Right to Work supporters who had gathered to picket the Old Bailey in support of Deason celebrated the acquittal by travelling to the Grunwick factory to stage what was to be the first mass picket there. One struggle fired another.

Marches continued over the next six years, and while they never made the same impact as the hunger marches of the 1930s, they did provide a focus for the continuing struggle against unemployment, and offered a field of activity for unemployed comrades who were unable to participate in trade union work.* The campaign fitted into Cliff's strategy of a turn towards militant young workers without traditions and organisational experience. The way in which the marches provided an opportunity for campaigning and fund-raising among organised workers showed that at this point it was the young workers who were giving a lead to the "experienced militants" and not the other way round.

Critics of the campaign called it "ultra-left". (The decision to hold it was one of the issues taken up by the IS Opposition at the time of the split; it was dismissed as "yet another get rich quick scheme".[198]) Undoubtedly there were ultra-left attitudes and slogans coming from some of the young marchers. But the willingness to fight contrasted sharply with the passivity of much of the rest of the left.

Roger Kline, a close ally of Cliff's in the 1973 conflict, decided at the time of the Right to Work Campaign that Cliff was putting the interests of the IS ahead of the needs of the broader movement. He discussed the matter amicably with Cliff, but when he spoke of leaving Cliff warned him, "It's cold out there." Cliff expected him to move to the right and was surprised, meeting him on a train a couple of years later, to learn that Kline had in fact moved left and joined the libertarian Marxist group Big Flame.[199] Another who left in 1976 was Richard Hyman. He believed Cliff was increasingly surrounded by yes-men and hatchet men; he was also developing a critique of Cliff's analysis of the rank and file and the trade union bureaucracy.[200]

The other major initiative of 1976 was less successful. In the autumn of 1976 the CC decided that the IS should begin to contest parliamentary by-elections. In the conditions of recession (Callaghan had now replaced Wilson as prime minister) and repeated spending cuts on the orders of the International Monetary Fund, the Labour government was becoming increasingly unpopular. Some of the discontent was reflected in electoral support for the racist National

---

* One indication of their impact on popular consciousness was a visit to Eton by the Right to Work marchers. *Socialist Worker* (17 June 1978) reported marchers pogoing through the streets of Eton to the sound of punk band Crisis, and presenting a giant silver spoon to the Eton Head Boy. These events were an inspiration for the Jam's "Eton Rifles", which reached number three in the charts (See J Wilson, "Chasing the blues away" (interview with Paul Weller), *New Statesman*, 15 May 2008).

Front. Electoral campaigns were also seen as a way of recruiting new members. Cliff was particularly enthusiastic for the electoral turn; Hallas was much more cautious. Cliff relentlessly argued his case and carried the organisation.[201]

The first seats chosen, in November 1976, were Walsall North (the constituency vacated by Labour MP John Stonehouse, who had faked his own death in a financial swindle), and Newcastle Central. The results were modest: 2 percent of the poll in Newcastle, and 1.6 percent in Walsall (more than the CP had got in that seat in October 1974). Fifty-six recruits joined the IS during the election campaigns,[202] but it proved difficult to maintain branches built around an election campaign. In Walsall, where there had been no real organisation on the ground prior to the election, most of the new members were quickly lost.[203]

A total of eight by-elections were contested, all with meagre results. By early 1978 it was apparent that the electoral strategy had been unsuccessful. The original intention of standing some 60 candidates in the general election was dropped, and it was eventually agreed not to stand any candidates at all.

Cliff had been one of the most enthusiastic advocates of the electoral strategy, but eventually he was obliged to face reality[204] and did so more quickly than other leading comrades. A document signed by Cliff and other CC members (and to judge from the style, drafted by him), stated:

> It is one thing to put a candidate or two every couple of months. Another thing to put 30-50 candidates at one go. The latter could just break our backs.[205]

The reason for the failure was twofold. Other left groups were standing candidates and there was a failure on all sides to agree not to stand against each other. So there were sometimes two and, on one occasion (Lambeth Central in 1978), three revolutionary socialist candidates in the same election. Voters could not be bothered to disentangle the differences between them.

More importantly, although Labour was doing badly in electoral terms, there was no substantial body of Labour support willing to break away to the left. Again the resilience of reformism had been underestimated. Cliff's long-term analysis of the historical decay of reformism was certainly valid, but in the short term it did not produce the anticipated results. Cliff's warning from 1969 was proved correct: "A declining interest in the traditional reformist organisations...does not mean the *overcoming* of reformist ideology".[206]

There were problems too with the trade union strategy. Shaun Doherty, editor of the teachers' paper *Rank and File*, had discussions with Cliff in the 1976-77 period; the teachers' rank and file group was already beginning to decline and was in danger of being no more than a front for the IS. Although Cliff was not yet using the term "downturn", he recognised that the movement had passed its zenith, and discussed frankly with Doherty the difficulties the movement now faced,[207] although he expected a revival of industrial struggle in the not too distant future.

At the end of 1976 it was decided to rename the organisation the Socialist Workers Party. There was some debate about what the new name should be. According to one account there was "a CC majority in favour of changing the name of the new party to 'the Socialist Party' on the grounds that the name SWP would represent a barrier to thousands of new potential recruits. Fortunately they could only muster a handful of votes among the delegates [to the December 1976 party council which made the decision]."[208] Cliff, who at this time still had an optimistic perspective for the future, was one of those who favoured the name Socialist Party, but he was defeated.[209] There was also the point that with a few strokes of a felt pen the graffiti NF (National Front) could be transformed into S\NF$^)$ = SWP.

The new name was a recognition of a change which had taken place over the preceding years rather than the announcement of a new strategy. With the abandonment of the Labour Party, the emphasis on rapid recruitment and the move to a more interventionist role through the Right to Work Campaign and the election candidacies, the IS was already functioning as a party. It made sense for the organisation to have a name which acknowledged this. As Cliff put it, "In the course of the last year, our organisation has become a party." He immediately added the necessity to beware of "illusions of grandeur", pointing out that "we are still in the fourth division".[210] In a phrase Cliff sometimes used around this time to draw out the contrast between the enormous tasks and the modest size of the organisation, the SWP was "the smallest mass party in the world".[211]

In an article in *Socialist Worker* Cliff explained the logic of the new name.[212] The SWP was now capable of electoral results at least as good as the CP's, and the November 1976 Right to Work Conference was bigger than recent conferences of the CP-led Liaison Committee for the Defence of Trade Unions. The CP was now seriously racked by disputes between Moscow loyalists and Eurocommunists (who wanted independence from Moscow and an openly social democratic orientation). There was a real possibility that the IS could replace the CP as the main left focus within the labour movement. Yet the ideas of the CP and the Labour left were still much stronger than those of the revolutionary current.

He noted that in the first two years of Labour government IS membership had fallen from 3,300 members to around 2,650. But in the previous seven months a thousand new members had joined. Cliff was preoccupied with numbers – because he knew from bitter experience that the best programme in the world was worthless without the forces able to fight for it. A substantial membership was necessary in order that rapid growth could take place in a crisis:

> If, when the revolutionary crisis comes to Britain, we have 40,000 members, there is no question that we can grow to 400,000 or perhaps half a million.
>
> If, on the other hand, the revolutionary organisation has only a few thousand members, it is even possible that the party appears as irrelevant and does not grow at all. A certain size *is* necessary for take-off.

All this was predicated on a situation of developing crisis. As he prophesied, "There is no doubt that in a few years' time, perhaps six, perhaps eight, perhaps ten, Britain will face a level of unemployment of three or four millions." In that situation there would be a choice between revolutionary socialism and "the fascist solution: 'If there are three million unemployed get rid of black workers, the Irish and the Jews'."

This was far from implausible. In fact official unemployment figures rose to over three million, for the first time since the 1930s, within just five years. The NF, though still relatively small, was enjoying greater electoral success than the IS/SWP, and had a dangerous presence on the streets in some areas. Cliff did not yet foresee a rather different right-wing outcome under Thatcher.

He was concerned to avoid any danger of triumphalism. Proclaiming the party was a recognition of a difficult task ahead, not a claim of what had already been achieved. He warned against making promises that could not be delivered, with an image he used frequently in speeches:

> Suppose I was in the business of making promises I couldn't deliver. I'd promise my child a gold-plated Rolls Royce in 1999. It is a safe promise.
>
> First I'll probably be dead by 1999. If not he'll probably forget my promise by then. And if those two things don't work, I'll have 22 years to think of excuses.

Cliff concluded with a stark warning about the dangers of elitism in the party and the labour movement. He valued youthful revolt more than experience, and warned members not to believe that just because they were in the party they were somehow superior to the workers outside. It was one of the most powerful statements of his vision, following directly from his writings on Rosa Luxemburg, his championing of the role of young workers in May 1968 and his efforts to reorient the organisation in 1973-75:

> The present members of our party are not the salt of the earth, the select few. If any elitism exists in our organisation it is necessary to uproot it completely.
>
> Some revolutionaries do suffer from elitist notions. They think of the barricades as follows: In the front row there is an Imperial Father of the Chapel representing craft workers in all their glory. He is wearing his gold chain of office to pay homage. Or is it perhaps to say you have nothing to lose but your chains.
>
> And then there are some representatives of section one of the Engineering Union.
>
> Only then if there is enough room in the street they would in their generosity allow some blacks, a few women and some youth – if they know their place, that is.
>
> Revolution has nothing at all to do with this hierarchical concept.
>
> Anyone who is in any doubt about it has no need to look further than the boys and girls of Soweto.*

---

* Soweto (South Western Township), an urban area of Johannesburg, was the scene of a rising against the apartheid regime in June 1976, described by Chanie's old comrade Baruch Hirson in his book *Year of Fire, Year of Ash*, London, 1979.

The SWP was launched with a booklet by Paul Foot entitled *Why You Should Be a Socialist – The Case for the Socialist Workers Party*. In the early months of 1977 the SWP launched a nationwide series of meetings to build the party under the title "The Case for Socialism". In the seven weeks from 26 January to 15 March Cliff addressed no fewer than 19 meetings – in Walsall, Dudley, Wolverhampton, Bristol, Sheffield, Bradford, Huddersfield, York, Portsmouth, Southampton, Oxford, Cambridge, Bedford, Reading, Tower Hamlets, Southall and Loughborough, and London meetings for civil servants and hospital workers.[213]

Most members participated enthusiastically in the party-building. There was, however, some dissent. One of Cliff's oldest associates, Peter Sedgwick, a brilliant writer but frequently an independent-minded and dissident member, refused to follow the move to the SWP, and wrote a sharp polemic against the style of leadership being offered by Cliff and the CC.

Stressing, against Cliff's analysis, that the present period was actually a difficult one for socialists, Sedgwick argued that the whole electoral strategy would merely expose the organisation's weakness:

> How easy it is in these circumstances to shoot off-course, trusting to the "intuition" which Comrade Cliff has celebrated in the life of Lenin but which is, at its worst, impressionism mingled with emotion.

He condemned the whole strategy of proclaiming the party:

> Since we cannot, in the present bad political climate, change class reality very much, the conclusion is drawn that we have to perform changes on the name of IS itself, in the delusion that this is some step towards the actual construction of a revolutionary socialist workers' party. If the CC decided that we should walk around with our bottoms painted bright green, doubtless it would have an electrifying effect on the morale of our membership (for a short time at least)... International Socialists are not yet a Socialist Workers Party, and will not get one whit nearer to that position in the working class by some fancy rallying and pseudo-inauguration. Forward with the IS![214]

It was splendid polemic, but somewhat unfair to Cliff. There were serious problems in the situation, but also real possibilities, and Cliff's merit was that he always stressed the opportunities available to be grasped. Rapid recruitment, even if many of the new members were not consolidated, showed that there was a layer of people open to revolutionary ideas. If the big battalions in the industrial struggle were temporarily quiescent, there was an important strike at Grunwick.* Above all there was the anti-fascist struggle. During 1977 there were three major NF mobilisations, at Wood Green, Lewisham and Manchester, and on each occasion the SWP played a large part in building the counter-demonstrations. Sedgwick was quite right about the electoral strategy, but it is easier to predict failure than point the way to success.

Another loss in this period was Mike Kidron, who dropped out so discreetly that it is hard to know exactly when he left. Nothing was more alien to Kidron's temperament than a noisy departure followed by denunciation of former comrades. In July 1977 he contributed an article to the 100th issue of *International Socialism*, whose founding editor he had been. Entitled "Two Insights Don't Make a Theory",[215] it was a critical assessment of the body of theory he and Cliff had developed over the preceding two decades. In effect it was his statement of resignation.

He paid tribute to Cliff's originality and insight in developing the theory of state capitalism: "He powerfully reasserted the prime inspiration of the socialist movement – that there can be no civilised future unless workers fight their way into becoming the subject of history." But he argued that the world had now reached a point where state capitalism was a description of the whole system and not just of the Eastern Bloc. The new world system required further study. Kidron dismissed as inadequate the theory of the permanent arms economy which he had done so much to develop.

Cliff must have profoundly disagreed with this. For him, since his abandonment of his book on the collectivisation of agriculture in favour of the incomes policy book, the need of the time had been for putting theory into practice through organisation. What most shocked Cliff was Kidron's argument that trade union struggle was increasingly irrelevant to the socialist struggle:

> If trade unions neither reflect the extent and composition of the working class nor fulfil their earlier role as independent representatives of

---

* The mass pickets at Grunwick caused real anxiety to prime minister Callaghan, who told a meeting at Chequers in June 1977, "If things continue on the present basis there could well be fatalities and in circumstances which might be in danger of bringing the government down." (C Andrew, *The Defence of the Realm*, p664)

working class interests, a political strategy structured around them is bound to fail. Yet that is what so much of our practice does: the issues we stress in our propaganda and agitation are the narrow defensive issues selected by the elite of the trade union world to which we add a gloss of revolutionary interpretation, not the problems created for the whole of the working class by its suicidal bondage to state capitalism.

Kidron came to the dismissive conclusion that:

> without theory no organisation can do more than ride the tides of working class consciousness, which might be exhilarating as sport but is irrelevant as revolutionary politics.*

The break with Kidron was a serious one for Cliff. For years in the 1950s and 1960s they had formed an intellectual partnership, and Kidron had influenced some of his most innovative thinking. Kidron was the bolder thinker of the two, less bound by the orthodoxies of Marxism or Trotskyism. For that very reason he lacked Cliff's unremitting commitment to revolutionary organisation.

Nigel Harris, who had been politically close to Kidron, thinks that Kidron always saw organisation as less important than ideas. He thought in terms of communists scattered throughout the movement, but not organisationally linked. After his break with Cliff, Kidron tried to pursue the same goal with Pluto Press.[216]

There was never any open polemic, but there was now a real break between the two men, though no hostility on Cliff's part. Indeed, he always spoke of Kidron with great respect[217] although Cliff, a shy man, felt ill at ease in Kidron's social circle.[218] Later he commented on Kidron's subsequent development, parodying Marx, "social consciousness is determined by the people you surround yourself with".[219] They met only for family occasions and there was little conversation between them – though in any case Cliff spoke little at such times, having no capacity for small talk.[220]

With the disappearance of Kidron, and Cliff preoccupied with *Lenin* and the day-to-day running of the organisation, Chris Harman came to occupy an increasingly important leadership role. His theoretical contribution was substantial and while it built on Cliff's work it made significant developments. Already his article "How the Revolution was Lost"[221] had dealt with the historical

---

* I recall Cliff citing this sentence with contemptuous fury; it was the day of one of the mass pickets at Grunwick.

origins of state capitalism, something largely missing from Cliff's account. His first book, *Bureaucracy and Revolution in Eastern Europe*,[222] had described the fightback by workers in Eastern Europe. He went on to write copiously on a range of subjects and, thanks to his special interest in student work, played a vital part in educating a new generation of party activists.

In the summer of 1977 the first "Marxism" event took place in the rather squalid basement of the Polytechnic of North London in Kentish Town. The idea was lifted from the CP's Communist University of London, and consisted of a week of meetings on a wide range of political, theoretical and cultural topics. The initiative and organisation had come from the SWP student committee (with strong encouragement from Chris Harman), and initially the event was aimed primarily at students.

Though Cliff played no part in initiating the event, he recognised the importance of activity among students[223] and was naturally one of the main speakers, addressing meetings on "Bolshevism, Menshevism, Lenin, Trotsky, Martov", "Lenin as a Philosopher" and "Portugal and the Revolutions of the West". Over the next few years Marxism developed from being a student event to being the SWP's main public showcase. (Meanwhile the Communist University of London declined into esoteric academicism and collapsed under the tensions of internal conflict.) Cliff spoke at every Marxism until his death.

In the late 1970s Cliff prepared another application for British citizenship. He was supported by Labour MPs Stan Newens, Eric Heffer and Norman Buchan,[224] and, as in 1964, by Michael Foot, who had become deputy leader of the Labour Party and Leader of the House of Commons. According to Cliff's own account, he was informed by a worker on the *Daily Mail* that the paper had got hold of the story, and was going to use it to attack Foot. (In 1977 the *Mail* had published an exposé of the SWP entitled "Their target is chaos".[225]) However, no story appeared. Cliff believed that Foot had used a D-Notice to prevent publication.[226]

What exactly happened is hard to disentangle. The *Daily Mail* has no archives relating to the matter,[227] and when approached in 2005 Michael Foot remembered "a whole series of quarrels with the *Daily Mail* on this subject and a number of others", but no details of this particular question.[228] There is no record of any such

D-Notice being issued, but some files from this period were destroyed in 1999. I am informed by the current Secretary of the Defence, Press and Broadcasting Advisory Committee that "it is highly improbable that any D-Notice guidance was sought, let alone issued, on this case" since this would not have been an appropriate use of a D-Notice.[229]

It was not just Foot's personal reputation that was at stake. At the time he was playing a key role propping up the Callaghan government, which no longer had a majority, and providing a left face for Callaghan's right-wing policies. Whether or not the formal D-Notice procedure was used, Foot could count on powerful allies to help him intimidate the *Mail*. But as Cliff wryly observed, Foot was powerful enough to cover his own back, but not strong enough to persuade the British state machine to grant citizenship to Cliff, who would die stateless.

In the course of 1977 the focus of SWP activity had switched towards anti-racism. In August the National Front organised a march through Lewisham, an area of London with a large black population. The SWP played a major role in building a counter-demonstration. There was street fighting, with the police protecting the fascists, but the National Front suffered a serious humiliation. Cliff was on holiday, but on the day of the demonstration he did not go to the beach but stayed watching television all day for the latest news.[230] The Nazis themselves were in no doubt about who had been responsible for their setback. At the end of August the Cotton's Gardens warehouse, which had been the IS/SWP headquarters since 1969, was petrol-bombed and partly destroyed.[231]

Cliff always found time for individual comrades. One member facing imprisonment after Lewisham was invited to meet Cliff. In the hour they spent talking Cliff did not waste a single minute on general expressions of sympathy: he immediately focused on the specific problems of organising in prison, based on his own experience in Palestine. When the comrade got to jail he faced serious physical threats and found Cliff's advice of great value.[232]

In October the fascists attempted to march in Manchester. A small demonstration was possible only with the protection of 9,500 police and despite secrecy and police protection the fascists were heavily outnumbered.[233]

Since the early 1960s the IS/SWP had advocated physical

confrontation with fascists.* The strategy had a real impact in the campaign against the NF. Over the previous couple of years the NF had enjoyed a small but significant electoral success; in May 1977 it won almost 250,000 votes in local elections across the country.[234] If the NF had transformed that passive support into active participation, it would have been a serious threat to the black population and eventually to the labour movement. Physical confrontation meant that only the most brutish thugs continued to march and the size of NF demonstrations fell rapidly.

This was not how the political mainstream saw it. In the weeks after Lewisham the SWP took a lot of stick for its role. Journalist Hugo Young described the SWP as "a forerunner of the forces of darkness", while the *Daily Mirror* said the SWP was "as bad as the National Front". Various Labour MPs accused the SWP of "red fascism", while Michael Foot, now deputy prime minister, declared, "You don't stop the Nazis by throwing bottles or bashing the police. The most ineffective way of fighting the fascists is to behave like them".[235]

In 1978 Richard Clutterbuck, an academic "expert" on political violence, assessed the threat posed by the SWP:

> They were not a serious political force in 1971-7, but they were a disruptive one and took part in some of the worst public disorders of the century... In 1976 they achieved what they had so long desired: a substantial working class involvement. They did this by recruiting immigrant and unemployed workers, who had good reason to be bitterly disgruntled with society and had time on their hands.[236]

All publicity is good publicity and this minor witch-hunt raised the SWP's profile. But the threat from the far right needed more than mere physical confrontation. In the summer of 1977 negotiations began to establish the Anti Nazi League (ANL).[237] This succeeded in establishing a broad anti-fascist organisation involving a number of prominent sportspersons, musicians and intellectuals as well as leading figures from the Labour Party such as Neil

---

* See the editorial (written by Mike Kidron) "Fists Against Fascists", *International Socialism* 10 (Autumn 1962).

Kinnock and Peter Hain.* Jim Nichol and Paul Holborow played the leading role in the process, but it was discussed thoroughly with Cliff,[238] who was supportive of the initiative while some other members of the CC were rather lukewarm. Holborow became secretary; while Cliff's political role was important, Holborow was left to operate on his own.[239] Likewise Jack Robertson, then working at the centre, recalls that Cliff gave comrades working in the ANL and Rock Against Racism (RAR) their head, trusted them and let them get on with the activity.[240]

The ANL took off rapidly, and involved a wide range of activities, mobilising the imagination and creativity of members. The high-points of 1978 were two carnivals, in Victoria Park and Brockwell Park, where anti-racist demonstrations were combined with huge open-air concerts featuring popular musicians, especially proponents of punk rock. The Clash were the main attraction at the first carnival.

The musical input to the ANL came from RAR, which had been founded in 1976 in protest at openly pro-racist statements by Eric Clapton and pro-fascist remarks by David Bowie.[241] This was a milieu very remote from Cliff, who had no musical tastes of any sort, and at 61 was too old to be enthused by punk. But when the Sex Pistols caused a major scandal with their record "God Save the Queen", Cliff's immediate response was, "Johnny Rotten is fantastic." He may not have actually heard the record, but he was impressed by the feeling of rebellion and sensed that revolutionaries ought to side with it. Yet the punk aesthetic remained totally alien to him. Red Saunders took a copy of *Temporary Hoarding*, the RAR paper, to show to Cliff, who began by giving him a "bollocking" about being overweight. When Cliff looked at the artwork he found it incomprehensible and thought it must be upside down.[242]

The SWP members who played a key role in founding RAR, Roger Huddle and Dave Widgery, alongside Red Saunders, who was not a party member but worked closely with the SWP,

---

* The ANL is sometimes described as being a "Popular Front", with the suggestion that the SWP had abandoned its Trotskyist principles. This is a misunderstanding. The Popular Fronts of the 1930s involved alliances with the *political organisations* of the bourgeoisie. The ANL contained people from a range of political positions, including some who were undoubtedly wealthy, but not the direct political representatives of the ruling class.

acknowledged Cliff as a key influence on their political formation. For Huddle the essence of RAR was unity against the common enemy, something he had taken from Cliff. Cliff never interfered with RAR or tried to tell those running it what they should be doing.[243] Widgery loved Cliff and was always talking about him, though he was not uncritical; sometimes he would say Cliff had gone bonkers, but shortly afterwards would declare he was brilliant. Saunders thinks that the IS attracted the best of the 1968 generation through its politics – "Neither Washington nor Moscow" – but also through the accessibility of its publications; it used ordinary language rather than the jargon of other far-left groups. It was recruits from 1968 who built the ANL and RAR.[244]

According to Huddle, "If Cliff had to book the music for the carnival, he would have booked the Bach string quartet, and no one else".[245] This is perhaps unfair; Cliff would certainly have handed the job over to Chanie – who would have booked the Bach string quartet. But though he was enthusiastic about the carnival, Cliff did not attend.[246] *

Immediately after the carnival Cliff wrote an article for *Socialist Worker* on the importance of linking the anti-racist struggle to the industrial struggle:

> In every workplace a branch of the ANL should be built.
>
> These branches should carry wide propaganda in their own workplaces, leaflet neighbouring workplaces, bring the anti-Nazi message to the trade unions to which the workers belong, organise mass leafleting of football grounds and so on.[247]

There is no doubt that it was the SWP initiative which was crucial in building the ANL. As the SWP's rivals and frequent critics in the IMG put it, "The Anti-Nazi League…was an initiative undertaken and launched by the comrades of the Socialist Workers Party… It would be crass sectarianism to try and underplay this fact".[248] Some of the party's critics accused it of simply using the ANL as a front organisation, the main purpose of which was to build the SWP. The reality is rather different. The Labour Party probably recruited more members out of the ANL than the SWP did – as Neil Kinnock put it, "The ANL performs a very important

---

* Contrary to the claim by Dave Renton (D Renton, *When We Touched the Sky*, p99).

function for the Labour Party".[249] For Labour politicians like Kinnock – who won the Labour leadership from the left in order to lead from the right – or Peter Hain, who was a minister in the government of Tony Blair, the ANL was an important means of establishing their left credentials. Despite Cliff's constant strictures on the need to build the party, it is arguable that the SWP actually underestimated the importance of party-building in the ANL period.

The strength of the ANL was its ability to draw together a wide range of participants. While Cliff wholeheartedly supported this breadth, on occasion he felt things were going too far. When the suggestion was raised that the ANL should reclaim 11 November as an anti-Nazi day, Cliff was fiercely hostile, seeing Remembrance Day as a celebration of British imperialism.[250]

The real achievement of the ANL was in stopping the rise of the far right. By the end of 1978 the NF had passed its peak electorally and was increasingly inhibited from demonstrating on the streets or even holding public meetings. In the 1979 general election the NF vote fell sharply.[251] The experience of other Western European countries showed that this was not inevitable. If the NF had reached a certain take-off point, it would have begun to establish itself in the political mainstream, as the Front National in France was to do a decade later.* That in turn would have made racist discourse respectable, and encouraged physical attacks on the black community. More than at any other time, the SWP made an impact on the course of British history.†

It was in the context of the Anti Nazi League that Cliff first wrote about gay oppression. The Gay Liberation Front had been formed in Britain in 1970, but it had made little impact on the IS. There was undoubtedly mild homophobia among many members, including some of the leadership. There was also a reluctance to challenge

---

* For a study of the rise of the French far right in the 1980s, and the relative failure of the left to block it, see P Fysh and J Wolfreys, *The Politics of Racism in France*, Basingstoke, 1998.

† For a range of assessments of the impact the ANL had on British political life, from Darcus Howe who claimed that ANL had created an atmosphere in which his youngest child could grow up "black and at ease", to Martin Webster, who admitted that the ANL "had made it impossible to get NF members on to the streets, had dashed recruitment and cut away at their vote", see D Renton, *When We Touched the Sky*, pp178-180).

prejudices widespread among many workers on what was seen as a "secondary" question.*

In 1973 the national committee agreed a document (drafted by Roger Protz) which strongly rejected prejudice against homosexuals, but resolved that members should withdraw from work in the Gay Liberation Front (the main gay organisation at the time).[252]

However, after extensive discussion, the 1976 conference reversed its position. *Socialist Worker* added to its regular "Where We Stand" column the words "We are for an end to all forms of discrimination against homosexuals", and a new IS Gay Group was established.

Cliff, though without any personal prejudice, had inherited attitudes from an earlier phase of the movement's history. Until 1967 homosexuality had been illegal in Britain and homosexuals were often seen as a security risk, being liable to blackmail. In the 1960s Cliff had stated[253] that he did not think homosexuals should be admitted to the IS for this reason.†

In the early 1970s Cliff had taken a rather dismissive attitude, arguing that there were many forms of suffering in the world, and no reason to give particular attention to that of homosexuals.[254] With the growth of the gay movement, he recognised the need to reconsider his position. He invited John Lindsay to his house for a discussion. Lindsay was a relatively new member of the party, active in the gay movement; he had joined the IS intending to argue on the gay question and expecting an uphill battle.

The meeting lasted for around eight hours. Lindsay did most of the talking, and Cliff listened carefully, showing that he took the argument seriously, for he was not always a patient man in such discussions. Lindsay argued his case on the basis of alienation and reification, pointing to the way that in capitalism a relationship between two people takes on the form of a commodity.[255]

Following this Cliff wrote an article for *Socialist Worker* called "Why socialists must support the gays",[256] which later appeared as the preface to the pamphlet *The Word is Gay*.[257] This began by

---

* For a critical account of IS attitudes in the early 1970s by an ex-member, see B Cant, "A Grim Tale: The IS Gay Group 1972-1975", *Gay Left* No 3, Autumn 1976.

† I know of no case where such a restriction was actually enforced, but also of no case where an IS member came out as gay.

arguing that socialists must fight all forms of oppression:

> In class-infested society there is oppressor and oppressed in all walks of life. Employer oppresses employee; man oppresses woman; white oppresses black; old oppresses young; heterosexual oppresses homosexual.
>
> The true socialist is able to overcome all these divisions. An engineering worker who can only identify with other engineering workers may be a good trade unionist but he has not proved himself to be a socialist. A socialist has to be able to identify with the struggles of all oppressed groups.

He then reiterated what he had been arguing for some time about hierarchy in the socialist movement; gay oppression was now integrated with the rest of his argument about elitism:

> It is as though the socialist revolution will be led by the Father of the Chapel in the print union, the NGA working on Fleet Street. Second in command will be an AUEW Convenor Section 1 from the toolroom in a big car factory. The lieutenants of the revolution will all be forty-year-old white male shop stewards.
>
> If there is enough space then we'll allow blacks and women and gays to take part – providing they stand quietly at the back!
>
> A lot of socialists still have difficulty believing that gays will be taking part in the revolution at all.
>
> *On the contrary we should look forward now to the first leader of the London workers' council being a 19-year-old black gay woman!*

He went on to argue that oppression engendered oppression. The Nazis sent gays to concentration camps, yet tens of thousands of gays supported Hitler. Being a Nazi gave an oppressed gay a sense of power. And so he concluded:

> For any oppressed group to fight back there is need for *hope*.
>
> If you are on the way *down* you feel despair. You look for a victim to kick.
>
> If you are on the way *up* you look for a back to pat.
>
> That's why only by building a socialist movement can you unite workers with oppressed blacks, women and gays.

It was a pertinent argument, linking gay oppression, the ANL and class struggle.

Around this time Cliff spoke to a fringe meeting in central London at the annual Gay Liberation Front march (later Gay Pride). About 30 or 40 people, many of them non-members, attended. Cliff spoke on the question of gay oppression and was well received.[258] One man stood up and told Cliff that gays didn't need him. Cliff responded by reminding him that in the Chilean coup of 1973 gays had been castrated in the stadium in Santiago.[259]

John Lindsay and gay comrades still faced incomprehension and even hostility from other leading members. But over the next few years opposition to gay oppression was taken up more widely in the party and incorporated into trade union work and the Right to Work Campaign. The uphill struggle had not been so bad as Lindsay had originally expected.[260]

The success of anti-fascist activity was accompanied by a far less cheerful situation in the industrial struggle. In the autumn of 1977 there was an all-out strike by firefighters. On 26 November a national Rank and File Conference in Manchester was attended by more than 500 delegates from 200 trade union organisations.[261] But though the firefighters' strike dominated the conference, it was unable to deliver any concrete solidarity. This failure angered Cliff (who said he had been forced to start smoking again during the conference), and probably contributed to his rethinking of the party's perspective.[262]

The experience of Lewisham and the ANL had a major impact inside the party. There were growing tensions inside the CC about perspectives. After Lewisham Steve Jefferys had argued that the membership could be doubled by Christmas 1977. This spilled over into a dispute about *Socialist Worker*.[263] The anti-fascist campaigning, together with the relative absence of industrial struggle, led to a decision to reorient *Socialist Worker* to the new audience emerging from the ANL. The editor, Chris Harman (who had taken over from Paul Foot in 1975), relinquished the post and was replaced by Jim Nichol. In February it was announced that "*Socialist Worker* is to be relaunched as an improved, livelier paper". The aim was to open the paper out to "reach and involve thousands more people who are not members of the *Socialist Workers Party*". A new team of journalists was announced; no editor was named but the list did not include Chris Harman, the editor up to that point.[264]

The new paper was often referred to as the "punk paper", but while there was extensive coverage of music, other features aimed beyond the punk milieu, notably regular sports and television coverage, and a serial story *The Faradays*. Perhaps the most striking example of the new approach was the issue produced for the football World Cup in Argentina. The front-page headline – "ENJOY THE GOALS – BUT REMEMBER THE JAILS" – referred to the repressive regime in Argentina, but while this theme was developed in the paper, there were also a couple of pages devoted to detailed apolitical coverage of the football.[265] The claim was that over the previous year or so the paper had become "boring" and "predictable", and that it should now be used to reach a new periphery.

Critics of the new paper alleged that the paper was giving insufficient attention to the industrial struggle; that important political questions were being oversimplified so much that the political content of the paper was diluted; and that the paper was simply reflecting and enthusing about the ANL, rather than arguing for the SWP's distinctive politics within that milieu.[266]

Cliff was sympathetic to the new orientation of the paper. At the same time he was keen to ensure that it did not stray from the primacy of the industrial struggle. During the first months of the new paper he made several contributions, all focused on workplace struggle as though he were gently bending the stick back again.

In March he wrote a piece on the impact of Labour's incomes policy, the dangers of productivity deals and predicted that the "bitterness, anger and frustration of workers" would lead to a sharp rise in struggle.[267] This was followed by a discussion of strategy towards pay differentials, urging socialists "to fight for the erosion of differentials and to oppose all craftism".[268] A third article dealt with the fight against redundancies in the steel industry.[269]

The issue immediately before the first ANL carnival was mainly devoted to material relevant to the anti-Nazi struggle. But Cliff wrote a full page devoted to a detailed examination of the fight against redundancies caused by the closure of two Thorns factories in Bradford. He urged the workers to occupy, and raised the stakes further by suggesting that the government should provide all pensioners with free colour television sets. "This would give workers years of work".[270] In June he wrote a more general piece on the fight against unemployment, arguing that factory occupations were the key to successful resistance.[271]

Cliff kept a keen eye on the content of the paper. When Martin Tomkinson wrote an article on how Muhammad Ali's career had been affected by racism and commercialism, Cliff sent a letter to the editor stressing that "Ali's decision to join the Black Muslims was really crucial to his political development", since this showed that "he was willing to defy completely the white American capitalist establishment". [272] For Cliff organisation was paramount.

The new paper was not popular in the party, and sales suffered a serious setback.[273] The paid sale in November 1978 was only 14,000, compared with 18,750 in November 1974.[274] However, the issue for the ANL carnival, with a full-colour front cover, had the second highest ever sale of 27,000. The debate over the paper carried on for some time, including an extensive discussion at the SWP conference that summer, which by a large majority passed a resolution pointing to the dangers of "diluting our politics" and the need to keep an "interventionist edge" with greater emphasis on industrial reports and SWP activities.[275] The CC attempted to implement the resolution by retaining the existing journalists but appointing Chris Harman political editor.[276] This proved unacceptable to the four writers who had been especially associated with the new line on the paper (Paul Foot, Jim Nichol, Laurie Flynn and Peter Marsden), and at the end of July they resigned as full-time journalists.[277] This created a difficult situation, with most of the burden falling on John Hodgman, who complained:

> The decline in commitment, enthusiasm and morale was very marked, with some of the other journalists talking about getting out as soon as possible.[278]

Chris Harman was now reappointed editor by the CC. But Cliff was determined to get his way:[*]

> It was then agreed that there would be a moratorium for six months on the argument about the direction of the paper to give Chris a chance to carry the conference line.

This last agreement turned out not to be worth the paper it was written on. On the day before Chris was due to start as editor, Cliff circulated

---

[*] The account is by Steve Jefferys, a participant in the events.

amongst the editorial staff [a document which] pretends to be a mere summary of an "opinion poll" about SW [*Socialist Worker*] conducted on Merseyside. But this was the first time Cliff had ever carried out such an exercise, and its appearance at that particular point in time was no accident. It was intended to strengthen the resolve of some of the editorial staff to ignore the conference decision.

Cliff wrote, "The decision of conference to include in every issue of the paper four pages on industry was probably taken in the same spirit as the decision to put up parliamentary candidates in every major area... *Such an attitude is obviously not serious and not responsible* (my emphasis [SJ])."

The following day Chris attended his first editorial meeting to find the whole staff confident that they had Cliff's backing against Chris over any changes he might suggest in line with conference policy... Through no fault of Chris's the atmosphere was poisoned. Anything Chris did or said could be construed as an attack on the true conception of the paper as argued by Jim, Paul, Laurie and endorsed by Cliff.[279]

Cliff's manoeuvre succeeded. Harman had undertaken discussions with a number of people about the paper, but when he came in to work the following Monday he was told he was out of touch.[280] The journalists demanded Harman's removal and Cliff and the CC backed them, with Harman, Callinicos, Jefferys and Jack Robertson voting against.[281]

Harman's response was remarkably philosophical. He found the situation "disturbing", but the positive side of this quarrel with Cliff – from whom he had learnt so much over the years – was that he now resolved to do what was necessary to build the party without going to Allerton Road twice a week. He had to think for himself.[282]

There was now a serious danger that the organisation could tear itself to pieces with an internal dispute. There was a deep antagonism between Cliff and Jefferys, and if Jefferys and Harman had responded with the same ruthlessness shown by Cliff, the conflict would have escalated dangerously.[283] Paul Foot recalled later that, "confused by the situation and reluctant to admit the truth, we turned on each other and came close to tearing the whole organisation apart".[284]

Cliff bore some of the responsibility for the way the dispute had developed. But now he realised that he himself was the only person in the party with the prestige to prevent a serious split. He had written and spoken a great deal over the past few years about the role of *Socialist Worker*; now he had the chance to put his money where his mouth was. Moreover, while he favoured a popular paper reaching out to a broader audience, he was also committed to hard politics and the centrality of the industrial struggle. He was therefore well placed to hold the situation together. What was more problematic was whether Cliff, with his other roles in the organisation, would have the time and energy to devote to the task of editorship.

In the issue dated 19 August 1978 Cliff announced himself editor (his deputy was John Hodgman) with a short piece about strike reports which had a "central role" in the paper. Here Cliff stressed attention to detail and the need to use the paper as an organiser:

> For these reports to be EFFECTIVE a special effort has to be made in SELLING the paper to those workers in dispute.
>
> For this reason we are introducing a new idea. A week or so after a comrade has sent a report to the paper about a strike and it has been published, he/she should send a short notice to us which includes the following information:
>
> Has the Socialist Worker been sold regularly at the workplace prior to the dispute? If so, how many copies were sold?
>
> HOW MANY copies have been sold since the dispute started?
>
> This report should be repeated until the end of the dispute.[285]

Two weeks later he contributed a piece which lamented the fact that many strike reports were written in "a boring fashion":

> You could almost believe they are written according to a standard formula, like painting by numbers, like filling in a form.
>
> Such a report is of hardly any use. Above all, every strike raises the spiritual level, and consciousness, the confidence, the enthusiasm of the workers involved and *this* is the embryo of the struggle for socialism.[286]

In the same issue Cliff gave an example of what he wanted to see with a short piece arguing that British workers should "be proud to learn" from Indian workers:

Transport workers in Britain can learn much from workers elsewhere how to run transport strikes. Ten years ago busworkers in Calcutta in India adopted a completely new strategy.

Instead of stopping the buses, they took them onto the streets as normal. Only they refused to collect the fares!

In other words the busmen offered free travel – which put the passengers firmly on their side. This action made their strike incomparably stronger than simply stopping the buses.

Workers on London's underground could do the same.[287]

In an Internal Bulletin piece written with Jack Robertson Cliff emphasised the need to improve the paper's industrial coverage, while recognising the unevenness of the readership:

> Of course, different readers will be interested in different aspects of the paper. One cannot expect a young unemployed or a young worker who holds a shitty job or is moving from one job to another to care about the industrial pages as much as an experienced active trade unionist. However, whatever part is read, the reader must find it easy to read, interesting and invigorating.[288]

In a number of issues in the autumn of 1978 the paper carried an editorial signed by Cliff. Some of these took up general economic arguments, like "Wages, profits and prices", where he rammed home the point that wage rises do not cause inflation.[289] In another editorial he set out the principles of the united front which underlay the ANL. To refuse to unite against the Nazis with those who do not share our final aims was "sectarianism and elitism of the worst order":

> There's a story about a number of oxen taken to the slaughterhouse. One ox said to his mates, "Let's unite and fight to save ourselves from the slaughterman." He was met with the argument of another ox saying, "The problem is not the slaughterer but the private ownership of cattle." The oxen heeded the "clever" ox and fell one by one under the knife.[290] *

The previous week Cliff showed that it was necessary for a leadership to acknowledge responsibility for its mistakes by personally signing a statement in which the SWP recognised that it had been

---

* The analogy was drawn from Trotsky. See L Trotsky, *The Struggle Against Fascism in Germany*, New York, 1971, p254.

wrong in failing to mobilise enough people to oppose the NF in Brick Lane in east London on the day of the Brockwell Park ANL carnival. While he argued that it was absolutely right for the carnival to go ahead to preserve the unity of the ANL, there had been an organisational failure which meant that not enough anti-fascists had got to Brick Lane in time to confront the NF.[291] *

The paper now regained its balance; it continued its cultural coverage, and had many articles written by workers, but the political and industrial content was strengthened.

But while Cliff had good ideas he showed little interest in the day-to-day running of the paper. Ralph Darlington, who sometimes wrote for the paper, describes him as a "completely and utterly useless" editor.[292] Those who worked with Cliff on the paper are unanimous in considering him a poor editor who would attend editorial board meetings on a Monday, but played no hands-on role whatsoever. He would simply sit in the office reading the daily papers and taking little interest in articles for *Socialist Worker*.[293] It was the journalists who actually ran the paper, but Cliff felt there were too many journalists and was angry when they spent time in the office rather than being out reporting activity.[294] John Rose recalls that Cliff "didn't have a clue about journalism" and was hopeless at the routine of the paper. Some of the journalists called him the "ayatollah". John Rose and Joanna Rollo were left effectively holding the baby.

Cliff himself did not want to keep the job for long and tried to pass on the job to Joanna Rollo, then to John Rose, who became editor in practice and was eventually appointed as such. Arguments about the paper persisted on the CC. Cliff tended to take a "liberal" position, for example favouring contributions from Dave Widgery, although he was completely unpredictable.[295]

Despite his involvement in so many other activities, Cliff remained committed to the importance of the industrial struggle. In December 1978 he published a short pamphlet for Chrysler workers

---

* Paul Holborow was initially in favour of cancelling the carnival and mobilising everyone to confront the Nazis at Brick Lane. Cliff persuaded him that this position was wrong. Holborow was oriented to the milieu of far-left militants, while Cliff saw things from the point of view of the broader support of the ANL, who would attend a carnival but not a physical confrontation. If the carnival had been cancelled the NF would have been able to veto any ANL activity any time they liked (Paul Holborow interview, July 2008).

– *Chrysler Workers: The fight for a future*.[296] This was short – 32 pages with cartoons by Phil Evans which wittily reinforced Cliff's main points – but was a beautiful example of Cliff's ability to integrate theory and practice, the totality of context and the specifics of resistance.

The starting point was the takeover by the French company PSA Peugeot-Citroën of Chrysler's operation in Britain, France and Spain, which would mean a major threat to the jobs of Chrysler workers. Cliff explained this by the pressure for rationalisation in the international car industry which meant only giants would survive, and by the particular problems of the declining British motor industry. He pointed to the "madness" of capitalist logic which meant car firms were increasing investment when there was already overcapacity. He then looked at the weakening of workers' organisation, and quoted rank and file workers on the ill effects of the incorporation of senior stewards into the management structure.

Cliff made a socialist critique of the irrationality of capitalism which produced for profit not for need. "The present car industry can be transformed to produce wheelchairs, safe invalid cars, trucks, tractors, combine harvesters, land movers, diesel engines...anything which millions of people round the world need".[297] But propaganda was not enough; the only way to save jobs was to demand nationalisation, and the best way to achieve that was through factory occupations. The pamphlet ended with detailed recommendations on how to organise an occupation – not spun out of Cliff's skull, but taken from the rank and file newspaper *Carworker*.

Surprisingly, he found time to show another skill, that of editing a book. John Molyneux was having disagreements with Pluto Press about his book *Marxism and the Party*.[298] Cliff was anxious to see the book published and, to resolve the situation, he agreed to edit the book, pruning it drastically to the required length, a job he carried out with great rapidity.[299]

Serious tensions persisted within the CC. The term "downturn" had been used in the mid-1970s, but only to indicate a temporary lull in struggle. When Cliff began to argue for the need to recognise a downturn in struggle in 1978 Chris Harman was resistant, while Steve Jefferys was developing a highly over-optimistic perspective based on the successes of the ANL.[300]

The perspective had not been adapted to the changing realities of struggle. To Mel Norris it felt like pushing jelly up a ladder. Cliff was upset by the fact that Harman and Jefferys seemed to be allying against him, and there was rivalry in the industrial department between Jefferys and Deason, something Cliff found hard to deal with.[301] Alex Callinicos, who had come onto the CC in 1977, remembers a stormy period, with the committee polarised and torn by bitter arguments. Callinicos was strongly opposed to the way Cliff had engineered the removal of Harman as editor, but remembers that Cliff always made efforts to persuade him, whereas Jefferys did not bother.[302]

Cliff continued to tour the country and draw in new members. Julie Waterson first met Cliff as a student in 1978. She was fascinated; she had never met anyone of his generation who was so political, with such empathy for younger people. Cliff was completely divorced from popular youth culture but despite his own background understood what it meant to be working class. He was never judgemental, never demanded respect for age or experience.[303]

Cliff was able to argue fiercely for his position without resorting to personal nastiness. In John Molyneux's words an argument with him could be like a "benign hurricane". On one occasion Cliff was having a heated argument with Molyneux when Molyneux's four-year-old son intervened: "Don't argue, Dad; can't you see he's just a little old man?"[304]

The state of the industrial struggle was still contradictory. As Chris Harman noted, the position publicly presented by the party was not quite the same as that argued by Cliff within the CC:

> The paper gave the impression that the industrial struggle had completely died out. The reality was, as Cliff argued, that the workers' offensive against the pay norms was being replaced by a bosses' offensive against jobs and conditions. The struggle had not ended, but there was a dip in the number of disputes...*and* a tendency for employers to win them.[305]

Alongside the disputes about *Socialist Worker*, 1978 saw increasing conflict between Cliff and Steve Jefferys. In September Jefferys complained of repeated personal attacks on him by Cliff, Simon Turner and Jim Nichol, and walked out of a CC meeting in protest. He explained his reading of the situation:

> The root cause of this personalisation is, I believe, the fact that over a

wide range of decisions taken at conference this year – on *Women's Voice*,* black work, youth work, *Socialist Worker*, elections – Cliff found himself in a minority. Seeking reasons for this other than in his own arguments, Cliff has decided that the problem is me.[306]

By the autumn of 1978 the prospects for a new wave of industrial struggle seemed favourable. In September Cliff predicted, accurately enough, a winter of strikes:

> But come what may, the coming winter will be one of industrial discontent.† The central role of the trade union bureaucracy in policing workers will be even more crucial than before.

He spelled out vividly the grim political choice in the impending general election:

> If you are on a ship on which the captain is incompetent and drunk day and night you do not jump overboard if there are sharks around. Seeing the teeth of Margaret Thatcher one is inclined to stick to skipper Callaghan. Up till now the revolutionary left, alas, has not been able to offer a lifeboat to the passengers.[307]

Shortly afterwards a national Ford strike began. Two more editorials were devoted to this. In the first Cliff argued that a Ford victory would help the low paid and the unemployed, but that a defeat would have political consequences:

> A defeat for the Ford workers will strain the loyalties of workers towards Labour and may well lead to demoralisation and abstentions in the coming general election, thus opening the door for Margaret Thatcher.[308]

In the second he noted that the Ford strikers were popular but urged other workers to take action immediately. Otherwise there was a grave danger that productivity deals would be used to divert the wages struggle.[309]

The Ford workers won a partial victory and by the New Year the struggle began to broaden. In the first two months of the year there was strike action by road haulage drivers, health workers, social workers, water workers, refuse collectors, gravediggers, other

---

* This was the SWP women's paper. There is a full account of its history in chapter ten.

† By early 1979 the phrase "winter of discontent" had become a journalistic cliché. Cliff was ahead of the field.

groups of low-paid public sector workers, journalists and many more. The widespread existence of militant picket lines represented an embryo of workers' control that produced hysterical responses from the mainstream press. Health workers blockaded hospital entrances so that many hospitals could take emergency patients only. Paul Foot later remembered "a sense of wonder and admiration at the way in which the transport drivers of Hull took control of their industry and ran it safely and properly in the best interests of the community".[310] This caused profound alarm among defenders of the established order, who wanted to put the blame on the Labour government which had served its purpose and could now be discarded.

The rank and file strategy, which had been dormant for some time, began to resume its relevance. In the first three months of 1979 *Socialist Worker* was full of material on disputes with contributions from rank and file leaders (some SWP, some not). On the front page of *Socialist Worker* on 6 January 1979 John Deason wrote:

> The key to future victories is *all-out* action. And for weaker sections of workers elementary solidarity is crucial.
>
> If all deliveries to Garners Steak Houses were stopped the Garners workers would soon win their strike for union recognition. If all printers honoured the journalists' picket lines, how much quicker they would win their claim.
>
> If other NALGO members were pulled out in sympathy with the social workers, their lengthening strike would soon produce results.

Yet if this was the revival of industrial struggle, it was only brief and in a sense marked the end of a period.* Callaghan's government had lost its majority some time ago, and had stayed in power only by a series of dishonourable deals first with the Liberals and then the Ulster Unionists. In March, Callaghan lost a vote of confidence and was compelled to call a general election.

---

*   MI5, keeping far-left involvement under scrutiny, noted, "Trotskyist groups are finding difficulty in keeping pace with events and in some places are being told by Party officials to concentrate their attention entirely on selling their newspapers. Deason, the industrial organiser of the Socialist Workers Party (SWP), believes that many of their members are daunted by the scale of the action and are not clear how to take advantage of it." (C Andrew, *The Defence of the Realm*, p666)

Also in March 1979 Jefferys resigned as industrial organiser. He characterised the position of Cliff and the CC majority as being:

> The decay of shop-floor working class organisation and the shift to the right in the trade union movement has gone so far that all we can do in this period is to make socialist propaganda as actively as possible.[311]

It was becoming clear that an argument largely confined to the CC would have to be taken to the membership as a whole.

In the course of the election campaign the NF, weakened but not crushed, took to the streets again. The ANL took part in a counter-demonstration in Southall on 23 April. At its end the Blair Peach, an east London teacher of New Zealand origin and an SWP member, was beaten to death police in the Special Patrol Group. Despite various enquiries, the full circumstances of his death have not been made public and only in 2010 did a police report accept partial responsibility.[312] Peach was the party's first martyr. At his funeral in June, attended by several thousand people, Ken Gill of the TUC General Council and Cliff spoke; they would have been unlikely to share a platform in any other circumstances. Cliff said, "Blair identified himself with all the oppressed, with the physically weak children,* with black people, with women, with the low paid workers. His heart was with the exploited and the oppressed. It is no use building monuments of brass and stone...let us mourn, but let us organise and mobilise".[313]

As the election approached, it was 11 years since the French General Strike. Much had changed. The secure world of full employment was long gone and capitalism was again revealed as a brutal, irrational system. The working class, which in the year of the Saltley picket and the Pentonville Five had held such power, was now less confident of its strength.

The SWP membership had shrunk, probably to below 2,000.[314] Although the party had some real roots in the workplaces, it was much smaller than had been expected five years earlier. The Anti Nazi League had been a resounding success but the electoral strategy had failed.

The great hopes of the early 1970s had not been realised and throughout Europe the generation of 1968 was in crisis.[315] In Italy and Germany some sections of the left turned to terrorism, while

---

* Blair Peach was a teacher at a special needs school.

groups like Avanguardia Operaia in Italy and the Ligue Communiste Révolutionnaire in France had been pulled to the right. In revolutionary Portugal and post-Franco Spain crisis had been resolved and the left was in disarray.

The SWP, despite internal disputes, had held together well, and Cliff could feel some satisfaction that, in comparison with many sections of the European left, his party was in reasonably good shape. Now, as Tory rule loomed, he faced some of the most difficult decisions of his life.

PART THREE
BUILDING FOR THE FUTURE

10

1979-84
Enforced Retreat

Since 1976 the SWP had held an annual Easter rally for members and sympathisers at the Derbyshire Miners' Holiday Camp at Skegness. There was a programme of political meetings and ample time for informal political discussion. There were children's activities, films and other entertainment as well as drunkenness, football and fornication. On the final morning, before comrades returned home, they gathered in the cinema to hear Cliff give an address. Each year he aimed to inspire, enthuse and orient them to the priorities of the coming months.

When Cliff came to speak in 1979 the general election was just weeks away. This time Cliff was nervous about the impact of his speech on the organisation. Before delivering it he walked round and round the camp with Andy Strouthous, going over what he was going to say.[1] All the indications were that the Tories would win and that Margaret Thatcher would become prime minister. Thatcher represented a more aggressive right-wing variant of Toryism than that which had dominated during the long post-war boom, and an attack on trade unionism and public services was imminent.[2]*

He began with the great successes of the early 1970s:

> The first five years [1969-74] was a period when the class struggle achieved a level unprecedented in British working class history for generations. We had two national miners' strikes. One of them smashed to pieces the incomes policy of the Tory government. The other forced the government to introduce a three-day week and then to lose power.

However, the Labour election victory in 1974 had marked a sharp turning point. After it "we did not have one national strike in any key section of the class". The unifying element up to 1974 was anti-Tory feeling. With Labour in power that general opposition

---

* Quotations are taken from an edited version of the speech published after the Tory victory. The original speech was given shortly before the election.

collapsed and the left union leaders backed the Social Contract. Scabbing had become respectable. He concluded ominously: "Labour laid the foundations and the Tories will now build the structure by using the law."

It was a grim message. Until now the perspective of the SWP had been essentially that developed in the early 1970s – the potential for rapid growth and the development of workplace organisation and a rank and file movement. In an interview a year earlier, Cliff recognised that there had been "serious" defeats, but insisted that "it is absolutely clear that workers are not demoralised". He predicted that in the event of a Tory election victory, within a few months "workers will burst into fight". Hence building rank and file organisation was central to the party's strategy.[3]

During the "winter of discontent" *Socialist Worker* had hailed the revival of struggle. A front-page headline proclaimed that "1979 is the year to win",[4] and an editorial stated that "we are witnessing the beginning of a new period of confrontation between workers and government, and between pickets and the law, of the sort that took place between 1969 and 1974", although it recognised that "there are important limitations to the present movement".[5]

Within the CC deep divisions were developing. But these disputes had been largely kept private; there had been no attempt to argue them before the membership as a whole. With his Skegness speech, Cliff was opening up an argument which would rage among the party's members for some time to come.

The new perspective outlined by Cliff rapidly acquired the shorthand label of "the downturn".[*] The development of the new analysis must have been painful for Cliff. He could not foresee the length of the downturn, but Cliff was now 62 years old and his hopes of living to see revolutionary change had sharply diminished.

Cliff had been raised in a tough school – one of his earliest memories was the way the Comintern had claimed that Hitler's coming to power was not a defeat for workers. So he faced the facts. If

---

[*] In his autobiography (T Cliff, *A World to Win*, p155) Cliff says that he first put the perspective forward in 1978. However, Cliff's articles for public consumption from late 1978 do not yet show a fully developed downturn analysis. In 1978-79 there were heated arguments about *Women's Voice* (see below) and *Flame* (a paper aimed at black workers) and their relation to the party. A a result, the question of the downturn did not become central till the spring of 1979.

things carried on in the same way, there was a danger of serious demoralisation. If comrades set their expectations too high, they could easily be afflicted with a sense of failure. Trying for too much could lead to humiliating defeat and victimisation.

He could be criticised for not having noticed the downturn earlier. From 1975 onwards there had been a sharp debate in the CP, with various "Gramscians" – Dave Purdy, Bill Warren, Mike Prior – challenging the CP's industrial strategy; this reflected an awareness that the wave of industrial militancy of the early 1970s had passed its peak.[6] Then in 1978 came Eric Hobsbawm's lecture "The Forward March of Labour Halted".[7] Though Hobsbawm would develop his ideas in a very different direction to Cliff, his starting point was an observation of the same phenomena, and a warning against any complacent belief that industrial militancy would continue its inexorable advance.

Cliff probably remembered Lenin's words in the aftermath of the 1905 revolution:

> The Marxist is the last to leave the path of direct revolutionary struggle, he leaves it only when all possibilities have been exhausted, when there is not a *shadow* of hope for a shorter way, when the basis for an appeal to prepare for mass strikes, an uprising, etc., is obviously disappearing.[8]

Cliff's downturn line brought him into direct conflict with Steve Jefferys, who had been one of the SWP's industrial organisers for five years in the 1970s. Jefferys had joined the IS at the LSE and then worked in a car factory in Glasgow for some years before coming to London to work as a full-timer. Though he had a somewhat abrasive manner he was a competent organiser and an independent-minded thinker. He had never been wholly uncritical of Cliff and now he came into head-on confrontation.

In the summer of 1979 Jefferys published a major article entitled "Striking into the 80s – modern British trade unionism, its limits and Potential".[9] This was not a direct attack on Cliff, who was mentioned only infrequently in the article, though one or two footnotes quoted Cliff with implied disagreement. The starting point was the debate taking place in the CP magazine *Marxism Today*, following the publication of Hobsbawm's lecture.

Jefferys set out a historical analysis of the British working class since the Second World War. He described the period 1975-76, with inflation, unemployment and support for the Social Contract by the trade union bureaucracy, as "the downturn". The following section, covering the years 1977 to 1979, was entitled "The dam breaks", where he claimed that the working class had won real victories. He cited Cliff's claim that "Wage drift, the difference between national wage rates and the 'going rate' on the shop floor, ten years ago was one of the most important expressions of the power of individual shop stewards. That has now practically disappeared from industry".[10] Jefferys responded, "Far from these years seeing a *decline* in shop-steward negotiated wage settlements, we are still witnessing a process in which *when the national wage controls are broken* it is the shop stewards and *job-based* trade unionism which breaches the dam."

Jefferys concluded that this was still a period of "onward march", and that the SWP rank and file strategy would continue to be valid under Thatcher:

> The task of revolutionaries in the 1980s is to raise this theoretical understanding to the level of practice. Our strategy must be to sharpen working class struggles, and to try and lock them into ongoing *rank-and-file* organisations which bridge the narrow horizons of the workplace. Ten years ago, the building of a *rank and file movement* clearly speaking and struggling for workers' interests *against* the "national interest" was merely a dream of a handful of revolutionaries. Today it is the property of a few thousand revolutionary trade unionists. As British trade unionism strikes into the 1980s, our task is to make it a political alternative for tens of thousands of workers.

The following issue of *International Socialism* contained Cliff's response, entitled "The balance of class forces in recent years".[11] It was a substantial article running to some 50 pages, but Jefferys' name never appeared in it. Cliff was anxious to avoid the dispute being seen in personal terms.

Jefferys' article had been thorough, clearly argued and well documented, as befitted a future Professor of European Employment Studies. Cliff's response was in a totally different style. As in *The Employers' Offensive* and the *Factory Branches* pamphlet, he allowed workers to speak for themselves. The article contained lengthy extracts from accounts written by militants and activists in the SWP – dockers Bob Light, Eddie Prevost and Mickey Fenn, engineering worker Roger Cox, Barnet Trades Council secretary Ken Montague, Chrysler shop steward Gerry Jones and several others. Though, like Jefferys, he used statistics and graphs to support his argument, he also made a devastating critique of the inadequacy of official statistics. For example, these did not record occupations and political strikes, and did not distinguish between strikes and lockouts. He noted that there was "often an inverse relation between growth of union membership and the strength of shop organisation". He drew on research by Dave Beecham on over 1,000 disputes in the period from 1977 to 1979. But his use of accounts by individual workers enabled him to give a picture of the *total* experience of workers.

A particularly vivid account was given in the testimony of health worker Bill Geddes. Geddes recalled the "sheer enthusiasm" of the strikers in 1973, and the weakness of the management. The latter was summed up in an incident where Geddes was reprimanded for giving out leaflets in breach of hospital rules:

> I demanded to see a copy of the rules (I knew there was no such thing). I pretended to be very angry at this attack on my behaviour and walked out, slamming the door behind me.
>
> The next day I got a letter *apologising* for the accusation over the leaflet incident. I fell off my chair laughing!

Yet by the end of the decade "the battle of the cuts was lost", Geddes himself had been sacked and there was "a great deal of demoralisation".

Cliff began by examining four industries which had been central to the big struggles of the early 1970s – shipyards, mining, docks and motor vehicle manufacturing. In each case he found evidence of downturn and demoralisation. In the case of the miners he argued that by 1974 the rank and file role was already much more tightly controlled by the union leadership. Subsequently serious divisions were caused by the acceptance of a productivity deal. In Yorkshire the Broad Left around Scargill was now "made up largely of officials or aspiring officials". Here he identified problems that would become apparent during the 1984-85 strike.

In engineering he showed the decline of wage drift and hence of shop stewards' strength. In general he showed that "never since the Second World War had the real wage of workers declined as much as under the Labour government of 1974-79". Taking into account unemployment and cuts in the "social wage" (public services) "the real standard of living of the working class as a whole was drastically slashed". He showed that the strikes of 1978-79 had come nowhere near the level of success of the early 1970s, and contrasted the solidarity with Grunwick with that achieved a decade earlier by the Roberts-Arundel strike in Manchester.

Cliff summarised his basic argument:

> In recent years: (1) disputes have been far more bitter and lengthy; (2) the employers were far more aggressive and quite often unready to concede anything except after a long battle; (3) lockouts were back with a vengeance; (4) the proportion of disputes ending with workers' defeats or partial defeats was much greater than in previous years.

There was no single cause for this state of affairs. He listed a number of factors which had contributed to the downturn: incomes policy, productivity deals, the move to the right of "left" trade union leaders, the impact of the economic crisis. He put particular emphasis on the incorporation of senior stewards into the management structure and the growing number of full-time convenors.

The crucial expression of the downturn was a lack of confidence on the part of workers:

> Lack of confidence to break, or at least loosen, the vice of government and employers is the key impediment to raising class consciousness. Class consciousness cannot exist independent of class confidence.*

In this situation struggles would necessarily be of a defensive

---

* This question of the relationship of confidence to consciousness was a common theme in Cliff's later years: "At the same time, however, workers have no confidence [that] they can achieve reforms by revolutionary struggle. They don't have enough confidence, enough unity, enough experience of a working class in struggle. Nor do they have confidence in achieving reforms by reformist efforts. This is why there is a very high level of apathy, and a very contradictory consciousness. Their consciousness is contradictory because of the situation. There is a lot of anger and at the same time this lack of confidence. The anger comes because the situation grows worse and worse with declining conditions and job insecurity. The lack of confidence comes from years of bureaucratic control, years of low level of struggle. And with that combination in these people when you say ,'Enough is enough'" they nod their heads. But when you say, 'Let's do something about it' then it's, 'Oh, wait, I'm not sure. I agree with you but our mates are not ready.'" (T Cliff, "50 Years of the International Socialist Tradition" (interview with Ahmed Shawki), *International Socialist Review*, 1 (Summer 1997))

nature; the upholding of elementary trade union principles was crucial. In particular Cliff referred to the "Code of Practice" adopted by the Rank and File "Defend Our Unions" conference in June 1979,[12] which emphasised basic principles: solidarity, respect for picket lines, collecting money, organising blacking.

He pointed to "a crisis of ideas" in the movement; there was a need for "socialist politics" on the shop floor: "Today, when world capitalism is in deep general crisis, industrial militancy alone is quite ineffective. General social and political questions have to be faced." Perhaps with a self-critical recollection of the *Incomes Policy* book, he warned, "Alas, there is no automatic transition from economic to political struggle."

The final section was headed grimly, "Hard slog ahead". It warned what the Thatcherite decade would mean for workers: "Attacks on living standards, cuts, redundancies, plant closures, are going to affect working people in a harsher and harsher way." But Cliff remained an incorrigible optimist and the final paragraph pointed to elements of hope:

> The dialectics of history, the general crisis of capitalism, are far more powerful than all the bureaucrats. If the crisis accelerates the death of the reformist forest, it will – if revolutionary socialists adopt a correct strategy and tactics – accelerate the growth of the green shoots of rank and file confidence, action and organisation.

The SWP conference in 1979, held in November in a central London hotel, was a lively event. Discussion centred around the downturn argument and its implications for the party's perspectives, especially on the questions of women's and black organisation. The whole of the first day was devoted to the downturn debate. Cliff warned that it would be dangerous to expect resistance to the Tories to follow the same lines that it had after the 1970 election.[13] He won the majority, but a number of trade union militants sided with Jefferys. The latter withdrew from the central committee, but there was no split.*

To win the argument required not just a conference vote but an extended and bitter argument within the party. Precisely because the impact of the downturn was uneven, experiences varied greatly and

---

* Jefferys remained in the party until the start of the miners' strike in 1984 though he was not particularly active.

there were sharp disagreements between comrades.[14] Glasgow was a particular problem. It was the most working class district in the party and had the best industrial base. Paper sales were impressive – during the 1970s some 200 papers a week were sold in the Chrysler factory branch. So Glasgow had real authority in arguing against the downturn and made Cliff's task more difficult.[15] Steve Jefferys had many supporters there, for he had won considerable respect a decade earlier when he had established himself, an Englishman, as a militant in a Scottish car factory. Willie Lee, who had worked with Jefferys at Chrysler, remembered him as an "amazing character", brilliant and single-minded. He thought Jefferys wanted to be the leading light in the party and realised that to achieve this he would have to remove Cliff, but his idea of his own importance and skill did not prove correct – Cliff was a tough man.[16]

Dave Sherry, the Glasgow organiser, opposed the downturn line and debated with Cliff at a Glasgow aggregate – in retrospect he thinks he must have been very cocky. Eventually he was convinced and Cliff gave him a lot of support. Cliff spent a whole afternoon in London arguing with him and making him realise that as organiser he didn't have to be popular with everyone. Sherry remembers that Cliff never ran away from an argument and that he always took people seriously, especially newer members. He warned comrades who overestimated their industrial strength that they would understand the downturn when the Linwood car factory closed.[17] (Linwood was closed in 1981.)

Mike Gonzalez remembers:

> The main meeting to discuss it was held in a community centre at the bottom of a tower block in the Gorbals. Cliff was at his furious and combative best – though he didn't win his argument on the day, in the longer term we recognised that he had been right on the downturn.

He was struck in particular by Cliff's "gift for hearing and understanding what working class people were saying".[18]

Despite his patience Cliff was angry with the Glasgow comrades, feeling that in refusing to accept the downturn perspective they were holding back the organisation, though his anger was political and not personal. Alan Borrell, who became Glasgow organiser, remembers Cliff taking him aside and laying down the law. It was "not a happy time".[19]

In Edinburgh, Willie Black had an argument with Cliff. He opposed the downturn thesis because he worked in a militant workplace and generalised from his own experience. Cliff told Black he would never be a "downturn person" and that he would have to wait for the upturn.[20]

Another problem area was the Lea Valley district in north London. This was where Jefferys lived and he had the support of a number of local activists on the questions of the downturn and *Women's Voice*. District organiser Simon Hester had the tough job of trying to win the district to the CC line. Cliff and Jefferys were paranoid about each other.* Hester had to take individual militants to Cliff's home, where Cliff would argue with them in vigorous terms, although not many were convinced. Eventually Cliff's line won the majority at the 1981 pre-conference aggregate. Cliff hugged Hester and promised him the "order of Lenin".[21]

In retrospect it is hard to argue that Cliff was mistaken. Some critics have put up a case against him. Jefferys has argued that if the rank and file organisations had survived until the struggles of the early 1980s, they could have made an effective intervention.[22] More recently Sheila Cohen has argued that the notion of the downturn was an oversimplification and that the IS/SWP should have continued with its rank and file strategy and not retreated into party-building.[23] But if one rereads Cliff's article 30 years later, the most striking thing is his depiction of the struggles of the late 1960s and early 1970s, which showed a level of militancy and solidarity almost inconceivable in Britain in a later period.

Willie Lee, a Linwood militant who later moved to London, believes that if Cliff had not carried the argument about the downturn the party would have smashed itself up.[24] It is interesting to compare Cliff's position to that of Ernest Mandel, who in the perspectives he presented to the 1979 World Congress of the Fourth International equivocated about whether the upturn had come to an end. According to his biographer, "Mandel recoiled from taking a definite stand, fearing demoralisation".[25] The organisation paid the price.

Certainly it must have taken enormous determination for Cliff to

---

* On one occasion Cliff even said that the biggest single problem facing the organisation was Jefferys (Pete Clark interview, July 2008).

argue the downturn thesis when, in fact, he was arguing for the abandonment of so many of his own hopes. Anyone else might have been accused of losing faith in the working class. Nobody, however, could have accused Cliff of that.[26]

The real argument in this period was not so much with those who denied the downturn, but with those who drew different conclusions from the facts. Hobsbawm's article "The Forward March of Labour Halted?"[27] and André Gorz's *Farewell to the Working Class*,[28] which argued that the working class as traditionally understood was now disappearing, had considerable currency on the left. Cliff had no sympathy whatsoever with this position. He was concerned with a shift in the balance of class forces, not with a change in the nature of society. Exploitation continued and, while it did, workers had the possibility of resisting. Till the day he died Cliff never abandoned the belief that the working class would change the world.

In fact, over the next few years Cliff produced a succession of articles and speeches in which he examined the ebbs and flows of the industrial struggle, looking for a favourable shift. From the beginning he stressed the need to resist the offensive: "We can only turn the tide if we start to close ranks now. We need to get back to the basics of trade union organisation – solidarity at every level between workers".[29]

With his eye for detail Cliff was not concerned simply with general analyses. He was always ready with advice for workers facing particular problems. In 1979 there was an 11-week strike at the Caterpillar earthmoving equipment factory in Newcastle. Dave Hayes was a 26-year-old newly elected steward. When a mass meeting was held to discuss a possible deal, Cliff spent the evening before in discussion with Hayes, advising him to resign as a steward because the deal was not good enough and to speak against it from the floor. Three years later Hayes was victimised and dismissed from Caterpillar. Cliff was in Newcastle and talked to him, giving him inspiration at this difficult time. Hayes spent a couple of days travelling round the North East with Cliff, and shortly afterwards became an SWP full-timer.[30]

Sometimes Cliff made misjudgements about individuals. In Manchester an enthusiastic young comrade promised he could double the paper sale. Cliff was impressed and encouraged him. The comrade failed, became demoralised and dropped out.[31]

With Jefferys having left the CC, and Cliff and Harman slowly becoming reconciled, a more stable leadership developed. There would be new arrivals and departures and sometimes fierce arguments (notably during the miners' strike), but Alex Callinicos recalls that "the CC was very much a collective, even though Cliff was much the strongest figure on it". Cliff developed important partnerships with individuals, particularly with successive national secretaries, often telephoning them at least daily, and also with some others – Lindsey German from the early 1980s onwards and Dave Hayes in the 1990s.[32]

The first major confrontation between Thatcher and the unions came with the defeated 13-week steel strike in early 1980. Cliff travelled the country speaking to steelworkers and other workers. In Ilkeston a Cliff meeting helped to turn a tiny group of three SWP members into a successful branch with a number of steelworker members. In Middlesbrough 40 people, including 26 steelworkers, heard Cliff and five were recruited. In Wolverhampton 70 people turned up to hear Cliff and two strikers from Bilston.[33] However, as Cliff noted later, whereas in 1972 he had addressed thousands of steel workers at Scunthorpe,* in 1980 "the biggest meeting of steel workers I spoke to was 100".[34]

At the end of the strike Cliff wrote a brutal assessment: "The strike had the worst leadership of any I can remember." He argued that if the rank and file had organised completely independently of the bureaucracy, victory could have been achieved.

> More steelworkers were actively and enthusiastically involved in this strike than dockers and probably even miners during their strikes in 1972. But they had no organisation.
>
> At the local level their organisation was neither cohesive nor clear cut. Throughout the strike you felt again and again that victory was at hand. But every time you felt the cavalry was coming, you also felt it was coming a little bit too late.[35]

On 14 May the TUC called a Day of Action against the proposed Tory Employment Bill, which aimed to limit trade union rights. But

---

* Cliff overstated the point, claiming, from memory, that he had spoken to "6,000 or 7,000" workers, though at the time *Socialist Worker* reported only 2,000 (see chapter eight).

the trade union leadership signally failed to encourage action in the form of strikes. For Cliff this showed the "bankruptcy of the leadership of the Labour movement". With the CP orienting itself more and more on the left union leaders, he argued:

> We have to replace the Communist Party by a socialist organisation with roots in the class. One of the main methods of achieving such a leadership is by the building of a united front – a unity in action against the Tories...
>
> There is real hatred for this Tory government. At the same time this hatred is accompanied by a very widespread impotence. There is a fantastic abyss between the feeling and the action.[36]

In the autumn of that year he was optimistic about a favourable shift after a successful Right to Work march:

> The march from Port Talbot was very much bigger than we had expected. So was the lobby on 10 October. And the anger was much more focused on unemployment than we expected... What I have said up to now does not point to any turning point in the immediate future. But I believe that there will be a turning point.[37]

The industrial struggle did not exist in a vacuum. On the contrary, the industrial downturn was accompanied by a political upturn. Cliff summed it up: "Because workers don't feel confident enough to fight for jobs or over wages in their own workplace, they look to Tony Benn".[38]

It was normal for the Labour Party to turn to the left after an electoral defeat. The left was freed of its obligations of loyalty to the government in office, and even the right welcomed an opportunity to reconnect with the activist base. In particular Tony Benn, who had been a cabinet minister throughout the 1974-79 government, now re-created himself as the major figure on the left and achieved considerable popularity with the Labour membership.

From the outset Cliff took a highly critical position, seeing the danger that activists could be sucked back into the Labour Party. The SWP's strategy was "steering left", that is, maintaining a critical distance from the movement around Benn, which had drawn in many revolutionaries and ex-revolutionaries.* Cliff pointed to the

---

* Thus Alan Freeman of the IMG promised, "The further Bennism advances against the old Labour Party tradition, the more likely are working class victories." He covered himself with the proviso that "Bennism itself contains the seeds of its own future failure" (A Freeman, *The Benn Heresy*, London, 1982, p1507.

limits of Benn's rhetoric: "Benn and his friends don't dare to oppose the union bureaucracy. They are parliamentarians through and through".[39]

However, Cliff remained interested in unity with other currents on the left. When Tariq Ali left the IMG in 1981 he told Paul Foot he would not join any other organisation. He immediately got a phone call from Cliff who said, "If you won't join us, will you at least write a column for *Socialist Worker*?" Tariq agreed[40] and a column appeared briefly.[41] Cliff had high hopes of recruiting Tariq, but they fell through very quickly.[42]

In November 1980 Michael Foot, a veteran Bevanite and Aldermaston marcher, was elected leader of the Labour Party. Cliff welcomed Foot's victory as "very good" – because it meant the Labour left's policies could be put to the test. But Foot and Benn had supported "terrible Irish policies" and immigration controls.[43]

The following year Benn announced he would stand for the deputy leadership of the Labour Party and ran a vigorous campaign, failing to win by a margin of less than 1 percent.[*] SWP members naturally voted for Benn if they were in Labour-affiliated unions, but otherwise maintained a sharply critical stance. [44][†]

In the summer of 1981 there were riots in urban centres throughout Britain. Cliff did not allow his downturn analysis to inhibit him or make him overcautious. He praised the rioters for their "fantastic discipline and…fantastic community feeling".[45] As the *Sunday Telegraph* reported with feigned outrage, he told a meeting in Liverpool:

> The riots and looting have been fantastic, but they have not gone far enough.
>
> Because they have not been organised, the kids have attacked shops when they should have been attacking factories. We must teach them to take the bakery, not just the bread.[46]

In April 1982 British forces were sent to recapture the Falkland

---

[*] Foot had been elected by the parliamentary party alone, but under new rules pushed through by the left in a bid to "democratise" the party, leadership contests were now extended to constituency and trade union members as well as MPs.

[†] Serious criticism was not a barrier to future unity. In the 1990s and afterwards Benn would cooperate with the SWP on many issues, notably in the anti-war movement, and he often spoke at the Marxism events.

Islands, which had been occupied by Argentina. Cliff was worried that the SWP might adapt to the Labour left. He emphasised that the main enemy was at home, that it was not enough to be anti-war, it was necessary to be anti-imperialist. For socialists in Britain the job was to attack British imperialism, not Argentina. He illustrated this with a joke. A Russian says to Stalin that in the US it is possible to criticise the president. Stalin replies that in Russia, too, it is possible to criticise the American president.[47]

Cliff argued that the Falklands War had "cruelly exposed the weakness of Tony Benn and the Labour left". Benn had "fantastically over-estimated" his support, claiming millions when the real figure was closer to 50,000.

> The block vote is like a hall of mirrors. It distorts the truth.
>
> If you assume your army is three million but it's really only 50,000, that produces massive demoralisation even among the 50,000.[48]

In the summer of 1982 a railway drivers' strike ended in defeat caused by the absence of solidarity from the rest of the labour movement. Cliff wrote a devastating analysis of the causes of defeat. The trade unions could be blamed, but they did not act in a vacuum; they would only fight under heavy pressure from the rank and file, and the rank and file suffered from the sectionalism which afflicted the leaders:

> The ruling class and the Tories don't suffer from this curse of sectionalism. On the contrary – they generalise all the time. They understand the downturn much better than the trade union leaders. Indeed they understand it much better than many shopfloor leaders…
>
> The individual train driver thinks he is so strong. There he is in charge of all those passengers travelling at high speed or pulling all that expensive freight.
>
> He thought no one would dare attack the train drivers. He didn't notice that only 14 percent of freight goes by rail. He didn't realise until it was too late that he couldn't win by himself.

He forecast more defeats to come:

> Again defeat feeds on defeat. The hospital workers will feel the defeat of the train drivers. And so will the miners. Arthur Scargill is going to have to do a lot of work amongst the rank and file miners if the Tories do

indeed decide to call his bluff.

He warned against the danger of believing "that masses of workers are ready to fight as long as you can manipulate the trade union or Labour Party machine".

> This approach will only deepen the rot – because it ignores the rank and file. Indeed it treats them with contempt...
>
> The call should be No Substitutionism! Don't substitute the leaders – even Tony Benn or Arthur Scargill – for the rank and file.[49]

In March 1983 the miners voted in a ballot not to take strike action against pit closures, a result Cliff described as "an *absolute* catastrophe". Scargill, the miners' president, was the most left-wing of all the current union leaders, but Cliff put a good deal of the blame on him:

> Even the style of Scargill, the way he speaks, shows he simply assumes he is the leader and he has the troops.
>
> He didn't just demand loyalty to the union, he told lies to the members and every member knew it. He said we can win the strike in seven to eight weeks, yet nobody in the country believed it. Why? Because the stocks at the power stations are enough for four or five months.[50]

Such weaknesses would become apparent in the 1984-85 strike.

Yet by June of the same year Cliff saw optimistic signs. A set of strikes at Halewood, Tilbury, Dundee and Cowley were seen as "not the upturn itself – more the prologue to the upturn". He observed that some groups of workers had "grown immune to the threat of unemployment". The decline of unionisation was "nothing like the 30s" and the crucial task was "rebuilding shop organisation".[51] The TUC conference that autumn marked "a massive shift to the right", and he stressed the need to orient on small struggles.[52]

As the 1980s progressed it became clear that Cliff had been right about the downturn and that the whole left was on the retreat. The SWP did not simply denounce the Labour left in a sectarian fashion, but tried to establish a dialogue. In late 1982 and early 1983 *Socialist Worker* published a series of interviews with Labour left activists – Peter Hain, Chris Mullin, Laurence Coates and Val Veness. Cliff wrote a final article summing up the arguments and responding to them. He was contemptuous of the "fantasy world" which considered internal disputes in the Labour Party more important than industrial struggles which actually mobilised mass workers' action.

> Above all they are building castles in the air. They are enamoured of resolutions. They, like the rest of the left, suffer from resolution-mongering... The Labour left learnt nothing from past experience of left-wing conference resolutions.[53]

In February 1983 Labour lost a disastrous by-election in Bermondsey in south London. The Labour candidate, Peter Tatchell, was a well-known left activist, but following a press witch-hunt the solidly Labour seat fell to the Liberal/Social Democratic alliance. Cliff described it as a "a cataclysmic event" and predicted that Labour would "shoot massively to the right".[54]

Here he was certainly correct. The Benn campaign of 1981 had been the high point for the Labour left. Michael Foot led Labour to electoral defeat in June 1983 and was replaced by Neil Kinnock, who had some left credentials but rapidly shifted the party to the right. Many of the Bennites moved right, while others dropped out in demoralisation. Benn himself became an increasingly isolated figure and lost his parliamentary seat in 1983 – although he would return to parliament.

Associated with the rise of Bennism was the rapid revival of the Campaign for Nuclear Disarmament in response to the aggressive anti-Communism of US president Reagan following the Russian invasion of Afghanistan. Thatcher gave ardent support to Reagan. There was an international wave of demonstrations, and in the autumn of 1981 200,000 marched through London (more than had taken part in any of the Aldermaston marches of the 1960s).

SWP members participated in building the campaign and tried to bring to it some of the imagination and creativity of the Anti Nazi League.* But by early 1983 Cliff was predicting that because CND had no political strategy and was even more remote from working class struggle than the Labour left, it would collapse after the 1983 election.[55] In fact the biggest CND mobilisation, with a claimed 400,000 in London, came just after the election, in October 1983.

---

* SWP members Bob Light and John Houston produced the very popular poster of Reagan and Thatcher based on the film *Gone With the Wind*; 100,000 were sold (see John Windsor, "Dear Maggie, wish you weren't here", *Independent*, 2 April 1994).

This was the last big demonstration and within a couple of years CND was beginning to decline.

Cliff was particularly hard on the Greenham Common women who had set up a permanent camp at a US base in Berkshire. They had achieved considerable popularity, but their campaign, based on feminist principles, positively discouraged mass participation. Cliff identified the weakness of their action in the fact that they were substituting themselves for mass action and so encouraging passivity. He even compared them to the terrorism which had characterised the decline of the left elsewhere in Europe:

> I don't want to compare the Greenham Common women to the Red Brigades in Italy too much. But there are elements in common. There is the general crisis of capitalism, the general move to the right of the movement, the industrial downturn and so there is a group of people who say "We will do it for you".
>
> The Red Brigades did this in Italy, and they did a massive amount of damage. In fact they ruined the movement. One of the tragedies of Italy was that the revolutionary left were a bunch of softies that felt guilty towards the Red Brigades because they thought the brigades were at least fighting.
>
> So when people say to me the Greenham Common women are fighting, I always ask exactly what are they doing?
>
> They tell us *they* will do it and stop the missiles while we remain at home.[56]

Such remarks were not calculated to win Cliff friends in CND or among feminists. But he considered that at this particular stage clarity was more important than unity.*

Cliff was extremely critical of what became known in the SWP as "movementism". This was summed up by Tony Benn when he urged:

> The Labour Party must align itself with the women's movement, the

---

* Again sharp criticism was not a barrier to future unity. In September 2001, three days after the attack on the World Trade Centre, the SWP held a London members' meeting to prepare a response, a meeting which led directly to the formation of the Stop the War Coalition. There was a guest speaker at the meeting – Helen John of CND, a former Greenham Common activist.

black movement, the environmental movement, the peace movement, the rural radical movement, the religious movements that object to monetarism and militarism... [57]

For Cliff nothing could be achieved by simply adding together various struggles against oppression and for good causes. Unless they were united by a central relation to the working class struggle, they could lead nowhere.

The sad course of events in the 1980s justified the pessimism of Cliff's downturn analysis. But predicting defeat alone would not build socialist organisation. Over the next few years Cliff argued vigorously, alongside other comrades, for important shifts in the strategy and organisation of the SWP. The process was different from the 1973-75 period. There were losses of members, but no serious split. A retreat certainly allowed rather more leisure than the race against time of the early 1970s, but Cliff had learnt some lessons about the need for patient persuasion.

The important shifts took place gradually over a period of almost three years. The NF had suffered a serious setback at the 1979 election and went into a decline marked by splits.* The ANL briefly revived, then was in effect wound up in 1981.[58] The Right to Work Campaign organised a successful demonstration against the Tory party conference in Blackpool in 1981, but since there was little resistance to redundancies it was wound up after a series of local marches in April and May 1982.[59]

With the decline of the broader organisations, there was much more concentration on direct recruitment to the SWP. This would be a slow process – Cliff stressed the importance of "talking to handfuls" of people.[60] As he put it, "We are not in a sprint – we are in a marathon".[61] In fact, SWP membership grew quite steadily in this period – from under 2,000 in 1980 to around 4,000 in 1984. Cliff opposed publicising the achievement on the grounds that it didn't fit the perspective.[62]

The industrial struggle remained at the centre of the picture, but by 1982 it was decided to wind up the rank and file groups, many of which had become shells with only SWP members and a few

---

* NF membership fell from 10,000 in 1979 to under 1,000 in 1985 (D Renton, *When We Touched the Sky*, p174).

fellow-travellers involved.* Cliff summed up his argument in the simple sentence "You can't have a rank and file movement if the factories are empty".† The objective conditions for a rank and file movement no longer existed: "The union bureaucracy at present is worse than it was ten years ago... But the opposition to it is much weaker and more fragmented".‡ Consequently "instead of recruiting people from rank and file groups into the party, comrades disappear into the rank and file groups".63

Again this involved Cliff in often sharp arguments with members of his own party. Dave Ayre recalls a meeting between Cliff and a group of six to ten building workers about the decision to close down the building workers' rank and file paper. Ayre felt that Cliff didn't have a proper political grasp of the situation and that he was oriented to students rather than to manual workers. He also remembers that though he was an inspiring speaker, some people found Cliff's style in meetings somewhat intimidating.64

Cliff stressed party intervention in industrial disputes:

> There are not going to be set-piece confrontations. The question of intervention means individual intervention in individual disputes. In ninety cases out of a hundred we will do it from outside. In ninety-nine cases out of a hundred we'll do it in a very low key.65

He argued that SWP members should still seek positions as shop stewards, but only on the basis of political honesty and openness:

> The central question is: how do we rebuild shop stewards' organisation? We are for socialists becoming shop stewards. The conditions we make are that they relate to their base and they are honest about their politics.
>
> That means fighting on issues your own base does not agree with – like for example, Ireland. Of course you will not get 100 percent agreement – you will get elected despite your position on Ireland, but everybody will know

---

* "The Rank and File groups, far from a body leading struggles, become a meeting place for often tired 'socialists' of frequently questionable hue – acting at times as little more than the left wing of the lower levels of the union bureaucracy. Our comrades are finding themselves high and dry with whoever else happens to be washed up on the beach." (Lindsey Greig, cited in A Callinicos, "The Rank and file Movement today" (*International Socialism* 17, Autumn 1982))

† A financial appeal from Cliff and Peter Clark dated January 1982 stated that "some 25 percent of the Party's members are now unemployed".

‡ A fuller argument, critical of aspects of the party's practice over the preceding years, was developed in A Callinicos, "The rank and file movement today".

what you stand for.⁶⁶

At the same time Cliff underlined the importance of political ideas. Only a high level of political understanding could hold the party together in a difficult period:

> In the cold world of the downturn the industrial militant cannot survive, cannot keep his or her spirit unless they are inspired by socialist ideas and are part of a community of militants.⁶⁷

In practice this meant much greater emphasis on branch meetings, with a political speaker coming first and a high level of political discussion. Cliff was impressed by the way Andy Strouthous had reorganised the Manchester district and made frequent phone calls to discuss details.⁶⁸ (Strouthous had amalgamated lots of rump "workplace branches" into larger geographical branches.⁶⁹)

He travelled tirelessly, speaking to branches around the country. In a 30-day period in January and February 1983 he addressed 11 meetings – three in Lancaster, two in Edinburgh, two in east London, and one each in Bradford, Leeds, Sheffield and Wolverhampton. Subjects included "Lenin, reform or revolution?", "How do we get rid of the bomb?", "Black struggles in Britain" and "Marx's view of history".⁷⁰

In Manchester a meeting with Cliff, two or three times a year, was prepared over a period of weeks and attracted hundreds, especially when he spoke jointly with Paul Foot. ⁷¹ * Cliff continued to exercise a powerful influence on those who heard him. Andy Wilson was a student with anarchist leanings who joined the SWP in 1983; though he later became more critical, his initial impression was that Cliff was a "genuinely awesome speaker" and he was "monumentally impressed".⁷² Yet Cliff's style in meetings was not designed to curry favour with his audience. He would sometimes pick on individuals in the audience, and he could be blunt in his responses: he once told Bob Light, who must have been 25 years his junior, "You're older than me".⁷³

He managed to bear his enormous workload at the price of an almost complete lack of interest in other aspects of life. On one occasion Cliff was staying with Ralph Darlington in his twelfth-floor council flat in Toxteth, which had a magnificent view across

---

* *Militant*, doubtless envious of such an impressive pair, used to refer to "Foot and Mouth meetings".

Liverpool. Early one morning Darlington noticed that a battleship was being launched and he drew Cliff's attention to this. Cliff did not even bother to cast a glance towards the spectacle, saying, "Ralph, I am not interested in battleships. I am interested in the branch, you bum." He had no time for conventional social graces. When Darlington thanked him for coming to Liverpool to speak to some meetings, Cliff simply responded, "Why thank me? Do you think I came here for you?"[74] Yet he was aware of his limitations and had a sense of self-parody; when Sabby Sagall told him he was writing an article on Beethoven, Cliff enquired, "Is he a member of our German organisation?"[75] *

The one exception to this single-mindedness was his family. He was a caring father and, later, was conscientious in looking after his grandchildren.[76]

He did not moralise about comrades' failings. If someone with responsibilities in the party was sexually promiscuous, was a heavy drinker or had an atrociously bad temper, it was of no concern to Cliff provided the job was done. Only in the context of a factional dispute could he sometimes be moralistic.

In this period Cliff became more tolerant towards intellectual activity. In the early 1980s George Paizis, a former North London district secretary, began a PhD on love in the novel.[77] He telephoned Cliff about it and found him encouraging. Cliff did not urge him to do a more explicitly political topic.[78]

Socialist Worker was central to the party's orientation. Some aspects of the "punk paper" style survived for quite a long time. Even in 1981 the headline to mark the royal wedding was "BIG EARS MARRIES NODDY".[79] But in the arguments on the CC, Harman more and more tended to be on the winning side. John Rose was still trying to marry a popular style of paper with hard politics, but in the circumstances of the downturn this became more and more difficult. In the conflict between imagination and politics, Cliff eventually opted for politics. In the spring of 1982 John Rose was removed from the editorship and replaced by Harman, who had

---

* While Cliff claimed he never listened to music, he respected hard work. Danny Gluckstein's cousin Tamar was training to be a concert pianist, and for a period of months she used to come and practise on the piano at Allerton Road, in the same room where Cliff was working on one of his books. Cliff never objected, but admired her industry (Danny Gluckstein interview, January 2009).

been Cliff's fiercest opponent during the debate on the paper in the late 1970s. Cliff's support for him now amounted to self-criticism. Cliff had learnt from his earlier tendency to drop former allies brutally. He spent hours trying to persuade John Rose to stay on the paper, working under Harman. Rose, who felt drained by the experience, decided to leave.[80]

Cliff and Harman now resumed the close cooperation that had been interrupted by the fierce disputes of the late 1970s. According to Alex Callinicos, "They formed a kind of tacit partnership that involved very little direct discussion between them but immense mutual reliance and respect".[81] Harman reoriented the paper so that it fitted more closely with the new perspectives of the party.

Another aspect of the growing emphasis on ideas was the increasing importance of the annual Marxism event, which shifted from being a largely student affair to being one of the main events in the calendar, an opportunity to educate members and win contacts. From 1983 it was held every summer in central London in the university area and gained a much higher profile. Cliff was originally somewhat puzzled by the idea of making Marxism such a major event, but when he saw the results he was enthusiastic.[82]

Cliff contributed on a wide range of topics, showing his commitment to developing an all-round political culture in the party. In 1980 his meetings included "The Balance Sheet of the Fight Against the Tories", "Labour in History", "Rosa Luxemburg" and "The Spanish Civil War". In 1981 it was "The English Suffragettes", "The Russian Revolution" and "The Working Class Family"; in 1982 "The Pentonville Five – Ten Years On [with docker Mickey Fenn]", "The Women's Movement in the Last 15 Years" and "Socialism Today, Building in the Downturn". In 1983 he spoke to no less than eight meetings: "Rebuilding Shop Stewards' Organisation", "What Next After the Election?", "Lenin and the Party", "Party and Class in the Russian Revolution", "The Rise and Fall of Bennism", "Syndicalism and the Working Class", "Zionism and the Middle East" and "Marx 100 Years On", as well as participating in a student forum.

On 11 March 1983 Cliff addressed a packed meeting in Camden Town Hall to mark the centenary of Karl Marx's death. Sharing the platform with him were Paul Foot, Jan Nielsen and Harry Wicks. Cliff stressed the centrality of Marxist theory to any proper understanding of the contemporary world. Far from the working class having disappeared, he argued that "the industrial working class is probably 100 times larger than when Marx died". But it was weakened by atomisation and the power of ideology. The growing integration of the world economy meant that not only was it impossible to have socialism in one country, but "it is stupid to speak even about capitalism in one country".

> That's why the nationalist and reformist ideas of the Labour Party and the idea of an alternative economic strategy are as effective in the face of world crisis as putting a brown paper bag on your head in the face of a nuclear explosion.

In conclusion he drew out the need for an organisation that was highly flexible in order to respond to unexpected developments, but at the same time sufficiently principled to avoid opportunism: "Only an organisation with a very clear sense of direction can veer and twist as the road veers and twists".[83]

To commemorate the centenary, Cliff and Pete Clark commissioned Alex Callinicos to write his book *The Revolutionary Ideas of Karl Marx*.[84] Cliff was helpful on technical points, showing that he retained his thorough knowledge of Marx's *Capital*. He defended Callinicos's approach against Chris Harman, who wanted it to be more geared to contemporary debates.[85] Cliff then wrote a highly favourable review.[86]

In a speech to the national committee just after this Cliff expressed himself largely satisfied with how the SWP was holding together in a difficult period: "The party is in a better state now than I remember for years".[87]

Amid all this activity Cliff still found time for individuals. In 1981 Clare Fermont returned to Britain after travelling in the Middle East, where she had become involved with Palestinian guerrillas. A mutual friend arranged for her to visit Cliff. When Cliff heard of her intention to return to guerrilla struggle in the Middle East, he told her she was a "very silly girl". Cliff argued with her that she should fight capitalism at its heart, not get herself killed to no purpose. He invited her back and, in all, they had three or four meetings during which he persuaded her to rethink her position, although he made no attempt to recruit her to the SWP. She now believes he probably saved her life, since all the guerrillas she had known were killed in 1983. Fermont joined the SWP some time later, although she did not accept the theory of state capitalism. Cliff got her to agree to speak on state capitalism at Marxism and, by working on the subject, she came to accept the position.[88]

He did not forget the comrades who had built the organisation in earlier years. In 1982 he learned that George Box, a member from Durham in the 1960s, was dying of cancer. Box had joined the Labour Party, but Cliff asked Jim Nichol to drive him to Nottingham to see Box. Cliff's approach was somewhat unconventional: he told Box that it was disgraceful that he had joined the Labour Party – how could he be a reformist if he knew he was dying? He urged him to rejoin the SWP and die a revolutionary. Box was greatly cheered up by the visit.[89]

The issue which produced the most internal debate in the downturn period, and to which Cliff was obliged, probably against his natural inclinations, to devote a great deal of time, was women's organisation within the SWP.

The question went back to the late 1960s when, inspired by the rising level of social struggle around the world, an international movement for women's liberation emerged. Its course did not run smoothly. It is scarcely surprising that, looking back at millennia of subordination, many women were angry and strident, and that ideas were put forward which, in retrospect, may appear bizarre. It is not surprising either that, faced with this new movement, many men, even some with impeccably left-wing credentials, were bewildered and alarmed.

The IS could not be untouched by such debates. Women had always played a part in the IS – not least the tireless Chanie Rosenberg – but it was nonetheless largely a male-dominated organisation and the working class it aspired to relate to was seen in overwhelmingly male terms, as the *Incomes Policy* book showed. There was only one woman (Constance Lever) out of 42 members of the first IS national committee elected in 1968. The first stormy debate on the question took place at the IS conference in 1970.

Cliff took part; one delegate summarised his contribution as follows:

> Cliff: cf. Marx after 1845 developing from alienation to exploitation. Emphasis as with blacks on collective rather than individual solution.[90]

Cliff was not naturally conservative on questions of sexual equality. The father of four children with a working wife, he had taken on many childcare responsibilities, and could be considered a pioneer "househusband". But in the early 1970s Cliff's overriding priority was to turn the IS into a workers' organisation and, with the limited resources available, he often saw demands for more activity around women's oppression as a diversion from the main task.

He could sometimes make sexist remarks, reflecting the male-dominated culture of the traditional labour movement. For example, Cliff would explain the need for realistic expectations by saying, "I'd like to sleep with Gina Lollobrigida, but I have to put up with what I've got".[91] But he was aware that the world was changing. During a visit to Belfast he made a passing sexist comment and was reprimanded by Goretti Horgan. Cliff immediately admitted she was right, and promised not to say such a thing again.[92]

Some 50 female IS members attended the Oxford Women's Liberation Conference early in 1970, which can be seen as one of the early landmarks of the movement in Britain. In June 1971 IS women comrades organised a conference on women attended by 300 people, although a report stated that "almost all of those who spoke were students, lecturers or teachers".[93]

The summer of 1972 saw the first issue of *Women's Voice*, an issue appearing every two months. Cliff did not show any great enthusiasm for this development, saying, "We'll have to let them do it or we'll lose some of our women members, but I think it's a disaster".[94] At the July national committee he recognised the case for a women's paper: "We take a certain advanced consciousness for granted in *Socialist Worker* readers. For most women we can't assume this consciousness, therefore a women's paper is a good idea." But he thought the paper was "flat and doesn't smell of working class women's experience".[95] In 1973 he suggested that "perhaps there is no place in IS for a women's group per se".[96]

Women's Voice acquired a higher profile in 1975 with the emergence of a mass movement against attempts to cut back on abortion rights. In June 1975 a demonstration of 40,000 in London demanded rejection of the Abortion (Amendment) Bill. IS comrades were active in the National Abortion Campaign.

Sheila McGregor was appointed the first full-time IS women's organiser. Cliff took little interest in what she was doing, whereas when she was in York and then full-time organiser in Sheffield he was constantly on the phone asking for detailed information. However, she did find his advice on united front work in the National Abortion Campaign useful.[97] In November 1975 a 600-strong *Women's Voice* rally was held in Manchester[98] and in June 1978 a *Women's Voice* rally in Sheffield attracted 1,000.[99]

Cliff remained sceptical. In 1978 Chris Harman noted that two members of the CC – Cliff and Jim Nichol – "tended to underestimate the way in which entry of women permanently into the labour force and the spread of the ideas of women's liberation have together opened up whole new layers of women to left wing ideas".[100]

The 1978 SWP conference decided that *Women's Voice* should not be simply a publication but an organisation and *Women's Voice* groups were set up in many localities.[101] The aim was to establish a campaigning organisation that could take up a variety of women's issues and was aimed at the small but significant periphery of women open to revolutionary politics who could not be won directly through *Socialist Worker*.

The success of *Women's Voice* as an organisation now led to a sharp debate about how far *Women's Voice* should be independent of the SWP. The CC majority made a compromise between Cliff's position (he would have liked to scrap *Women's Voice* immediately) and that of Harman and Callinicos who wanted to keep it as a party women's organisation.[102] This provoked sharp antagonism from many of the women activists in the party and there was considerable discussion in the pre-conference bulletins, leading to a stormy debate at the conference which decided that, within the limits of the present level of struggle, *Women's Voice* could not be "politically independent" of the SWP.

A great many women activists in the party, including Sheila McGregor – the former women's organiser – and Joan Smith, opposed Cliff. McGregor thought the SWP leadership had not understood the nature of modern women's oppression and believed it was necessary to have a women's organisation to make sure the question was taken seriously.[103]

Cliff had learnt some of the lessons of his impatience in earlier disputes and spent much time arguing to try to bring women comrades over to his side. Lindsey German thinks that at this stage Cliff did not really understand the argument – he thought one must either oppose *Women's Voice* or capitulate to bourgeois feminism.[104]

Penny Krantz remembers a debate between Cliff and Joan Smith in Manchester. She had been involved in *Women's Voice* and turned up expecting to be annoyed by Cliff, but was convinced in the course of the debate, in particular by Cliff's argument that in the present circumstances *Women's Voice* was not a bridge into the party, but a bridge out of it.[105]

Cliff was determined to wind down *Women's Voice* eventually, but was nervous of having a fight about it; he was terrified of losing some of the women activists who supported *Women's Voice*. So he wanted to let the debate go on as long as necessary. (This was common practice with Cliff. He would often ask, "Have you got a side?" and insist that until you were sure your side had 75 percent, you should not move against the opposition.[106]) He depended on a number of allies, in particular Lindsey German, who became a key member of the leadership at this time.[107]

Sue Caldwell was a relatively new recruit when she attended a caucus for trade unionists in the civil service at which Cliff was present. At the end of the meeting Cliff approached her and asked her view on *Women's Voice*. When she expressed disagreement with the CC line, he argued with her. She was not immediately convinced and went to the 1981 conference as an opponent of the CC line, where she was convinced by the arguments in the course of the conference. She was impressed by the way Cliff seemed to know everyone in every district and encouraged an argument because he knew the question had to be won politically in the branches. She now thinks that Cliff had been aware of her position before he approached her at the meeting.[108]

Women's Voice continued as a magazine and it was only in 1982 that the decision was taken to close that down too. Again there was a fierce argument, although Cliff had won over some of his former opponents. There was some loss of women activists, but no major split.

Cliff spent a good deal of time in this period speaking, writing and reading about the question of women's oppression and women's organisation in the socialist movement. The final fruit of his labours came in early 1984 with the publication of his book *Class Struggle and Women's Liberation*.[109] In many ways it was a remarkable achievement. Cliff was 66 years old when he finished the book and it covered fields of history and social analysis which had never previously interested him. He ploughed his way through well over 200 volumes and articles in order to complete his study. Perhaps it was the fact that anti-racism had always been central to his Marxism that enabled Cliff to develop a critique of other forms of oppression to which he had originally not been sensitive.[110]

The theme of the book was not women's oppression, but women's resistance. He began by setting out his fundamental argument in a stark fashion, insisting on the fundamental antagonism between Marxism and feminism:

> Feminism sees the basic division in the world as that between men and women. The cause of women's oppression is men's urge to dominate and control them. History is the story of the unchanging patriarchal structures through which men have subjugated women. The only way to abolish these structures is for women, of whatever social class, to unite against men, of whatever class.
>
> For Marxism, however, the fundamental antagonism in society is that between classes, not sexes. For thousands of years a minority of men and women have cooperated to live off the labour of the overwhelming majority of working men and women. The class struggle between exploiter and exploited, whatever their sex, is the driving force of historical change. Women's oppression can only be understood in the context of the wider relations of class exploitation.
>
> There can be no compromise between these two views, even though some "socialist feminists" have in recent years tried to bridge the gap between them.[111]

In order to develop this argument, necessarily a provocative one to feminist readers, Cliff began with a brief chapter on the Levellers, Diggers and Ranters of the English Revolution, and then moved on to the French Revolution. Drawing heavily on the work of Daniel Guérin, he brought out the dual nature of the revolution, the struggle of the bourgeoisie against the nobility, and the struggle of the embryonic working class against the bourgeoisie, and showed how the bourgeois Jacobins betrayed working women.

Class Struggle and Women's Liberation then took the story forward with episodes from the history of women's struggles in the US,

Britain, France, Germany and Russia. Cliff's heroines were women from the working class movement, such as Elizabeth Gurley Flynn and "Mother" Jones in the US, Louise Michel and the women of the Paris Commune, and Clara Zetkin in Germany. He showed that it was the women workers of Petrograd who had begun the Russian Revolution – while the Bolsheviks tried to hold them back. He cited with great enthusiasm the words of Domitila Barrio, a Bolivian miner's wife, denouncing middle class feminists:

> Senora, I've known you for a week. Every morning you show up in a different outfit and on the other hand I don't... And in order to show up here like you do, I'm sure you live in a really elegant home, in an elegant neighbourhood, no? And yet we miners' wives only have a small house on loan to us, and when our husbands die or get sick or are fired from the company, we have ninety days to leave the house and then we're in the street. Now, senora, tell me: is your situation at all similar to mine? Is my situation at all similar to yours? So what equality are we going to speak of between the two of us? If you and I aren't alike, if you and I are so different?[112]

He showed that the modern women's movement in Britain had begun with the 1968 sewing machinists' strike at Ford Dagenham and the creation of the National Joint Action Campaign for Women's Equal Rights, rather than with the Oxford Women's Liberation Conference in 1970, as was often claimed.

He also showed just how deeply sexist attitudes had permeated the socialist tradition. He condemned the reactionary ideas of Proudhon and the "outrageous" views of Belfort Bax, who had opposed votes for women.[113] He pointed out that the Amalgamated Society of Engineers (the British engineering union) did not admit women until 1943, and he gave examples of the "gross sexism" which characterised the American new left that emerged in the 1960s.[114]

Even the greatest Marxists had neglected women's oppression. He described as "astonishing" the fact that Marx had referred to "universal suffrage" in the Paris Commune, even though women did not have the vote, and that Lenin had repeated this in *State and Revolution*.[115] Marx and Engels had been wrong to predict the withering away of the working class family under capitalism; on the contrary, working class women had actively re-created the family.

Cliff was scathing about bourgeois feminists. He showed the deep racism of the American women's movement in the 19th century, and observed how post-1968 feminism became respectable and offered a basis for careerism. He was particularly hard on the British suffragettes, showing how the Pankhursts capitulated to chauvinism at the outbreak of the First World War. Even Sylvia Pankhurst, who broke with her family to take an anti-war line and became a communist, was dealt with harshly, although – or perhaps because – she had been popular in *Women's Voice* circles. Cliff dismissed her period as a socialist as "short and confused".[116]

Cliff's assessment of the suffragettes in *Class Struggle and Women's Liberation* was extremely negative and can only be seen as an example of the "stick-bending" in which he often indulged. He concluded:

> Seeing the revolutionary upheavals following the Russian Revolution, the ruling classes decided to try to block the road to workers' power by diverting the growing militancy on to the parliamentary road... If in general, as Lenin argued, serious reforms are the by-products of revolutionary struggle, the establishment of the Weimar Republic in Germany and the granting of universal suffrage in Germany, Austria, Hungary, Poland, the Baltic States...and Britain, was the by-product of the revolutionary struggle of workers and a measure to block this struggle. Votes were granted to women as a reaction to the struggle of the millions of workers led by Lenin, Trotsky, Luxemburg and Liebknecht, and not as a result of the pressure of the suffragettes in Britain or the women's movement in Germany.[117]

It was one of Cliff's less convincing arguments. Certainly the post-war crisis provided the essential context, but if there had been no movement for women's suffrage, why would there have been any necessity for concessions to be made on this particular front? Just over the Channel in France, where there had been no significant suffrage movement, women had to wait another quarter of a century before getting the right to vote, even though the revolutionary threat, in the form of a mass Communist Party, was more real there. Cliff's concern was with directing the present rather than interpreting the past. Perhaps he feared that SWP women comrades would start chaining themselves to railings or leaping under racehorses instead of building in the labour movement.*

Cliff stressed that there could be no unity of all women across class boundaries. He recalled the brutality of the Versailles ladies against the women of the Paris Commune and mocked "the unity of ladies with their maids".[118] The development of the women's liberation movement was more closely linked to the experience of the new middle class than to the working class.

For Cliff the development of women's struggle could not be abstracted from the total situation. The reversal of the gains made by women in the Russian Revolution was not attributable to mistaken or male-dominated policies, but to the material conditions which led to the defeat of the revolution. Likewise the current decline in the women's movement was inseparable from the general context of the downturn.

Cliff did not directly deal with the role of women in the SWP, but merely cited various historical points which had a direct bearing on current disputes. The Bolsheviks had produced a separate paper for women workers, *Rabotnitsa*, at moments of rising struggle, in 1913 and 1917. Because the overall struggle was more important than any sectional struggles, women's organisation had to be subordinated to the party's democratic centralism.

He was scathing about the trend to separatism, and particularly about the enthusiasm for "consciousness-raising" in the women's movement:

> Many women, especially socialist feminists in Britain, argued that consciousness-raising was important not because it improved women's lives but because it gives women the confidence to take part in political activity. Alas, it doesn't. You don't build your confidence by separating yourself off from the struggle going on in the world around you. If you do, then just the opposite happens: you never get the chance to develop the skills and arguments necessary for political activity. As the experience showed, women tended to cling more and more to their small groups, and when these broke up, to drop out completely.[119]

It was in changing the world that people changed themselves: "Only in the struggle to transform social relations do people change.

---

* The chapter on the suffragettes entitled "Women" in Paul Foot's *The Vote* (pp171-237) is a sustained posthumous polemic against his old comrade. They had argued fiercely about the question for many years (Clare Fermont interview, September 2008).

It is the workplace that opens up to women the widest opportunities to struggle to organise and hence to change themselves".[120]

Towards the end of *Class Struggle and Women's Liberation*, in one of the most interesting sections, Cliff dealt with the question of the family. Against those feminists who argued for the abolition of the family, he showed how women had often seen the family as a form of defence against the brutalities of capitalist society. He argued that the working class family was contradictory, "both protective and oppressive, both a haven from an alienating world, and a prison".[121] Here Cliff was drawing on Marx's account of religion as both the "heart of a heartless world" and "opium of the people".[122] He was also probably influenced by his own happy childhood and his deep devotion to Chanie and their children. Perhaps too he drew on some of the many articles on women's oppression that had appeared in party publications – already back in 1974 Kathy Ennis had argued that many people saw the family as a "place of retreat", somewhere for "emotions which have no place in the cut-throat world of capitalist competition", but that the capitalist family could never live up to this ideal because it was "riddled with contradictions".[123]

As for the future, Cliff observed that different Marxists had held different views about the future of the family and he concluded agnostically, "We simply do not know. There is no crystal ball to tell us how people will feel and act in their personal relations under communism".[124] Since communism was about freedom, individuals would choose from a variety of lifestyles.

Sheila McGregor thinks Cliff was changed by the experience of writing the book. In the 1970s his attitude had been egalitarian and profoundly humanitarian, but he had thought that the Marxist tradition was sufficiently developed in relation to women's oppression and was reluctant to work on the topic. When he did write the book it provided an excellent account of the relation between class and oppression.[125] He had to argue with Chanie, who in particular disagreed with him over the inclusion of a passage which Cliff wanted to cut, and persuaded him that it must stay.[126]

There was much useful material in *Class Struggle and Women's Liberation*, but it had flaws. It was not his natural territory, rather a task he felt he had to accomplish because of difficulties in the party. Sometimes polemical zeal led him to overstatement, as with the suffragettes; sometimes he lapsed into pedantry or over-literal interpretation, and seemed to be trying to push as much as possible of the socialist tradition into the wrong camp. He sneered at "lesbian feminists" for their use of the word "herstory" instead of history, accusing them of ignorance of the word's etymology.* [127] It is curious that someone with a sense of humour like Cliff should not recognise a pun when he saw one.

The greatest weakness was that, unlike his best works, it did not draw on the experience of the organisation. The strength of *The Employers' Offensive* and other writings on the industrial struggle from the 1970s was the way Cliff drew on the experience of workers in the organisation and let them speak in their own words. *Class Struggle and Women's Liberation* contained a few references to articles from the SWP press, but there was no attempt to draw on the experience of women in the party.

The book made a certain impact beyond the SWP. Each week the London magazine *City Limits* published a list of "alternative bestsellers", based on sales at left, feminist and alternative bookshops in London, of which there were then a fair number. In the week 1-7 June 1984 Cliff's book appeared at number five in the non-fiction list.

Cliff's uncompromising polemic was not designed to win friends, even among socialist feminists. Judith Williamson responded in kind with a vigorously critical review:

> His claimed intent is to show "that women's liberation is impossible without the victory of socialism and that socialism is impossible without women's liberation" – which might sound like a socialist feminist project. But his real purpose is to refute the entire feminist movement of the last 15 years, while at the same time taking ground from it: "feminism" is to be proved bourgeois and individualist, yet its impact is manifest in the book's very existence, its need to colonise areas of consciousness feminism has opened up.
>
> Although supposedly about class struggle and women's liberation "from 1640 to the present day", the historical material is wheeled on to substantiate the contemporary subtext, the battle around feminism and the position of women in left groups: which makes the book weak as history,

---

* *Women's Voice* had also used the "herstory" pun – e.g. No 12, December 1977.

though strong as a polemic. Its emphasis on class politics and its criticism of bourgeois feminism are valid (i.e. I agree); but *feminists* have made these points too, and this Cliff will not allow. Here the book is fundamentally dishonest, for it sets up feminism as nothing but a crass battle-cry on the very first page: "Feminism sees the cause of women's oppression as men's urge to dominate and control them". Few feminists would say anything as simplistic, yet on this hangs Cliff's whole position.[128]

SWP member Norah Carlin responded equally vigorously. She quoted feminist literature to show that the positions attacked by Cliff were current among feminists, and argued that women were playing a stronger role in the SWP since the closure of *Women's Voice*:

> Readers of Judith Williamson's review...may be surprised to know that there are women in the Socialist Workers Party, that we welcome Cliff's book, and that we don't feel our voice is being "replaced" by his.
>
> The review gives no idea of what the bulk of the book is about: a history of revolutionary socialists' commitment to women's liberation on the one hand, and a critique of *both* bourgeois feminism *and* the sexist politics of much of the history of the labour movement on the other.
>
> In stating that there is an alternative, in revolutionary socialism committed to women's liberation, Cliff's polemic is timely, and I hope that women not blinded by "feminist" subjectivism *will* read it and perhaps join us in the fight. Our voices are still here – and are heard a lot more in *Socialist Worker* and *Socialist Review* nowadays than when we were ghettoised in our "own" corner.[129]

Another question which Cliff took up around this time was the question of whether men benefit from the oppression of women. This was discussed only briefly in the book,[130] though it was implicit in the whole argument. Cliff did not participate in the debate on this published in *International Socialism*,[131] but he always considered this question to be of great importance and referred to it in his autobiography as a major question.[132] He often argued, "If men benefit from women's oppression, then unity is impossible".[133]

Cliff's main opponent in the debate was John Molyneux, who considers that it was Cliff who made this into a major issue for debate, seeing it as a key argument against feminism. Molyneux was heavily defeated in a conference debate on the question, and put under pressure to agree not to pursue it.[134]

Class Struggle and Women's Liberation appeared in April 1984. The previous month had seen the start of what was to be the biggest class confrontation of the 1980s.

11
1984-89
Digging Deep

On 12 March 1984 there began a bitter year-long miners' strike against pit closures. Many who hated Thatcher but did not have the confidence to fight themselves invested their hopes in the miners winning again as they had in 1972 and 1974. But it was a strike the Tories were determined to win. Careful preparations had been made and Thatcher was looking not just for revenge, but for a means of weakening and demoralising the whole working class. There were massive deployments of police against miners' pickets and frequent instances of police violence.

The miners had a president in Arthur Scargill who was a militant of the left, a man committed to aggressive mass picketing. In style he appeared far more radical than even the most left-wing trade union leaders of previous years. But the miners suffered from serious weaknesses. Incentive schemes, a form of productivity deal introduced under the Labour government, had created deep divisions between the different areas. Many Nottinghamshire miners, despite pickets from Yorkshire, continued to work throughout the dispute.

For Cliff and the whole SWP, the strike meant going onto a war footing. A defeat for the miners would be a disaster for the whole working class movement. From 10 March 1984 to 9 March 1985 every issue but one of *Socialist Worker* had a front page on the strike. SWP members were active in collecting money and winning support in the labour movement.

From the beginning Cliff addressed meetings around the country and made an impression on miners and their supporters. In the first months of the strike the SWP organised rallies under the slogan "Victory to the Miners". In a period of ten weeks Cliff spoke at meetings in Liverpool, Nottingham, Derby, Barnsley, Sheffield, Swansea, Cardiff, Brighton and Manchester, and addressed two rallies in Leeds and eight district meetings in London.[1] He carried on travelling the country for the duration of the strike. Eileen Boyle, aged 18, heard Cliff speak. He stormed around the stage; she had never heard anything like it and was totally enthralled. She joined the party soon afterwards and remained a member for 25 years.[2] While he was speaking at one meeting a man stood up and began to heckle in Hebrew. Without hesitation Cliff shouted something back in Hebrew and the heckler sat down. He then told the audience, "I was just correcting his grammar".[3]

One militant described the impact of first hearing Cliff speak in Sheffield in the first month of the strike:

> At lunchtime I was persuaded to attend a fringe meeting to be addressed by someone called Tony Cliff… He was an old guy, short and stocky with wiry grey hair sticking out from either side of his head, and wearing glasses. He had a strong foreign accent which I found hard to understand at first. However, once I was tuned in I found myself agreeing with almost everything he said. He wasn't like the other speakers I had heard because he openly criticised Scargill and the NUM leadership saying they were tactically naive! He drew comparisons between the '72 and '74 strikes and now, saying we couldn't win this one just by closing down power stations, mainly because of the time of year but also because we would not get support from other trade unionists unless we began campaigning for support now amongst the rank and file… He said our only hope was to appeal to workers directly by going to their meetings and explaining exactly what the strike was about. He got a tremendous round of applause and I for one thought what he had to say made sense, even if it did depress me a bit![4]

In April Cliff surveyed the first month of the strike:

> The strike has been running for four weeks and we are still waiting for a decisive breakthrough. It is like a car that stalls at every set of traffic lights. The Tories and the Coal Board haven't turned the strike back, but the miners haven't yet built up the momentum to carry them to victory.

He pointed to the serious weaknesses on the miners' side:

> So far, the level of picketing and involvement is lower than during the 1972 strike when an estimated 40,000 pickets were out every day. In Yorkshire, strike committees still haven't been set up. And there is a danger that the active militant minority will become an isolated self-contained group, not generalising the fight to bring in other miners and other workers.[5]

The SWP had only about eight miner members at the beginning of the strike, though many more were drawn around it in the course of the struggle.[6] After the first month of the strike a meeting was held of 35 miners from eight pits who supported *Socialist Worker*. Cliff spoke, stressing the need for "initiative from the rank and file in the picketing" and calling for honesty in recognising weaknesses on the miners' side:

> There are all sorts of horror stories about how badly the picketing has been organised.
>
> Of course people don't talk about these things at big rallies like those held on Saturday. They say things are marvellous, we're winning and so on. But razamataz like that doesn't win strikes.
>
> The people who come to these rallies are the people who agree anyhow. We have to know what the truth is, however horrible, but then draw the conclusions.[7]

In the first months of the strike the SWP emphasis was on how the strike could be won. The collection of money was important, but in itself it would not win the strike, merely enable the strikers to stay out longer. A great many trade unionists were willing to put their hands in their pockets for the miners, but did not feel the confidence to take action in their support. The SWP was often accused of being sectarian in the first months of the strike for not simply putting all their efforts into the support committees which were growing up across the country. But Cliff and the central committee thought that they had a duty to point to how victory might be achieved. Initially Cliff believed the strike could be won by mass pickets of key coal users, especially steel plants. He proposed organising a petition to get the NUM to picket the Ravenscraig steelworks in Scotland. This led to a quite unpleasant disagreement with Peter Alexander and other CC members, who thought he was going behind their backs.[8]

While some sections of the left were concentrating on collecting food for the striking miners, the SWP emphasised the importance of militant picketing. At one point Cliff said that the only thing we should do with a tin of beans was to throw it at the police. Ian Mitchell, a young miner who had joined the SWP at the beginning of the strike, admits that this was "a tad ultra-left", but says it chimed with himself and other militants at the time, because the branch officials were trying to hold back militancy.[9] *

In Birmingham there was a large miners' support group run by the trades council, in which the SWP participated from the outset. Cliff was keen to discuss this experience with John Rees, the Birmingham organiser, showing that he was already thinking about the need for a more defensive strategy.[10]

The crunch came three months into the strike, at the end of May, with mass pickets of the British Steel coking plant at Orgreave, near Sheffield. Miners turned up in substantial numbers, but were outnumbered by police in riot gear who attacked the miners in brutal fashion. Unlike most union leaders Scargill put his head on the line, participating actively in the pickets, being arrested on one occasion and hospitalised on another.

Scargill's aim was that Orgreave should be the Saltley of the 1984 strike. This hope was doomed to failure. Whereas the Birmingham engineers were essential for the Saltley victory, Sheffield steel and engineering workers were not mobilised. The miners were left to fight alone and were unable to stand up to the forces of the state.

After Orgreave Cliff wrote another article for *Socialist Worker*, drawing out the political weakness of the leadership in the working class movement:

> The debacle at Orgreave shows that you can't expect miners to suddenly flock to picket steel if you've been telling them to leave steel alone for 12 weeks.
>
> The rank and file appear as a stage army to the trade union bureaucrats and every action they sanction is too little, too late.[11]

At a meeting in June of more than 50 SWP-supporting miners from 16 pits, Cliff argued that the area leaderships were sabotaging the effectiveness of the strike:

> Scargill is like a general who depends upon his colonels to give orders to his army. And the colonels are saying to him, "Jump in the river".[12]

In July there was a possibility that dockers would join the miners in

---

* A cartoon by Tim Sanders (*Socialist Worker*, 21 July 1984) showed a miner throwing a tin of beans at a policeman. Tim may well have got the idea from Cliff, but later Cliff used Tim's cartoon to illustrate the follies of ultra-leftism (communication from Tim Sanders, March 2010).

confronting the government. The Marxism event was closed a day early and Cliff addressed a special rally urging all comrades to get involved. However, the dock strike crumbled after ten days and the opportunity was lost.

The emphasis was now shifting. The possibility of a reasonably quick victory was evaporating. It was still vital to support the strike as long as it lasted, to prevent the possibility of a humiliating defeat. SWP members now became more active in the local support committees, raising money for the miners and their families. In particular they argued for the twinning of support committees and workplaces with particular pits, though this was not encouraged by the NUM leadership.

In some unpublished notes Cliff attempted to analyse the significance of Orgreave and its impact on the day-to-day practice of the SWP:

> Many comrades and branches made the change of gear very well. Some cases showed terrible divorcement from reality of life of miners, and changing gear made terrible noises.
>
> The auspices: in some case comrades resisted the move from SW [*Socialist Worker*] collecting sheets to official collecting sheets. Sign of substitutionism. Role of revolutionary party. Raise activity of workers...
>
> After Orgreave – with a couple of weeks' pause – we concluded that the strike is completely defensive. Miners are going to picket *only* their pits, with some token, tiny pickets elsewhere...
>
> The word "downturn" has become worn from use. It has lost its concrete content, and is obviously inadequate for analysing the post-Orgreave stage.
>
> The concept of the downturn is not a master key that unlocks all tactical problems. No, it does not free us from the necessity of concrete analysis of every stage of the downturn. On the contrary it forces us to make just such an analysis. But it goes on to serve as a correct starting point in understanding the dynamics of the class struggle at present.
>
> If one proceeds only on the basis of the characterisation of the present situation as the downturn and nothing more, ignoring its concrete states, one might easily lapse into schematism. Orgreave was a central turning point...

Orgreave was a decisive turning point in the struggle. Always a crisis in the working class must cause contradictions, tension, difficulties in any healthy revolutionary party – and that, I believe, is in fact what happened to us.[13]

The problems caused by the strike were reflected within the CC. Several of those on the CC at the time remember it as a difficult period, marked by many disagreements and tensions. Despite the enormous commitment and energy he put into the strike, Cliff bore some of the responsibility for this. Indeed on one occasion other CC members actually held a caucus without Cliff.[14] Cliff knew that a defeat for the miners would set back working class struggle for several years, and he was well aware that, at his age, this was going to be his last chance to intervene actively in a major struggle.[15]

At times it seemed that Cliff thought he was running the strike. Once he argued that the miners should do the same when facing the police as workers in Japan, where they had crash helmets and long poles.[16] He had a voluntarist attitude to the strike, and was too upbeat, not doing enough to prepare miners and the membership for the defeat ahead of them.[17] He thought the main thing was not to prepare for defeat, but to stand with those miners who wanted to fight. While he accepted central committee discipline, Cliff found himself having a different emphasis to other comrades.[18]

The CC had to strike a difficult balance: throwing the party into the strike but trying simultaneously to maintain the general approach to the downturn evolved over the previous few years, designed to cope with a situation that was tough (as the strike was to confirm).[19]

In the last few months of the strike there was a very nasty row on the CC, although this was kept from the membership. Cliff was highly critical of the party's earlier sectarianism, despite having been one of those most suspicious about the miners' support groups in the early months of the strike.[20] Other CC members thought he was passing himself off as having been a non-sectarian all along and failing to defend his CC comrades.[21] The situation was unstable and sharp antagonisms were developing, threatening a serious split in the CC.[22]

Yet there is a striking contrast between the recollections of CC members and the memories of striking miners. Militants such as Ian

Mitchell and Steve Hammill have a much more positive view of Cliff's involvement. He kept in close touch with the miners who were active in the strike. He visited Yorkshire frequently and the SWP miners went to London for various meetings. Ian Mitchell found himself in a number of one-to-one discussions with Cliff during the strike and found Cliff "very attentive" and willing to find time to explain arguments.[23] Clearly Cliff was much happier close to the struggle than he was in committee meetings.

Nonetheless, by the end of the strike Cliff was aware defeat was inevitable and that this was a shattering defeat for the whole working class. Briefly he appeared to lose his enthusiasm: at a public meeting in Portsmouth he spoke sitting down (something he never otherwise did) and sent his audience away demoralised.[24]

Martin Smith attended a meeting addressed by Cliff towards the end of the strike. He was a Labour Party member and still firmly convinced the miners would win, so he was shocked when Cliff said the strike would be defeated. He argued fiercely against Cliff and shouted at him; Cliff explained patiently and at the end of the meeting put his arm round Smith and told him people like him were needed in the SWP. Smith joined at the end of the strike.[25]

One year on, the strike was defeated. Scargill, with some courage, led a united return to work. Cliff was now a few months short of his sixty-seventh birthday. The defeat of the strike was a major turning point. The hope of revolutionary change within his lifetime, which he had believed in until very recently, had now become remote. Most people in Cliff's situation would have been sorely tempted to feel they had done their bit, to step down from a leadership role and to spend the rest of their lives doing some leisurely writing.

Such a course would have been quite foreign to Cliff's nature. He immediately began to address public meetings. The message was simple. The defeat had not been inevitable, but was the result of reformist politics. Hence the imperative was to build a revolutionary alternative.* Despite the general mood of defeat Cliff was able to recruit quite a few new members in the aftermath of the strike.[26] For

---

* Though it was small consolation for the defeat, the SWP's patient work during the strike had led to a growth in membership and much greater paper sales; the financial situation improved and by the end of 1985 it was possible to move to a larger printshop in Bow (communication from Alex Callinicos, August 2010).

example he addressed a successful north London public meeting just after the strike. He assessed the meaning of the defeat, drew parallels with 1926 and made an honest, realistic evaluation of the prospects ahead; several new members were recruited.[27] This new wave of recruits was important in lifting the low morale of the organisation after the defeat of the miners,[28] and some of those who joined during and after the strike would become the mainstay of the party in the subsequent quarter-century.[29]

Cliff continued to take a close personal interest in individual miners who had gone through the strike, as they faced victimisation and had to grapple with the problem of whether to take redundancy payments.[30]

Only now did Cliff apply himself to an analysis of the weaknesses of the strike, and an understanding of these in a broader historical context. Late in 1985 he published a long article entitled "Patterns of mass strike".[31]

This began with the affirmation that the recent strike had been "radically different" to the strike of 1972. In order to explain the differences Cliff presented a wide-ranging analysis of mass strikes in the 20th century. He began with Luxemburg's book *The Mass Strike, The Political Party and The Trade Unions*, which showed "the role of the mass strike in forging the working class into a fighting unit...changing them so that they become able to change society". For Luxemburg the mass strike overcame "the separation of economics and politics" and was "a bridge between the here and now and the socialist future".

He then went on to contrast Luxemburg's picture, based on Russia before and during 1905, with situations in which strikes were more tightly controlled by the union bureaucracy. Cliff provided two historical examples, the general strikes of 1909 in Sweden and 1913 in Belgium. Here, he showed, there was "no spontaneity, no independent rank and file action, complete separation of politics from economics, no economic challenge to the capitalists, and no real political challenge to the state".

Cliff moved on to the British General Strike of 1926, pointing out that it came after a long period of downturn, and that Trotsky greatly exaggerated workers' combativity. He contrasted it with 1919, when offensive strikes brought Britain "closer to revolution than at any time in modern history". A section on France in 1968 drew mainly on his pamphlet from that year.

He then looked at the three miners' strikes. For Cliff, 1972 was the high-point; it was a "a rank and file strike" with a high level of active involvement – perhaps two-thirds of strikers being involved in picketing. Moreover, "The miners won not only by their own efforts but by the help they received from other workers." That such help was lacking in the later strike had a simple explanation: "Workers who lack the confidence to stand up to their own bosses cannot be expected to come out in support of other workers."

The 1974 strike, though successful, was "radically different" from 1972, being held in the "stranglehold" of the bureaucracy. The 1984-85 strike showed even greater weaknesses: "The level of activity of rank and file miners was lower and, crucially, they showed much less initiative and independence of the bureaucracy." Lying behind the weaknesses of the strike was "the ideology of Labourism". Cliff stressed the "conservative social and political attitudes" of the British working class. During the long boom reformism had delivered real improvements, and reformist ideas had not disappeared: "Even though reformism cannot protect the working class from the ravages of the crisis, if no credible revolutionary alternative is available, masses of workers will cling to reformist ideas for want of anything better." As a result, the only prospect for socialists was "long haul".

Like Cliff's other articles on working class history, the analysis was packed with detail and full of illuminating insights. It contained the seeds of his next two books.

Cliff wrote one other article directly inspired by the great strike, although it was characterised by a rather strange double silence. At the Skegness rally at Easter 1985 Paul Foot had addressed a meeting on AJ Cook, the miners' leader at the time of the 1926 strike. In January 1986 this was produced as a pamphlet under the title *An Agitator of the Worst Type*.[32] Foot had a glorious lyrical style and a slight tendency to hero-worship, and he produced a highly favourable portrait of a man whom he saw as a great working class leader. He praised Cook's pamphlets as "hot with the struggle of the times". He did not deny Cook's "waverings", and noted his political retreat in his last years, accepting that his praise for the Prince of Wales made him appear to be "yet another groveller before royalty", although Foot excused it as "warm-hearted impetuousness".

Foot pointed to the limits of Cook's syndicalism and showed that his retreats were a product of the defeat of the mass movement. He made clear the parallels between the situation after 1926 and those now faced by the SWP. After 1926 the only organised left force, the CP, had become "monkish and fanatical". Foot concluded with a ringing denunciation of sectarianism and declared that "one of the important tests of socialists' behaviour is how we relate to, and how we criticise, great working class leaders who can lead their class in the heat of the struggle, impervious to the most awful onslaught from the other side".

Foot's treatment of Cook stung Cliff and he responded almost immediately with a substantial article entitled "The Tragedy of AJ Cook".[33] He began with a recognition of Cook's strengths, showing that his popularity among miners was rooted in an ability "to touch the profound feelings and aspirations of his audience". But he stressed the political limitations of the revolutionary syndicalist tradition which had formed Cook, and pointed to Cook's "woolliness" and "semi-pacifist definition of revolution".

Cliff's main point was to draw out the nature of the trade union bureaucracy, described as "an *inevitable* product of the role of trade unions under capitalism". Hence he argued that "while the line of division between left and right union officials is of importance, the cleavage between the bureaucracy and the rank and file is of even greater consequence".* Cliff praised Cook's efforts during the 1926 strike, yet pointed to his "isolation", which he attributed to the fact that he was not a member of a revolutionary party:

> The lack of a party to support Cook led him to vacillations that sometimes bordered on capriciousness. The revolutionary party gives one a sense of realism. Being rooted in the class, made up of the most advanced workers, it allows elasticity and adaptation without falling into unprincipled opportunism.

Cliff was scathing about Cook's move to the right after 1926 and made no excuses for him. He insisted, "Trotsky was absolutely right

---

* This represented a shift of emphasis on Cliff's part. A little earlier, when Mike Simons and Alex Callinicos were writing their history of the strike ("The Great Strike", *International Socialism* 27-28, 1985) Cliff urged them to stress the TUC's failure to support the miners rather than be too critical of the left bureaucracy in the NUM (communication from Alex Callinicos, August 2010).

in making no concession to any of the left bureaucrats, not even to Cook, who was the most radical of them."

There were two absences in this exchange which made it different from normal polemics in the revolutionary movement. Cliff did not polemicise with Foot; on the contrary, there was no reference to Foot's pamphlet at any point. As in his earlier polemic with Steve Jefferys, Cliff was anxious not to personalise the debate. The second absence was Arthur Scargill. The parallels between Cook and Scargill were obvious,* and Cliff's concern was not with a dead historical figure, but to orient the party away from any softness on the left trade union leaders. Yet Foot mentioned Scargill only once in passing and Cliff did not name him at all. In Cliff's case it may have been so as not to be seen publicly attacking a workers' leader who had been subjected to the most appalling abuse in the press.

Foot's intervention was motivated by a concern that the SWP strategy for the deepened downturn which followed the miners' defeat could lead to propagandist sectarianism. During the strike he had registered some sharp disagreements with Cliff, arguing that the party must throw itself into the movement before criticising. At one national meeting during the strike he had called the entire CC "Stalinist".[34] Cliff responded by "bending the stick" towards the need to build the party on the basis of clarity about the nature of the bureaucracy. There was a problem of balance here, but the debate did not spill over into a broader argument.

It was an episode in the often complex relationship between Foot and Cliff. They worked together over four decades and, despite their great mutual respect and affection, there was a certain tension between them. Foot has recorded that Cliff would frequently jibe that he was "soft",[35] and over the years they had furious rows about a whole number of issues, from proportional representation, which Cliff opposed, to the Balkans where Foot found Cliff soft on Serbia. Foot tested his ideas out on Cliff and despite constant sparring they deeply influenced each other. Foot recognised Cliff as a genius while Cliff tended to see Foot as an errant son. Foot was never afraid to challenge Cliff if he thought him wrong. Although they frequently shared platforms at public meetings, Cliff never let Foot speak last

---

* Foot had been in regular telephone contact with Scargill during the strike (communication from Alex Callinicos, August 2010).

so that he could correct him if necessary – but he also often adapted what he argued to take account of what Foot had said previously.[36] At one national meeting where Foot was critical of a tendency to sectarianism, Cliff began shouting at him that it was necessary to "keep clear of the swamp".[37]

The miners' defeat did not put an end to resistance, but it shifted the balance of forces. The next major confrontation came with the print unions. The Murdoch press moved production out of Fleet Street to Wapping, using new technology. It was a head-on confrontation with the print unions, whose members had traditionally enjoyed good wages and strong organisation. (During the miners' strike printers at the *Sun* had refused to print a front page calling miners "the scum of the earth".[38]) For a full year there were mass pickets, sometimes attacked by mounted police. Large numbers of SWP members took part in the pickets and demonstrations. The struggle went down to defeat.

In the spring of 1986 Cliff gave an interview surveying the current state of struggle,[39] aiming to draw out positive features in a bleak situation. The left should not concentrate on looking at its own weaknesses, but see that the other side had problems. The Tories had "won a lot of individual battles – they didn't win the war". Real wages had risen since 1979 and trade union organisation was largely intact:

> It is very important for socialists in general principle to despise the enemy – we are the many; they are the few. But in terms of the specific we have to show great respect to them – because we can be the few and they are the many. So fighting for individual shop organisation, collecting money – all the small things – are terribly important. Unless you tactically respect the enemy you are lost.*

He referred in particular to the "new realism" then being advocated by trade union leaders. While recognising that outside of a revolutionary situation most workers would be passive, he rejected as "stupidity" the claim by Eric Hobsbawm and others that the working class was finished. The South Korean working class alone

---

* As Cliff often acknowledged, the maxim "strategically we should despise all our enemies, but tactically we should take them all seriously" came from Mao Tse-tung's speech at the Moscow Meeting of Communist and Workers' Parties (18 November 1957).

was now bigger than the world working class at the time of Marx. So Cliff attacked what he called "the manic depressive people" who retreated into passivity because of recent defeats:

> Instead of accepting from Gramsci optimism of the will and pessimism of the intellect, they accept optimism of the intellect and pessimism of the will. So everything is marvellous in the garden, but there is nothing we can do about it. Instead we say, "Everything in the garden is terrible, but there are things we can do."
>
> In this situation the perspective must be to "increase our membership marginally. Can we grow to 6,000 instead of 4,000? Yes, but 50,000 doesn't fit the level of struggle." (As he used to put it, "If you recruit one that is good, two is very good, three you're a liar".[40]) He rejected abstract propagandism; the SWP must intervene where it could. In mobilising for the Wapping pickets the SWP could bring out as many people as the much larger, but much more passive Labour Party. "We are not insignificant. Why? Because an organisation of 4,000 is not as small as all that if it intervenes correctly in the specific struggles."

In November 1986 he told the SWP conference that, unlike the early 1980s when there had been "a political upturn in an industrial downturn", now "the shift to the right – both industrially and politically – is *massive*". The message, however, was not despair or accommodation, rather:

> It means working hard and enthusiastically in the here and now, but being honest, keeping our expectations low and not exaggerating the possibilities.[41]

Labour's heavy election defeat in 1983, followed by the miners' strike, had largely demoralised the Labour left. After Michael Foot's ineffective display as leader, Neil Kinnock, who replaced him, had won the leadership as the left candidate, but was steering the party rightwards. The Bennites had largely disintegrated and many had gone over to the right, although Benn himself was moving left. Efforts were made to regroup around the Chesterfield conferences in the late 1980s (in which the SWP participated), but they were on a much smaller scale than the Bennism of 1981.

This situation caused problems for the revolutionary left. The *Militant* group, whose history, like Cliff's, went back to the RCP of the 1940s, had established a significant membership in the

Labour Party and for a time had a leading role on Liverpool City Council, though it suffered a major defeat in confronting the government over spending limits. Now Kinnock launched a witch-hunt against *Militant*. Many *Militant* supporters were expelled and, in an effort to safeguard their positions, others claimed they were not revolutionaries but believed in a parliamentary transition to socialism.

The SWP now addressed unity proposals to *Militant*. Cliff explained this in a speech to the SWP conference in November 1985:

> The right wing of the Labour party, Kinnock and the centre and the soft left have all gone for unity and are attempting to cement it with the blood of *Militant*...
>
> So we've seen a wholesale drift to the right with *Militant* as the one group which hasn't shifted like this.
>
> So under such conditions you can't concentrate on the differences between us and *Militant*.[42]

In the situation after the miners' strike a united organisation could have attracted thousands of activists. The CC discussed the possibility of a positive response from *Militant* and envisaged transforming the SWP into a tendency in a larger organisation. *Militant* refused to take the proposals seriously and all the SWP could do was try to win some of the *Militant* membership when it suffered what Cliff described as "fraying at the edges".[43]

Cliff rejected any suggestion that the SWP should enter the Labour Party (as some sections of the far left, notably the former International Marxist Group, had done). Because of the trade union block vote an entrist group would be able to achieve very little:

> The left in the Labour Party are dreamers, utopians, completely unrealistic, because they say they can use the block vote if they take it under their control.
>
> Revolutionaries can take control over a district of a union or individual workplace organisation. They cannot take over the whole union machine. To do that you need the majority of workers to be activists and you can't expect it in a non-revolutionary situation.[44]

A more dramatic illustration of the crisis of the far left came with the explosion in the Workers Revolutionary Party, successor to the

SLL. Gerry Healy was accused of various offences against women members and was expelled from the organisation. Cliff may have felt some satisfaction that his old rival had got his just deserts, but he pointed to the political causes of the WRP crisis:

> Because of the wrong perspective about the miners' strike, expectations rose, and when those expectations were not realised then they started tearing one another to pieces... When conditions are tough, people who don't fit disintegrate. The fact that we didn't shows that we were right.* It's nothing to do with psychological toughness – in terms of toughness the WRP are the toughest in the world, but they disintegrated completely because they issued statements which didn't fit the situation at all.[45]

In 1992 Ted Grant was expelled from *Militant* after the majority decided to abandon work in the Labour Party. Of the three historic leaders of British Trotskyism from the generation of the 1940s, Cliff was the only one not to be expelled by his own organisation.

Cliff considered political clarity and the education of members to be vital. There was a shift to branch-based educationals. In the 1970s the term "education" had been discouraged in the party, because many workers had bad experiences of school, and it was replaced by the term "training"; now education was very much back and branches were urged to establish educational programmes for both new and experienced members.[46]

Cliff contributed to the educational task by continuing to travel tirelessly around the country, although he was now nearing 70 years of age. In February and March 1987 he spoke in Brighton, Kilburn, Westminster, Lewisham, Cardiff, Sheffield (two meetings), Lambeth, Colchester and Holborn, on topics ranging from "The revolutionary road to socialism" to "AIDS and the new morality" and "Lessons of the BT dispute".[47] He had cheap rail travel as a pensioner and boasted to other comrades that he was a more popular speaker because he cost less.[48]

While travelling, Cliff observed the state of the organisation. In some unpublished notes, probably written around 1987, he gave a candid and often highly critical account of the life of many SWP branches:

---

* The SWP did suffer losses of individuals and small groups on political grounds during this period, but the membership held together well.

In some cases I found political discussion abstract. Practice doesn't relate to the *real* branch members.

Discussions boring, regimented, humourless – main aim to show how high you can put SWP profile.

Discipline is crucial for a revolutionary party. Blind, bureaucratic discipline crumbles to dust when radical changes are necessary.

Abstract concept of democratic centralism. Party democracy is necessary to develop party members, but can only be achieved if healthy relations between the party and workers outside it exist.

World outside very cold and oppressive. Branch must be warm and friendly.

No second-class citizens in the branch. If young working class boy or girl find it unpleasant, if housewife finds it unpleasant, the attitude of all the workers will not be different.

A lot of what I said will be to many comrades old hat. But really all of us, even those with many years' experience, are quite rusty. And the young need experience.

Crucial task of branch to merge young with old. Youthful experience could lead it to a cul-de-sac.

Healthy ultra-leftism of the youth. Young enthusiasts can bump their heads against reality – not understanding reality, and turn quickly to become wise opportunists. Disappointed ultra-lefts turn in a short time into conservative bureaucrats just as a robber settles down and becomes transformed into an excellent policeman…

Last conference warned against the two-branch syndrome – a branch committee that discusses everything, decides everything, then at a later stage gets a managed discussion in the branch…

Workers, above all manual workers, must be pushed to the front…

Clique: depresses those outside it.[49]

Pat Stack, who often shared a platform with Cliff and sometimes had the unenviable job of speaking after Cliff, was impressed with his phenomenal ability to connect with an audience. Cliff was good at reading a meeting and making the necessary adjustments to fit the mood of those listening to him. On one occasion after only a couple of minutes Cliff passed Stack a note reading "bad atmosphere – difficult audience".[50]

Weyman Bennett was a student at Hull University in 1987 and a friend of Cliff's daughter Anna; he was a black nationalist. He went to hear Cliff speak on the Russian Revolution and it transformed his view of what the revolution had been. Then he had a discussion with Cliff about black nationalism. Cliff presented him with simple but vivid arguments, such as: if there are three people in a boat and they throw one out it makes it more difficult for the others to survive. Cliff predicted that one day skin colour would be no more significant than wearing glasses. Weyman joined the party and a couple of years later Cliff encouraged him to become a full-time organiser.[51]

Cliff played an active role in the annual Marxism events, now a major focus for party-building and attracting several thousand people; he usually spoke at around six meetings each year. He was always one of the speakers at the closing rally, generally entitled "Reform or Revolution?" or "The Socialist Alternative". Other meetings were often on the heritage of Lenin, Trotsky and Luxemburg and the main features of the SWP's tradition.

He played an active role in the regular meetings of full-time organisers. He was well informed and very hard on the need for organisers to take responsibility. He didn't tolerate moaning, and would quote the proverb "Fish rots from the head".[52] He urged organisers to follow their instincts; he didn't tell them what to do but gave them the confidence to try things out.[53] When Dave Hayes became national treasurer and printshop manager in 1988 Cliff would telephone him every day to ask for news.[54]

Cliff never forgot the need to encourage young comrades. He once summed up his approach as, "If someone does something well, praise them more than once. If they do something bad, only mention it once".[55] It was good advice, even if he did not always practise what he preached.

Eileen Boyle was working at the printshop. One evening Cliff had spoken at her branch in Harlesden, and she had contributed to the discussion. The next day she met Cliff on the stairs at the printshop and he congratulated her on what she had said, making her feel ten feet tall. She recalled his ability to talk to young people with a combination of politics, humour and self-assurance. But the encouragement was mixed with political hardness. Cliff would tell how the Bolsheviks had to wade through icy cold rivers holding their papers above their heads in order to distribute their publications – and would add that if they could do that, we could surely get out of bed to sell papers.[56]

Martin Smith remembers a number of hard arguments with Cliff when he was a young militant in the civil service. Cliff could be hard and would say things that comrades would not accept from anyone else, but he could recognise that he was wrong and change his position quickly. He could have a vigorous row with you, but he didn't bear grudges and was pleasant the next time he saw you. Smith thinks Cliff respected him for disagreeing. When Smith differed with him about policy towards promotions in the civil service, Cliff argued – but said it was good to have the argument. On another occasion Smith was involved in a dispute about which of two demonstrations should be supported. He was called to Cliff's home, expecting a "bollocking", but after listening agreed Cliff was right.[57] Sean Vernell agrees that learning and listening were central to Cliff's leadership style; he could demolish your argument without making you feel bad.[58]

Cliff was often supportive to comrades facing difficult situations amid the low level of struggle. Shaun Doherty was a leading activist in the NUT which was operating a policy of refusing to cover for absent colleagues. When management threatened to sack members who refused to cover, Doherty had to argue for ending the action, since they were not strong enough to defend anyone who was victimised. Many members saw this as a retreat, and Doherty was heckled at a meeting. Cliff consoled him by saying, "The day you become popular is the day we expel you from the party".[59]

Though encouraging, Cliff had not lost his critical edge. When he stayed at Mark Krantz's home, he took Mark's copy of *Capital* from the bookshelf and flicked through it till he found pencil marks, apparently checking to see if Mark had actually read it.[60] And he still had a tendency to make favourites – and drop them. John Rees remembered being warned by his friend Kevin Murphy, "When Cliff loves you, try and ignore it; when Cliff hates you, try and ignore it".[61]

He kept a close eye on party publications, sometimes writing letters to the editor if he felt comrades had put a wrong argument. When Colin Sparks published a book review which contained a paragraph apparently critical of Lenin's opposition to the demand for "peace" during the First World War, Cliff responded straight away in defence of the orthodoxy.[62]

In 1987 Nigel Harris wrote an article on the role of business in oppositional movements in South Korea and Panama. Cliff responded even more sharply, criticising Harris for neglecting the Korean working class and opening the door to popular frontism.[63] Harris left the SWP later that year. Cliff would have liked to keep him, and he and Duncan Hallas asked Harris what his differences were. Harris replied that he believed the SWP in the 1980s had stopped producing new ideas.[64]

But if Cliff could be hard, he was never callous. Several comrades remember that he found time for those with personal problems. Told of a comrade with psychosomatic illness, he insisted, "Psychosomatic pain is real pain." For a time Duncan Hallas, who was having difficulty finding somewhere to live, came to stay with Cliff and Chanie. This caused some problems, since Hallas's lifestyle – especially his drinking – was very different from Cliff's. Yet Cliff got on well with Hallas and despite the friction they never quarrelled.[65]

Cliff became involved in a debate about the work of his son Donny Gluckstein, who had written an article, "The missing party", in which he attempted to explain why nobody in Western Europe, even Rosa Luxemburg, had been able to build the kind of party needed to take advantage of the revolutionary situation that developed after 1917. Alex Callinicos wrote a sharp response, accusing Donny of absolving Rosa Luxemburg for her failure to build a revolutionary party and tending to give priority to soviets over the party.[66] This led to a vigorous debate at Marxism 1984. Callinicos's emphasis on the centrality of the party reflected the mainstream view in the SWP at the time, but Cliff intervened from the floor on his son's side, not from family loyalty but to advance his view on the nature of the revolutionary party. While agreeing that Lenin was in advance of Luxemburg, he argued that the real point was not to contrast Lenin to Luxemburg, but to juxtapose Lenin to Luxemburg. It had taken Lenin nearly 20 years longer than Luxemburg to make the break with Kautsky. Lenin had got it wrong about Western

Europe because he had to learn from the class: "Leadership learns from the class; leadership is shaped by the class".[67] When Donny subsequently made a written reply to Callinicos, Cliff helped him by providing relevant quotations from Lenin.[68]

More bizarrely, Cliff, who claimed he never listened to music, found himself in the popular music charts. The Redskins, a punk soul band consisting of members and sympathisers with the SWP which had been active doing gigs in support of the miners' strike, produced their first – and only – album, entitled *Neither Washington nor Moscow*.[69] The sleeve credited "Bootleg Propaganda: Tony Cliff of the SWP". Brief extracts from Cliff's speeches were inserted between some of the tracks. The album entered the *Music Week* chart on 22 March 1986, peaking at number 31.

Even when engaged on historical work Cliff's concern was primarily with the present. When he wrote a preface to the translation of the memoirs of a veteran Bolshevik, AY Badayev's *Bolsheviks in the Tsarist Duma*,[70] he devoted a good part of his contribution to arguing that the Labour Party was "the most extreme, purest antithesis of Bolshevism" and polemicising against *The Class Struggle in Parliament*[71] by left Labour MP Eric Heffer, because it neglected the industrial struggles of 1972 in favour of parliamentary debates.

Another growing preoccupation in the period after the end of the miners' strike was with the SWP's international tendency. There were now a number of groups, some with only a handful of members, in various countries around the world, and Cliff was anxious to pass on the experience of the early years of the International Socialists. His contribution was often similar to the way he had nurtured a new generation of activists in the 1960s – spending many hours discussing and arguing with individuals and small groups. Alex Callinicos remembers his peculiar ability to insult people and charm them at the same time.[72]

Unlike almost anyone else in the SWP, Cliff had experience of clandestine work. This enabled him to be much firmer in criticising people who allowed a concern for security to lead to passivity. Operating illegally meant hiding the comrades but revealing the ideas.[73]

Around 1985 Ron Margulies was in touch with a small group of Turkish exiles in London who had split from a larger group and who were moving away from Stalinism. For some years Margulies would go with the leaders of the group to Cliff's home where there would be long discussions lasting several hours, with Cliff particularly concerned to convince them of the importance of the theory of state capitalism. In 1989 he was furious that the Turkish comrades had missed their opportunity to use state capitalism to explain the crisis around the fall of the Berlin Wall. Finally in the early 1990s, they were won into the International Socialist Tendency.[74]

Much of Cliff's time in the late 1980s was devoted to two major books on the British labour movement, one on the trade union bureaucracy, the other on the Labour Party. The books stemmed directly out of his considerations on the downturn and the miners' strike, and were his contribution to the ideological struggle within the labour movement. He wanted to leave a legacy to SWP members, warning them against the continuing dangers of capitulation to reformism.

The books were written in collaboration with his elder son Donny, now an established historian in his own right. The first, *Marxism and Trade Union Struggle: The General Strike of 1926*[75] dealt with the British labour movement in the period up to 1926 and brought together Cliff's earlier work on trade union struggle and on the Comintern.

After the miners' defeat Cliff had recognised that the party was in for a long haul and was concerned at the danger of assimilation to the bureaucracy. He had proposed a book on the trade union bureaucracy and Gluckstein suggested centring it on the General Strike. Gluckstein wrote everything up to the outbreak of the strike, and Cliff everything from the outbreak of the strike onwards. They discussed the general approach and read each other's contributions. There were no major disagreements and since they had similar styles, the work fitted together well.[76]

They began by contrasting the different experiences of trade unions in Russia and Britain. Russia had avoided the dangers of bureaucracy, which in Britain had so often blocked workers' struggles. Hence Lenin, with his theory of the labour aristocracy, had not adequately appreciated the nature of reformism and the role of trade unions in the West.

This meant sharp criticism of the Comintern's main organisational approach to trade unions in the West – the Red International of Labour Unions (RILU).[77] The pair argued, "The trouble with the whole concept of RILU was not merely that it was ambiguous, but that it was fundamentally wrong." They blamed this on the fact that "its founders did not understand Western trade unions".[78]

The authors were sharply critical of the early CP and its attitude to reformism and the union machine. They emphasised the difference between revolutionary leadership – "the art of encouraging rank and file self-reliance" – and reformist leadership "which consists of spurring bureaucrats to act on behalf of the rank and file".[79]

They recalled Marx's views on the limitations of purely trade union struggle, insisting that revolutionaries must wage a political struggle within the unions, and laid down principles for a revolutionary attitude to trade union elections:

> It must be understood that the decision to become a shop steward, trade union branch official, member of a trades council or its secretary, depends on whether, by doing so, it assists the *activity* of the rank and file, or removes obstacles to this. Union office cannot substitute for this activity. The decisive factor in looking for any union position, therefore, is the possibility of raising the level of combativity of the workers one represents.[80]

Cliff and Gluckstein emphasised the need to distrust the trade union bureaucracy, which they saw as "a distinct, basically conservative, social formation". Union officials were "managers of discontent" who held back and controlled workers' struggle.[81] They made clear they wanted the lessons of the 1920s to illuminate the struggle in the present, and this assertion of the importance of maintaining independence from the union bureaucracy was the main theme of the book.

The account of the General Strike in *Marxism and Trade Union Struggle* differed somewhat from that often provided by writers drawing on Trotsky's writings on the period.[82] The authors paid tribute to the clarity and pertinence of Trotsky's writings on the British labour movement, but drew out their disagreement with Trotsky, who argued that 1926 was a "missed revolutionary opportunity". Rather they claimed that a retreat had begun after the high point of struggle in 1919, and that "the 1922 lockout of engineers killed the shop stewards' movement stone dead". In 1919-20 the government had "feared an outbreak of revolution"; there had been no comparable fear in 1926.* The strike was a genuine mass workers' movement, showing determination and creativity, with the potential for workers' control. The 1926 defeat was "the end of an era".[83]

The second collaboration was more ambitious: a comprehensive history of the Labour Party from the late 19th century to the present.[84] Though Bennism was finished and Labour moving rapidly rightwards under Kinnock, Cliff was still anxious that comrades might develop illusions in the Labour Party. More than 400 pages long, *The Labour Party: A Marxist History* was scholarly but politically hard, comprehensively documented from a range of primary sources, including *Hansard*, cabinet minutes, the minutes of Labour Party conferences, and the diaries and biographies of Labour leaders. Gluckstein wrote the chapters on the period up to 1931 and a short conclusion, while Cliff wrote the chapters covering 1931 to the 1980s. There were few problems because they were both thinking along similar lines.[85]

The authors began with a definition of the Labour Party, derived from Lenin, as a "capitalist workers' party" that is, a party which "defends the interests of capitalism (particularly when in government) but has the mass support of workers".[86] The analysis hammered home two main themes which distinguished it from the many other histories of the Labour Party. Firstly, the authors stressed the division between reformism and revolution; there was a clear line between revolutionary socialists and even the most militantly left-wing reformist. Secondly, the Labour Party could not be understood simply through parliamentary history, but must be located in

---

* The argument had something in common with the position argued by James Hinton and Richard Hyman in their book *Trade Unions and Revolution: The Industrial Politics of the early British Communist Party* (London, 1975), which also claimed that the early years of the CP did not offer revolutionary possibilities. But Cliff and his son dismissed the argument that the British CP would have done better to build "a cadre party placing primary emphasis on the *quality* rather than the quantity of its membership" (*Trade Unions and Revolution,* p73). As they pointed out, cadre could not be developed separately from the struggle for mass influence (Cliff and Gluckstein, *Marxism and Trade Union Struggle,* p125).

a broader history of class struggle.*

The pair began by attacking the myth, widespread among Labour leftists, that there had been a "golden age" of the Labour Party, arguing it had been reformist since its inception. The founding of the Independent Labour Party (ILP) had been "a genuine step forward for the class",[87] but far from being "independent", the ILP had been highly dependent for its theory on sources outside the working class.

The Labour Party had grown out of the trade unions; while the union bureaucracy was at one remove from the class struggle, the Labour Party was "twice removed". For the minority of advanced workers, the Labour Party was "a millstone around their necks". During the "Labour Unrest" which preceded the First World War, the Labour Party was "totally and utterly irrelevant". Compared with the "do-it-yourself reformism" of direct action, the Labour Party's efforts were "dismal".[88]

Likewise, Cliff and Gluckstein were scathing about Labour's role in the struggles that followed the First World War. In 1918 Labour adopted the famous Clause Four, which committed it to common ownership. While recognising that, 70 years later, Clause Four had to be defended as a sign of "commitment to a minimal anti-capitalist position", they saw the original clause advocated by Sidney Webb and Arthur Henderson as "a conscious means of staving off revolution". Labour gave more importance to the means (parliamentary success) than to the achievement of the socialist end. At the high-point of struggle in 1919 it was the union bureaucrats who were "the chief obstacle to revolution", but the Labour Party was an important auxiliary. [89]

Labour in the 1930s got a similar treatment. Of George Lansbury, often seen as a saintly figure, they wrote, "It is difficult to think of any other working class party in the world that could produce a leader with the muddleheadedness and reactionary ideas of Lansbury".[90]

---

* On this point they differed from Ralph Miliband, author of one of the best and most critical studies of the Labour Party, which widely influenced IS members in the 1960s: *Parliamentary Socialism* (London, 1961). Miliband had failed to grasp the point that "the willingness of both right and left Labour and trade union leaders to use extra-parliamentary means proves that the point of reference for reformists is not this or that institution but the function of mediation between classes" (Cliff and Gluckstein, *The Labour Party*, pp89-90).

They tackled the myths surrounding the Attlee government of 1945-51, generally perceived by left and right as the high-point of Labour's achievement, conceding it was "the most effective reformist Labour government of them all". Yet they adopted a sharply critical attitude to Labour's reforms in the form of nationalisation and the welfare state, arguing that "state ownership in no way implies socialism". The National Health Service meant real gains for working people, but at the same time it was "an efficient method of maintaining a fit and able workforce at minimum cost", while "the health of workers was subordinated to the health of capitalism". They noted Attlee's frequent use of troops to break strikes and showed that Indian independence was not a result of Labour's "magnanimity", but was brought about by the mutiny of the Indian navy in 1946.[91]

The pair explained Labour's policies after 1945 by the fact that Keynesianism had become accepted by the Labour leaders, and by many Tories. Consequently the mixed economy came to dominate Labour policy. But Keynesianism was based on a trade-off between inflation and unemployment; by the 1970s inflation and unemployment were coming together. Keynesianism had proved bankrupt and was abandoned in favour of monetarism.

They looked at the problematic relationship between reform and revolution. This was not a simple alternative: "Our criticism of the Labour Party is not solely that Labour can never bring socialism, but that for most of the time *it is an obstacle to the struggle for reforms.*" By the 1950s and 1960s workers were winning reforms, not through parliament but through workplace organisation, what the authors called "do-it-yourself reformism": "Do-it-yourself reformism is not socialism, but it is the necessary process by which the working class maintains its basic collective organisation." By the 1980s the Labour Party was ever less capable of responding to working class aspirations. But this did not mean the end of reformism, certainly not the victory of revolutionary socialism: "Reformist consciousness...is not dependent on the actual prospect of winning reforms...Labour can survive *as reformism without reforms*".[92] *

---

* The phrase "reformism without reforms" came from Trotsky's 1938 *Transitional Programme* ("Against Opportunism and Unprincipled Revisionism"). I recall it being used in the 1960s by Mike Kidron, but have been unable to find it in his published work.

The authors were particularly concerned to deflate the claims of the Labour left. While they recognised there were real differences between left and right, nonetheless there was a "fundamental unity". They minimised the importance of Bevanism in the 1950s, seen by some historians as the "high tide" of the Labour left.[93] Bevan and his followers had "no link with rank and file workers' struggles" and were mainly concerned with foreign policy issues, on which they "shared the basic assumptions of Labour's foreign policy", especially with regard to NATO.[94]

The same was true of the Bennite left, which had won the enthusiastic support of much of the far left in the early 1980s. Benn's record in government was carefully dissected; his attempt to be the star of the left while serving in the cabinet was dismissed as the manoeuvring of a "political acrobat". In the early 1980s the rise of Bennism was actually a sign of weakness: "Since workers did not have the confidence to take on their employers *in the workplace*, many of the activists looked for a political solution *outside the workplace* from a saviour on high: the Labour Party." Bennism's base was limited and its achievements illusory; its politics were essentially substitutionist: "The Bennites, who fell into the substitutionist trap of claiming to speak for workers they had not brought into active agreement with themselves, were open to the hammerings of the media and the right wing".[95]

The point of *The Labour Party: A Marxist History* was not simply to recount the history, but to draw tactical and strategic lessons. The authors gave particular importance to the period just after the First World War when the CP was founded. They rejected a position commonly held on the revolutionary left: "There is a theory which states that when workers move in a revolutionary direction they will turn to the Labour Party and remake it. 1919 proved this to be arrant nonsense. Even the most left-wing section – the ILP – stood entirely on the sidelines".* They endorsed Lenin's argument that the newborn British Communist Party should seek affiliation to the Labour Party, stressing that this was "simply a means to the end" and that the CP would retain full political independence. In the context of the immediate prospect of European revolution,

---

* Something similar to this scenario did take place in those European countries where Communist parties were formed from splits in the mass social democratic parties.

"affiliation was therefore a short-term policy for winning workers to the Communist Party, not a long-term one for becoming an integral part of Labour". As for the question of Communists standing against the Labour Party in elections, the authors doubtless reflected on the SWP's own experience of electoral politics a decade earlier: "The decision to stand depends on *whether or not this will assist workers' self-activity and build the revolutionary party*. A campaign which produced a derisory vote could only demoralise the left".[96]

This position was a firm rejection of entrism. In the downturn of the 1980s, entrism in the Labour Party had attracted various groups on the far left and the *Militant* group had won significant support, sufficient for it to be witch-hunted by the Labour leadership. While condemning the witch-hunt, the authors were dismissive of *Militant*, describing it as a "centrist sect" which "did not support any campaign unless this was organised through the Labour Party or by itself", and which was guilty of "fantastic triumphalism" and a failure to face reality. They rejected *Militant*'s demand for "Labour to power on a socialist programme" since "no socialist programme is possible for a reformist parliamentary party". The only form of entrism they approved was that practised by the Socialist Review Group in the 1950s and 1960s:[*]

> This did not involve a public declaration of revolutionary intent, or insistence on official recognition of the right to free criticism and organisational autonomy. Such entrism had to be recognised as a tactic imposed by great weakness. As soon as it had served the purpose of helping revolutionaries to stand on their own feet, entrism had to be abandoned. As a long-term policy it could only lead to absorption by the reformist milieu or the abandonment of genuine class struggle (which has always been outside the confines of the Labour Party organisation).[97]

The authors stressed the importance of ideology. Reformism was not just a question of organisation, but of ideas in workers' heads. Those ideas (separation of politics and economics, the existence of cross-class interests, the neutrality of the state) served to protect the existing order, but had sufficient basis in experience for them to appear plausible: "the reformist view of the world is *false consciousness*, but it has an indirect yet genuine link with the

---

[*] Cliff would frequently recommend such entrism to small groups in the International Socialist Tendency.

outside world, is influenced by the outside world and in turn influences it". Quoting Trotsky's words about the "inner policeman", they pointed to the importance of reformist ideology in a crisis situation such as 1919: "When the real policemen were about to strike, the existence of ideological ones was crucial to the system".[98]

The Labour Party: A Marxist History was not calculated to please Marxists who still advocated that revolutionaries should work within the Labour Party. Al Richardson directed a furious polemic against what he called "the two Cliffs" for alleged "selective misrepresentation" of the views of Lenin and Trotsky. He had much less to say about how the Labour Party had changed since the days of the classic Marxists.[99]

In a situation of downturn, aggravated by the defeat of the miners, there was great pressure on revolutionaries to move to the right, to accommodate to the left reformists. The two books served to warn SWP members and supporters of the dangers of any such accommodation.

In 1987 Cliff celebrated his seventieth birthday. A party was arranged on 16 May at the Institute of Education, a joyful occasion to which members and ex-members from various stages of his life were invited. Cliff's speech dealt with the past and the future.[100] He gave no indication of wanting to retire; on the contrary, he assured comrades he would be with them for some time to come. "I come from a long-lived family. My father died at the age of 92 after choking on a prune. I tell you, when I am 90, I stop eating prunes".[101]

In July 1987 the *Guardian* published a version of one of Cliff's Marxism talks, reflecting on Labour's recent election defeat, under the title "Why the Workers did not Fight for Labour".[102] Cutting through the verbiage produced by journalists and psephologists since the election, Cliff insisted that the election result could be understood only in the context of the class struggle:

> The real reason for the dreadfully low Labour vote in 1987 is the level of class struggle. Workers' confidence rises when their struggle rises and is successful. If the standard of living is rising as a result of workers' collective effort, everything is marvellous. People have high hopes of change – and this is reflected in a high Labour vote. But if you are unemployed and don't have a roof over your head, or if you're worried about being unemployed and not having a roof over your head, you look after

number one. When everything is lousy, workers forget one another and tend to think only of themselves.

He was contemptuous of Kinnock's belief that Labour could improve its fortunes by becoming more respectable, and mocked Kinnock's recent visit to US President Reagan:

> It reminds me of the story of two soldiers in the First World War. One said to the other proudly, "Do you know, the general spoke to me today."
>
> "The general?" said his companion. "But that's impossible. What did he say?"
>
> "Oh, he said, 'Piss off, pig'."

His conclusion was agnostic but practical. We could not predict what attacks would come and how the working class would respond:

> It's no good saying I wish there was rain. What we can do is to organise to build the irrigation canals for when the rain comes.

This was water off a duck's back for Labour loyalists. Walter Cairns, a *Tribune* supporter, responded by accusing Cliff of "outdated notions of class struggle" and "unblemished purity of ideological perfection".[103]

Cliff's central concern was with building the organisation. In November 1987 he told SWP conference delegates that they were entering a new stage of the downturn, since the Labour Party had moved qualitatively to the right, and they must start preparing for the upturn. He combined irrepressible optimism with concrete realism:

> It is very easy to be enthusiastic about big things. To expect very little and to do very little is even easier. To do a lot for a very little is extremely difficult. But that's what the situation demands.
>
> When the upturn comes we'll have the shock of our lives. Why? Because tens of thousands, maybe millions, of people who at present are passive will begin to move.
>
> It is terribly important that we prepare ourselves for such circumstances.
>
> Trotsky wrote of a lesson he learned from a group of workers which he retained for the rest of his life. One worker was raring to go, really a

fighter. One worker was a real reactionary. The few workers in between could be won to either side.

The key in leadership is how to influence the people in between to follow one pole instead of the other. And this is the problem you face whether there are ten workers in struggle or a million.[104]

In the spring of 1988 Cliff gave another interview to *Socialist Review* on the current perspective. Nothing fundamental had changed; workers were still engaged in a "war of attrition" with the employers. But the working class was proving to be resilient. Working class organisation was intact, and the number of shop stewards was actually growing. The *British Social Attitudes 1987* survey showed that Thatcherite values had not triumphed; 76 percent of the population believed the nation's wealth was shared unfairly and 65 percent said management and workers were on opposite sides. The situation was still volatile, but when the Tories attacked social services, it offered possibilities of generalisation: "The majority of workers don't give a damn about Ford's. Workers care about the NHS; they have a stake in it".[105]

In 1988 Cliff addressed a meeting of the SWP national committee. He began by noting a "new mood" among workers, which he contrasted to the "new realism" of the union leaders. The term "new mood" rapidly acquired widespread currency among SWP members to indicate a greater willingness to fight. This derived largely from the new Tory strategy. Until 1987 the Tories had used "salami" tactics, attacking one section of organised working class at a time. Now the attack became general, with Health Service cuts and the proposed poll tax (which attacked the poorest by replacing the old local authority rates based on property values with a flat-rate tax, thus attacking the poorest). While many workers still accepted the "new realism", their attitude was different to that of the union leaders: "Ron Todd is not too worried about this lack of fight. Some union leaders like Hammond or Laird are even happy about it. But workers are bitter because they can't fight".* The situation was still uneven and contradictory – hence Cliff's

---

* Ron Todd was general secretary of the Transport and General Workers Union; Eric Hammond and Gavin Laird were, respectively, the right-wing general secretaries of the Electrical, Electronic, Telecommunications and Plumbing Union and the Amalgamated Engineering Union.

metaphor of "dark clouds and silver linings" – and the perspective was still modest: developing regular sales of *Socialist Worker* to individual shop stewards and Labour Party members.

Cliff stressed the need for a change of attitude in the party. "The legacy of recent years", marked mainly by defeat, meant that there was a tendency for comrades to be "too dismissive of struggles that do arise". There was a danger of sectarianism and political purism, leading socialists "to argue about how they differ from those in struggle, rather than talk [about] what they have in common".[106]

In November Cliff followed this up by leading a session on party-building at the SWP conference. Leadership meant being involved in struggle and learning from the experience:

> We have to be the people who get stuck into a fight and the last to give up on it. Even if we lose then it is better to lose with a fight than without.
>
> Another danger is to talk *at* people instead of *to* them. We have to learn to listen to what people are saying and respond. We can't always choose the terms of discussion.[107]

He continued to intervene vigorously in party debates. When Mark Krantz went to SWP conference as a young delegate, he criticised an SWP pamphlet on the poll tax. Cliff, sitting in the front row, began to point at him and to heckle, shouting, "Write your own pamphlet!"[108]

In a speech to an SWP national meeting in the summer of 1989 Cliff again pointed to the way the situation was changing: "The industrial situation today is like a kaleidoscope. Everything is shifting very quickly and with tremendous unevenness." Current strikes showed "a combination of defensive and offensive struggle". It was therefore necessary "to change very quickly to adapt to the rapid changes taking place in the class". While he recognised the danger of exaggerating the possibilities of a dispute, the far greater danger was abstention.[109]

On one question Cliff and the central committee were mistaken. They rightly recognised that the poll tax would be a major area of conflict. But they believed that the fight against the poll tax would have to be spearheaded by local authority workers responsible for its collection. Cliff acknowledged that this put the struggle in a weak position:

> The most extreme example of where the power of delivery of workers' action is extremely weak is the poll tax campaign. Millions of people reject the tax but fighting against the tax depends on a few groups of NALGO workers in the council in the finance department, or in the DSS in the CPSA. Because of this we get massive vacillation.[110]

At the end of the year he reiterated this position even more forcefully:

> The struggle against the tax will be a long-term one in which it is still difficult to argue for the correct strategy. Nevertheless, we have to insist on the importance of industrial action since individual non-payment can't win in the long term.[111]

This insistence on industrial action was a longstanding commitment to the principle that workers' power lay essentially in the workplace, not in the community. In addition there was the experience of the Fares Fair campaign of 1982 in London. Ken Livingstone and the Greater London Council had introduced a policy designed to cheapen public transport. The scheme was ruled illegal. Some of Livingstone's friends urged individual passengers to refuse the new fares – but rejected the only method which could have won: industrial action by transport workers. Resistance had collapsed in a few days. It was easy to believe the same would apply to non-payment of the poll tax. In 1989 Cliff told Newcastle students, "The non-payment campaign does not exist. Not paying the poll tax is like getting on a bus and not paying your fare; all that will happen is you'll get thrown off".[112] He forgot that it was a lot easier to put a bill in the bin than to have a face-to-face confrontation with a bus conductor. As the movement against the poll tax grew, the SWP initially appeared to be taking a sectarian position.

In Scotland, where the poll tax was introduced first, the line argued by Cliff caused real problems. Mike Gonzalez remembers the SWP had a dangerously sectarian position which "gave *Militant* a new lease of life, at our expense". Gonzalez believes that this was partly a result of Cliff's position in the organisation: precisely because he was a well-respected leader, it was difficult to oppose him when he got something wrong:

> My feeling was that Cliff attracted admiration and loyalty, but his enormous authority made it very difficult to question his views. Many of the people around him at the centre I felt pandered to him rather than

arguing – and in return he accepted their judgement.[113]

In the next couple of years adaptations would have to be made. But momentous events were now occurring on a world scale.

12
1989-97
Excited About The Future

In November 1989 there were mass demonstrations in East Germany which culminated in the opening of checkpoints in the Berlin Wall, that had divided the city since 1961, and the subsequent demolition of parts of the wall. Within a year the process of reuniting Germany, under the political and economic structures of the West, was carried through. There was now a chain reaction across Eastern Europe as the various pro-Russian regimes toppled one after the other.

Russia itself was not immune. Mikhail Gorbachev, General Secretary of the Communist Party of the Soviet Union and later President of the Soviet Union, had embarked on a series of ambitious reforms under the slogans of restructuring (*perestroika*) and openness (*glasnost*), but these proved insufficient to preserve the old order. Following a failed coup attempt in August 1991 the Soviet Union was dissolved. In Russia, under president Boris Yeltsin, state capitalism gave way to a society based on the free market and a rather dubious variant of parliamentary democracy. China too began to move towards a market economy, and by the middle of the 1990s the only regimes where command economies survived were Cuba and North Korea.

It was a momentous period of change which no section of the left had anticipated. During the Cold War both supporters and opponents of Stalinism had believed the economic and political system of the Eastern Bloc to be permanently established and irreversible. Ten years earlier Ernest Mandel had claimed that "the restoration of capitalism [in the so-called 'workers' states'] could occur only through new and disastrous defeats for the Soviet and international proletariat, through violent social and political upheavals".[1] Now the right were triumphant, claiming socialism was dead. The old Stalinist parties went into crisis: the British Communist Party wound itself up in 1991 and the Italian Communist Party, the biggest in the

West, changed its name and became a social democratic party.

For the orthodox Trotskyist left it was a period of crisis. The "workers' states", seen as economically superior to the market capitalism of the West and in transition to a higher form of society, had vanished into thin air. The state of disillusion was neatly summed up by long-time activist Tariq Ali in his cynically satirical novel *Redemption*,[2] which caricatured various leading Trotskyists such as Ezra Einstein (Mandel). Cliff appeared as "Jimmy Rock", whose wife Sugar Brink was "at least two feet taller than he was". Rock was shown "waging a campaign of predatory seduction, known in the trade as a 'unity offensive', towards the Burrowers [*Militant*]".

For Cliff the events posed rather less of a problem. Since he had never considered state capitalism more progressive than Western capitalism, or as a gain to be defended, the events were perceived not as a defeat, but the opening of a new historical phase.

At the end of 1989 Cliff made his first preliminary assessment of the situation in an article entitled "Earthquake in the East".[3] He began by recognising the significance of the events, comparing 1989 to 1848 and 1917 as a year of international revolution. He argued that state capitalism had become "a brake on the development of the productive forces", leading to a rapid decline in rates of growth. He was in no doubt that the "reforms" promised in Russia would be to the detriment of the working class. Comparing Gorbachev's *perestroika* to the role of the Thatcher government in the 1980s, he noted that "in Britain they closed 20 to 25 percent of manufacturing capacity. In Russia they will have to do more."

Yet politically *glasnost* was encouraging radical demands on the part of workers. The situation was complicated by the fact that the very idea of communism was contaminated by its association with the old repressive regime, so "the process of clarification will take time". Cliff commented that in the short term the crisis in the East would be "a massive boost to the right wing", and that those who had believed the claims made by Mandel and Deutscher about the superiority of the Eastern economies would be demoralised.

His conclusion was optimistic: "Ideas cannot be smashed by tanks, by force alone… The stream disappears from sight and then reappears miles later." Citing Trotsky's contention that "the vengeance of history is much more terrible than the vengeance of the most powerful general secretary",[4] he declared, "Trotsky is smiling and

Stalin is dead."

After the failed coup in Russia in August 1991 Cliff returned to the subject.[5] He saw the key to the situation in the crisis of the Russian economy, which was trapped because "the command economy is not yet dead and the market economy is stillborn". Again he observed that the introduction of a market economy would mean massive unemployment. The only alternative lay with independent workers' organisation, but that depended on the degree of class confidence: "Empty stomachs can lead to rebellion or they can lead to submission".*

Cliff felt, with some self-satisfaction, that the collapse of state capitalism vindicated the position he had been arguing since 1947. He liked to quote the statement by Nina Temple of the CP that Russia had never been socialist; he compared this to the Pope saying God did not exist.[6] † Certainly Cliff had been right to maintain – against the Stalinist apologists, against those coming from the Trotskyist tradition like Mandel and Deutscher, and against social democratic admirers of the Russian economic system like Harold Wilson[7] – that the regimes of the Eastern Bloc were both exploitative and prone to crisis. The theory of state capitalism had protected a significant section of the left from the sense of defeat that followed the collapse of so-called communism.

Cliff had not predicted everything; history reserved a few surprises for him. In his writings from the 1940s Cliff had asserted that the only force that could overthrow state capitalism was the working class.[8] The Hungarian Revolution of 1956 seemed concrete proof of this. But in the changes that befell Russia after 1991 the working class was largely the victim. Certainly there were a number of strikes, but not enough to challenge the regime, and in the following years the working class suffered a substantial fall in living

---

* The fullest analysis of the changes in the Eastern Bloc came in Chris Harman's article "The Storm Breaks" (*International Socialism* 46 (Spring 1990)), which drew on Cliff's earlier analyses and concluded, "The transition from state capitalism to multinational capitalism is neither a step forward nor a step backwards, but a step sidewards." (p82)

† I have been unable to find a source for this statement by Temple.

standards.[9] * Later he would argue, citing a phrase from Chris Harman's "The Storm Breaks", that "for the people at the top the years 1989-91 did not mark a step backward or a step forward, but simply a step sideways".[10]

But Cliff left the detailed examination of developments in the Eastern Bloc to those like Chris Harman and Mike Haynes who had built on his analyses. His main concern continued to be with building the organisation. The Thatcher regime, which had enjoyed such hegemony throughout the 1980s, was now encountering serious difficulties. The poll tax, precisely because it was a generalised attack on all workers, provoked generalised resistance. Contrary to Cliff's predictions, it was not industrial action but widespread non-payment that made the tax unworkable. Cliff sensed this shift, and it was largely due to his urging that the SWP adjusted to the reality reasonably quickly and became deeply involved in local committees against the poll tax.[11] Several members were jailed and many more were involved in resisting bailiffs. Cliff and Chanie did not pay, but were not troubled by the bailiffs.[12]

In the spring of 1990 a massive demonstration in London turned into a riot. Many sections of the left hastily dissociated themselves from the violence. *Socialist Worker* responded with an editorial headed "No Wonder They Fight Back": "Of course no socialist believes rioting will beat the poll tax, but neither should any socialist condemn the howl of rage which filled the fashionable West End last Saturday".[13]

By the autumn Thatcher was forced to resign when her own colleagues lost confidence in her. She was replaced by John Major, a much weaker figure who presided over a number of years of Tory division. The poll tax was rapidly withdrawn and replaced by the marginally fairer Council Tax, a clear – but rare – working class victory.

---

* Chris Harman's article "The Stalinist States" (*International Socialism* 42 (February-March 1970)) took a rather more agnostic view of the possible outcome of a crisis in the Eastern Bloc: "The chronic crises of state capitalism will inevitably reach a nodal point at which the whole system is threatened. What happens then will depend upon the ability of the different classes to mobilise around programmes reflecting their own genuine interests. In such a situation, the most dangerous development from the point of view of the working class would be a 'Polish' one, in which the ideological confusion of the masses permitted the reforming bureaucracy to retain power." This had been adopted as a national committee document for the IS conference in 1970, and would therefore have had Cliff's endorsement.

At SWP conferences and at innumerable meetings around the country Cliff reiterated the main message – although the upturn had not yet come, the worst of the downturn was over; there were great opportunities ahead and the task was to build the party. He was desperately impatient to see the end of the downturn.[14] He told the 1990 SWP conference that, though there was not massive struggle, there was a "sense of things bubbling".[15]

In 1991 he told the conference that the collapse of Stalinism and the decline of Bennism and of *Militant* had left a "vacuum on the left". There was great anger among working people: "We won't miss big struggles when they arise. The danger for us is that we miss the small events, that express the general anger...our active members must relate to people who are less active, and those in turn to people outside the party".[16]

At the time of the poll tax demonstration in 1990 Labour had a massive opinion poll lead, but Neil Kinnock's inept leadership managed to take Labour to defeat in the 1992 election; as Cliff pointed out, "the Labour Party campaign did not reflect the massive anger which exists against the Tories".[17]

Cliff's general message in this period was one of hope. At a meeting at Marxism in 1992 he attacked the current fashion for arguing that there was a long-term decline in the working class movement, calling it "a lot of rubbish". Citing trade union membership figures he argued there were clear indications of the "strength and resilience of the working class movement". The class was being restructured and new sections needed time to develop confidence and organisation. The present period was a "war of attrition" but the balance could not continue indefinitely. So building the party was crucial: "Before any upturn we will be marginal. But when an upturn comes, what socialists do can be fundamental. We have to prepare." Often he would refer to the job of revolutionaries as being to "create facts" – that is, not to accept the world simply as given, but to create successes and thereby change the objective situation.[18]

He concluded, "I'm excited about the future, because I believe the other side is in terrible trouble".[19] Proof of this trouble came a few months after the election, in October of 1992. To consolidate the defeat inflicted at the end of the 1984-85 strike, Major's government announced the closure of 31 pits, with a loss of 30,000 jobs, in effect destroying most of what remained of Britain's mining industry.

It was a profoundly unpopular move. Even right-wing papers like the *Sun* were scathing in their criticism of the government. In an echo of the great strike of the 1980s, there was massive support for the miners in the labour movement. In two demonstrations in London miners were joined by huge numbers of other trade unionists.

Cliff and the central committee decided that in this climate a call for a general strike would be a realistic demand. *Socialist Worker* appeared with the headline "General Strike Now!"[20] This was based on the leadership's ability to listen to the membership. Sean Vernell was one of the organisers who reported to Cliff that workers in Sheffield were talking about the possibility of a general strike.[21] The call proved popular and sales of *Socialist Worker* shot up. But in the end the left proved to be neither large enough nor well enough organised and the government rode the storm.

In an interview early in 1993 Cliff stressed that British capitalism was in a much deeper crisis than in the 1980s and that, unlike Thatcher, Major was heading "an extremely weak government". Generalisation was possible because the threat of job losses did not just affect the miners, but all groups of workers. "If everybody's job was safe there would be sympathy for the miners but not such deep anger. People are angry because they feel they are in the same boat." Hence the call for a general strike had fitted the mood. But the leadership of the TUC and the Labour Party had failed to rise to the challenge. The SWP, despite recent growth, was not big enough to fill the vacuum:

> The role of socialists is crucial.
>
> Imagine if we had 15,000 members of the SWP and 30,000 supporters: the 21 October miners' demonstration could have been different. Instead of marching round Hyde Park, socialists could have taken 40 or 50,000 people to parliament.
>
> If that had happened, the Tory MPs wouldn't have dared vote with Michael Heseltine [the minister responsible for the pit closures]. The government would have collapsed.

In concluding he stressed the importance of even the smallest struggles: "All the small battles are important...you can't live by waiting for the revolution".[22]

The lesson was clear. The enemy was weak, but the key task was to build an organisation big enough to intervene in such crises. That was Cliff's message to the SWP conference in 1992:

> Over the last three weeks we have recruited 1,000 new members...
>
> But the situation is so explosive we run the danger of missing opportunities. It is difficult to break the habits that have built up over the last 15 years of defeats for workers.
>
> But if we break those habits another 1,000 and more can join the socialist party over the next few months.
>
> We need to tell new people, "Join and bring your mates."

He added a warning against oversimplification, saying political ideas were still crucial:

> The world is very complicated. The answers to issues aren't simple.
>
> The new people joining our party will teach us all how to explain clearly what we say about Russia, Ireland, socialism and so on.[23]

The following year at the SWP conference he argued that the British working class was too strong for the employers to make a major attack; the problem was a lack of confidence. So he looked to the younger members to give a lead:

> Many people around the SWP are serious about the need to fight and to build an alternative political organisation.
>
> These people are often more angry and active than socialists who have been around a bit longer...
>
> There is a massive audience for socialist ideas. We must get to it.[24]

The central question was the need to build a revolutionary party, because that was the key to effective activity. He spelt it out in a talk at Marxism 1994:

> Why do we need a revolutionary party? The basic reason is in two statements Marx made. He stated that "the emancipation of the working class is the act of the working class" and at the same time he said "the prevailing ideas of every society are the ideas of the ruling class".
>
> There is a contradiction between those two statements. But the contradiction is not in Marx's head. It exists in reality. If "the emancipation of the working class is the act of the working class" then to be honest we can do nothing about it – let's sit with folded arms and smile. The

workers will emancipate themselves!

If on the other hand "the prevailing ideas of every society are the ideas of the working class" and that's all, workers will always accept the ideas of the rulers. Then we can sit with folded arms and cry because nothing can be done.

On this basis he analysed the dangers between which revolutionaries had to steer a course:

The conflict in consciousness is the problem. You can stand on a picket line and next to you is a worker who makes racist comments. You can do one of three things. You can come and say, "I'm not standing with him on a picket line. I'm going home because there no one makes racist comments." That is sectarianism because if "the emancipation of the working class is the act of the working class" I have to stand with him on a picket line.

Another possibility is simply avoiding the question. Someone makes a racist comment and you pretend you haven't heard and say, "The weather is quite nice today!" That's opportunism.

The third position is that you argue with this person against racism, against the prevailing ideas of the ruling class. You argue and argue. If you convince him, excellent. But if you don't, still when the scab lorry comes you close arms to stop the scabs because "the emancipation of the working class is the act of the working class".[25]

Cliff's optimism in this period, especially his often repeated comment that the present period was like "the 1930s in slow motion" provoked a number of critics, who felt that the perspective – small branches, push for rapid recruitment – did not fit reality. Pete Green felt that an observation had been changed into a fetish; he annoyed Cliff by urging him to reread his own earlier articles, in particular "All that glitters is not gold", which he saw as a model of how to look at what was actually happening. But Green remembers that whereas other comrades simply told him to shut up, Cliff was always willing to have an argument. Eventually, following disagreements in the Hackney district, Green was called to Cliff's home for a discussion with Cliff and another CC member. Though Cliff was now in his late seventies, he was concerned to involve himself even in relatively minor disciplinary matters. Green left the party a year later, but when he saw Cliff subsequently, Cliff was always pleasant to him – unlike some other former comrades.[26]

Likewise, when Andy Wilson proposed to launch a cultural journal, he was threatened with expulsion by the CC. Wilson was called for a two-hour discussion with Cliff and another CC member. Cliff did not take the lead in pushing for his expulsion, but waited to see whether the accusation that such a journal would become factional was justified. He appeared uninterested in Wilson's ideas but was concerned to deal with a dispute that could damage the party.[27] Wilson was instructed not to go ahead with the journal and was expelled when he refused to accept discipline.

Julie Waterson, who joined the CC in the early 1990s, recalls that Cliff was still "sharp as a knife", and that he continued to play an active part in the leadership until close to his death. He kept in regular contact with key party members by telephone. Waterson described him as a "telephone terrorist" and threatened to resign from the CC if anyone gave him a mobile phone for his eightieth birthday.[28] Chris Bambery, who was national organiser from 1987 to the time of Cliff's death, remembers that Cliff would telephone him more or less every day.[29]

As the organisation became larger and more complex, Cliff only gave direct attention to certain aspects of the party's work. He took a close interest in the numbers attending Marxism, and who was coming from where, but took relatively little interest in planning the meetings, apart from the large debates. He would decide what topics he wanted to speak on, usually key party-building topics.[30]

From some arguments Cliff stood back. At several Marxisms there were heated debates about whether the laws of dialectics applied to the natural world or only to human history. Cliff never expressed a view, though John Rees is confident that Cliff did believe there was a dialectic in nature. Cliff read the first draft of Rees's book *The Algebra of Revolution*[31] and had no basic disagreements with it.[32] Probably he was reluctant to use his authority in the party to intervene on a philosophical matter.

Though the industrial struggle was central, the SWP was also involved in a range of other activities in this period. In 1991 the US, enthusiastically backed by the British Tory government, launched a war against Iraq, and a substantial opposition movement arose although the war lasted only six weeks. Cliff showed remarkable energy in addressing SWP rallies against the war and the Tory government. In the two months after the outbreak of the war he spoke in Edinburgh, Doncaster, Coventry, Brighton, Liverpool, Glasgow, Norwich, Colchester, Cardiff, Canterbury, Southampton, Leicester, York, Swansea, Hull, Rochdale, Birmingham and four districts of London. In Sheffield, where he spoke with Reservists Against the War, the rally drew 350 people. He failed to get to a rally in Luton because of snow. In Barnsley he spoke at a united front meeting against the war with Peter Heathfield of the NUM and Marjorie Thompson of CND.[33]

In 1993 the British National Party (BNP) won a by-election in east London. Martin Smith, who was the East London organiser, remembers Cliff took the situation very seriously and would phone him every two days to talk about the situation; in particular, they had detailed discussions about tactics for defending paper sales against the BNP.[34]

All this sparked off a revival of the Anti Nazi League, which in October 1993 helped to organise a vigorous 60,000-strong demonstration at the BNP's headquarters at Welling, confronted by considerable police violence.[35] In May 1994 a highly successful ANL carnival drew 150,000 people.[36]

Also in 1994 the Tory government carried through the Criminal Justice Act. This increased police powers, brought in measures against raves and squatting, and imposed restrictions on various kinds of protest action. There were large demonstrations in London against the new laws, which mobilised a different milieu from the normal political demonstration, bringing in what one participant described as "ravers, squatters, travellers, eco-activists and civil libertarians".[37] In many ways this was a precursor of what became known as the "anti-capitalist movement" of the early 21st century. Cliff was keen on involvement in this campaign as a means of reaching a new, younger audience,[38] although it was Chris Bambery who was the first on the CC to spot the significance of the anti-capitalist movement.[39] Weyman Bennett, who was involved in organising a demonstration jointly with anarchists and others, found Cliff supportive; his comments about the "spirit of the united front" were helpful.[40]

During the early 1990s the SWP recruited considerably. It was during the activity around the Criminal Justice Bill that the party reached a membership of 10,000, though many of the new recruits did not last very long.[41]

Between 1989 and 1993 Cliff published his last major work, a four-volume study of *Trotsky*. More than 1,200 pages long and drawing heavily on recently published material, it was a substantial achievement for a man of his age, since the writing was combined with a punishing schedule of speaking and other organisational tasks.

In writing the book Cliff was, in a sense, returning to his roots. He had identified with the Trotskyist tradition since the age of about 15, and whatever the absurdities of organised Trotskyism, he had always remained fiercely loyal to Trotsky. Nearing the end of his life, he was determined to pass on to a new generation the tradition which had nurtured him.

Yet for the most part this was not Cliff at his best. In his earlier writings Cliff had been concerned to develop Marxism in order to interpret the modern world. Now it seemed he was going onto the defensive. As the 20th century approached its end, the Russian Revolution, despite its later distortions and betrayals, remained the solitary success story for revolutionary socialism. That Cliff in his last years had to return to the inspiration of 1917 (rather than, say, examining the changing nature of the British working class) was a sign of the weakness of the movement.

One example of this was a meeting in the late 1980s at which Cliff criticised Mike Haynes in a discussion about the peasantry. Colin Barker spoke in support of Haynes, and Cliff responded by asking, "Do you agree with Lenin?" To Cliff's consternation, Barker responded that he agreed with what Cliff had written in the 1960s.[42]

There were other problems. Anyone writing the biography of Trotsky does so in the shadow of Isaac Deutscher's great trilogy. Many of those who had joined the IS or SWP in the preceding 30 years had gained their knowledge of Trotsky through Deutscher. Cliff had written a demolition of Deutscher's politics in 1963,[43] and in the introduction to the first volume of his biography he repeated his claim that Deutscher had capitulated to Stalinism.[44] But though Cliff presented a divergent interpretation from Deutscher's at many points, the main lines of the story remained the same and to most readers Cliff's differences would seem relatively minor.

Moreover, in the first two volumes of *Trotsky* Cliff was covering ground already dealt with in his biography of Lenin. Cliff's works frequently contained borrowing from his own writings (he had no inhibitions about repeating himself) and in the Trotsky study he repeated substantial chunks of his own earlier works. Additionally, he had the declared intention of letting Trotsky speak in his own words, which meant a large number of extensive quotations, making the book at times appear more like an anthology than a biography.

Cliff made clear from the outset that his study of Trotsky would be critical and would avoid hagiography. In particular he repeatedly drew attention to the differences between Lenin and Trotsky. Traditionally, Trotskyist accounts – beginning with Trotsky's own *My Life* – had sought to minimise the differences, in face of Stalinist slanders that Trotsky was an enemy of Leninism. Cliff was at pains to show that neither man was infallible and each could be used to criticise the other. He showed how each could, on occasion, complement the other's inadequacies.

In the first volume, however, he unequivocally gave the verdict to Lenin on the debate about party organisation, and observed, "It is frustrating, nay, depressing, that in writing the present biography one has to deal – and at length – with the faction fight in the RSDRP, before dealing with the great events of 1905." Later he described the period from 1907 to 1914 as "seven long wasted years" for Trotsky.[45] This was entirely consistent with the central role Cliff gave the revolutionary party, but it was hardly an appealing invitation to the reader.

Cliff also sided with Lenin over the debate on revolutionary defeatism in the First World War. But when it came to the October Revolution he was more critical towards Lenin. He observed, as he had done in *Lenin*, that all parties have an element of conservatism, and he was quite critical about Lenin's argument that the revolution should be carried out in the name of the party rather than of the soviets.[46]

The second volume of *Trotsky* was devoted to the critical years immediately after the revolution. Here Cliff drew out the many points on which Lenin and Trotsky had been in disagreement. On Brest-Litovsk he showed that while Lenin was proved right, Trotsky's case for "Neither war nor peace" was far from implausible. On a number of military questions Trotsky was in the right, and Cliff claimed Lenin was "out of touch" with the military situation.[47]

Cliff showed the rise of bureaucracy from the early years of the revolution and the important role played in this process by the Red Army. In the chapters on the civil war and the Red Army, Cliff drew on a good deal of new material not available when he had written his books on Lenin. Trotsky had been an advocate of the New Economic Policy some time before Lenin was converted to the idea. On Kronstadt Cliff described the rising as "counter-revolutionary", but dismissed as "pure myth" the "anarchists' story" that Trotsky played a part in suppressing the rebellion.[48]

Cliff described Trotsky's role trying to build the Comintern and showed the failure to create authentic mass revolutionary parties, which in turn produced the rise of Stalinism. He concluded:

> Of course one could argue that Communist parties could not be expected to come into existence fully fledged even in the most acute revolutionary situation, which is true; or that time would have welded the parties into real, consistent revolutionary organisations. That is also possibly true. But time was the one thing history did not grant.[49]

Here one can sense Cliff justifying his own impatience in the early 1970s. If only the party had been built more rapidly before the onset of the downturn, could things have been different? Perhaps under the influence of this thought Cliff, rather untypically, lapsed into a little romantic hagiography. He told of how Stalin and Zinoviev had blocked a request from the German Communists to send Trotsky to Germany in 1923, and asked, "If Trotsky, the organiser of the Russian October insurrection, had taken hold of the German party, who knows whether the German October would not have ended in victory instead of defeat?"[50] There were deep-rooted historical reasons for the failure of the German Communists in 1923, and it is unlikely that one individual, even one with Trotsky's talents, could have overcome these in a matter of months.

In the third volume of *Trotsky* Cliff traced Trotsky's struggle against Stalin and his eventual defeat. Here he was going over the old ground of his theory of state capitalism, although this time looking at it in a historical perspective rather than in a structural fashion as he had in his 1948 document.

Cliff was strongly influenced by John Molyneux's book *Leon Trotsky's Theory of Revolution*.[51] Molyneux had argued that Trotsky's hesitations in opposing Stalin had resulted not from psychological factors, but from a false political analysis of the situation. In particular Trotsky had been too willing to compromise with Stalin because he saw Bukharin as the main enemy. Because Cliff perceived this weakness in Trotsky, he was very hard on Trotsky in his account of the 1923-27 period, much harder than Deutscher had been.[52] Hence he was critical of Trotsky's tactics in the dispute, accusing him of "conciliationism" manifested by "going into battle against the ruling group in party and state, then stopping, retreating, keeping quiet, then starting again".[53]

Elsewhere Cliff repeatedly emphasised the necessity of a disciplined revolutionary party, but saw the party as a means to an end, not an end in itself, and here he blamed Trotsky for not being "ready to go to the mass of the workers outside of the party".[54]

In the end it was objective factors that led to Stalin's victory and the defeat of the revolution. No theoretical insight or organisational prowess on Trotsky's part could have enabled the victory of socialism in a single, isolated and economically backward country. Yet Cliff rejected fatalism; what Trotsky did mattered:

> While his *strategic* direction was correct, he made a number of serious *tactical* blunders and compromises. The point is not that had he been firmer he would have been able to beat Stalin, but that he would have laid firmer bases for the growth of the Opposition, not allowing the 1923 Opposition to wither on the vine, not disorienting his followers in the foreign Communist Parties (this being especially important in view of what was to come), and so on.[55]

The first three volumes contained much valuable information and analysis, but it was only with the fourth volume that the biography really came to life. Cliff himself said Volume Four was the most important part of *Trotsky*, just as Volume One had been in the case of *Lenin*.[56] In his study of Trotsky and Trotskyism in the 1930s, Cliff was returning to his roots; this was where he had started, the grim world of Hitler's rise to power and the Spanish Civil War. Cliff had never seen mass insurrection or civil war, but the world of minuscule groups, factional disputes and splits was one he was all too familiar with. When he described the clandestine distribution of leaflets by the Russian Left Opposition – "the light suddenly went off and leaflets started flying"[57] – he must have remembered similar episodes from his youth in Palestine. He was constantly concerned to understand why Trotsky had failed to win wider forces around him.[58]

Though he was now in his mid-seventies, Cliff's prodigious energy and curiosity were as powerful as ever, and the final volume revealed a formidable amount of research. Before 1968 there had been little serious historical work on the history of Trotskyism; with the re-emergence of an anti-Stalinist left there had been a flourishing of work on the subject in the 1970s and 1980s, and Cliff was able to draw on a wide range of material. There were journals like the *Cahiers Léon Trotsky* and *Revolutionary History*; the works of veterans like Yvan Craipeau and Cliff's old comrade Sam Bornstein (who with Al Richardson had written two invaluable volumes on British Trotskyism); the writings of the great historian Pierre Broué,* and of scholars from various currents of the left such as Isabelle Longuet, Reiner Tosstorff, Alan Wald, Andy Durgan and Robert Alexander. These and many more were used as sources.

The fourth volume of *Trotsky* was longer than the other three, and Cliff spent over two years completing it, whereas the other volumes had appeared at yearly intervals. It contained a wealth of detail, both on Trotsky's life and on the problems of organising small groups. Two main themes ran through the work.

Firstly the failure of the Left Opposition was not simply a result of persecution, however brutal that might have been: "It was the ideological crisis, far more than police pressure, that broke the spirit of the Trotskyists in the prisons and camps of exile... One of the reasons why the Trotskyists in the USSR in 1928-30 were so hesitant and why the morale of so many collapsed was the lack of theoretical clarity".[59] Likewise the destructive role of Stalinist infiltrators was a result of the movement's weakness: "agents provocateurs are only

---

* Though Cliff admired Broué and drew on his books on Germany and Spain, he apparently did not read Broué's life of Trotsky (Paris, 1988), and only referred to Broué's work on the papers in the Harvard archives at second hand in a quotation from another author (*Trotsky*, Vol 4, p150).

effective if the situation lends itself to provocation".*

Central to this lack of clarity was the fact that Trotsky "completely misunderstood" the Stalinist bureaucracy, seeing it as comparable to the bureaucracy in the trade unions and social democratic parties, and failing to see that the Russian bureaucracy controlled the national economy and was in process of becoming a class in its own right. Moreover, Trotsky made misleading comparisons with the French bourgeois revolution of 1789 and confused issues by his use of the terms Thermidor and Bonapartism.[60]

But however important clarity was, Cliff knew it was not enough. Ideas were not self-sufficient; they required "a body, that of the party within the wider proletariat, to be transformed into a material force". The real tragedy of Trotskyism was "the gaping abyss between Trotsky's grand ideas, and the actual means, the personnel to carry out those ideas".[61]

Hence the failure to grow even in favourable circumstances, such as the mass strike in France in 1936: "Green shoots do grow in fertile soil. But if the shoots are weak, they can still wither before maturing".[62] In times of rapid change delay could be fatal. The international application of the entry tactic had highly mediocre results.

Cliff concluded that the whole strategy of Trotskyism in the late 1930s was based on false assumptions. Trotsky believed that the Stalinist regime in Russia was unstable, and that reformism in the West had no future. By 1945 these assumptions were shown to be false. Transitional demands, which fitted a period of deep slump, became "at best meaningless, and at worst reactionary" when capitalism expanded massively. Trotsky had been absolutely right to try

---

* Cliff, while well aware of problems of security, generally took a relaxed attitude to the possibility of police agents in the organisation, arguing that infiltrators would always work hard in order to ensure their position, so they should be given lots of jobs. According to Peter Branston, "When I was a member of the International Socialists, we were told to work hard to hang on to any police spies in the branch... They had more time than any one else, were more reliable and went out at all hours to sell the *Socialist Worker*. As Tony Cliff used to say, 'You've got someone from MI5...you've got a full timer, for nothing, comrades.'" (Letter in the *Guardian*, 31 October 2002) However, former MI5 officer Peter Wright claimed that officers could not be infiltrated into organisations like the SWP and WRP "since many of them lived promiscuous lives, and there were some sacrifices even an MI5 officer would not make for his country" (P Wright, *Spycatcher*, New York, 1987, p360).

to build an organisation, however unfavourable the circumstances, but the "over-ambitious" structure of the Fourth International did not fit the needs of the time, and the very decision to establish the Fourth International was "almost certainly a mistake".[63]

Despite the succession of defeats which he related, despite the "horror without end" of the destruction of Trotsky's family, Cliff's conclusion was optimistic: "The last six decades belonged to Stalin. The coming decades will belong to Lenin, Luxemburg and Trotsky".[64] Nothing could suppress Cliff's faith in the future. But it was symptomatic that he looked backwards, above all to 1917, for a source of hope.

It is interesting to compare Cliff's *Trotsky* to Pierre Broué's near-contemporaneous 945-page *Trotsky*.[65] Cliff and Broué came from different wings of the Trotskyist movement, but they had a number of preoccupations in common. Both were deeply hostile to Deutscher's depiction of Trotsky, especially in the way he separated theory from practice and downgraded the importance of Trotsky's political activity in his final decade. Broué had worked extensively on the closed section of the Trotsky archives in Harvard; he provided a mass of detailed information, notably on the size and state of the opposition in Russia. Considered purely as historical scholarship, Broué's book might be considered superior to Cliff's. But there were certain political weaknesses in Broué's account. Since he adhered to the orthodox Trotskyist view of the nature of Russian society under Stalin, he was unable to give an adequate account of the limitations of Trotsky's analysis. While Broué fully recognised the importance of Trotsky's struggle to form the Fourth International, the actual treatment of the Fourth International was thin and uncritical. Broué was apparently not prepared to defend the detailed political perspective that lay behind the founding of the Fourth International, but not willing to subject it to rigorous criticism.

For most of his life Cliff's work got relatively little attention in academic circles; academics generally tend to regard anything not produced within their own closed world of scholarship as not worth noticing. But towards the end of his life Cliff received a number of hostile reviews in the academic journals *Soviet Studies* and *Revolutionary Russia*, from such scholars as James D White, Ian D Thatcher and Geoff Swain. The reason why is shown in a review of the reissue of Cliff's *Lenin* by Swain. Having dismissed the work as "devoid of interest to historians" he ruefully noted that "some of Cliff's theories appear in undergraduate essays".[66] Apparently students found Cliff's attempt to relate history to the tasks of the present more appealing than the dispassionate subtleties of their lecturers. James D White, despite finding Cliff's scholarship inferior to Deutscher's and Broué's, conceded that the first volume of Cliff's *Trotsky* was "undeniably a stimulating book, and one which captures admirably the spirit of radical politics in which Trotskii thrived".[67]

But though the critics made much of alleged lapses of scholarship, the ultimate problem was political and went to the heart of Cliff's project. Ian D Thatcher thought one of Cliff's main weaknesses was the fact that he uncritically accepted "Trotsky's view of the Russian Revolution as a workers' revolution".[68] James D White concluded that the third volume of *Trotsky* did "no service...to the cause of socialism" because it encouraged the "illusion" that there was a viable "Trotskyist alternative" to Stalinism.[69]

During this period Cliff continued to travel tirelessly, addressing meetings all over the country. In the first three months of 1993 he spoke to no fewer than 18 rallies on "The Revolutionary Road to Socialism" and "Get the Tories Out – Fight for Socialism". Six were in different parts of London, but he travelled to Birkenhead, St Helens, Hull, Leicester, Thanet, Aylesbury, Sunderland, Oxford, Stoke, Wolverhampton, Wakefield and Mansfield. In September and October of the same year the SWP held a series of anti-Tory rallies, mainly under the title "Racist, corrupt and cornered – can we finish off the Tories?" Over a period of seven weeks Cliff, now aged 76, addressed meetings in Lowestoft, Norwich, Cambridge, Doncaster, Birmingham, Swansea, Cardiff, Tower Hamlets, Edinburgh, Hull, Sheffield and Bradford.[70]

Imperceptibly but remorselessly he was growing older. He tended to leave some of the detailed work to other comrades. The CC had to work hard to ensure that he did not tire himself too much. Cliff never liked to refuse invitations to speak and the party centre had to turn them down on his behalf. Pat Stack recalls sitting in a cafe with Cliff, who had his radio clamped to his ear. The waitress clearly saw him as just an old man and would have been astonished to see him a couple of hours later, able to keep an audience enthralled.[71]

After her retirement Chanie became active in the pensioners' movement, and Cliff accompanied her on one or two demonstrations. On one occasion pensioners staged a sit-down in Oxford Street. Chanie sat down but Cliff, still stateless at the end of his life and nervous about arrest, did not.[72]

Cliff was regarded throughout the organisation with great respect and affection, but remained a modest and even shy man. When Willie Black made a video of Cliff at a Skegness rally, Cliff was hostile to being videoed, because he hated anything resembling a personality cult.[73] Likewise he firmly refused the proposal of photographer Red Saunders to do a portrait of him next to Marx's grave.[74]

He was incapable of hypocrisy and found it hard to adapt to the conventions of social politeness.[75] Though he was always polite to his children's friends, he had no small talk. If he had to go to a party, he would ask if Lindsey German would be there so he would have someone to talk to. He hated parties and sometimes would take a book and sit in a corner reading.[76]

Certainly he sought no particular privileges for himself. The author remembers meeting him in the early 1990s late one night in King's Cross tube station, on his way home from speaking at a meeting somewhere in the Midlands. He was about 75 years old, and exhausted, yet it never seemed to have crossed his mind to get a taxi and charge it to the party.

Cliff had no hobbies, no cultural interests to balance his political commitment. But for occasional relaxation he was fond of popular television programmes. He loved *Dad's Army*, *'Allo 'Allo!*, Morecambe and Wise and cowboy films.[77] He was also fond of *The Rockford Files*.[78]

He continued to show a remarkable capacity for detail. Before a meeting in Leicester he asked the organiser how many people were expected. When the organiser said about 35, Cliff demanded to know why 100 chairs had been put out. As he pointed out, if there are only 20 chairs and 30 turn up, it creates a good atmosphere.[79]

Likewise John Rees remembered that when he was editing *International Socialism* Cliff would always comment, not just on the general content, but on typographical detail, saying, "How can I trust the journal if I can't trust the footnotes?"[80]

He took a deep interest in the development of the international tendency. Choi Il-bung from South Korea first met Cliff in 1990 when he attended Marxism in London; he was a syndicalist though he didn't realise it. He spent four hours talking to Cliff, then accompanied him to a branch meeting. He remembered Cliff as the most impressive person he had ever met. Cliff persuaded him that the group around him was too small to involve itself in industrial struggles and should become a propaganda organisation, focusing on basic ideas and especially the theory of state capitalism. As a result, the organisation was later able to play a leading role in campaigns.

A couple of years later there was a wave of repression and Choi Il-bung was jailed. He received a letter from Cliff telling him not to despair because people in Britain and elsewhere were supporting him. This greatly boosted his spirits.[81]

Cliff spent a lot of time on the SAG in Germany. A sense of Cliff's passionate interest and his concern with matters of detail is shown by a letter he wrote to veteran SAG member Volkhard Mosler in 1993.

He began by calling the proposed appointment of a full-timer "absolute madness". He went on to question Mosler's conception of leadership:

> You believe that like Mother Hen you have to look after the flock. You have to keep the peace in the group. That is the worst method of leadership. To lead is to do the right thing and not simply to be the peace-maker. Peace-making leads to squabbling, paralysis, waste.

He recalled his own involvement in building the IS in the 1960s and urged that similar work in Germany would require full-timers:

> They will have to work seven days a week… But if it is done half-cock, it is better not to do it at all. Let the SAG go on drifting! If these two have to spend all that time they must be full-timers.

He picked up on a minor administrative question, the holding of a weekly Political Committee meeting in Berlin, and used this to criticise what he saw as dangerous formalism in the SAG's organisation:

> I tell you straight, if I had to travel seven hours each direction for a PK [Political Committee] meeting, you'd have to count me out; it's a waste of time… Why the hell this formal, heavy burden in Germany? Do you

1989-97: EXCITED ABOUT THE FUTURE 527

have such a lot of decisions to take every week that you need everybody present? Can't you consult on the phone? This formal set-up not only wastes time – which is serious as time is precious – but makes also for flabby thinking.[82]

Whether Cliff was right on particular questions is secondary; what was significant was his detailed involvement in the day-to-day life of the international tendency.

Cliff continued to be a major speaker at the Marxism events, where he would normally address five or six meetings each year, on topics ranging from Lenin and Trotsky to "Marxism and Oppression" and "The Changing Nature of Labourism", as well as giving an inspiring concluding speech at the final rally.

Certainly he showed signs of tiredness and not all meetings were equally well prepared. In 1992 Dave Widgery, one of the SWP's most talented writers, died suddenly and in December the party held a memorial meeting at the LSE. Cliff was the final speaker; he began by declaring "Dave's fight is our fight", and then spoke for another 20 minutes, not mentioning Widgery at all and repeating almost *verbatim* the speech he had given the previous evening at a north London rally on "The revolutionary road to socialism".[83] (Widgery had an acute sense of the absurd, rooted in his love of surrealism; he would have taken great delight in writing up his own memorial meeting.)

But when he put his mind to it, Cliff was still capable of giving a powerful and thought-provoking lecture. In 1995, to commemorate the centenary of Engels's death, he spoke at Marxism (and at various public meetings) about Engels. It was a *tour de force*, summing up a lifetime's thought about the nature of Marxism and the relation of theory and practice.[84]

He began by dismissing Engels's own claim that he was merely "second fiddle" to Marx: "To be second fiddle to Marx is quite an achievement. Even to be fiddle 150 to Marx is an achievement!" Engels was an important thinker in his own right and had often been ahead of Marx in the development of his ideas.

Cliff drew out the way Engels had been influenced by the experience of the English working class, notably the general strike of 1842 in which, Cliff claimed, the idea of the flying picket had been "invented". Engels grasped before Marx "the centrality of the working class" and for him "workers appear, not as the victims of history, but as the subject of history".

Here Cliff drew out a fundamental point – that the whole history of Marxism was about learning from the working class. In 1848 Marx had said virtually nothing about the dictatorship of the proletariat, but in 1871 he had defined it much more precisely:

> You might say to yourself, "This shows that Marx has been working very hard in the British Museum. In 1848 he said nothing like this, but in 1871 he does!" Not at all. His views in 1871 were shaped by the Paris Commune of that year, which was a fact of life. The workers of Paris created their Commune without bureaucracy, without a standing army, and so on.

Moreover, he argued, "ideas are like a river and a river is formed from lots of streams. Engels is one of the streams contributing to Marxism." Cliff made the point simply and in everyday language; the lecture was easily comprehensible and a fine introduction for someone who had never previously heard of Engels. At the same time he made a devastating critique of views of Marxism that were current in the academic milieu, especially among the followers of Althusser (whom Cliff scorned*), who held that Marxism was the product of an "epistemological break", a conceptual shift inside Marx's skull in abstraction from the evolution of the working class movement.

Cliff emphasised Engels's commitment to the self-emancipation of the working class, citing the passage where he wrote that the revolutionary class "can only in a revolution succeed in ridding itself of all the muck of ages and become fit to found society anew". In changing the world the working class changed itself.

Cliff drew out Engels's intellectual originality, showing that Engels had written about "permanent revolution", rejected the idea of socialism in one country and, after Marx's death, had explored new areas such as the origin of the family. He rubbished the notion, again common in academic circles, that Engels was a mechanical determinist. Cliff also paid tribute to Engels's willingness to work as a factory manager: "He bloody hated it, and you know why he did

---

* At Marxism 1983 Cliff had a heated argument with Alex Callinicos, author of *Althusser's Marxism* (London, 1976), in which he insisted that Althusser was a Stalinist (Alex Callinicos interview, July 2008).

it? Only for one reason. He did it for Marx, because Marx never earned anything in his life." (Perhaps he was thinking of the sacrifices Chanie had made for him.)

Finally, Cliff explored the question of the unity of theory and practice. He argued that Engels was "a man of action" who had fought on the barricades in 1848 while Marx was writing "marvellous articles". He argued that those who stressed the difference between Marx and Engels did so "because they want to separate theory from practice".

It was common in the SWP – and Cliff was certainly one of those primarily responsible – to talk of the unity of theory and practice primarily in order to stress the centrality of practice. Cliff detested academic Marxism which never led to action; he put it here in a phrase he often used: "The idea of unity of theory and practice is not, as it is sometimes presented, that someone writes a book – that is theory; and you read the book – that is practice."

But here he pointed out that the relationship between theory and practice was more complex: "If you have a too direct relationship to the action, you do not have the distance." He illustrated the point with the difference between Marx and Engels over the American Civil War. Engels was convinced that the South would win because, in purely military terms, it had the advantage. "Yet Marx said, no question about it, the North is going to win. Why? Because wage labour is more productive than slave labour. Full stop!" He concluded that "despite all Engels's technical military expertise Marx was right about the war, while Engels was wrong".

At the end of the lecture the themes came together in a powerful assertion of what Cliff meant by Marxism:

> I can never understand the idea that is put forward that the party teaches the class. What the hell is the party? Who teaches the teacher? The dialectic means there is a two-way street. Theory by itself is absolutely useless. Practice by itself is blind.

In 1994 the leader of the Labour Party, John Smith, had died suddenly and Tony Blair was elected to replace him. Smith had been a traditional right-winger, but Blair was a radical right-winger of a new sort. He and his associates proclaimed themselves "New Labour" to dissociate themselves from the minimal attachment that traditional Labour had shown to the working class. In particular Blair campaigned successfully to change Labour's constitution and get rid of the celebrated "Clause Four" which committed Labour to nationalisation.

For Cliff the main feature in defining the period was the state of industrial struggle rather than purely political developments. At the SWP conference in 1994 he set out his analysis of the balance of class forces:

> Today we face a weak government which is forced to take on all workers – through tax rises and wage controls.
>
> It makes workers angry, but cautious about taking action, particularly in opposition to the union leaders. It is a period of working class recuperation where we must inject socialist politics.[85]

Early the next year he argued that while the downturn proper was over, there was still no upturn. "In the industrial struggle we have had three stages over the past 25 years: the period of upturn, the period of downturn and now the third stage – a period of transition." There would be no rapid victories, but a slow recovery: "two steps forward, one step back".[86]

> We cannot build the house of today with the bricks of tomorrow. But we can make the bricks today for the house of tomorrow.[87]

He continued to be one of the group's main public speakers; at the NUT teachers' union conference in 1995, 120 people attended a fringe meeting addressed by Cliff.[88]

By 1996 everything was overshadowed by the coming general election. The Tories were still in disarray and it was fairly clear Labour would win. In an interview in November 1996 Cliff gave his predictions for a Blair government. He observed that since 1945 every Labour government had been more right wing than its predecessors. Blair was looking to reduce expectations, so "the betrayal from Blair is coming before he gets into office".

Therefore he expected rapid opposition to Blair. Referring to the debates from 1974 about how long the honeymoon would last, he commented, "I don't think we should be talking about a honeymoon. I doubt whether there will even be a consummation." Between 1974 and 1979 Labour had lost 13 out of 31 by-elections: "That's what happens when Labour gets in and disappoints. It will be worse next time".* This offered great opportunities for the SWP:

> Tony Blair fights on all fronts – he's highly ideological, highly political and he intervenes in industrial affairs. He tends to cement all three things together, which makes the situation more favourable for us.

Cliff noted the decline of the Labour left, the collapse of the CP and the likelihood that Scargill's newly launched Socialist Labour Party would not make much headway.† The SWP's strength was as an interventionist organisation: "When it comes to fighting the BNP we are more effective. We collected far more money for the signal workers‡ than the Labour Party." The SWP's weakness lay within itself, its failure to respond to change:

> We have to change radically. I believe the SWP can be the most conservative organisation in the country. It was important in the 1980s to keep our sights low. We talked quite rightly about growing by ones and twos. Now we must shift our sights.

He believed that rapid growth was possible, but this would need greater decentralisation and greater accountability. After a Labour victory "there will be a race between the far right and the far left to win workers to their politics".[89] At Marxism 1995, he rashly predicted that the SWP could grow by 500 members a week when Blair came to power.[90] Yet at the same time Cliff insisted the SWP must not isolate itself from the anti-Tory mood which would carry Blair into power. He argued vigorously for the slogan "Hate the Tories, Don't Trust Blair, Join the Socialists". All this contributed to a mood of real urgency in the party, though it sometimes overstated the possibilities; older members were sometimes alienated by attacks on their alleged conservatism.[91]

In the summer of 1996 Bookmarks published a second edition of *The Labour Party: A Marxist History*.[92] This contained a substantial new section on the emergence of New Labour, written by Donny

---

* In fact, although Labour had some poor by-election results, it did not actually lose a single by-election between 1997 and 2001, and in 2001 won only six fewer seats than in 1997.

† When the SLP was launched some CC members thought it had potential, but Cliff was contemptuous of it from the start, certain that it was going nowhere (Lindsey German interview, September 2008).

‡ There was a series of strikes by railway signal workers in the summer of 1994.

Gluckstein, but approved by Cliff.[93] It traced in remorseless detail Labour's inexorable move to the right under Kinnock and then Blair. Ostensibly Labour was driven by electoral considerations, yet it did not respond to radical attitudes among its followers: "Labour policies are not primarily shaped by public opinion. The dictates of capitalism are far more important".[94] So those who had turned to Labour in disgust at Tory policies would find Labour following those same policies. Echoing Kidron's formulation about "reformism without reforms", Cliff and his son argued that "the Labour Party today is a reformist organisation that cannot deliver reforms, only destroy them".[95] The conclusion was an uncompromising call for a revolutionary alternative: "In Britain the main political obstacle in the way of demolishing capitalism is the Labour Party. To win the working class we must get past the obstacle".[96]

In an interview given around the time of the 1997 election, Cliff placed the situation in a broader context. Both the collapse of Stalinism and the international crisis of social democracy had opened up more space for the revolutionary left. Now the left faced "reformist parties which don't deliver reforms". He concluded with a comment he made frequently in meetings and which was widely quoted within the SWP:

> I remember the 1930s and I have the feeling that I'm seeing the same film for the second time – mass unemployment, a rise in racism, the growth of the fascists. But this time the film goes much slower.[97]

As an observation by a survivor of the 1930s this made a valid point. As a perspective it had distinct limitations; to describe the 1990s as "the thirties in slow motion" could be misleading.* Cliff knew well that history did not repeat itself. The Blair experience had a number of surprises in store.

---

* For a brave attempt to theorise the metaphor, stressing the differences as much as the similarities between the 1930s and the 1990s, see A Callinicos, "Crisis and Class Struggle in Europe Today", *International Socialism* 63 (Summer 1994).

13

1997-2000
Still Fighting

The election of 1 May 1997 produced a landslide victory for Blair's Labour. The size of the majority surprised most on the left and was an indication of the sheer hatred for the Tories that had developed over the previous years. Blair's policies promised no significant reforms in the interests of the working class, but offered a continuation of Tory policies and an increasing distancing of the Labour Party from any hint of industrial militancy. It was not yet clear just how reactionary Blair's foreign policy would be and how slavishly he would support US aggression.

Cliff's analysis of how right-wing Labour had become proved absolutely accurate, but not his predictions of rapid resistance. In a speech to an SWP national meeting later in May Cliff gave his first response to the situation after the election. He pointed to the contrast between Labour's victory in 1945 and the present situation:

> Their promises are miserable. In 1945 Labour "thought the unthinkable" and set up the welfare state. Now thinking the unthinkable means finding ways of getting rid of it...

> Tony Blair comes into office after three recessions in 20 years. Under such conditions the path to reform is closed.[1]

The argument was developed in the next month's *Socialist Review*. On the question of the honeymoon Cliff had dropped his optimism of the previous year and took a more nuanced position: "It would be a mistake to speak simply about a honeymoon, this will be a honeymoon racked or intertwined with conflicts." Because many people had split consciousness, it was necessary to employ "both common action and argument". There were possibilities of growth, though he warned that in the long run "either industrial struggle will rise to the level of the ideas or the ideas will go down to the level of the struggle". He concluded that the present period was "very promising for socialists".[2]

On 31 May 1997 Cliff celebrated his eightieth birthday with a party at the Irish Centre in Camden Town. It was a cheerful occasion with many old friends and comrades. Cliff detested personality cults, and there was a gently self-mocking atmosphere about the occasion. There was an exhibition of family photographs to which satirical captions had been added by Cliff's younger son Danny and one of his friends – later reproduced in a booklet.[3]

Cliff gave a highly political speech, recalling his 65 years as a Trotskyist. But as he reached this landmark in his life, he knew that time was beginning to run out, that he was not going to see the fulfilment of his dreams. There was resistance to Blair – the SWP helped to organise a successful lobby of the Labour Party conference in Brighton in 1997.[4] But the government had a huge majority, and the level of industrial struggle remained low. Cliff told the opening rally at Marxism, two months after Blair's victory, that he read pages 14 and 15 of *Socialist Worker* – the industrial reports – "religiously", and read everything twice to make sure he had understood.[5] He was determined not to miss any sign of a fightback.

When the death of Princess Diana in August 1997 produced a vast expression of public grief, the reaction of most SWP members was one of cynicism, feeling no need to mourn a royal parasite. Cliff was more sympathetic to the public mood, seeing it as somehow linked to an aspiration for a more caring world, and he was critical of aspects of the treatment of the event in *Socialist Worker*.[6]

Sometimes Cliff seemed torn between two timescales. He never took his eye off the day-to-day struggle, stressing the urgency of the next target. At the same time he was aware that he was engaged in activity directed to a future he would not see. He told an interviewer, "In history 50 years is nothing".[7] Sometimes this could be handled with one of his customary jokes: "It is good to be a professional revolutionary; the revolution never comes, so you have a job for life".[8] In meetings, and in one of the last articles he wrote, he pointed out that the transition from feudalism to capitalism had been a process lasting several centuries; he was reminding his successors that they had a long road ahead of them:

Again, when we speak about the transition from feudalism to capitalism, quite often it sounds like a very smooth process. One can spend half an hour reading a chapter on feudalism, and then move on to a chapter on capitalism. But the process was much less smooth, much more contradictory. Feudalism survived for over a millennium in Europe. When it was in decline and capitalism was rising in the cracks of feudal society, it was not a one-way street leading upwards.[9]

In a speech to the final rally at Marxism 1998 he affirmed:

> The future belongs to the working class. If the workers' revolution will be defeated, I'll tell you straight, the next generation will fight on. If they'll be defeated, we'll fight on, because we are the many, they are the few.[10]

Balanced against this philosophical sense of the long term, and in constant tension with it, was a determination not to miss any opportunity to advance the cause. There was a peculiar combination of patience and impatience; he longed to see revolution immediately, but put great effort into things that would not show rapid results.[11] But he never abandoned his focus on action in the present. He scornfully dismissed people who say, "I'll be on the barricades when the revolution comes." He responded, "Who the hell needs you? When the revolution comes there will be a million on the barricades. What matters is what you're prepared to do now. Are you ready to get up at 5am to sell two *Socialist Workers*?" He repeated, "Nothing is inevitable... Everything is to play for".[12]

In the autumn of 1998 Cliff addressed a meeting of SWP delegates and linked the economic situation to developments in Indonesia:

> The fall of Suharto in Indonesia is obviously linked to the economic collapse.
>
> The economic catastrophe leads to fury from below. In Indonesia now there are 96 million people with no income, half the population.
>
> The crisis also causes deep splits inside the ruling class across the world as leaders are uncertain whether they should keep screaming, "No retreat! No U-turns," or offer a few reforms in an effort to buy off the anger.
>
> When the splits at the top occur at the same time as the immense explosion from below, that is the condition for revolution.[13]

In Indonesia in May 1998 demonstrations, strikes and riots by workers, students and the urban poor had overthrown the brutal and reactionary dictator Suharto. The protests continued and Suharto's successor, Habibie, had no solution to the deep economic crisis. At the time it seemed that a potentially revolutionary situation was developing. The SWP had made contacts with some of the left groupings in Indonesia. Cliff decided to write a short pamphlet aimed at socialists in the country.

"Revolution and Counter-Revolution: Lessons for Indonesia"[14] was not comparable to Cliff's earlier writings on France and Portugal. There was none of the careful analysis of social struggle that had marked those two studies. Only at the end did he refer briefly to the specific history of Indonesia and he contemptuously dismissed the two main contenders for power from the moderate opposition:

> Megawati [Sukarno's daughter] and Amien Rais are pygmies compared to Robespierre or Danton and in no way more militant than the cowardly bourgeoisie in Germany in 1848 that Marx so sharply castigated.[*]

The main thrust of the pamphlet was to reiterate some of the basic lessons of the revolutionary tradition. It was the debate between reform and revolution which was the central issue for the Indonesian left. He gave a brief account of the contrasting experiences of Russia in 1917 and France in 1968, emphasising the need for a revolutionary party: "The working class, not the party, makes the revolution, but the party guides the working class."

Socialism was neither inevitable nor impossible, so what socialists did mattered. Lenin had understood that:

> The development of the party requires very different tactics and forms of organisation tailored according to the size of the organisation, the composition of its membership, and the tasks required of it by the balance of forces in the wider society.

In particular he drew out the difference between the party and the trade unions, important in a situation where unions were just emerging from illegality: "The trade union movement is a blunt axe but a large one. The revolutionary party is a sharp axe even if it is

---

[*] Cliff's perspective was confirmed, but only negatively. The left was unable to take its opportunities. Megawati became president in 2001, but failed to be re-elected in 2004. Poverty, unemployment and corruption persisted.

relatively small." He concluded with a warning:

> In a whole number of countries where the bourgeoisie is young and the political regime is either autocratic or only recently became democratic, such as Indonesia, there is a danger that the proletariat will tail the bourgeois democrats.

The 21-page pamphlet was produced in a special edition for Indonesian readers; it had a cover with the innocuous title *The Internet – Guidelines for Helplines*. Weyman Bennett took 1,500 copies to Indonesia. The police examined the pamphlet but the whole country was in such turmoil that they let him through – nobody knew how things were going to turn out. Bennett distributed the 1,500 pamphlets and did three meetings on reform or revolution. When he got home Cliff quizzed him for three and a half hours about every detail of the experience and about how the left had grown again after the 1965 massacre.[15]

Cliff continued to take a keen interest in the international tendency. He never allowed personal relations to modify his political judgement, and on occasion appeared to be ruthless. In 1997 there was a split in the Turkish organisation. Ron Margulies took the opposite side to Cliff, and went to see him to argue about the question. The discussion went on for five hours – Cliff began by praising him, then laughed at him and insulted him. Although Margulies had worked closely with Cliff over a number of years when the Turkish group was being won over, this was the end of the relationship and they did not speak again.[16]

He put a huge amount of time and energy into the SWP's sister organisation in Germany. He encouraged a new young leadership and then directed by almost daily phone conversations the reorientation of the organisation towards entry into the Social Democratic Party youth organisation and the launch of the paper *Linksruck*. In some ways Cliff seemed to be re-enacting the way he had worked with young organisers in the IS in the early 1970s. The German organisation was transformed and a new young cadre emerged. But Cliff also showed some of his weaknesses, making misjudgements about individuals, and some of the older comrades he had tried to sideline later helped rescue the group when it encountered difficulties.[17]

He continued to show support for individuals in difficult situations. Shaun Doherty faced victimisation in his school. He discussed the situation with Cliff, who agreed that it would be reasonable for Shaun to leave the job after the dispute was resolved.[18]

At the same time Cliff was working on another book, his first since he completed *Trotsky* in 1993. *Trotskyism after Trotsky* [19] was in a way a conclusion to the Trotsky biography. While there were a few side-swipes at old adversaries, Cliff was primarily concerned to analyse the crisis of Trotskyism after the death of its founder, and to present his own role in offering a way out of that crisis.

The book was structured around what Cliff, in a reversion to his Russian mother-tongue, called the "troika" – the trio – of theories: state capitalism, the permanent arms economy, and deflected permanent revolution. It was a mixture of theory and autobiography, a reflection on his own intellectual achievement and an attempt to discover a unity in it. Much in the book was a reiteration of points Cliff had made time and again over the preceding 50 years.

He reminded a younger generation for whom Trotskyism had all too often appeared only in grotesque and caricatured manifestations just how important Trotsky had been for an isolated and threatened left:

> With the Nazis' terrifying advance and the Moscow show trials that condemned the leaders of the October Revolution, the Bolshevik Party and the Comintern as Nazi agents, our dependence ideologically and emotionally was deep and understandable. We were quite convinced, and rightly, of the genius of his analysis of the total situation and of the strategy and tactics needed to face it that he developed.[20]

Cliff recalled that after 1945 the Fourth International had to face "a new and decisive challenge – how to react to a situation radically different to that visualised by its founder".[21] Some of Trotsky's predictions had proved false and it was necessary to revise Trotskyism in order to defend it.

He restated his positions, with substantial quotations from his own works, and was able, with the benefit of hindsight, to assess the validity of his own theories. As for the arms economy, Cliff noted that he been right to point both to the reality of the exceptional post-war boom, but also to its temporary nature. He pointed to the factors – Vietnam, followed by the oil crisis – which had brought the boom to an end, and argued that his analysis had been essentially correct although "it was not Russia which forced the United

States to cut its military budget, but primarily West Germany and Japan". The theory had pointed to the terrible irrationality of capitalism: the fact that economic prosperity could only be ensured by the production of the means of mass slaughter revealed "the most extreme expression of the bestiality and barbarity of the system".[22]

In retrospect, Cliff argued, his various theoretical innovations had an interconnected unity. In particular he traced the roots of the argument about the arms economy to his discussion of the role of arms production in his 1948 document.

Cliff had written both a political testament and an introduction to his own theoretical work. The book was also a reflection on the nature of the Marxist method. Marxism was concerned to analyse an ever-changing world and therefore must itself constantly change: "the moment Marxism stops changing, it is dead". Hence in the period after 1945 "to repeat Trotsky's words literally while avoiding facing the real situation was to give too much honour to Trotsky, but also too much insult".[23]

Such a position could easily drift into a form of sceptical relativism in which there were no fixed points of reference. But Cliff's position was rooted in what he saw as the unchanging core of Marxism. His criticism of Trotsky was based on "the classical Marxist tradition which identified socialism as the self-emancipation of the working class". Hence "Marxism as a living theory must continue as it is, and change at the same time".[24]

Although the world had changed greatly since the end of the long boom and the collapse of the Eastern Bloc, Cliff argued his theoretical contribution remained relevant to the tasks of socialists. "The idea that state ownership of industry and economic planning, even without workers' democracy, is equal to socialism, is still alive," Keynesianism was "alive and kicking", and Maoism and Che Guevara still exercised a great attraction.[25]

The logic of Cliff's position was that if Marxism is to remain a "guide to action"[26] in the modern world, a whole series of troikas may be needed, as successive generations relate Marxism to the realities of their particular epoch. Socialists in the 21st century face new patterns of employment, the revolution in communications produced by the internet, the challenge of globalisation and the threat of disaster from climate change.

For Cliff this meant a constant struggle to preserve what is essential in Marxism while adapting it constantly to the realities of the epoch. As he put it at a meeting at Marxism 1999:

> If you sit on Marx's shoulders you see far, but if you sit on Marx's shoulders and close your eyes, you don't see very far at all.[27]

In this sense, Cliff's work can serve as a source of enlightenment and encouragement for a new generation of Marxists.

There was, however, a strange ambiguity to the conclusion of the book. After developing his argument that Marxism must constantly change, Cliff insisted in his conclusion that Trotskyism "is coming into its own" again. So he claimed:

> the words of the 1938 *Transitional Programme* that "there can be no discussion of systematic social reforms and the raising of the masses' living standards" fits reality again. The classic theory of permanent revolution, as argued by Trotsky, is back on the agenda, as shown by the Indonesian Revolution in 1998.[28]

This seems bizarre.* Certainly capitalism has continued to deliver war and destruction, economic instability and terrible oppression in all parts of the world. Whether Trotsky's 1938 perspective applies is a rather different question. Sometimes in his last years Cliff seemed to retreat to a defensive stance, holding on to the achievements of 1917 as the one certain point of reference that proved the validity of revolutionary Marxism. At his best Cliff was a supremely non-defensive Marxist, but in his last years he occasionally lapsed into defensiveness. Here he seemed to imply that "orthodox Trotskyism", whose inadequacies Cliff had so acutely exposed in his earlier years, was due for a new lease of life.

But at the very end Cliff quoted Marx from the *Eighteenth Brumaire*: "Eventually quantity changes into quality and the system as a whole is racked by crises and instability. Then, as Marx put it, humanity 'will leap from its seat and exultantly exclaim, Well burrowed, old mole!'"[29] This was the true spirit of Cliff – a critical, open Marxism with an unshakeable faith in the future.

As Cliff concluded this summation of his career, his health finally began to break down. For some time he had begun to take more

---

* In 1973 Cliff had argued that a transitional programme was inappropriate because we "do not live in a period which excludes the possibility of serious reforms" (T Cliff and A Nagliatti, "Main Features of the Programme We Need", IS Internal Bulletin, January 1973).

care of himself, doing regular exercise. Before that he had taken no care of his body for many years, having more important things to do. Now he tried to correct that, asking his son Danny for advice on exercise, but it was too late.[30] He and Chanie could be seen "speed-walking" round Clissold Park, near their home.[31] But the remorseless energy he had shown was declining. He suffered a lot of pain in his last years and had to sleep in the afternoon. Chris Bambery, who often travelled by train to meetings with Cliff, remembers that in the early 1990s Cliff would always spend train journeys reading in order not to waste time, but by the later 1990s he would be very tired, and would pass the time talking and joking.[32] He hated spending the night away from home and would insist on being driven back home from meetings outside London so he could sleep in his own bed.[33]

He remained an impressive speaker. If on occasion he hesitated, misread his notes or forgot a name, he would rapidly incorporate his own lapses into the performance, commenting, "Senility starts," or, "I've a good excuse – Alzheimer's disease." He commented sourly, "Wine improves with age, human beings deteriorate and I am the witness of it".[34] Cliff still took a keen interest in the world, and not only in the strictly political. He was excited when France won the World Cup in 1998 because the team contained several black players, and he saw this as a blow against Le Pen.[35]

For 80 years the sickly child had endured jail, clandestinity, exile, poverty, tireless activism and the emotional strain of holding an organisation together. The medication he was taking was ceasing to be effective. When he went to the London Chest Hospital in Bonner Road, London E2 he was normally accompanied by Chanie or Anna, since if he went on his own he would always say he was fine, however ill he had been, as he hated bothering people about himself.

Initially the hospital was reluctant to operate, since Cliff was over 80. But a letter from Paul Foot, explaining Cliff's significance, persuaded them to go ahead.[36] The operation for a heart valve replacement required five months leave of absence from the central committee, the first time in 50 years that Cliff had been away from his position in the organisation for so long. His absence came at a difficult time for the party. Paul Foot was also seriously ill and the war in Kosovo was demanding increased activity.

Cliff faced the prospect with his normal good humour. To friends enquiring about his health, he responded, "The Chief Rabbi has given permission for me to have a pig's heart transplanted".[37] The operation was a great strain for a man of his age. In the immediate aftermath he became delusional, his early break with Zionism returning to haunt him. At one point he thought one of the nurses was trying to kill him because of his anti-Zionism. On another occasion he had a vivid dream that he had written an article for the *Financial Times* explaining why Zionists were right, and he awoke in great distress.[38] William Morris compared becoming a revolutionary to crossing "a river of fire that will put all that tries to swim across to a hard proof indeed".[39] Cliff had suffered his "hard proof", and the memories of those early struggles were implanted deep within his brain.

Though he must have known he had not long to live, he never talked about his impending death.[40] A considerable period of convalescence was necessary. To be obliged to stay at home and rest was something he was utterly unaccustomed to, so he found a new occupation. At the suggestion of his two daughters[41] he decided to write his autobiography. Written largely from memory, since he could not travel to consult libraries, *A World to Win* gave a vivid account of his political trajectory as he had experienced it. The material on the years in Palestine was largely new, even to those who had known him for many years. Sometimes he neglected to give sufficient acknowledgement to the contribution of other comrades who had assisted in the building of the organisation; some of his judgements caused offence to former comrades.* But the book was fresh, lively, sometimes humorous, often perceptive; it gave a picture not only of Cliff's life, but of the ups and downs of class struggle over seven decades. It was his last address to the comrades who would carry on without him.

The operation achieved its purpose; Cliff made a good recovery,

---

* Jim Higgins, who never forgave Cliff for the 1973-75 dispute, described it as "clever but naive, cunning but transparently obvious, and a mine of misinformation" (*Revolutionary History*, 7/4 (2000), p220). Ray Challinor, who had known Cliff since 1947, acknowledged his "colossal contribution", but rejected, with some justice, as "complete fantasy" the suggestion that Cliff "did all the work almost single-handedly in these early years" (*Revolutionary History*, 7/4 (2000), pp185-187). Among SWP members Paul Foot was also very critical of Cliff's account (communication from Alex Callinicos, August 2010).

though he had lost weight and was a lot frailer. On 27 July 1999 both he and Chanie received certificates for completing a Cardiac Rehabilitation Course. He was given an advice sheet on "Stress Management". Some of the points would have seemed ironic to anyone who knew Cliff:

> Avoid trying to do too many things at once.
>
> Recognise your limitations and stick to them.
>
> Don't harbour grudges; forgive and forget.
>
> Learn to be assertive.
>
> Look at criticisms constructively.[42]

On recovering from the operation Cliff tried to take up where he had left off. In July 1999 he was, as ever, one of the main speakers at Marxism. He gave a set of three lectures based on *Trotskyism after Trotsky*, recapitulating his theoretical contribution. The old verve and wit were still there; he told his audience, "When I was sick, I thought I'll join the Conservative Party. I want them to lose a member and not us."

In explaining the permanent arms economy he gave a basic introduction to Marxist economics. He was assisted by Chanie, who wrote some of Marx's equations on an overhead projector. When she failed to keep up, he joked, "You are slow; you'll get the sack," and, "Slave, do your job – women's oppression, that's a demonstration".[43]

In addressing what he may have realised would be his last final rally, he cited James Connolly's words: "The only prophets today are those that shape the future," and added, "The future starts, not in five years time, not in five months time, it starts here and now. We have to shape the future".[44]

For a time he seemed full of life. At a demonstration at the Labour Party conference that autumn he challenged Jim Cronin – a veteran from the 1960s who had also had heart problems – to a hundred yards race.[45] He was pleased to see old comrades, even if they had moved away from the party. At that demonstration he met Gerry Norris, whom he hadn't seen for 20 years; she told him she didn't agree with the SWP line on Kosovo, and he spent half an hour discussing with her.[46]

He continued to address public meetings and party gatherings.

His efforts were still devoted to passing on a tradition of Marxism to a new generation. He gave particular attention to encouraging new members. A new generation of students and young members was emerging, and on some of these he made a powerful impression. For Richard Seymour:

> There are three things I remember distinctly about Cliff's speech. First of all, his unassuming demeanour didn't identify him as an "inspiring speaker". And as it turned out, he was not a "firebrand", and he did not pander to sentiment. Secondly, he was incredibly funny. Much of the humour was directed at the kinds of hubris and overstatement that revolutionaries are sometimes given to. He was most sardonic, as I recall, about the temptation to retreat to grandiose fantasies. Thirdly, despite the hard-headedness and the refusal of cheap sanguinity, he left us confident and optimistic. Cliff insisted on a particular analysis and a strategy, and it was this that empowered us to engage in a political situation that for most on the Left at the time was still deeply discouraging.[47]

For Christian Hogsbjerg:

> Firstly, it was clear he was an outstanding "populariser" of Marxism – after hearing him speak you felt really confident as though you now grasped the essence of what Marx was saying however little you had actually read. And yet secondly, as a perfect complement, I remember him clearly imploring us students to "read, read, and read" – he did not want us to take what he was saying on trust – he wanted us to discover why this was the case for ourselves.[48]

In November 1999 Cliff attended his last party conference. He argued that the present period was not one of either upturn like the early 1970s or downturn like the 1980s: "The strike situation remains very low, but people hold very political ideas. People's ideas have moved to the left. But the class struggle doesn't remain in the realm of ideas forever".[49] It was a mixture of realism and hope that characterised what was to be a farewell message to the party.

He continued to write. In the last year of his life he produced a series of articles for the papers of the International Socialist Tendency groups in Germany and Turkey. After his death a selection of these were collected in a small book entitled *Marxism at the Millennium*.[50] There were no theoretical innovations here; instead he set out to put forward some of the basic arguments for socialism. Many of the points he made, and the concrete illustrations – and jokes – he used were familiar to those who had heard his public speaking.

Perhaps he now felt slightly freer of organisational responsibilities, of the need to defend the apparatus which had so often fallen on him. The critical, innovative strain in his Marxism was particularly visible in some of these articles. The revolutionary party was vital – but it carried its own dangers of conservatism:

> The problem with revolutionaries is that we need a routine to survive. But the routine enters into you. You take it for granted that you are in advance of the working class. But when the workers start moving you find you are so bloody backward! The revolutionary party has to catch up with the working class.[51]

He illustrated with Lenin's response to the creation of soviets in 1905: "When workers established the first soviet in Petrograd in 1905, Lenin wrote four days later – what the hell is that for?"[52] * The account was much starker – and less complimentary to Lenin – than that in his biography.[53]

There was also a passionate defence of intellectuals. On occasion in the SWP there had been currents of workerism and anti-intellectualism, and Cliff himself had sometimes been guilty of encouraging them. Now he argued:

> The worst damage that can be done inside a revolutionary party is if there is an attack on the intellectuals inside the party, in the name of a proletarian attitude. As a matter of fact such an attack is not so much on the intellectuals but on the workers in the party. It is an insult to the workers as it assumes the workers are unable to grasp theory.[54]

He argued that "the most important aspect of the revolution is the spiritual changes of the working class" – workers change themselves in the process of changing the world. He pointed to the responsibilities that revolutionaries bore: "Only revolutionaries can fight at present consistently for reforms".[55]

History was still open. Engels and Luxemburg had pointed to the

---

* Cliff's colourful paraphrase may refer to Lenin's article "The Zemstvo Congress" of October 1905, which condemns the "erroneousness" of the Menshevik call for St Petersburg workers to elect committees in their factories (Lenin, *Collected Works*, IX 306). See also J-J Marie, *Lénine*, Paris, 2004, pp117-118. For the way Lenin observed and learned from the soviet see "Gorev Remembers Lenin", *Revolutionary History* 9/1 (2005), pp121-123.

choice between socialism and barbarism:

> Neither knew as much about barbarism as we do. Engels died in 1895; Rosa Luxemburg was murdered in January 1919. Both did not know about the gas chambers, about Hiroshima and Nagasaki, about the mass famine in Africa, etc.

There were dangers but also enormous hope:

> As a matter of fact the working class of South Korea is larger than the total working class of the world when Marx died. And South Korea is only the eleventh economy in the world. Add to them the American, Japanese, Russian, German, British workers, etc., and the potential for socialism is greater than ever.[56]

He returned to the tricky subject of the timescale which ran through many of the contradictions of his final years. He was determined to remind comrades to seize the time, not to miss any opportunity that might arise; yet he also wanted to communicate the need for patience, the recognition of a long-term perspective: "It will take time to overcome the depression left by decades of reaction, of Stalinism and fascism. But the path is open for the authentic permanent revolution to come into its own".[57]

Patience was never an excuse for missing opportunities. In the last months of his life Cliff had to respond to his final challenge. In November 1999 a huge demonstration in Seattle against the World Trade Organisation brought together protesters from many different backgrounds, from trade unionists to ecological campaigners. They all learned in action. As one demonstrator put it, "I came here to protest the killing of turtles. I'm going home determined to turn the world upside down".[58]

Many of those involved in what rapidly became known as the "anti-capitalist" movement came from traditions and forms of activity that were foreign to Cliff. But for Cliff, in the spirit of Rosa Luxemburg, a real movement was more important than any abstract formulation, and he felt immediate enthusiasm for the new activists. He wrote in one of his last articles:

> The Battle of Seattle demonstrated massive anger against the capitalist corporations. The German mass circulation paper *Der Spiegel*, commenting about the demonstration in Seattle, said that it shows that the next millennium will begin with a war against capitalism. For many

years the word anti-capitalism was part of the vocabulary of small revolutionary organisations. Now it is part of the language of millions.[59]

Unfortunately Seattle sharpened the tensions between the SWP and its fraternal organisation in the US, the International Socialist Organization (ISO). There had already been an exchange of views over the 1999 Kosovo War, with the SWP CC claiming that the ISO had failed to relate adequately to the anti-war movement.[60] While the ISO thought the SWP had accommodated to the reformist left, Cliff was concerned that the ISO might develop into a propagandist sect.[61] In the autumn before Seattle there had been a meeting between the SWP CC and some ISO representatives, including Ahmed Shawki, which had turned into a hostile confrontation. Cliff had always been fond of Shawki, but now he was uncompromising.[62]

He became convinced that the ISO had failed to respond to the opportunities offered by the Seattle demonstrations, and insisted that there must be an open debate.[63] For the last time in his life, he entered the arena of internal polemic. Writing jointly with Alex Callinicos, he stated bluntly:

> Your National Committee Bulletin, while analysing at length the mood after Seattle, does not acknowledge, let alone discuss the fact that the ISO leadership had failed the test of Seattle.
>
> This failure…comes after your weak intervention in the movement against last year's Balkan War. The greatest test of every revolutionary organisation is war. The ISO passed that test magnificently during the 1991 Gulf War, but failed the test of the 1999 Balkan War.[64] *

Just three days later a second letter followed, stating that "we regard it as quite tragic that the ISO Steering Committee failed to mobilise for Seattle, when it is clear that activists from all over the United States did so", and calling for a "frank and open debate" with the ISO membership.[65] A heated exchange ensued.[66]

On 29 March Cliff and Callinicos wrote another letter. They repeated their analysis of events:

> Throughout the advanced capitalist world an anti-capitalist mood is developing among a significant and rapidly growing minority. Seattle is the

---

* Cliff drafted this first document, which was revised by Callinicos. In particular the words "failed the test of Seattle" were Cliff's. The later documents were written by Callinicos, but he continued to discuss the ISO with Cliff right up to his death (Alex Callinicos interview, July 2008).

most spectacular example of this phenomenon so far.

Their critique of the ISO was even more blunt:

> The reason why [the ISO Steering Committee] aren't too worried about their failure at Seattle is that they don't think that Seattle was such a big deal.[67]

The details of the ISO's response to Seattle remain a matter of dispute and are probably of little general interest. Ahmed Shawki of the ISO feels that Seattle was a "smokescreen" and the issue was used to hide other differences that had developed in the 1990s. He thinks that the SWP was happier to have no fraternal organisation in the US than one which disagreed with them. Shawki felt disappointed in Cliff, from whom he had learnt so much in the past.[68] Likewise Joel Geier feels there was no question of political principle dividing the SWP and the ISO and that the real motive was that the SWP didn't want the political independence of the ISO.[69] Alex Callinicos, however, recalls that the SWP CC was desperately worried about losing its most important sister organisation. Cliff drafted and insisted on sending the first letter. But he didn't want flunkies, as was reflected in the enormous respect he had for the comrades in Greece, despite the way they had defended the independence of their group during some serious disagreements.[70]

Cliff, old, frail and well aware that he could be dead within weeks, was determined to make his final intervention, to fight his "last struggle". He had sensed that a new period was opening, and he was committed to persuading the organisations he had helped to build that they must not miss their opportunities. For the last time the stick was bent.

In principle the different assessments of the anti-capitalist movement could have been contained within the international tendency. But the following year, after a split in the Greek sister organisation SEK, blamed on ISO intervention, there was an open break between the SWP and the ISO.[71] The indisputable reality of the anti-capitalist mood was shown by the demonstration in Prague in September 2000 and the 300,000-strong march in Genoa in July 2001.

Meanwhile developments in Britain were opening up new possibilities. Though there was no mass revolt against the Labour government, there was considerable disaffection. In the London mayoral election of 2000, Ken Livingstone, a well-known figure of the

Labour left, announced that he would stand against the official Labour candidate for mayor. Meanwhile a number of groupings of the far left came together to establish an electoral coalition called the Socialist Alliance. The possibility of establishing a current to the left of the Labour Party was becoming a reality, though many difficulties lay ahead. On 22 February Cliff attended a rally in the Camden Centre to launch the London Socialist Alliance's election campaign, sitting in the front row.[72] When his son Donny saw him for the last time, only a few weeks before his death, Cliff was excited at the prospect of Ken Livingstone making a break with the Labour Party.[73]

There were signs of a revival of industrial struggle. In the face of widespread job losses, notably 2,500 at the Rover Longbridge factory in Birmingham, there was a 100,000-strong demonstration in Birmingham on 1 April. Martin Smith had particular responsibility for this on the CC. Although Cliff was seriously ill and in and out of hospital, he took a keen interest in the developing situation and had long discussions with Smith about it.[74] When Chris Bambery visited Cliff in hospital just before his death, he was anxious to have details of paper sales on the Longbridge demonstration.[75]

He continued to attend the CC and to speak at meetings right up to the last time he went into hospital just before his death. He appeared tired, but some of the old spark was still there. Sean Vernell, the first of the 1980s generation to join the CC shortly before Cliff's death, remembers Cliff in his last months; he was tired, but still passionately interested in developments in the US and Zimbabwe.[76]

Cliff still kept up a strong outward image – he was incapable of simply resting. He eased up a bit, watching more television – but not much more. He was now deteriorating rapidly; he was in and out of hospital and by April he was unable to walk upstairs. His son Danny, who still lived with his parents, found himself wondering if Cliff was still alive any time he was out of his sight.

On Friday 7 April 2000 John Rees and Lindsey German visited him in hospital, where he was still asking detailed questions about what was happening in the party. He was then allowed to return home.[77] On Sunday morning, 9 April, he came downstairs, then went back to bed. Ten minutes later Danny had a feeling that something was not right and felt he should check. He went into Cliff's room; his father seemed to be asleep, but Danny realised he was not breathing. He ran downstairs and an ambulance was called.

Resuscitation was attempted, but it was too late.[78]

"Many die too late, and some die too early".[79] Among Cliff's closest colleagues Paul Foot was to die suddenly four days after giving one of the best meetings of his life, while Duncan Hallas would spend his last years confined to a wheelchair in an old people's home in Hackney. With Cliff there was a tremendous sense of loss, a feeling that he had died when he had more to give. Yet he would have found it insufferable if he had spent his last days condemned to inactivity. Of nobody more than Cliff were Voltaire's words true: "Man is born for action as fire rises upwards and stone falls downwards".[80]

The news spread rapidly among Cliff's comrades. John Charlton, who had worked closely with Cliff in the 1960s and 1970s, was in New York, staying in the apartment of a young feminist, where he was telephoned. She handed him the phone and he just wept. She thought it must have been a close relative.[81]

Tributes came in from friends and from political opponents. Many were collected in a little booklet prepared for a memorial meeting on 7 May. Monty Johnstone of the Communist Party judged that "the Marxist left as a whole will be the poorer for his passing", while the United Secretariat of the Fourth International wrote that "we belonged to branches of the same family, having much more in common – if compared with other left-wing political tendencies – than areas of disagreement". There were messages from Australia, Denmark, Germany, Italy, New Zealand, Norway, Poland, South Africa, Spain, South Korea, the United States, Turkey and the Czech Republic. Richard Kirkwood, one of those expelled after the 1975 split, wrote, "To say that he 'taught me' my revolutionary socialism would miss the point. Like any good (especially socialist) educator he helped me to learn it for myself." Of veteran members, Shaun Doherty remembered that "during the last 28 years I've learned more in your front room than anywhere else", and Colin Barker recalled that "in the 1960s and early 1970s he was the most amazing teacher for me". Perhaps closest to Cliff's spirit was Pete Glatter's simple tribute to "a great revolutionary who did his job".[82]

In the *Guardian* Paul Foot remembered his long friendship, concluding, "'Don't mourn, organise!' was one of Cliff's most consistent slogans, and somehow we must try to live up to it".[83] In the *Independent* Lindsey German paid tribute to Cliff's "theoretical clarity and...his insistence that socialists have to stand up for their politics and organise".[84] Even an old opponent like Jim Higgins praised his "intellectual eminence, allied to tremendous energy, persistence and intuition"[85] – though he would make sharper judgements later.[86] One sour note was struck by the attention-seeking journalist Julie Burchill, who claimed that Cliff's use of a pseudonym indicated he was a "self-loathing" Jew. His four children wrote an angry reply, dismissing Burchill's suggestion as "petty and contemptible"; they insisted that "the loathing dad had was not for himself, but for racism in any form, be it anti-Semitic, anti-Arab or any other".[87]

The funeral took place on 19 April. About 3,000, including some who had travelled from abroad, gathered near Golders Green tube station and marched to Golders Green crematorium. Lindsey German, Chris Harman, Ahmed Shah from Germany, and Cliff's children Donny and Anna spoke. They paid tribute to his enormous political contribution – but in keeping with Cliff's own spirit, there were jokes.

Anna summed up Cliff as a human being, recalling his sense of humour; she "urged people to continue to fight for a world full of love, warmth and laughter, which he would have loved".[88] Cliff's niece Tamar Swade played Beethoven's *Appassionata* and mourners left to the sound of *Joe Hill* – "What they can never kill went on to organise".

It was April 2000. Ken Livingstone was expelled from the Labour Party; he would go on to be elected Mayor of London as an independent. In the US George W Bush had in effect ensured his selection as presidential candidate. Ford announced the end of saloon car assembly at Dagenham, while negotiations for the sale of the Rover plant at Longbridge in Birmingham collapsed. American and British aircraft continued to attack Iraqi air defences. President Clinton was back in the US after a visit to Pakistan where he had urged General Musharraf to assist in the effort to secure the arrest of Osama bin Laden. New reports measured the extent of global warming during the 20th century and showed that the loss of ozone over the Arctic in 1999-2000 was the worst ever recorded, yet the US and Canada blocked the fixing of a deadline for ratifying the Kyoto protocol. Thirty-five thousand anti-capitalists, trade unionists and environmentalists gathered in Washington to demonstrate against the IMF and the World Bank. An old world was dying; a new one was being born.

14

Conclusion

Cliff did not see the revolution he had hoped for and to which all his efforts were devoted. For the sneering cynics among his political enemies this will suffice to show that his long and full life was a waste of effort, that all his sacrifices were futile. So it is worthwhile to remember the things that Cliff got right and which now, ten years on from his death, are more self-evidently right than ever.

Firstly Cliff was right about capitalism. From his earliest years he hated capitalism for the way it bred poverty and oppression, racism and war. Capitalism has survived a lot longer than he expected, but it has not changed for the better. The rich get richer while the poor get poorer.* Those rich live in obscene luxury while millions die for want of the most elementary necessities. The spectres of nuclear annihilation and ecological disaster loom ever larger. The current economic crisis merely confirms that capitalism has failed to overcome its contradictions. Quite correctly, Cliff never saw any reason to revise his judgement that the only hope for humanity was a root-and-branch overthrow of the whole capitalist order.

Secondly Cliff was right about Stalinism. In the 1950s and 1960s the so-called "planned economies" of the Eastern Bloc had millions upon millions of admirers around the world, far beyond the ranks of the organised Communist parties. That the whole bloc would collapse in a discreditable shambles can scarcely have crossed the minds of either its friends or its enemies. Cliff's insistence that the whole Stalinist system had nothing in common with socialism beyond an illicit appropriation of the name pushed him into a tiny

---

* In Britain under 18 years of Tory rule from 1979 to 1997-98, the share of national income taken by the richest tenth of the population rose from 21 percent to 28.5 percent; the share taken by the poorest tenth fell from 4 percent to 1.8 percent. Under Labour from 1997-98 to 2007-08 the richest tenth increased their share from 28.5 percent to nearly 30.8 percent, while the share taken by the poorest tenth fell to 1.4 percent (letter from Professor Ruth Levitas, Bristol University, *Guardian*, 23 November 2009).

disregarded minority. Fifty years on it is hard to imagine how many were taken in by the great lie of the Stalinist system.

Thirdly he was right about reformism. The collapse of parliamentary socialism has been less dramatic but equally thoroughgoing. Throughout the world labour parties and social democratic parties have been transformed into the open and unashamed advocates of privatisation, inequality and aggressive war. If many people retain the belief that the Labour Party has policies marginally superior to those of the Tories, few have any illusion that it might usher in socialism.

The revolution that Cliff envisaged began to seem a real possibility in the stormy years from 1968 to 1975; both the hopes of an aspiring generation and the fears of those who saw their privileges under threat bear witness to that. Those revolutionary possibilities were aborted, and we are still paying the price.

Since Cliff was so clear-sighted in the negative critique of capitalism, Stalinism and reformism, it is surely worth taking his theoretical and organisational work seriously. Cliff's major theoretical contribution was the analysis of state capitalism. He wrote three major books on the subject and his book on Russia has been translated into at least a dozen languages. The issue remains controversial among Marxists, but in the period of the Cold War Cliff's theory enabled him to argue for a position independent of both Washington and Moscow. By insisting that state ownership and centrally controlled economies had, in themselves, absolutely nothing to do with socialism, Cliff helped to preserve the idea of socialism based on human freedom and workers' control.

The collapse of "actually existing socialism" after 1989 led to demoralisation among many sections of the left, but Cliff's followers were relatively immune to any sense of defeat. The argument about the social nature of Russia and China is now largely an academic question, and Cliff's work remains a contribution to that debate. For a new generation coming to socialism in the 21st century important questions remain. Did Bolshevism and, more generally, revolutionary politics lead inevitably to Stalinism? Did the USSR play an overall progressive role on a world scale? The enemies of socialism continue to deploy the experience of Stalinism as a knock-down argument against any attempt to revolutionise the human condition and, for as long as they do, Cliff's work will remain an important contribution to the argument.

The other two components of what Cliff described as the "troika" of his theoretical achievement were slighter. Mike Kidron and, later, Chris Harman developed the arguments about the permanent arms economy in much greater detail than Cliff himself ever did. He did not return to the ideas developed in the article on "deflected permanent revolution", although they inspired the work of several of his followers.

But the importance of Cliff's various theoretical writings was not so much their specific content as the method he employed, the way in which he combined adherence to basic principles with constant openness to new facts and changing realities. In his non-defensive deployment of Marxist categories, Cliff provided a model for the future of Marxism as revolutionary theory.

Of Cliff's other writings, the two short books on incomes policy and productivity deals relate to a stage of working class history that is now in many ways remote. But it was a period of a high level of working class struggle and deserves to be remembered, for the working class has not spoken its last word and when an upturn in struggle occurs there will be many lessons to be learnt. In the way Cliff drew on and quoted at length the concrete experience of workers he made a real contribution to "history from below".

Cliff's works on the socialist movement were written as "activist history". His insistence on mining the past for lessons for the present was not calculated to win the approval of more academic historians. But he made some important contributions. His little book on Rosa Luxemburg rescued an important figure who risked disappearing into obscurity and contributed to the revival of interest in a great revolutionary. His much longer study of Lenin pioneered a new approach to the history of Bolshevism. Cliff tried to rescue Lenin from both enemies and friends by rejecting the Stalinist stereotypes. At the same time he broke with the defensiveness which had all too often characterised Trotskyist historical writing. In defending wholeheartedly the basic principles of the Bolshevik revolution, Cliff felt no obligation to defend every twist and turn of policy, and he made some wide-ranging criticisms of the infant Soviet Republic and the early years of the Communist International. There are interesting parallels between the non-defensive spirit of Cliff's work and more recent studies by historians such as Pierre Broué, Jean-Jacques Marie, Jean-François Fayet and Reiner Tosstorff.[1]

There is much else of value in Cliff's writings. He wrote prolifically for more than 60 years, and produced some 20 volumes and several hundred articles. His work on the Middle East, France and Portugal remains of considerable historical interest.

Yet if he took considerable pride in his writings, he did not regard them as essential. He never considered books an end in themselves and scorned those who did. For Cliff writing was a guide to action. Among writers of the anti-Stalinist left who built on Trotsky's heritage in the second half of the 20th century, Isaac Deutscher, CLR James and Hal Draper produced books comparable in quality to Cliff's, but their organisational legacy was negligible.

For Cliff, action meant organisation. He had a rare ability to combine the theoretical, the political and the tactical.[2] For the last 50 years of his life, Cliff's central preoccupation was the building of an organisation – the Socialist Review Group, the International Socialists, the Socialist Workers Party. Many others played a part, but Cliff's role was, as Duncan Hallas wrote on the occasion of his death, "absolutely central at every stage".[3] Those seeking a monument for Cliff will find it not in a row of books on a library shelf, but in an organisation of living people.

Cliff's achievement cannot be separated from that of his organisation. Its most visible success was the Anti Nazi League, which would never have come into existence without the initiative and hard work of SWP members. And without the ANL the racist far right in Britain might well have reached take-off point and become part of the political mainstream, as has happened in other European countries with serious consequences.

After Cliff's death the SWP was to play a key role in building the Stop the War Coalition. SWP members have been at the heart of hundreds of local campaigns and industrial struggles. In many workplaces SWP members have kept the structures of trade unionism alive when they might otherwise have perished.

On an international level the International Socialist Tendency has groups, some small, some larger, in at least 28 countries, which have played their part in the international anti-war movement and the various World and European Social Forums, as well as being involved in struggles in their own countries.

The SWP has contributed to the whole culture of the British left. The annual Marxism event provides an opportunity for many currents of the left to debate and confront each other's positions. Testimony to its role comes from the assorted groups who set up their stalls on its fringes, even while they denounce it. Bookmarks publishers have produced a long string of original analyses and reprints of Marxist classics; it is in part thanks to Bookmarks that writers such as Rosa Luxemburg and Victor Serge are still available. A whole series of writers who have enriched the British left – David Widgery, Paul Foot, Alex Callinicos – owe or owed a substantial debt to Cliff.

Though many others have contributed to the building of the SWP, Cliff's insistence on the unity of theory and practice has undoubtedly influenced the party's particular style of activism. As one member who joined in the 1970s put it, he was attracted to the IS by the "combination of competent organisation and coherent ideas".[4] In the 1980s someone from one of the SWP's rivals characterised the party's mode of operation as, "If it moves, recruit it; if it doesn't move, stick a poster on it." It was meant as a slander, but may serve as a tribute.

For those who worked with him, even this does not sum up Cliff's significance. Those who know Cliff merely through his writings only half know him. As a public speaker he was unique; he conformed to none of the rules, presented a persona which combined elements of the Jewish orator with aspects of the stand-up comedian, all united by an unquenchable political purpose. He showed that being serious did not mean being humourless. No wonder his meetings were something special; a former Newcastle activist recalls, "What should be stressed is the appeal of a 'Cliff meeting'. I remember oh-so-many badly attended and often boring IS meetings in Newcastle. Yet everything changed when Tony Cliff was booked to speak. We could easily fill the venue... And folk not seen for months would suddenly materialise".[5]

It was not just public meetings. Cliff spent innumerable hours with comrades, face to face or on the telephone, arguing and persuading, listening and learning. It was this that earned him the fierce and undying loyalty of so many whose political development he shaped. (Inevitably he was selective about who he listened to, which meant he incurred enmities.) There are hundreds of activists who can look at their lives and consider how different – and in most cases how much less interesting and worthwhile – they would have been if they had not encountered Cliff.*

In researching this book I have been struck by the fact that I have met a number of people who remember being enthused and educated by Cliff, and who, 30, 40 and even 50 years later, are still active, some in the SWP, some elsewhere. They are walking refutations of the myth that leftists become more moderate as they grow older and acquire mortgages.

Many who left the SWP and pursued other paths within the labour movement still have positive memories of Cliff. Ian Gibson left the SWP in the early 1980s and later became a Labour MP. But he never regretted his time in the IS/SWP, where he got a political education he could never have obtained in the Labour Party.[6] Paul Mackney, former general secretary of NATFHE, is glad he met Cliff, who motivated him and pointed him towards trying to change the world; Cliff helped him to see that industrialisation and nationalisation are not the same as socialism. He also learned from Cliff the value of making jokes in speeches.[7] Lord Macdonald of Tradeston, for a time transport minister in Tony Blair's government, has moved far from the revolutionary politics of his youth, but he does not regret his involvement with Cliff; he remembers it as a "very instructive period", when Cliff got him to read seriously.[8]

Cliff was remorselessly single-minded. Sport, music, entertainment, gardening – all the things that enrich most people's lives – left him cold. (He once jokingly called Tirril Harris a peasant when he saw her gardening.[9]) In 70 years of political activism he probably never let a single day go by without applying his mind to how the socialist cause could be advanced. Yet he was no puritan, no ascetic, never hard-faced or sour-faced; his speeches, like his conversation, sparkled with humour. Above all he had the capacity to enthuse and inspire and few whom he encouraged will ever forget the experience.

---

* For David Widgery, one of the finest radical writers of his generation, "Without 1968 and the SWP I would, no doubt, in the conventional manner of the educationally upwardly mobile, be ensconced in the Department of Community Medicine of a cathedral town with my children down for public school and a sub to the SDP. Instead I got involved in the socialist Left, in medical trade unionism and am still plugging away as a GP in the council flats of east London."
(D Widgery, *Preserving Disorder* (London, 1989), pxiv)

Cliff, like all of us, had his weaknesses. His "stick-bending" could lead him to exaggeration and overstatement which produced errors of judgement. He was not always a good judge of character, adopting comrades as favourites – when it was often obvious to others that they had serious limitations – and then dropping them again. He could be impatient and operated best when others took care of details he could not be bothered with. He was sometimes unkind and even ruthless. In his later years he largely concentrated on defending the Marxist tradition rather than developing a critical Marxism appropriate to new conditions, as he had done in the 1950s and 1960s.

All revolutions are surprises and the future of socialism in the 21st century will have many surprises that fall outside the framework of Cliff's analyses. Yet some basic truths remain which were at the centre of Cliff's understanding. Capitalism is a cruel and vicious system which produces war, poverty and growing inequality, which wrecks and destroys human lives. It can only be changed by those who are exploited by it and have no interest in its survival, by those whose role in the collective organisation of production gives them the power to transform the world. Without conscious organisation that power cannot be put into practice.

One phrase quoted in Cliff's study of Rosa Luxemburg looms over the 21st century as it did over the 20th: Socialism or barbarism. Cliff's generation lived through the Holocaust and faced the threat of nuclear war. Now global warming comes, not to replace the old dangers, but to join them – for the social upheavals and mass migrations caused by climate change can easily provoke the revival of fascism or spark off nuclear annihilation.

If the socialist revolution is made, it will be made by people who, in Victor Serge's words, are "infinitely different from us, infinitely like us".[10] When they look back at their forebears they will recognise as a kindred spirit Ygael Gluckstein who, in his long journey from Zikhron Yaakov to Hackney, never lost sight of his goal.

Bibliography of Cliff's works

This is a revised and extended version of the bibliography which has been available for some years at http://www.modkraft.dk/spip.php?article5553 There are about a hundred additional items, mainly manuscripts, internal documents and circulars, and translations. It remains seriously incomplete. I have found only a very small number of Cliff's writings from the period of his activity in Palestine. Cliff did not take great care of his papers, and much correspondence and abandoned writing projects have simply disappeared. He used a variety of pseudonyms, not all of which are known. I hope nonetheless that this bibliography will be of some use to those wishing to research Cliff's ideas or the history of the British left.

I have listed as far as possible all of Cliff's books, pamphlets and articles. Since article titles are often not self-explanatory, I have added short notes on the context and/or content, but have kept these extremely brief and not attempted to add a political commentary.

Cliff played a very active role in the leading bodies of the organisation. In the 1960s and 1970s extensive minutes were kept of these meetings. I have tried to list Cliff's major contributions to political and organisational discussions, while omitting brief interventions and trivial and routine matters. In later years his contributions to conferences and national meetings were often reported in *Socialist Worker*, and again I have listed significant items. I have attempted to list translations, but this section is necessarily very incomplete. My ignorance of many of the languages in question meant I had to rely on a number of informants; this accounts for the inconsistencies in the presentation of bibliographical information. In a few cases I have listed items on the basis of second-hand information without knowing where the originals may be located. These are marked [NOT SEEN] and I should be grateful to hear from anyone who knows the location of any of these items. Cliff spoke at thousands of meetings. I have merely listed topics he spoke on at Marxism over 23 years – recordings of many of these exist.

Cliff's own papers, such as they are, are now available for consultation at the Modern Records Centre (University of Warwick) [MRC]. Much relevant material is also available at Senate House, London, in the Richardson Collection [Rich] and the Will Fancy Papers [Fancy]. References are given where appropriate. I am grateful to a large number of people who have helped me locate various items, and in particular to John Rudge, who pointed out a number of errors and omissions in the original version.

Ian Birchall

Key

The following abbreviations are used to indicate publications for which Cliff wrote frequently:

LW   Labour Worker (1962-68)
SW   Socialist Worker (1968-)
SR1 Socialist Review – first series 1950-62
SR2 Socialist Review – second series 1978-
IS1 International Socialism – first series 1960-1978
IS2 International Socialism – second series 1978-

The following indicate anthologies of Cliff's works or of party writings. Where these appear in brackets after an item they indicate that the item was reproduced therein:

NWNM Neither Washington nor Moscow 1982
W1   Cliff: *Writings* vol 1, 2001
W2   Cliff: *Writings* vol 2, 2002
W3   Cliff; *Writings* vol 3, 2003
ASR1 *A Socialist Review* (introduced by J Higgins) 1965
ITHOS *In the Heat of the Struggle* (edited by C Harman) 1994
ASR2 *A Socialist Review* (edited by L German and R Hoveman) 1998

Where no author's name is listed the item appeared under the name T Cliff or Tony Cliff, or initials TC. Where Cliff used one of his many pseudonyms, or wrote jointly with comrades, the authorship is indicated in square brackets before the title.

Pseudonyms

During his life Cliff used a great many pseudonyms, not all of which are known. The following are the main ones found in the bibliography.

Yga(e)l Gluckstein
Y Tsur
Y Sakhry
L Rock
R(oger) Tennant
C Tariq (?)
L, M, and N Turov
F Delroux (?)
L Miguel
Harry Jones

A: Books, pamphlets, prefaces

Books

[Ygael Gluckstein]: *Stalin's Satellites in Europe*
Allen and Unwin, London, 1952, 333pp.
The Beacon Press, Boston, 1952, 333pp.

Stalinist Russia: A Marxist Analysis
Michael Kidron, London, 1955, xiii, 273pp.
This is based on *The Nature of Stalinist Russia* (Internal Bulletin, Revolutionary Communist Party, June 1948: see section H) but (according to C Harman, Introduction to 1988 edition) differs "mainly in terms of chapter order, but also by the addition of material referring to the split between Yugoslavia and Russia in 1948, and amendments to the section dealing with crisis in state capitalism".

Russia: A Marxist Analysis
International Socialism, London, 1964, 384pp.
Book I (pp17-191) is a revised version of *Stalinist Russia. A Marxist Analysis*, 1955
Book II (pp195-349) *Russia after Stalin* was published for the first time.
The main changes in Book 1 concern chapter order. A section on Trotsky's idea of the "degenerated workers' state", which was an appendix in the 1955 edition, is incorporated into Book I as chapter 7, while a modified version of the final chapter of the 1955 edition becomes the conclusion to Book 2.

State Capitalism in Russia
Pluto Press, London, 1974, 309pp.
Reprint of *Stalinist Russia* from 1955.

State Capitalism in Russia
Bookmarks, London, 1988, 377pp.

Introduction and postscript by C Harman.
pp309-331: "Appendix I – An examination of Trotsky's definition of Russia as a Degenerated Workers' State" was chapter 7 in earlier versions.
pp333-53: The theory of bureaucratic collectivism: a critique [see section H].

[Ygael Gluckstein]: *Mao's China: Economic and Political Survey*
Allen and Unwin, London, 1957, 438pp.
The Beacon Press, Boston, 1957, 438pp.

Rosa Luxemburg: A Study [W1]
International Socialism, London, 1959, 96pp.
(*International Socialism*, Nos 2-3)
Reprinted January 1968.
Reissued April 1969 (International Socialism, London).
The 1969 edition is printed from a photocopy of the first edition, but two significant changes are made on pp53-54, reflecting Cliff's changing views on the question of the revolutionary party. The two versions are published side by side in W1, p113.
Reissued July 1980 (Bookmarks, London).
The 1980 edition follows the 1969 version, with a few purely stylistic changes (eg "epigones" become "followers").

[Tony Cliff and Colin Barker]: *Incomes Policy, Legislation and Shop Stewards* [W2]
London Industrial Shop Stewards Defence Committee, Harrow Weald, 1966, 136pp.

[Tony Cliff and Ian Birchall]: *France: The Struggle Goes On* [W1]
Socialist Review Publishing Co, London, 1968, 80pp.
International Socialism special

The Employers' Offensive, Productivity Deals and how to fight them [W2]
Pluto Press, London, 1970, 234pp.

BIBLIOGRAPHY 563

The Crisis: Social Contract or Socialism,
Pluto Press for Socialist Worker,
London, 1975, 192pp.

Lenin Vol 1: Building the Party
Pluto Press, London, 1975, 398pp.

Lenin Vol 2: All Power to the Soviets
Pluto Press, London, 1976, 412pp.

Lenin Vol 3: Revolution Besieged
Pluto Press, London, 1978, x + 230pp.

Lenin Vol 4: The Bolsheviks and World Communism
Pluto Press, London, 1979, xi + 251pp.

Lenin: Building the Party 1893-1914
Bookmarks, London, 1986, 398pp.
Reissued Bookmarks, 2010.
Reprint of Pluto, 1975.

Lenin: All Power to the Soviets 1914-1917
Bookmarks, London, 1985, 412pp.
Reprint of Pluto, 1976.

Lenin: Revolution Besieged 1917-1923
Bookmarks, London, 1986, xvi + 480pp.
Reprint of Pluto 1978 and 1979.

Class Struggle and Women's Liberation, 1640 to Today
Bookmarks, London, 1984, 271pp.
[chapter 14 reproduced in W3]

[Tony Cliff and Donny Gluckstein]:
Marxism and Trade Union Struggle, the General Strike of 1926
Bookmarks, London, 1986, 320pp.

[Tony Cliff and Donny Gluckstein]: *The Labour Party, A Marxist History*
Bookmarks, London, 1988, 427pp.
Second edition, with new chapter on Blair and New Labour.
Bookmarks, London, 1996.

Trotsky Vol 1: Towards October 1879-1917
Bookmarks, London, 1989, 314pp.

Trotsky Vol 2: The Sword of the Revolution 1917-1923
Bookmarks, London, 1990, 309pp.

Trotsky Vol 3: Fighting the Rising Stalinist Bureaucracy 1923-1927
Bookmarks, London, 1991, 306pp.

Trotsky Vol 4: The Darker the Night, the Brighter the Star 1927-1940
Bookmarks, London, 1993, 427pp.

Trotskyism after Trotsky, the Origins of the International Socialists
Bookmarks, London, 1999, 95pp.

A World to Win: Life of a Revolutionary
Bookmarks, London, 2000, 247pp.

Marxism at the Millennium
Bookmarks, London, 2000, 86pp.
Collection of articles written for IS tendency publications in Germany and Turkey.

Pamphlets

Middle East at the Crossroads
Workers International News Pamphlet, London, 1946, 24pp.
Dated Jerusalem, 12 November 1945.
Compilation of three articles which appeared in *Workers International News* December 1945, January and February 1946, also in *Fourth International* December 1945, January and February 1946 [see section B].

Russia from Stalin to Khrushchev
Published by Michael Kidron, London, 24pp.
First impression: April 1956.
Second impression: May 1956.
Analyses destalinisation before "secret speech"; concludes "Stalin is dead, Stalinism lives".

"Why We Left the Communist Party"
Nottingham Marxist Group, Stapleford,
Notts, [March 1957], 8pp.
Said to be statement by 12 CP members,
but no names. According to Ken Coates,
written by Cliff.

*Socialist Theory: A Series of Twelve
Weekly Lectures on Socialist Theory
and Practice*
Syllabus 1/- [one shilling]
National Council of Labour Colleges
c 1960 [revised version in W3].

The Struggle in the Middle East
[shortened version in W1]
International Socialism pamphlet,
London, [1967], 4 pp, newspaper
format.
Analysis of situation after Six Day War
in June 1967.

IS Internal Bulletin, December 1969,
reports that Cambridge IS have produced a pamphlet containing
"Permanent Revolution" [IS1 12] and
Kidron's *Imperialism*. [NOT SEEN]

*Permanent Revolution, a
Re-examination* [IS1 12]
Bookmarks for the SWP, London, 1983,
21pp.
Reissued as: *Deflected Permanent
Revolution*,
Socialist Workers Party, 1990, 28pp.

[Tony Cliff and Chris Harman]:
*Portugal: The lessons of the 25th
November* [NWNM]
1975, 8pp.

*Chrysler Workers: The Fight for a
Future*
Socialist Worker pamphlet, London,
[1978], 32pp.
*Marxism and the Collectivisation of
Agriculture*
Socialists Unlimited, London, 1980, 36
pp, from IS1 19.
International Socialism reprint No 1.

Permanent Revolution
London, 1981, 36 pp, from IS1 61.
International Socialism reprint No 5.

*Permanent Revolution, a
Re-examination*
from IS1 12. Bookmarks for the SWP,
London, 1983, 21pp.

Deflected Permanent Revolution
from IS1 12
Socialist Workers Party, 1986, 24pp.

*Revolution and Counter-revolution:
lessons for Indonesia*
21pp, from IS2 80. Produced for
Indonesia: outer cover reads: "The
Internet – Guidelines for Helplines".

Prefaces, etc.

Paul Frölich, *Rosa Luxemburg*
Pluto Press, London, 1972, reissued
1981
ppix-xi: Introduction.
Argues Luxemburg's critique of reformism superior to Lenin's.

*The Bolsheviks and the October
Revolution*: Minutes of the Central
Committee of the Russian Social-
Democratic Labour Party (Bolsheviks)
August 1917-February 1918
Pluto Press, London, 1974.
pp253-323: Notes prepared by Institute
of Marxism-Leninism for second
Russian edition, Moscow, 1958, plus, in
different typeface, additional notes by T
Cliff, correcting Stalinist distortions.

Rosa Luxemburg: *The Mass Strike*
Bookmarks, London, 1986.
pp5-10: Introduction by Tony Cliff.

[Peter Binns, Tony Cliff, Chris Harman]
*Russia: From Workers' State to State
Capitalism*
Bookmarks, London, 1987.
pp7-12: Workers' Revolution and
Beyond. Introduction to reprints of

BIBLIOGRAPHY 565

articles by Harman and Binns.

AY Badayev: *Bolsheviks in the Tsarist Duma*
Bookmarks, London, 1987.
pp7-15: Introduction by Tony Cliff.
Partly polemic against Eric Heffer: *The Class Struggle in Parliament* (1973).

Chris Harman: *Russia: How the Revolution was Lost*
SWP, London, 1988.
pp4-6: Introduction by Tony Cliff.

Leon Trotsky: *The History of the Russian Revolution*
Pluto, London, 1997.
ppv-xii: Introduction by Tony Cliff.

Socialist Workers Party Gay Group: *The Word is Gay*
Socialists Unlimited, London, 1979.
pp3-4: Introduction by Tony Cliff.
Article from SW 593, 26 August 1978.
Articles in Books and Pamphlets.

Tariq Ali (ed): *New Revolutionaries*
Peter Owen, London, 1969.
pp219-37: "The Struggle in the Middle East"
1967 pamphlet listed above.

N Harris and J Palmer (eds): *World Crisis*
Hutchinson, London, 1971.
pp225-50: "The Class Struggle in Britain" [NWNM]

R Kuper (ed): *The Fourth International, Stalinism and the Origins of the International Socialists – Some Documents*
Pluto, London, 1971.
pp14-64: "On the Class Nature of the People's Democracies [NWNM]".
pp79-94: "The Theory of Bureaucratic Collectivism – a critique" [IS1 32 and NWNM].
Both were originally internal documents; the bureaucratic collectivism piece was substantially revised [see section H].

[Tony Cliff, Duncan Hallas, Chris Harman and Leon Trotsky]: *Party and Class*
Pluto Press for the International Socialists, London, 1971.
pp26-46 Trotsky on Substitutionism. (from IS1 2).

The Emerging Crisis of Capitalism
International Socialist Publishing Company, Michigan, US, 1974
pp57-75: "On Perspectives" from IS1 36.

David Widgery: *The Left in Britain 1956-68*
Peregrine, Harmondsworth, 1976.
pp92-97: "Revolutionary Traditions"
Transcript of talk given to IS aggregate at Wortley Hall, Sheffield, 22 April 1967.
pp437-47: Nothing So Romantic
From *Idiot International* No 6, June 1970 [see section I].

What do we Mean by Revolution?
Socialist Workers Party pamphlet 1996
pp13-17: "Soviets: the Lessons of 1905" [SR2 72].

Party and Class (introduction by Alex Callinicos)
Bookmarks, London, 1996.
Contains "Trotsky on Substitutionism" from IS1 2.

Socialist Worker, "Fighting to Change the World"
SWP, London, 2002.
pp11-19: "*Pravda* - the Legal Newspaper"
Edited version of chapter 19 from *Lenin* vol 1 (1975).
pp42-45: "The Use of *Socialist Worker* as an Organiser " from IS Internal Bulletin, April 1974 [NWNM].

The Socialist Experience: The Chinese Revolution
International Socialists (US) no date or place. Number 3 in a series of educational reprints.
pp32-37: [Ygael Gluckstein] "Mao and the Peasantry: Historical Retrospect" from *Mao's China*, 1957, chapter 9.
pp37-44: [Ygael Gluckstein] "Regimentation of the Working Class" from *Mao's China*, 1957, chapter 11.
pp51-54: "Mao Tse-Tung and Stalinism", from *Socialist Review*, April 1957. [NWNM] [ASR1] [W3].

Translations

A World to Win (p26) reports that in Palestine Cliff translated two books into Hebrew: Lewis Corey, *The Decline of American Capitalism*, and a book by Fritz Sternberg. The former was for the Hashomer Hatzair publishing house, but Corey blocked publication [NOT SEEN].

NB The British Library catalogue lists the pamphlet by Steve Berry: *The Prevention of Terrorism Act* (1977) under Cliff's name as "personal author". This is a mistake; there is no evidence of any involvement by Cliff.

B: Fourth International publications

New International

October 1938: pp311-12 [W1]
L Rock: "British Policy in Palestine"

November 1938: pp335-7 [W1]
L Rock: "The Jewish-Arab Conflict",
Argues for struggle against Zionism, Arab national exclusivism and imperialism.
(January 1939, p31: letter from Paul Koston (Cape Town) accusing Rock of being insufficiently critical of Zionism; February 1939, pp41-44: article from *The Spark* (Cape Town) urging support for Arabs against Zionism.)

June 1939, pp169-73 [W1]
L Rock: "Class Politics in Palestine"
Response to article from *The Spark*.
(October 1939, pp313-14: further article from *The Spark* responding to Rock.)

Fourth International (SWP US)

December 1945, pp361-366 [NWNM]
"The Middle East at the Crossroads: Part I"

January 1946, pp10-13
"The Middle East at the Crossroads: Part II"

February 1946, pp50-53
"The Middle East at the Crossroads: Part III"
All three parts translated by R Bod. These three articles also appeared in *Workers International News*, December 1945, January and February 1946, then as a pamphlet *Middle East at the Crossroads* [1946 – see section A]

September 1946, pp282-84
A New British Provocation in Palestine
Common and antagonistic interests of imperialism and Zionism.

April 1947, pp114-17
Some Features of Capitalist Economy in the Colonies
Mainly on role of banks in Egypt.

June 1947, pp190-91
The World Struggle for Oil
Reprinted from *Socialist Appeal*, January 1947.

Workers International News

December 1945, pp72-79
"Imperialism in the Middle East – I"
January 1946, pp106-13
"Imperialism in the Middle East – II

On Zionism".

February-March 1946, pp153-60
Imperialism in the Middle East – III
On Stalinism"; all three translated by R Bod.
These three articles also appeared in *Fourth International*, December 1945, January and February 1946, then as a pamphlet *Middle East at the Crossroads* [1946 – see section A].

January-February 1947, pp27-32
"Conflict in India"
Muslims not a nation; need for Hindu-Muslim unity.
(There are two versions of this issue, one dated January-February 1947, one dated February 1947; contents are identical.)

October 1947 (issue 7/3), pp12-21
"The United States in World Economy: The Basis of the Marshall Plan"
This is advertised as the first of a series of three articles; however, issue 7/4 is missing from the Socialist Platform archive; issue 7/5 (August 1948) contains nothing by Cliff and is mainly concerned with the Stalin-Tito split.

Socialist Appeal

Mid-May 1946, p3
"Palestine Strike – Arabs and Jews Unite"
Cliff described as "Our Middle East Correspondent".

December 1946, p3
"Are the Terrorists Anti-Imperialist?"
Argues Stern gang, Irgun, etc. opposed to interests of Jews and Arabs alike.

January 1947, pp1-4
"World Struggle for Oil".
February 1947, pp3-4
"The Bureaucrats in Industry"
This and the next five items part of a series called "What is Happening in Stalinist Russia?"

Mid-February 1947, pp3-4
"Piece Work in Russia"

April 1947, pp3-4
"Punishments and Fines in USSR"

Mid-April 1947: pp3-4
"Housing in Russia"

Mid-May 1947, pp1-4
"*Daily Worker* Defends Inequalities in Russia"
Response to *Daily Worker* articles of 8 and 9 May 1947.

Mid-July 1947, pp3-4
"Women in the USSR"
"The degree of humanity's progress is measured by the condition of women."

February, 1948
"The Franc Devaluation"
Slump can be delayed only a few years.

C: Socialist Review – series one (1950-62)

Vol 1, No 1, November 1950
pp1-7 [R Tennant]: "The Struggle of the Powers"
Background to Korea, though not explicitly on war; stresses parallel mechanisms of US and Russian imperialism. Ends with slogan "Neither Washington nor Moscow, but International Socialism".

Vol 1, No 2, January 1951
pp6-10: "Stalinist Russia – The Facts: The Bureaucrats in Industry"
Crushing of workers' control; managers' privileges. Said to be from a series of articles appearing in *Information Digest*, March, April, May 1949. I have been unable to locate a collection of *Information Digest*.

Vol 1, No 3, March 1951
pp9-13: "Stalinist Russia - The Facts: Piece-work in Russia"
End of collective agreements; piece-work and Stakhanovism. From *Information Digest*.

Vol 1, No 4, May 1951
pp12-13, 21: "Stalinist Russia – The Facts: Punishment and Fines in the USSR"
Labour discipline and numbers in concentration camps. From *Information Digest*.

Vol 1, No 6, November-December 1951
pp11-15 [C Tariq]: "Britain and Egypt"
Possibly by Cliff; cites Corey (whom Cliff had translated); statistics mainly 1938-44.

pp17-18, 25 [Roger Tennant]: "The Tsarist Empire through Stalinist Eyes"
Recent Russian sources give sympathetic account of Tsarist Empire.
pp19-21: "Stalinist Russia – The Facts: Housing in Russia"
Poor quality and overcrowding in Russian housing. From *Information Digest*.

Vol 2, No 6, December 1952-January 1953
pp7-8 [L Turov]: "Yes-Men on Parade"
19th Congress of Russian CP; social composition of party.

Vol 3, No 1, February-March 1953
pp5-7 [unsigned]: "The Kremlin's 'Jewish Plot'"
Style and approach suggest Cliff's authorship. Growing anti-Semitism in Russia, its roots and limits.

Vol 3, No 2, May 1953
pp1-4 [L Turov]: "A Russian Socialist Asks – What Lies Behind Malenkov's Moves?"
Situation after Stalin's death; Sino-Russian friction. No indication of source or why Turov has become "Russian socialist".

Vol 3, No 3, October 1953
pp8-10 [N Turov]: "Recent Russian Developements" [sic]
Limits of Malenkov concessions; disappearance of Stalin leader-cult.

Vol 3, No 8, April 1954
pp5-6 [L Miguel]: "Puerto Rico"
Poverty in Puerto Rico; background to recent terrorism.

Vol 3, No 10, June 1954
pp5-6 [L Turov]: "Russia's War Budget"
Russian arms spending shown to be higher than claimed by CPGB.

Vol 3, No 12, August 1954
pp4-6: F Delroux: "The Permanent Crisis in France"
Role of PCF at Liberation and after. [In *A World to Win* (p62) Cliff states that he wrote on France in *Socialist Review* under the pseudonym De Lacroix. There are no articles under this name in SR, but there are two pieces signed F Delroux (here and October 1954) which could well be by Cliff.]

Vol 4, No 2, October 1954
pp6, 8: F Delroux: "The Crisis in French Foreign Policy"
Mendès-France and the EDC.

Vol 4, No 7, March 1955
pp1-2, 8 [unsigned]: "The Fall of Malenkov"
No real liberalisation under Khrushchev. Written in name of "we the editors of *Socialist Review*", claiming to have predicted post-Stalin developments in Russia, and quoting from L Turov piece in Vol 3 No 2.

Vol 4, No 9, May 1955
pp4-6 [L Turov]: "Purges in China"
Expulsion and suicide of Kao Kang

Vol 5, No 4, December 1955
[L Turov]: "Who Controls Soviet Factories – Workers or a Boss Class?" Crushing of post-Revolutionary workers' control; one-man management and powerless unions. Turov described as "an expert on Soviet affairs".

Vol 5, No 5, January 1956
pp6-7 [L Turov]: Examples of Russian imperialism. Russian treatment of nationalities.

Vol 5, No 9, June 1956
pp6-7: "Life in Russia". Anecdotes from the Russian press.

Vol 6, No 3, December 1956
pp3-4, 6: "The Future of the Russian Empire: Reform or Revolution?" [NWNM] [ASR1]
Published by *Labor Action* (Independent Socialist League) in collaboration with *Socialist Review*; these pages printed in New York.

Vol 6, No 4, January 1957
p6: "Plekhanov: The Father of Russian Marxism" [ASR1]
Commemorating centenary of Plekhanov's birth.

Vol 6, No 5, February 1957
pp5-6: Forum
Lucio Libertini of Italian Unione Socialista Independente writes criticising section on Titoism in "Future of the Russian Empire" (Vol 6, No 3), arguing Russia is bureaucratic collectivist but Yugoslavia is in some ways progressive. Cliff responds arguing limits of workers' control in Yugoslavia.

Vol 6, No 6, March 1957
pp3-4: Forum: "The Nature of Modern Capitalism. One: State Capitalism" [ASR1]
A reply to critics (Ken Coates and John McLaren). Followed by sections on British and US capitalism by Seymour Papert and Gordon Haskell.

Vol 6, No 7, April 1957
pp5-6 Forum: "Mao Tse-Tung and Stalinism" [NWNM] [ASR1] [W3]
Economic backwardness, arms burden, personality cult, etc.

Vol 6, No 8, May 1957
pp5-6: Forum: "Perspectives of the Permanent War Economy" [NWNM] [ASR1] [W3]
Effects of arms spending and prediction of crisis.

Vol 6, No 9, June 1957
pp3-5: Forum: "Probing into the Economic Roots of Reformism, Tony Cliff shows What Makes Right-Wing Labour Tick". [NWNM] [ASR1][W3]
Critique of Lenin on aristocracy of labour.

8th Year, No 11, 1 June 1958
p7: "Background to the French Crisis" [ASR1]
De Gaulle's return; failings of PCF and SFIO.

8th Year, No 13, 1 July 1958
pp6-7: "Background to Hungary" [ASR1]
Nagy murder, Titoism, rise of Khrushchev, Hundred Flowers.

8th Year, No 15, August 1958
pp7-8, 3: "Background to the Middle East Crisis" [ASR1]
Oil as key; withdraw British troops from Jordan.

9th Year, No 2, Mid-January 1959
pp4-5: "40 Years to the Death of Rosa Luxemburg – Revolutionary Socialist". First chapter of book [see section A]

9th Year, No 7, Mid-April 1959
p7: Letter
Response to article by John Rex, "Welensky's Racial Dictatorship" (SR,

9th year, No 6, Easter 1959). Cliff challenges Rex's suggestion of sending British troops to Nyasaland, arguing from Algerian experience that imperialist troops will side with settlers.

9th Year, No 9, mid-May 1959
pp4-5: "China: The Hundred Flowers Wilt" [ASR1]
Impact of Hungary in China.

10th Year, No 3, March 1960
p5: "What was Behind Mac's Africa Tour?"
Political independence not synonymous with economic and social freedom.

10th Year, No 4, April 1960
p3: "International Notebook"
Khrushchev and Asia, Germany, South Africa, US.

10th Year, No 5, May 1960
pp4-5: "International Notebook – Khrushchev, De Gaulle and Algeria"
Various aspects of Algerian crisis.

10th Year, No 8, August 1960
p8 [M Turov]: "The Russian Organisation Man"
Review of D Granick, *The Red Executive*, Macmillan, 1960.

10th Year, No 11, November 1960
p5: "The Truth about Hiroshima"
Japanese surrender offer before bomb used; CP attitudes.

11th Year, No 2, February 1961
pp4-5, 8: "The Belgian General Strike" [ASR1]
Many passages identical to article in IS1 4, but several important differences, notably a section defending *La Gauche* and Mandel.

November 1961
pp4-6: "The 22nd Congress of the CPSU" [ASR1]
Economic roots of Sino-Soviet split.

December 1961
pp4-5: "Why were Krupps Not Expropriated?"
Bevin's failure to nationalise; anti-German chauvinism in British labour movement.

January 1962
pp6-7 [unsigned]: "Pages from Khrushchev's Biography"
Style suggests Cliff.

April 1962
pp4-5 [unsigned]: "Algerians Betrayed"
Response to reader's enquiry for information on role of PCF and SFIO on Algeria. Style and content suggest Cliff.

11th Year, No 6, June 1961
pp1, 7: "Stalinism not Dead"
Russian law puts property before people.

D: International Socialism – series one

No 1: September 1958
pp19-56: "Changes in Stalinist Russia: I Changes in the Management of Industry"
Billed as first of a series of five articles on post-Stalin Russia.
NOTE: Nos 2 and 3 were Cliff's *Rosa Luxemburg* (see section A). The journal was then relaunched in 1960, beginning again with No 1.

No 1: Spring 1960
pp20-28 [Ygael Gluckstein]: "The Chinese People's Communes"
The "Great Leap Forward" and subsequent retreat.

No 2: Autumn 1960
pp14-16, 21-27: "The Revolutionary Party and the Class or Trotsky on Substitutionism" [NWNM] [W1]
Veiled polemic against SLL-type

organisation.

No 3: Winter 1960-1
p 29: "Ephemeral Flora"
Review of R MacFarquhar (ed), *The Hundred Flowers* (Stevens and Sons).
p30 [M Turov]: "On the Line"
Review of Giuseppe Boffa, *Inside the Khrushchev Era* (Allen and Unwin).

No 4: Spring 1961
pp10-17: "Belgium 2: Strike to Revolution" [W1]
Many sections similar to article in SR1, February 1961, but significant differences; ᵃsee section C).

No 5: Summer 1961
pp28-29: "Regrouping"
Review of AA Berle, *Power without Property* (Sidgwick and Jackson).
p31 [M Turov]: "China"
Review of Chao Kuo-chun, *Agrarian Policy of the Chinese Communist Party* (Asia Publishing House) and R Hughes, *The Chinese Communes* (Bodley Head).

No 6: Autumn 1961
p33: "Bureaucracy"
Review of E Strauss, *The Ruling Servants* (Allen and Unwin).

No 7: Winter 1961
p30 [M Turov]: "The Divide"
Review of H Feis, *Between War and Peace* (OUP).
p31: "Soviet Studies"
Review of A Nove, *The Soviet Economy* (Allen and Unwin) and RV Daniels, *The Conscience of the Revolution* (OUP).

No 8: Spring 1962
pp18-22: "The Decline of the Chinese Communes"
Changes since Gluckstein article in IS1 1.

No 9: Summer 1962
pp4-14: "The Labour Party in Perspective" [W1]

Argument for entrism in 1960s conditions.
p31: Sovietology
Review of *Soviet Affairs* No 3 (Chatto and Windus).
pp31-2: Peron
Review of G Pendle, *Argentine* (OUP).

No 11: Winter 1962-3
p28: "Kremlinology"
Reviews of R Conquest, *The Lost Empire* (Ampersand) and W Leonhard, *The Kremlin since Stalin* (OUP).

No 12: Spring 1963
pp15-22: "Permanent Revolution" [W3]
Theory of "Deflected permanent revolution".

No 14: Autumn 1963
pp3-16, 24: "China-Russia: The Monolith Cracks"
Sino-Soviet split.

No 15: Winter 1963
pp10-20: "The End of the Road: Deutscher's Capitulation to Stalinism" [NWNM]
Assessment of Deutscher's work after completion of Trotsky trilogy.
pp38-9 [M Turov]: "1925-7"
Review of RC North and XJ Eudin, *MN Roy's Mission to China* (University of California Press).
p39: "Kremlinology"
Review of R Pethybridge, *A Key to Soviet Politics* (Allen and Unwin).

No 17: Summer 1964
p31 [Y Sakhry]: "Catalogue"
Review of G Baer, *Population and Society in the Arab East* (Routledge and Kegan Paul). Book by a former comrade gone astray; hence Cliff uses an old Palestine pseudonym.
pp31-2: "Splits"
Reviews of K Mehnert, *Peking and Moscow* (Weidenfeld and Nicolson) and

D Floyd, Mao against Khrushchev (Praeger).
p 32: "Useful Placidities"
Review of R Hiscocks, *Poland, Bridge for the Abyss* (OUP).
p32 [M Turov]: " Little Profit"
Review of KE McKenzie, *Comintern and World Revolution, 1928-43* (Columbia UP).

No 18: Autumn 1964
p32: "Facts"
Review of A Nove, *Was Stalin Really Necessary?* (Allen and Unwin), A Zauberman, *Industrial Progress in Poland, Czechoslovakia and East Germany 1937-1962* (OUP), HP Shaffer (ed), *The Soviet Economy* (Methuen) and G Ionescu, *Communism in Rumania 1944-1962* (OUP).
pp32-33: "Inadequate"
Review of R Pethybridge (ed), Witnesses to the Russian Revolution (Allen and Unwin) and J Keep (ed), *Contemporary History in the Soviet Mirror* (Allen and Unwin).

No 19: Winter 1964-65
pp4-16: "Marxism and the Collectivisation of Agriculture" [W3]
Critical review of Marxist theories.

No 21: Summer 1965
p24 [unsigned]: Introduction to extract from Rosa Luxemburg, *Mass Strike, Party and Trade Union*
Style suggests this is by Cliff.
p32: "Figures of Fun"
Review of D Ingram, *The Communist Economic Challenge* (Allen and Unwin).
p32 [M Turov]: "How to Grow?"
Review of JW Hulse, *The Forming of the Communist International* (Stanford UP). Importance of fact that CPs grew from splits in existing mass parties.
p32 [R Tennant]: "Barton is Best"
Review of S Swianicwicz, *Forced Labour and Economic Development* (Chatham House/OUP).
p32: "Change of Sign"

Review of L Fischer, *The Life of Lenin* (Weidenfeld and Nicolson).

No 29: Summer 1967
pp7-16: "Crisis in China" [NWNM] [W3]
The Cultural Revolution; Maoist voluntarism against Bukharinism.

No 32: Spring 1968
pp13-18: "The Theory of Bureaucratic Collectivism - a Critique" [NWNM]
Significantly revised version of duplicated document dated 1948 [see section H]; also reproduced in *The Fourth International, Stalinism and the Origins of the International Socialists* (1971) [See section A].

No 36: April-May 1969
pp15-21: On Perspectives [W2]

No 37: June-July 1969
pp23-24: Introduction
Introduces Sheng-wu-lien document "Whither China?"

No 48: June-July 1971
pp31-3: "The Bureaucracy Today"
Conclusion to a special issue on *The Trade Union Bureaucracy in Britain*.

No 52: July September 1972
pp16-22: "From Marxist Circle to Agitation"
Abbreviated chapter 2 from *Lenin* vol 1.

No 61: Summer 1973
pp18-29: "Permanent Revolution" reprint from IS1 12 with slight variations.
pp30-39: "Crisis in China" reprint from IS1 29.

No 63: October 1973
pp29-30: review of T Deutscher (ed), Not by politics alone: the other Lenin (Allen and Unwin)
There was no unpolitical Lenin.
No 67: March 1974
pp10-14: "Lenin's Pravda"

From *Lenin* vol 1, chapter 19; a contribution to the internal debate on the role of *Socialist Worker*.

No 74: January 1975
pp28-9: Lenin's Central Committee.
Review of *The Bolsheviks and the October Revolution*, Central Committee Minutes of the Russian Social-Democratic Labour Party (Bolsheviks), Pluto *1974*. Cliff contributed notes to this volume [see section A].

Nos 81-82: September 1975
Portugal at the Crossroads [W1]
Special double issue entirely by Cliff.

No 87: March-April 1976
pp10-19: [Tony Cliff and Robin Peterson] "Portugal: The Last Three Months"
Retreat after 25 November.

No 95: February 1977
pp19-24: Portugal at the impasse.
Retreat in 1976; critique of PRP.

E: *Labour Worker, Socialist Worker*

Labour Worker

Vol 2, No 1 (1963)
pp4-5: "Peking – Moscow: The Widening Gulf"
Why Mao opposes peaceful coexistence.

Vol 2, No 2 (1963)
pp6-7: "Peking – Moscow: The Widening Gulf" (concluding from last month)
Economic roots of Sino-Soviet split.

Vol 2, No 4: June 1963
p3: "How Hitler's Bosses Kept Power"
Why German steel industry was not nationalised after 1945.

Vol 3, No 8: November 1964
pp3-4: "Maurice Thorez – Communist Dinosaur"
Obituary of French Communist leader; role at Liberation and over Algeria.

Vol 3, No 9 [wrongly numbered 4]: December 1964
p3: "Why was Khrushchev removed?"
Fall of Khrushchev and crisis of Russian agriculture.

No 30: 1 February 1965
p2 [unsigned]: "Churchill"
Brief chronology of Churchill's inglorious career.

No 35: Mid-April 1965
p3: "Permanent War Economy"
Extracts from *Socialist Review* article (SR1, April 1957); edited by I Birchall; Cliff found the editing highly unsatisfactory and described it as an "abortion".

No 41: Mid-July 1965
p2: Letter
Response to article by John Palmer in LW 40; Palmer's alleged claim that Britain could be insulated from world slump is dismissed as "not revolutionary". See also letter from Paul Foot in LW 42.

No 47: Mid-November 1965
p4: "Profit Without Honour"
Critique of Labour Government's "National Economic Plan"

No 62: 5 August 1966
p4: Letter
Reply to Tony Young's comment on *Incomes Policy* book in LW 61; why Britain cannot emulate economic "miracles in continental Europe.

No 64: 28 September 1966
p3 [Tony Cliff and Chris Harman]: "End of the Parliamentary Road to Socialism?"
Crisis of Wilson government and need

for revolutionary alternative.

No 66: December 1966
pp4-5: Palest pink in word and deed
History of Labour Party to 1931; why
Labour has never been a socialist party.

No 67: January 1967
p6: "Labour's Addiction to the "Rubber
Stamp" [NWNM] [W2]
Economic change means Labour no
longer even reformist.

No 68: February 1967
p7: "The Sad Saga of the Soggies'
Decline"
Decline of Labour left from Lansbury to
Michael Foot.

No 70: April 1967
p2: "Mao and the Workers"
The Chinese working class and the
Cultural Revolution.

No 72: June 1967
p2: "Sneaky Old Chu Te!"
Mao's purge of Chu Te comparable to
Moscow trials.

No 73: July 1967
pp4-5: "Middle East: Powder Keg with
a Zionist Fuse"
Precis of pamphlet *The Struggle in the
Middle East* (1967) [see section A].

No 77: November 1967
pp4-5: October: "The Unfinished
Revolution".
Fiftieth anniversary of Russian
Revolution.

Socialist Worker (from June 1968)

No 132: 24 July 1969
pp2-3: "The Nigerian Bloodbath"
Against support for Biafra; cf article by
P Sedgwick in SW 130 and letters in SW
133.

No 144: 30 October 1969
pp2-3 [Harry Jones]: "CP: Down the
Slippery Slope..."
Critique of Communist Party industrial
policy; style and compiler's memory
suggest attribution to Cliff.

No 156: 29 January 1970
p3: "Time and Motion Study:
'Scientific' way of squeezing more
profit"
Fighting scientific pretensions of time
and motion study on the shop floor;
taster for *The Employers' Offensive*.

No 158: 12 February 1970
p4: "Shift Work"
Another taster for *The Employers'
Offensive*.

No 266: 8 April 1972
p11: "The Irish Struggle: Which Way
Ahead?"
IS conference intervention; unconditional
but critical support for IRA.

No 283: 5 August 1972
pp5, 7: "The Battle is Won but War
Goes On" [NWNM] [W2]
Situation after freeing of Pentonville
dockers; three cogs – party, rank and
file, trade unions.

No 287: 2 September 1972
p5: "Balance Sheet on Docks Battle"
Situation after Aldington-Jones
agreement; need to involve rank and file.

No 293: 14 October 1972
p5: Heath's Pay Fraud Must be Smashed
No incomes policy under capitalism.

No 300: 2 December 1972
p1: [unsigned] IS members speak to
mass meeting
Brief account of Scunthorpe strike for
higher pensions including quote from
Cliff; full report p15.
p15 [Bill Message]: "2,000 Strike to
Back Higher Pensions Call" [ITHOS]
Includes speech by Cliff to 2,000 strik-

ing workers in Scunthorpe advocating industrial action to raise pensions.

No 302: 16 December 1972
p7: *International Socialism*
Plug for new monthly *International Socialism*, "a real weapon in the struggle".

No 304: 6 January 1973
p5: "1972: Tremendous Year for the Workers" [NWNM] [W2]
Organisational implications of the successful strikes in 1972.

No 305: 13 January 1973
p1: "IS Fund: Get the Message from this Cartoon!"
Financial appeal made by Cliff after treasurer Jim Nichol injured in road accident.

No 314: 17 March 1973
pp8-9: "Gale that can blow down the Tories..."
Unevenness of struggle and need to go beyond sectionalism.

No 315: 24 March 1973
pp2-3: "Build Workers' Party: IS Conference Keynote"
p2: "History is Knocking on our Door, says Cliff"
Introduction to conference debate on perspectives; also short intervention on "rising scale of wages".
p3: Programme adopted

No 319: 21 April 1973
p7: "Now Rank and File must Pick up the Gauntlet"
Retreats by TU bureaucracy and need for rank and file organisation.

No 328: 23 June 1973
p9: "Grasp Nettle of Factory Power"
Need to build IS factory branches.
No 332: 21 July 1973
p10: "Membership in Yorkshire Doubles in Two Months"
Cliff's report to NC on factory branches.

No 336: 18 August 1973
p10: "Membership Boom: 1260 since March"
Cliff's report to NC on factory branches.

No 344: 13 October 1973
p14: "Struggle that Lies Ahead"
Rave review of Roger Rosewell's pamphlet *The Struggle for Workers' Power*.

No 347: 3 November 1973
p9: "Phase 3 Must Go"
Attack on Tory wages policy; importance of SW Industrial Conference on 11 November.

No 349: 17 November 1973
p2: "Build New leadership – with Socialist Politics"
Speech to SW Industrial Conference at Manchester.

No 355: 5 January 1974
p5: "Heath's Blackmail"
How to fight three-day week imposed by Heath in response to miners' overtime ban.

No 357: 19 January 1974
p7: "How Far will the Bosses Go?"
Deepening crisis of British capitalism.

No 359: 2 February 1974
pp8-9: "Lenin – His Ideas are the Future" [NWNM]
Fiftieth anniversary of Lenin's death; first volume of biography promised for later in year.

No 364: 9 March 1974
p3: "Minority: Alibi for Union Chiefs"
Perspectives for newly elected Labour government.
No 380: 29 June 1974 (wrongly dated 1975)
pp8-9: "Lessons for the Revolution"

[ITHOS]
How to develop the pre-revolutionary situation in Portugal.

No 394: 5 October 1974
p14: "We have the Muscle, we Need the Brain!"
Introductory speech at IS conference.

No 404: 14 December 1974
p7: "Stagflation!"
Extract from *The Crisis*.

No 405: 21 December 1974
p7: "The Great Incomes Policy Con-Trick" [NWNM]
Extract from *The Crisis*.

No 406: 4 January 1975
p9: "The Revolutionary Party – Midwife of Socialism"
Extract from *The Crisis*.

No 413: 22 February 1975
p2: "We've Planted the Seed – Now we must Make it Grow"
Second IS factory branches conference to be held in Manchester, 22 February.

No 418: 7 June 1975
p10: "IS Conference 1975"
Opening speech at conference.

No 446: 11 October 1975
p11: "Portugal: An Open Letter to the Revolution"
Extracts from pamphlet *Portugal – o caminho a frente* [see section K] distributed in Portugal.

No 448: 25 October 1975
p5: "Portugal: The Great Danger"
Soldiers cannot substitute for workers; critique of PRP.

No 454: 6 December 1975
p7 [Tony Cliff and Chris Harman]:
"Portugal: Reaction has Won a Battle"
Situation in Portugal after 25 November.

No 479: 5 June 1976
p10: "Link with the Party – in Action!"
p13: "Racism"
Contributions to IS Conference on united front and on exploitation and oppression.

No 509: 8 January 1977
p10: "Why we need a socialist workers' Party" [NWNM]
International Socialists become the SWP.

No 521: 2 April 1977
pp8-9: "Phase 3...or Phase-Free?"
Fighting new phase of Labour's Social Contract.

No 546: 24 September 1977
p8: "Build the Socialist Workers Party in the Workplace!"
Situation after Grunwick's strike and Lewisham anti-NF demonstration.

No 568: 4 March 1978
p7: "Scenario for the Future?"
First of a series on the present state of the class struggle.

No 571: 25 March 1978
p5: "Divide and Rule!"
Differentials and craftism.

No 573 (wrongly numbered 523): 8 April 1978
p7: "Steel: These Jobs *Can* be Fought for"
Analysis of situation in the steel industry.

No 576: 29 April 1978
p6: "Thorns: the Great Switch-Off"
How to fight redundancies at Thorns in Bradford.

No 578: 13 May 1978
p4: "Build the Anti Nazi League"
Perspectives after first ANL carnival.

No 579: 20 May 1978
p9: "King Canute would be Just as Effective..."

BIBLIOGRAPHY 577

Inadequacy of CP and Labour left policies against unemployment.

No 581: 3 June 1978
p4: "Unemployment: Building the Resistance"
Experience of fighting sackings in 1930s and 1970s.

No 582: 10 June 1978
p6: Letters
Comment on Martin Tomkinsons's article on Muhammad Ali in SW 580, stressing importance of joining Black Muslims.

No 591: 12 August 1978
p11: "Shooting it out in Paris and London"
Attacks on PLO offices have roots in Arab states' dependency on imperialism.

No 592 (wrongly numbered 560): 19 August 1978
p12: "News from the Socialist Workers Party"
Statement by Cliff, now SW editor, on role of strike reports and sales to strikers.

No 593 (wrongly numbered 592): 26 August 1978
p2: "For the Right to Work"
Editorial on socialist answer to unemployment.
p9: "Why Socialists must Support the Gays" [NWNM] [W3]
Part of centre spread on "Coming Out"; London workers' council will be led by "19 year old black gay woman". Also published as preface to *The Word is Gay* (see section A).

No 594 (not numbered); 2 September 1978
p12: "Getting Away from Boring Reports"
Call from editor for more imagination in strike reports.
p16: "From Calcutta to King's Cross"
We can learn from Indian bus workers who ran buses but refused to collect fares.

No 596: 16 September 1978
p2: "Stormy Weather for Ship of State"
Editorial forecasting winter of industrial discontent.

No 598: 30 September 1978
p2: "Ford Fight for Us All"
Editorial: Ford victory will help low paid; Ford defeat will open door for Thatcher.
p7: "Still United!"
Second ANL carnival; admission of mistake in not mobilising enough people to oppose NF in Brick Lane.

No 599: 7 October 1978
p2: "100,000 Plus"
Editorial on need to keep ANL broad, but fight for socialist ideas within it.

No 600: 14 October 1978
p10: "The Prod Fraud"
Ford strikers popular but other workers should take action now.

No 601: 21 October 1978
p2: "Wages, Profits and Prices"
Editorial – wages do not cause inflation.

No 605: 18 November 1978
p3: "Healey's Hammer"
Labour government raises interest rates.

No 606: 25 November 1978
p2: "The Whip"
Editorial – Labour government drops humane rhetoric and becomes more openly anti working class.

No 631: 26 May 1979
pp8-9: "Ten Years On" [NWNM] [W2] [ITHOS]
Class struggle 1969-79 – based on speech at Skegness rally, Easter 1979.
No 635: 23 June 1979
p4: "No More Murders"
Extract from speech at Blair

Peach funeral.

No 647 (wrongly numbered 674): 15 September 1979
p8: "These Words are Weapons Against the Cuts"
Review of Dave Widgery, *Health in Danger* (Macmillan), and Noreen Branson, *Poplarism 1919-1925* (Lawrence and Wishart).

No 656: 17 November 1979
p10: "What They Said"
Speech to SWP conference on downturn and Code of Practice.

No 657: 24 November 1979
p6: "*Socialist Worker*"
Editor's introduction to debate on SW at SWP conference.

No 660: 15 December 1979
p2: "It's Time to Close Ranks"
Editorial on need for unity in face of employers' offensive.

No 664: 19 January 1980
p13: "Get a Hold on the Present"
Plug for new issue of *Socialist Review*.

No 676: 12 April 1980
pp2-3: "Steel – Time to Stoke the Fires Down Below"
Assessment of the steel strike after return to work.

No 677: 19 April 1980
p11: "The £62,000 Misprint"
Letter correcting misprint in SW 676 article.

No 681: 17 May 1980
p3: "After May 14..."
Limits of TUC Day of Action on 14 May.

No 685: 14 June 1980
p2: "Who's Left to Back Benn?"
Editorial – Benn does not dare challenge TU bureaucracy.

No 698: 13 September 1980 [NB subsequent issue also numbered 698]
p4 "Poland: How Long can the Deal Last?"
Polish unions challenge state capitalism.

No 709: 29 November 1980
p10: "In the Fight Against This...is he Hoing to be Any Help?"
Michael Foot elected Labour leader; limits of Labour's challenge to Tories.

No 741: 18 July 1981
p3: "After the Riots we say Jobs not Jails"
1981 riots.

No 765: 9 January 1982
pp8-9: "Benn's Campaign Faces Collapse"
Decline of the Labour left.

No 767: 23 January 1982
p13: "Poland: Read All About it in *Socialist Review*"
Review of *Socialist Review* [SR2 23 January - 19 February 1982] issue on Poland.

No 787: 12 June 1982
pp8-9: "Labour Left in Retreat"
Bennism and the Falklands War.

No 790: 3 July 1982
pp8-9: "The Road from Zionism to Genocide"
Personal recollections of origins of Zionism.

No 793: 24 July 1982
pp8-9: "Picking up the Pieces"
Lessons of the train drivers' defeat.

No 794: 31 July 1982
p12 [Tony Cliff and Peter Clark]: "The SWP – Building in the Next Nine Months"
Organising in the downturn.

No 809: 13 November 1982
pp8-9: "Russia 1917 – When the

BIBLIOGRAPHY 579

Workers Took Over"
Sixty fifth anniversary of October Revolution

No 812: 4 December 1982
p10: "To Understand Ireland Today you have to Start with Connolly"
From speech to SWP Conference.

No 819: 5 February 1983
p13: "Building Castles in the Air"
Summing up and response to series of interviews ("Where do we Go from Here?") with representatives of Labour left: Peter Hain (11 December 1982); Chris Mullin (18 December 1982); Laurence Coates (8 January 1983); Val Veness (15 January 1983).

No 822: 26 February 1983
p11: "*The Revolutionary Ideas of Karl Marx*"
Review of Callinicos book.

No 823: 5 March 1983
p13: "Water Workers: Lessons of the Dispute"
Water workers' dispute ends in victory.

No 824: 12 March 1983
Marx Special supplement pp7-8: "There Cannot be a Revolutionary Movement without a Revolutionary Theory, And this Theory is Marxism"
Marx centenary.

No 880: 14 April 1984
p10: "Neither Side has Broken Through"
First month of the miners' strike.

No 881: 21 April 1984 (wrongly numbered/dated 880/14 April)
p5: "Taking the Initiative"
Summing up of meeting of SWP supporting miners.

No 888: 9 June 1984
p10: "A Crisis of Leadership"
Miners' strike after three months.

No 889: 16 June 1984
pp4-5: "Weighing up the Problems Sizing up the Tasks"
Introduction to meeting of SWP supporting miners.

No 962: 16 November 1985
p10: "Militant – the Scapegoat"
SWP conference speech – unity appeal to Militant.

No 1103: 15 November 1986
p11: "Election will Solve Nothing for our Rulers"
Introduction to discussion on tasks for socialists at SWP conference.

No 1023: 7 February 1987
p10: "BT Strike: Strength and Weaknesses"
Socialist strategy in a sectional dispute.

No 1064: 21 November 1987
p11: "Winning an Audience for Revolutionary Ideas"
SWP conference – New stage of the downturn; preparing for the upturn.

No 1065: 28 November 1987
p10: "Nationalism"
Contribution to conference debate on Iran; military but not political support.

No 1066: 5 December 1987
p10: "Fighting Racism"
Contribution to conference debate: black nationalism as reformism without reforms.

No 1114: 19 November 1988
p11: "Learning to Lead"
Introduction to party-building session at SWP conference.

No 1118: 17 December 1988
pp8-9: [Interview with Tony Cliff and Duncan Hallas] "Which Way Forward for the left?"
Labour Party and anti-Tory mood.

No 1202: 18 August 1990
p10: "As Long as I Breathe I Hope"
Fiftieth anniversary of Trotsky's death.

No 1215: 17 November 1990
p11: "Opportunities Ahead"
Introduction to SWP conference debate on *Socialist Worker* and building the SWP.

No 1266: 16 November 1991
pp10-11: "Building the Party"
Report of speech to SWP conference.

No 1300: 18 July 1992
p7: "Class Struggle in the 90s" [ITHOS]
Text of Marxism meeting.

No 1317: 14 November 1992
p11: "Build the Socialists"
Report of speech from SWP conference.

No 1326: 23 January 1993
p10: [Interview] "Shape the Future"
Perspectives after pit closures.

No 1368: 13 November 1993
p10: [Tony Cliff and Chris Bambery] "Get Stuck in and Build"
Introduction to session at SWP conference.

No 1418: 12 November 1994
p10: "Balance of Forces"
SWP conference – introduction to discussion on state of class struggle.

No 1433: 11 March 1995
p5: "We Can Learn from Each Other"
Reasons to support SW trade union conference

No 1468: 11 November 1995
p10: "Socialist Workers Party Conference"
Introduction to first session on year ahead.

No 1520: 16 November 1996
p10: "Our Historic Opportunity"
Introduction to opening session of SWP conference.

No 1545: 17 May 1997
p13: "Moving on After the Celebrations"
Speech to SWP national meeting after Labour election victory.

No 1566: 11 October 1997
p13: "Our Politics can Bridge the Gap"
Speech to SWP national meeting.

No 1571: 15 November 1997
p10: "Politics Can win a Big Audience"
Speech to SWP conference on discontent with Blair government.

No 1617: 10 October 1998
p14: "A Bold Response to the Economic Crisis"
Speech to SWP national meeting on Indonesia and conditions for revolution.

No 1673: 20 November 1999
p11: "Politics is Vital"
Speech to SWP conference on nature of present period.

No 1743: 14 April 2001
p10: "Roots of Israel's Violence"
Written 1982; [reprint of SW 3 July 1982]

F: *Socialist Review* – series two

No 1, April 1978
pp12-15: "Where Do we Go From Here?"
Interview with Alex Callinicos; analysis of state of labour movement showing origins of "downturn" thesis.
1981:1, January-February
p36 [Tony Cliff interviewed by Simon Turner]: "T is for Trotsky the Hero who Had to Take all of the Blame"

Contribution to back-page series "The Socialist ABC"

1981:4, April-May
p29: contribution to SWP National Committee discussion on failure to resist Linwood closure. Downturn not an excuse for passivity; need to relate to minority.

1982:6, May-June
pp18-19: "You Can't have a Rank and File Movement if the Factories are Empty'
Reasons for winding up the rank and file movement.

No 53, April 1983
pp3-5: "Building in the Downturn"
Extracts of speech to SWP National Committee.

No 55, June 1983
pp16-19: "Prologue to an Upturn"
Speech to SWP National Committee; small revival of industrial struggle.

No 58 (misnumbered 57), October 1983
pp5-7: "The Charge of the Right Brigade
Speech to SWP National Committee on TUC move to right.

January 1985 Issue 1 (No 72)
pp15-17: "1905"
Eightieth anniversary of 1905 revolution in Russia.

No 76, May 1985
p34: Letter: "In Defence of Lenin"
Response to book review by Colin Sparks ("Lenin and the Patriots" in SR2, No 75, April 1985, pp28-9) which had made criticisms of Lenin's positions during the First World War.

No 85, March 1986
pp32-3: "Unclear Pictures"
Review of HA Clegg, *A History of British Trade Unions since 1899*, Vol II, 1911-35, OUP
Praise for Clegg's "impeccable scholarship".

No 86, April 1986
pp17-20: "The State of Struggle Today" [W2]
Interview with Lindsey German; balance of forces at time of Wapping print dispute; need to be realistic.

No 88, June 1986
pp20-22: "Another Tale of Betrayal"
Career of Stafford Cripps used as a means of criticising modern Labour left.

No 100, July/August 1987
pp14-19: "Fifty-Five Years a Revolutionary" [ASR2]
Interview with Alex Callinicos and Lindsey German; review of life on occasion of seventieth birthday.

No 101, September 1987
pp18-22: "The Working Class and the Oppressed"
From speech at Marxism 87.

No 102, October 1987
p34: Letter: "Where are the Workers?"
Response to article on South Korea by Nigel Harris in SR 101 (September 1987, p10), criticising Harris for neglecting Korean working class and opening door to popular frontism.

No 107, March 1988
pp17-20: "In Fighting Mood"
Interview on current balance of class forces.

No 113, October 1988
pp10-11: "Dark Clouds and Silver Linings"
Speech to SWP National Committee analysing "new mood" of hostility to Thatcher.

No 126, December 1989
pp11-14: "Earthquake in the East" [ASR2] [W3]

Extract from recent speech; continuing crisis in Eastern bloc.
p26: report of speech at SWP Conference. Individual non-payment cannot defeat poll tax.

No 133, July/August 1990
pp19-20: "The revolution changed to a sword the pen of its best publicist"
Extracts from volume 2 of *Trotsky, The Sword of the Revolution*.

No 135, October 1990
pp15-18: "The Struggle in the Middle East" [W1]
Edited and shortened version of *The Struggle in the Middle East* (1967) [see section A].

No 145, September 1991
pp10-11: "Balance of Powerlessness" [W3]
Crisis in Russia continues after failure of August coup.

No 183, February 1995
pp16-19: "In the Balance" [W2]
Revival of industrial struggle with signal workers' victory.

No 202, November 1996
pp9-11: "Labour's Crisis and the Revolutionary Alternative"
Interview with Chris Nineham; perspectives for SWP in run-up to 1997 election.

No 209, June 1997
pp9-11: "Change is Going to Come – but how?" [W2]
Speech to SWP national meeting on illusions and contradictions in consciousness after Blair victory.

No 219, May 1998
pp20-22: "The Jews, Israel and the Holocaust" [W1]
Roots of Zionism; need for working class revolution in Arab states to resolve Palestinian question.

No 221, July/August 1998
pp20-21: "The Test of Time"
Theory of state capitalism proved correct by history.

No 241, May 2000
pp16-20: "Nothing So Romantic"
Interview with Nicolas Walter from *Idiot International* (June 1970) reprinted on occasion of Cliff's death.

No 260, February 2002
pp12-13: 1972: "A Great Year for the Workers"
Reprinted from SW 6 January 1973.

G: *International Socialism* – series two

No 6: Autumn 1979
pp1-50: "The Balance of Class Forces in Recent Years" [W2]
Said to be extract from forthcoming book "*The Employers' Offensive and the Fightback*". Analyses extent of workers' retreat, the "downturn". A response – though not explicitly – to Steve Jefferys "Striking into the 80s" in IS 5.

No 13: Summer 1981
pp29-72: "Clara Zetkin and the German Socialist Feminist Movement".
Some of this forms chapter 5 of *Women and the Struggle for Socialism* but also contains much additional material not in book. See also polemics by Juliet Ash and Janet Vaux in IS2 14, pp120-27, showing how this relates to internal debate in the SWP on women's organisation.

No 14: Autumn 1981
pp75-104: "Alexandra Kollontai: Russian Marxists and Women Workers".
Substantially the same as chapter 6 of *Women and the Struggle for Socialism*, but contains additional material.

BIBLIOGRAPHY 583

No 29: Summer 1985
pp3-61: "Patterns of mass strike".
1984-85 miners' strike in historical context.

No 31: Spring 1986
pp69-111: "The Tragedy of AJ Cook"
Although it is never made explicit, this article is clearly a response to Paul Foot's pamphlet *An Agitator of the Worst Type* (SWP, January 1986, based on a talk at the Skegness Rally, Easter 1985). Foot is much more sympathetic to Cook. The parallels with Scargill are unstated but obvious.

No 55: Summer 1992
pp65-76 [Lindsey German and Peter Morgan]: "The prospects for socialists – an Interview with Tony Cliff".
1992 election and underlying class relations.

No 80: Autumn 1998
pp53-70: "Revolution and Counter-revolution: Lessons for Indonesia" [W1]
Historical analogies for Indonesian revolution.

H: Internal bulletins, party circulars, etc.

Period prior to Formation of Socialist Review group

"All that Glitters is not Gold" [NWNM] [W3]
Revolutionary Communist Party Internal Document, September 1947
Polemic against Germain (Mandel), arguing that there is currently a boom in Britain.
"The Nature of Stalinist Russia". [W3]
Internal Bulletin, Revolutionary Communist, Party June 1948
Translated by C Dallas

"Marxism and the Theory of Bureaucratic Collectivism" [revised version in W3]
24 pp duplicated document – no date [1948] Translated by C Dallas
[Rich MS 1117/box 118/file 9.]
Has 13 sections:
1. What determines the place of Any Regime in History?
2. The Nature of the Working Class in Russia
3. The Historical Function of the Stalinist Bureaucracy
4. The Motive of Exploitation in Bureaucratic Collectivist Society
5. Is Bureaucratic Collectivism more Progressive than Capitalism?
6. Bruno R on Bureaucratic Collectivism
7. Can Slaves Make the Socialist Revolution?
8. "The Managerial Revolution"
9. A Comparison of Nazi German Economy and Russian Economy and the Theory of Bureaucratic Collectivism
10. Shachtman and the Question of the Inevitability of Socialism
11. Dialectics and Bureaucratic Collectivism
12. Is the Rise of Bureaucratic Collectivism Accidental?
13. In Conclusion

There are a number of major differences between this and the version published in 1968. The sections on dialectics and inevitability have disappeared and been replaced by a section on the Stalinist Parties. Some references have been updated.
Revised version appears in IS1 32 and in *The Fourth International, Stalinism and the Origins of the International Socialists* (1971) [See section A]
[No name]: "On the class nature of the people's democracies" (39 pp duplicated document, July 1950) Reprinted in *The Fourth International, Stalinism and the Origins of the International Socialists*

(1971) [See section A] [NWNM].

Socialist Review Group

Minutes

Minutes of National Committee held 22 and 23 September 1951 at Birmingham
International perspectives
RT [Roger Tennant] gave "comprehensive report covering state capitalist connections in many countries" [MRC MSS.75/1/1/1].

Minutes of SR EC, 7-8 October 1961
Cliff on Work in the Labour movement: the Blackpool Conference and After [Fancy MS 1171/box 1/4]

Minutes of the Quarterly Meeting of the SRG, 10 and 11 February 1962
Cliff on Work in the Nuclear Disarmament Movement. [Fancy MS 1171/box 1/4]

Miscellaneous Documents

On Social Democratic Illusions
Internal documents [1957/1958].
Signed by four SR branch secretaries, but according to Stan Newens inspired by and probably written by Cliff. Attack on illusions in Labour Party work. [Stan Newens archive]

NOTES FOR AGGREGATE DISCUSSION
[1960?]: "Suggested Changes in What We Stand For "by T Cliff [Fancy MS 1171/box 24/SR]
Detailed amendments.

"Prospects and Tasks"
[1960?] 2pp
Perspectives for Labour Party and activity elsewhere [Fancy MS 1171/box 24/SR].
"Some Remarks on the Regroupment of Marxists"
[1960?] single sheet.

Possible bases for left unity. [Fancy MS 1171/box 24/SR]

"Suggestions for Changes in SR"
to be raised before October EC [1961?]
Role of *Socialist Review* now that other publications exist [Fancy MS 1171/box 1/4].

International Socialists

International Socialism Internal Bulletin

IS Internal Bulletin, January 1963
[TC]: Cuba
More or less the same as Section 3 (Castro's Revolution) of "Permanent Revolution" (IS 12). [Rich. MS 1117/box 222/file 5].

IS Bulletin No 7, 22 October 1965
p1: report by Tony Cliff on visit to various branches in North of England.

IS Bulletin No 8, 5 December 1965
pp1-2: further report by TC on visit to various branches in north of England.
pp8-15: [unsigned, in name of NC]: Document entitled "Metropolitan Countries" [c February 1970]
Apparently drafted by Cliff. One of three documents on metropolitan countries, Stalinist states and the Third World produced for 1970 conference. Some passages taken verbatim from "On perspectives" (IS1 36)

(Autumn 1971) (Special bulletin before December 1971 conference to exclude Workers' Fight)
pp10-12: "For the Record"
Defence of IS position on troops in Ireland in August 1969 against Workers' Fight criticisms.
[Tony Cliff and Chris Harman]: Theses on the Common Market for June National Committee International Socialism Internal Bulletin

BIBLIOGRAPHY 585

June 1971
pp6-7 [Tony Cliff and Chris Harman]: Theses on the Common Market for June National Committee
Argues for dropping previous abstentionist position and voting in TUs for opposition to Common Market (Adopted by June NC).

January 1973
pp18-20 [Tony Cliff and Andreas Nagliatti]: "Main Features of the Programme We Need"
Contribution to debate on draft programme for annual conference.

IS Bulletin May/June 1973
pp3-5: "On Recruitment"
Possibility of quick recruitment; need for sales inside factories.

Undated June 1973
pp3-4: [Tony Cliff and John Charlton]: "Further Remarks on Recruitment"
Yorkshire experience; batch recruitment and public meetings.

April 1974
pp3-4 "The Use of *Socialist Worker* as an Organiser" [NWNM]
Argues that buyers of SW should become sellers.

[May 1974]
p3: Introduction to "Organisation Perspectives"
Argues audience is mainly younger workers without traditions; need for Organisation Commission to examine restructuring of organisation.
pp8-9: "The Way Ahead for IS"
Factory branches, SW a workers' paper, worker leadership.

Internal Bulletin November 1976
The role of *Socialist Worker* (document submitted to SW Organisers Conference).

Minutes of leading committees

IS Working Committee Minutes, 4 July 1964
Cliff on two traps: Labour Party cretinism and Open Party [Rich MS 1117/box 209/file 6].

Minutes of an ISEC, 19-9-64
[The "EC" was in fact a quarterly delegate meeting]
p2: Intervention by TC.
YS "no longer a horizon of growth"; turn to industry.

IS Northern Weekend School 28.3.65
Discussion on building organisation.
Cliff on experiment, *Young Guard,* etc. [Rich. MS 1117/box 221/file 1].

ISEC – 10-11 April 1965
Cliff: *International Socialism* "the most important journal of the group". [Rich. MS 1117/box 221/file 1].

IS Working Committee Minutes 14 May 1966
Document signed Chris Harman and Tony Cliff for the Nottingham Workers' Control Conference, 25-26 June.
Full workers' control requires political power in the hands of the working class [Rich. MS 1117/box 209/file 6].

[NOTE: From 1969 to 1975 IS had a National Committee (NC) elected by conference and meeting monthly, and a London-based Executive Committee (EC) elected by the NC and meeting weekly. For most of this period minutes of both bodies were circulated to the membership, at times as part of the Internal Bulletin.]

EC Minutes, 27/1/69
Discussion on perspectives
Cliff – must build on fragments, but not talk *only* of fragments. [Rich. MS 1117/box 223/file 1].
NC minutes, 11 October 1969
Discussion on Left Unity
Cliff – don't expel Workers' Fight, but use to educate [Rich. MS 1117/box

222/file 2].

EC Minutes, 23.2.1970
TC reports speaking tour by himself and Chris Davison to promote *Employers' Offensive*.

NC minutes, 22 August 1970
p4: Report on Pilkington dispute; need to oppose breakaway unions and for IS to have more centralised industrial intervention.

EC minutes 12.5.69
p2: Interventions by TC arguing that LSE students should "fight to the end", and that *Socialist Worker* should become six-pages, with middle two pages "devoted to theory".

NC minutes, 19 December 1970
p1: TC report: January 12th Preparing for TUC day of protest against Tory anti-union laws on 12 January.
Cliff on "General Strike" slogan [Fancy MS 1171/box 17/1970].
NC minutes, 27 February 1971
pp1-2: TC intervention re fighting Tories.

NC minutes 10 July 1971 (in Internal Bulletin July 1971)
pp1-2: TC report: "IS and the Labour Party"
How IS should relate to LP in TUs and in recruitment.

NC minutes, 14 August 1971 (in Internal Bulletin, August 1971)
p3: TC intervention re Upper Clyde Shipbuilders occupation.
Warns of dangers of demoralisation.
p5: TC intervention re Ireland.
Weakness of left in North; suggests that "Irish comrades go home".
NC minutes, October 1971 (in special Internal Bulletin of Discussion material for 4 December Conference
p3: TC intervention – why Trotskyist Tendency should be excluded.
Opening of debate culminating in exclusion of "Workers' Fight" grouping.

NC minutes, 11 December 1971 (in December 1971 Internal Bulletin)
p4: TC intervention in education discussion.
Need for worker-intellectuals; role of cadre schools [Rich. MS 1117/box 212/file 2].

NC minutes, March [1972]
p3: TC on downturn after miners' strike.

NC minutes, 12 August 1972
p4: TC on rightward move of Communist Party in docks dispute.

NC minutes, November [1972]
p6: TC on Tory freeze and split consciousness.

EC minutes, 11 December 1972
p2: TC on rise of National Front. Argues conditions for a fascist movement not present.

NC minutes, 10 March 1973
pp1-2: TC introduction on "The Freeze and the TUC"
pp4-5: TC intervention re parliamentary elections – against candidates at this stage.

EC minutes, 26 March 1973
p2: TC intervention – to oppose National Front IS must call for Labour vote.

EC minutes, 2 April 1973
pp1-2, 4: TC introduction and summing up on "Proposed United Front with the CP"
Long-term perspective – overtake CP over 2-3 years.

EC minutes, 9 April 1973
pp1-2: TC introduction on "Political

Perspectives"
Inflation and TU bureaucracy retreat will mean large unofficial strikes.

NC minutes, April [1973]
pp2-3, 5: TC introduction and conclusion on "Political Perspectives"
Short downturn in struggle; need to recruit; preparing united front strategy towards CP.

EC minutes, 8 May 1973
p1: TC introduction on "Recruitment"
Unevenness in organisation; need to recruit quickly in present period.

NC minutes, May [1973]
pp1-3: TC report on recruitment,
Stress on recruiting workers in bunches and not as individuals.
(Appended) [Andreas Nagliatti and Tony Cliff]: Birmingham Commission Report to May NC
Proposals for district reorganisation to deal with problems caused by Left Faction.

EC minutes, 28 May 1973
pp2-3: TC interventions on improving London organisation and introducing flat rate subs.

EC minutes, 25 June 1973
pp3, 4-5: TC interventions about recruitment
Argues worker members should be encouraged to recruit fellow workers.

EC minutes 30 July 1973
pp2, 4, 5: TC on need for *International Socialism* to relate to needs of present membership.
Discussion with Mike Kidron, at that time about to take on editorship of journal (he did not in fact do so).

NC minutes, October [1973]
pp1-2: TC introduction on "Phase 3: Perspectives"New stage of Tory incomes policy; preparing for IS Manchester rally on 11 November.

NC minutes, November [1973]
pp1-2, 3: TC report and conclusion on "Political Perspectives"
Deep crisis caused by miners; "we must put politics forward more"
There is a somewhat different report of these speeches in "National Secretary's Report" dated 27 November 1973.
pp5, 7: TC interventions on rank and file conference and recruiting black workers.

NC minutes, December [1973]
p3: TC intervention in "Political Perspectives" discussion
Problems of generalising in current crisis.

NC minutes April [1974]
pp5-6, 8: TC introduction and conclusion on *Socialist Worker*
Most readers are young workers without traditions; we need workers' paper not paper for workers. Debate led to removal of Roger Protz as SW editor.
Minutes of May National Committee, Saturday 11 May 1974
pp2-4, 13-14: Cliff: Organisational Perspectives
Orientation to young workers; worker leadership [Rich. MS 1117/box 209/file 5].

NC minutes, 30 May [1974]
p2: TC introduction and conclusion re "Threshold/Incomes Policy"
Prospect of new incomes policy based on threshold agreements

NC minutes, July 1974
p3: TC intervention defending Steve Jefferys' Industrial Perspectives document against reference back moved by Andreas Nagliatti.
Danger of demoralisation.
Internal Pamphlet
Factory Branches [W2]
International Socialists, [1973], 22pp

Published in summer of 1973 for first Factory Branches conference in September 1973; IS formed factory branches following conference decision in March 1973.

Miscellaneous documents and circulars

20 June 1968
"Notes on Democratic Centralism" [NWNM]
Arguing for transition to a democratic centralist structure, finally agreed November 1968.

"Notes on the Industrial Scene and the Tasks Ahead"
5pp, apparently August 1969.
25 points on strategy for opposing productivity deals. [Rich. MS 1117/box 222/file 2]

December 1969
"Some Preliminary Notes on Perspectives for Western Capitalism", 5pp.
Document for NC, December 1969

July 1970
p1: [Tony Cliff and Duncan Hallas] Introduction to "Organizational Notes 1"
This was a four-page duplicated bulletin with reports on selling *The Employers' Offensive* and the teachers' fraction.

[Cliff, Hallas, Higgins] Letter dated 21.8.70
Appeal to raise £5,000 in ten days to buy printing machine. [Fancy MS 1171/box 17/1970].

[March] 1971
[T Cliff, D Hallas, C Harman]: "The Current Situation and Immediate Perspectives in Industry and the Unions"
Document for 1971 Easter conference on strategy in trade unions following defeat of postal strike.

22 June 1972
Suggestions re Autumn/Winter Campaign
Proposals for party-building campaign in late 1972.

Undated [July 1972]
[JH (Jim Higgins) and TC]: Security response to fears of repression during industrial conflicts of 1972. Various measures to minimise circulation of names and addresses.

22 August 1972
IS Building Workers Group
four-page document for IS Building Workers Conference, 2 September 1972, at time of strikes during which Shrewsbury pickets were arrested.

January 1973
Letter to members of ATTI and AUT requesting donation of £100 to Fighting Fund.

Undated (probably Spring 1973)
Letter to I Birchall and D Hallas redrafting of programme after 1973 conference.

4 May 1973
Branch circular [73/83] re procedures for reporting membership to centre. Cliff was at this point Membership Secretary of IS.

Branch circular 73/124, 19 September 1973
Circular from Cliff, Membership Secretary, asking branches for accurate membership details. [Rich. MS 1117/box 209/file 5].

20 December 1973
[Tony Cliff, Jim Nichol, Dave Peers]
Financial appeal to members in various white-collar unions, asking all earning over £2,000 a year to donate £100.

16 May 1974
Letter asking for information and

BIBLIOGRAPHY 589

suggestions for Organisation Commission. The Organisation Commission was established following heated May NC which brought out deep divisions in organisation. [Rich. MS 1117/box 223/file3].

3 June 1974
Letter apparently to members of Organisation Commission asking for suggestions. [Rich. MS 1117/box 222/file 2].

9 June [1974]
Notes of Organisation Commission discussion
Contains many comments by TC

11 June 1974
Circular to branches requesting statistics on membership for Organisation Commission. [Rich. MS 1117/box 211/file 3].

13 June 1974
Covering letter sent out with minutes of first Organisation Commission meeting.

23 June [1974]
Notes of Organisation Commission discussion 23 June [1974]
Contains many comments by TC, in particular on roles of NC and EC.

MEETING HELD BETWEEN IS MEMBERS ON THE R&F ORGANISING COMMITTEE, Tony Cliff, Steve Jefferys and John Deason, 30 June [1974]
Long contribution by Cliff on politics and rank and file organisation of hospital workers. [Fancy MS 1171/box 17 (National R&F Conference)].

13 July 1974
Letter to all NC members asking for amendments to report of Organisation Commission. [Rich. MS 1117/box 221/file 1].
Undated [June 1974]
[P Bain, T Cliff, J Deason, D Hallas]:

Report of the Commission Appointed... Commission into disputes in Manchester district following May NC.

Undated [June-July 1974]
Organisation Commission Questionnaire No 2
Questions on workplace SW sales and leaflets. [Rich. MS 1117/box 211/file 3].

Notes of ORGANISATION COMMISSION discussion [1974]
Cliff on factory branches, discipline etc. [Rich. MS 1117/box 220/file 1].

[Cliff and Paul Foot]: Making *Socialist Worker* into a Workers' Paper [1974?]
Very similar to piece in April 1974 Internal Bulletin; need for greater worker involvement in SW. [Rich. MS 1117/box 209/file 2].
Second part of Cliff-Foot document on improving the content of the paper No date; probably summer-autumn 1974 After removal of Roger Protz as editor; Need to encourage worker writers.

Socialist Workers Party

SWP Internal Bulletin

No 1: February 1977
[Tony Cliff and Duncan Hallas]: "The devolution referenda"
Advocates abstention in Scottish and Welsh referenda.

No 6 [1978]
p4 [Tony Cliff and Jack Robertson]: "The Future of *Socialist Worker*"
How to improve industrial coverage in post-ANL period.
Pre-conference Bulletin No 2, 1994 pp8-12: "Why do we need a revolutionary party?"
Transcript of talk at Marxism 94.
Spring 2000
pp20-21 [Tony Cliff and Alex

Callinicos]: Letter to ISO (20 February 2000)
p22 [Tony Cliff and Alex Callinicos]: Letter to ISO Steering Committee (23 February 2000)
pp40-41 [Tony Cliff and Alex Callinicos]: Letter to ISO Steering Committee (20 March 2000)
pp41-47 [Tony Cliff and Alex Callinicos]: Letter to ISO Steering Committee (29 March 2000).
Polemic with ISO (US) re inadequate response to Seattle and anti-capitalist movement.

Miscellaneous Documents and Circulars

March 1977
[Paul Foot, Jim Nichol, Tony Cliff]: Financial Appeal to the Trade Union and Labour movement following the award of damages to Clive Jenkins of ASTMS SW sued for £10,000 for criticising Jenkins for organising holidays in Franco's Spain.

"Our Election Tactics in the General Election"
Document for National Advisory Committee signed by Cliff and five other comrades. Style suggests drafted by Cliff. Apparently late 1977.
Advocates retreat from electoral strategy. [MRC MSS.244/2/1/2].

Steve Jefferys: "The politics behind the row on the paper"
[late 1978]
Contains extracts from document circulated by Cliff to SW staff before removal of Harman as editor. [MRC MSS.244/2/1/2].

19 January 1982
[Tony Cliff and Peter Clark]: Individually addressed appeal to lecturers to donate to Fighting Fund.

3 March 1983
[Peter Clark, Nasreen Tabrizi, Tony Cliff]: Appeal for money to publish Farsi translation of Cliff's *State Capitalism in Russia*.

I: Miscellaneous articles

New Politics (US)
No 2: Winter 1962
"The 22nd Congress of the Russian Communist Party" [NOT SEEN]
Reprinted from SR1 November 1961.

Solidarity
Vol 3, No 10: August 1965
pp22-25: Report of the Cardan-MacIntyre debate, with account of Cliff's contribution, including many verbatim quotations.

Speak Out (Detroit)
No 12: June 1967
pp13-15: "Mao and the Workers"
Reprinted from LW April 1967.

Workers' Fight (A Trotskyist journal for members of the IS Group)
New Series No 1, 1969
Cliff on substitutionism
Reprint from IS1: 2.

Idiot International
No 6, June 1970
pp8-10: Tony Cliff – interview by Nick Walter
Interview on IS politics, especially role of party.

Radical America
Vol 9, No 6, November-December 1975
pp9-44: "Portugal at the Crossroads"
Shortened version of IS1 81-82. There was a disagreement between Cliff and *Radical America* about the editing; see letter from *RA* to Cliff [The Women's Library: 7SHR/A/5 Box 2].

The Leveller
No 29, August 1979

BIBLIOGRAPHY 591

pp12-13 [David Clark and Tim Gopsill]: "Taking on the Tories – 'Defend Our Unions'"
Report on the Defend Our Unions conference, Manchester, 23 June 1979. Contains extracts from an interview with Cliff on the Rank and File movement.

No 30, September 1979
pp20-21 [Tony Cliff interviewed by Dave Clark and Mike Prest]: "Sell the Paper! Build the Party!"
On politics of SWP; approach to CP and Bennism.

The Guardian
20 July 1987
p20: "Why the Workers did not Fight for Labour"
Based on Marxism talk "Elections 87 – Lessons for Socialists"; see also the *Guardian*, 22 July, Letters, p12 for response.

New Statesman and *Society*
16 September 1994
p13: Influences (questionnaire)
Says "I don't listen to music"; trusts nobody in the world other than Chris Harman and Lindsey German; most admired political figures listed as: "Karl Marx, Friedrich Engels, Leon Trotsky and Rosa Luxemburg". Cliff claimed "Leon Trotsky" was misheard over telephone, should have been "Lenin, Trotsky".

International Socialist Review (ISO - US)
Issue 01: Summer 1997
pp27-31 [Ahmed Shawki interviews Cliff]: "50 Years of the International Socialist Tradition".
Fiftieth anniversary of document on state capitalism.

Other Items

In an article in SWP Internal Bulletin No 6 [1978], p4, Cliff refers to the fact that he wrote his first strike leaflet 45 years previously, that is, in 1934. [NOT SEEN]

Revolutionary History
Volume 6, no 2/3, Summer 1996
pp4-48: Ciaran Crossey and James Monaghan: "The Origins of Trotskyism in Ireland"
On pp43-44 the authors refer to and quote a leaflet issued in Dublin in May 1948 entitled "Who Wears Connolly's Mantle?" They speculate that this may have been written or influenced by Cliff who was in Dublin at the time. [NOT SEEN]

Isis (Oxford University)
No 1452: 13 November 1963
p7 [Richard Condon]: "Colourful Mixture"
Detailed report of meeting of Oxford University Labour Club addressed by Cliff on "The Limits of De-Stalinization".
EC minutes of 23 February 1970 report that Cliff had signed on behalf of IS an ISRACA leaflet making the following points: against persecution of Jews in Russia: against the slogan of calling for Jews to return to Israel: in favour of Palestinian Arabs being able to return to Israel [NOT SEEN]

Redskins: Neither Washington nor Moscow (Decca FLP 1)
This album contains some extracts from a speech by Cliff; it entered the *Music Week* chart on 22 March 1986, peaking at No 31.

J: Manuscripts, correspondence

The Tony Cliff archive at Warwick [MRC MSS.459] contains a large number of manuscripts, draft articles and notes for meetings etc. Only some of the most interesting and significant are listed here.

Books

Middle East
210 pp typescript, plus bibliography, May 1946.
Six parts:
1. Historical Background
2. Imperialism in the Arab East
3. The Economic Structure of the Arab East
4. The National Movement in the Arab East
5. Zionism
6. The Working Class Movement in the Arab East [MRC MSS.459/box 6].

[Ygael Gluckstein]: *Collectivisation of Agriculture*
292pp typescript, c. 1962
Seven parts:
1. General Analysis
2. Russian Collectivization
3. The Chinese People's Communes
4. Communist Regime Upholds Individual Farming
5. Castro's Transformation of Agriculture
6. The Israeli Communal Farm (Kibbutz)
7. Communism and the Peasantry
More than one version of some sections. [MRC MSS.459/2/1/1-11].

Articles and Manuscripts

[Y Tsur]: "The managerial revolution. The theory of counter-revolution of monopoly capitalism".
5pp; in Hebrew
No date (late 1930s, early 1940s). Apparently published, but no record of which journal it appeared in. English translation has been made. Critique of James Burnham, *The Managerial Revolution* (1943). Postscript promises a further article on the nature of the Russian regime. [MRC, MSS.459/box 10] English translation at http://www.marxists.org/archive/cliff/works/1943/xx/burnham.html

"The Crisis of Society is the Crisis of the Leadership"
4pp typescript, no date.
French Revolution and Lenin; critique of voluntarism. [MRC MSS.459/2/17].

"An Idea Transformed into its Opposite"
5pp, no date.
Parallel between history of Christianity and transformation of Marxism into Stalinism. [MRC MSS.459/2/17].

"The Russian Revolution"
4pp in note form no date. [MRC MSS.459/2/21]

A very rough draft of a synopsis of a book on Trotsky.
4 typewritten sheet. Probably 1960. Ten chapters on aspects of Trotsky's thought. [MRC MSS.459/2/14].
Notes on Revolutionaries and Reformism
[MRC MSS.459/2/21]

Single untitled sheet, numbered "8". no date but later than 1984.
Some thoughts on sectarianism. [MRC MSS.459/2/17].

Untitled, undated notes from 1980s – incomplete.
On miners' strike and party organisation. [MRC MSS.459/3/3].

Letters

Letter to V Mosler, 29.7.93
Organisational problems of SAG. [MRC MSS.459/3/30].

Part of letter to Turkish comrade
Economism not a danger at present.
[MRC MSS.459/2/21]

Notebook

Notebook 346pp.
Mostly Hebrew, some English. Statistics re Russian agriculture, etc.
Contains offer of reward of £5 if found.
[MRC MSS.459/3/22].

K: Translations

Arabic

State Capitalism in Russia (cf *A World to Win* p201)

Bengali

Russiay Rashtriya Pujibad
Social Education and Alternative Research, Kalikata, 1992, xxvii + 251p
State Capitalism in Russia

Danish

Rosa Luxemburg. En politisk biografi
Politisk Revy, Copenhagen, 1973
Translation of 1959 edition of *Rosa Luxemburg*
Contains foreword for Danish edition by Cliff, dated 1972.

"Trotsky on Substitutionism" (IS1 2)
Proletar No 6, November 1974, pp24-34.

Portugal at the Crossroads
1975/1976 [?]
Produced in Denmark [see IS Bulletin February 1976] [NOT SEEN]

Dutch

"De strijd in het Midden-Oosten"
in Tariq Ali (ed), Nieuwe revolutionairen. Linkse oppositie (Bussum, 1969) 213-33
("The Struggle in the Middle East", in T Ali, *New Revolutionaries*, London, 1969). 1967 pamphlet – see section A.

"Rosa Luxemburg's verdediging van het marxisme"
in *Rosa Luxemburg, Dubblernummer te elfder ure. 18e jaargang nr. 7 en 8* (Nijmegen 1971), pp312-22.

"De opvatting van Rosa Luxemburg over de massastaking"
in *Rosa Luxemburg, Dubblernummer te elfder ure. 18e jaargang nr. 7 en 8* (Nijmegen 1971), pp364-76.
(Chapters on "Reform or Revolution" and "Mass strikes and revolution" in *Rosa Luxemburg*; translated from German edition of 1969).

"Revolutie en contra-revolutie, lessen voor Indonesie"
in C Harman, T Cliff, P Brandon, *Marxisme en de partij* (Amsterdam 1999), pp6-139.
"Revolution and counter-revolution: lessons for Indonesia" (IS2 80).

Farsi

State Capitalism in Russia [March 1983]
Printed in Britain, "Socialist Publications".

Deflected Permanent Revolution, Bookmarks, 1990.

French

Quatrième Internationale
August-September 1946: pp38-46
"Le Proche et le Moyen-Orient à la croisée des chemins: Part I"
October-November 1946: [Not seen] presumably contains Part II.
December 1946: pp20-25
"Le Proche-Orient au carrefour: Part III".
These three articles are a French translation of *The Middle East at the*

Crossroads (*Fourth International*, December 1945, January and February 1946) subsequently published as a pamphlet *Middle East at the Cross Roads* [1946 - see section A]

[Y Gluckstein] *Les satellites européens de Staline*
Les îles d'or, Paris, 1953
Stalin's satellites in Eastern Europe.

"L'avenir de l'empire russe: réforme ou révolution?"
In *Correspondance socialiste* (Pivertiste), No 69, December 1956, pp9-11.
Résumé from "The Future of the Russian Empire" (SR1 December 1956).

Portugal au Carrefour [1975]
Portugal at the Crossroads [IS1/81-82]
IS International Department

La Pravda de Lénine [1977?]
"Lenin's Pravda" [IS1/67]
IS International Department
Prepared for sale at Lutte Ouvrière fête

Le Capitalisme d'état en URSS de Staline à Gorbatchev
Etudes et documentation internationales, Paris, 1990
State Capitalism in Russia – contains introduction and conclusion by C Harman, also contains (pp261-276): "The theory of bureaucratic collectivism: a critique" (IS1 32).

"La Révolution permanente"
"Permanent Revolution" [IS1/12]
Referred to in an internal document of the Canadian IS; date not known [NOT SEEN]
"Traits communs et differences entre le capitalisme d'État et un État ouvrier", [extract from *Russia*], *Socialisme International* No 10, Summer 2004.

German

[Rock, L] *Palästina: seine*

Arbeiterbewegung und ihre Aufgaben.
n.p., 1938, 61pp.
Trotsky Papers Cataloging Records (MS Russ 13.11). Houghton Library, Harvard University, item 17140.
Rock articles from *New International*, 1938-39. [NOT SEEN]

Revolte der Arbeiter
Oberbaumpresse, Berlin, 1968.
Incomes policy, legislation and shop stewards.

[Tony Cliff, Rosa Luxemburg, Paul Frölich and Peter Nettl]: *Rosa Luxemburg und die Oktoberrevolution 1917*. Published by Arbeitstexte Verlag O, Hamburg, 1970 pp1-10: "Rosa Luxemburgs Kritik an der bolschewistischen Regierung". This is the chapter "Rosa Luxemburg's criticism of the Bolsheviks in power", pp61-70 from *Studie über Rosa Luxemburg*, Neue Kritik, Frankfurt-am-Main, 1969.

Studie über Rosa Luxemburg
Neue Kritik, Frankfurt-am-Main, 1969, 92pp.
Rosa Luxemburg (from 1969 version) Also another edition of the same book: Linden-Druck, Hanover
Jahrbuch Arbeiterbewegung Band II: Marxistische Revolutionstheorie (ed) C Pozzoli Fischer, Frankfurt-am-Main, 1974, pp93-113: "Revolution und revolutionäre Organisation" (Trotsky on Substitutionism – IS1 2)

Portugal vor der Entscheidung
Sozialistische Arbeitergruppe, Frankfurt am Main 1975.
Portugal at the Crossroads.

Staatskapitalismus in Russland
SAG, Frankfurt-am-Main 1975, 283pp.
State Capitalism in Russia

Greek

Rosa Luxemburg

(includes two chapters from Cliff's *Rosa Luxemburg*)
November 1972 (out of print)
Ydrohoos, 125pp.

Portugal at the Crossroads: early 1976.
No publisher named; contact address: 6 Cottons Gardens, London. Joint effort by Greek and Greek Cypriot comrades.

State capitalism in Russia (two editions)
1st edition Bookmarks, 1983, 326pp.
2nd edition Marxistiko Vivliopolio, December 1991, 290pp.

Russia – from Workers' State to State Capitalism (two editions)
1st chapter: "Workers' revolution and beyond", from Binns, Cliff, Harman, *Russia: From Workers' State to State Capitalism* (1987)
1st edition Athens 1989, ESSD, pp20-26
2nd edition 1991 (out of print)
Marxistiko Vivliopolio

Deflected Permanent Revolution
October 1991, Marxistiko Vivliopolio, 40pp.

Lenin Vol 1: 1893-1914
March 1995, Marxistiko Vivliopolio, 382pp.

Lenin Vol 2: 1914-1917
October 1997, Marxistiko Vivliopolio, 430pp.

Lenin Vol 3: 1917-1924
February 2000, Marxistiko Vivliopolio, 492pp.

Spain 1936: Revolution against fascism
(includes chapter on Spanish Revolution from *Trotsky* Vol 4)
1st edition October 1995; 2nd edition January 2000, Marxistiko Vivliopolio, 70pp.

June 1936: The factory occupations in France
(includes chapter on France from *Trotsky* Vol 4)
May 1996, Marxistiko Vivliopolio, 60pp.

"We have a World to Win"
(last chapter of Cliff's autobiography)
Socialism from below journal No 35, April 2000.

Indonesian

Revolusi dan kontra-revolusi
Henry Marten, London, 22pp.
"Revolution and counter-revolution: Lessons for Indonesia" (IS2 80).

Italian

Portugal at the Crossroads [IS1/81-82]
IS International Department, 1975.

Capitalismo di stato in Russia
Prospettiva, Rome, 1999, 242pp.
State Capitalism in Russia.

Japanese

Socialist Review (March 1960), p5 reports that Tadayuki Tsushima's latest work, *A Criticism of Soviet 'Socialism'* contains two articles from SR1: "The Future of the Russian Empire" (December 1956) and "Mao-Tse tung and Stalin" (April 1957), plus a chapter from *Stalinist Russia*.

France – the Struggle Goes On
Gendaishichosha, 1968
Also contains texts by Raya Dunayevskaya and Eugene Walker.

Stalinist Russia: A Marxist Analysis

State Capitalism in Russia

Portugal at the Crossroads
1975/1976 [?]
Produced in Japan [see IS Bulletin February 1976] [NOT SEEN]

Rosa Luxemburg
Two editions: 1988 and 1993.

NB: Cliff's personal library contains three other volumes in Japanese which I was unable to identify.

Korean

T'ŭrochŭk'iŭsahu ŭi T'ŭrochŭk'ijuŭi – kukche sahoejuŭi kyŏnghyang ŭi kiwon [*Trotskyism after Trotsky: the origins of the International Socialist Tendency*]. (Seoul: Ch'aekkalp'i, 2010). Translated by Yi Suhyŏn.

Lenin p'yŏngjŏn 1 [*Lenin* 1]. (Seoul: Ch'aekkalp'i, 1996/2004/2010). Translated by Choi Il-bung.

Lenin p'yŏngjŏn 2 [*Lenin* 2]. (Seoul: Ch'aekkalp'i, 2009). Translated by Yi Suhyŏn.

Lenin p'yŏngjŏn 3 [*Lenin* 3]. (Seoul: Ch'aekkalp'i, 2010). Translated by Yi Suhyŏn.

Yŏsŏng haebang kwa hyŏngmyŏng [*Class struggle and women's liberation*]. (Seoul: Ch'aekkalp'i, 2008). Translated by Yi Nara and Chŏng Chinhŭi.
Saech'ŏnnyŏn ŭi Marŭk'ŭsŭjuŭi [*Marxism at the Millennium*]. (Seoul: Pukmaksŭ, 2002). Translated by Chŏng Yŏng-uk.

Marŭk'ŭsŭjuŭi esŏ pon yŏngguk no-dongdang ŭi yŏksa [*The Labour Party: A Marxist History*]. (Seoul: Ch'aekkalp'i, 2008). Translated by Yi Suhyŏn.

Marŭk'ŭsŭjuŭi wa nodong chohap t'ujaeng [*Marxism and trade union struggle*]. (Seoul: Pulmujil, 1995). Translated by C'hoe Kyujin.
Roja Ruksemburŭkŭ [*Rosa Luxemburg*]. (Seoul: Pukmaksŭ, 1992/2001). Translated by Cho Hyorae.

Soryŏn kukka chabonjuŭi [*State capitalism in Russia*]. (Seoul: Ch'aekkalp'i, 1993). Translated by Jeong Seongjin.

Norwegian

Trotskij om substitusjonismen
Internasjonale Sosialister, Oslo 1994. 19pp.
"Trotsky on Substitutionism" (IS1 2)

50 år med den Internasjonale Sosialistiske tradisjonen
Internasjonal Sosialisme 2-1998, pp90-101.
Interview with Ahmed Shawki from *International Socialist Review* Summer 1997 [see section I]

"Regimene var ikke sosialistiske"
Sosialistisk Arbeideravis 22-1999 (16 November 1999).
Source unknown.

Trotskisme etter Trotski
Internasjonale Sosialister, Oslo, 1999, 88pp.
Trotskyism after Trotsky.
"'Globalisiering" – myter og virkelighet"
Sosialistisk Arbeideravis, 24-2000 (15 December 2000).
Chapter 4, "'Globalisation' – myths and realities", from *Marxism at the Millennium*.

Polish

Pánstwowy Kapitalizm W Rosji
Warsaw, 316pp.
State Capitalism in Russia.

Portuguese

Portugal en la Encrucijada
IS International Department, 1975, 48pp.
"Portugal at the Crossroads" [IS1/81-82].

Portugal – O Caminho a Frente

BIBLIOGRAPHY 597

London, 28 September 1975
According to SW 11 October 1975
2500 copies had been sent to Portugal; an extract from the pamphlet appears in this issue of SW.

Lições do 25 de Novembro
Printed/Published London, IS International Department, 1975, 8pp.
Portugal: The Lessons of the 25th November (with Chris Harman).

Russian

State Capitalism in Russia
Leningrad, 1991.
Contains (pp3-5) Cliff's preface to Russian edition.
This translation was originally made by the KGB in 1956, printed and kept in a sealed section of the library. (See *A World to Win*, p201).

Russian paper (*Sosialisticheskaya Solidarnost* No 12, June 1996) announces Rusian translations of:
"Economic Roots of Reformism" (SR1 June 1957);
"Permanent Revolution" (IS1 12);
"Permanent War Economy" (SR1 April 1957).

Spanish

La Batalla
10 January 1948
"La condición de la mujer en la Rusia de Stalin"
"Women in the USSR", *Socialist Appeal*, mid-July 1947.

20 February 1952
[C Tariq]: "Inglaterra y Egipto"
"Britain and Egypt", *Socialist Review* November-December 1951.

8 April 1951
"La Burocracia en la Industria"
"Stalinist Russia - The Facts: The Bureaucrats in Industry", *Socialist Review*, January 1951.

[Ygael Gluckstein]: *Los Satélites de Rusia en Europa*
Artola editor, Madrid, 1955.
Stalin's Satellites in Europe.

Primavera
"Portugal at the Crossroads" [IS1/81-82]
IS International Department, 1975
Published under misleading title ("Springtime") and without author's name for clandestine distribution in Franco's Spain.

Capitalismo de estado en Rusia,
Ediciones En Lucha, Barcelona, 2000.
247pp. Translated by Mike Gonzalez.

Turkish

Lenin 1: Partinin Insasi
(*Lenin 1, Building the Party*)
Translated by Tarik Kaya
1st ed. Yeni gün Yayinlari, London, 1987;
2nd ed. Z Yayinlari, Istanbul, 1994.

Rusya'da devlet kapitalizmi
(*State Capitalism in Russia*)
Translated by Ronnie Margulies and Tarik Kaya
Metis Yayinlari, Istanbul, 1990
Sürekli Devrim: Bir Degerlendirme
(*Deflected Permanent Revolution*)
Translated by Ronnie Margulies and Tarik Kaya
Koral Yayinlari, Istanbul, 1990.

Kadinlarin Özgürlügü ve Sinif Mücadelesi
(*Class Struggle and Women's Liberation*)
Translated by Samil Bestoy
Ataol Yayinlari, Istanbul, 1991

Lenin 2, Bütün Iktidar Sovyetlere
(*Lenin 2, All Power to the Soviets*)
Translated by Tarik Kaya and Bernar Kutlug
Z Yayinlari, Istanbul, 1994.

Lenin 3, Kusatilmis Devrim
(*Lenin 3, The Revolution Besieged*)
Translated by Bernar Kutlug
Z Yayinlari, Istanbul, 1996.

"Uluslararasi Sosyalizm Akimi'nin 50 Yili"
Interview with Ahmed Shawki: "Fifty Years of the International Socialism Tendency"
from *International Socialist Review* Summer 1997 [see section I]
Translated by Ronnie Margulies
Enternasyonal Sosyalizm, No 1, September 1997

Rosa Lüksemburg
(*Rosa Luxemburg*)
Translated by Metin Firtina
Z Yayinlari, Istanbul, 1998.

Lenin 4, Bolsevikler ve Dünya Devrimi
(*Lenin 4, The Bolsheviks and World Revolution*)
Translated by Bernar Kutlug
Z Yayinlari, Istanbul, 2001

Ukrainian

Vpered
No 3(12), 1950
T Cliff: "The Class Struggle in Russia" (from *The Nature of Stalinist Russia*).

Vpered
No 7-8 (19-20), 1951
T Cliff: "The imperialist expansion of Russia" (from *The Nature of Stalinist Russia*).

L: Marxism

Recordings of Marxism meetings from 1992 onwards are in the British Library Sound Archive, C 797. Lists for some of the early years may be incomplete.

1977
Bolshevism, Menshevism, Lenin, Trotsky, Martov
Lenin as a Philosopher
Portugal and the Revolutions of the West

1978
Building an International

1979
Luxemburg
Labour in Irish History
Spain
Deutscher

1980
When they were all Social Democrats
Labour in Irish History
Luxemburg
Rise of Russian Revolutionary Movement
The Struggle Against British Imperialism 1917-1947
Spanish Civil War
Balance Sheet of the Fight Against the Tories

1981
The English Suffragettes
Russian Revolution
The Working Class Family

1982
The Pentonville Five – Ten Years On [with Micky Fenn]
The Women's Movement in the last 15 Years
Zionism
Socialism Today, Building in the Downturn

1983
Rebuilding Shop Stewards' Organisation
What Next After the Election?
Lenin and the Party
Party and Class in the Russian Revolution
Student Forum
The Rise and Fall of Bennism
Syndicalism and the Working Class
Zionism and the Middle East

Marx 100 Years On

1984
The Class Struggle today
Women's Liberation and the Class Struggle
The General Strike and the Lessons of 1926
The Russian Revolution
Deflected Permanent Revolution
SWP: Tactics and Strategy Today (Forum)

1985
Changing Balance of Class Forces 1945-1985
The Revolutionary Party
Zionism
The General Strike
The Revolution (Russian)
Reform or Revolution? (Rally)

1986
Marxism and the Trade Union Struggle
Lenin and the Revolutionary Party
Socialist Question Time [with Chris Harman and Sheila McGregor]
Cripps, Bevan and Benn – Leaders of the Labour Left
The Socialist Alternative (Rally)

1987
Elections 87 – Lessons for Socialists
Lessons of October
1951-67 – Building in the Boom
The Accumulation of Capital (Luxemburg)
The Working Class and the Oppressed
The Case for a Socialist Alternative (Rally)

1988
Revolutionaries and the Class Struggle Today
State Capitalism
Permanent Revolution
Lenin, Trotsky, Luxemburg and the Party
The Revolutionary Road to Socialism (Rally)

1989
Where Our Politics Come From [SWP]
Trotsky and the Russian Revolution
Trotsky and the Red Army
The Crisis of Labourism
The Foundation of Mao's China
Reform or Revolution? (Rally).

1990
State Capitalism
How do we Build the Revolutionary Party?
50 Years Since Trotsky's Assassination – a Commemoration
International Forum
Socialism into the 1990s (Rally)

1991
State Capitalism
Trotsky and the Fourth International
Revolutionaries and the Class Struggle Today
Can Socialism Come Through Parliament?
Lenin and the Party
Build the Socialist Alternative (Rally)

1992
The Class Struggle in the 90s.
State Capitalism
The Legacy of Trotsky
Marxism and Oppression
Spain 1936
Stopping the Nazis Today (Forum)
Build the Socialist Alternative (Rally)

1993
The New Militancy
The Changing Nature of Labourism
Trotsky's Fight Against Stalinism
State Capitalism
The Working Class and the Oppressed
Final Rally

1994
Build the Resistance. Opening Rally
Marxism and the Oppressed
Prospects for Building the SWP Today
Trotsky's Fight for Internationalism

The Theory of State Capitalism
What is the Revolutionary Party?

1995
Engels: Centenary of a Revolutionary [W1]
The Revolutionary Party
The Theory of State Capitalism
Why do Workers Look to Blair?
Marxism and Oppression
Final Rally

1996
The Relevance of Marxism
Can Blair deliver?
Lenin and the Party
Final Rally

1997
Socialists under Blair
What are Rank and File Politics? (Trade Unions)
State Capitalism
Lenin on Revolutionary Strategy and Tactics
Could Trotsky have won?
Final Rally

1998
Israel: Fifty Years of the Zionist state
The International Socialist Tradition
Globalisation: Fact and Fiction
James Connolly and the Limits of Syndicalism
Final Rally

1999
State Capitalism
Deflected Permanent Revolution
The Permanent Arms Economy
Final Rally

M: Compilations

Volumes of Cliff's writings

Neither Washington nor Moscow, (introduction by D Hallas), Bookmarks, 1982
pp11-23: The Middle East at the crossroads (*Fourth International*, December 1945)
pp24-39: All that glitters is not gold (RCP Internal Document, September 1947)
pp40-85: On the class nature of the people's democracies (Duplicated document July 1950)
pp86-100: The theory of bureaucratic collectivism: A critique (Duplicated document 1948)
pp101-07: Perspectives for the permanent war economy. (SR1 March 1957)
pp108-17: Economic roots of reformism (SR1 June 1957)
pp118-34: The future of the Russian empire: Reform or revolution? (SR1 December 1956)
pp135-42: Mao Tse-Tung and Stalin (SR1 April 1957)
pp143-65: Crisis in China (IS1 29)
pp166-91: The end of the road: Deutscher's capitulation to Stalinism (IS1 15)
pp192-209: Trotsky on substitutionism (IS1 2)
pp210-14: Labour's addiction to the rubber stamp (LW January 1967)
pp215-17: Notes on democratic centralism (IS internal document June 1968)
pp218-38: On perspectives: the class struggle in Britain (Harris and Palmer (eds.) *World Crisis*, and not, as stated in volume, IS1 36)
pp239-45: After Pentonville: the battle is won but the war goes on (SW 5 August 1972)
pp245-49: 1972: A tremendous year for the workers (SW 6 January 1973)
pp249-52: The use of Socialist Worker as an organiser (International Socialists Internal Bulletin April 1974)
pp253-56: Lenin: His ideas are the future (SW 2 February 1974)
pp257-59: The great incomes policy con-trick (SW 21 December 1974)
pp260-73: Portugal: the lessons of the 25th November (pamphlet 1975, written with Chris Harman)

pp274-77: Why we need a socialist workers party (SW 8 January 1977)
pp278-79: Why socialists must support gays (SW 26 August 1978)
pp279-83: Ten years on: 1969 to 1979 (SW 26 May 1979)

Selected Writings Volume 1: *International Struggle and the Marxist Tradition*, Bookmarks, 2001
pp7-25: The Palestine Question (New International October, November 1938, June 1939)
pp27-41: Industry and banking in Egypt (Part three, chapter eight, from unpublished book *Imperialism and the Arab East*)
pp43-51: The Struggle in the Middle East (from edited and shortened version of 1967 pamphlet in SR2 October 1990)
pp53-57: The Jews, Israel and the Holocaust (SR2 May 1998)
pp59-116: Rosa Luxemburg (1959 and 1969; main variants between two editions given)
pp117-32: Trotsky on Substitutionism (IS1 2)
pp133-42: Engels (Marxism 1995)
pp143-57: Belgium: strike to revolution? (IS1 4)
pp159-217: [Tony Cliff and Ian Birchall] France - the struggle goes on (1968)
pp219-310: Portugal at the Crossroads (IS1 81-2)
pp311-26: Revolution and counter-revolution: lessons for Indonesia (IS2 80)

Selected Writings Volume 2: *In the Thick of Workers' Struggle*, Bookmarks 2002
pp1-22: The Labour Party in perspective (IS1 9)
pp23-122: [Tony Cliff and Colin Barker]: Incomes policy, legislation and shop stewards (1966)
pp123-28: Labour's addiction to the rubber stamp (LW January 1967)
pp129-44: On perspectives (IS1 36)

pp145-328: The employers' offensive (1970)
pp329-34: After Pentonville: the battle is won but the war goes on (SW 5 August 1972)
pp335-38: 1972: a tremendous year for the workers (SW 6 January 1973)
pp339-68: Factory branches (International Socialists internal pamphlet)
pp369-72: Ten years on: 1969 to 1979 (SW 26 May 1979)
pp373-422: The balance of class forces in recent years (IS2 6)
pp423-30: The state of the struggle today (SR2 April 1986)
pp431-36: In the balance (SR2 February 1995)
pp437-42: Change is going to come: but how? (SR2 June 1997)

Selected Writings Volume 3: *Marxist Theory After Trotsky*, Bookmarks 2003
pp1-138: The nature of Stalinist Russia (RCP Internal Bulletin, June 1948)
pp139-154: All that glitters is not gold (RCP internal document, September 1947)
pp155-168: The theory of bureaucratic collectivism: a critique (IS1 32 – a considerably revised version of the original 1948 document)
pp169-176: Perspectives for the permanent war economy (SR1 May 1957)
pp177-186: Economic roots of reformism (SR1 June 1957)
pp187-202: Permanent revolution (IS1 12)
pp203-210: Mao Tse-Tung and Stalin (SR1 April 1957)
pp211-232: Crisis in China (IS1 29)
pp233-260: Marxism and the collectivisation of agriculture (IS1 19)
pp261-267: Earthquake in the East (SR2 December 1989)
pp269-272: Balance of powerlessness (SR2 September 1991)
pp273-292: The family: haven in a heartless world? (chapter 14 (pp205-

223 of *Class Struggle and Women's Liberation*)
pp293-294: Why socialists must support the gays (SW 26 August 1978)
pp295-310: Lecture notes on Marxist theory (revised and updated version of NCLC pamphlet from early sixties)

Anthologies of SWP publications

A Socialist Review, J Higgins (intro), International Socialism [1965]
pp34-40: Perspectives of the Permanent War Economy
SR1 May 1957
pp48-58: Economic Roots of Reformism
SR1 June 1957
pp75-82: Background to Middle East Crisis
SR1 August 1958
pp191-98: The Nature of State Capitalism
SR1 March 1957
pp199-215: The Future of the Russian Empire: Reform or Revolution?
SR1 December 1956
pp222-28: Background to Hungary
SR1 1 July 1958
pp228-35: Mao Tse-Tung and Stalinism
SR1 April 1957
pp236-41: China: The Hundred Flowers Wilt
SR1 Mid-May 1959
pp241-48: The 22nd. Congress
SR1 November 1961
pp296-300: Plekhanov: The Father of Russian Marxism
SR1 January 1957
pp312-16: Background to the French Crisis
SR1 1 June 1958
pp316-26: The Belgian General Strike
SR1 February 1961

In the Heat of the Struggle, C Harman (ed), Bookmarks 1993
p91: 2000 strike to back higher pensions
SW 2 December 1972

p128: Lessons for the revolution
SW 29 June 1974
pp181-2: Ten years on
SW 26 May 1979 [This is an edited and abridged version]
p277: Class struggle in the 90s
SW 18 July 1992

A Socialist Review, Lindsey German and Rob Hoveman (eds), Bookmarks 1998
pp15-28: Fifty five years a revolutionary
SR2 July 1987
pp46-53: Earthquake in the East
SR2 December 1989

Notes

INTRODUCTION
1. See the comprehensive account of the debate in M van der Linden, *Western Marxism and the Soviet Union*, Leiden, 2007.
2. T Cliff, "Marxism and the Collectivisation of Agriculture", *International Socialism* 19 (Winter 1964-65).
3. L Trotsky, *My Life*, London, 1930; I Deutscher, *Stalin*, London, 1949, *The Prophet Armed*, New York, 1954, *The Prophet Unarmed*, New York, 1959, *The Prophet Outcast*, New York, 1963; P Broué, *Trotsky*, Paris, 1988; J-J Marie, *Staline*, Paris, 2001, *Lénine*, Paris, 2004, *Trotsky*, Paris, 2006.
4. K Marx, "Comments on Latest Prussian Censorship Instruction", in K Marx and F Engels, *Collected Works*, London and Moscow, 1975-2005, vol 1, p112.
5. V Serge, *Birth of Our Power*, Harmondsworth, 1970, p157.
6. L Trotsky, *The History of the Russian Revolution*, London, 1997, p20.
7. T Cliff, "Engels", in T Cliff, *Selected Writings* vol 1: *International Struggle and the Marxist Tradition*, London, 2001, pp117-32 (pp140-41).
8. The papers are now available in the Tony Cliff Archive, Modern Records Centre, University of Warwick.
9. See A Machon, *Spies, Lies and Whistleblowers*, Lewes, 2005, p39.
10. I Birchall, *The Spectre of Babeuf*, Basingstoke, 1997, *Sartre Against Stalinism*, New York and Oxford, 2004.
11. Cliff, "Engels", p135.

CHAPTER 1
1. Naomi Gunn interview, April 2005.
2. Y Sarneh, "A Revolutionary Life", *International Socialism* 87 (Summer 2000), p140.
3. S Schama, *Two Rothschilds and the Land of Israel*, London, 1978, pp68, 71, 121, 153.
4. Schama, *Two Rothschilds*, p131.
5. H Halkin, *A Strange Death*, London, 2006, p30.
6. Note in Stan Newens archive.
7. Halkin, *A Strange Death*, p29.
8. T Cliff, *A World to Win*, London, 2000, p5.
9. *The Letters and Papers of Chaim Weizmann*, London, 1968ff, vol 1, p426.
10. R Tourret, *Hedjaz Railway*, Abingdon, 1989.
11. Naomi Gunn interview, April 2005.
12. Mary Phillips interview, June 2005.
13. Cliff, "Engels", p136.
14. Naomi Gunn interview, April 2005.
15. Anna Gluckstein interview, October 2008.
16. Mickey Loeb interview, July 2005.
17. Cliff, *A World to Win*, p6.
18. Mary Phillips interview, June 2005.
19. T Segev, *One Palestine, Complete*, London, 2000, in particular pp5, 9, 158.
20. N Nardi, *Education in Palestine 1920-1945*, Washington DC, 1945, p144.
21. R Kramer, *Maria Montessori*, London, 1989.
22. Communication from Donny Gluckstein, July 2003.
23. Hanna Ben Dov interview, June 2005.
24. Nardi, *Education in Palestine*, pp35-8.
25. Cliff, *A World to Win*, p6.
26. A Koestler, *Arrow in the Blue*, London, 1952, pp126, 137.

27 Naomi Gunn interview, April 2005.
28 E Hobsbawm, *Interesting Times*, London, 2002, pp15, 21.
29 FL Carsten, *The First Austrian Republic 1918-1938*, Aldershot, 1986, pp46-7, 72.
30 V Serge, *Witness to the German Revolution*, London, 2000, pp4-5.
31 Cliff, *A World to Win*, p16.
32 D Carpi and G Yogev, *Zionism*, Tel Aviv, 1975, pp161-4.
33 Mickey Loeb interview, July 2005.
34 Chanie Rosenberg interview, December 2003.
35 Danny Gluckstein interview, January 2009.
36 Communication from Anna Gluckstein, June 2009.
37 Nardi, *Education in Palestine*, p44.
38 Cliff, *A World to Win*, p4.
39 J Rees, "Tony Cliff: Theory and Practice", *International Socialism* 87 (Summer 2000), p134; VI Lenin, *Collected Works*, Moscow, 1960ff, vol 24, p45.
40 E.g. Y Gluckstein, *Stalin's Satellites in Europe*, London, 1952, p265.
41 "Influences", *New Statesman and Society*, 16 September 1994, p13.
42 Letter to Margaret Harkness, April 1888, in Marx and Engels, *Collected Works*, vol 48, p168.
43 H Heine, *Selected Prose*, Harmondsworth, 1993, p270.
44 H Heine, *Complete Poems*, Boston, 1982, p544.
45 Heine, *Complete Poems*, p398.
46 T Cliff, *Trotsky* vol 3: *Fighting the Rising Stalinist Bureaucracy 1923-1927*, London, 1991, pp9, 98-123.
47 T Cliff, "Crisis in China", *International Socialism* 29 (Summer 1967).
48 Thanks to Leon Yudkin for advice on this point.
49 *Numbers*, chapters 13 and 14, in particular chapter 13 verse 7.
50 Schama, *Two Rothschilds*, pp167-70, 255.
51 Segev, *One Palestine, Complete*, pp276-7.
52 Cliff, *A World to Win*, p7.
53 F Kafka, *Wedding Preparations in the Country*, Harmondsworth, 1978, pp37-8.
54 J-P Sartre, *Les Mots*, Paris, 1964, p66.
55 Koestler, *Arrow in the Blue*, p105.
56 Cliff, *A World to Win*, pp6-7.
57 Naomi Gunn interview, April 2005.
58 I Deutscher, *The Non-Jewish Jew*, London, 1968, p51.
59 Cliff, *A World to Win*, p7.

CHAPTER 2
1 T Cliff, *Lenin* vol 1: *Building the Party*, London, 1975, p7.
2 Cliff, *A World to Win*, p17.
3 See A Rosmer, *Lenin's Moscow*, London, 1987, pp101-4.
4 P Broué, *Histoire de l'internationale communiste*, Paris, 1997, pp181-2.
5 Quoted in I Spector, *The Soviet Union and the Muslim World 1917-1958*, Seattle, 1959, p292.
6 Broué, *Histoire de l'internationale communiste*, p271; J Degras (ed), *The Communist International 1919-1943*, vol 1, London, 1971, pp365-6.
7 Broué, *Histoire de l'internationale communiste*, p510.
8 Quoted in Spector, *The Soviet Union and the Muslim World*, p156.
9 WZ Laqueur, *Communism and Nationalism in the Middle East*, London, 1956, p88.
10 M Budeiri, *The Palestine Communist Party 1919-1948*, London, 1979, pp37, 78, 97, 115.
11 DH Nahas, *The Israeli Communist Party*, London, 1976, p20.
12 Budeiri, *The Palestine Communist Party*, p7.
13 Broué, *Histoire de l'internationale communiste*, p727; J Berger, *Shipwreck of a Generation*, London, 1971.
14 Laqueur, *Communism and

  Nationalism in the Middle East, p99.
15 Budeiri, *The Palestine Communist Party*, p73.
16 Cliff, *A World to Win*, p15.
17 Y Sarneh, "A Revolutionary Life", *International Socialism* 87 (Summer 2000), p143.
18 Alex Callinicos interview, July 2008.
19 Cliff, *A World to Win*, p15.
20 Sarneh, "A Revolutionary Life", p142.
21 Sarneh, "A Revolutionary Life", pp142-3.
22 SWP Internal Bulletin 6 [1978], p4: T Cliff and Jack Robertson, "The Future of *Socialist Worker*".
23 Y Schwartz, "Arab-Jewish workers' joint struggles prior to the partition of Palestine", Part 1, http://www.marxist.com/MiddleEast/arab_jewish_struggles1.html
24 Communication from Moshé Machover, June 2007.
25 Cliff, *A World to Win*, p18.
26 Cliff, *A World to Win*, p23.
27 Author's recollection.
28 Hanna Ben Dov interview, June 2005.
29 Cliff, *A World to Win*, p26.
30 Chanie Rosenberg interview, July 2007.
31 See D Renton, "Bread and Freedom: British Soldiers and Egyptian Trotskyism", http://www.dkrenton.co.uk/research/egypt.html
32 Hanna Ben Dov interview, June 2005.
33 Hanna Ben Dov interview, June 2005.
34 Cliff, *A World to Win*, p16.
35 *Ha-Mesheq Ha-Shittufi* [The Cooperative Economy], issue 3(11), 1935, pp183-188. An English translation is available at http://www.marxists.org/archive/cliff/works/1935/xx/egypt.htm

36 Cliff, *A World to Win*, p33.
37 Communication from Moshé Machover, August 2005.
38 Communication from Anne Alexander, July, 2005.
39 Communication from Pete Glatter, August 2005.
40 A Alexander, *Nasser*, London, 2005, pp37-52.
41 Sarneh, "A Revolutionary Life", p143. (Original article not yet located.)
42 T Cliff, *Trotsky* vol 4: *The Darker the Night, the Brighter the Star 1927-1940*, London, 1993, pp176-83.
43 S Bornstein and A Richardson, *Against the Stream*, London, 1986, pp222-8.
44 Bornstein and Richardson, *Against the Stream*, pp183-5.
45 Cliff, *Trotsky* vol 4, p186.
46 W Reisner (ed), *Documents of the Fourth International: The Formative Years (1933-40)*, New York, 1973, p97.
47 Cliff, *Trotsky* vol 4, p183; Reisner (ed), *Documents of the Fourth International*, p307.
48 Cliff, *A World to Win*, p86.
49 J Rose, *The Myths of Zionism*, London, 2004, pp129-31.
50 Cliff, *A World to Win*, pp20-21.
51 L Rock, "Class Politics in Palestine", *New International*, June 1939.
52 Hansard Vol 34, 2058-67, 24 November 1938; cf *La Lutte ouvrière* (Paris), 10 March 1939.
53 Obituary (unsigned), *The Times*, 27 October 1947.
54 Cliff, *A World to Win*, p17.
55 Sarneh, "A Revolutionary Life", p143.
56 Author's recollection.
57 Cliff, *A World to Win*, p23.
58 Interview with Misha of Matzpen in *Permanent Revolution* 1 (Spring 1973).
59 Reisner (ed), *Documents of the*

Fourth International, pp157, 288-9.
60 Reisner (ed), *Documents of the Fourth International*, pp157, 288-9.
61 Reisner (ed), *Documents of the Fourth International*, p149.
62 See B Knei-Paz, *The Social and Political Thought of Leon Trotsky*, Oxford, 1978, pp533-55.
63 "On the Jewish Problem", February 1934.
64 "Thermidor and Anti-Semitism", written February 22, 1937, from *New International*, May 1941.
65 "On the Jewish Problem", February 1934.
66 *Fourth International*, December 1945, p379. (This single-paragraph statement, described as "from the archives of Leon Trotsky" is not included in Trotsky's collected *Writings*.)
67 The two articles, plus a third responding to criticisms, appeared in *New International* October 1938, November 1938 and June 1939. They are reproduced in Cliff, *Selected Writings* vol 1, pp7-25.
68 *New International*, February 1939, pp41-44 (originally published in *The Spark*, November 1938).
69 See also B Hirson, *Revolutions in My Life*, Johannesburg, 1995, p136.
70 *New International*, June 1939, p166.
71 *New International*, June 1939, pp173-6.
72 *New International*, October 1939, pp313-4.
73 Cliff, *A World to Win*, p28; Sarneh, "A Revolutionary Life", p142.
74 See also Segev, *One Palestine, Complete*, pp377-8.
75 Testimony of Chanie Rosenberg at a meeting at Marxism, July 2006, recorded on the CD of the meeting.
76 *La Lutte ouvrière*, 10 March 1939.
77 T Cliff, "The Road from Zionism to Genocide", *Socialist Worker*, 3 July 1982.
78 See Schwartz, "Arab-Jewish workers' joint struggles prior to the partition of Palestine", Parts 1 and 2.
79 *Writings of Leon Trotsky 1938-39*, New York, 1974, pp207-13.
80 Sarneh, "A Revolutionary Life", p144; Naomi Gunn interview, April 2005.
81 Chanie Rosenberg interview, July 2007.
82 *Palestine Post*, 11 September 1939.
83 Chanie Rosenberg interview, July 2007.
84 Cliff, *A World to Win*, pp30-31; Naomi Gunn interview, April 2005.
85 Jakob Moneta interview, March 2005; see also J Moneta, *Mehr Macht für die Ohnmächtigen*, Frankfurt am Main, 1991 and "Jakob Moneta wird 85", *Avanti*, November 1999.
86 Moneta, *Mehr Macht für die Ohnmächtigen*, pp119-20.
87 Moneta interview, March 2005.
88 Cliff, *A World to Win*, p29.
89 T Cliff, "Are the Terrorists Anti-Imperialist?", *Socialist Appeal*, December 1946.
90 Naomi Gunn interview, April 2005.
91 Communication from Anna Gluckstein, March 2010.
92 Reisner (ed), *Documents of the Fourth International*, p306.
93 Rudolf Segall interview, March 2005.
94 Jakob Moneta interview, March 2005.
95 Budeiri, *The Palestine Communist Party*, p133.
96 T Cliff, "Background to the Middle East Crisis ", *Socialist Review*, August 1958, pp7-8, 3.
97 http://www.marxists.org/archive/cliff/works/1943/xx/burnham.html, translated by Moshé Machover; Hebrew original at *Managerial*

Revolution, Tony Cliff Archive, MRC MSS.459/box 10.
98 Dov Shas interview, April 2005; Tuvia Shlonsky interview, April 2005.
99 G Baer, *Fellah and Townsman in the Middle East*, London, 1982.
100 GR Warburg, "In Memoriam Gabriel Baer, 1919-1982", *Asian and African Studies* 15 (1981), pp161-3; "In Memoriam: Professor Gabriel Baer", *International Journal of Middle East Studies*, 15/1 (1983), pp129-130.
101 *International Socialism* 17 (Summer 1964); author's recollection.
102 "Jabra Nicola (1912-1974)", *Intercontinental Press,* 27 January 1975 (translated from *Rouge*, 5 January 1975).
103 Budeiri, *The Palestine Communist Party*, pp67, 277.
104 Cliff, *A World to Win*, p24.
105 M Warschawski, *Sur la Frontière*, Paris, 2002, p45.
106 Cliff, *A World to Win*, p23.
107 *Intercontinental Press*, 27 January 1975; communication from Susi Scheller, October 2006.
108 "Jakob Moneta wird 85", *Avanti,* November 1999.
109 Communication from Moshé Machover, September 2004.
110 Chanie Rosenberg at a meeting at Marxism, July 2006, recorded on the CD of the meeting.
111 E Mandel, *Revolutionary Marxism Today*, London, 1979, pxii.
112 *Socialist Worker*, 25 January 1975.
113 A Brossat and S Klingberg, *Le Yiddishland révolutionnaire*, Paris, 1983, pp309-11; J Moneta, "Jakob Taut (1913-2001)", *Sozialistische Zeitung* 23, 8 November 2001, p15.
114 Brossat and Klingberg, *Le Yiddishland révolutionnaire*, pp317-9.
115 Moneta, "Jakob Taut (1913-2001)".
116 Communication from Susi Scheller, October 2006.
117 Communication from Daniel Gaido, September 2004; communication from Susi Scheller, October 2006.
118 Jean and Danny Tait interview, February 2004; interview by John Charlton with Jean and Danny Tait.
119 This account of the RCL is based on interviews with Danny Tait (see previous note) and Dov Shas (April 2005), and a communication from Susi Scheller (October 2006).
120 M Warshawski, "On the development of Trotskyism in Palestine until the decade of the Sixties", unpublished document.
121 Chanie Rosenberg interview, December 2003.
122 Cliff, *A World to Win*, p27.
123 Cliff, *A World to Win*, p26.
124 Hanna Ben Dov interview, June 2005.
125 Chanie Rosenberg at a meeting at Marxism, July 2006, recorded on the CD of the meeting.
126 Cliff, *A World to Win*, p3.
127 M Warshawski, "On the development of Trotskyism in Palestine until the decade of the Sixties".
128 T Cliff, "On the Irresponsible Handling of the Palestine Question", Revolutionary Communist Party Internal Bulletin, [no date but early 1947]. (Thanks to Mike Pearn for locating this item.) http://www.marxists.org/archive/cliff/works/1947/xx/palestine.htm
129 As reported by Dov Shas – communication from Daniel Gaido, September 2004.
130 Schwartz, "Arab-Jewish workers' joint struggles prior to the partition of Palestine", Part 2.
131 "The Fight for Trotskyism in

Palestine", *The Internationalist*, Summer 2001.
132 Schwartz, "Arab-Jewish workers' joint struggles prior to the partition of Palestine", Part 2.
133 Hirson, *Revolutions in My Life*, pp112-4, 123, 132-3, 155-6.
134 C Rosenberg, "The Time of My Life", *Socialist Review*, April 1992, p24.
135 Cliff, *A World to Win*, pp13-14.
136 Chanie Rosenberg interview, July 2007.
137 Tuvia Shlonsky interview, April 2005.
138 Tuvia Shlonsky interview, April 2005.
139 Jean and Danny Tait interview, February 2004.
140 Mickey Loeb interview, July 2005.
141 Danny Gluckstein interview, January 2009.
142 Mickey Loeb interview, July 2005.
143 Mickey Loeb interview, July 2005.
144 Tuvia Shlonsky interview, April 2005.
145 Chanie Rosenberg interview, July 2007.
146 J Newsinger, *The Blood Never Dried*, London, 2006, pp139-40.
147 See Rose, *The Myths of Zionism*, pp135-53.
148 T Cliff, "The Jews, Israel and the Holocaust", *Socialist Review*, May 1998, p21.
149 *Workers International News*, vol 5, no 7 (December 1944), pp4-11.
150 H Dalton, *The Fateful Years*, London, 1957, pp425-7, 431-2.
151 Jean and Danny Tait interview, February 2004; interview by John Charlton with Jean and Danny Tait.
152 *Fourth International*, December 1945, January 1946, February 1946; *Workers International News*, December 1945, January and February 1946; *Middle East at the Cross Roads*, Workers International News Pamphlet, London, 1946; *Quatrième Internationale*, August-September 1946, October-November 1946, December 1946.
153 Sarneh, "A Revolutionary Life", p144.
154 Chanie Rosenberg interview, July 2007.
155 Quoted in "Manager's Column", *Fourth International*, February 1946.
156 "Manager's Column", *Fourth International*, March 1946.
157 Albert Gates (pseudonym of Glotzer), "The Meaning of Self-Determination: A Reply to Leon Shields", *New International*, August 1946.
158 Cliff, "A New British Provocation in Palestine", *Fourth International*, September 1946.
159 Cliff, "On the Irresponsible Handling of the Palestine Question", Revolutionary Communist Party Internal Bulletin.
160 *Middle East* – drafts of book, Tony Cliff Archive, MRC MSS.459/box 6. The Hebrew original was completed in July 1945, but was updated during the process of translation into English. The manuscript is dated May 1946.
161 *Middle East* – drafts of book, pi.
162 *Middle East* – drafts of book, pp1, 5.
163 *Middle East* – drafts of book, p27.
164 *Middle East* – drafts of book, pi.
165 *Middle East* – drafts of book, pp39-43.
166 *Middle East* – drafts of book, pp195, 120.
167 A Callinicos, "Introduction" to T Cliff, *Selected Writings* vol 1, pp1-2.
168 *Middle East* – drafts of book, p175.
169 *Middle East* – drafts of book, pp164, 97.
170 *Middle East* – drafts of book, p49.
171 *Middle East* – drafts of book,

pp203-4.
172 *Middle East – drafts of book* pp 210ff, i.
173 Cliff, *A World to Win*, p26.
174 PM Buhle, *A Dreamer's Paradise Lost*, New Jersey, 1995, p119.
175 T Cliff, "Fifty-Five Years a Revolutionary", *Socialist Review*, July-August 1987.
176 Moneta, *Mehr Macht für die Ohnmächtigen*, p121.
177 Cliff, *A World to Win*, pp34-5.
178 "Against the stream", *Fourth International*, May 1948, p88.
179 Cliff, *Trotsky* vol 4, p306.

CHAPTER 3
1 Chanie Rosenberg interview, July 2007.
2 Chanie Rosenberg interview, July 2007.
3 Passport at MRC MSS 459/6/1.
4 Chanie Rosenberg interview, July 2007.
5 Cliff, "Fifty-Five Years a Revolutionary".
6 Terry Conway, obituary of Charlie Van Gelderen at http://www.geocities.com/youth4sa/charlie.html
7 Chanie Rosenberg interview, July 2007.
8 File on Charles van Gelderen, NA KV2/2177.
9 Interview by Dave Renton with Chanie Rosenberg, October 1996.
10 Chanie Rosenberg interview, July 2007.
11 Sheila Leslie interview, January 2004.
12 Chanie Rosenberg interview, July 2007.
13 Chanie Rosenberg interview, March 2009.
14 L Trotsky, "The Workers' State, Thermidor and Bonapartism" (1935), *Writings (1934-35)*, New York, 1971, pp181-82.
15 L Trotsky, *Writings (1939-40)*, New York, 1973, p43.
16 See Broué, *Histoire de l'internationale communiste*, p351.
17 P Broué and R Vacheron, *Meurtres au Maquis*, Paris, 1997.
18 T Cliff, *Trotskyism after Trotsky*, London, 1999, p14.
19 S Bornstein and A Richardson, *War and the International*, London, 1986, pp97-159.
20 RCP Conference Documents 1947, quoted in Bornstein and Richardson, *War and the International*, p207.
21 Bornstein and Richardson, *War and the International*, pp178-9, 189.
22 See Bornstein and Richardson, *War and the International*, p33.
23 Bornstein and Richardson, *War and the International*, p188.
24 Jean and Danny Tait interview, February 2004.
25 Cliff, *A World to Win*, p50.
26 R Challinor, "Tony Cliff's Early Years in Britain", *Revolutionary History* 7/4 (2000), p185.
27 Chanie Rosenberg interview, July 2007.
28 Cliff, *A World to Win*, p51.
29 *Socialist Appeal*, January 1947, pp1-4.
30 *Fourth International*, April 1947, pp114-17.
31 *Workers International News*, January-February 1947, pp27-32.
32 RCP Internal Document, September 1947.
33 RCP Internal Bulletin, September 1947, quoted in Bornstein and Richardson, *War and the International*, p190.
34 "The Economic Breakdown of Great Britain", *Fourth International*, March 1947, p70.
35 M Kidron, "Imperialism – Highest Stage but One", *International Socialism* 9 (Summer 1962).
36 T Cliff, "The United States in World Economy: The Basis of the Marshall Plan", *Worker*

International News, 7/3 (October 1947).
37 See Cliff, *Trotsky*, vol 4, pp299-300.
38 Charlie van Gelderen in *Socialist Outlook*, May 2000.
39 J Haston, "The Dual Character Of The USSR", RCP Conference Documents, 1946.
40 Bornstein and Richardson, *War and the International*, pp182-7.
41 T Grant, *History of British Trotskyism*, London, 2002, p144.
42 T Cliff, "What is Happening in Stalinist Russia?", six-part series in *Socialist Appeal*, February-July 1947.
43 Cliff, *A World to Win*, p42.
44 T Cliff, "50 Years of the International Socialist Tradition", *International Socialist Review* 1 (Summer 1997).
45 Tony Cliff interviewed, "Sell the Paper! Build the Party!", *The Leveller*, no 30, September 1979, pp20-21.
46 Marx and Engels, *Collected Works*, vol 25, p266.
47 W E Walling, *Socialism As It Is*, New York, 1912, pp44-45.
48 Van der Linden, *Western Marxism*, pp12-20.
49 Van der Linden, *Western Marxism*, p47; E Farl, "The State Capitalist Genealogy", *International*, vol 2, no 1 (Spring 1973).
50 See Van der Linden, *Western Marxism*, pp54, 69; Farl, "The State Capitalist Genealogy"; D Bell, *The End of Ideology*, New York and London, 1965, p429.
51 Van der Linden, *Western Marxism*, pp36-41.
52 R Barltrop, *The Monument*, London, 1975, pp61-68.
53 Quoted in RV Daniels, *The Conscience of the Revolution*, Boulder and London, 1988, pp85-86.
54 Van der Linden, *Western Marxism*, p50.
55 See T Cliff, *Lenin* vol 3: *Revolution Besieged*, London, 1978, pp69-71.
56 Daniels, *The Conscience of the Revolution*, pp255, 261.
57 J-F Fayet, *Karl Radek (1885-1939)*, Bern, 2004, p620.
58 P Broué, *Communistes contre Staline*, Paris, 2003, pp71, 179.
59 Daniels, *The Conscience of the Revolution*, p87.
60 Broué, *Communistes contre Staline*, p71.
61 Van der Linden, *Western Marxism*, pp51-52.
62 V Serge, *The Case of Comrade Tulayev*, London, 1993, p80.
63 P Flewers, *The New Civilisation?*, London n.d. [2008], pp144, 251.
64 L Laurat, *L'Économie soviétique*, Paris, 1931, p178; van der Linden, *Western Marxism*, pp69-73.
65 Y Craipeau, *Le Mouvement trotskyste en France*, Paris, 1971, p196.
66 L Trotsky, "Once Again: the USSR and its Defense", in *Writings of Leon Trotsky 1937-38*, New York, 1976, pp34-46; Y Craipeau, "La Quatrième Internationale et la Contre-Révolution Russe", *Quatrième Internationale*, June 1938, pp81-5.
67 Van der Linden, *Western Marxism*, pp74-90.
68 Van der Linden, *Western Marxism*, pp57-60.
69 Van der Linden, *Western Marxism*, pp122-26; A Bordiga, *Russie et révolution dans la théorie marxiste*, Paris, 1978.
70 Van der Linden, *Western Marxism*, pp108-110; G Munis, *Les révolutionnaires devant la Russie et le stalinisme mondial*, Mexico DF, 1946, especially p42.
71 "Natalia Trotsky Breaks with the Fourth International", *The Fourth International, Stalinism and the Origins of the International*

     Socialists, London, 1971, pp101-4.
72 B Péret and G Munis, *Les syndicats contre la révolution*, Paris, 1968, pp51-2, 82.
73 Freddie James (Dunayevskaya), "The Union of Soviet Socialist Republics is a Capitalist Society", Internal Discussion Bulletin of the Workers Party, March 1941.
74 F Forest (Dunayevskaya), "An Analysis of Russian Economy", *New International*, December 1942, January and February 1943.
75 R Dunayevskaya, "A New Revision of Marxian Economics", *American Economic Review*, 34/3 (September 1944).
76 R Dunayevskaya, "The Nature of the Russian Economy", *New International*, December 1946/January 1947.
77 CLR James, *State Capitalism and World Revolution*, Chicago 1986 (first published 1950).
78 James, 1984 Foreword to *State Capitalism*, pvii.
79 James, *State Capitalism*, pp41, 113.
80 Letters dated 25 July to 7 August 1947, made available by the Raya Dunayevskaya Collection at the Wayne State University Archives of Labour and Urban Affairs in Detroit.
81 R Dunayevskaya, letter to Ray Challinor, 8 June 1976, quoted in JD Young, *The World of CLR James*, Glasgow, 1999, p213.
82 Raya Dunayevskaya to Sheila Rowbotham, 29 June 1978, Women's Library, Rowbotham correspondence, 7SHR/A/6 – Box 2.
83 R Dunayevskaya, Introduction to the Second Edition, *Marxism and Freedom*, New York, 1964, p13.
84 T Cliff, *Selected Writings* vol 3: *Marxist Theory After Trotsky*, London, 2003, pp94, 136.
85 SRG NC minutes 2-23 September 1951, 23-24 February 1952, MRC MSS 75/1/1/1.
86 R Dunayevskaya, *Marxism and Freedom*, New York, 1958.
87 Author's recollection.
88 R Dunayevskaya, "Marxism and 'the party'" (letter of 4 September 1980), *News and Letters*, April 1998.
89 GL Boggs, *Living for Change*, Minneapolis, 1998, pp100-103.
90 Sheila Leslie interview, January 2004.
91 Chanie Rosenberg interview, July 2007.
92 *The Times*, 27 October 1947.
93 Chanie Rosenberg interview, March 2009.
94 Aliens Order 1935 Certificate of Registration, MRC MSS 459/6/2.
95 Chanie Rosenberg interview, July 2007.
96 Cliff, *A World to Win*, p53.
97 Chanie Rosenberg interview, July 2007.
98 Chanie Rosenberg interview, December 2003.
99 Aliens Order 1935 Certificate of Registration, MRC MSS 459/6/2.
100 Interview by Dave Renton with Chanie Rosenberg, October 1996; see also Bornstein and Richardson, *War and the International*, p201 and D Renton, *This Rough Game*, Stroud, 2001, pp168-80.
101 Chanie Rosenberg interview, December 2003.
102 Communication from Anna Gluckstein 27 June 2009.
103 MRC MSS 459/3/21.
104 Cliff, *A World to Win*, p55.
105 Cliff, *Selected Writings* vol 3, p2.
106 Cliff, *Trotskyism after Trotsky*, p37.
107 Cliff, *Selected Writings* vol 3, p5.
108 Cliff, *Selected Writings* vol 3, pp62, 105-7.
109 Cliff, *Selected Writings* vol 3, pp83-4.
110 Cliff, *Selected Writings* vol 3,

pp25, 90-91.
111 Cliff, *Selected Writings* vol 3, pp24, 43, 79, 122.
112 Cliff, *Selected Writings* vol 3, p48.
113 Cliff, *Selected Writings* vol 3, p16.
114 K Marx and F Engels, *Collected Works*, vol 6, p486.
115 Cliff, *Selected Writings* vol 3, pp94-5.
116 Cliff, *Selected Writings* vol 3, pp91-2, 110-13.
117 Cliff, *Selected Writings* vol 3, p59.
118 Cliff, *Selected Writings* vol 3, pp60-61.
119 Cliff, *Selected Writings* vol 3, pp129-30.
120 Cliff, *Selected Writings* vol 3, p2.
121 K Tarbuck, *Ever Hopeful – Never Sure: Reminiscences of a Some-time Trotskyist*, 1995, chapter 6 at http://www.revolutionaryhistory.co.uk/autobiography-of-ken-tarbuck-to-1964.html. Quoted by kind permission of Marion Tarbuck.
122 Sheila Leslie interview, January 2004.
123 See *Revolutionary History* 7/3 (2000), pp164-5.
124 *Socialisme ou Barbarie* 4, October-December 1949, p93.
125 Rich. MS 1117/box 211/file 3.
126 *Socialist Review* 6 (November-December 1951).
127 See C Ford, "Socialism, Stalinism and National Liberation: Coming to Terms with a Changed World, The Ideas of the URDP (*Vpered* Group) in the Post-War Era", *Debatte: Journal of Contemporary Central and Eastern Europe*, 14:2 (2006), pp119-143. (Thanks to Chris Ford for drawing this material to my attention.)
128 *Vpered* 3 (12), 1950 and 7-8 (19-20), 1951.
129 Vs Felix, "In the Mirror of Stalin's Parliament", *Socialist Review* vol 1, no 1 (November 1950).
130 T Cliff, *Stalinist Russia: A Marxist Analysis*, London, 1955, p230.
131 Socialist Worker International Fund Appeal [c1991]; Cliff, *A World to Win*, p201.
132 English translation, New York and London, 1957.
133 Author's recollection.
134 Email from Dr Aleksa Djilas to Dragan Plavšić, June 2005.
135 Joel Geier interview, March 2009.
136 T Grant, "Against the Theory of State Capitalism", *The Unbroken Thread*, London, 1989, pp197-246. Originally published as two pamphlets: E Grant, *Against the theory of State Capitalism, In answer to Cliff* [n.d.] and T Grant, *The Marxist Theory of the State as applied to the Stalinist states: reply to Cliff*, August 1949.
137 Grant, "Against the Theory of State Capitalism", p210.
138 Grant, "Against the Theory of State Capitalism", pp199, 242.
139 Grant, "Against the Theory of State Capitalism", pp231, 244.
140 Grant, "Against the Theory of State Capitalism", pp234, 245.
141 Bornstein and Richardson, *War and the International*, pp194-6.
142 See C Harman, *Bureaucracy and Revolution in Eastern Europe*, London, 1974, pp46-48
143 *Socialist Appeal*, March 1948.
144 R Prager (ed), *Les Congrès de la IVe Internationale*, tome 3, Montreuil, 1988.
145 Bornstein and Richardson, *War and the International*, pp218-21.
146 Sheila Leslie interview, January 2004.
147 Bornstein and Richardson, *War and the International*, pp226-30.
148 T Grant, *History of British Trotskyism*, London, 2002, p195.
149 Bornstein and Richardson, *War and the International*, p230.
150 Annual Congress of the Revolutionary Communist Party,

NA HO 45/25486.
151 M Milotte, *Communism in Modern Ireland*, Dublin, 1984, pp218-19.
152 A Sheehy-Skeffington, *Skeff: The Life of Owen Sheehy-Skeffington 1909-1970*, Dublin, 1991, pp137-38.
153 The fullest account of the early years of Irish Trotskyism is C Crossey and J Monaghan, "The Origins of Trotskyism in Ireland", *Revolutionary History*, 6/2-3 (1996), pp4-57. See also Milotte, *Communism in Modern Ireland*, pp188, 213-15.
154 Quoted in Crossey and Monaghan, "The Origins of Trotskyism in Ireland", pp46-47.
155 Sheehy-Skeffington, *Skeff*, p98.
156 Chanie Rosenberg interview, July 2007.
157 Crossey and Monaghan, "The Origins of Trotskyism in Ireland", pp43-44.
158 Sheehy-Skeffington, *Skeff*, pp1, 21.
159 Sheehy-Skeffington, *Skeff*, pp140, 161, 144-45, 104, 251, 94, 95-98.
160 Chanie Rosenberg interview, December 2003.
161 Sheehy-Skeffington, *Skeff*, p101.
162 Gluckstein, *Stalin's Satellites in Europe*, pvi.
163 Undated [1961?] circular from John Phillips, Fancy MS 1171/box 1/4.
164 Communication from Alasdair MacIntyre, January 2004.
165 Sheehy-Skeffington, *Skeff*, p116.
166 Cliff, *A World to Win*, p53.
167 See P Luke (ed), *Enter Certain Players*, Dublin, 1978 and H Hunt, *The Abbey: Ireland's National Theatre 1904-1978*, Dublin, 1979.
168 S O'Casey, *Collected Plays* vol 1, London, 1952, pp197, 203.
169 *New Statesman and Society*, 16 September 1994.
170 *Marxism and the theory of bureaucratic collectivism* (24pp duplicated document – no date [1948], Rich. MS 1117/box 118/file 9). The text published in *International Socialism* 32 (Spring 1968) was a substantially revised version of this.
171 Duplicated document July 1950; reproduced in T Cliff, *Neither Washington nor Moscow*, London, 1982, pp40-85.
172 Cliff, *Neither Washington nor Moscow*, pp65-66.
173 Cliff, *Neither Washington nor Moscow*, pp63-64, quoting Marx and Engels, *Collected Works*, vol 25, p270 (different translation).

CHAPTER 4
1 B Cumings, *The Origins of the Korean War*, Princeton NJ, 1981-1990, vol 2, p621.
2 Cumings, *The Origins of the Korean War*, vol 2, p550.
3 Chanie Rosenberg interview, March 2009.
4 Tarbuck, *Ever Hopeful – Never Sure*, chapter 6.
5 B Pitt, *The Rise and Fall of Gerry Healy*, chapter 2, at http://www.whatnextjournal.co.uk/Pages/Healy/Chap2.html. See also Bornstein and Richardson, *The War and the International*, pp230-2, and John Walters [pseudonym of Ken Tarbuck], "Some Notes on British Trotskyist History", *Marxist Studies* 2/1 (Winter 1969-70).
6 "British Perspectives 1950", internal document of "The Club"; quoted in Bornstein and Richardson, *The War and the International*, p231.
7 Tarbuck, *Ever Hopeful – Never Sure*, chapter 6.
8 Tarbuck, *Ever Hopeful – Never Sure*, chapter 7.
9 Tarbuck, *Ever Hopeful – Never Sure*, chapter 7.
10 Agenda, Rich. MS 1117/box 211/

file 3.
11. Chanie Rosenberg interview, December 2003.
12. Letter from "Jane" [not identified] to Bill Ainsworth, 17 October 1950, Rich. MS 1117/box 211/file 3.
13. NC minutes, MRC MSS 75/1/1/1.
14. Letter from Bill Ainsworth to the International Secretariat, 30 October 1950, Rich. MS 1117/box 211/file 3.
15. Minutes of [Birmingham] branch meeting, 9 October and 27 November 1950, Rich. MS 1117/box 88/file 2.
16. Minutes of [Birmingham] branch meeting, 18 December 1950, Rich. MS 1117/box 88/file 2.
17. MRC MSS 75/3/7/32.
18. *Socialist Review*, November 1950, pp1-7.
19. R Challinor, "Tony Cliff's Early Years in Britain", *Revolutionary History* 7/4 (2000), p186.
20. NC minutes, 29-30 November 1952, Rich. MS1117/box 88/file 2.
21. Cliff, *A World to Win*, p56.
22. NC minutes book, MRC MSS 75/1/1/1.
23. R Challinor, "The Perspective of the long haul", *Workers' Liberty* 21, May 1995.
24. MRC MSS 75/3/7/32.
25. "Statement to all Branches", MRC MSS 75/3/7/28.
26. NC minutes 29-30 November 1952, MRC MSS 75/1/1/1.
27. J Plant, "Marking the Death of Cyril Smith", *Revolutionary History* 10/2 (2010), pp378, 380.
28. NC minutes 17-18 November 1951, MRC MSS 75/1/1/1.
29. NC minutes 29-30 November 1952, MRC MSS 75/1/1/1.
30. Birmingham branch minutes, MRC MSS 75/1/2.
31. NC minutes 22-23 September 1951, MRC MSS 75/1/1/1; NC minutes 23-24 February 1952, MRC MSS 75/1/1/1; MRC MSS 75/3/7/20.
32. NC minutes 23-24 February 1952, MRC MSS 75/1/1/1.
33. Undated letter from K Tarbuck, MRC MSS 75/3/7/16; NC minutes 17-18 November 1951, MRC MSS 75/1/1/1.
34. *La Batalla*, 1 August 1953.
35. N Harris, "Duncan Hallas: Death of a Trotskyist", *Revolutionary History* 8/4 (2004), pp259-72.
36. "An Agitator of the Best Kind", *Socialist Review*, November 2002.
37. D Hallas, "Optimism of the Will", *Socialist Review*, May 2000.
38. D Hallas, "The Stalinist Parties", in D Hallas (ed), *The Fourth International, Stalinism and the Origins of the International Socialists*, London, 1971, pp65-75.
39. *Socialist Review*, May 1951.
40. See R Challinor, "State Capitalism – a New Order", *Left* 140 (June 1948).
41. Bornstein and Richardson, *The War and the International*, p226.
42. J Rosser and C Barker, "A Working Class Defeat: The ENV Story", *International Socialism* 31 (Winter 1967/68).
43. Jean and Danny Tait interview, February 2004; John Charlton interview with Jean and Danny Tait.
44. See letter to Jean Tait, MRC MSS 75/3/7/41.
45. Stan Newens interview, July 2005.
46. Sheila Leslie interview, January 2004.
47. Rich. MS1117/box 88/file2.
48. John Charlton interview with Jean and Danny Tait.
49. NA HO 45/25486.
50. "One Way Only? But Which Way?", *Socialist Review*, April-May 1952.
51. Notes on Foundation Conference, Rich. MS 1117/box 211/file 3.

52 E Hillman, *The Nature of the Stalinist Parties* (May 1951). Rich. MS1117/box 209/file 6.
53 Author's recollection of conversation with Cliff.
54 See A Mason, "Korea: End This 'Liberating'!", *Socialist Review*, December 1952-January 1953.
55 *Socialist Review*, November-December 1951.
56 NC minutes 22-23 September 1951, MRC MSS 75/1/1/1.
57 Naomi Gunn interview, April 2005.
58 Certificate of Registration Aliens Order 1920, MRC MSS 459/6/2.
59 Passports, MRC MSS 459/6/1.
60 Chanie Rosenberg interview, December 2003.
61 Gluckstein, *Stalin's Satellites*, pp41-2.
62 Gluckstein, *Stalin's Satellites*, pp78, 126, 228, 86.
63 Gluckstein, *Stalin's Satellites*, pp105-9, 93.
64 Gluckstein, *Stalin's Satellites*, pp55, 143-50, 206-21.
65 Gluckstein, *Stalin's Satellites*, pp65-6, 242-3.
66 Gluckstein, *Stalin's Satellites*, pp273, 276-7.
67 Gluckstein, *Stalin's Satellites*, p321.
68 M Gayn, "East of Europe", *The Nation*, 16 August 1952.
69 *The Russian Review*, 11/4 (October 1952), pp247-50. (I am grateful to Paul Flewers for providing me with a copy of this.)
70 *Preuves*, November 1953; translated in *International Socialism* 103 (Summer 2004).
71 Tarbuck, *Ever Hopeful – Never Sure*, chapter 7.
72 Y Gluckstein, *Les satellites européens de Staline*, Paris, 1953.
73 Y Gluckstein, *Los Satélites de Rusia en Europa*, Artola, Madrid, 1955.
74 Stan Newens interview, July 2005.
75 Bornstein and Richardson, *The War and the International*, p39.
76 *Stalin: A Political Biography* and *The Prophet Armed: Trotsky 1879-1921*.
77 I Deutscher, *Heretics and Renegades*, London, 1955, p20.
78 NC minutes, 9-10 August 1952, Rich. MS 1117/box 88/file 2.
79 E.g. L Turov, "Yes-Men on Parade", *Socialist Review*, December 1952-January 1953; N Turov, "Recent Russian Developements" [*sic*], *Socialist Review*, October 1953; M Turov, "The Russian Organisation Man", *Socialist Review*, August 1960.
80 L Miguel, "Puerto Rico", *Socialist Review*, April 1954.
81 Sarah Cox interview, July 2005.
82 Jean and Danny Tait interview, February 2004.
83 A Rosmer, "Letters to Stan Newens", *Revolutionary History* 7/4 (2000), pp159-61.
84 Cliff, *A World to Win*, p57.
85 Cliff, *A World to Win*, p57.
86 D Breen, "Soccer for Suckers", *Socialist Review*, January 1954.
87 R Kuper, "Michael Kidron", *The Guardian*, 27 March 2003.
88 Chanie Rosenberg interview, March 2009.
89 Cliff, *A World to Win*, pp56-57.
90 G Thayer, *The British Political Fringe*, London, 1965, p142.
91 M Kidron, "Her Majesty's Humble Petitioners", *Socialist Review*, July 1954.
92 John Phillips interview, July 2005.
93 Author's recollection.
94 Richard Kirkwood interview, October 2008.
95 Geoff Carlsson, "An Open Letter to John Gollan", *Socialist Review*, February 1955.
96 L Turov, "What Lies Behind Malenkov's Moves?", *Socialist Review*, May 1953.
97 Minutes of SR Aggregate, 19

January 1957; letter from Stan Newens to Duncan Hallas, 16 January 1957 [Stan Newens archive].
98 H Draper, "A matter of terminological taste", *Labor Action*, 16 January 1956; reproduced in *Workers' Liberty* 49, September 1998.
99 P Morgan, "Russia with the Lid Off", *Socialist Review*, August 1955.
100 T Cliff, *Russia from Stalin to Khrushchev*, London 1956.
101 Cliff, *Russia from Stalin to Khrushchev*, p5.
102 Cliff, *Russia from Stalin to Khrushchev*, pp9, 11.
103 Cliff, *Russia from Stalin to Khrushchev*, pp16-7, 18.
104 Cliff, *Russia from Stalin to Khrushchev*, p22.
105 P Fryer, *Hungarian Tragedy*. London, 1956, p51.
106 Cliff, *A World to Win*, p64.
107 S Newens, "Memories of a seminal year", *International Socialism* 112 (Autumn 2006), p158.
108 Thanks to Stan Newens for this leaflet from his archives.
109 I Deutscher, "Russia in transition", *Universities and Left Review*, 1/1 (Spring 1957).
110 *Socialist Review*, December 1956.
111 See S Parsons, "Nineteen Fifty-Six", *Revolutionary History*, 9/3 (2006), pp72-83.
112 Stan Newens interview, July 2005.
113 Published by the Nottingham Marxist Group, Stapleford, Notts [March 1957?].
114 Ken Coates interview, October 2008.
115 Y Gluckstein, *Mao's China: Economic and Political Survey*, London, 1957.
116 Author's recollection.
117 Gluckstein, *Mao's China*, pp8, 83-4.
118 Gluckstein, *Mao's China*, p42.
119 Gluckstein, *Mao's China*, p224.
120 Gluckstein, *Mao's China*, pp209-13.
121 Gluckstein, *Mao's China*, pp178, 183.
122 T Cliff, "Permanent Revolution", *International Socialism* 12 (Spring 1963).
123 Gluckstein, *Mao's China*, p422.
124 Gluckstein, *Mao's China*, p415.
125 Notably Ygael Gluckstein, "The Chinese People's Communes", *International Socialism* 1 (Spring 1960); T Cliff, "Crisis in China", *International Socialism* 29 (Summer 1967).
126 Gluckstein, *Mao's China*, p119.
127 Communication from Charlie Hore, September 2006.
128 S de Beauvoir, *The Long March* London, 1958.
129 De Beauvoir, *The Long March*, pp501, 200-01.
130 *Problems of Communism*, 7/4 (July 1958), pp50-53.
131 "Red China Up to Date", *The New Leader*, 23 December 1957. (Thanks to Paul Flewers for this reference.)
132 M Dobb, *Capitalism Yesterday and Today*, London, 1958, p62.
133 P Fryer, *The Battle for Socialism*, London, 1959, pp63, 33.
134 A Crosland, *The Future of Socialism*, London, 1956.
135 K Popper, *Conjectures and Refutations*, London, 1972, pp370-71.
136 *Socialist Review*, May 1957.
137 "International Capitalism", *International Socialism* 20 (Spring 1965); "A Permanent Arms Economy", *International Socialism* 28 (Spring 1967).
138 M Kidron, *Western Capitalism Since the War*, London, 1968; revised edition, Harmondsworth 1970.
139 E.g. van der Linden, *Western*

Marxism and the Soviet Union, pp160-61; Higgins, *More Years for the Locust*, p137.

140 TN Vance, "The Permanent War Economy", *New International*, 17/1-6 (January-December 1951); see also W J Oakes, "Toward a Permanent War Economy?", *Politics*, February 1944.

141 See G Pozo, "Reassessing the permanent arms economy", *International Socialism* 127 (Summer 2010).

142 Communications from Pete Green and Joseph Choonara, May 2010.

143 M Kidron, "Two Insights Don't Make a Theory", *International Socialism* 100 (July 1977).

144 C Harman, *Explaining the Crisis*, London, 1984.

145 *Socialist Review*, June 1957.

146 See K Corr and A Brown, "The labour aristocracy and the roots of reformism", *International Socialism* 59 (Summer 1993).

147 Minutes of SR Aggregate, 19 January 1957 [Stan Newens archive].

148 Report of visit, September [1957/1958?] [Stan Newens archive].

149 Minutes of SR Aggregate, 19 January 1957; correspondence (1957) between Stan Newens and Duncan Hallas; statement of Revolutionary Socialist Unity Committee (January 1958) [all in Stan Newens archive].

150 Zena Maddison interview, October 2008; Stan Newens interview, July 2005.

151 D Widgery, *The Left in Britain*, Harmondsworth, 1976, pp78-85.

152 See V Clark, "It was PEOPLE who made me a socialist", *Socialist Worker*, 1 December 1973.

153 Letter from John Palmer to Jim Higgins, 30 May 1996, Rich. MS 1117/box 223/file 3.

154 See S Hall, "Life and Times of the First New Left", *New Left Review* 61 (Jan-Feb 2010), p189.

155 Nick Howard interview, December 2008.

156 Higgins, *More Years for the Locust*, p46.

157 J Higgins, "1956 and All That", *New Interventions*, 1993.

158 Higgins, *More Years for the Locust*, p47.

159 Pitt, *The Rise and Fall of Gerry Healy*, chapter 4.

160 Higgins, *More Years for the Locust*, pp51-2, quoted in conversation with Cliff.

161 Stan Newens interview, July 2005.

162 Letters of 10 May and 26 June 1958, Rich.MS 1117/box 117/file 4.

163 Ken Coates interview, October 2008.

164 Zena Maddison interview, October 2008; John Witzenfeld interview, October 2008.

165 S Papert, "The Strike Movement", *Socialist Review*, July 1957, "Strikes and Socialist Tactics", *Socialist Review*, October 1957.

166 JD Young, *Making Trouble*, Glasgow, 1987, p49.

167 JD Young, "Comrades were 'history's instruments'", *Workers' Liberty*, no 20, April 1995.

168 Zena Maddison interview, October 2008; John Witzenfeld interview, October 2008.

169 Mary Phillips interview, June 2005.

170 Roger and Sarah Cox interview, July 2005.

171 John Phillips interview, July 2005.

172 See http://www.marxists.org/archive/sedgwick/index.htm

173 Richard Kuper interview, February 2009.

174 Stan Newens interview, July 2005.

175 Mary Phillips interview, June 2005.

176 John Phillips interview, July 2005.

177 Mickey Loeb interview, July 2005.

178 Ray Challinor interview, October 2003.
179 Discussion with Stan Newens, May 2010.
180 "On Social Democratic Illusions", [early 1958] [Stan Newens archive].
181 Letter from Stan Newens to Wilf Albrighton, 10 January 1958 [Stan Newens archive].
182 Stan Newens interview, July 2005.
183 B Hagg, "Notebook", *Socialist Review*, mid-June 1958.
184 Information from *Plebs*, monthly journal of the NCLC 1955-1960; see in particular May 1957.
185 Cliff, *A World to Win*, p81.
186 *Socialist Review*, 1 April 1958.
187 *Socialist Review*, mid-April 1958.
188 Zena Maddison interview, October 2008.
189 *Socialist Review*, May Day 1958.
190 "To all...", *Socialist Review*, 1 January 1958.
191 "Letter to Readers", *Socialist Review*, 1 January 1959.
192 John Phillips interview, July 2005.
193 W Roy Nash, "The New Revolutionaries", *News Chronicle*, 23 and 24 September 1958.
194 "Stop hiding comrades!", *Socialist Review*, 1 October 1958.
195 Quoted in G Carlsson, "Carron – the noble knight", *Socialist Worker*, 11 December 1969.
196 W Podmore, *Reg Birch: Engineer, Trade Unionist and Communist*, London, 2004, pp51-2.
197 Higgins, *More Years for the Locust*, p70; Cliff, *A World to Win*, p61.
198 Roger Cox interview, July 2005.
199 T Cliff, *Rosa Luxemburg*, Harrow Weald, 1959.
200 JV Stalin, "Some Questions Concerning the History of Bolshevism", *Works*, vol 13, Moscow, 1955, pp86-104.
201 EJ Hobsbawm, "The Writing on the Wall", *New Central European Observer*, 3/18, 16 September 1950.
202 *The Socialist Leader*, 10 January, 25 April, 6, 13, 20 and 27 June 1959.
203 JP Nettl, *Rosa Luxemburg*, 2 vols, London, 1966.
204 Daniel Guérin, *Rosa Luxembourg et la spontanéité révolutionnaire*, Paris, 1971.
205 Cliff, *Rosa Luxemburg*, p7.
206 Cliff, *Rosa Luxemburg*, p95.
207 Cliff, *Rosa Luxemburg*, p30.
208 Cliff, *Rosa Luxemburg*, p37.
209 Cliff, *Rosa Luxemburg*, p26.
210 Cliff, *Rosa Luxemburg*, p27.
211 Cliff, *Rosa Luxemburg*, p36.
212 Cliff, *Rosa Luxemburg*, p61.
213 Cliff, *Rosa Luxemburg*, p64.
214 Cliff, *Rosa Luxemburg*, pp87-91.
215 Cliff, *Rosa Luxemburg*, p39.
216 Cliff, *Rosa Luxemburg*, p47.
217 Cliff, *Rosa Luxemburg*, p45.
218 Cliff, *Rosa Luxemburg*, p49.
219 Cliff, *Rosa Luxemburg*, p23.
220 Cliff, *Rosa Luxemburg*, p92.
221 Cliff, *Rosa Luxemburg*, p93.
222 Cliff, *Rosa Luxemburg*, p54.
223 Cliff, *Rosa Luxemburg*, p40.
224 Cliff, *Rosa Luxemburg*, p41.
225 Cliff, *Rosa Luxemburg*, p41.
226 Cliff, *Rosa Luxemburg*, p42.
227 See Cliff, *Lenin*, vol 1, pp66-8.
228 Cliff, *Rosa Luxemburg*, p37.
229 Cliff, *Neither Washington nor Moscow*, pp63-64.
230 Cliff, *Rosa Luxemburg*, p38.
231 Cliff, *Rosa Luxemburg*, p22.
232 Quotations from *The Holy Family* and *Capital*, Marx and Engels, *Collected Works*, vol 4, p131 and vol 35, p88.
233 Cliff, *Rosa Luxemburg*, p95.
234 Cliff, *Rosa Luxemburg*, p32.
235 Minutes of SR EC 21 January 1960, Rich. MS 1117/box 224/file 1; Chanie Rosenberg interview, March 2009.
236 *Socialist Review*, October 1959.

237 Naomi Gunn interview, April 2005.
238 Certificate of Registration Aliens Order 1920, MRC MSS 459/6/2.
239 T Cliff, *Prospects and Tasks* [1960], Fancy MS 1171/box 24/SR.
240 T Cliff, *Some remarks on the regroupment of Marxists* [1960], Fancy MS 1171/box 24/SR.

CHAPTER 5
1 Minutes of SR EC 7-8 October, 1961, Fancy MS 1171/box 1/4.
2 Minutes of the Quarterly Meeting of the SRG, 10-11 February 1962, Fancy MS 1171/box 1/4.
3 Higgins, *More Years for the Locust*, p12.
4 Nigel Coward interview, May 2008.
5 A MacIntyre, *Marxism: An Interpretation*, London, 1953.
6 Author's recollection.
7 See the collection of MacIntyre's Marxist writings in P Blackledge and N Davidson (eds), *Alasdair MacIntyre's Engagement with Marxism: Selected Writings 1953-1974*, Leiden, 2008.
8 A MacIntyre, *After Virtue*, London, 1981.
9 Author's recollection.
10 *International Socialism* 13 (Summer 1963).
11 *International Socialism* 15 (Winter 1963-64).
12 Author's recollection.
13 MRC MSS 459/2/17.
14 T Cliff, *Marxism and the Theory of Bureaucratic Collectivism*, Rich. MS 1117/box 118/file 9.
15 Communication from Samuel Farber, March 2009.
16 Communication from Alasdair MacIntyre, January 2004.
17 Author's recollection.
18 EP Thompson et al, *Out of Apathy*, London, 1960.
19 "Two Left Feet", *International Socialism* 2 (Autumn 1960).
20 EP Thompson, "Revolution Again!", *New Left Review* 6 (Nov-Dec 1960), pp18-31.
21 *International Socialism* 6-9 (Autumn 1961 to Summer 1962); contributions by Henry Collins, Alasdair MacIntyre, Michael Kidron, Ken Coates, Peter van Oertzen.
22 Nick Howard interview, December 2008.
23 Ken Coates interview, October 2008.
24 Bill Thomson interview, January 2009.
25 Notes on ISEB [1961?], Rich. MS 1117/box 230/file 1.
26 See M Coggins, *The Young Socialists: Labour's Lost Youth*, London, 1965.
27 Minutes of Hackney-Shoreditch SR, 17 June 1960, Fancy MS 1171/box 24/SR.
28 P Sirockin, *The Story of Labour's Youth*, Edgware, 1960.
29 Mary Phillips interview, June 2005.
30 John Phillips interview, July 2005.
31 John Palmer interview, June 2008.
32 Chris Davison interview, November 2008.
33 Mary Phillips interview, June 2005.
34 Will Fancy and John Phillips, "The Young Socialists", *International Socialism* 10 (Autumn 1962).
35 Fancy and Phillips, "The Young Socialists".
36 *Labour Review* 7/2 (Summer 1962).
37 Quoted in Coggins, *The Young Socialists*, p17.
38 Letter from Chris Davison, 29 July 1962, Fancy MS 1171/box 1/1.
39 Working Committee Minutes, 7 April 1963, Rich. MS1117/box 209/file 6.
40 *International Socialism* 14 (Autumn 1963).

41 Labour Party Archives, People's History Museum, Manchester, The General Secretary's Papers, Proscribed Organisations LP/GS/PROS: Miscellaneous Trotskyites.
42 IS Working Committee, 20 June 1964, Rich. MS 1117/box 209/file 6.
43 M Caffoor, "A weekend with the lumpentrots", *Young Guard*, June 1964.
44 Chris Davison interview, November 2008.
45 Eric Morse, "The Workers' Bomb", *Solidarity* vol 1, no 5, 1961.
46 IS Working Committee Minutes, 9 February 1963, Rich. MS 1117/box 209/file 6.
47 John Charlton interview, October 2008.
48 Jim Nichol interview, June 2008.
49 Jim Cronin interview, May 2008.
50 Alan Woodward interview, May 2008.
51 Alan Watts interview, October 2008.
52 Fergus Nicol interview, October 2008.
53 Communication from Noel Tracy, December 2008.
54 Dave Peers interview, October 2008.
55 Roger Rosewell interview, February 2009.
56 Roger Huddle interview, July 2008.
57 Lord Macdonald interview, February 2009.
58 Communication from Jimmy McCallum, January 2009.
59 Cliff, *A World to Win*, p72.
60 Lord Macdonald interview, February 2009.
61 IS Working Committee Minutes, 5 October 1963, 4 January 1964. Rich. MS 1117/box 209/file 6.
62 P Foot, "Tony Cliff", *The Guardian*, 11 April 2000.
63 Nigel and Tirril Harris interview, September 2008.
64 Richard Kirkwood interview, October 2008.
65 Fred Lindop interview, November 2008.
66 Richard Hyman interview, September 2008.
67 Colin Barker interview, May 2008.
68 Chris Harman interview, April 2009.
69 Richard Kuper interview, February 2009.
70 Ewa Barker interview, May 2008.
71 Author's recollection.
72 Mickey Loeb interview, July 2005.
73 Chris Davison interview, November 2008.
74 Jim Nichol interview, June 2008.
75 See Sarneh, "A Revolutionary Life", pp142-3.
76 *Plebs*, May 1962, August 1962, July 1963, August 1963, August 1964.
77 Minutes of ISEC June 22-23 [1963], Fancy MS 1171/box 1/2.
78 Working Committee minutes, 29 May 1963, Rich. MS 1117/box 209/file 6.
79 Telephone interview with Naomi Gunn, February 2004.
80 Communication from Paul Mackney, August 2008.
81 Ron Margulies interview, December 2008.
82 Roger Kline interview, February 2009.
83 Author's recollection.
84 See R Learsi, *Filled with Laughter*, New York and London, 1961, pp197-8.
85 Donny Gluckstein interview, February 2009.
86 Working Committee minutes, 9 November 1963, Rich. MS 1117/box 209/file 6.
87 R Condon, "Colourful Mixture", *Isis* (Oxford University), 13 November 1963, p7. The author was at that time a member of the Oxford IS. It is quoted with his

88 Minutes of EC 8-9 December 1962; Fancy MS 1171/box 1/4.
89 Y Gluckstein, "The Chinese People's Communes", *International Socialism* 1 (Spring 1960).
90 *International Socialism* 2 (Autumn 1960).
91 MRC MSS 459/2/14.
92 In T Cliff, D Hallas, C Harman and L Trotsky, *Party and Class*, London, 1971.
93 I Deutscher, *The Prophet Armed*, Oxford, 1970, pp88-97.
94 Author's recollection.
95 *International Socialism* 9 (Summer 1962).
96 Ted Crawford, "Harry Selby again", *Revolutionary History* 1/2 (1988), p57.
97 R Challinor and P Mansell, "Socialism at the Parish Pump", *International Socialism* 11 (Winter 1962).
98 R Miliband, *Parliamentary Socialism*, London, 1961.
99 *International Socialism* 12 (Spring 1963).
100 *International Socialism* 9 (Summer 1962).
101 N Harris, "India: Part One", *International Socialism* 17 (Summer 1964).
102 L Zeilig, "Tony Cliff: Deflected permanent revolution in Africa", *International Socialism* 126 (Spring 2010).
103 Communication from Mike Gonzalez, March 2010.
104 K Coates, "Caribbean Pilgrim", *International Socialism* 6 (Autumn 1961).
105 S Junco assisted by N Howard, "Yanqui No! Castro No! Cuba Si!", *International Socialism* 7 (Winter 1961).
106 Communication from Samuel Farber, March 2009.
107 TC, "Cuba", IS Internal Bulletin, January 1963.
108 SJ, "A criticism of TC's analysis of the Cuban situation", *A Socialist Survey* [1963].
109 S Farber, "Cuban Myths", *International Socialism* 112 (Autumn 2006).
110 Communication from Samuel Farber, March 2009.
111 *International Socialism* 14 (Autumn 1963).
112 T Cliff, "The Hundred Flowers Wilt", *Socialist Review*, mid-May 1959; Y Gluckstein, "The Chinese People's Communes", *International Socialism* 1 (Spring 1960); T Cliff, "The Decline of the Chinese Communes", *International Socialism* 8 (Spring 1962).
113 *International Socialism* 15 (Winter 1963).
114 Cliff quoting Deutscher, *The Prophet Outcast*, p518.
115 Cliff quoting Deutscher in *Universities and Left Review* 1/1 (Spring 1957), p10.
116 MRC MSS 459/2/1/1-11.
117 *International Socialism* 19 (Winter 1964-65).
118 T Cliff, *Russia: A Marxist Analysis*, London, 1964.
119 IS Working Committee Minutes, 2 November 1963, Rich. MS 1117/box 209/file 6.
120 Cliff, *Russia: A Marxist Analysis*, p198.
121 Cliff, *Russia: A Marxist Analysis*, p199.
122 Cliff, *Russia: A Marxist Analysis*, pp200, 280.
123 Cliff, *Russia: A Marxist Analysis*, p289.
124 Cliff, *Russia: A Marxist Analysis*, p201.
125 Cliff, *Russia: A Marxist Analysis*, pp309-10.
126 Cliff, *Russia: A Marxist Analysis*, p333.
127 Cliff, *Russia: A Marxist Analysis*,

      p335.
128 E Germain [Mandel], "Le 6e. plan quinquennal", *Quatrième Internationale*, vol 14, no 1/3, 1956, quoted in JW Stutje, *Ernest Mandel*, London, 2009, p349.
129 Cliff, *Russia: A Marxist Analysis*, pp340-41.
130 Cliff, *Russia: A Marxist Analysis*, p347.
131 Cliff, *Russia: A Marxist Analysis*, p345.
132 *Soviet Studies* 16/3 (January 1965), pp368-9. (Thanks to Paul Flewers for pointing this out and suggesting possible authorship.)
133 IS Working Committee minutes, 26 September 1963, Rich. MS1117/box 209/file 6.
134 Invoice from George Ellis and Sons, Rich. MS 1117/box 227/file 3.
135 Author's recollection.
136 Bill Thomson interview, January 2009.
137 Jim Nichol interview, June 2008.
138 IS Newsletter no 2, September 1964, Fancy MS 1171/box 1/2.
139 Author's recollection.
140 IS Working Committee minutes, 18 July 1965, Rich. MS1117/box 209/file 6.
141 Donny Gluckstein interview, February 2009.
142 Correspondence at MRC MSS 459 6/3.
143 Communication from Donny Gluckstein, February 2010.
144 NA HO 213/2381.

CHAPTER 6

1 See P Foot, *The Politics of Harold Wilson*, Harmondsworth, 1968.
2 Foot, *The Politics of Harold Wilson*, p305.
3 M Foot, *Harold Wilson: A Pictorial Biography*, Oxford, 1964, p75.
4 A MacIntyre, "Labour policy and capitalist planning", *International Socialism* 15 (Winter 1963-64).
5 *The Economist*, 10 October 1964.
6 K Alexander and J Hughes, *A Socialist Wages Plan*, London and Halifax, 1959.
7 E Heffer, "Socialist Wages Policy", *Socialist Review*, mid-April 1959; K Alexander, "Socialist Wages Plan", *Socialist Review*, 1 June 1959; M Kidron, "The Limits of Reform", *Socialist Review*, mid-June 1959; J Hughes and K Alexander, "Kidron and the Limits of Revolution", *Socialist Review*, February 1960; M Kidron, "A Note on the Limitations of Reforming 'Realism'", *Socialist Review*, February 1960.
8 Editorial: "Labour: Advise or Dissent", *International Socialism* 18 (Autumn 1964); Pat Jordan, "From Our Readers", *International Socialism* 19 (Winter 1964/5).
9 *Labour Worker*, September 1964.
10 Editorial: "The Future Offered Labour", *International Socialism* 17 (Summer 1964).
11 IS Working Committee Minutes, 4 July 1964, Rich. MS 1117/box 209/file 6.
12 The IS Group and a Labour government [1964], Rich. MS 1117/box 224/file 5.
13 Minutes of an ISEC 19-9-64. [The 'EC' was in fact a quarterly delegate meeting.]
14 IS Working Committee Minutes, 10 October 1964, Rich. MS 1117/box 209/file 6.
15 Minutes of ISEC, 10-11 April 1965, Rich. MS 1117/box 221/file 1.
16 *Labour Worker*, 1 February 1966.
17 *Labour Worker*, 7 June 1966.
18 "Churchill", *Labour Worker*, 1 February 1965.
19 "The money behind God", *Labour Worker*, Mid-May 1965,

20. and "Letter", *Labour Worker*, 1 June 1965.
20. P Foot, *Immigration and Race in British Politics*, Harmondsworth, 1965, p44.
21. "Immigration: Wilson Surrenders", *Labour Worker*, 15 February 1965; Paul Foot, "Labour Panders to Racialists", *Labour Worker*, mid-July 1965.
22. A Woodward, "CARD", *Labour Worker*, 15 March 1965.
23. R Protz, "Young Socialists' Great Victory", *Labour Worker*, December 1965.
24. *The Times*, 29 and 30 March 1966.
25. *Guardian*, 16 March 1966.
26. IS Working Committee minutes, 14 May 1966, Rich. MS 1117/box 209/file 6; see also J McIlroy, "Adrift in the Rapids of Racism", pp152-6.
27. *Lancashire Evening Post*, 31 May, 8 June 1965; S Castles and G Kosack, *Immigrant Workers and Class Struggle in Western Europe*, Oxford, 1985, pp153-5.
28. IS Working Committee minutes, 6 June 1965, Rich. MS 1117/box 209/file 6.
29. *Labour Worker*, mid-June and 1 July 1965.
30. Author's recollection.
31. Richard Kirkwood interview, October 2008.
32. Minutes of ISEC 24 July 1965, Rich. MS 1117/box 221/file 1.
33. IS Northern Weekend School, 28 March 1965, Rich. MS 1117/box 221/file 1.
34. Author's recollection.
35. IS Working Committee minutes, 20 March 1965, Rich. MS 1117/box 209/file 6.
36. IS Working Committee minutes, 19 June 1965, Rich. MS 1117/box 209/file 6.
37. IS Working Committee minutes, 8 January 1966, Rich. MS 1117/box 209/file 6.
38. IS Bulletin No 7, 22 October 1965.
39. IS Bulletin No 8, 5 December 1965, pp1-2.
40. See Joyce Rosser and Colin Barker, "A Working class Defeat: The ENV Story", *International Socialism* 31 (Winter 1967-68).
41. Author's recollection.
42. *Labour Worker*, mid-November 1965.
43. C Davison and P Finch, *What Happened at Woolf's*, London, 1966.
44. IS Working Committee Minutes, 10 September 1966, Rich. MS 1117/box 209/file 6.
45. House of Commons, 20 June 1966.
46. See P Foot, "The Seamen's Struggle", in R Blackburn and A Cockburn (eds), *The Incompatibles*, Harmondsworth, 1967, pp192-3, 201.
47. *Labour Worker*, 7 and 20 June 1966.
48. Working Committee minutes, 20 May 1967, Rich. MS 1117/box 209/file 6.
49. T Cliff and C Barker, *Incomes Policy, Legislation and Shop Stewards*, Harrow Weald, 1966.
50. M Didron and A Shonfield, *Modern Capitalism*, London, 1965.
51. Colin Barker interview, May 2008.
52. Cliff and Barker, *Incomes Policy*, p6.
53. Cliff and Barker, *Incomes Policy*, pp16, 7.
54. Cliff and Barker, *Incomes Policy*, p24.
55. Cliff and Barker, *Incomes Policy*, p48.
56. Cliff and Barker, *Incomes Policy*, p65.
57. Cliff and Barker, *Incomes Policy*, p76.

58 Cliff and Barker, *Incomes Policy*, pp75, 85.
59 Cliff and Barker, *Incomes Policy*, pp105-6.
60 Cliff and Barker, *Incomes Policy*, pp135, 128.
61 Cliff and Barker, *Incomes Policy*, pp131-2.
62 Cliff and Barker, *Incomes Policy*, pp135-6.
63 Cliff and Barker, *Incomes Policy*, p90.
64 Cliff and Barker, *Incomes Policy*, p105.
65 "Introduction" to Cliff and Barker, *Incomes Policy*, p3.
66 London Industrial Shop Stewards Defence Committee Circular, 31 May 1966; Fancy MS1171/box 1/2.
67 Working Committee minutes, 16 July 1966, Rich. MS 1117/box 209/file 6.
68 Roger Cox interview, July 2005.
69 IS Working Committee minutes, 30 April 1966, Rich. MS 1117/box 209/file 6. See *Royal Commission on Trade Unions and Employers' Associations 1965-1968*, London, 1968, p322.
70 Colin Barker interview, May 2008.
71 Mel Norris interview, November 2008.
72 Rosser and Barker, "A Working class Defeat".
73 Higgins, *More Years for the Locust*, p70.
74 Colin Barker interview, May 2008.
75 Nigel Coward interview, May 2008.
76 Document included in IS Working Committee Minutes, 14 May 1966, Rich. MS 1117/box 209/file 6.
77 "Revolt of the 'Rubbish People'", *Labour Worker*, 20 June 1966.
78 Richard Kirkwood interview, October 2008.
79 Ian Macdonald interview, March 2009.
80 Ian Macdonald interview, March 2009.
81 Dave Peers interview, October 2008.
82 John Palmer interview, June 2008.
83 *Labour Worker*, December 1966.
84 *Labour Worker*, January 1967, p6.
85 *Labour Worker*, February 1967, p7.
86 Working Committee minutes, 24 September 1966, Rich. MS 1117/box 209/file 6.
87 *Common Cause Bulletin*, no 113, Winter 1965-66.
88 T Cliff, "Revolutionary traditions", in D Widgery, *The Left in Britain*, pp92-7.
89 John Charlton interview, October 2008.
90 Nick Howard interview, December 2008.
91 Volkhard Mosler interview, March 2005.
92 Ewa Barker interview, May 2008.
93 Donny Gluckstein interview, February 2009.
94 Nigel Coward interview, May 2008.
95 Nigel and Tirril Harris interview, September 2008.
96 *Daily Worker*, 15 February 1965.
97 "Vultures Over the Swamp", *Labour Worker*, 1 June and mid-June 1965.
98 M Kidron, "International Capitalism", *International Socialism* 20 (Spring 1965).
99 Author's recollection.
100 Unsigned article in *Labour Worker*, 1 January 1966.
101 Author's recollection.
102 Chris Harman interview, April 2009; minutes of VSC National Executive, 11 July 1967.
103 *Morning Star*, 21 October 1967.
104 *The Times*, 23 October 1967.
105 Fred Lindop interview, November

2008.
106 Author's recollection.
107 Naomi Gunn interview, April 2005.
108 Tariq Ali interview, February 2009.
109 International Socialism pamphlet, London [1967].
110 Werner Cohn, "From Victim to Shylock and Oppressor: The New Image of the Jew in the Trotskyist Movement", *Journal of Communist Studies* (London), vol 7, no 1, March 1991, pp46-68.
111 *Jewish Chronicle*, 14 July 1967.
112 *Tribune*, 2 June and 9 June 1967.
113 Working Committee minutes, 1 July 1967, Rich. MS 1117/box 209/file 6.
114 Fred Lindop interview, November 2008.
115 Sean Matgamna interview, November 2008.
116 Eamonn McCann interview, July 2008.
117 Cliff, *A World to Win*, pp92-5.
118 Author's recollection.
119 *LSE – what it is and how we fought it*, Agitator pamphlet, London, 1967.
120 Chris Harman interview, April 2009.
121 Sabby Sagall interview, May 2008.
122 George Paizis interview, October 2008.
123 Sabby Sagall interview, May 2008.
124 Martin Tomkinson interview, August 2008.
125 J Rose, "Debate sparked by Six Day War 1967 transformed a generation", *Socialist Worker*, 9 June 2007.
126 Passport: MRC MSS 459/6/1.
127 "Rencontre avec 'International Socialism'", *Pouvoir Ouvrier* 84 (May-June 1967).
128 Colin Barker interview, May 2008.

CHAPTER 7

1 J-P Sartre, *Situations VIII*, Paris, 1972, p273.
2 Communication from Noel Tracy, December 2008.
3 International Socialism Group Secretary's Report, 6 January 1968, Fancy MS 1171/box 16/1967-69.
4 Sabby Sagall interview, May 2008.
5 Telephone conversation with Akiva Orr, April 2005.
6 *The Times*, 18 March 1968.
7 *The Times*, 25 March 1968.
8 "The War in Vietnam and in Britain", leaflet, London, undated.
9 F Lindop, "Racism and the working class: strikes in support of Enoch Powell in 1968", *Labour History Review* 66/1 (Spring 2001), p91.
10 Eddie Prevost interview, June 2008.
11 F Lindop, "Racism and the working class", p94.
12 *International Socialism* 33 (Summer 1968).
13 Cliff, *A World to Win*, p91.
14 Roger Cox interview, July 2005.
15 Jim Nichol interview, June 2008.
16 Quoted in I Birchall, *The Smallest Mass Party in the World*, London, 1981, p15.
17 Nigel Coward interview, May 2008.
18 IS Working Committee minutes, 18 March and 4 December 1967, Rich.MS 1117/box 209/file 6
19 ISEC minutes, 1 June 1968, Fancy MS 1171/ box 16.
20 Tariq Ali interview, February 2009.
21 Chris Harman interview, April 2009.
22 Document "On Unity", adopted by the January 1972 IS National Committee, and published in the IS Bulletin, January 1972.
23 *The Economist*, 18 May 1968.

24   A Gorz, "Reform and Revolution", in R Miliband and J Saville (eds), *The Socialist Register 1968*, London, 1968, p111. (Gorz's article was based on a lecture series originally delivered in Sweden in April 1966.)
25   T Cliff and I Birchall, *France: The Struggle Goes On*, London, 1968, pp4-5.
26   Bob Clay interview, November 2008.
27   M Brinton, *Paris May 1968*, Bromley, 1968.
28   Author's recollection.
29   Author's recollection.
30   Cliff and Birchall, *France*, p50.
31   John Palmer interview, June 2008.
32   IS internal document, June 1968. Reprinted in Cliff, *Neither Washington nor Moscow*, pp215-7.
33   Author's recollection.
34   Higgins, *More Years for the Locust*, p81.
35   Nigel Harris interview, September 2008.
36   Richard Kirkwood interview, October 2008.
37   T Cliff, *Lenin* vol 2: *All Power to the Soviets*, London, 1976, pp140-43. The reference was to the pamphlet *The Tasks of the Proletariat in Our Revolution*, in Lenin, *Collected Works* 24, pp55-91.
38   Joel Geier interview, March 2009.
39   Sean Matgamna interview, November 2008.
40   Higgins, *More Years for the Locust*, p80.
41   London, 1968.
42   Brinton, *Paris May 1968*.
43   P Seale and M McConville, *French Revolution 1968*, Harmondsworth, 1968.
44   Cliff and Birchall, *France*, pp22, 28, 29.
45   Cliff and Birchall, *France*, p61.
46   *Black Dwarf*, 5 July 1968.
47   Cliff and Birchall, *France*, p11.
48   Cliff and Birchall, *France*, p12.
49   Cliff and Birchall, *France*, pp15, 13.
50   See for example C Harman, R Kuper, D Clark, A Sayers and M Shaw, *Education, Capitalism and the Student Revolt*, London, 1968; A Cockburn and R Blackburn (eds), *Student Power*, Harmondsworth, 1969.
51   Cliff and Birchall, *France*, pp72, 77, 78.
52   Cliff and Birchall, *France*, pp49-50.
53   Cliff and Birchall, *France*, p80.
54   Cliff and Birchall, *France*, pp33, 36-7.
55   Cliff and Birchall, *France*, pp50, 76, 77.
56   *New Left Review* 52 (Nov-Dec 1968), p8.
57   *Gendaishichosha 1968*.
58   *The Struggle for self-management: An Open Letter to IS Comrades, Solidarity Special*, September 1968.
59   P Sedgwick, "The French May...", *International Socialism* 36 (April/May 1969).
60   Richard Kuper interview, February 2009; Admin Committee Minutes, 26 August 1968, Fancy MS 1171/box 16/1967-69.
61   P Barker, "Portrait of a Protest", *New Society*, 31 October 1968.
62   Chanie Rosenberg interview, December 2003.
63   Tariq Ali interview, February 2008.
64   John Molyneux interview, September 2008.
65   J Nichol, "Ross Pritchard: in memoriam", *Fragments* 3 (Haringey TUC), London, 2001, p40.
66   *Socialist Worker*, 13 May 2006.
67   *Socialist Worker* sales, Fancy MS 1171/box 16/1967-69.

68 Cliff, *A World to Win*, p101.
69 "Towards a Fighting Theory", Rich. MS 1117/box 220/file 1.
70 "Towards a Revolutionary Strategy", a document of the Democratic Centralist Faction, 1969.
71 "Platform Four", Rich. MS 1117/box 209/file 5.
72 Document in the name of Hull IS, October 1968. Reproduced in Higgins, *More Years for the Locust*, pp 145-6.
73 See "Letter to Readers", *International Socialism* 33 (Summer 1968).
74 See "Statement to the Appeals Commission", July 1973, signed by 14 members of the "Right Faction", Fancy MS 1171/box 17/IS Appeals Commission.
75 Bill Thomson interview, January 2009.
76 Author's recollection.
77 John Palmer interview, June 2008.

CHAPTER 8

1 *International Socialism* 36 (April-May 1969).
2 IS Perspectives Document, January 1970, Rich. MS 1117/box 88/file 2.
3 Sabby Sagall interview, May 2008.
4 Report to National Committee, 17 May 1969, Rich. MS 1117/box 209/file 6.
5 H Jones, "CP: down the slippery slope…", *Socialist Worker*, 30 October 1969.
6 *Socialist Worker*, 22 January 1970.
7 T Cliff, *The Employers' Offensive: productivity deals and how to fight them*, London, 1970.
8 NC minutes, 17 May 1969, Fancy MS 1171/box 16 (1969).
9 Chanie Rosenberg interview, September 2010.
10 Richard Hyman interview, September 2008.
11 Cliff, *The Employers' Offensive*, p3.
12 Cliff, *The Employers' Offensive*, pp3, 46.
13 Cliff, *The Employers' Offensive*, p203.
14 Cliff, *The Employers' Offensive*, pp218-30.
15 Cliff, *The Employers' Offensive*, p215.
16 Cliff, *The Employers' Offensive*, p3.
17 Cliff, *The Employers' Offensive*, pp11-13.
18 Cliff, *The Employers' Offensive*, pp42-5.
19 Cliff, *The Employers' Offensive*, pp110-11.
20 Cliff, *The Employers' Offensive*, p53.
21 Cliff, *The Employers' Offensive*, p63.
22 Cliff, *The Employers' Offensive*, pp107-8.
23 Cliff, *The Employers' Offensive*, pp133-4.
24 Cliff, *The Employers' Offensive*, p32.
25 Cliff, *The Employers' Offensive*, pp90, 95.
26 Cliff, *The Employers' Offensive*, p217.
27 Cliff, *The Employers' Offensive*, p207.
28 Cliff, *The Employers' Offensive*, p208.
29 EC minutes, 16 March 1970, Rich. MS 1117/box 224/file 1.
30 Richard Kuper interview, February 2009.
31 Chanie Rosenberg interview, September 2010.
32 F Henderson, *Life on the Track*, London, 2009, p70.
33 Sammy Morris interview, January 2009.
34 Alan Watts interview, October 2008.
35 As announced in *Socialist Worker*.

36 Granville Williams interview, January 2009.
37 Paul Holborow interview, July 2008.
38 J Bugler, "Battle manual", *New Society*, 9 April 1970.
39 Cliff, *The Employers' Offensive*, p143.
40 P Jay, "Militants' handbook", *The Times*, 25 March 1970.
41 C Mansell, "Counter Productive Argument", *Management Today*, May 1970, pp134-5.
42 Quoted in *Organizational Notes* 2, Rich. MS1117/box 209/file 4.
43 Richard Hyman interview, September 2008.
44 Willie Lee interview, January 2009.
45 Bob Clay interview, November 2008.
46 Dave Sherry interview, January 2009.
47 Paul Mackney interview, June 2008.
48 Shaun Doherty interview, November 2008.
49 Fancy MS 1171/box 17/1970.
50 Sheila McGregor interview, January 2009.
51 Paul Holborow interview, July 2008.
52 Pete Clark interview, July 2008.
53 Peter Alexander interview, July 2004.
54 Bob Clay interview, November 2008.
55 Red Saunders interview, May 2008.
56 John Rose interview, June 2008.
57 NC Minutes, 11 December 1971, Rich. MS 1117/box 212/file 2.
58 Bob Clay interview, November 2008.
59 Roger Rosewell interview, February 2009.
60 Sabby Sagall interview, May 2008.
61 John Palmer interview, June 2008.
62 NC minutes, 11 October 1969, Rich. MS 1117/box 226/file 4.
63 TC, "For the Record", Special Bulletin (Autumn 1971) before December 1971 conference to exclude Workers' Fight.
64 *Socialist Worker*, 5 February 1972.
65 *Socialist Worker*, 26 February 1972.
66 *Socialist Worker*, 25 March 1972.
67 *Socialist Worker*, 8 April 1972.
68 Eamonn McCann interview, July 2008.
69 *Socialist Worker*, 16 January 1971.
70 John Molyneux interview, September 2008.
71 Communication from Noel Tracy, December 2008.
72 NC minutes, 12 July 1969, Fancy MS 1171/box 16.
73 "The Nigerian bloodbath", *Socialist Worker*, 24 July 1969; F Forsyth, *The Biafra Story*, Harmondsworth, 1969.
74 J Greenlark, "The Cliff versus Healy Debate", *The Bulletin of Marxist Studies*, vol 1, no 5, 1969.
75 T Ali, *The Coming British Revolution*, London, 1972, p135.
76 Executive Committee minutes, 16 November 1970, Fancy MS 1171/box 17/1970.
77 See *International Bulletin of Revolutionary Socialists*, London and Paris, June 1971.
78 Joel Geier interview, March 2009.
79 A McSmith, *Faces of Labour*, London, 1996, p130.
80 "Britain and Europe", *International Socialism* 6 (Autumn 1961).
81 T Cliff and C Harman, "Theses on the Common Market for June National Committee", International Socialism Internal Bulletin, June 1971, pp6-7.
82 NC Minutes, 11 October 1969, Rich. MS 1117/box222/file 2.

83   Minutes of Special Conference, Rich. MS 1117/box212/file 2.
84   Tape of the debate, Bookmarks c. 2000.
85   *Socialist Worker*, 19 December 1970.
86   NC minutes, 19 December 1970, Fancy MS 1171/box 17/1970.
87   Cliff, *A World to Win*, p124.
88   O Woods, P Routledge, B MacArthur, "The Revolutionaries", *The Times*, 15, 16, 17 and 18 February 1971.
89   N Harris and J Palmer (eds), *World Crisis*, London, 1971.
90   *Times Literary Supplement*, 4 June 1971.
91   John Palmer interview, June 2008.
92   *Socialist Worker*, 19 January 1972.
93   Pete Green interview, August 2008.
94   John Charlton interview, October 2008.
95   Granville Williams interview, January 2009.
96   Granville Williams interview, January 2009.
97   T Cliff, "1972 Tremendous year for the workers", *Socialist Worker*, 6 January 1973.
98   T Cliff, "In the balance", *Socialist Review* 183, February 1995.
99   See R Darlington and D Lyddon, *Glorious Summer*, London, 2001, for a full account of the struggles of 1972.
100 T Cliff, "1972 Tremendous year for the workers".
101 Communication from Dave Lyddon, February 2010.
102 *Socialist Worker* Docks Special, 22 July 1972.
103 T Cliff, "The battle is won but war goes on", *Socialist Worker*, 5 August 1972.
104 J McIlroy, "Notes on the Communist Party and Industrial Politics", in J McIlroy, N Fishman and A Campbell, *British Trade Unions and Industrial Politic* vol 2, Aldershot, 1999, pp241-45.
105 *Socialist Worker*, 17 June 1972.
106 *Socialist Worker*, 14 April 1973.
107 J McIlroy, "Notes on the Communist Party and Industrial Politics", p239.
108 Eddie Prevost interview, June 2008.
109 "IS Building Workers Group", 22 August 1972.
110 Nick Howard interview, December 2008.
111 Bill Message, "2000 strike to back 'higher pensions' call", *Socialist Worker*, 2 December 1972.
112 Jack Robertson interview, November 2008.
113 Dave Sherry interview, January 2009.
114 *Socialist Worker*, 24 March 1973.
115 *Socialist Worker*, 17 March, 21 April, 23 June 1973.
116 Bob Clay interview, November 2008.
117 "Membership report to June NC", IS Bulletin [June 1973].
118 T Cliff, "Grasp Nettle of Factory Power", *Socialist Worker*, 23 June 1973.
119 Tony Cliff and John Charlton, "Further Remarks on Recruitment", IS Bulletin [June 1973].
120 "Membership Boom: 1260 since March", *Socialist Worker*, 18 August 1973.
121 Jim Nichol interview, June 2008.
122 Author's recollection.
123 *Socialist Worker*, 8 April 1972.
124 Sabby Sagall interview, May 2008.
125 T Cliff, *Factory Branches*, London [1973]; reproduced in T Cliff, *Selected Writings* vol 2: *In the Thick of Workers' Struggle*, London, 2002, pp339-68.
126 Pete Clark interview, July 2008.
127 Jim Nichol interview, June 2008.

128 Helen Blair interview, January 2009.
129 Alex Callinicos interview, July 2008.
130 See R Protz and N Fountain, "Jim Higgins", *The Guardian*, 21 October 2002.
131 NC minutes, 8 January 1972; author's recollection.
132 Roger Cox interview, July 2005.
133 Penny Krantz interview, May 2008.
134 *Socialist Worker*, 24 March 1973.
135 Jim Nichol interview, June 2008.
136 EC minutes, 30 July 1973.
137 Richard Kuper interview, February 2009.
138 NC minutes, July 1973.
139 EC minutes, 16 July 1973.
140 Author's recollection.
141 Roger Rosewell interview, February 2009.
142 Roger Kline interview, February 2009.
143 Jim Nichol interview, June 2008.
144 Dave Peers interview, October 2008.
145 Roger Rosewell interview, February 2009.
146 John Charlton interview, October 2008.
147 Roger Kline interview, February 2009.
148 Granville Williams interview, January 2009.
149 Paul Holborow interview, July 2008.
150 Higgins, *More Years for the Locust*, pp100, 103-4; John Palmer interview, June 2008.
151 EC minutes, 28 May 1973.
152 NC minutes June [1973].
153 NC minutes October [1973].
154 T Cliff, "Phase 3 Must Go", *Socialist Worker*, 3 November 1973.
155 NC minutes, November [1973], Rich. MS 1117/box 227/file 3.
156 *Socialist Worker*, 17 November 1973.
157 *Socialist Worker*, 5 January 1974.
158 See D Ayre, T Barker, J French, J Graham and D Harker, *The Flying Pickets*, n.p. 2008, especially pp375-9.
159 D Ayre et al, *The Flying Pickets*, p224.
160 D Ayre et al, *The Flying Pickets*, p238.
161 As announced in *Socialist Worker*.
162 National Secretary's Report, 22 January 1974, Rich. MS 1117/box 226/file 4.
163 T Cliff, "Heath's blackmail", *Socialist Worker*, 5 January 1974.
164 T Cliff, "How far will the bosses go?", *Socialist Worker*, 19 January 1974.
165 As announced in *Socialist Worker*.
166 Contribution by Tony Goodchild in meeting on Cliff at Marxism 2006.
167 Paul Holborow interview, July 2008.
168 John Rose interview, June 2008.
169 George Paizis interview, October 2008.
170 *Socialist Worker*, 6 April 1974.
171 "Trotskyist rival to Liaison Committee", *Morning Star*, 1 April 1974.
172 George Bishop, "The Rank and File Movement", *New Statesman*, 5 April 1974.

CHAPTER 9
1 Paul Holborow interview, July 2008.
2 Steve Hammill interview, July 2008.
3 Dave Hayes interview, December 2008.
4 Andy Strouthous interview, July 2008.
5 T Cliff, "On Perspectives", *International Socialism* 36 (April-May 1969).
6 *Socialist Worker*, 16 March 1974.

7   *Socialist Worker*, 6 April 1974.
8   Letter from J Higgins to Alan, Mike and Brian, 25 April 1974, Rich. MS1117/box 223/file 2.
9   "The International Socialists – Our Traditions", reproduced in J Higgins, *Speak One More Time*, London, 2004, p91.
10 Edward Crawford interview, September, 2008.
11 Protz et al, "Socialist Worker – Perspectives and Organisation", IS Internal Bulletin, April 1974, Rich. MS 1117/box 211/file 1.
12 IS Internal Bulletin, April 1974.
13 L Trotsky, *In Defense of Marxism*, New York, 1965, p112.
14 "Socialist Worker – Perspectives and Organisation", IS Internal Bulletin, April 1974, pp18-24, Rich. MS 1117/box 211/file 1.
15 Communication from Roger Huddle, February 2010.
16 *Socialist Worker*, 13 April 1974.
17 *Socialist Worker*, 20 April, 18 May 1974.
18 "National Committee report", IS Internal Bulletin, [May 1974].
19 IS Internal Bulletin, [May 1974].
20 NC, 11 May 1974.
21 NC minutes, 11 May 1974, Rich. MS 1117/box 209/file 5.
22 EC minutes, 18 May 1974.
23 Author's recollection.
24 Documents of May 1974 National Committee.
25 NC minutes, 11 May 1974, Rich. MS 1117/box 209/file 5.
26 NC minutes, May 1974, Rich. MS 1117/box 221/file 1.
27 IS Internal Bulletin, June 1974, reproduced Higgins, *More Years for the Locust*, pp152-4.
28 J Higgins, "The End of the 'Rank and File'", *Workers Liberty* 19, March 1995.
29 May NC, 11 May 1974.
30 M Sheridan, "Sean Hallahan (1946-2000)", *Revolutionary History* 8/1 (2001), pp270-2.
31 Ian Gibson interview, June 2008.
32 *Socialist Worker*, 6 July 1974.
33 *Socialist Worker*, 26 October 1974.
34 C Andrew, *The Defence of the Realm: The Authorized History of MI5*, London, 2009, pp660-8.
35 *Socialist Worker*, 20 July 1974.
36 I Gibson, "The stars face a fight", *Socialist Worker*, 11 May 1974.
37 Ian Gibson interview, June 2008.
38 R Rosewell, *The Struggle for Socialism*, London 1970; London, 1973.
39 Letter dated 21 April 1974, Rich. MS 1117/box 209/file 6.
40 *Socialist Worker*, 17 November 1973.
41 Roger Rosewell interview, February 2009.
42 Author's recollection.
43 *Guardian*, 16 February 1994.
44 John Palmer interview, June 2008.
45 Richard Kirkwood interview, October 2008.
46 Pete Green interview, August 2008.
47 Pat Stack interview, September 2008.
48 *Workers' Liberty*, September 1995, p35.
49 Alex Callinicos interview, July 2008.
50 A Nagliatti, "Letter of resignation", IS Internal Bulletin [May 1974].
51 NC minutes, July [1974], Rich. MS 1117/box 227/file 3.
52 See M Balfour, "Italy: The Unions and Rank and File Power", *International Socialism* 57 (April 1973).
53 NC minutes, 11 May 1974, Rich. MS 1117/box 209/file 5.
54 Dave Peers interview, October 2008.
55 Meeting held between IS members on the R&F Organising Committee, Tony Cliff, Steve Jefferys and John Deason, 30 June [1974],

56　Fancy MS 1171/box 17 (National R&F Conference).
56　Notes of Organisation Commission discussion, 9 June [1974], Rich. MS 1117/box 220/file 1; notes of Organisation Commission, 23 June 1974.
57　*Socialist Worker*, 5 October 1974.
58　IS Bulletin, April 1975, Rich. MS 1117/box 212/file 2.
59　"Industrial Perspectives", IS Internal Bulletin, Pre-Conference issue, 1974.
60　Report of the National Committee to Conference 1974, Rich. MS 1117/box 209/ file 4.
61　Dave Peers interview, October 2008.
62　*Socialist Worker*, 29 March 1975.
63　*The Agitators: Extremist Activities in British Industries*, London [1974], p34.
64　*Daily Telegraph*, 7 March, 10 March 1975.
65　*Hansard*, 26 February 1975, Lords Sitting, vol 357 cc820-956.
66　T Cliff, *The Crisis: Social Contract or Socialism*, London 1975.
67　According to the "What's On" column of *Socialist Worker*.
68　Cliff, *The Crisis*, p32.
69　Cliff, *The Crisis*, pp55-6.
70　Cliff, *The Crisis*, pp59-60.
71　Cliff, *The Crisis*, pp59, 61.
72　Cliff, *The Crisis*, p192.
73　Cliff, *The Crisis*, pp188-9.
74　"False demons of the revolution", *Financial Times*, 7 January 1975.
75　"The struggle for socialism", *Socialist Worker*, 15 March 1975.
76　*Socialist Worker*, 31 May 1975.
77　*Socialist Worker*, 22 February 1975.
78　Author's recollection.
79　Chris Bambery interview October 2008.
80　Pat Stack interview, September 2008.
81　*The Economist*, 5 July 1975.
82　*The Economist*, 11 January 1975.
83　Higgins, *More Years for the Locust*, p116.
84　M Shaw, "The Making of a Party?", in R Miliband and J Saville (eds), *The Socialist Register 1978*, London, 1978, p132.
85　*Socialist Worker*, 13 July 1974.
86　T Cliff, "Portugal: Lessons for the revolution", *Socialist Worker*, 29 June 1974.
87　*International Socialism* 81-82 (September 1975), p48.
88　Peter Robinson interview, June 2008.
89　*International Socialism* 81-82 (September 1975), pp48, 8.
90　*International Socialism* 81-82 (September 1975), p11.
91　*International Socialism* 81-82 (September 1975), p29.
92　*Insight on Portugal*, London, 1975.
93　*Insight on Portugal*, pp11, 120, 153, 7.
94　*International Socialism* 81-82 (September 1975), p40.
95　Chris Harman interview, April 2009.
96　*International Socialism* 81-82 (September 1975), pp17, 42.
97　*International Socialism* 81-82 (September 1975), pp47-8.
98　*International Socialism* 81-82 (September 1975), p19.
99　Joel Geier interview, March 2009.
100　Danny Gluckstein interview, January 2009.
101　Peter Robinson interview, June 2008.
102　*Socialist Worker*, 11 October 1975.
103　*Socialist Worker*, 25 October 1975.
104　Peter Robinson interview, June 2008.
105　Peter Robinson interview, June 2008.
106　*International Socialism* 87

107 T Cliff, "Portugal at the Impasse", *International Socialism* 95 (February 1977).
108 Communications from Einde O'Callaghan and Panos Garganas, April-May 2010.
109 According to "International Work", IS Bulletin, February 1976.
110 *Radical America*, vol 9, no 6 (November-December 1975).
111 Author's recollection.
112 S Jefferys, "How the SWP narrowed into a sect", *Workers' Liberty* 22, June 1995.
113 Peter Robinson interview, June 2008.
114 Author's recollection.
115 Joel Geier interview, March 2009.
116 Cliff, *A World to Win*, p114.
117 Danny Gluckstein interview, January 2009.
118 Anna Gluckstein interview, October 2008.
119 Bob Clay interview, November 2008.
120 Paul Mackney interview, June 2008.
121 J Sullivan, *Go Fourth and Multiply / When this Pub Closes*, London, 2004, p3.
122 Jim Higgins, review of *A World to Win*, *Revolutionary History* 7/4 (2000), p217.
123 Q Skinner, "Meaning and understanding in the history of ideas", in J Tully (ed.), *Meaning and Context: Quentin Skinner and his Critics*, Princeton NJ, 1988, p65.
124 D Hallas, "Building the Revolutionary Party", *International Socialism* 79 (June 1975).
125 Author's recollection.
126 Author's recollection.
127 Cliff, *Lenin* vol 1, p67.
128 S T Possony, *Lenin: The Compulsive Revolutionary*, London, 1966, pp 19, 478.
129 Eg *The Ulyanov Family*, (March-April 1976).
Moscow, 1968.
130 C Hill, *Lenin and the Russian Revolution*, London, 1947, eg p213.
131 Cliff, *Lenin* vol 1, pp67-8.
132 Cliff, *Lenin* vol 1, pp92, 301, 137.
133 Cliff, *Lenin* vol 1, p80.
134 Cliff, *Lenin* vol 1, p87, quoted in Lenin, *Collected Works* 1, p298.
135 Lih, *Lenin Rediscovered*, pp14-5, 19-21, 491, 526-7.
136 Lih, *Lenin Rediscovered*, pp490, 540, 555.
137 Lih, *Lenin Rediscovered*, pp25, 27.
138 Cliff, *Lenin* vol 1, p75.
139 Cliff, *Lenin* vol 1, pp262-3.
140 For some more general considerations on stick-bending, see Lih, *Lenin Rediscovered*, pp26-7.
141 Andy Wilson interview, June 2008.
142 J Molyneux, "Lih's Lenin – a review of Lars T Lih, 'Lenin Rediscovered'", http://johnmolyneux.blogspot.com/2006/11/lihs-lenin-review-of-lars-t-lih-lenin.html
143 Cliff, *Lenin* vol 1, p77.
144 Cliff, *Lenin* vol 1, p117.
145 Cliff, *Lenin* vol 1, p164.
146 Cliff, *Lenin* vol 1, p226.
147 Cliff, *Lenin* vol 1, pp253-72.
148 Cliff, *Lenin* vol 2, London, 1976, pp59-61.
149 Cliff, *Lenin* vol 2, pp83, 157-8.
150 Cliff, *Lenin* vol 2, p376.
151 Cliff, *Lenin* vol 2, pp368-9.
152 Cliff, *Lenin* vol 2, pp256, 378.
153 T Cliff, *Lenin* vol 3: *Revolution Besieged*, London, 1978, pp6-7, 184.
154 S Courtois et al, *The Black Book of Communism*, London/Cambridge Mass., 1999.
155 Cliff, *Lenin* vol 3, p19.
156 Cliff, *Lenin* vol 3, p190.
157 Cliff, *Lenin* vol 3, pp 20-21.
158 Cliff, *Lenin* vol 3, p194.
159 Cliff, *Lenin* vol 3, pp177-8.

160 D Widgery, "Post-Electronic Leninism", *Socialist Review*, March 1979.
161 C L R James, *World Revolution 1917-1936*, London, 1937.
162 D Hallas, *The Comintern*, London, 1985. See also P Frank, *Histoire de l'internationale communiste*, Paris, 1979.
163 A Rosmer, *Lenin's Moscow*; V Serge, *Memoirs of a Revolutionary 1901-1941*, London, 1967.
164 T Cliff, *Lenin* vol 4: *The Bolsheviks and World Communism*, London, 1979, pp55-6.
165 Cliff, *Lenin* vol 4, p47.
166 Cliff, *Lenin* vol 4, p46.
167 Cliff, *Lenin* vol 4, p57.
168 Cliff, *Lenin* vol 4, pp58-63.
169 Cliff, *Lenin* vol 4, p187.
170 P Broué, *Révolution en Allemagne 1917-1923*, Paris, 1971; translated as *The German Revolution 1917-1923*, Leiden, 2005.
171 Cliff, *Lenin*, vol 4, p166.
172 Broué, *Histoire de l'Internationale Communiste*.
173 Cliff, *Lenin*, vol 4, p172.
174 Cliff, *Lenin*, vol 4, p216.
175 Jefferys, "How the SWP narrowed into a sect"; Higgins, *More Years for the Locust*, p120.
176 Jefferys, "How the SWP narrowed into a sect".
177 Jim Nichol interview, June 2008.
178 Letter from Paul Mackney (for the IS Opposition Steering Committee), 14 December 1975.
179 Paul Mackney interview, June 2008.
180 John Rose interview, June 2008; Pete Clark interview, July 2008.
181 Paul Holborow interview, July 2008.
182 Cliff, *A World to Win*, p135.
183 Granville Williams interview, January 2009.
184 Communication from Alex Callinicos, August 2010.
185 John Palmer interview, June 2008.
186 Richard Kirkwood interview, October 2008.
187 Higgins, *Speak One More Time*, p119.
188 Willie Lee interview, January 2009.
189 John Phillips interview, July 2005.
190 Ron Senchak interview, May 2008.
191 Roger Huddle interview, July 2008.
192 Jim Nichol interview, June 2008.
193 John Rees interview, October 2008.
194 *Englandbericht und meine Konsequenzen daraus für die SAG*, [author unknown].
195 "Preliminary Political Perspectives", IS Bulletin March 1976.
196 Communication from Jimmy McCallum, January 2009.
197 Dave Hayes interview, December 2008.
198 "The IS Crisis Deepens", undated document of the IS Opposition [late 1975], Rich. MS 1117/box 117/file 4.
199 Roger Kline interview, February 2009.
200 Richard Hyman interview, September 2008; see R Hyman, "The Politics of Workplace Trade Unionism: Recent Tendencies and some Problems for Theory", *Capital and Class* 8, Summer 1979, pp54-67.
201 Pete Clark interview, July 2008.
202 *Socialist Worker*, 13 November 1976.
203 D Hallas, "Elections – We Have to Think Again", 21 April 1978, Steve Jefferys Archive, MRC, MSS.244/2/1/2.
204 Cliff, *A World to Win*, pp140-2.
205 Our Election Tactics in the General Election [1977?], Steve Jefferys Archive MRC MSS. 244/2/1/2.
206 T Cliff, "On Perspectives",

International Socialism 36 (April-May 1969).
207 Shaun Doherty interview, November 2008.
208 Untitled document [apparently by Steve Jefferys, 1978], Steve Jefferys Archive, MRC MSS.244/2/1/2.
209 Dave Sherry interview, January 2009.
210 T Cliff, "Why we need a Socialist Workers Party", *Socialist Worker*, 8 January 1977.
211 Author's recollection.
212 Cliff, "Why we need a Socialist Workers Party".
213 As announced in *Socialist Worker*.
214 P Sedgwick, "The SWP Fraud", Socialist Workers Party Bulletin, No 1, February 1977.
215 *International Socialism* 100 (July 1977).
216 Nigel Harris interview, September 2008.
217 Shaun Doherty interview, November 2008.
218 Lindsey German interview, September 2008.
219 Nick Howard interview, December 2008.
220 Donny Gluckstein interview, February 2009.
221 *International Socialism* 30 (Autumn 1967).
222 C Harman, *Bureaucracy and Resistance in Eastern Europe*, London, 1974.
223 Communication from Andy Strouthous, January 2010.
224 Extract from Stan Newens' diary for 13 January 1976 [Stan Newens archive].
225 *Daily Mail*, 18 August 1977.
226 Cliff, *A World to Win*, p52.
227 Communication from Joanne Norbury, Associated Newspapers librarian, April 2010.
228 Communication from Michael Foot, February 2005.
229 Communications from Air Vice-Marshal Andrew Vallance, April 2010.
230 Anna Gluckstein interview, October 2008.
231 *Socialist Worker*, 3 September 1977.
232 Contribution from the floor at a meeting on Cliff at Marxism 2009.
233 *Socialist Worker*, 15 October 1977.
234 D Renton, *When We Touched the Sky*, Cheltenham, 2006, p1.
235 Quotations from Renton, *When We Touched the Sky*, p69.
236 R Clutterbuck, *Britain in Agony*, London, 1978, p236.
237 See Renton, *When We Touched the Sky*, pp75-80.
238 Jim Nichol interview, June 2008.
239 Paul Holborow interview, July 2008.
240 Jack Robertson interview, November 2008.
241 See I Goodyer, *Crisis Music*, Manchester, 2009.
242 Red Saunders interview, May 2008.
243 Roger Huddle interview, July 2008.
244 Red Saunders interview, May 2008.
245 Renton, *When We Touched the Sky*, p99.
246 Chanie Rosenberg interview, March 2009.
247 T Cliff, "Build the Anti Nazi League", *Socialist Worker*, 13 May 1978.
248 *Socialist Challenge*, 4 May 1978.
249 Quoted in D Widgery, *Beating Time*, London, 1986, p113.
250 Paul Holborow interview, July 2008.
251 Renton, *When We Touched the Sky*, pp156-63.
252 NC Attitude to Gay Work [1973].
253 Author's recollection.
254 Author's recollection.
255 John Lindsay interview, May 2008.

256 *Socialist Worker*, 26 August 1978.
257 Written by the Socialist Workers Party Gay Group, London, 1979.
258 John Lindsay interview, May 2008.
259 See T Cliff, "Marxism and Oppression", Marxism 1995, BLSA C797/04/41.
260 John Lindsay interview, May 2008.
261 *Socialist Worker*, 3 December 1977.
262 Communication from Alex Callinicos, August 2010.
263 Communication from Alex Callinicos, August 2010.
264 *Socialist Worker*, 11 February 1978.
265 *Socialist Worker*, 3 June 1978.
266 C Harman, "Time to Resume Course", SWP Pre-Conference Bulletin No 3, May 1978.
267 T Cliff, "Scenario for the Future?", *Socialist Worker*, 4 March 1978.
268 T Cliff, "Divide and Rule!", *Socialist Worker*, 25 March 1978.
269 T Cliff, "Steel: These jobs *can* be fought for", *Socialist Worker*, 8 April 1978.
270 T Cliff, "Thorns: The Great Switch-Off", *Socialist Worker*, 29 April 1978.
271 T Cliff, "Unemployment: Building the resistance", *Socialist Worker*, 3 June 1978.
272 *Socialist Worker*, 27 May, 10 June 1978.
273 Pete Clark interview, July 2008.
274 State of the Organisation, December 1978, Steve Jefferys Archive, MRC MSS. 244/2/1/2.
275 *Socialist Worker*, 24 June 1978.
276 Letter from John Hodgman to CC, 5 August 1978, Steve Jefferys Archive, MRC MSS. 244/2/1/2.
277 P Foot, "Continued next week", *Socialist Worker*, 5 August 1978.
278 Letter from John Hodgman, 23 July 1978, Steve Jefferys Archive, MRC MSS. 244/2/1/2.
279 Steve Jefferys, "The politics behind the row on the paper" [undated], Steve Jefferys Archive, MRC MSS. 244/2/1/2.
280 Chris Harman interview, April 2009.
281 Communication from Alex Callinicos, August 2010.
282 Chris Harman interview, April 2009.
283 Communication from Alex Callinicos, August 2010.
284 Letter from Paul Foot to Cliff [1999?], Tony Cliff Archive, MRC MSS.459/2/21.
285 *Socialist Worker*, 19 August 1978.
286 T Cliff, "Getting away from boring reports", *Socialist Worker*, 2 September 1978.
287 T Cliff, "From Calcutta to Kings Cross", *Socialist Worker*, 2 September 1978.
288 T Cliff and J Robertson, "The Future of Socialist Worker", *SWP Bulletin* No 6, 1978.
289 *Socialist Worker*, 21 October, 1978.
290 T Cliff, "100,000 Plus", *Socialist Worker*, 7 October 1978.
291 T Cliff, "Still United", *Socialist Worker*, 30 September 1978.
292 Ralph Darlington interview, May 2008.
293 Roger Huddle interview, July 2008.
294 Mary Phillips interview, June 2005.
295 John Rose interview, June 2008.
296 T Cliff, *Chrysler Workers: the fight for a future*, London, 1978.
297 Cliff, *Chrysler Workers: The fight for a future*, p23.
298 J Molyneux, *Marxism and the Party*, London, 1978.
299 John Molyneux interview, September 2008.
300 Chris Harman interview, April 2009.
301 Mel Norris interview, November

302 Alex Callinicos interview, July 2008.
303 Julie Waterson interview, November 2008.
304 John Molyneux interview, September 2008.
305 Untitled typescript by Chris Harman [1978?], Steve Jefferys Archive, MRC MSS.244/2/1/2.
306 Letter from Steve Jefferys to Duncan Hallas, 21 September 1978, Steve Jefferys Archive, MRC MSS. 244/2/1/2.
307 T Cliff, "Stormy weather for ship of state", *Socialist Worker*, 16 September 1978.
308 T Cliff, "Ford fight for us all", *Socialist Worker*, 30 September 1978.
309 T Cliff, "The Prod Fraud", *Socialist Worker*, 14 October 1978.
310 P Foot, *The Vote: How It Was Won and How It Was Undermined*, London, 2005, p396.
311 Untitled draft, Steve Jefferys Archive, MRC MSS. 244/2/1/2.
312 *Guardian*, 27 April 2010.
313 *Socialist Worker*, 23 June 1979.
314 Communication from Peter Alexander, December 2008.
315 See C Harman, "The crisis of the European revolutionary left", *International Socialism* 4 (Spring 1979).

CHAPTER 10

1 Andy Strouthous interview, July 2008.
2 T Cliff, "Ten years on", *Socialist Worker*, 26 May 1979.
3 T Cliff, "Where do we go from here?", *Socialist Review* 1, April 1978.
4 *Socialist Worker*, 6 January 1979.
5 *Socialist Worker*, 3 February 1979.
6 W Thompson, *The Good Old Cause*, London, 1992, p164; G Andrews, *Endgames and New Times*, London, 2004, pp145-8.
7 *Marxism Today*, September 1978.
8 T Cliff, *Lenin* vol 1, p236, quoting Lenin, *Collected Works* 11, p351.
9 *International Socialism* 5 (Summer 1979).
10 T Cliff, "Ten Years On: 1969 to 1979", *Socialist Worker*, 26 May 1979.
11 *International Socialism* 6 (Autumn 1979).
12 *Socialist Worker*, 30 June 1979.
13 *Socialist Worker*, 17 November 1979.
14 Jack Robertson interview, November 2008.
15 Helen Blair interview, January 2009.
16 Willie Lee interview, January 2009.
17 Dave Sherry interview, January 2009.
18 Communication from Mike Gonzalez, March 2010.
19 Alan Borrell interview, January 2009.
20 Willie Black interview, July 2008.
21 Simon Hester interview, July 2008.
22 Steve Jefferys, "How the SWP narrowed into a sect".
23 S Cohen, *Ramparts of Resistance*, London, 2006, pp30, 212.
24 Willie Lee interview, January 2009.
25 JW Stutje, *Ernest Mandel*, London, 2009, p204.
26 John Molyneux interview, September 2008.
27 Reprinted and discussed in M Jacques and F Mulhern (eds), *The Forward March of Labour Halted?*, London, 1981.
28 A Gorz, *Farewell to the Working Class*, London, 1982.
29 T Cliff, "It's time to close ranks", *Socialist Worker*, 15 December 1979.

30 Dave Hayes interview, December 2008.
31 Andy Strouthous interview, July 2008.
32 Communication from Alex Callinicos, August 2010.
33 *Socialist Worker*, 26 January, 2 February, 1 March, 22 March 1980.
34 T Cliff, "The state of the struggle today", *Socialist Review*, April 1986.
35 T Cliff, "Steel: Time to stoke the fires down below", *Socialist Worker*, 12 April 1980.
36 T Cliff, "After May 14...", *Socialist Worker*, 17 May 1980.
37 T Cliff, "The Right to Work: A new stage?", *Socialist Review*, 15 October-14 December 1980.
38 Cliff, "Building in the downturn".
39 T Cliff, "Who's left to back Benn?", *Socialist Worker*, 14 June 1980.
40 Tariq Ali interview, February 2009.
41 *Socialist Worker*, 16 January to 20 February 1982.
42 Andy Strouthous interview, July 2008.
43 T Cliff, "In the fight against this... Is he going to be any help?", *Socialist Worker*, 29 November 1980.
44 D Hallas and A Callinicos, "The end of the Labour Party as we know it?", *Socialist Worker*, 6 June 1981.
45 T Cliff, "After the riots we say Jobs not Jails", *Socialist Worker*, 18 July 1981.
46 *Sunday Telegraph*, 12 July 1981.
47 Dave Sherry interview, January 2009.
48 T Cliff, "Labour Left in Retreat", *Socialist Worker*, 12 June 1982.
49 T Cliff, "Picking up the Pieces", *Socialist Worker*, 24 July 1982.
50 T Cliff, "Building in the downturn", *Socialist Review*, April 1983.
51 T Cliff, "Prologue to an upturn", *Socialist Review*, June 1983.
52 T Cliff, "The charge of the right brigade", *Socialist Review*, October 1983.
53 *Socialist Worker*, 5 February 1983.
54 Cliff, "Building in the downturn".
55 Cliff, "Building in the downturn".
56 Cliff, "Building in the downturn".
57 Jacques and Mulhern (eds), *The Forward March of Labour Halted?*, p89.
58 Renton, *When We Touched the Sky*, pp173-4.
59 *Socialist Worker*, 17 April 1982; communication from Geoff Collier, May 2008.
60 T Cliff and P Clark, "The SWP – building in the next nine months", *Socialist Worker*, 31 July 1982.
61 Cliff, "Building in the downturn".
62 Communication from Peter Alexander, December 2008.
63 T Cliff, "You can't have a rank and file movement if the factories are empty", *Socialist Review*, 20 May-17 June 1982.
64 Dave Ayre interview, July 2008.
65 Cliff, "Building in the downturn".
66 Cliff, "The charge of the right brigade".
67 Cliff, "Prologue to an upturn".
68 Andy Strouthous interview, July 2008.
69 Communication from Alex Callinicos, August 2010.
70 As announced in *Socialist Worker*.
71 Geoff Brown interview, May 2008.
72 Andy Wilson interview, June 2008.
73 Eddie Prevost interview, June 2008.
74 Ralph Darlington interview, May 2008.
75 Sabby Sagall interview, May 2008.
76 Donny Gluckstein interview, February 2009.

77 See G Paizis, *Love and the Novel*, Basingstoke, 1998.
78 George Paizis interview, October 2008.
79 *Socialist Worker*, 25 July 1981.
80 John Rose interview, June 2008.
81 Communication from Alex Callinicos, August 2010.
82 Pete Clark interview, July 2008.
83 *Socialist Worker*, 12 March 1983.
84 A Callinicos, *The Revolutionary Ideas of Karl Marx*, London, 1983.
85 Alex Callinicos interview, July 2008.
86 *Socialist Worker*, 26 February 1983.
87 T Cliff, "Building in the downturn".
88 Clare Fermont interview, September 2008.
89 Jim Nichol interview, June 2008.
90 Will Fancy's notes on copy of 1970 Conference resolutions, Fancy MS 1171/box 17/1970.
91 Geoff Brown interview, May 2008.
92 Eamonn McCann interview, July 2008.
93 "Conference on Women", IS Bulletin, June 1971.
94 Mary Phillips interview, June 2005.
95 NC minutes, July 1972.
96 EC minutes, 14 May 1973.
97 Sheila McGregor interview, January 2009.
98 *Socialist Worker*, 6 December 1975.
99 *Socialist Worker*, 17 June 1978.
100 Untitled typescript, apparently by Harman, 1978, Steve Jefferys Archive, MRC MSS. 244/2/1/2.
101 *Socialist Worker*, 1 July 1978.
102 Communication from Alex Callinicos, August 2010.
103 Sheila McGregor interview, January 2009.
104 Lindsey German interview, September 2008.
105 Penny Krantz interview, May 2008.
106 Andy Strouthous interview, July 2008.
107 Communication from Alex Callinicos, August 2010.
108 Sue Caldwell interview, September 2008.
109 T Cliff, *Class Struggle and Women's Liberation: 1640 to today*, London, 1984.
110 Communication from Alex Callinicos, August 2010.
111 Cliff, *Class Struggle and Women's Liberation*, p7.
112 Ciff, *Class Struggle and Women's Liberation*, p161, quoting D Barrio, *Let Me Speak!*, London 1978, pp198-9.
113 Cliff, *Class Struggle and Women's Liberation*, p118.
114 Cliff, *Class Struggle and Women's Liberation*, p158.
115 Cliff, *Class Struggle and Women's Liberation*, p245.
116 Cliff, *Class Struggle and Women's Liberation*, p128.
117 Cliff, *Class Struggle and Women's Liberation*, p132.
118 Cliff, *Class Struggle and Women's Liberation*, p66.
119 Cliff, *Class Struggle and Women's Liberation*, p163.
120 Cliff, *Class Struggle and Women's Liberation*, p233.
121 Cliff, *Class Struggle and Women's Liberation*, p206.
122 K Marx, "Contribution to the Critique of Hegel's Philosophy of Law", in Marx and Engels, *Collected Works*, vol 3, p175.
123 K Ennis, "Women's Consciousness", *International Socialism* 68 (April 1974).
124 Cliff, *Class Struggle and Women's Liberation*, p240.
125 Sheila McGregor interview, January 2009.
126 Chanie Rosenberg interview, March 2009.

127 Cliff, *Class Struggle and Women's Liberation*, p261.
128 J Williamson, "The Woman Question", *City Limits* 139, 1-7 June 1984.
129 N Carlin, "Women and the Left", *City Limits* 141, 15-21 June 1984.
130 Cliff, *Class Struggle and Women's Liberation*, pp228-9.
131 J Molyneux, "Do working class men benefit from women's oppression?", *International Socialism* 25 (Autumn 1984); S McGregor, "A reply to John Molyneux on women's oppression", *International Socialism* 30 (Autumn 1985); J Molyneux, "Marxism and male benefits – a reply to Sheila McGregor", L German, "Oppression, individuals and classes: a rejoinder to John Molyneux", *International Socialism* 32 (Summer 1986).
132 Cliff, *A World to Win*, p146.
133 T Cliff, "The Working Class and the Oppressed", Marxism 1993, BLSA C797/02/116.
134 John Molyneux interview, September 2008.

CHAPTER 11

1 As advertised in *Socialist Worker*.
2 Eileen Boyle interview, January 2009.
3 Joe Hartney, letter to *The Guardian*, 15 April 2000.
4 N Strike, *Strike by Name*, London, 2009, p22.
5 T Cliff, "Neither side has broken through", *Socialist Worker*, 14 April 1984.
6 Steve Hammill interview, July 2008.
7 *Socialist Worker*, 21 April 1984.
8 Peter Alexander interview, July 2004; communication from Alex Callinicos, August 2010.
9 Ian Mitchell interview, January 2009.
10 John Rees interview, October 2008.
11 T Cliff, "A crisis of leadership", *Socialist Worker*, 9 June 1984.
12 *Socialist Worker*, 16 June 1984.
13 Undated notes, Tony Cliff Archive, MRC MSS. 459/3/3.
14 Communication from Peter Alexander, December 2008.
15 Peter Alexander interview, July 2004.
16 Andy Strouthous interview, July 2008.
17 Sheila McGregor interview, January 2009.
18 Dave Hayes interview, December 2008.
19 Communication from Alex Callinicos, August 2010.
20 Alex Callinicos interview, June 2008.
21 Pat Stack interview, September 2008.
22 Andy Strouthous interview, July 2008.
23 Ian Mitchell interview, January 2009; Steve Hammill interview, July 2008.
24 John Molyneux interview, September 2008.
25 Martin Smith interview, October 2008.
26 Simon Hester interview, July 2008.
27 Chris Bambery interview, October 2008.
28 Pat Stack interview, September 2008.
29 Communication from Alex Callinicos, August 2010.
30 Ian Mitchell interview, January 2009.
31 *International Socialism* 29 (Summer 1985), pp3-61.
32 P Foot, *An Agitator of the Worst Type*, London, 1986.
33 *International Socialism* 31, Spring 1986, pp69-111.
34 Clare Fermont interview, September 2008.

35 Foot, *The Vote*, pxii.
36 Clare Fermont interview, September 2008.
37 Simon Hester interview, July 2008.
38 "Stopping the Filth", *Socialist Worker*, 6 October 1984.
39 T Cliff, "The state of the struggle today", *Socialist Review*, April 1986.
40 Weyman Bennett interview, November 2008.
41 *Socialist Worker*, 15 November 1986.
42 *Socialist Worker*, 16 November 1985.
43 Communication from Alex Callinicos, August 2010.
44 Cliff, "The state of the struggle today".
45 Cliff, "The state of the struggle today".
46 "Education document", Socialist Workers Party Conference 1986 Report; A Strouthous, "Packing it in", *Socialist Review*, April 1986.
47 As advertised in *Socialist Worker*.
48 Author's recollection.
49 Undated notes, Tony Cliff Archive, MRC MSS. 459/3/3.
50 Pat Stack interview, September 2008.
51 Weyman Bennett interview, November 2008.
52 Sue Caldwell interview, September 2008.
53 Sean Vernell interview, September 2008.
54 Dave Hayes interview, December 2008.
55 Peter Alexander interview, July 2004.
56 Eileen Boyle interview, January 2009.
57 Martin Smith interview, October 2008.
58 Sean Vernell interview, September 2008.
59 Shaun Doherty interview, November 2008.
60 Mark Krantz interview, May 2008.
61 John Rees interview, October 2008.
62 C Sparks, "Lenin and the patriots", *Socialist Review*, April 1985; T Cliff, "In defence of Lenin", *Socialist Review*, May 1985.
63 N Harris, untitled column, *Socialist Review*, September 1987; T Cliff, "Where are the Workers?", *Socialist Review*, October 1987.
64 Nigel Harris interview, September 2008.
65 Danny Gluckstein interview, January 2009.
66 D Gluckstein, "The missing party", *International Socialism* 22 (Winter 1984); A Callinicos, "Party and class before 1917", *International Socialism* 24 (Summer 1984).
67 Tape of the debate. (Thanks to Annie Nehmad.)
68 D Gluckstein, "A rejoinder to Alex Callinicos", *International Socialism* 25 (Autumn 1984); Donny Gluckstein interview, February 2009.
69 Decca FLP 1.
70 A Y Badayev, *Bolsheviks in the Tsarist Duma*, London, 1987.
71 E Heffer, *The Class Struggle in Parliament*, London, 1973.
72 Alex Callinicos interview, June 2008.
73 Communication from Alex Callinicos, June 2008.
74 Ron Margulies interview, December 2008.
75 T Cliff and D Gluckstein, *Marxism and Trade Union Struggle*, London, 1986, especially pp9-10.
76 Donny Gluckstein interview, February 2009.
77 The definitive study of the RILU, published since Cliff's death, is R

Tosstorff, *Profintern: Die Rote Gewerkschaftsinternationale 1920-1937*, Paderborn, 2004.
78 Cliff and Gluckstein, *Marxism and Trade Union Struggle*, pp49, 9.
79 Cliff and Gluckstein, *Marxism and Trade Union Struggle*, p99.
80 Cliff and Gluckstein, *Marxism and Trade Union Struggle*, p33.
81 Cliff and Gluckstein, *Marxism and Trade Union Struggle*, p27.
82 See for example the accounts given by J Redman (Brian Pearce), "The Early Years of the CPGB", *Labour Review*, vol 3, no 1, (January-February 1958), and D Hallas, "The Communist Party and the General Strike", *International Socialism* 88 (May 1976).
83 Cliff and Gluckstein, *Marxism and Trade Union Struggle*, pp91, 285-6, 282.
84 T Cliff and D Gluckstein, *The Labour Party: A Marxist History*, London, 1988.
85 Donny Gluckstein interview, February 2009.
86 Cliff and Gluckstein, *The Labour Party*, p2.
87 Cliff and Gluckstein, *The Labour Party*, p14.
88 Cliff and Gluckstein, *The Labour Party*, pp31, 37, 48, 53.
89 Cliff and Gluckstein, *The Labour Party*, pp72, 81.
90 Cliff and Gluckstein, *The Labour Party*, p180.
91 Cliff and Gluckstein, *The Labour Party*, pp218, 219, 237, 242-3.
92 Cliff and Gluckstein, *The Labour Party*, pp131, 278, 390.
93 M Jenkins, *Bevanism, Labour's High Tide*, Nottingham, 1979.
94 Cliff and Gluckstein, *The Labour Party*, pp247, 266, 263.
95 Cliff and Gluckstein, *The Labour Party*, pp342, 349, 355.
96 Cliff and Gluckstein, *The Labour Party*, pp85, 107-8, 111.
97 Cliff and Gluckstein, *The Labour Party*, pp363-4, 110, 108.
98 Cliff and Gluckstein, *The Labour Party*, pp31, 83.
99 A Richardson, review of Cliff and Gluckstein, *The Labour Party*, *Revolutionary History* 2/3 (Autumn 1989).
100 See also an interview reviewing his life: T Cliff, "Fifty-Five years a revolutionary", *Socialist Review*, July 1987.
101 Author's recollection.
102 "Monday Agenda", *Guardian*, 20 July 1987.
103 "Letters", *Guardian*, 22 July 1987.
104 *Socialist Worker*, 21 November 1987.
105 T Cliff, "In fighting mood", *Socialist Worker Review*, March 1988.
106 T Cliff, "Dark clouds and silver linings", *Socialist Worker Review*, October 1988.
107 *Socialist Worker*, 19 November 1988.
108 Mark Krantz interview, May 2008.
109 T Cliff, "First stirrings", *Socialist Worker Review* 121, June 1989.
110 T Cliff, "First stirrings".
111 T Cliff, "Building for the Future", *Socialist Worker Review*, December 1989.
112 Peter Taaffe, The great anti-poll tax victory, http://socialistworld.net/eng/2010/02/2601.html.
113 Communication from Mike Gonzalez, March 2010.

CHAPTER 12

1 Mandel, *Revolutionary Marxism Today*, p150.
2 T Ali, *Redemption*, London, 1990, pp180-1.
3 *Socialist Review* 126, December 1989
4 L Trotski, *Stalin*, London, 1947,

p383.
5   T Cliff, "Balance of Powerlessness", *Socialist Review*, December 1991.
6   T Cliff, "Socialists under Blair", Marxism 1997, BLSA C797/06/43.
7   See Foot, *The Politics of Harold Wilson*, p111.
8   Cliff, *Writings* vol 3, pp129-30.
9   M Haynes and P Glatter, "The Russian Catastrophe", *International Socialism* 81(Winter 1998).
10 T Cliff, "The Test of Time", *Socialist Review*, July 1998.
11 Chris Bambery interview, October 2008.
12 Chanie Rosenberg interview, March 2009.
13 *Socialist Worker*, 7 April 1990.
14 Chris Bambery interview, October 2008.
15 *Socialist Worker*, 17 November, 1990.
16 *Socialist Worker*, 16 November 1991.
17 L German and P Morgan, "The prospects for socialists – an interview with Tony Cliff", *International Socialism* 55 (Summer 1992).
18 Chris Bambery interview, October 2008.
19 T Cliff, "Class Struggle in the 90s", *Socialist Worker*, 18 July 1992.
20 *Socialist Worker*, 24 October 1992.
21 Sean Vernell interview, September 2008.
22 T Cliff, "Shape the future", *Socialist Worker*, 23 January 1993.
23 *Socialist Worker*, 14 November 1992.
24 *Socialist Worker*, 13 November 1993.
25 T Cliff, "Why do we need a revolutionary party?", SWP Pre-Conference Bulletin no 2, 1994.
26 Pete Green interview, August 2008.
27 Andy Wilson interview, June 2008.
28 Julie Waterson interview, November 2008.
29 Chris Bambery interview, October 2008.
30 Julie Waterson interview, November 2008.
31 J Rees, *The Algebra of Revolution*, London, 1998.
32 John Rees interview, October 2008.
33 As announced and reported in *Socialist Worker*.
34 Martin Smith interview, October 2008.
35 *Socialist Worker*, 23 October 1993.
36 *Socialist Worker*, 4 June 1994.
37 A Fogg, "The prophecy of 1994", *Guardian*, 21 July 2009.
38 Chris Bambery interview, October 2008.
39 Alex Callinicos interview, July 2008.
40 Weyman Bennett interview, November 2008.
41 Communication from Alex Callinicos, August 2010.
42 Colin Barker interview, May 2008.
43 "The End of the Road: Deutscher's Capitulation to Stalinism", *International Socialism* 15 (Winter 1963).
44 T Cliff, *Trotsky* vol 1: *Towards October 1879-1917*, London, 1989, pp14-17.
45 Cliff, *Trotsky*, vol 1, pp37, 174.
46 Cliff, *Trotsky*, vol 1, pp251, 261; cf. *Lenin*, vol 2, pp376-7, 368-9.
47 T Cliff, *Trotsky*, vol 2: *The Sword of the Revolution 1917-1923*, London, 1990, p115.
48 Cliff, *Trotsky*, vol 2, pp185-6.
49 Cliff, *Trotsky*, vol 2, pp235-6.

50 Cliff, *Trotsky*, vol 2, p274.
51 J Molyneux, *Leon Trotsky's Theory of Revolution*, Brighton, 1981, especially pp87-112 (Chapter 3: Resisting the Degeneration)
52 John Molyneux interview, September 2008.
53 Cliff, *Trotsky*, vol 3, p17.
54 Cliff, *Trotsky*, vol 3: *Fighting the Rising Stalinist Bureaucracy 1923-1927*, London, 1991, p59.
55 Cliff, *Trotsky*, vol 3, p278.
56 Sean Vernell interview, September 2008.
57 Cliff, *Trotsky*, vol 4, p71.
58 Lindsey German interview, September 2008.
59 Cliff, *Trotsky*, vol 4, pp14, 19.
60 Cliff, *Trotsky*, vol 4, pp49-50, 64-7.
61 Cliff, *Trotsky*, vol 4, pp233, 139.
62 Cliff, *Trotsky*, vol 4, p224.
63 Cliff, *Trotsky*, vol 4, pp300, 306.
64 Cliff, *Trotsky*, vol 4, pp367, 384.
65 P Broué, *Trotsky*, Paris, 1988.
66 *Revolutionary Russia*, 1/2 (December 1988), pp225-7.
67 *Revolutionary Russia*, 3/1 (June 1990), pp134-6.
68 *Revolutionary Russia*, 4/2 (December 1991), pp293-6; see also Thatcher's review of the third vol of *Trotsky* in *Soviet Studies*, 44/1 (1992), p164.
69 *Revolutionary Russia*, 5/2 (December 1992), pp232-4. (Thanks to Paul Flewers for drawing my attention to this group of reviews.)
70 As announced in *Socialist Worker*.
71 Pat Stack interview, September 2008.
72 Chanie Rosenberg interview, March 2009.
73 Willie Black interview, July 2008.
74 Red Saunders interview, May 2008.
75 Geoff Brown interview, May 2008.
76 Anna Gluckstein interview, October 2008.
77 Anna Gluckstein interview, October 2008; Danny Gluckstein interview, January 2009.
78 John Rees interview, October 2008.
79 Ian Mitchell interview, January 2009.
80 John Rees interview, October 2008.
81 Choi Il-bung interview, August 2008.
82 Letter to Volkhard Mosler, 29 July 1993, Tony Cliff Archive, MRC MSS. 459/3/30.
83 Author's recollection.
84 T Cliff, "Engels".
85 *Socialist Worker*, 12 November 1994.
86 T Cliff, "In the balance", *Socialist Review*, February 1995.
87 T Cliff, "'We can learn from each other'", *Socialist Worker*, 11 March 1995.
88 North London District Notes, 26 April 1995.
89 T Cliff, "Labour's Crisis and the Revolutionary Alternative", *Socialist Review*, November 1996.
90 T Cliff, "Why Do Workers Look to Blair?", Marxism 1995, BLSA C797/04/44.
91 Communication from Joseph Choonara, September 2010.
92 Cliff and Gluckstein, *The Labour Party*, pp389-433.
93 Donny Gluckstein interview, February 2009.
94 Cliff and Gluckstein, *The Labour Party*, p395.
95 Cliff and Gluckstein, *The Labour Party*, pp430-31.
96 Cliff and Gluckstein, *The Labour Party*, p433.
97 T Cliff, "50 Years of the International Socialist Tradition", *International Socialist Review* (Summer 1997).

CHAPTER 13

1. *Socialist Worker*, 17 May 1997.
2. T Cliff, "Change is going to come: but how?", *Socialist Review*, June 1997.
3. *Tony Cliff's 80th Birthday*, London [1997].
4. *Socialist Worker*, 4 October 1997.
5. T Cliff, "Socialists under Blair", Marxism 1997, BLSA C797/06/43.
6. Lindsey German interview, September 2008.
7. Tony Cliff interviewed by Daniel Lak, 1992, BLSA C1377/46.
8. Author's recollection.
9. T Cliff, *Marxism at the Millennium*, London 2000, p83.
10. T Cliff et al, "Final Rally", Marxism 1998, BLSA C797/07/41.
11. Alex Callinicos interview, July 2008.
12. Cliff, "Socialists under Blair", Marxism 1997, BLSA C797/06/43.
13. *Socialist Worker*, 10 October 1998.
14. *International Socialism* 80 (Autumn 1998).
15. Weyman Bennett interview, November 2008.
16. Ron Margulies interview, December 2008.
17. Communication from Alex Callinicos, August 2010.
18. Shaun Doherty interview, November 2008.
19. T Cliff, *Trotskyism after Trotsky*, London, 1999.
20. Cliff, *Trotskyism after Trotsky*, p14.
21. Cliff, *Trotskyism after Trotsky*, p8.
22. Cliff, *Trotskyism after Trotsky*, pp57, 59.
23. Cliff, *Trotskyism after Trotsky*, pp7, 14.
24. Cliff, *Trotskyism after Trotsky*, pp46, 79.
25. Cliff, *Trotskyism after Trotsky*, p80.
26. V I Lenin, "Certain Features of the Historical Development of Marxism" (1910), *Collected Works*, vol 17, pp39-44.
27. T Cliff, "The Permanent Arms Economy", Marxism 1999, BLSA C797/08/51.
28. Cliff, *Trotskyism after Trotsky*, pp81-2.
29. Cliff, *Trotskyism after Trotsky*, p82.
30. Danny Gluckstein interview, January 2009.
31. Red Saunders interview, May 2008.
32. Chris Bambery interview, October 2008.
33. Lindsey German interview, September 2008.
34. T Cliff, "James Connolly and the Limits of Syndicalism", Marxism 1998, BLSA C797/07/44; T Cliff et al, "Final rally", Marxism 1999, BLSA C797/08/48.
35. Lindsey German interview, September 2008.
36. Anna Gluckstein interview, October 2008.
37. Author's recollection.
38. Anna Gluckstein interview, October 2008.
39. Quoted in EP Thompson, *William Morris: Romantic to Revolutionary*, London, 1977, p244.
40. Anna Gluckstein interview, October 2008.
41. Cliff, *A World to Win*, p1.
42. MRC MSS 459/6/9.
43. Cliff, "The Permanent Arms Economy", Marxism 1999, BLSA C797/08/51.
44. T Cliff et al, "Final Rally", Marxism 1999, BLSA C797/08/48.
45. Jim Cronin interview, May 2008.
46. Mel Norris interview, November 2008.

47 Communication from Richard Seymour, October 2008.
48 Communication from Christian Hogsbjerg, June 2008.
49 *Socialist Worker*, 20 November 1999.
50 T Cliff, *Marxism at the Millennium*, London, 2000.
51 Cliff, *Marxism at the Millennium*, pp12-13.
52 Cliff, *Marxism at the Millennium*, p12.
53 Cliff, *Lenin* vol I, pp163-8.
54 Cliff, *Marxism at the Millennium*, p20.
55 Cliff, *Marxism at the Millennium*, pp4, 27.
56 Cliff, *Marxism at the Millennium*, pp5, 6.
57 Cliff, *Marxism at the Millennium*, p47.
58 Quoted in J Charlton, "Talking Seattle", *International Socialism* 86 (Spring 2000), p16
59 Cliff, *Marxism at the Millennium*, p86.
60 See documents in SWP Internal Bulletin, Spring 2000.
61 Alex Callinicos interview, July 2008.
62 Lindsey German interview, September 2008.
63 Alex Callinicos interview, July 2008.
64 "Letter to ISO from Alex Callinicos and Tony Cliff", 20 February 2000, SWP Internal Bulletin, Spring 2000.
65 "Letter to ISO Committee from Alex Callinicos and Tony Cliff", 23 February 2000, SWP Internal Bulletin, Spring 2000.
66 See SWP Internal Bulletin, Spring 2000.
67 "Letter from Alex Callinicos and Tony Cliff to ISO Steering Committee", 29 March 2000, SWP Internal Bulletin, Spring 2000.
68 Ahmed Shawki interview, November 2008.
69 Joel Geier interview, March 2009.
70 Communication from Alex Callinicos, August 2010.
71 A Callinicos and P Garganas, "ISO breaks with IS Tendency", SWP International Bulletin, March 2001.
72 John Rees interview, October 2008.
73 Donny Gluckstein interview, February 2009.
74 Martin Smith interview, October 2008.
75 Chris Bambery interview, October 2008.
76 Sean Vernell interview, September 2008.
77 Lindsey German interview, September 2008.
78 Danny Gluckstein interview, January 2009.
79 F Nietzsche, *Thus Spoke Zarathustra*, Oxford, 2005, p62.
80 Voltaire, *Lettres philosophiques*, Paris, 1964, p159.
81 Communication from John Charlton, December 2010.
82 *Tony Cliff 1917-2000*, London, 2000.
83 *Guardian,* 11 April 2000.
84 L German, "Tony Cliff", *The Independent,* 5 April 2000.
85 J Higgins, "Tony Cliff: A Man of his Time", *Weekly Worker*, 20 April 2000.
86 *Revolutionary History*, 7/4 (2000), pp212-20.
87 *Guardian*, 13 April 2000, 14 April 2000.
88 *Socialist Worker*, 29 April 2000.

CHAPTER 14
1 Broué, *Histoire de l'internationale communiste*; J-J Marie, *Lénine*; J-F Fayet, *Karl Radek (1885-1939)*; R Tosstorff, *Profintern: Die Rote Gewerkschaftsinternationale 1920-1937*.

2   Joel Geier interview, March 2009.
3   "Optimism of the Will", *Socialist Review*, May 2000.
4   John Lindsay interview, May 2008.
5   Communication from Sandy Irvine, September 2007.
6   Ian Gibson interview, June 2008.
7   Paul Mackney interview, June 2008.
8   Lord MacDonald interview, February 2009.
9   Tirril Harris interview, September 2008.
10 Serge, *Birth of Our Power*, p66.

Name index

Tony Cliff/Ygael Gluckstein is not included in the index, except for a list of books and major articles. Since Socialist Review Group, International Socialists, Socialist Workers Party, *Socialist Worker*, *Socialist Review* and *International Socialism* occur very frequently in the text, index references are only to significant mentions.

Abern, Martin, 35
Abramovich, 22
Acción Comunista, 326
Adenauer, Konrad, 61, 144
Aesop, 217
AEU (Amalgamated Engineering Union), 178-80, 257-8, 263
Affleck, Arthur, 318
Ainsworth, Bill, 133-4, 137, 142
Al Ittihad, 58
Alexander II, 220-1
Alexander, Ken, 246
Alexander, Peter, 320, 477
Alexander, Robert, 522
Ali, Muhammad, 428
Ali, Tariq, 272, 275, 284, 287, 298, 338, 452, 509
Allenby, Edmund, 2
Althusser, Louis, 529
Angry Brigade, 324
Anti Nazi League, i, 366, 404, 420-3, 425-8, 431-3, 437, 455, 457, 517, 556
Archer, Jeffrey, 327
Armstrong, Bob, 120, 122
Armstrong, Elsie, 122
ASTMS (Association of Scientific, Technical and Managerial Staffs), 367-8
Atkinson, Bert, 98
Attlee, Clement, 69, 89, 94, 143, 245, 499
AUEW (Amalgamated Union of Engineering Workers), 317, 338, 403, 425
Avanguardia Operaia, 326, 370-1, 388, 438
Ayre, Dave, 458

Baader-Meinhof, 324
Babeuf, Gracchus, x
Bach, Johann Sebastian, 422
Badayev, AY, 494
Baer, Gabriel, 34, 56-8, 60, 62, 81, 83
Bain, Peter, 210, 364
Bakunin, Mikhail, 291
Balfour, Arthur, 2
Balzac, Honoré de, 11
Bambery, Chris, 377-8, 516-7, 542, 550
Bammifneh, 22, 31
Bandaranaike, Sirimavo, 141
Barcia, Robert, 326
Barker, Colin, 212, 259-65, 272, 280, 292, 311, 518, 551
Barrett, Terry, 266, 285, 311
Barrio, Domitila, 468
Batalla, La, 139
Bauer, Otto, 100, 220
Bax, Ernest Belfort, 468
Beatles, The, 269, 277
Beauvoir, Simone de, 163
Beba, 25
Beecham, Dave, 444
Beethoven, Ludwig van, 460, 552
Behan, Brian, 171-2
Ben Dov, Hanna, 22, 25-7, 34, 63
Ben-Gurion, David, 5, 21
Benn, Tony, 356, 377, 451-3, 455-6, 487, 497, 500, 512
Bennett, Les, 180, 257
Bennett, Weyman, 491, 517, 538
Benns, F Lee, 147
Bentwich, Norman, 53
Berger, Joseph, 20
Bernstein, Eduard, 183, 187
Bettelheim, Charles, 112
Bevan, Aneurin, 143, 169, 179, 245, 500
Bidwell, Syd, 141, 178, 228, 250

NAME INDEX 649

Big Flame, 410
Bin Laden, Osama, 552
Binyamin, Rabbi, 22
Birch, Reg, 180-1, 263, 265
Birchall, Ian, 212, 248-9, 273, 275, 293-8, 325, 347, 374, 389
Birmingham Post, 318
Black Dwarf, 295
Black Muslims, 428
Black, Willie, 448, 526
Blackburn, Robin, 272
Blair, Tony, 530-5, 558
Blauweiss, Hava, 61
Blauweiss, Theodor, 61-2
Blum, Léon, 89
BNP (British National Party), (1960s) 250, (1990s) 517, 532
Boggs, Grace Lee *see* Lee, Grace
Bolshevik Party, 2, 7, 223, 291, 393-5, 398-400, 418, 470, 492, 494, 539
Bookmarks, 532, 557
Bordiga, Amadeo, 104
Bornstein, Sam, 99, 108, 160, 522
Borrell, Alan, 447
Bowie, David, 421
Box, George, 463
Boyle, Eileen, 476, 491
Brailsford, Henry Noel, 273
Brandler, Heinrich, 37, 59, 151
Branston, Peter, 523
Brit Kommunistim Mahapchanim, *see* Revolutionary Communist League
Brit Shalom, 22
British Council for Peace in Vietnam, 273
British Sociological Association, x
Broué, Pierre, iii, 393, 402, 522, 524-5, 556
Brown, George, 245, 269
Buchan, Norman, 418
Bugler, Jeremy, 317
Bukharin, Nikolai, 102, 112, 239, 397, 521
Burchill, Julie, 552
Burnham, James, 54-6
Bush, George W, 552
Byrne, Johnny, 122-4

Cadogan, Peter, 194
Caffoor, Mike, 206, 250
Cagney, James, 336
Cahiers Léon Trotsky, 522
Cairns, Walter, 503
Caldwell, Sue, 466
Callaghan, James, 205, 410, 416, 435-6
Callinicos, Alex, 80, 344, 429, 434, 450, 461-2, 465, 484, 493-4, 529, 533, 548-9, 557
Campaign Against Racial Discrimination, 250
Campbell, Frank, 324
Cannon, James P, 90
Cant, Bob, 424
Carlin, Norah, 275, 473
Carlsson, Geoff, 133, 140, 143, 175, 178, 180-1, 257-8, 265-6
Carlsson, Renée, 133
Carpenter, John, 352
Carr, Robert, 324
Carroll, Lewis, 11
Carron, William, 181-2
Cartoon Archetypical Slogan Theatre, 320
Carvalho, Otelo Saraiva de, 383
Carver, Glyn, 352
Carworker, The, 334-5, 341, 404, 435
Castoriadis, Cornelius, 120, 253-4
Castro, Fidel, 231, 233, 235, 238
Chalfont, Lord, 374
Challinor, Ray, 92, 106, 133, 137, 140, 170-1, 179, 251, 543
Charlton, John, 207, 272, 331, 338, 346-8, 350, 551
Chernyshevsky, v
Choi Il-bung, 527
Churchill, Winston, 7, 249
CIA (Central Intelligence Agency), 198, 382-3
Citrine, Walter, 103
City Limits, 472
Clapton, Eric, 421
Clark, Peter, 320, 404, 458, 462
Clash, The, 367, 421
Clay, Bob, 289, 390
Clegg, Hugh, 313
Cliff, Tony, writings of:
"All that glitters is not gold" 95-7, 515
"Balance of Class Forces, The", 443-6, 448
"British Policy in Palestine" etc., 41-9, 71

Chrysler Workers: The fight for a future, 432-3
Class Struggle and Women's Liberation, 467-74
Crisis, The, 374-6
"Deflected Permanent Revolution", 230-4
"Deutscher's Capitulation to Stalinism", 235-7
"Economic Roots of Reformism, The", 167-9, 229
Employers' Offensive, The, 310-8, 320, 336, 340, 365, 376, 381, 443, 472, 555
Factory Branches, 340-4, 443
France: The Struggle Goes On, i, 293-9, 302, 306, 363, 382, 482, 537
"Future of the Russian Empire, The", 158-9
Incomes Policy, Legislation and Shop Stewards, 259-65, 365, 376, 416, 463, 553
Labour Party: A Marxist History, The, 497-502, 532-3
"Labour Party in Perspective, The", 228-30
Lenin, i, iv, 18, 302, 328, 360, 390-403, 417, 519-21, 524, 555
"Lessons of the 25th November, The", 385-6
"Managerial Revolution, The", 54-6
Mao's China, 135, 160-4, 172, 231, 234
Marxism and Trade Union Struggle, 495-7
Marxism at the Millennium, 396, 545-7
Middle East – drafts of book, 4, 79-82
Middle East at the Crossroads, The, 73-6, 92, 380
"Nature of Stalinist Russia, The", 110-9, 139, 302
"On Perspectives", 306-9
"People's Democracies, The", 127, 145, 187
"Perspectives of the Permanent War Economy", 165-7
Portugal at the Crossroads, i, 73, 380-8, 537
"Present Agrarian Crisis in Egypt, The", 27-31, 42
"Revolution and Counter-Revolution: Lessons for Indonesia", 537-8
Rosa Luxemburg, 171, 181-8, 222, 302-4, 555, 559
Russia from Stalin to Khrushchev, 155-6
Russia: A Marxist Analysis, ii, 239-43
Stalin's Satellites in Europe, 125-6, 145-8, 150, 154, 235
Stalinist Russia: A Marxist Analysis, ii, 154-5, 239
Struggle in the Middle East, The, 275-7
"Struggle of the Powers, The", 135-6
Trotsky, i, iv, 12, 83-4, 518-25, 539
"Trotsky on Substitutionism", 221-5, 303
Trotskyism after Trotsky, 90, 539-41, 544
Why We Left the Communist Party, 160
World to Win, A, iv, ix, 13, 27, 58, 404, 406, 441, 543
Clinton, William, 552
Club, The, 121, 129-32, 188
Clutterbuck, Richard, 420
CND (Campaign for Nuclear Disarmament), 167, 178-9, 190, 193-5, 201, 206, 208, 211, 228, 245, 256, 274, 283, 455-6
Coates, Ken, 160, 172, 200, 233, 311
Coates, Laurence, 454
Cogniot, Georges, 393
Cohen, Sheila, 448
Cohn, Werner, 276
Collier, The, 331-2, 334-5
Committee of 100, 195-6, 210, 234
Committee to Defeat Revisionism for Communist Unity, 235
Common Cause Bulletin, 270
Communist International, 9, 18-21, 32, 38, 46, 79, 150-1, 388, 400-2, 441, 495, 520, 539, 555
Communist Party (Britain), i, 89, 91-2, 98, 129, 142-3, 152, 154, 157, 159-60, 164, 170, 191, 194, 196, 256-8, 263, 265, 272-3, 275, 283-5, 308-10, 314-7, 331, 335, 337, 348-50, 352, 357, 366-7, 369, 373, 409, 411, 413, 418, 442, 451, 484, 496-7, 500, 508
Communist Party, French, 85, 150, 288, 290, 296, 306, 469

NAME INDEX

Communist Party, German, 23, 59, 151, 402, 520
Communist Party, Italian, 104, 508-9
Communist Party, Palestine, 19-21, 38, 43, 51, 54, 57-9, 62-3, 65
Communist Party of Britain Marxist-Leninist, 263
Communist Party of Ireland, 125
Communist University of London, 418
Connolly, James, 123-4, 544
Conrad, Joseph, 149
Cook, AJ, 483-5
Cooley, Mike, 317
Corey, Lewis, 55, 82, 100
Coward, Nigel, 266, 272, 286
Cox, Roger, 174-5, 202, 265, 299, 311, 368, 444
Craipeau, Yvan, 104, 522
Crawford, Edward, 406
Crisis (band), 410
Cronin, Jim, 207-8, 544
Crosland, Anthony, 165
Crossman, Richard, 144
Cumings, Bruce, 128

Daily Mail, 369, 418-9
Daily Mirror, 420
Daily Telegraph, 87, 374
Daily Worker, 156-7, 171
Dallas, Elana, 6, 109, 127, 139, 140, 150, 174, 543
Daniels, Robert, 103
Danton, Georges, 537
Darlington, Ralph, 432, 459-60
Davison, Chris, 203, 205-6, 215
Deason, John, 379, 408-9, 434, 436
Dedijer, Vladimir, 118
Demby, Frank, *see* Vance, TN
Deutscher, Isaac, iii, 16, 148-49, 158, 198, 220, 223, 235-7, 272, 279, 509-10, 518, 521, 525, 556
Deutscher, Tamara, 396
Devlin, Bernadette, 323-4, 389
Devlin, Patrick, 266
Diana, Princess, 535
Dickens, Charles, 11
Dix, Bernard, 176-7
Djilas, Milovan, 117
Dobb, Maurice, 110, 164
Dockworker, 341

Doherty, Shaun, 319, 390, 412, 492, 538-9, 551
Dollfuss, Engelbert, 9
Douglas-Home, Alec, 245-6
Downey, Percy, 132-3
Draper, Hal, 12, 154, 198, 393, 556
Dreyfus, Alfred, 15
Dubček, Alexander, 298
Dunayevskaya, Raya, 105-6, 120, 141, 187, 210, 403
Dunbar, Karl, 221
Duncan, Arthur, 270
Durgan, Andy, 522

Eaton, Ken, 182
Economic, League, 374
Economist, The, 96, 149, 246, 288, 378
El-Nur/El-Nour, 47, 58
Encounter, 198, 252
Engels, Friedrich, viii, 11, 21, 27, 100, 111, 127, 140, 213, 468, 528-30, 546-7
Ennals, David, 284
Ennis, Kathy, 471
Evans, Phil, 435

Farber, Samuel, 233-4
Farrell, Michael, 277
Faulkner, John, 352
Fayet, Jean-François, 556
Feldman, *see* Talmi, Alon
Felix, Vs, 117
Fenn, Michael, 335, 443
Fermont, Clare, 462-3
Financial Times, 376, 543
Finch, Harry, 132
Fior, Reuben, 174, 178, 194, 201
Fiszman, Joseph R, 163-4
Flame, 441
Flaubert, Gustave, 5
Flynn, Elizabeth Gurley, 468
Flynn, Laurie, 278-9, 352, 359, 428-9
Foot, Hugh, 211
Foot, Michael, 244, 246, 270, 356, 377, 418-20, 452, 455, 487
Foot, Paul, x, 209, 211, 221, 244-5, 247, 250-1, 285, 352, 358-9, 361-2, 367, 415, 426, 428-9, 436, 452, 459, 461, 470, 483-6, 542-3, 551, 557

Forsyth, Frederick, 325
Fourth International, 10, 32-3, 35-8, 41, 47, 50, 54, 59, 61, 64, 73, 77, 79, 85-6, 88, 90-2, 95, 98, 104-6, 111, 115-6, 119-20, 122-4, 126-7, 129-30, 134, 137, 147, 150, 184, 273, 277, 286, 292, 326, 448, 524, 539, 551
Fourth International (journal), 73, 76, 95
Franco, Francisco, 148
Frank, Pierre, 120
Fraser, Ronald, 313
Free Speech Movement, 278
Freedman, Harold, 175
Freeman, Alan, 451
Frölich, Paul, 182, 304
Fryer, Peter, 156, 164, 171, 237

Gaitskell, Hugh, 193, 229, 245
Gallienne, Jacques, 120
Garbett, Geoff, 336
Gately, Kevin, 367
Gauche, La, 226-8
Gaulle, Charles de, 288
Gay Liberation Front, 424, 426
Geddes, Bill, 444
Geier, Joel, 117-8, 293, 388-9, 549
Germain, *see* Mandel, Ernest
German, Lindsey, 450, 466, 526, 550-2
Gibson, Ian, 367-8, 558
Gill, Ken, 373, 437
Gisborough, Lord, 374
Glatter, Pete, xi, 551
Glotzer, Albert, 76
Gluckstein, Akiva, 2-6, 10, 15, 68, 502
Gluckstein, Alexandra, 5
Gluckstein, Anna, 6, 248, 389-90, 491, 542-3, 552
Gluckstein, Chaim, 2, 5, 10, 34, 51, 53
Gluckstein, Danny, 6, 210, 389-90, 460, 535, 542, 550
Gluckstein, Donny, 6, 150, 179, 218, 243-4, 272, 345, 493-502, 532-3, 550, 552
Gluckstein, Esther, 2, 4-6, 10-1, 13, 68
Gluckstein, Shimon, 5
Goethe, Johann Wolfgang von, 11
Gollancz, Victor, 182
Gonzalez, Mike, 232-3, 447, 506

Gomulka, Władysław, 127
Gorbachev, Mikhail, 508-9
Gordon, Sam, 85-6
Gordon Walker, Patrick, 249
Gorter, Herman, 101
Gorz, André, 288, 449
Gott, Richard, 254, 274
Gramsci, Antonio, 184, 217, 303, 442, 487
Grant, Ted, 91, 98, 118-19, 121, 129-30, 132, 159-60, 170, 202, 255, 489
Green, George, 180
Green, Pete, 330-1, 369, 515
Greig, Lindsey, 458
Griffiths, Peter, 249
Guardian, The, 502, 551
Guérin, Daniel, 182, 467
Guevara, Che, 378, 540
Gunn, Naomi, 13, 53
Gunter, Ray, 170

Habibie, BJ, 537
Hain, Peter, 421, 454
Halkin, Hillel, 3
Hall, Philip, 279
Hallahan, Sean, 366
Hallas, Duncan, xi, 137, 139-40, 154, 166, 170-1, 287, 301, 320-3, 334, 344-8, 359, 362, 365, 369-70, 379, 389, 391, 400, 411, 493, 551, 556
Hammill, Steve, 356-7, 481
Hammond, Eric, 504
Hansard, 497
Haor, 48
Harman, Chris, xi, 112, 165, 167, 212-3, 247, 254, 266, 274-5, 278, 286-7, 302-3, 321, 327, 347, 379, 385, 389, 417-8, 426, 428-9, 433-4, 450, 460-2, 465, 510-1, 552, 555
Harper, Arthur, 331
Harris, Nigel, 163, 171, 201, 209, 211, 213, 254, 273, 278, 292, 302, 328, 347, 367, 417, 493
Harris, Tirril, 211, 273, 558
Hashomer Hatzair, 19, 37, 61, 66, 78, 82
Haston, Jock, 91-2, 98-99, 119, 121-2, 131, 178
Hayes, Dave, 357, 449-50, 491
Haynes, Mike, 511, 518

Healey, Denis, 378
Healy, Gerry, 91-2, 98, 121-2, 129-34, 138, 141, 149, 159, 171-2, 189, 195, 202, 204-5, 210, 224, 326, 352, 354, 356, 489
Heath, Edward, 262, 284, 327, 329, 350, 353, 357, 373
Heathfield, Peter, 517
Heffer, Eric, 170, 246, 418, 494
Hegel, GWF, 397
Heine, Heinrich, 11-2, 217
Henderson, Arthur, 498
Henderson, Frank, xi, 316
Henein, Georges, 26
Henry VIII, 147
Herzen, Alexander, 158
Herzl, Theodor, 15
Heseltine, Michael, 513
Hester, Simon, 448
Heyerdahl, Thor, 145
Heym, Mike, 202, 213, 299
Higgins, Jim, xi, 171, 195-7, 201, 206, 247, 254, 292-3, 300-1, 310-1, 344-8, 358-9, 361-2, 364-6, 368-71, 373, 378, 390, 403-5, 543, 552
Hilferding, Rudolf, 112, 397
Hill, Christopher, 160, 392
Hillier, Tom, 325
Hillman, Ellis, 140, 143-4
Hinton, James, 497
Hirson, Baruch, 61, 66, 414
Histadrut, 20, 64, 68, 78
Historical Materialism, x
Hitchens, Christopher, 331
Hitler, Adolf, 20, 23, 40, 50-1, 54, 58-59, 89, 136, 146, 218, 425, 441, 521
Hoban, Jeanne, 133
Hobsbawm, Eric, 8, 169, 181, 442, 449, 486
Hodgman, John, 428, 430
Hogsbjerg, Christian, 545
Holborow, Paul, 316, 319, 348, 404, 421, 432
Holubnychy, Vsevolod, *see* Felix, Vs
Horgan, Goretti, 464
Hospital Worker, 335, 371-2
Houston, John, 455
Howard, Nick, 171, 200, 233, 272, 336
Howe, Darcus, 423

Hoyles, Andrée, 294
Huddle, Roger, 209, 406-7, 421-2
Hudson, Rock, 318
Hughes, Brendan, 323
Hughes, Celia, 273, 298
Hughes, Dave, 316
Hughes, John, 246
Hutchinson, Jim, 207
Hyman, Richard, 212, 311, 313, 318, 410, 497

ILP (Independent Labour Party), 32, 34, 87-8, 91, 140, 170, 182, 498, 500
IMG (International Marxist Group), 286-7, 298, 302, 326, 367, 422, 451-2, 488
Independent, The, 551
Industrial Worker, 221
Ingrams, Richard, 251
Institute for Workers Control, 266, 311
International Monetary Fund, 410, 552
International Socialism (journal), 11, 181, 191, 198, 200-1, 213, 221, 244, 246, 252, 254, 302, 346, 526
International Socialism (organisation), International Socialists, i, iii, vii, 171, 201, 206-16, 264-5, 270-1, 282-3, 290, 299, 309, 311, 338-48, 355, 363-73, 378-9, 556
International Socialist Organization (ISO), 548-9
International Socialists of the United States, 326, 388-9
IRA (Irish Republican Army), 323-4
Irish Workers Group, 277
Isis, 219
ISL (Independent Socialist League), 139, 160
Israelite Colonisation Association, 3, 14

Jam, The, 410
James, CLR, 105-6, 120, 139, 268, 280, 400, 403, 556
James, David, 127
Jaurès, Jean, 391
Jay, Peter, 318
Jefferys, Steve, 279, 311, 348, 370, 373, 379, 403, 426, 428-9, 433-4, 436, 442-4, 446-8, 450, 485
Jenkins, Clive, 368

Jesus Christ, 390
Jeunes Gardes Socialistes, 203
Jewers, Jimmy, 180
John, Helen, 456,
John the Baptist, 390
Johnson-Forest, 105-7, 139, 143 *see also* Dunayevskaya, Raya; James, CLR
Johnstone, Monty, 310, 551
Jones, Bill, 202
Jones, Gerry, 368, 444
Jones, Jack, 310, 337, 373
Jones, Janie, 367
Jones, "Mother", 468
Jones, Sergeant W, 121
Jordan, Pat, 160

Kafka, Franz, 14-5
Kalvarisky, Chaim, 14
Kamenev, Lev, 220
Kant, Immanuel, 12
KAPD (Communist Workers Party of Germany), 101
Kasrils, Ronnie, 279-80
Katz, Moi, 61
Kautsky, Karl, 27, 100, 239, 303-4, 401, 493
Keep Left, 202-6, 222, 255
Kelly, George, 352
Kelly, Gerry, 352
Kemp, Gerard, 374
Kemp, Tom, 171, 237
Kendall, Walter, 182
Kennedy, John F, 234
Kerr, Sandra, 352
Keynes, John Maynard, 110, 239, 259
KGB (Committee for State Security, USSR), 117
Khrushchev, Nikita, 117, 155-6, 159, 181, 219-21, 234, 240-1
Khushi, Abba, 24
Kidron, Michael, xi, 68, 96, 151-2, 154, 158, 160, 165-7, 169, 171, 173-4, 178, 180-1, 197, 200-1, 203, 209, 211-2, 221, 226, 232, 244, 246, 252, 254, 259, 274, 301, 316, 327, 346, 363, 377, 380, 390, 416-7, 420, 499, 533, 555
Kim Ha-yong, 128
Kinder, Tony, 330

Kinnock, Neil, 421-2, 455, 487-8, 497, 503, 512, 533
Kirkwood, Richard, 152, 212, 405-6, 551
Kline, Roger, 347-8, 410
Knight, Ted, 209
Koestler, Arthur, 8, 15
Koston, Paul, 43
KPO (Communist Party Opposition, Germany), 37, 59
Krantz, Mark, 492, 505
Krantz, Penny, 345, 466
Kropotkin, Peter, 391
Krupskaya, Nadezhda, 396
Kumarin, Anil *see* Moonesinghe, Anil
Kun, Bela, 402
Kuper, Richard, 151, 213, 278, 316, 405

La Fontaine, Jean de, v, 217
Labor Action, 139, 158
Labour Friends of Israel, 277
Labour League of Youth, 135, 143
Labour Party (Britain), i, 70-1, 87, 91-2, 100, 108, 119, 121, 127, 129, 142, 144, 165, 170, 174, 176-7, 186, 189-90, 193, 195, 201-2, 217, 228-30, 245-6, 249, 252, 254, 264, 269-70, 286, 296, 300, 303, 306, 351, 356-7, 373, 411, 422, 451-6, 488-9, 494, 497-503, 512, 530-4, 550, 554
Labour Party, Irish, 123-4
Labour Review, 172, 196
Labour Worker, v, 221, 243, 246-51, 254-6, 290
Labour's Northern Voice, 203
Laird, Gavin, 504
Lambert, Pierre, 120
Lansbury, George, 270, 498
Laurat, Lucien, 103
Lawless, Gery, 277, 280
LCDTU (Liaison Committee for the Defence of Trade Unions), 258, 335, 349-50, 354, 413
Le Pen, Jean-Marie, 542
Lee, Grace, 106-7, 120
Lee, Willie, 318, 406, 447-8
Lenin, Vladimir Ilyich, i, iii, viii, 2, 6, 7, 11, 18, 26-7, 31, 50, 81, 90, 97, 100-4, 111, 118, 123, 138, 140,

150, 167, 169, 181-3, 185-7, 191, 208, 223, 226-7, 229, 231, 239, 302-4, 306, 317, 328, 333, 354, 360, 389-404, 418, 442, 468-9, 487, 491, 493-45, 497, 500, 502, 513, 518-20, 524, 528, 537, 546, 555
Leslie, George, 142
Leslie, Sheila, 87, 107, 116, 121, 142
Lever, Constance, 293, 325, 463
Levi, Paul, 402
Lewis, Wyndham, 103
Liebknecht, Karl, 51, 469
Light, Bob, 335, 352, 380, 443, 455, 459
Ligue Communiste Révolutionnaire, 437
Lih, Lars T, 393-4
Linden, Marcel van der, 100, 114
Lindop, Fred, 212, 247, 277, 284, 322, 325
Lindsay, John, 424, 426
Linksruck, 538
Livingstone, Ken, 506, 549-50, 552
Llywarch, John, 352
Locke, John, 344
Loeb, Mickey, 68, 151
Lollobrigida, Gina, 464
Lomax, Willie, 206
London Bureau, 32-3, 37
London Industrial Shop Stewards Defence Committee, 258-9, 264-5
London Socialist Historians Group, x
Longuet, Isabelle, 522
LSE (London School of Economics), 142, 171, 266, 273-4, 278, 301, 318, 442, 528
Lukács, Georg, 9, 184
Lutte, La, 116
Lutte Ouvrière, 293, 326-7
Luxemburg, Rosa, 39, 82, 181-8, 302-4, 315, 394, 397, 399, 414, 469, 482, 491, 493, 524, 546-7, 555, 557, 559
Lyons, Danny, 284
Lyons, Leo, 77-8

Macdonald, Gus, 205, 209-11, 558
Macdonald, Ian, 268
MacDonald, Ramsay, 229
Machover, Moshé, 2, 46
MacIntyre, Alasdair, 125, 171, 196-8, 201, 203-4, 221, 244, 246, 252-4, 290, 301
Mackney, Paul, 404, 406, 558
Macmillan, Harold, 245
Maddison, Mike, 170, 173
Maddison, Zena, 170, 172-3, 179
Magnes, Judah, 14
Major, John, 511-3
Malenkov, Georgy, 153
Management Today, 318
Mandel, Ernest, 59, 86, 91, 95-6, 120, 226-8, 241, 326, 377-8, 448, 508-10
Mansell, Christopher, 318
Mao Tse-tung, 24, 127, 151, 160-3, 178, 220, 231, 279, 486
Mapai, 21-4
Mapam, 65
Margulies, Ron, 494-5, 538
Marie, Jean-Jacques, iii, 399, 556
Marsden, Peter, 428
Marsh, Dick, 201
Martov, Julius, 418
Marx, Karl, iv, 11-2, 21, 27, 51, 55, 60, 78, 81, 96, 104, 110-1, 113-4, 127, 183, 186, 188, 213, 220, 236, 238-9, 253, 271, 291, 293, 295, 344, 417, 461-3, 468, 471, 486, 496, 514, 526, 528-30, 537, 541, 547
Marxism (event), viii, x, 418, 452, 461, 479, 491, 493, 502, 512, 514, 516, 527-8, 532, 535-6, 541, 544, 557
Marxism Today, 442
Marxist Circles, 22-3, 25, 27, 30-2, 34-7, 56, 87
Matgamna, Sean, 292-3, 320
Matzpen, 59-61, 83
May Day Manifesto, 287
McCallum, Jimmy, 210
McCann, Eamonn, 277, 324
McConville, Maureen, 294
McCreery, Michael, 235
McFadyen, Gavin, 234
McGovern, John, 34
McGregor, Sheila, 319, 465, 471
McKenna, Mike, 279
McShane, Harry, 210, 221
Megawati, 537
Mellish, Bob, 284
Mestre, Michèle, 120

MFA (Armed Forces Movement), 381
MI5, 244, 367, 436, 523
Miasnikov, GT, 103
Michel, Louise, 468
Mikardo, Ian, 277, 284
Miliband, Ralph, 228-9, 498
Militant (Britain), 255, 258, 278, 292, 302, 368, 459, 487-9, 501, 506, 509, 512
Militant, The (US), 35
Miller, Arthur, 126
Miller, Owen, 128
Mills, Stan, 180
Minority Movement, 348
Mitchell, Adrian, 201
Mitchell, Geoff, 257-8, 266
Mitchell, Ian, 477, 481
Molyneux, John, 299, 395-6, 433-4, 473, 520-1.
Moneta, Jakob, 52, 58, 82
Montague, Ken, 444
Montessori, Maria, 7
Moonesinghe, Anil, 133, 141
Mooney, Ian, 210
Moore, Barrington, 57
Morecambe, Eric, 526
Morgan, Peter, 133, 154-5, 170
Morning Star, 310, 354, 373
Morris, Sammy, 317
Morris, William, 543
Moses, 13
Moshaev, Jacob, 34
Moshaev, Yitzhak, 22
Mosler, Volkhard, 272, 527
Mosley, Oswald, 103, 109, 250
Mourre, Xavier, 228
Mousnier, Roland, 59.
Mufti, The, 76
Mullin, Chris, 454
Munis, Grandizo, 104-5, 120
Murphy, Kevin, 492
Murray, Jim, 327
Musharraf, Pervez, 552
Music Week, 494
Muslim Brotherhood, 76
Mussolini, Benito, 32, 50

Nadel, Baruch, 22
Nadel, Menahem, 22
Nagliatti, Andreas, 322, 347, 353, 370-1
Nagy, Imre, 157
Nalgo Action Group, 374
Napoleon, 80, 397
Nash, W Roy, 180
Nasser, Gamal Abdel, 31, 276, 280
National Abortion Campaign, 465
National Association of Labour Student Organisations, 278
National Caucus of Labor Committees, 326
National Front, 367, 410, 412-3, 419-20, 423, 432, 437, 457
National Joint Action Campaign for Women's Equal Rights, 468
National Liberation Front (Vietnam), 273, 282
National Unemployed Workers' Movement, 409
Naville, Pierre, 36
NCLC (National Council of Labour Colleges), 140-1, 178, 195, 215, 250
Nearing, Scott, 76
Nehmad, Annie, 385
Neilsen, Jan, 461
Nelson, Ruth, 365
Nettl, JP, 182
New Advance, 203-4
New International, 34-6, 41, 43-5, 47, 50, 54, 139, 158
New Left Review, 170-1, 197, 200, 203, 246, 297, 313
New Outlook, 57
New Reasoner, 170, 190
New Society, 317
New Statesman, 11, 126, 173, 354
Newens, Stan, 141-2, 150, 154, 156-7, 160, 169-70, 172, 176-7, 418
News Chronicle, 180
Newsletter, 171-2, 179
Nichol, Jim, 207, 215, 300, 302, 347-8, 353, 362, 364, 373, 379, 403, 421, 426, 428-9, 434, 463, 465
Nicol, Fergus, 208-9
Nicola, Jabra, 51, 57-60, 83, 152
Nikolai I, 220
Nilsen, Dennis, 389
Norris, Gerry, 544
Norris, Mel, 208, 265, 433
Nottingham Marxist Group, 160, 170

NUS (National Union of Students), 308
NUT (National Union of Teachers), 301, 334, 338, 492, 531

O'Callaghan, Einde, viii
O'Casey, Sean, 125-6
O'Shea, Clarrie, 314
Oakes, Walter J *see* Vance, TN
Observer, The, 149
Orr, Akiva, 283
Orwell, George, 103
Osborne, John, 195
Osinsky, VV, 101

Pablo, Michel, 91, 96, 120, 130, 149
Paisley, Ian, 323
Paizis, George, 279, 354, 460
Pallis, Chris, 195, 223, 228, 253, 272, 289, 294, 297
Palmer, John, 171, 203, 209, 228, 254, 273, 290, 301, 322, 324, 330, 346-7, 362, 370, 373, 403-6
Pankhurst, Sylvia, 469
Pannekoek, Anton, 101
Papert, Seymour, 172-3, 179
Parker, Ted, 278
Partido Obrero Revolucionario (Cuba), 116
PAWS (Palestinian Arab Workers' Society), 66
Peach, Blair, 437
Pearce, Brian, 171
Peers, Dave, 209, 259, 269, 348, 353, 362, 371, 373
Pelling, Henry, 159
People's Democracy (Ireland), 277, 323, 326
Péret, Benjamin, 104
Petty, William, 344
Phillips, John, 175, 180, 202, 406
Phillips, Mary, 173-4, 202
Pink Floyd, 320
Piratin, Phil, 337
Pitt, Bob, 130
Pivert, Marceau, 158
Plekhanov, Georgi, 27
Pluto Press, 316, 346, 390, 417, 433
Poale Zion, 19-23, 37
Pollitt, Harry, 89
Popper, Karl, 9, 165

Porat, Yehoshua, 31
Porter, Lady Shirley, 369
Possony, Stefan T, 392
Potere Operaio, 326
POUM (Workers Party of Marxist Unity, Spain), 32, 139, 387
Pouvoir Ouvrier, 281
Powell, Enoch, 284-6, 288-9
Pravda, 360, 394
Preston, Wally, 336
Preuves, 148
Prevost, Eddie, 335-6, 443
Prior, Mike, 442
Pritchard, Ross, xi, 210, 299, 365
Private Eye, 245
Problems of Communism, 163-4
Profumo, John, 245
Protz, Roger, 204, 255-6, 299, 347, 353, 361-2, 364, 368, 403, 424
Proudhon, Pierre-Joseph, 291, 468
PRP (Proletarian Revolutionary Party – Revolutionary Brigades), 384-9
Purdy, Dave, 442
Pushkin, Alexander, 11

Qol, Ha'am, 63
Qol, Hamma'amad, 63
Quatrième, Internationale, 73

Rabotnitsa, 470
Radek, Karl, 19, 102
Radical America, 388
Rais, Amien, 537
Rally, 202-3, 206
Ramelson, Bert, 310, 369
Rank and File, 334, 412
Rank and File Movement, 354-5, 408, 426, 446
RAR (Rock Against Racism), 421-2
RCP (Revolutionary Communist Party), 87, 91-2, 96-8, 106, 108-10, 115, 118-9, 121, 127, 134, 137, 140-2, 159, 164, 184, 189, 223, 228, 244, 257, 282, 301, 487
Reagan, Ronald, 455, 503
Rebel, 202-3, 206, 255
Red Brigades, 324, 456
Red Mole, 326
Redskins, The, 494
Reed, Gwynn, 336

Rees, John, 11, 407, 478, 492, 516, 526, 550
Reid, Betty, 309
Reilly, Tommy, 109
Renard, André, 227
Renton, Dave, 391, 422
Resistance, 258
Révolution!, 388
Révolution Prolétarienne, 150
Revolutionary Communist League (Palestine), 37, 53, 56-66, 70, 83-4
Revolutionary History, x, 43, 522
Revolutionary Russia, 524
Revolutionary Socialist Party (Ireland), 122-4
Rhee, Syngman, 144
Richardson, Al, xi, 99, 502, 522
Ridley, FA, 182
Right to Work Campaign, 408-10, 412-3, 426, 451, 457
RILU (Red International of Labour Unions), 150, 393, 495-6
Rizzi, Bruno, 104
Robertson, Jack, 421, 429, 431
Robertson, John, 204, 206
Robespierre, Maximilien, 12, 537
Robinson, Edward G, 336
Robinson, Peter, 383, 385-6
Rollo, Joanna, 388, 432
Rose, John, 278-80, 404, 432, 460-1
Rosenberg, Chanie, v, xi, 6, 12, 61-4, 66-69, 73, 83-8, 92, 99, 108-10, 121, 127, 129, 133, 139, 141, 145, 150-2, 173, 189, 197, 205, 207, 210-3, 215, 234, 237, 243, 248, 268, 272-3, 279, 334, 389-90, 409, 414, 422, 463, 471, 493, 511, 525-6, 530, 542, 544
Rosenberg, Isaac, 67
Rosewell, Roger, 209, 247, 273, 302, 321, 323, 342, 346-8, 350, 352, 364, 368-71
Rosmer, Alfred, 116, 147-8, 150, 388, 401
Rothschild, Edmond de, 3-4
Rothschild, James de, 3
Rothschild, Sigi, 61
Rotten, Johnny, 421
Roosevelt, Franklin D, 55
Rousset, David, 120

Routledge, Paul, 330
Rowbotham, Sheila, 106
RSDLP, RSDRP (Russian Social-Democratic Labour Party), 393, 519
Rühle, Otto, 101
Russell, Bertrand, 195, 273
Russian Review, The, 147

SAG (Socialist Workers Group, Germany), 272, 387, 407, 527-8, 538
Sagall, Sabby, 279, 283, 309, 321, 340, 460
Sanders, Tim, 478
SAP (Socialist Workers Party, Germany), 32, 82
Sapronov, TV, 102
Sard Ed *see* Vance TN
Sarneh, Ygal, 22, 24, 31
Sartre, Jean-Paul, x, 5, 15, 120, 279, 282
Saunders, Red, 320, 421-2, 526
Sawbridge, Ben, 206
Scanlon, Hugh, 310, 373
Scargill, Arthur, 331-2, 444, 453-4, 475-6, 478, 481, 485, 532
Schama, Simon, 3, 14
Scheller, Dov, 60-1
Scheller, Susi, 60-1
Schlesinger, Rudolf, 242
Schoenman, Ralph, 210, 273
Schwartz, Yossi, 65-6
Scott, Jim, 273
SDS (Socialist German Student Union), 272
Seale, Patrick, 294
Sedgwick, Peter, 171, 175, 195, 201, 203, 209, 237, 297, 339, 415-6
Sedova, Natalia, 105, 139, 144
Segall, Rudolf, 37
Selby, Harry, 228
Serge, Victor, v, 9, 103, 175, 401, 557, 559
Seton-Watson, Hugh, 145
Sewell, Rob, 121
Sex Pistols, 421
Seymour, Richard, 545
Shaberman, Ralph *or* Renée, 133
Shachtman, Max, 54, 98, 104-5, 107, 120, 126, 136, 140, 146, 199, 270

Shah, Ahmed, 552
Shakespeare, William, 11, 26
Shas, Dov, 56, 61-6, 83
Shaw, Martin, 379
Shawki, Ahmed, 548-9
Sheehy-Skeffington, Andrée, 123-5
Sheehy-Skeffington, Owen, 122-4
Sherry, Dave, 319, 447
Shlonsky, Tuvia, 56, 67-8
Shohat, Ana, 61
Shonfield, Andrew, 259
Silverman, Sidney, 277
Simon, Serge, 228
Simons, Mike, 484
Skinner, Quentin, 391
Slaughter, Cliff, 171, 184
SLL (Socialist Labour League), 164, 171, 180, 184, 186, 192, 196-7, 200, 202, 205, 222, 224, 228, 269, 272, 278, 286, 292, 302, 312, 404, 489
Smith, Cyril, 138
Smith, Joan, 319, 465-6
Smith, John, 530
Smith, Martin, 481, 492, 517, 550
Soares, Mário, 383
Social Democratic Party, German, 83, 182, 188, 303, 401, 538
Socialisme ou Barbarie, 116, 120, 222-3, 253, 281
Socialist Alliance, 550
Socialist Appeal (Britain) 119
Socialist Appeal (US), 35, 361
Socialist Labour Party, 532
Socialist Leader, 182
Socialist Outlook, 131
Socialist Party (Belgium), 203, 227
Socialist Party (Portugal), 382-3
Socialist Review Group, i, 107, 109, 116, 125, 134, 137-39, 141-4, 148, 150, 156-8, 160, 164, 170-8, 184, 188-91, 195-6, 228, 501, 556
Socialist Review, 116, 134, 137, 139-42, 149-52, 176-7, 179-80, 191, 197, 221, 246
Socialist Worker, 290, 299-300, 309, 341, 359-64, 367, 378, 426-32, 460-1, 475, 513, 535
Solidarity, 223, 228, 253, 283, 289, 297
Soviet Studies, 242, 524

Spark, The, 43-5, 47-49
Sparks, Colin, 493
SPGB (Socialist Party of Great Britain), 98, 101, 329
Spiegel, Der, 547
Spinoza, Baruch, 16
Stack, Pat, 370, 378, 490-1, 525
Stalin, Joseph, iii, 20, 32, 51, 55, 58, 69, 88, 90, 102-3, 112-3, 117-8, 120, 135-6, 146-7, 149, 151-3, 155-6, 159, 161, 171, 181, 219, 236, 239-41, 329, 453, 510, 520-1, 524
Stein, Mordechai, 38, 47
Stendhal, 51
Stephen, Campbell, 34, 88, 108
Stern, Avraham, 52-3, 62
Sternberg, Fritz, 82
Stokes, Donald, 318
Stonehouse, John, 411
Stop the War Coalition, i, 456, 556
Strindberg, August, 126
Strouthous, Andy, 357, 440, 459
Stutje, Jan Willem, 228
Suharto, 536-7
Sun, The, 486, 513
Sunday Telegraph, 452
Sunday Times, 381
Sverdlov, Yakov, 397
Sviták, Ivan, 118
Swade, Tamar, 460, 552
Swain, Geoffrey, 393, 524
SWP (Socialist Workers Party, Britain), i, iii, iv, v, vi, x, 412-6, 437-8, 457, 462, 479-80, 489-90, 514, 516-7, 523, 532, 556
SWP (Socialist Workers Party, US), 34-5, 47, 54, 64, 73, 77, 85, 105, 120, 171

Tait, Danny, 61-3, 68, 73, 133, 140-1, 150
Tait, Jean, 133, 140-1, 150
Tallantire, Malcolm, 175
Talmi, Alon, 22, 24
Tarbuck, Ken, 115, 129-33, 137
Tarbuck, Rhoda, 133-4, 137
Tatchell, Peter, 455
Taut, Jakob, 58-60, 62, 64-6, 83
Taylor, George E, 164
Taylor, Robert, 355

Tearse, Roy, 301
Temple, Nina, 510
Temporary Hoarding, 421
Thackray, Jake, 352
Thatcher, Ian D, 524-5
Thatcher, Margaret, 262, 413, 435, 440, 443, 446, 450, 455, 475, 509, 511, 513
Thompson, Edward, 160, 200, 261
Thompson, Marjorie, 517
Thomson, Bill, 210, 243
Thorez, Maurice, 89
Times Literary Supplement, 330
Times, The, 318, 329
Tito, Josip Broz, 120, 127, 146-7
Todd, Ron, 504
Tomkinson, Martin, 279, 428
Torrance, Sheila, 206
Tosstorff, Reiner, 522, 556
Tracy, Noel, 209, 293, 325
Trench, Paddy, 124
Tribune, 143, 210, 212, 248, 503
Trotsky, Leon, i, ii, iii, vi, vii, viii, 7, 11-2, 21, 26, 29, 31, 39-41, 50, 63, 69, 81, 83, 88-90, 97-100, 102-4, 111, 118-19, 123, 149-51, 154, 158, 169, 171, 182, 186, 199, 221-5, 229-32, 235-6, 239, 271, 308, 334, 361, 392, 396-8, 400, 418, 431, 469, 482, 484, 491, 496, 499, 502-3, 509, 518-25, 528, 539-41, 556
Truman, Harry S, 136, 144
TUC (Trades Union Congress), 329, 332, 373, 450, 484, 513
Turner, Simon, 434

Ukrainian Revolutionary Democratic Party, 116
ULR (*Universities and Left Review*), 170, 190
UPA (Ukrainian Resurgent Army), 117

Van Gelderen, Charles, 87, 98, 121
Vance, TN, 165-6
Vashee, Basker, 279
Veness, Val, 454
Vernell, Sean, 492, 513, 550
Voix Ouvrière, 293
Voltaire, 551
Voyseisky, Esther (SEE Gluckstein, Esther)
Vpered, 116
VSC (Vietnam Solidarity Campaign), 273, 275, 283, 286-7

Wafd Party, 30
Wainwright, William, 89
Wald, Alan, 522
Walling, William English, 100
Warburg, Gabriel, 56
Warren, Bill, 442
Warshawski, Michel, 36, 38
Waterson, Julie, 434, 516
Watts, Alan, 208, 317
Webb, Sidney, 498
Weber, Max, 299
Webster, Martin, 423
Week, The, 246
Weigler, Otto, 61
Weizmann, Chaim, 2, 4-5
Weizmann, Yehiel Mikhail, 4-5
Wesker, Arnold, 195
White, James D, 524-5
Wicks, Harry, 24, 280, 461
Widgery, Dave, 399-400, 421-2, 432, 528, 557-8
Widowson, Ewa, 12, 272
Williams, Granville, 319, 331, 348, 403, 406
Williams, Len, 205
Williams, Raymond, 171
Williamson, Colwyn, 211
Williamson, Judith, 472-3
Wilson, Andy, 459, 516
Wilson, Harold, 245, 247, 256, 258, 260, 262, 269, 273, 284, 292, 327, 356, 375, 377-8, 410, 510
Wingate, Orde, 33
Wise, Ernie, 526
Wittfogel, Karl, 160
Witzenfeld, John, 173
Women's Voice, 435, 441, 448, 464-6, 469, 472-3
Woodward, Alan, 208, 335
Workers' Fight, 292-3, 323, 325, 328, 345, 400
Workers International News, 69, 73
Workers' League, 404-6
Workers Party, 105, 120
Workers Party of South Africa, 43-4

Workers' Republic, 292
World Events, 76
Worrall, Ryan, 104
Wright, Peter, 523
WRP (Workers Revolutionary Party), 367, 403, 488-9, 523

X, Malcolm, 273

Yaffe, Hillel, 2
Yeltsin, Boris, 508
Yitzhaki, 22
Young Chartist, 143
Young Guard, 203-6, 213, 234, 243, 255
Young, Hugo, 420
Young, James D, 173, 178-9
Young Socialists, 201-11, 215, 221, 228, 247, 250, 255, 257, 274

Zalutsky, Pyotr, 102
Zeilig, Leo, 232
Zetkin, Clara, 468
Zinoviev, Grigory, 19, 102, 220, 402, 520

Subject index

The terms Marxism, socialism and working class have been omitted since they appear throughout the book.

anti-capitalism, iii, 517, 547-9
arms economy *see* permanent arms economy

Balkan War(1999) 274, 485, 542, 544, 548
black nationalism, 183, 251-2, 491
bureaucratic collectivism, 54, 98, 103-4, 126, 139, 154

Chilean coup (1973), 290, 349, 382-3, 386, 426
Cold War, 122, 124, 129, 256, 508

deflected permanent revolution, 31, 161-2, 200, 222, 23-234, 539, 555
democratic centralism, 268, 290-2, 300-1, 490
dialectics, 124, 271, 308-9, 397, 516
downturn, 292, 412, 433, 440-9, 457, 463, 479, 502

electoral strategy, 91, 274, 410-11, 415, 501
entrism, 91-2, 119, 121, 127, 140, 142, 170, 176-7, 186, 189-90, 201-7, 217, 228-30, 247, 252, 264, 269-70, 290, 300, 303, 330, 488-9, 501

factory branches, 339, 44, 363, 459
factory occupations, 288, 294, 332, 433
Falklands War (1982), 274, 452-3
falling rate of profit, 82, 166, 234
fascism, ii, 9, 24, 26, 42, 50, 55, 74, 109, 286, 533, 547

female labour, 96-7, 161
feminism *see* women's oppression
First World War, 2-3, 13, 18, 50-1, 63, 89, 397, 469, 493, 498, 500, 519
French general strike (1968), i, 288-90, 293-8, 306, 537, 556
French Revolution, 61, 127, 220, 297, 391, 467, 523

gay oppression, 277, 423-6
Gulf War (1991), 274, 516-7, 548

Holocaust, 23, 48, 69, 71, 74, 547, 559
Hungarian Revolution (1956), 156-60, 171, 179-81, 183, 220, 237, 242, 256, 289, 294, 510

immigration, 41-2, 46, 48-49, 71, 247, 249-51, 284, 286
imperialism, 7, 19-20, 26, 28, 31, 34, 40-5, 48, 51-2, 66, 69, 73-4, 76, 78-81, 83, 92-4, 130, 135-6, 184, 226, 232, 235, 274, 276, 286, 323, 380, 397
incomes policy, 246, 256, 259-65, 350, 375, 378

Keynesianism, 82, 165, 499, 540
Korean War, 128-9, 131, 135, 144, 179, 273

labour aristocracy, 45-6, 81, 167-9, 229, 495
labour discipline, 161, 240-1, 312
left unity, 170, 172, 190-1, 203, 285-8, 326, 488, 550

Maoism, 12, 163, 235, 256-7, 265, 371, 388, 540
miners' strike (1984-5), 376, 475-86, 488, 495, 512

New Left, 170, 196, 211, 237, 246, 287
nuclear war, 136, 166, 178, 183, 191, 206, 234, 455, 547, 553, 559

Paris Commune, 24, 186, 293, 468, 470
peasantry, 161-2, 219, 237-9, 518
permanent arms economy, 113, 136, 164-7, 181, 184, 203, 307, 416,

539-40, 544, 555
permanent revolution, ii, 29, 31, 42, 77, 89, 94, 161, 396, 529, 541 *see* also deflected permanent revolution)
poll tax, 505-6, 511
popular front, 21, 38, 63, 421 *see* also united front
Portuguese Revolution (1975), i, 375, 379-89, 556
post-war boom, 91, 95-7, 164-7, 257, 260, 349 *see* also permanent arms economy
productivity deals, 309-18, 435, 445

racism, 16, 249-52, 262, 284-5, 419-23, 515, 552
rank and file organisation, 333-5, 341, 349-51, 354-5, 371-2, 448, 454, 457-8
rate of profit *see* falling rate of profit
reformism, 167-69, 177, 229, 304, 308, 357, 375, 383, 405, 411-2, 483, 499, 501-2, 533, 554
religion, 52, 146, 249, 251
revolutionary party, 177, 184-7, 222-5, 281, 285, 290-2, 296-7, 333, 337, 341, 372, 383-6, 393-5, 397-400, 403, 493, 514, 530, 537-8, 546
Russian Revolution (1905), 183, 394, 396, 482, 491, 546
Russian Revolution (1917), iii, 2, 18, 29, 88, 100-1, 111, 184, 224, 231, 280, 294, 297, 302, 306, 397-400, 468-70, 518-9, 525, 537, 539, 555

Second World War, ii, 23, 33, 47, 50-4, 58, 60, 64, 69, 74, 80, 88-90
shop stewards, 173, 257, 259-65, 269, 296, 365-6, 443-5, 458, 496
Sino-Soviet split, 153-4, 162-3, 220, 234-5, 241, 256
socialism or barbarism, 199, 546-7, 559
Stalinism, 23-4, 27, 35, 89, 100, 131, 136, 143, 145-6, 224, 290, 508, 512, 520, 525, 547, 553, 554
state capitalism, i, 55-6, 97-108, 110-20, 126-7, 129-31, 136, 138-40, 143, 145-8, 152-6, 160-4, 172, 174, 191, 203, 232-3, 236, 238-42, 271, 302, 326, 416, 418, 463, 495, 509-11, 520, 527, 539, 554-5
state in modern capitalism, 100, 112-3, 140, 145-6, 155, 176-7, 246, 260
students, 211-3, 274, 278-80, 288-9, 294-5, 320, 418
syndicalism, 307, 388, 484

terrorism, 73-4, 76, 324
theory and practice, unity of, 270, 308, 321, 326, 416, 528, 530, 556-7
trade union bureaucracy, 185-6, 261, 304, 310, 317, 350, 353, 356, 368, 373, 445, 458, 484, 495-7
transitional demands, 308, 523, 541
Transitional Programme, 50, 97, 169, 222, 229, 308, 499, 541
Trotskyism, ii, v, viii, 27, 32-3, 37-8, 41, 44-5, 49, 54, 58, 60, 62, 69, 77, 81, 83-5, 88-92, 95, 98, 101, 104, 108, 111-2, 118, 122-4, 127, 129, 134, 142, 152, 160, 164, 169, 171, 200, 216, 229, 286, 292, 346, 367-8, 392, 400, 417, 489, 509, 518, 521-4, 539-41

united front (*see* also Popular Front), 26, 143, 465, 517

Vietnam War, 183, 273-6, 282-3, 286, 298

women's oppression, women's liberation, 239, 263, 315, 343, 446, 463-74 (*see* also female labour)
workers' control, 227, 266-7, 286, 312, 554

Zionism, iv, 2-3, 5-7, 12-16, 18-24, 27-8, 31, 33-4, 39-44, 47-49, 51-2, 59, 61, 67, 69-79, 81-3, 238, 276-7, 279-80, 349, 543